THE GREAT INCOME TAX HOAX

Irwin Schiff

THE GREAT INCOME TAX HOAX

Why You Can Immediately Stop Paying This Illegally Enforced Tax

with Peter Schiff

Freedom Books

Hamden, Connecticut

This book is designed to provide the author's findings and opinions based on research and analysis of the subject matter covered. This information is not provided for purposes of rendering legal or other professional services, which can only be provided by knowledgeable professionals on a fee basis.

Further, there is always an element of risk in standing up for one's lawful rights in the face of an oppressive taxing authority backed by a biased judiciary.

Therefore, the author and publisher disclaim any responsibility for any liability of loss incurred as a consequence of the use and application, either directly or indirectly, of any advice or information presented herein.

Sections of the Internal Revenue Code reprinted by permission from the Tax and Professional Services Division, The Research Institute of America, Inc. Copyright ©1984.

Copyright© 1985 by Irwin A. Schiff

Library of Congress Catalog Card No. 85-070036

ISBN-0-930374-05-3

85 86 87 88 10 9 8 7 6 5 4 3 2 1

TO

Melville Weston Fuller, Chief Justice of the United States from 1888–1910, and Stephen Johnson Field, Associate Supreme Court Justice from 1863–1897, for the judicial integrity they displayed in holding an income tax unconstitutional; and for their magnificent opinions which, by contrast, clearly reveal the criminal nature of today's Federal judiciary.

BOOKS BY IRWIN SCHIFF

The Great Income Tax Hoax

How An Economy Grows and Why It Doesn't

The Social Security Swindle — How Anyone Can Drop Out

How Anyone Can Stop Paying Income Taxes

The Kingdom of Moltz

The Biggest Con: How The Government Is Fleecing You

CONTENTS

INTRODUCTION

This book will shock you. It will convince you that for over seventy years the Federal government has been illegally collecting income taxes and that the courts (if not Congress) know it. Federal judges allow property to be illegally confiscated and knowingly send innocent people to jail in order to intimidate an uninformed public and to aid the IRS in illegally enforcing Federal tax law. The reason the public can be duped and intimidated is because it *does not know the law or even the legal meaning of income*. Most Americans do not realize they have *no income that can be legally taxed under our income tax laws.*

This book will clearly explain the law to you so that you will know why *you can legally stop paying income taxes immediately* and how you can protect yourself from IRS harrassment and control.

In essence, history has repeated itself and America now finds itself in the same circumstances as Thirteenth Century Egypt. In the Twelfth Century, slaves known as Mamelukes (literally "owned men") were brought to Egypt to serve as soldiers to the Sultan. In 1250 they overthrew the government they were supposed to serve, installed one of their own as Sultan and ruled Egypt for the next two hundred and fifty years. America has essentially the same problem.

The Federal government was created (with limited power) by the people of America in order to protect their unalienable rights to life, liberty, and property. Federal employees were recruited and sent to Washington to administer the laws commensurate with this limited grant of power. Initially, these employees were conceived as servants of the people; however, as the Mamelukes before them, the Federal bureaucracy has now illegally installed itself as the master while the people have become their servants.

In order to manage this, America's Mamelukes had to destroy the very document designed to limit their power and keep them in check. This was largely achieved by those assigned the role of "judges." In addition, the key ingredient in the expansion and preservation of Mameluke control of America has been their success in installing and *illegally* enforcing the income tax.

Many Americans are now united in a struggle to depose American Mamelukes and to retrieve and reestablish both the document and the freedoms they have destroyed. The days of Mameluke control of America are numbered. More and more Americans are learning to recognize our

Mamelukes for the usurpers they are. They are learning how to successfully fight them. This book was written to help in that struggle and to persuade *you* to join the battle. The faster we get rid of our Mameluke masters and their illegal income tax the better off we will all be.

Not only is the battle to free America from Mameluke control exciting, it will also allow you to have *more money to spend while enjoying life, your new-found liberty, and your increased ability to pursue your own happiness.* According to the April, 1983 issue of *Life* magazine some 20,000,000 working Americans have stopped filing income tax returns — WE NOW HAVE THE MAMELUKES ON THE RUN!

1

Direct vs Indirect Taxes

In an 1819 decision Chief Justice John Marshall wrote: "The power to tax involves the power to destroy." History agrees. From the beginning of organized government, kings and ruling castes used taxation as an instrument and a weapon. Throughout recorded history, moreover, capricious or heavy-handed taxation led to insurrection or, less dramatically, to the dissolution of the ties which bind people to their government. In Twelfth Century England, outrageous taxation inspired the Peasants' Revolt which rampaged until Richard II skewered the head of Wat Tyler, its leader, on a pole. It was the very issue of taxes that sparked the American Revolution and today the tax system in America is as violative of the rule of law and the Constitution as the "judges" who administer it.

In ancient times, kings and emperors needed taxes for the support of their courts and armies. Men-at-arms and the nobility produced no wealth so they had to be supported by those who did. Historically, governments have been run by non-producers and non-producers generally gravitate to government service. But to the extent that government performs its limited social function — that of protecting society from external enemies and maintaining internal peace and order by eliminating social predators — the cost of supporting government workers can be born out of the increased productivity that a limited, well-run government will generate.

The first 150 years of America bears excellent testimony to this principle. Unfortunately, history demonstrates the accuracy of Lord Acton's observation that "power corrupts and absolute power corrupts absolutely." As government acquires more power[1] it becomes arbitrary and corrupt. Taxes are increasingly raised for the support of entrenched government, not for the benefit of society. Eventually, the growing army

---

[1] In America this unconstitutional expansion of federal power was achieved by the government, illegally maintaining and exercising (in peacetime) numerous emergency powers it acquired as "temporary" war-time measures.

of government created non-producers will no longer be able to be supported by the ever dwindling number of producers and the economic and social structure of society will ultimately give way.

This is the story of Rome and provides the explanation for what is happening in America today. The parallel between the decline of Rome and the decline of America is so sharp that only government-run schools could fail to make the connection.

Only People Pay Taxes

How should government extract taxes? Citizens could be required to pay a certain sum to the "royal" tax collector — but how much? Since some citizens can afford to pay more than others, governments devised methods for taxing citizens according to their supposed ability to pay or, in simpler terms, according to their wealth which became one of the earliest forms of taxation. However, while such taxes *appear* to tax wealth, it is the citizen that is being taxed, not his wealth. He is being taxed *according to his wealth*. It is important to keep this distinction in mind. As you will see, the government seeks to fool the public on this *simple* issue. For example, property taxes are not really taxes *on property* but taxes *on individuals* based on the property they own. All such taxes fall within the constitutional category of "direct taxes."

The Importance of Tax Classes

The Constitution recognizes two classes of taxes and imposes different restrictions on the Federal government's right and ability to impose either. It is important, therefore, that the taxpayer be able to identify both classes in order to determine whether they are being levied constitutionally. The government and the courts have evaded the issue by claiming that the differences between the two taxing categories are unclear — that the Founding Fathers (who were so *specific* in *everything* else) did not know what they were talking about and that their proscriptions on the power of taxation were the result of confusion and lack of clear thinking. This is self-serving nonsense. The courts know, as we all do, what great texts the Founding Fathers consulted, what they were influenced by, and how they debated the system they embodied in the Constitution. Not only were the framers of the Constitution keenly cognizant of the issues before them, they also had studied Adam Smith's definitive work, *The Wealth of Nations*, published in 1776 — the same year the Declaration of Independence was written. I will quote extensively from this material so there can be no doubt in anyone's mind regarding *exactly* what the Founding Fathers had in mind when they wrote these taxing restrictions into the Constitution.

Capitation Taxes

The first category of taxes taken up in the Constitution were "capitation and direct taxes." This is what Smith had to say about them.

> Capitation taxes, if it is attempted to proportion them to the *fortune or revenue of each contributor,* become altogether arbitrary. The state of a man's fortune varies from day to day, and without an inquisition more intolerable than any tax, and renewed at least once every year, can only be guessed at. His assessment, therefore, must in most cases depend upon the good or bad humour of his assessors, and must, therefore, be altogether arbitrary and uncertain.
>
> Capitation taxes, if they are proportioned not to the supposed fortune, but to the rank of each contributor, become altogether unequal; the degree of fortune being frequently unequal in the same degree of rank.
>
> Such taxes, therefore, if it is attempted to render them equal, become altogether arbitrary and uncertain; and if it is attempted to render them certain and not arbitrary, become altogether unequal. Let the tax be light or heavy, uncertainty is always a great grievance. In a light tax a considerable degree of inequality may be supported; in a heavy one it is altogether intolerable.
>
> In the different poll-taxes which took place in England during the reign of William III. the contributors were, the greater part of them, assessed according to the degree of their rank; as dukes, marquisses, earls, viscounts, barons, esquires, gentlemen, the eldest and youngest sons of peers, etc. All shopkeepers and tradesmen worth more than three hundred pounds, that is, the better sort of them, were subject to the same assessment, how great soever might be the difference in their fortunes. *Their rank was more considered than their fortune.* Several of those who *in the first poll-tax were rated according to their supposed fortune, were afterwards rated according to their rank.* Serjeants, attornies, and proctors at law, *who in the first poll-tax were assessed at three shillings in the pound of their supposed income* were afterwards assessed as gentlemen. In the assessment of a tax which was not very heavy, a considerable degree of inequality had been found less insupportable than any degree of uncertainty.
>
> In the capitation which has been levied in France without any interruption since the beginning of the present century, the highest orders of people are rated according to their rank, by an invariable tariff; the lower orders of people, according to what is supposed to be their fortune, by an assessment which varies from year to year. The officers of the king's court, the judges and other officers in the superior courts of justice, the officers

of the troops, etc. are assessed in the first manner. The inferior ranks of people in the provinces are assessed in the second. In France the great easily submit to a considerable degree of inequality in a tax which, so far as it affects them, is not a very heavy one; but could not brook the arbitrary assessment of an intendant. The inferior ranks of people must, in that country, suffer patiently the usage which their superiors think proper to give them.

In England the different poll-taxes never produced the sum which had been expected from them, or which, it was supposed, they might have produced, had they been exactly levied. In France the capitation always produces the sum expected from it. The mild government of England, when it assessed the different ranks of people to the poll-tax, contented itself with what that assessment happened to produce; and required no compensation for the loss which the state might sustain either by those who could not pay, or by those who would not pay (for there were many such), and who, by the indulgent execution of the law, were not forced to pay. The more severe government of France assesses upon each generality a certain sum, which the intendant must find as he can. If any province complains of being assessed too high, it may, in the assessment of next year, obtain an abatement proportioned to the overcharge of the year before. But it must pay in the mean time. The intendant, in order to be sure of finding the sum assessed upon his generality, was impowered to assess it in a larger sum, that the failure or inability of some of the contributors might be compensated by the over-charge of the rest; and till 1765, the fixation of this surplus assessment was left altogether to his discretion. In that year indeed the council assumed this power to itself. In the capitation of the provinces, it is observed by the perfectly well-informed author of the Memoirs upon the impositions in France, the proportion which falls upon the nobility, and upon those whose privileges exempt them from the taille, is the least considerable. The largest falls upon those subject to the taille, who are assessed to the capitation at so much a pound of what they pay to that other tax.

Capitation taxes, so far as they are levied upon the lower ranks of people, are direct taxes upon the wages of labour and are attended with all the inconveniencies of such taxes.

Capitation taxes are levied at little expence; and, where they are rigorously exacted, afford a very sure revenue to the state. It is upon this account that in countries where the ease, comfort, and security of the inferior ranks of people are little attended to, capitation taxes are very common. It is in general, however, but a small part of the public revenue, which, in a great empire, has ever been drawn from such taxes; and the greatest sum which they have ever afforded, might always have been found in some other way much more convenient to the people. (Emphasis added)

Examples of Capitation And Direct Taxes

As explained by Adam Smith there are a variety of capitation taxes[2] and each can be levied according to different criteria: wealth, revenue, rank, occupation or even "upon the wages of labor." Note that Smith (whose ideas were a major guide to the framers of the Constitution) stated that capitation taxes attempted to "proportion" taxes to either the fortune or the revenue of each contributor." He made it absolutely clear that taxes related to income were *direct* taxes which is extremely relevant since the U.S. Supreme Court ruled that an income tax was not a capitation tax on the absurd claim that "Smith's work as to the meaning of such a tax" made no distinction between direct and indirect taxes (see page 105). This claim was patently false since Smith not only made a definitive distinction he also *specifically* labelled taxes related to income as being capitation or direct taxes!

There is no question that an income tax is clearly a capitation tax whereby the government seeks to tax individuals directly according to their income. It is important to remember, however, that in all capitation taxes (perhaps they should have been called *decapitation* taxes) it is not wealth, revenue, rank, or occupations that are being taxed but the *individual* — and he is being taxed according to some arbitrary yardstick the government believes measures his ability to pay. If you think an "income" tax is a tax on "income" then let your "income" calculate and pay the tax! Instead of taxing you according to your income, the government could conceivably tax you according to your weight, say at $1.00 per pound. Someone who weighs one hundred pounds would pay a $100.00 "weight tax" and someone who weighs two hundred pounds would pay $200.00. But would such a tax actually be a tax *on* "weight"? No, it would be a tax *on* the individual *measured by* his weight. For the same reason an "income" tax is not a tax on "income" — it is a tax *on* the individual *measured by* his "income."

Taxing People Directly

If a government decides to tax people *directly* according to their wealth, there remains the problem of how to determine that wealth. Will citizens be compelled to disclose the amount and nature of what they possess to the tax collector so they can be properly taxed? Under

---

[2] Note that Smith uses "poll" and "capitation" taxes interchangeably and says that either can relate to rank or fortune.

the Constitution, citizens cannot be compelled to provide information that can be used against them and they are further presumed to have a right to privacy. Yet all information on a tax return can be used against taxpayers — and can even be given to other Federal agencies as well as to state and foreign governments to be used against them. Exactly how much privacy does a citizen have after giving all the information required on a 1040?[3] Requiring Americans to file income tax returns violates the First and Ninth Amendments which is why (though few people seem to know this) *no such filing requirement is contained in the law.*

In England, direct taxes were once levied on chimneys and windows, the theory being that the more windows and chimneys a house had the wealthier the owner and the more taxes he could pay. Again, the tax was not actually *on* windows or chimneys but was, rather, *on* the *individual* who owned the home *measured by* the number of chimneys and windows he had (which presumably measured his ability to pay). In *The Wealth of Nations* Adam Smith gives an interesting description of how such taxes worked.

> The contrivers of the several taxes which in England have, at different times, been imposed upon houses, seem to have imagined that there was some great difficulty in ascertaining, with tolerable exactness, what was the real rent of every house. They have regulated their taxes, therefore, according to some more obvious circumstance, such as they had probably imagined would, in most cases, bear some proportion to the rent.
>
> The first tax of this kind was hearth-money; or a tax of two shillings upon every hearth. In order to ascertain how many hearths were in the house, it was necessary that the tax-gatherer *should enter every room in it. This odious visit rendered the tax odious.* Soon after the revolution, therefore, *it was abolished as a badge of slavery.*
>
> The next tax of this kind was, a tax of two shillings upon every dwelling house inhabited. A house with ten windows to pay four shillings more. A house with twenty windows and upwards to pay eight shillings. This tax was afterwards so far altered, that houses with twenty windows, and with less than thirty, were ordered to pay ten shillings, and those with thirty windows and upwards to pay twenty shillings. The number of windows can, in most cases, be counted from the outside, and, in all cases, without entering every room in the house. The visit of the tax-gatherer, therefore, was less offensive in this tax than in the hearth-money.
>
> This tax was afterwards repealed, and in the room of it was established the window-tax, which has undergone too several alterations and

---

[3] The full details on this can be found in *How Anyone Can Stop Paying Income Taxes* by Irwin Schiff (FREEDOM BOOKS: 1982).

augmentations. The window-tax, as it stands at present (January, 1775), over and above the duty of three shillings upon every house in England, and of one shilling upon every house in Scotland, lays a duty upon every window, which, in England, augments gradually from two-pence, the lowest rate, upon houses with not more than seven windows; to two shillings, the highest rate, upon houses with twenty-five windows and upwards.

The principal objection to all such taxes is their inequality, an inequality of the worst kind, as they must frequently fall much heavier upon the poor than upon the rich. A house of ten pounds rent in a country town may sometimes have more windows than a house of five hundred pounds rent in London; and though the inhabitant of the former is likely to be a much poorer man than that of the latter, yet so far as his contribution is regulated by the window-tax, he must contribute more to the support of the state. (Emphasis added)

In Eighteenth Century England, the fact that tax collectors could enter one's home to count the hearths was considered such an "odious visit" that the tax was abolished as "a badge of slavery." If such a visit was a "badge of slavery, " how much more odious is a visit today from the IRS to search a taxpayer's papers, books, and private records — in clear violation of the Fourth Amendment — and to make them prove every expenditure?

In the final analysis, for any government to tax *directly*, it must first find the individual in order to tax him/her — regardless of what yardstick (wealth, income, rank, occupation, etc.) is used. Governments, however, have discovered another way to tax individuals without having to catch them, or without even knowing they exist which leads us to the other category of taxes provided for in the Constitution.

Indirect Taxes

Since individuals use a variety of products, governments have discovered another, easier way to levy taxes — by putting taxes on the products they buy. The more a person buys, the more taxes he pays. Such taxes are not paid *directly* to the government; they are paid *indirectly* through the merchants who sell the products. Indirect taxes are relatively easy to levy and collect and are placed on products as they are produced within a country or imported. The manufacturer or importer pays such "excises" or "duties" and adds them to the price of the product, thus passing the tax on to the consumer.

An important distinction between indirect taxes and capitation (direct) taxes is that indirect taxes are avoidable. If the individual does not buy the taxed products he avoids paying the taxes imposed. Capitation taxes, on the other hand, are not avoidable since they are levied *directly* on the individual. Since direct taxes are not avoidable they are subject to far greater tyrannical abuse than indirect taxes — which is why the Constitution makes them subject to special conditions not applicable to indirect taxes.

The following passage from *The Wealth of Nations* will provide a clear understanding of the meaning of indirect taxes as understood by those who wrote our Constitution.

> The impossibility of taxing the people, *in proportion to their revenue, by any capitation,* seems to have given occasion to the invention of taxes upon *consumable commodities.* The state not knowing how *to tax, directly and proportionably, the revenue of its subjects,* endeavours to tax it *indirectly by taxing their expence,* which, it is supposed, will in most cases be nearly in proportion to their revenue. Their expence is taxed by taxing the consumable commodities upon which it is laid out. (Emphasis added)

Note that Smith makes as clear a distinction as can be made that taxing people "in proportion to their revenue" is clearly a type of capitation tax as opposed to the taxes on "consumable commodities" which obviously fall into the category of indirect (excise) taxes. Here his statement clearly proves that the numerous claims by U.S. judges that "income" taxes are not capitation taxes (falling, rather, within the category of excise taxes) have been a cynical perversion of logic and law.

Government Now Fools The Public

It is crucial that the American public *rediscover* the distinction between direct and indirect taxes because the Constitution lays down different provisions regarding how each is to be lawfully levied. The Federal government (with the help of a perfidious Federal judiciary) now *completely disregards* these constitutional distinctions and is, therefore, able to collect taxes in a blatantly illegal manner.

2

Constitutional Restrictions Regarding Direct And Indirect Taxes

The Constitutional provision regarding how indirect taxes are to be levied is found in Article 1, Section 8, Clause 1, of the Constitution and also defines the Federal government's general taxing powers:

> . . . Congress shall have the power to lay and collect *taxes, duties, imposts,* and *excises,* to pay the debts and provide for the common defense and *general welfare* of the United States; but all *duties, imposts* and *excises shall be uniform throughout* the United States. . . (Emphasis added)

Note that in the first portion of this paragraph Congress is given the power to lay: a) taxes, b) duties, c) imposts and d) excises but the word "taxes" is later deliberately omitted from the requirement that all such listed taxes be "uniform throughout the United States." Only "duties, imposts and excises" were made subject to the requirement that they be uniform throughout the United States. Why? The reason the word "taxes" was specifically omitted from the latter phrase, is because the Constitution already provided (in Article 1, Section 2) for a different method of levying "taxes" which, in colonial times, generally meant *direct* taxes. So Article 1, Section 8 only sought to establish a constitutional method for levying "duties," "imposts," and "excises," all of which are indirect taxes, since other sections of the Constitution provided the legal basis by which direct taxes were to be levied.

So, for excises, imposts and duties to be constitutional, they have to be levied on the basis of uniformity, while direct taxes must be levied according to another standard. Uniformity means that if the government levies a tax of 10¢ on a pack of cigarettes, the tax must apply equally to cigarettes manufactured in every state. It would be unconstitutional for the government to levy an excise or duty on a product in one state but exclude certain manufacturers or importers in other states from the same duty or tax. The government, however, can discriminate *between* products when imposing excises and import duties. It can tax one product and not another, or one type of manufacturer and not another. As long as all similar manufacturers and similar products are equally taxed in all states, the tax is uniform and, therefore, constitutional.

Direct Taxes Are To Be Apportioned

Article 1, Section 2, Clause 3 of the Constitution says:

> . . . Representatives and *direct* taxes shall be apportioned among the several States which may be included within this Union, according to their respective numbers. . . (Emphasis added)

This requirement of apportionment of direct taxes is repeated in Article 1, Section 9, Clause 4 as follows:

> . . . No *capitation,* or other *direct* tax shall be laid unless in proportion to the *census* or enumeration herein before directed to be taken. (Emphasis added)

The "herein before directed to be taken" refers to the prior reference contained in Article 1, Section 2, Clause 3.

Though not dealing directly with taxation, The Bill of Rights further protected citizens from the arbitrary use of taxing power. For example, the Fourth Amendment guaranteed that the right of the people to be "secure in their persons, houses, *papers and effects* . . . shall not be violated" and that any searches and seizures must be supported by "oath or affirmation" and be court ordered only "upon probable cause." And the Fifth Amendment guaranteed that: ". . . no person shall be held to answer" for an infamous[1] crime "unless on a presentment or *indictment of a Grand Jury* . . . nor shall he be compelled in any criminal case to be *a witness against himself,* nor be *deprived of* life, liberty, or *property without due process of law,* nor shall private property be taken for public use without just compensation." (Emphasis added in both quotes.) Today these constitutional guarantees are totally ignored by the "courts" and the IRS. Individuals are put to trial for tax "crimes" without indictments and without *any* probable cause being established; are jailed for refusing to turn over "papers and effects" to the IRS and

---

[1] The Supreme Court has ruled that an "infamous crime" is one punishable by imprisonment. *Ex parte Wilson* 114 US 417, *Mackin vs US* 117 US 348.

for refusing (in tax matters) to be "witnesses against themselves"; and are routinely deprived of property without "due process of law."

You will note that the Founding Fathers, unlike Smith, drew a distinction between capitation taxes and all other direct taxes. This was because they regarded capitation taxes as direct taxes levied specifically *on people* (and therefore particularly abhorrent because they could be levied arbitrarily), as opposed to other forms of direct taxes levied on property (both real and personal). In either case, people pay the tax directly to the government and, as such, both are (by definition) direct taxes. Therefore, though (in a constitutional sense) a capitation is a direct tax, not all direct taxes are capitations.

Apportionment

The requirement of apportionment of direct taxes is the only provision in the Constitution stated *twice*. It was written into the Constitution only after extensive debate and probably represents the most important compromise of the entire Constitutional Convention, and their inclusion most likely created more controversy and debate at the state ratifying conventions than any other provision. No less than five states recommended in their ratifying statements that these two provisions should be removed and the Federal government's direct taxing power be eliminated entirely. Yet today these two provisions (though their force is still as undiminished and binding as the day they were written) are totally ignored by the U.S. government — as if the limitations imposed upon the government by them did not exist at all!

In contrast to excises, imposts, and duties (indirect taxes), the Constitution requires that all *capitation* and other *direct taxes* be "apportioned among the states" (according to population) as opposed to the principle of *uniformity*. This means that for a Federal direct tax to be lawful it must be levied so that the total tax collected from the residents of each state must be proportional to each state's population (in that the amount collected from each state must bear the same proportion to the total tax as that state's population bears to the nation's total population). If any Federal direct tax is not levied in this manner it is unconstitutional and, therefore, illegal!

How Apportionment Works

The state of Arkansas has a population roughly equivalent to 1% of the nation so its citizens must (constitutionally) pay 1% of any direct tax imposed by the Federal government. If the Federal government imposes a direct tax (based on "income," for example) of $100 billion, the citizens of Arkansas must (collectively) pay $1 billion of that tax.

Californians, on the other hand, constitute 10% of the nation and would, therefore, have to (collectively) pay $10 billion of such a tax. As you see, another important distinction between direct and indirect taxes is that before direct taxes can be lawfully extracted (on a compulsory basis) the *total amount* to be extracted must be exactly *determined beforehand* so that the correct apportionment can be made. The amount to be collected by indirect taxes, on the other hand, does not have to be predetermined but can be imposed to *generate whatever revenue they can bring in*.

Based on the 1970 census, California had forty-three representatives in Congress and Arkansas had four. Californians would, therefore, have to pay ten times as much of any direct Federal tax as do the people of Arkansas. If they did this they would be paying the tax in direct proportion to their representation in Congress (as required by Article 1, Section 2, Clause 3 of the United States Constitution). As I stated previously, if any Federal direct tax is not imposed in this specific manner, it is imposed unconstitutionally and no American need take any notice of it.[2] Since the concept of apportionment is so crucial for an understanding of the Federal government's *legitimate* taxing powers (and since this principle is practically unknown today — *let alone understood*), we should nail it down even further.

If two states have the same population then citizens of both states have to *(collectively)* pay *the same total amount of any* direct Federal tax. If the tax concerned property (the Federal government *can* tax property, see Chapter 6), and if State A had half the amount of taxable property as did State B, the Federal property tax rate in State A would have to be *twice as high* as that in State B in order for both states to generate the same total Federal property tax. If the tax concerned "income" — and the citizens of State A have half the taxable income as those of State B — then the Federal income tax rates in State A have to be *twice as high* as those in State B in order, again, for both states to generate the same total "income" tax revenue. On the basis of population, since both states are represented equally in Congress, both states have to pay the same (equal) amount of any direct tax, making taxation and representation directly proportional — on a state-to-state basis![3]

---

[2] A fundamental principle of American law is "...anything repugnant to the Constitution is null and void..." This principle was laid down by John Marshall in *Marbury vs Madison* 1CR 137, and means that all citizens are free to disregard all Federal "laws" promulgated in obvious disregard of the Constitution. Such "laws" are, in reality, not laws at all but are born dead.

[3] A state's taxing power, for example, is not limited by any such consideration, though no state can lawfully compel payment of state income taxes for a variety of *other* reasons!

A Compulsory Income Tax Must Be Related To State Population

Since the income tax is currently levied as a direct tax it must be based on state population. Since it is not, the tax is collected in a totally unconstitutional manner. When direct taxation was linked to state population and representation in Congress, a fundamental principle of the American Revolution ("taxation without representation is tyranny") was preserved and consciously incorporated into the U.S. Constitution. The Federal government, however, illegally destroyed this principle and that linkage (when it realized that the American public did not understand, nor was even aware of it) and, in so doing, completely destroyed the "federal" character of the American Republic. Tying direct taxation to state representation is, essentially, what Federalism is all about. Destroy that linkage and you no longer have a Federal republic.[4]

America — No Longer A Federal Republic

The Federal establishment succeeded in engineering this fundamental change in the nature of our country with the help of a lawless Federal judiciary[5] that is itself a part of that establishment. Federal employees thus increased their own power by illegally converting America from what started out as a democratic, *federal republic* into what we now have, which is essentially a centralized democracy — a form of government never imagined, conceived, or contemplated by the framers of the Constitution. Such a form of government was, in fact, abhorent to and feared by them (see pages 43, 44). For this reason, we should never, logically, refer to the nation's government as the "Federal" government since what we now have is a *monolithic central government* with almost no remaining constitutional checks and balances.[6]

---

[4] For a practical example of how this works, see Chapter 6.

[5] Someone once defined a judge as a lawyer who knew a governor. I believe this is accurate and helps explain the sorry state of our judicial system.

[6] To the extent that I use the term "Federal government" I do so reluctantly and only because of style and clarity. But the term itself has ceased to have any meaning.

3

The Intent Of The Constitution

To determine whether our understanding of the government's consitutional taxing powers is indeed correct, we need only refer to the published statements of those who wrote and ratified that document. One of the most authoritative works, *The Federalist Papers,* contains a collection of essays written by three of the most knowledgeable and influential men of their day: Alexander Hamilton, James Madison and John Jay. Hamilton served as our first Secretary of Treasury and was one of the most indefatigable workers on behalf of ratification. If not for the efforts and energy expended by Alexander Hamilton, the Constitution may never have been ratified. James Madison is, of course, regarded as the "Father of the Constitution" while John Jay served as the nation's first Chief Justice and presided over a number of sessions of the Constitutional Convention.

This towering triumverate combined to write *The Federalist Papers* (actually a series of essays that first appeared in New York newspapers between October, 1787 and March, 1788, written to rally public support for the proposed Constitution in a state where considerable opposition existed). New York was a crucial and influential state and if it had failed to ratify the Constitution we can only speculate as to the consequences.

The Federalist Papers (because of the depth and lucidity of their explanations and the influence of their authors) provide the best source for revealing the clear intent of those who wrote and ratified the Constitution.[1] In *Federalist Paper #21* Hamilton writes:

> There is no method of steering clear of this inconvenience, but by authorizing the national government to raise its own revenues in its own way. *Imposts, excises, and, in general, all duties upon articles of consumption,*

[1] "The opinion of the Federalist has always been considered as of great authority. It is a complete commentary on our Constitution; and is appealed to by all parties in the questions to which that instrument has given birth." *Cohens vs Virginia* 6 Wheat 2 (1821).

may be compared to a fluid, which will in time find its level with the means of paying them. The amount to be contributed by each citizen will in a degree be at his own option, and can be regulated by an attention to his resources. The rich may be extravagant, the poor can be frugal; and *private oppression may always be avoided by a judicious selection of objects proper for such impositions.* If inequalities should arise in some States from duties on particular objects, these will in all probability be counterbalanced by proportional inequalities in other States, from the duties on other objects. In the course of time and things, an equilibrium, as far as it is attainable in so complicated a subject, will be established everywhere. Or, if *inequalities* should still *exist*, they would neither be so great in their degree, so uniform in their operation, nor *so odious* in their appearance, as those which would necessarily spring from quotas upon any scale that can possibly be devised.

It is *a signal advantage of taxes on articles of consumption that they contain in their own nature a security against excess.* They prescribe their own limit, which cannot be exceeded without defeating the end proposed — that is, an extension of the revenue. When applied to this object, the saying is as just as it is witty that, "in political arithmetic, two and two do not always make four." If duties are too high, they lessen the consumption; the collection is eluded; and the product to the treasury is not so great as when they are confined within *proper* and *moderate* bounds. *This forms a complete barrier against any material oppression of the citizens by taxes of this class,* and is itself a *natural limitation* of the power of imposing them.

Impositions of this kind usually fall under the denomination of *indirect taxes*, and must for a long time constitute the chief part of the revenue raised in this country. Those of the *direct kind,* which *principally* relate to land and buildings,[2] *may admit of a rule of apportionment.* Either the value of land, or the number of the people, may serve as a standard. The state of agriculture and the populousness of a country are considered as having a near relation with each other. And, as a rule, for the purpose intended, numbers, in the view of simplicity and certainty, are entitled to a prefer-

---

[2] Here Hamilton clearly reveals that our Founding Fathers related capitation (direct) taxes "principally...to land and buildings (i.e. one's accumulated wealth). Our Founding Fathers did not even conceive of an income tax but obviously thought that any taxes other than those on consumption would be related to wealth, principally real estate. Presumably a tax on "income" is a tax on wealth though, in reality, it is not. An individual with considerable wealth could conceivably liquidate a portion of it in exchange for food, clothing and shelter. Another individual, however, with a lot less wealth might be forced to work in order to supply himself with the funds necessary to buy food, clothing and shelter. Thus, the second citizen might find himself paying more in "income" taxes than he would if a tax were directly related to wealth. This passage by Hamilton proves that our Founding Fathers believed that indirect taxes only applied to articles of consumption, while direct taxes were related to wealth. They never thought they were giving the Federal government authority to tax a citizen's "income", nor his estate at death, nor his right to transfer property during his lifetime since none of these taxes (i.e. income, estate and gift) relate to consumption nor are they imposed equally on all property.

ence. In every country it is an *herculean task* to obtain a *valuation* of the land; in a country imperfectly settled and progressive in improvement, the difficulties are increased almost to impracticability. The expense of *an accurate valuation is, in all situations, a formidable objection.* In a branch of taxation where *no limits to the discretion of the government are to be found in the nature of the thing,* the establishment of a fixed rule, not incompatible with the end, may be attended with fewer inconveniences than to leave that discretion altogether at large. (Emphasis added)

It is clear from this passage that our Founding Fathers were far more knowledgeable about the nature of taxes than contemporary Americans who make no distinctions *whatsoever* concerning them. They understood, for example, that direct taxes were not avoidable, that they did not "prescribe their own limit," but were a "branch of taxation where no limits to the discretion of the government are to be found in the nature of the thing." This principle — which was obviously well understood by the statesmen responsible for our Constitution (which is why they included careful restrictions over the Federal government's power to levy direct taxes) — is totally foreign to the mentality of those who now dominate most of America's legislative bodies. America's current state of affairs tragically confirms the taxing principles so well understood, explained, and warned of by Hamilton in this passage.

Government Must Look To Indirect Taxation

In *Federalist Paper #12,* Hamilton uses Britain to explain why the new government must look to indirect taxes for the largest part of its revenue and why direct taxes would "yield but scanty supplies". It is also important to note that while in the former quote Hamilton suggests that direct taxes "principally relate to land and buildings", in the following passage he definitely acknowledges that direct taxes also apply to personal property. When he states "...and personal property is too precarious and invisible a fund to be laid hold of in any other way than by the imperceptible agency of taxes on consumption..., " he means that the only way the state could conceivably tax the money hidden away in a citizen's strong box (compatible with constitutional rights) is for the state to tax the consumable products that might be purchased with that money.

It is evident from the state of the country, from the habits of the people, from the experience we have had on the point itself that it is *impracticable to raise any very considerable sums by direct taxation.* Tax laws have in vain been multiplied; new methods to enforce the collection have in vain been tried; the public expectation has been uniformly disappointed, and the treasuries of the States have remained empty. The popular system of administration inherent in the nature of popular government, coinciding with the real scarcity of money incident to a languid and mutilated state of trade, has hitherto defeated every experiment for extensive collections, and has at length taught the different legislatures the folly of attempting them.

No person acquainted with what happens in other countries will be surprised at this circumstance. In so opulent a nation as that of Britain, where *direct taxes* from superior wealth must be much more tolerable, and from the vigor of the government, much more practicable than in America, far the greatest part of the national revenue is derived *from taxes of the indirect kind,* from imposts and from excises. Duties on imported articles form a large branch of this latter description.

In America it is evident that we must a long time depend for the means of revenue chiefly on such duties. In most parts of it excises must be confined within a narrow compass. The genius of the people will ill brook the inquisitive and peremptory spirit of excise laws. *The pockets of the farmers, on the other hand, will reluctantly yield but scanty supplies in the unwelcome shape of impositions on their houses and lands; and personal property is too precarious and invisible a fund to be laid hold of in any other way than by the imperceptible agency of taxes on consumption.* (Emphasis added)

Many Against Giving Federal Goverment Any Direct Taxing Power

Federalist Paper #30 further demonstrates how hard Hamilton had to work to persuade his contemporaries to give direct taxing powers to the new government. Many of his contemporaries argued that the new government should have powers to levy direct taxes only after requisitions had failed.

The more intelligent adversaries of the new Constitution admit the force of this reasoning; but they qualify their admission by a distinction between what they call internal and external taxation. The former they would reserve to the State governments; the latter, which they explain into commercial imposts, or rather duties on imported articles, they declare themselves willing to concede to the federal head. This distinction, however, would violate that fundamental maxim of good sense and sound policy, which dictates that every POWER ought to be proportionate to its OBJECT; and would still leave the general government in a kind of tutelage to the State governments, inconsistent with every idea of vigor or efficiency. Who can pretend that commercial imposts are, or would be, alone equal to the present and future exigencies of the Union?

Let us attend to what would be the effects of this situation in the very *first war* in which we should happen to be engaged. We will presume, for argument's sake, that the revenue arising from the impost duties answers the purposes of a provision for the public debt and of a peace establishment for the Union. Thus circumstanced, *a war breaks out.* What would be the probable conduct of the government in such an emergency? Taught by experience that proper dependence could not be placed on *the success of requisitions,* unable by *its own authority* to lay hold of *fresh resources,* and urged by considerations of national danger, would it not be driven to the expedient of diverting the funds already appropriated from their proper objects to the defense of the State? It is not easy to see how a step of this kind could be avoided; and if it should be taken, it is evident that it would prove the destruction of public credit at the very moment that it was becoming essential to the public safety. To imagine that at such a crisis credit might be dispensed with would be the extreme of infatuation. In the modern system of *war,* nations the most wealthy are obliged to have recourse to large loans. A country so little opulent as ours must feel this necessity in a much stronger degree. But *who would lend to a government* that prefaced its overtures for borrowing by an act *which demonstrated* that *no reliance* could be placed *on the steadiness of its measures for paying?* The loans it might be able to procure would be as limited in their extent as burdensome in their conditions. They would be made upon the same principles that usurers commonly lend to bankrupt and fraudulent debtors — with a sparing hand and at enormous premiums. (Emphasis added)

This would have been a logical enlargement of the taxing powers written into the Articles of Confederation. The Articles provided for the Federal government to make "requisitions" of funds from the various states, but the Federal government (under the Articles) had no recourse if the states failed to meet their requisitions.[3]

Apportionment Necessary To Keep States Honest

In *Federalist Paper #54,* Madison touches on another reason for relating direct taxation to representation. States would be less likely to inflate their population figures (to gain added political representation) since this would also increase their tax burdens if a direct tax were imposed.

---

[3] A requisition was a specific levy made by the Federal government on the states themselves with each state expected to use its own taxing power to collect the money from its own citizens and was provided for in the Articles of Confederation. The Articles, however, did not give the Federal government any independent taxing powers to collect the tax directly from individual citizens if any state ignored the "requisition". So, giving the new government direct taxing powers to be used if requisitions failed would still be a substantial grant of new taxing power over that contained in the Articles. But, is it logical (considering all the opposition to the proposed new Constitution) that those favoring it would have proposed going from a situation where the Federal government had *no independent taxing powers whatsoever* to one where it would have the seemingly unlimited power it exercises today?

In one respect, the establishment of a *common measure for representation and taxation* will have a very salutary effect. As the *accuracy of the census* to be obtained by the Congress will necessarily depend, in a considerable degree, on the disposition, if not on the co-operation of the States, it is of great importance that the States should feel as little *bias* as possible to *swell* or to *reduce the amount of their numbers*. Were their share of representation alone to be governed by this rule, they would have an interest in *exaggerating* their inhabitants. Were the rule to decide their share of taxation alone, a *contrary temptation* would prevail. By extending the rule to *both objects*, the States will have opposite interests which will control and balance each other and produce the requisite impartiality. (Emphasis added)

Therefore, another important purpose for the apportionment of direct taxes was to keep the states honest in reporting their population for the purpose of Congressional representation and to prevent poorer states from using their votes in Congress to simply drain wealth away from richer states. This they could accomplish by passing taxing bills that would allow their constituents to escape their proportional burden of the tax![4] This, of course, is exactly what has been happening — poorer western and southern states used their disproportionate Congressional power to drain wealth away from richer northern states. Our Founding Fathers put the apportionment provisions into the Constitution to insure that this would not happen — that taxation and representation would go hand-in-hand (regardless of wealth) and that Federal taxation could never be used to redistribute the nation's wealth. But this is *precisely* how income, estate, and gift taxes are being used today. As a result, the entire country — North and South, rich and poor — is suffering the economic consequences of such an unconstitutional practice.[5]

---

[4] To see how this was ultimately accomplished, see the words of Representative Hill on page 176.

[5] For additional historical references and supporting documentation regarding the constitutional meaning of direct and indirect taxes, see Appendix C.

4

The Federal Government's General Taxing Powers

Up to now we have examined the Federal government's specific constitutional taxing powers. Let us now examine its overall, legitimate taxing powers.

The people turned over general taxing power to the new government so it could achieve certain specific national objectives spelled out in Article 1, Section 8, Clause 1 of the Constitution (see Chapter 2) which limits the U.S. government's use of taxes to three specific areas. The U.S. government can levy taxes:

1. to pay the debts of the United States;
2. to provide for the common defense of the United States; and
3. to provide for the general welfare of the United States.

Note that the first limitation on the government's taxing powers is that it can only tax Americans to pay "the debts of the United States." It obviously has no constitutional authority to tax Americans to pay anyone else's debts such as those of U.S. corporations (i.e. Chrysler), or of individuals (i.e. FHA mortgage or college loan guarantees), or the debts of individual states, and certainly not those of foreign countries (i.e. the interest on Polish Bonds owed to U.S. banks which was paid by the U.S. government). Government can only *lawfully* tax Americans to pay *the debts of the United States.*

The U.S. Constitution simply does not authorize the U.S. government to tax Americans for anything and everything that vote-seeking politicians and free-spending Washington lobbyists want them to pay for. The debts of private citizens and corporations as well as the debts of individual states and foreign governments are not the debts of the United States, and the U.S. Constitution does not give the U.S. government any authority to tax working Americans to pay for such things. All such payments are illegal and a blatant abuse by the U.S. government of its taxing powers.

U.S. Government Not Authorized to Lend Money

This constitutional restriction (allowing the U.S. government to tax Americans only to pay the debts of the United States) is further complemented by another constitutional provision contained in Article 1, Section 8, Clause 2 of the Constitution which states "Congress shall have the power. . . to borrow money on the credit of The United States." Notice that the Constitution specifically authorizes the Federal government to borrow money, but nowhere does it allow the Federal government to *lend* money, or to guarantee private or corporate loans or the debts of individual states.

The Constitution also does not allow the U.S. government to tax working Americans for funds to give to a World Bank or an Export-Import Bank to use to finance private, commercial transactions and the grandiose schemes of foreign governments. The U.S. Constitution provides no such grant of power (either express or implied) so all Federal taxes levied for such "banking" purposes obviously represent a clear-cut usurpation of power by the Federal government and are totally illegal and Americans need not submit to it according to *Marbury vs. Madison* 1 Cr. 137.

Taxes For The Defense "Of The United States"

The Constitution next grants the Federal government the power to tax Americans "to provide for the common defense of the United States." Those, therefore, who refuse to pay income taxes because they object to this or that war or because they believe that too much of the nation's budget goes for armaments are on untenable ground. The Federal government has the constitutional authority to tax for these purposes. One might object to such expenditures as wasteful or even stupid and ill- advised but, at least, they are constitutional! Whether such expenditures are *proper* is a political question that should be resolved at the ballot box. Americans, however, have no lawful basis for not paying income taxes because they do not like political decisions. It is one thing not to pay income taxes because the law itself does not require it or because the levy is unconstitutional. It is another thing not to pay income taxes because one simply disapproves of the nature or amount of constitutional expenditures.

Americans Not Required to Pay Taxes for Unconstitutional Purposes

It makes greater legal sense for such individuals to stop paying U.S. income taxes because such taxes are raised unconstitutionally for unconstitutional purposes since Americans are legally free to refuse to pay taxes for purposes not authorized by the Constitution. Ironically, those Americans who have refused to pay U.S. taxes because of antipathy to military spending have generally been enthusiastic supporters of government subsidies to private individuals (euphemistically called "social programs") — thereby supporting *illegal* government expenditures and objecting to legal ones.

What is the "Defense of the United States"?

There are circumstances when what constitutes "the defense of the United States" can be open to question or interpretation. Can the U.S., for example, tax Americans for the defense of some foreign country? The answer to that is obviously no. However, if the defense of that foreign country is related to the defense of America or for the protection of America's vital interests, then the answer is yes. What should be noted, though, is that in this instance it is not the law that is being "interpreted" but the facts as they apply to the law. The facts can be open to "interpretation" but the law itself must be clear or it is not even law! Every freshman law student knows of the legal principle "void for vagueness" which means that if a law is vague (i.e. open to varied interpretation) "it must be void." If laws (including the Constitution) had to be "interpreted" then those laws (and the Constitution) would be "void for vagueness." The legal profession is continually misleading the public about the court's alleged authority to "interpret" the law. [1] Any such "authority" is nonsense.

The General Welfare

It is, however, a total perversion of this last provision that has enabled the U.S. government to escape every restraint placed upon it by the Constitution. The government — and supporters of more government — have completely misled the public concerning the meaning of the "general welfare" clause of the Constitution. This has enabled the government to invade all areas it wishes to, regardless of what the Constitution has to say about it.

This provision should make clear, however, that the "welfare" intended is the "general welfare" of the nation *as a whole* and not the "welfare" of *specific* individuals, *specific* companies, or *specific* segments of society no matter how deserving those individuals, companies or segments of society might be.

[1] For a fuller discussion of such "interpretation," see *How Anyone Can Stop Paying Income Taxes,* pages 148–151.

If the United States, for example, builds a foreign embassy, such an expenditure is obviously for the benefit of all Americans. If the government launches a weather satellite, presumably it is for the benefit of all Americans (though some might benefit more than others from the increased accuracy of weather forecasting). Such expenditures would be constitutionally lawful since they are made for the "general welfare" of all the people.

When the U.S. government (through taxation) takes money away from some and hands it over to others (disguised as "subsidies," "grants," "rent supplements," etc.), such activities are not to "promote the general welfare of the United States" but rather for the *specific* welfare of some at the expense of others. Of course, such expenditures do promote the welfare of many politicians (and the U.S. bureaucracy) who gain public office by promising to provide benefits (literally stealing the property of some in order to buy votes from others) under the guise of promoting the "general welfare." Not only are such payments not authorized by the Constitution, they also obviously violate the equal protection clause of that document.

If it is sophistically argued that such "grants," "subsidies," "supplements," etc. are indeed for the "general welfare of the United States" (when such is obviously not the case) it is because it is *possible* to argue or attempt to justify *just about anything!* Spanish inquisitors argued that burning people at the stake saved their souls and was thus in their best interest. All attempts to rationalize farm subsidies and other "entitlement" payments as being for the "general welfare of the United States" fall into this category.

When farm subsidies (paying grown men not to produce) were first introduced it was argued that without such subsidies small farmers would go under, leaving fewer farmers who would then be free to raise farm prices. The hypocrisy of the farm subsidy argument was revealed when Congress refused to end tobacco subsidies. Congressmen in favor of this subsidy argued that eliminating it would force tobacco farmers to grow *more tobacco* (to make up for the lost subsidy) causing tobacco and cigarette prices to fall which, in turn, would encourage more smokers (cigarettes now being cheaper) and thus cause even more cancer in the long run! Therefore, those lobbying for the continuation of tobacco subsidies argued *exactly opposite* to those who had proposed agricultural subsidies in the first place — and Congress bought their argument, too!

So we have the spectacle of the U.S. government spending millions on tobacco subsidies and millions trying to persuade Americans *not to use* the product they are taxed to subsidize. Presumably, subsidizing the spread of cancer is in "the general welfare of the United States!"

To further demonstrate the utter hypocrisy and illegality of such government payments and subsidies, the Supreme Court recently ruled that the Federal government could actually confiscate the home of a Dallas woman to satisfy alleged taxes owed by her late husband though her home was presumably protected by Texas homesteading laws. I get routine calls from individuals telling me that the IRS is trying to seize their homes in payment of back taxes. On the other hand, the Federal government purchased homes for the residents of Love Canal and provides rent subsidies to millions more. So here we have the U.S. government taking homes away from some in order to provide homes and rent supplements for others — all in the guise of doing it for the "general welfare." Such government activity not only violates the taxing power and equal protection clauses of the Constitution, it also violates all logic, decency, and common sense.

The government has literally forced businesses to close because of IRS liens for back taxes. It also routinely lends money to other businesses (either to expand or to provide start-up capital). Can it be lawful or logical for the government to be able to tax some businesses out of existence in order to get the funds to launch or expand the businesses of others?

A Land of Serfs

When the Constitution was written, serfdom still existed in parts of Europe. It existed in Russia until 1861 and continued within the Hapsburg monarchy as late as 1781. Serfdom was a state of half-freedom with serfs owing the "lord and master" approximately 25 percent of their productivity. Taxation also existed in Europe, but tax paying Europeans were hardly serfs and it was certainly not the intent of America's Founding Fathers to establish serfdom in America under the tutelage of the Federal government. What was the nature of taxation in Europe when Americans gave the government the power to levy direct taxes? Insight into this subject can be found in Smith's *The Wealth of Nations:*

> *In all countries a severe inquisition* into the circumstances of *private persons* has been carefully *avoided.*[2]

> At Hamburgh every inhabitant is obliged to pay to the state, one-fourth per cent. of all that he possesses; and as the wealth of the people of Hamburgh consists principally in stock, this tax may be considered as a tax upon stock. Every man *assesses himself*[3] and, in the presence of the magistrate, puts annually into the public coffer a certain sum of money,

[2] Not so in America!

[3] See *How Anyone Can Stop Paying Income Taxes,* pages 13, 14 and 107.

which he *declares upon oath* to be one-fourth per cent. of all that he possesses, but without declaring what it amounts to, or being *liable to any examination upon that subject*. This tax is generally supposed to be paid with great fidelity. In a small republic, where the people have entire confidence in their magistrates, are convinced of the necessity of the tax for the support of the states, and believe that it will be faithfully applied to that purpose, such conscientious and *voluntary payment*[4] may sometimes be expected. It is not peculiar to the people of Hamburgh. (Emphasis added)

Incredibly, this is how America's current income tax system is also supposed to operate — on the basis of "voluntary payment" and "self-assessment." But most Americans do not know this. The current Internal Revenue Code only allows American citizens to assess themselves and gives the IRS no authority to do so if citizens refuse (see pages 256, 257). Of course the IRS (with the protection of U.S. courts) violates both the law and the principle of self-assessment and collects taxes on the basis of fraudulent and illegal assessments which the government has no authority to make. The IRS then proceeds to enforce payment by deceit, intimidation and extortion — all under the protection of the U.S. Department of Justice and both Federal and States courts!

Note that the good citizens of Hamburgh "volunteered" (*under oath*) as to what they owed. Note further that they were "not liable to any examination upon that subject." Their sworn statements were considered good enough! Not so for 20th century Americans. Like so many robots, Americans line up and swear *under penalty of perjury* what they believe (incorrectly) they owe and then submit to exhaustive tax audits, thereby surrendering both 4th and 5th Amendment rights, which expose them to possible prosecution and conviction for tax evasion if their sworn statements are shown to be incorrect! If the U.S. government (as even 19th century Hamburghers must have known) is not going to accept a sworn statement as correct, why bother giving one in the first place?

It is obvious that 20th century Americans (despite all their apparent schooling) do not possess the understanding shown by 19th century Hamburghers. The tax paid by those good citizens of Hamburgh constituted only one quarter of one percent of their assets. Thus a citizen worth $100,000 need only have paid $250. Such citizens could afford to be honest!

---

[4] See Chapter 1 ("Surprise! The Income Tax Is Voluntary!") of *How Anyone Can Stop Paying Income Taxes* and pages 242–244 of this book.

How High Should Direct Taxes Be?

The Wealth of Nations, which deeply influenced America's Founding Fathers, comments thusly:

> In Holland, soon after the exaltation of the late prince of Orange to the stadtholdership, a tax of *two per cent.* or the fiftieth penny, as it was called, was imposed upon the whole substance of every citizen. Every citizen *assessed himself* and paid his tax *in the same manner as at Hamburgh;* and it was in general supposed to have been paid with great fidelity. The people had at that time the greatest affection for their new government, which they had just established by a general insurrection. The tax was to be paid but *once;* in order to relieve the state in a particular exigency. It was, indeed, *too heavy to be permanent.* In a country where the market rate of interest seldom exceeds three per cent. a tax of two per cent. amounts to thirteen shillings and fourpence in the pound upon the highest neat revenue which is commonly drawn from stock. It is a tax which very few people could pay without encroaching more or less upon their capitals. In a particular *exigency* the people may, from great public zeal, make a great effort, and give up even *a part of their capital, in order to relieve the state. But it is impossible that they should continue to do so for any considerable time; and if they did, the tax would soon ruin them so completely as to render them altogether incapable of supporting the state.* (Emphasis added)

A tax of 2 percent on capital was believed by Smith to be "too heavy to be permanent." Moreover, a tax of $2,000 paid by an individual worth $100,000 was believed to be so heavy a tax burden that it could not continue "for any considerable time" and would "ruin taxpayers so completely as to render them altogether incapable of supporting the state." This, of course, is exactly what is happening to America today. Smith believed a tax of $2,000 paid by a person with $100,000 was too severe to be permanent, yet many Americans today pay $5,000 in income taxes when they do not have $15,000 to their name. That's more than one-third of their worth! Some people actually have to borrow money in order to pay income taxes.

When the framers of the Constitution thought of direct taxes (as opposed to "duties," "imposts," and "excises") they were obviously thinking of a direct tax that might take from one quarter to perhaps two percent of an individual's capital. They certainly did not envision a type of direct tax that would take away more from Americans than what was taken from serfs by their lord and master — or more than the total wealth they possessed!

U.S. Government Now Presumes to Own All Private Wealth

From time to time the U.S. government releases studies purporting to show how much revenue it loses because of certain tax exemptions and deductions. These studies invariably show how much the government (theoretically) "loses" because of interest, medical or charitable deductions, personal exemptions, etc. All such studies reflect the thinking that any money the government does not *take* in taxes it has theoretically *lost*! In essence, this philosophy reflects the thinking that any money taxpayers get to keep for themselves has somehow been given to them by a *charitable* government. Such reasoning could justify requiring citizens to send in all their money to the government — with the government returning whatever it thinks the citizen deserves.

Sadly, our nation has arrived at a situation where (despite Constitutional safeguards to the contrary) working Americans are held in a form of feudal bondage by the U.S. government for the benefit of an illegal, parasitic, Washington-based, bureaucratic complex.[5]

[5]Indeed, the Federal government has literally established a "slave state," see page 389.

5

What The U.S. Government And America Are All About

The U.S. government was created by people who did not, for a moment, believe they were creating a "new" government capable of destroying the sovereignty of the states and/or capable of intruding into practically every facet of a citizen's private life as the U.S. government now does. Such an undertaking was the farthest thing from their minds. Indeed, had they thought this possibility existed, the Constitution never would have been adopted at all. They believed they were creating a new government primarily to attend to the external affairs and needs of the thirteen states (and those destined to follow) and for a few important, *but limited,* internal matters. The problem facing them was how to give the new government enough power to accomplish these goals without making it so powerful that it could intrude and interfere with each state's sovereignty and the private lives of individuals. This presented a difficult problem and the document that emerged to solve it was the Constitution.

In preparing the Constitution our Founding Fathers studied the various forms of government that had, from time to time, flourished on this planet: the Cantons of Switzerland, the German Confederation, the Italian city-state, the Roman republic, and the Ionian League to name only a few. They sought to protect the American public from the problems, mistakes, and dangers they perceived in these and other forms of government. They also understood the power of demogogues and the danger of mob rule with which they associated "democracy" and they sought to protect America from this as well. Incidentally, Americans are now taught to believe that America is a "democracy." Such a belief, however, is false. America was created as a *democratic republic,* and tragically most Americans do not have the slightest idea of what that term means or how it differs from a "democracy." The following excerpts from *Federalist Paper #10,* written by James Madison, reveal why the Founding Fathers never intended to create a democracy. They also reveal the level of insight, understanding, and sense of justice that existed among those who established our great Republic and the wide gulf that separates them from the charlatans who now run it. Such insights and concerns as expressed by Madison are totally foreign to the thinking of America's present-day legislators, while most of the barriers carefully thought out and erected by our Founding Fathers to protect the public and minority factions from the evils referred to by Madison, have long since been removed.

AMONG the numerous advantages promised by a well-constructed Union, none deserves to be more accurately developed than its tendency to break and control the violence of faction. The friend of popular governments never finds himself so much alarmed for their character and fate as when he contemplates their propensity to this dangerous vice. He will not fail, therefore, to set a due value on any plan which, without violating the principles to which he is attached, provides a proper cure for it. The *instability, injustice, and confusion introduced into the public councils have, in truth, been the mortal diseases under which popular governments have everywhere perished,* as they continue to be the favorite and fruitful topics from which the adversaries to liberty derive their most specious declamations. The valuable *improvements* made by the American constitutions on the popular models, *both ancient and modern,* cannot certainly be too much admired; but it would be an unwarrantable partiality to contend that they have as effectually obviated the danger on this side, as was wished and expected. Complaints are everywhere heard from our most considerate and virtuous citizens, equally the friends of public and private faith and of public and personal liberty, that our governments are too unstable, that the public good is disregarded in the conflicts of rival parties, and that measures are too often decided, not according to the rules of justice and the rights of the minor party, but by the superior force of an interested and overbearing majority. However anxiously we may wish that these complaints had no foundation, the evidence of known facts will not permit us to deny that they are in some degree true. It will be found, indeed, on a candid review of our situation, that some of the distresses under which we labor have been erroneously charged on the operation of our governments; but it will be found, at the same time, that other, causes will not alone account for many of our heaviest misfortunes; and, particularly, for that prevailing and increasing distrust of public engagements and alarm for private rights which are echoed from one end of the continent to the other. . .

The latent *causes of faction* are thus sown in the nature of man; and we see them everywhere brought into different degrees of activity, according to the different circumstances of civil society. A zeal for different opinions concerning religion, concerning government, and many other points, as well of speculation as of practice; an attachment to different leaders ambitiously contending for pre-eminence and power; or to persons of other descriptions whose fortunes have been interesting to the human passions, have, in turn, divided man kind into parties, inflamed them with mutual animosity, and rendered them much more disposed to vex and oppress each other than to co-operate for their common good. So strong is this propensity of mankind to fall into mutual animosities that where no substantial occasion presents itself the most frivolous and fanciful distinctions have been sufficient to kindle their unfriendly passions and excite their most violent conflicts. *But the most common and durable source of factions has been the verious and unequal distribution of property.* Those who hold and those who are without property have ever formed *distinct interests to society. Those who are creditors, and those who are debtors, fall under a like discrimination. A landed interest, a manufacturing interest, a mercantile interest, a moneyed interest, with many lesser interests, grow up of necessity in civilized nations, and divide them into different classes, actuated by different sentiments and views.* The *regulation* of these *various and interfering interests forms the principal task of modern legislation* and involves the spirit of party and faction in the necessary and ordinary operations of government.

No man is allowed to be a judge in his own cause, because his interest would certainly bias his judgment, and not improbably, corrupt his integrity. With equal, nay with greater reason, a body of men are *unfit to be both judges and parties at the same time;* yet what are many of the *most important acts of legislation* but so many judicial determinations, not indeed concerning the rights of single persons, but concerning the rights of large bodies of citizens? *And what are the different classes of legislators but advocates and parties to the causes which they determine?* Is a law proposed concerning private debts? It is a question to which the creditors are parties on one side and the debtors on the other. *Justice ought to hold the balance between them.* Yet the parties are, and must be, themselves the judges; and the most numerous party, or in other words, the most powerful faction must be expected to prevail. Shall domestic manufacturers be encouraged, and in what degree, by restrictions on foreign manufacturers? are questions which would be differently decided by the landed and the manufacturing classes, and probably by neither with a sole regard to justice and the public good. *The apportionment of taxes on the various descriptions of property is an act which seems to require the most exact impartiality; yet there is, perhaps, no legislative act in which greater opportunity and temptation are given to a predominant party to trample on the rules of justice. Every shilling with which they overburden the inferior number is a shilling saved to their own pockets.*

It is in vain to say that enlightened statesmen will be able to adjust these clashing interests and render them all subservient to the public good. Enlightened statesmen will not always be at the helm. Nor, in many cases, can such an adjustment be made at all without taking into view indirect and remote considerations, which will rarely prevail over the immediate interest which one party may find in disregarding the rights of another or the good of the whole.

The inference to which we are brought is that the causes of faction cannot be removed and that relief is only to be sought in the means of controlling it effects.

If a faction consists of less than a majority, *relief is supplied by the republican principle,* which enables the majority to defeat its sinister views by regular vote. It may clog the administration, it may convulse the society; but it will be unable to execute and mask its violence under the forms of the Constitution. *When a majority is included in a faction, the form of popular government, on the other hand, enables it to sacrifice to its ruling passion or interest both the public good and the rights of other citizens. To secure the public good and private rights against the danger of such a faction, and at the same time to preserve the spirit and the form of popular government, is then the great object to which our inquiries are directed.* Let me add that it is the great desideratum by which alone this form of government can be rescued from the opprobrium under which it has so long labored and be recommended to the esteem and adoption of mankind.

By what means is this object attainable? Evidently by one of two only. Either the existence of the same *passion or interest in a majority at the same time must be prevented,* or the *majority,* having such coexistent passion or interest, *must be rendered, by their number and local situation, unable to concert and carry into effect schemes of oppression.* If the impulse and the opportunity be suffered to coincide, we well know that neither moral nor religious motives can be relied on as an adequate control. . .

. . . From this view of the subject it may be concluded that a pure *democracy,* by which I mean a society consisting of a small number of citizens, who assemble and administer the government in person, *can admit of no cure for the mischiefs of faction.* A common passion or interest will, in almost every case, be felt by a majority of the whole; a communication and concert results from the form of government itself; and there is nothing to check the inducements to sacrifice the weaker party or an obnoxious individual. Hence it is that such *democracies have ever been spectacles of turbulence and contention; have ever been found incompatible with personal security or the rights of property; and have in general been as short in their lives as they have been violent in their deaths.* Theoretic politicians, who have patronized this species of government, have *erroneously* supposed that by *reducing mankind to a perfect equality in their political rights,* they would at the same time be perfectly *equalized* and assimilated in their possessions, their *opinions,* and their *passions.*

A *republic,* by which I mean a government in which the scheme of representation takes place, opens a *different prospect and promises the cure for which we are seeking.* Let us examine the points in which it varies from *pure democracy,* and we shall comprehend both the nature of the cure and the efficacy which it must derive from the union.

The two great points of difference between a democracy and a republic are: first, the delegation of the government, in the latter, to a small number of citizens elected by the rest; secondly, the greater number of citizens and greater sphere of country over which the latter may be extended.

The effect of the first difference is, on the one hand, to *refine* and enlarge *the public views by passing them through the medium of a chosen body of citizens, whose wisdom may best discern the true interest of their country* and whose *patriotism* and *love of justice* will be *least likely to sacrifice it to temporary or partial considerations*. Under such a regulation it may well happen that the public voice, pronounced by the representatives of the people, will be *more* consonant to the pubic good than *if pronounced by the people themselves*, convened for the purpose. . .[1]

. . . It must be confessed that in this, as in most other cases, there is a mean, on both sides of which incoveniencies will be found to lie. By enlarging too much the number of electors, you render the representative too little acquainted with all their local circumstances and lesser interests; as by reducing it too much, you render him unduly attached to these, and too little fit to comprehend and pursue great and national objects. The federal Constitution forms a happy combination in this respect; the great and aggregate interests being referred to the national, the local and particular to the State legislatures.

The other point of difference is the greater number of citizens and extent of territory which may be brought within the compass of *republican* than of *democratic* government; and it is this circumstance principally which renders factious combinations *less to be dreaded in the former than in the latter*. . .

. . . Hence, it clearly appears that the same **advantage which a republic has over a democracy in controlling the effects of faction** is enjoyed by a large over a small republic — is enjoyed by the Union over the States composing it. Does this advantage consist in the substitution of representatives whose enlightened views and virtuous sentiments render them superior to local prejudices and to schemes of injustice? It will not be denied that the representation of the Union will be most likely to possess these requisite endowments. Does it consist in the greater security afforded by a greater variety of parties, against the event of any one party being able to outnumber and oppress the rest? In an equal degree does the increased variety of parties comprised within the Union increase this security. Does it, in fine, consist in the greater obstacles opposed to the concert and accomplishment of the *secret wishes of an unjust and interested majority?* Here again the extent of the Union gives it the most palpable advantage.

---

[1] Thus Congressional representatives are not supposed to vote in the way even a majority of their constituents want them to. They are supposed to be smarter and more knowledgeable than those they represent. Yet some Congressmen make a big thing out of polling their constituents (seeking their views) prior to voting on an issue.

The influence of *factious* leaders may kindle a flame within their particular States but will be *unable to spread* a general conflagration through
the other States. A religious sect may degenerate into a political faction in
a part of the Confederacy; but the variety of sects dispersed over the entire
face of it must secure the national councils against any danger from that
source. *A rage for paper money, for an abolition of debts, for an*
equal division of property, or for any other improper or wicked
project will be less apt to pervade the whole body of the Union than a particular member of it, in the same proportion as such a malady is more
likely to taint a particular county or district than an entire State. [2]

In the extent and proper structure of the Union, therefore, we behold
a *republican* remedy for the diseases most incident to *republican* government. And according to the degree of pleasure and pride we feel in being
republicans ought to be our zeal in cherishing the spirit and supporting
the character of federalists. (Emphasis added)

In the final analysis, our Founding Fathers viewed government as
a protection from bullies and other forms of social and political predators (both foreign and domestic) that would interfere with their liberty
and pursuit of happiness as they viewed it. It should also be noted that
the American Revolution was the only revolution where the revolution-
ists did not seek any property or favors for themselves but only sought
their own personal freedom as compared to, for example, the Russian or
Cuban revolutions.

America Is Different

Americans today have no concept of what makes America different
from all other countries. In Europe, for instance, through century after
century, kings and emperors ruled and commoners had practically no
rights at all. Bit by bit over the centuries, though, Europeans gained
the rights they now have (though in many European countries, even today, individual rights as we know them — such as *habeas corpus* — are
still unknown). After the American Revolution, however, Americans
had all their rights and did not have to contend with a sovereignty other
than that of their own state governments.

Unlike Europe (and most other places on earth) the U.S government did not give the people their rights — it was the other way around.
The people gave the Federal government its power, limiting it to certain
restricted areas. These restrictions are what the U.S government has

---

[2] Note that America eventually got all three of the "wicked projects" referred to by Madison: 1) paper money, 2) abolition of debt via government-created inflation and, at
times, specific legislation suspending debt payments, and 3) legislation designed to
equalize wealth via confiscatory estate, gift and income taxes.

constantly, over the years, sought to throw off. The U.S. government would like to operate like other interfering foreign governments, but *our* Constitution *forbids* it!

The Purpose Of Government In America

American politicians (along with many of our nation's "educators" and media representatives) have thoroughly misled the American public concerning the legitimate role of government in America. Government now attempts to tell us what we can and cannot eat, who we can and cannot hire, what we must pay our employees, and how we must save for our old age. And now, according to the IRS, Americans are expected to keep daily logs of how they use their automobiles and home computors to justify tax deductions. Great numbers of Americans ("factions" as Madison would say) want something for nothing, and American politicians — in exchange for votes — seek to get it for them.

But, as worthwhile as some of these projects might appear, pursuing them is simply not the legitimate role of government in America. The real role of government in America is the protection of individual rights — not the pursuit of economic or social goals. The forces of free enterprise and private social agencies (which free citizens always create) will deliver more goods faster, better, and cheaper than any collection of politicians and bureaucrats. The real problem is keeping them out of the way.

The Declaration Of Independence Defines The Role Of Government In America

A fundamental principle of American jurisprudence is "The intent of the lawmaker is the law." Since the U.S Constitution is our supreme law, the intent of the lawmakers who drew it up is, therefore, as important as the law itself. That intent is clearly and eloquently revealed in the second paragraph of the Declaration of Independence:

> We hold these Truths to be self-evident, that all Men are created equal, that they are endowed by their Creator with certain unalienable Rights, that among these are Life, Liberty, and the pursuit of Happiness — *That to secure these Rights, Governments are instituted among Men...* (Emphasis added)

So, in America, the proper role of government is to protect and "secure" our unalienable rights, not to try and provide us with all manner of economic services or to dictate how we should live or conduct our affairs (so long as we do not interfere with the rights of others).

If, however, our government's role is to protect both an individual's life and right to happiness, then it must also protect his property, since without property one can be deprived of both life and happiness.[3]

And, if individuals have an unalienable right to their property, how can the U.S government lay claim to so much of it under the guise of legitimate taxation and give it to others under various and sundry government programs such as farm subsidies, business loans, and "welfare" payments, to name only a few? It cannot. The U.S. government was not created so that politicians and bureaucrats could run our lives or the American economy.

The U.S. government was created to protect rights, period.[4] The American economy, operating on the principles of free-enterprise, was expected to do the rest. The following citations from two authoritative sources will help illustrate this. The first comes from Grover Cleveland's *Second Annual Message to Congress*, delivered in December, 1886. The second is from the Supreme Court case of *Loan Association vs. Topeka (1874)*.

> When more of the people's sustenance is exacted through the form of taxation than is necessary to meet the just obligations of *government* and expenses of its *economical administration*, such exaction becomes ruthless extortion and a violation of the fundamental principles of a free Government. (Emphasis added)

And this is what the Supreme Court had to say on the subject:

> To lay with one hand the power of the government on the property of the citizen, and with the other to bestow it on favored individuals . . .is none the less robbery because it is done under the forms of law and is called taxation.

---

[3] If one has a right to life then one surely has a right to sustain that life. But it takes food, clothing and shelter to sustain life. Without such property one could die of starvation or of the elements. So depriving an individual of his property is tantamount to depriving him of his life and right to happiness. Liberals often talk about "human" rights as somehow being superior and often opposed to "property" rights. But "property" rights *are* "human" rights – they are a human's right to his own property and it is just as sacred and important as one's right to life. If, for example, slaves on a Southern plantation had all the rights with which we are generally so concerned (such as the right of free speech, of religion, of assembly, etc.) but all their productivity still belonged to their master, what good would all their other "rights" be? The difference between a slave and a free person is that a free person owns what he produces and a slave does not.

[4] The U.S. Constitution did authorize the government to "establish post offices and post roads" but every other grant of power under the Constitution involved the protection of rights and/or the government's authority to regulate trade between the states, foreign governments or with the Indians.

Forgetting about the economic merits of free-enterprise over bureaucratic planning, what is clear is that the intent of the framers of the Constitution was to write a document that would protect an American's unalienable right to both his life and his property so he could pursue his own happiness — free of both private and public interference. Today the average working American has 60 percent of his spendable income taken to support government and its activities.[5] How can Americans pursue their own happiness when government takes away more than half of their spendable income? It was the absence of such taxes prior to World War II that accounted for America's spectacular growth and its economic superiority and moral power — both of which are now largely gone.

The U.S. Constitution

Our Founding Fathers understood and distrusted the nature of government and knew the danger of endowing it with too much power. Almost to a man each understood what the famous British historian Lord Acton was to say generations later, "The government that governs best is the government that governs least." Thomas Paine (whose pamphlet, *Common Sense,* paved the way for the Declaration of Independence) observed that "Government, even in its best state, is but a necessary evil; in its worst state, an intolerable one." And Thomas Jefferson summed up the purpose of the Constitution with these words, "In questions of power, then, let no more be heard of confidence in man, but bind him down from mischief by the chains of the Constitution."

Laws That Apply To Government

The U.S. Constitution is "...the *supreme law* of the land, and the *judges* in every state shall be *bound* thereby..." In addition, all members of Congress and all executive and judicial officers both of the United States and "of the several states, shall be bound by oath or affirmation to support this Constitution..."[6] Americans forget that this document is a body of law *directed at government, not at individuals*. It was designed to protect the people from too much government! It imposes no restraints on the people, only restraints on government.[7] These restraints

[5] See Appendix A.

[6] United States Constitution, Article 6, Clause 2, emphasis added.

[7] The problem is, how do we prosecute U.S. government law-breakers when these law-breakers have now taken over control of the courts and all Federal law enforcement activities?

and the Federal government's legitimate role is clearly and concisely explained in the following quote from James Madison, taken from *Federalist Paper #45:*

> The powers delegated by the proposed Constitution to the Federal Government are *few and defined.* Those which are to remain in the State Governments are numerous and indefinite. The former will be exercised principally on external objects as war, peace, negotiations, and foreign commerce; with which the last, the power of taxation will, for the most part, be connected. The powers reserved to the several States will extend to all the objects which, in the ordinary course of affairs, concern the lives, liberties, and properties of the people and the internal order, improvement and prosperity of the State.
>
> The operations of the Federal Government will be most extensive and important in times of war and danger; those of State Government in times of peace and security.[8] (Emphasis added)

The U.S. Government's Constitutional Taxing Powers

With respect to the government's constitutional taxing powers, the intent of the Founding Fathers can be summarized as follows:

1. Taxes paid by the public directly to government are capitation or direct taxes and fall squarely within Article 1, Sections 2 and 9 of the Constitution and must be levied on the basis of apportionment.
2. All indirect taxes apply only to articles of consumption and fall within the provisions of Article 1 Section 8 of the Constitution and must be levied on the basis of geographic uniformity.
3. It was assumed that the Federal government's direct taxing powers would be used sparingly only during emergencies (principally war) and it was *for that reason only* that the new government was even given direct taxing powers.
4. The overwhelming majority of those who wrote and ratified the Constitution were totally opposed to the idea of the Federal government having direct taxing powers, but such authority was provided solely to enable it to raise revenue in times of war.
5. Those ratifying the Constitution fully believed that the new government would finance its normal, peace-time activities solely through indirect taxes (derived from taxing items of consumption).
6. Our Founding Fathers never would have given the new government taxing powers that would enable it to create "a Multitude of new Offices" containing "Swarms of Officers to harass our People and eat out their Substance" as is now the case.

[8] How many people in the U.S. think of the powers of the Federal government as being "few and defined"? If the powers of the government are indeed "few and defined," how is it possible that it can now control so much of our personal and business lives?

7. The Constitution granted no taxing powers to the new Federal government for the purpose of redistributing wealth or for carrying out social and economic programs (thus establishing the unconstitutional and illegal nature of 60 percent of Federal expenditures).

The Constitution (Article 1, Section 8) only gives Congress power in sixteen clauses, seven of which deal directly with either military or foreign affairs. The so-called "elastic" clause (appearing at the end of that section) under which Congress is authorized to "make all laws which shall be necessary and proper for carrying into execution the foregoing powers," was clearly explained by Madison in *Federalist Paper #44* as applying only to the enumerated powers listed in the previous sixteen clauses. Any attempts by the U.S. government to expand these enumerated powers under the "elastic" clause, would be, according to Madison, acts of "usurpation." This clause, however, is continually used by "educators" to justify U.S. involvement in almost any area it chooses to enter on the grounds that it made the Constitution a "living" and "adaptable" document. The 10th Amendment proves that no such "elasticity" was ever intended. And further proves that much of the power now wielded by the U.S. government is wielded illegally. It states:

> The powers not delegated to the United States by the Constitution, nor prohibited by it to the States, are reserved to the States respectively, or to the people.

You can clearly see that the only powers the U.S. government can legally exercise are those limited powers given to it in the Constitution with the States and individuals retaining all the rest.

The Bill of Rights

As added protection against any attempt on the part of the Federal government to encroach on individual rights, a *Bill of Rights* was immediately added to the Constitution listing specific rights (such as freedom of speech, of assembly, to petition, to bear arms, etc.), rights which the Federal government could make "no laws" prohibiting. These rights, however, are by no means all the rights secured under the Constitution as the 9th Amendment makes abundantly clear:

> The enumeration of the Constitution of certain rights shall not be construed to deny or disparage others retained by the people.

Thus Americans are free to claim and assert numerous other rights not specifically mentioned in the *Bill of Rights*. For example, the *Bill of Rights* does not specifically list "privacy" as a protected right. You can, however, assert this right as retained and protected under the 9th Amendment. Other rights can, of course, be claimed as 9th Amendment rights, such as one's right to take the type of medication one wants and not the type that government feels (however correctly) is appropriate.

A Brainwashed Public

Most Americans believe they must do everything the U.S. government tells them; that they have no rights that politicians, lawless U.S. judges, or the IRS cannot take away. For example, in 1971 three Connecticut chicken farmers were shown on television drowning baby chicks in a large tub. When asked by the reporter why they were doing this, they explained that the Nixon Administration's mandatory price ceilings on chickens would force them to sell their chickens below the cost of bringing them to market. So they destroyed them rather than lose money by marketing them. Incredibly these Americans believed that if it cost them $2.00 to produce a chicken the U.S. government could still compel them to sell it for $1.50. The very idea that the U.S. government has the legal authority to compel anyone to sell a product or service below cost is doubly ridiculous because, in addition to anything else, such an act would be in violation of the 5th Amendment, since it would deprive individuals of property without due process of law. Where in the Constitution, though, is the U.S. government even remotely authorized to dictate to anyone the price at which they can sell their wares? Yet this piece of legislation was passed by a "conservative" administration with a supposed bias for free-enterprise! But what is even more ridiculous is that the American public (including the media) accepted this outrageous piece of legislation without a murmur.

The Interstate Commerce Clause

A substantial amount of the U.S. government's illegally exercised power comes from its total perversion of the so-called "commerce" clause of the Constitution. This appears as the third clause of Article 1, Section 8 and states:

> Congress shall have the power. . . to regulate commerce with foreign nations, and among the several states, and with the Indian tribes.

First of all, it is obvious why the U.S. government was empowered to regulate foreign commerce since one of the express responsibilities of the new government was in the area of foreign affairs, of which foreign commerce is obviously a part. The Indian tribes were treated as foreign nations (we made treaties with them) so trade with them would also come under foreign affairs. The Federal government was given the power to regulate commerce "among the several states" to prevent individual states from raising tariffs or other trade barriers on the transshipment of goods across state boundaries. Such power was absolutely necessary to insure a free flow of goods between all the states. That this was the sole purpose and intent of this provision is made abundantly clear by Madison in the following passages from *Federalist Paper #42*:

> The defect of power in the existing Confederacy to regulate the commerce between its several members is in the number of those which have been clearly pointed out by experience. To the proofs and remarks which former papers have brought into view on this subject, it may be added that without this supplemental provision, the great and essential power of *regulating foreign commerce* would have been incomplete and ineffectual. A very material object of this power was *the relief of the States which import and export through other States from the improper contributions levied on them by the latter.* Were these at liberty to *regulate* the trade between State and State, it must be foreseen that *ways would be found out to load the articles of import and export, during the passage through their jurisdiction, with duties which would fall on the makers of the latter and the consumers of the former.* We may be assured by *past experience* that such a practice would be *introduced* by future contrivances; and both by that and a common knowledge of human affairs that it would *nourish unceasing animosities*, and not improbably terminate in serious interruptions of the public tranquillity. To those who do not view the question through the medium of passion or of interest, the *desire of the commercial States to collect, in any form, an indirect revenue from their uncommercial neighbors* must appear not less impolitic than it is unfair; since it would stimulate the injured party by resentment as well as interest to resort to less convenient channels for their foreign trade. But the mild voice of reason, pleading the cause of an enlarged and permanent interest, is but too often drowned, before public bodies as well as individuals, by the clamors of an impatient avidity for immediate and immoderate gain.
>
> The necessity of a superintending authority over the *reciprocal* trade of confederated States has been illustrated by *other* examples *as well as our own*. In Switzerland, where the Union is so very slight, each canton is obliged to allow to merchandises a *passage through its jurisdiction* into other cantons, without an *augmentation of the tolls*. In Germany it is a law of the empire that the princes and states *shall not lay tolls or customs on* bridges, rivers, or passages, without the *consent* of the emperor and the diet; though it appears from a quotation in an antecedent paper that the practice in this, as in many other instances in that confederacy, has not followed the law, and has produced there the *mischiefs which have been foreseen here*. Among the *restraints* imposed by the Union of the Netherlands on its members, one is that they shall *not establish imposts* disadvanta-

geous to their neighbors without the *general permission*. (Emphasis added)

The sole purpose of this clause was to prevent the states from laying "tolls or customs" on goods shipped across state lines. Yet with this simple and limited clause the U.S. government has now taken centralized, bureaucratic control over the nation's entire economy, and with it, has reduced each state to a mere geographic expression.[9]

Note that the clause does not say the U.S. government can regulate any or all business *engaged* in commerce — it only gave the U.S. government authority to regulate the "commerce" (i.e. shipment) itself. The dictionary defines "commerce" as "an interchange of goods, usually on a large scale, between cities, states, or countries." What was clearly intended was the regulation of the actual shipment of goods across state lines. There is absolutely nothing in the wording of the clause that even remotely suggests that the law was to apply to the regulation of the businesses *engaged in such commerce!* No such thought ever entered the minds of those who wrote this clause into the Constitution.

Because the U.S. government was given the power to regulate "tolls and customs" between states, it has "interpreted" this *limited* power to mean that it can broadly regulate the working conditions and internal affairs of practically every American business — not just those that operate across state lines, but even those that merely use the products and services of out-of-state companies.

In 1976, for example, I operated an insurance agency that did business solely in the state of Connecticut. One day I received a notice from the U.S. Labor Department regarding the new increase in the Federal minimum wage law. Since I did not sell insurance in other states I could not see how I came under Federal labor laws but I decided to check with the Department of Labor anyway. I was asked if I sold insurance issued by out-of-state companies. I said yes.[10] "In that case, " I was told, "you come under U.S. Labor law." Such an extension of the "commerce" clause of the Constitution is, of course, totally erroneous and an obvious perversion of both the law as written and the lawmaker's clear intent. But this is what U.S. judges have been allowing the U.S. government to do. Such "judges" have not been "interpreting" the Constitution, they have simply been ignoring it. In so doing they not only have violated their sworn oaths but they have become nothing less than subverters of the Republic.

---

[9] The U.S. government now dictates state highway speeds through the withholding of subsidies. Today states have so little power they cannot even control their own speed limits!

[10] It is practically impossible to run an insurance agency limited to the sale of policies issued only by in-state carriers.

U.S. Government's Power Illegally Acquired

Where did the U.S. government get most of the power it now wields if not from the Constitution? It usurped it . Apart from merely ignoring the law and clear intent of the interstate commerce clause, the U.S government "acquired" much of its illegal power by never relinquishing "temporary" emergency powers acquired during times of war.

For example, the U.S government only issued gold and silver coin until 1862 (pursuant to clauses in Sections 8 and 10 of Article 1 of the Constitution) when, for the first time, the government issued a limited amount of paper currency as a "temporary" war-time measure to finance the Civil War. From that moment on, the nation got paper currency on a permanent basis, even though the U.S. Constitution not only did not give the government any power to issue it, but it was specifically designed to eliminate such instruments from ever circulating. A provision allowing the Federal government to issue note currency (paper money) was actually included in the first two drafts of the Constitution, but it was stricken by a vote of ten to two. It was Madison who decided the vote for Virginia and he left this testimony:

> The pretext for a paper currency, and particularly for making the bill a tender, either for public or private debts, was cut off.

Commenting on this aspect of the Constitution, Robert Bancroft wrote:[11]

> So the adoption of the Constitution is to be the end forever of paper money, whether issued by the several States or by the United States, if the Constitution shall be rightly interpreted and honestly obeyed.

Obviously, the Constitution is neither being "rightly interpreted" nor "honestly obeyed." And, because of it, the U.S. government is able to use fiat paper money to loot billions from the savings of an unsuspecting American public. Our Founding Fathers had first-hand experience with the financial tradgedies that stem from the use of such money. They had seen it become totally worthless. Similar currency had been issued by the Continental Congress (known as "continentals") and led to the saying "as worthless as a Continental." Some states also issued such currency. Rhode Island, for example, practically brought its entire economy to a standstill with repeated issues of paper money. Fully knowledgeable of the dangers of issuing paper currency, the framers of the Constitution sought to forever ban its use in America. Despite all

---

[11] *Bancroft's History of the Formation of the Constitution,* 2 Vol., page 137.

their precautions (and the monetary restrictions written into the Constitution), however, the nation is now flooded with "continentals" — only now they are called "Federal Reserve notes."[12] Franklin Roosevelt also ilegally nationalized gold in 1934 by resurrecting an "emergency" power created in 1918 in connection with World War I.

Witholding taxes were first imposed in 1942 as a temporary, World War II "Victory" tax. Subsequently it, too, became permanent and gave the U.S. government far more peacetime influence (since it now had substantially more money) and power than it ever had before. It is obvious that practically all of the monetary and fiscal powers currently exercised by the U.S. government were acquired as "temporary" war-time measures and are currently being illegally exercised in peace-time.

This gradual but relentless usurpation of power by the U.S government (and with it the erosion of both state and individual rights) was accomplished with the help of U.S judges who were far more interested in accommodating their employers (the U.S. government) than they were in enforcing the Constitution, so they continually bent the Constitution out of shape to help them do it. In the past U.S. judges merely *bent* the Constitution out of shape, today, however, (especially in tax matters) they have made it a dead letter.

Since our Founding Fathers never intended to give the Federal government more power than it needed to achieve its limited purpose (as explained by Madison), the American people are not bound by "laws" that obviously exceed the Federal government's "few and defined" legitimate powers. Regardless of what self-serving Federal judges say, Americans must now, en masse, heed the advice from James Madison as expressed in *Federalist Paper #33:*

> If the federal government should overpass the just bounds of its authority and make a tyrannical use of its powers, *the people* whose creature it is, *must appeal to the standard they have formed, and take such measures to redress the injury done to the Constitution* as the exigency may suggest and prudence justify. . .it will not follow from this doctrine that acts of a larger society which are *not pursuant* to its constitutional powers, but which are invasions of the residuary authorities of the smaller societies will become the supreme law of the land. These will be merely acts of usurpation and will deserve to be treated as such. (Emphasis added)

---

[12] For an in-depth discussion of this, see Chapter 1 ("The U.S. Money Swindle") of *The Biggest Con: How the Government is Fleecing You,* by Irwin Schiff (FREEDOM BOOKS: 1977).

6

Federal Real Estate Taxes — How They Were Levied and Collected

Now that we know the difference between direct and indirect taxes and the restrictions placed upon the Federal government's taxing powers by the Constitution, let us examine early Federal taxing statutes since they will reveal how the Federal government is still supposed to collect taxes (other than taxes on articles of consumption) even today. The first direct Federal tax was enacted on July 14, 1798 when war with France appeared imminent. This, at least, fulfilled the expectations of those who argued that the Federal government needed an independent, direct taxing power since the tax was levied in response to an exigency. To prepare for that contingency Congress levied a direct tax of two million dollars.[1] Much of the language and principles incorporated into that first direct tax act are still incorporated (though completely disregarded) in today's Internal Revenue Code. By analyzing and understanding this first direct tax law a better understanding of today's Internal Revenue Code, with less likelihood of being hoodwinked by the IRS, becomes possible.

Tax Apportioned To Each State

Under this first statute, the tax was apportioned to each state, right down to the pennies and mills. New Hampshire, for example, was apportioned the sum of $77,705.362, while New York was apportioned a tax of $181,680.707. So, in addition to New York's having to pay some $104,000 more, the state also had to come up with five more mills. The following, moreover, should be noted with respect to this first direct tax:

---

[1] For the full text of this first tax statute, see Appendix C.

1. The tax was a direct tax based upon wealth, but the form of wealth was limited to "dwellings, lands and slaves." These forms of wealth were the easiest to identify and thus the easiest to assess because houses and lands are out in the open (with their ownership recorded in town records) and slaves can be counted. But how could the government pry open a citizen's strongbox and see how much gold and silver coin he had? Under this Act no citizen had to prepare his own tax return (listing his taxable assets) and swear "under the penalty of perjury" that such a "return" was true and correct and that he had computed his tax correctly. Assessing and computing U.S. taxes was the government's job (and still is today though Americans have been led to believe the opposite).

2. The law provided that the tax had to be first assessed before it could be owed. In other words, until an assessment was made no tax was due. The Internal Revenue Code, even today, provides for such assessments, but again, few Americans know this. Today the IRS even confiscates property in payment of taxes which have never been assessed pursuant to law. This first direct taxing statute clearly demonstrates that all taxes collected prior to an assessment being made are illegal, yet this is done today with the full knowledge and cooperation of U.S. courts.

3. In Section 2 the Act provided that dwelling houses "with the out-houses appurtenant thereto" on not more than two acres were to be valued at between $100 and $500, and were to be taxed at the rate of 20¢ per $100 of assessed valuation. So the minimum tax in this category could be 20¢ and the maximum tax $1.00.

4. Taxes were then graduated from 30¢ per $100 on dwellings valued over $500 to a maximum rate of $1.00 per hundred on dwellings over $30,000.

5. A dwelling valued at $5,000 (which, in those days was a substantial one) would be taxed $25.00.

6. Slaves were to be taxed at the rate of 50¢ per slave.

7. The above amounts were to be "deducted from the sum . . . apportioned to (each) state" and the rest was to be assessed upon the lands within each state "at such rate per centum as will be sufficient to produce the said remainder." Thus the tax rate that was to apply to land had to be set locally in order to produce the exact amount of the apportionment.

8. No tax was to be assessed upon properties which were "exempted from taxes by the laws of the states respectively." Thus the Federal government was careful not to conflict with the taxing laws set up within each state.

This gives us a concrete understanding of how apportionment was supposed to work and what direct taxes are all about. Note that the tax rates themselves were well within (actually lower than) the limits referred to by Adam Smith. No one had to take out a loan to pay his taxes. Also note that all dwellings were taxed (albeit on a graduated basis) and no household escaped the tax because of an initial exemption. In addition, the Act did not provide for any deductions or exemptions. Though the tax was graduated, all those who had dwellings would pay something, even if it was only 20¢. A variable tax rate (set locally) was needed to produce the apportioned amount.

For the Federal government to *legally* collect direct taxes, these elements had to be present:

1. the total amount to be collected from all states had to be exactly determined;
2. specific sums then had to be exactly apportioned to each state, based on their congressional representation; and
3. variable rates of tax (of necessity) had to apply to each state to produce the apportioned amount.

It is therefore obvious that the Federal government, in levying direct taxes, cannot use a simple and uniform rate of tax to apply to all citizens throughout the country as it does today but, rather, must call on the states to develop their own variable tax rates.

How The Tax Was To Be Collected

1. Assessments were to be made by "supervisors of the several districts within the U.S." pursuant to instruction from the Secretary of the Treasury, "as soon as the valuations and enumerations had been completed in the state to which such supervisor belongs."
2. The tax became due and payable "after the expiration of three months after these instructions were received" by the supervisors.
3. The supervisors were authorized to reduce the tax rates if the sums assessed "will exceed the sum hereby apportioned." This re-emphasises the principle that individual tax rates must vary from state to state depending on the amount of each state's taxable wealth Lower tax rates would prevail in states with greater per capita wealth and higher tax rates would apply in states with lower per capita wealth. Though this way

seems unfair, it was designed to insure that Federal taxation would be directly related to representation. If a tax would be particularly burdensome to citizens of poorer states their legislators could work to defeat the tax. But our Founding Fathers were determined to make the constituents of voting congressmen directly responsible for the taxes their representatives voted to impose, and not be irresponsible as is the case today. This, again, was to prevent poorer states from using their congressional votes to drain wealth away from richer states (a principle that is reversed today). Thus rates (other than indirect ones on articles of consumption) when applied by the Federal government to the country as a whole, were to vary from state to state in order to fulfill the requirement of apportionment. The laws requiring apportionment are still in force today — that is if the Constitution is still in force. The fact that these laws are disregarded by the Federal government is merely indicative of all the other laws it now disregards.

4. The supervisors were "authorized and required" to appoint their own tax collectors "within their collection districts" who would then collect the tax under the direction of the supervisors according to regulations.

5. After the assessments had been made the supervisors would "by special warrants . . . cause the surveyors of the revenue" to make out "lists" containing the amounts payable for "every dwelling house, tract or lot of land, and slave within each collection district, " and containing such other information as provided in the act. There were therefore three individuals involved in the collection of this tax: a) supervisors, b) collectors, and c) surveyors of the revenue. The surveyors also had to prepare a separate list of "lands, dwelling-houses and slaves" for property that was "not owned, or occupied by, or under the care or superintendance of any persons resident therein" of such owners "where known."

6. The collectors were to be furnished by the surveyors of the revenue "with one or more of said lists signed and certified by such surveyor." Before a citizen could be liable for any tax there had to be *on record* a "signed and certified" statement as to what he owed. Today the government (through the IRS) sends out notices of alleged income tax due that are not certified and, in many cases, are not even signed! Now what Federal official takes the responsibility for *certifying* that the income taxes the IRS claims is owed is legally owed? The reason for this is that no one can legally "owe" Federal "income" taxes since no such liability for them is written into the law!

7. Each collector, "on receiving a list, " was to make three copies: one for the surveyor of the revenue acknowledging the "full and correct copy of such list" (said list to be open to "inspection of any person who may apply to inspect the same"); a second copy to be kept by the "inspector of the survey"; and the third copy to be kept by the "supervisor of the district." Thus all valuations and all taxes due were open to public inspection in much the same way as local property tax records are open to the public today.

8. The collectors were to be bonded "in at least double the amount of the taxes assessed on the collection district for which he may be appointed." This is one area where tax collection has substantially changed. Tax collectors are now full-time government employees.

9. Such assessed taxes would become "a lien upon all lands, and other real estate, and all slaves, of the individual for the same, during two years after the time when it shall become due and payable according to the act." Interestingly no such provision appears in the Code in connection with income taxes. No provision establishes a lien for such taxes or even states that such taxes "shall becomes due and payable." The reason is that the taxes provided for by the Fifth Congress were levied lawfully, pursuant to the Constitution, and did not violate anyone's constitutional rights. Being lawfully levied they could be collected by distraint (i.e. force). Since current income taxes are not levied pursuant to any taxing clause in the Constitution and *do* violate a number of constitutional rights, they cannot be legally mandatory or legally collected by distraint. That is why there is no requirement for paying income taxes, nor any penalties, nor any provisions for collecting them by distraint anywhere in the Internal Revenue Code. This being the case, the Federal government cannot legally confiscate property (as it now does) in payment of U.S. "income" taxes.[2] However, Federal judges (in league with the U.S. Justice Department) allow the IRS to fraudulently use (in connection with income taxes) enforcement provisions that, by law, can only apply to certain valid excise taxes — such as tobacco and alcohol — and the public is none the wiser. Of course, the law is deliberately writ-

[2] While the Code does provide for liens in general, the provision restricts their application to taxes for which one is liable, thereby excluding liens for "income" taxes (see pages 254–256).

ten in such a confusing manner as to make this outrageous
scam almost impossible to detect.[3]
10. After the collectors got their lists they were to post them "in at
least four public places in each collection district, (to note) that
the said tax has become due and payable and the times and
places at which they will attend to receive same."

The Revenue Act of 1813

Some fifteen years elapsed before Congress again exercised its
power of direct taxation. This occurred on July 22, 1813 when, as a result of the War of 1812, Congress levied a direct tax of three million dollars. An examination of that Act will show how the government again
attempted to collect direct taxes expediently and lawfully and will
bring us even closer to the language and principles contained in today's
Internal Revenue Code. The Act differed from the Act of 1798 in four significant ways:

1. It provided for the apportionment of the tax down to the county
   as well as state level;
2. it did not contain any overall tax rates at all but left their determination to local assessors;
3. it provided for the making of "lists" by taxpayers; and
4. it provided that the states themselves could pay their apportioned amount and take a 15% discount.[4]

Federal Collection Districts

The Act created 382 Federal collection districts which conformed to
county districts and apportioned the tax right down to these collection
districts. The first page of this thirteen page Act (see Appendix C)
shows how it provided for such districts in the eighteen states that made
up the Union. It also provided for "one collector and one principal assessor" for each of these districts.

A Companion Act of August 2, 1813 provided for the exact apportionment of the three million dollar Federal tax both by state and district (county) level. This district breakdown accounted for seventeen of

---

[3] For in-depth proof of this deception (and a discussion of how Treasury Regulations deliberately misstate the law) see *The Schiff Report*, Volume 1, Numbers 2, 3, 5 and 6
and Volume 2, Numbers 4, 5 and 6.

[4] For relevant sections of this Act see Appendix C.

the nineteen pages in the bill. The Act also provided for the appointment by the principal assessor of assistant assessors. All assessors were required to take an oath that they would execute their office "without favor or partiality" and that they would seek to do "justice in every case." It further provided for penalties against those assessors who did not take this oath. These penalties were to be in favor of both the United States and "to him who shall first sue for same, to be recovered with costs of suit, in any court having competent jurisdiction." This penalty provision was further supplemented by Section 29 which provided for penalties against collectors who shall "be guilty of any extortion or oppression under color of law." Note that Congress attempted to keep the assessors and collectors honest and within the law. No such consideration now even enters the minds (let alone the law) of the Federal government. In providing that individuals could sue in "any court having competent jurisdiction, " the Federal government apparently made no attempt to limit such suits to Federal courts but allowed citizens to bring them in state courts — where they belong.[5] Today if a citizen sues an IRS agent in a state court the Federal government sees to it that it is removed to a Federal District Court where it is assured that its own judges will "bag" the case by seeing to it that the charges are arbitrarily dismissed.[6]

Lists

This Act established a new procedure requiring taxpayers to furnish the assessors with written "lists" of their taxable property. Such lists (while entirely different from today's tax "return") obviously served as their forerunner.

First, note that Section 5 specifies that the tax provided for is a direct tax and further states that such a tax "shall be assessed." This demonstrates that a taxing statute should identify the type of tax it is and, before anyone can be liable for the tax, it must be assessed by the government. The Internal Revenue Code today, however, does not give the government any power to assess income taxes on its own. Unlike excise taxes, income taxes (by law) are based on self-assessment. The gov-

---

[5] Challenges to Federal taxes should be heard in state courts and vice versa since state and Federal judges cannot be impartial concerning the taxes in which they have a direct stake. Judges, by definition, must be impartial, but such impartiality simply *does not exist* among Federal Judges sitting on Federal tax cases.

[6] In case after case Federal judges routinely dismiss as "frivolous" or rule "these issues have already been decided, case dismissed" when the grievance concerns the IRS's illegal enforcement of income taxes.

ernment and Federal courts, however, allow the IRS to contrive assessments on their own in violation of law. And, unlike the Act, nowhere does today's Code identify whether the income tax is a direct or an indirect (excise) tax. Code Section 4986, for example, clearly identifies the windfall profit tax as being an indirect, *excise* tax[7], while numerous other Federal taxes are grouped in the Code in sections specifically labelled as excise taxes. But nowhere is the income tax identified in the Code (as is shown in Section 5) as being either an excise or a direct tax.

Let me repeat that Section 6 required that "all persons owning, possessing, or having the care or management of any land, lots of ground, dwelling-houses or slaves . . ." had to deliver "written lists of the same" to the assistant assessors, "in such manner as may be directed by the principal assessor." This was a significant departure from the Act of 1798 since no such lists were required of taxpayers under that Act.

Section 7 further provided that if individuals did not provide these lists, but should "consent to disclose" such information, then "it shall be the duty of the officer to make such list, which being distinctly read and consented to, shall be received as the list of such person." This wording is almost identical to the current wording of Code Section 6020 which covers the voluntary making of tax returns.

Note further that Section 8 provided for a civil penalty if anyone submitted a "false or fraudulent list, with intent to defeat or evade" the tax. There were no criminal penalties for filing fraudulent lists or for failing to file any lists at all. The government criminally prosecutes individuals today for such tax "crimes." These "crimes" were not enumerated in this Act because tax statutes are civil statutes and the government cannot, by civil statute, create "crimes." In fact, nothing in today's Criminal Code (Title 18) gives Federal courts criminal jurisdiction over "crimes" enumerated in the Internal Revenue Code (Title 26), which is why the Code does not even refer to criminal jurisdiction. In contrast, civil jurisdiction (which is clearly provided for in Section 1340 of Title 28 — the rules of civil procedure) is repeatedly mentioned in the Code. For example, Section 7402(f) states that Federal District courts have jurisdiction in "civil actions involving internal revenue."

However, when this matter is raised by *pro se* litigants in the tax resistance movement when fighting false, criminal charges such as failing to file income tax returns — there is no such *requirement* in the

---

[7] The windfall profits tax is an illegal excise because it is not levied on a consumable product or even on a contrived privilege. In addition, it is not levied on the basis of geographic uniformity since Alaskan oil is excluded from the tax.

Code nor is there any provision making that a crime — Federal judges simply ignore the matter and/or fabricate jurisdiction. But Section 8 of the Act of 1813 clearly shows that all criminal prosecutions for alleged tax crimes are illegal and that no criminal penalties in connection with such "crimes" were ever intended.

Section 10 provided that if taxpayers failed to submit lists of their own then it was to "be the duty of the assessor . . . to enter upon the lands, dwelling-houses and premises . . . of such persons . . . to make . . . his own . . . list." Taxpayers refusing to provide their own list could be fined $100.00. Note again that there were no criminal penalties for not filing, only civil ones. Also note that the government could not simply levy the fine but had to bring suit in court. Today the government levies $500 fines for allegedly filing "frivolous" tax returns or incorrect W-4s (employee withholding forms) *without hearings of any kind* and then proceeds illegally to collect these "fines" by garnishing wages and bank accounts without court orders.

Difference Between A List And A Return

There are tremendous differences between a list and a return. For one thing, a list enumerated the individual's taxable property and no attempt was made either to value the property or to determine the tax due. The list only included the real estate owned and the number of one's slaves. In addition, a list did not ask for any personal financial information or require that taxpayers provide other personal information such as medical expenses or charitable contributions in order to arrive at their proper tax. As mentioned above, the most important distinction between a return and a list is that there was no attempt on a list to value the property listed or to calculate the tax due.

No Specific Tax Rates Applied

Another interesting aspect of this tax Act was that it made no attempt to establish *specific tax rates!* All applicable rates were to be established *locally* as provided in Section 16. The principal assessors were to "make out lists containing the sums payable according to the assessment . . . so as to raise upon the county or counties . . . the quota of the direct tax laid by the United States." Thus it became apparent that it was futile (due to the requirement of apportionment) to attempt to establish any uniform tax rate since the applicable rate would depend on the taxable wealth contained in each collection district.

Let us say, for example, there were 500 families in the county of Rockingham, New Hampshire, all living in houses worth approximately $3,000 each. This would amount to $1.5 million worth of "dwelling-houses." Suppose the value of all land in Rockingham County was $500,000, making the total value of all land and real estate $2 million. The tax rate would have to be $12.65 per $1,000 to generate the total Federal tax due. Therefore, the average dwelling would be taxed at $37.95 and, if we assume that the land value was ten percent of the dwelling, we would get a total tax of $41.74 for the typical lot and house.

Suppose, however, that in Strafford County (which had to raise $17,698.60) there were only 300 dwellings worth approximately $2,000 each with all other land in the county worth $200,000. The tax rate in this county would have to be $22.10 per $1,000 to generate the apportioned tax. Therefore, in Strafford County the average household would pay $48.60 ($44.20 for the dwelling and $4.42 for the land) versus the average tax in Rockingham County of $41.74. So, while the average homeowner in Strafford was poorer than the average homeowner in Rockingham County, Strafford residents would have to pay a higher tax. A homeowner in Strafford County (having the same value dwelling and lot as a resident in Rockingham) would pay $72.93 as opposed to the Rockingham resident's tax of $41.74 — or 74 percent more. However, the Act provided that the States, by an act of their legislatures, could equalize the apportionments between the collection districts within their state! And even the assessors, in certain cases, were permitted to equalize the valuations between assessment districts. So every effort was made to assess the tax equitably within each state, and the Act provided for local authority to do it.

A State's 15 Percent Discount

The companion Act of August 2, 1813 contained another interesting provision. It allowed each state to take a 15 percent deduction if it paid its quota before the 10th of February, and ten percent if paid before May 1st. This almost converted the Federal tax to a requisition (as provided for in the Articles of Confederation) and forcefully drove home the principle of apportionment. So individual states, if they so chose, could eliminate Federal tax collectors completely — and get a 15 percent discount to boot.

These were the major changes in the Act of 1813 over the Act of 1796, though the Act also contained more extensive provisions for hearings and appeals before assessments became final and prior to any tax becoming due. This is a big departure from today's method of collecting Federal taxes with individuals expected to pay such taxes before any assessments are made and before any hearings take place.

The third direct tax was for $6 million and was enacted on January 9, 1815. This tax also was levied because of the War of 1812 and was similar to the Act of 1813 except that the Act made no attempt to apportion taxes down to the assessment districts, although the districts themselves were still maintained. The act provided for a "board of principal assessors" who would be responsible for equitably establishing the assessment for each district and the rate of tax in order to equalize assessments and tax rates within the state.

With respect to persons who did not pay up, the collector was to go at "once to their respective dwellings . . . and there demand the taxes payable." If the taxes were not paid within twenty days, collectors were authorized to collect them by distress sale, for which they could keep an 8 percent commission. Certain items such as "tools or implements of a trade or profession . . . and household utensils" were to be exempt from such distress sales. There is no comparable section (relating to income taxes) in the current Internal Revenue Code. The Code actually establishes that property cannot be taken except by court order, but this provision is totally ignored by the IRS, the U.S. Department of Justice and the courts. IRS revenue officers routinely seize property for income taxes allegedly owed without court orders or hearings of any kind. For the constitutionally required due process and the requirements of the statute, the IRS has substituted intimidation—aided and abetted by the courts.

The Act also provided for dismissal of collectors and included specific penalties if any one of them willfully refused or neglected "to surrender his collection list and to render a true account of all monies collected". More importantly, it provided for specific penalties in lawsuits brought against collectors who resorted to "extortion or oppression under color of this act or shall demand other or greater sums than shall be authorized by law . . . " This was an important provision since it sought to protect the public from unlawful acts of tax collectors, a class who historically have a reputation for such abuses, and would serve to deter them from breaking the law.

Today the public apparently has no comparable protection. IRS agents now break both Federal and state law with impunity and the public tamely accepts it[8]. There is no comparable section in the Internal Revenue Code for the protection of the public. On the contrary, Section 7422 (c) of the Internal Revenue Code actually seeks to protect IRS lawbreakers and interposes the doctrine of *res judicata* in suits "against any officer or employee of the United States . . . for the recovery of any internal revenue tax alleged to have been wrongfully collected, or of any

---

[8] Effective measures that citizens can take to fight back are discussed in Chapter 18.

penalty claimed to have been collected without authority, or any sum alleged to have been wrongfully collected." So where the Fifth Congress sought to protect the public from the abuses of tax collectors, present legislation does everything possible to protect tax collectors who engage in abusive and illegal acts. Indeed, all the enforcement activities of the IRS are practiced illegally and designed to terrorize the public into believing that our income tax system is really compulsory.

7

The Civil War: The Seeds Of Tax Tyranny Are Sown

Some forty-five years passed before America got another direct tax. This one was for $20 million and was enacted on August 5, 1861 during the Civil War. Fort Sumter had been bombarded four months previously and the North had already suffered its first major military defeat at the first Battle of Bull Run in July. It was under such circumstances that the tax was passed.

The Act containing the tax also provided for another type of tax never before levied in America — a Federal income tax. This tax was plainly unconstitutional on its very face and never could have been adopted except for the War (just as withholding tax never could have been foisted on the people had America not been in the throes of World War II). In passing this "income" tax, Congress contrived it as an *indirect* tax in order, it hoped, to circumvent the apportionment provisions of the Constitution, even as it flagrantly violated the Bill of Rights. The 1861 income tax was allowed to stand even after the war was over, until 1871, and set the stage for a pattern of complicity between the Federal judiciary and power-hungry Washington politicians who have since used it to expand the power of the U.S. government while eroding the rights of citizens and the lawful authority of state governments.

The Direct Tax Aspects of the Act of 1861

Since three prior direct tax acts had already been passed in which constitutional rights and procedures were preserved, this war-time Congress must have labored long to so radically subvert the taxing powers in the Constitution.

The Act (similar to all prior acts) apportioned the tax among all thirty-four states that then constituted the Union — *including the states in the Confederacy* — plus seven territories and the District of Columbia. Again, *no rate of tax was established in the Act.* Tax rates were to be set locally (depending on the amount of taxable property) to produce the apportioned amount. The provisions for levying and collecting the tax were similar in almost every respect to the provisions of the Act of 1815, in sharp contrast to its "income" tax provisions.

No Criminal Penalties Applied to Public

First of all, the Act stated that it was a direct tax to be "assessed and laid on the value of all lands and lots of ground, with their improvements and dwelling-houses" but unlike all prior Acts, did not provide for the inclusion of slaves when determining the tax due. Taxpayers were required to submit lists of their taxable property while the collectors were authorized to enter the "lands, buildings, dwelling-houses, and premises" and make lists of their own in cases where no lists were submitted. In addition, the Act only provided for civil penalties for those who filed either fraudulent lists or filed no lists at all. The President was authorized to appoint, for each assessment district, an assessor and collector who had to be "freeholders and residents within same." All collectors were required to be bonded and they (as well as the assessors) were authorized to appoint assistants who also had to be "freeholders." All assessors and assistant assessors were required to take the same oath as covered on page 61, and were liable to both the government and the public if they did not. A board of assessors was provided for and it was authorized 1) to establish the rate of tax, based upon the amount of taxable property in each collection district, 2) to hear appeals, and 3) to equalize assessments. The Act provided that if any inequality were found in the apportionment, it was to be reported to Congress so that it could be corrected. Section 22 established an appeals procedure wherein the assessors were to "receive, hear, and determine, in a summary way, according to law and right, upon any and all appeals. . ." In addition, Section 12 provided that the assessors, in preparing their lists of taxable property, were to do so "by all other lawful ways and means." The only criminal penalties provided by the Act were to apply to the collectors themselves — those who did not turn over or account for the monies collected (as explained on page 65) while taxpayers were further protected by provisions in Section 47.

Pay for the assessors and assistant assessors was provided for in Section 30 while collectors were to be paid according to Section 48. The Act also contained provisions in Section 53 that allowed each State to pay its total quota of the direct tax and to deduct either 10 percent or 15 percent from the amount due, depending upon when the tax was paid. Thus the wording of the direct tax act of 1861 was almost verbatim to that of the Act of 1815.

The Income Tax Rears Its Ugly Head

The income tax portion of the Revenue Act of 1861 took up less than four pages and was covered in seven sections. For that feat we can, at least, take off our hats to the 34th Congress. Today's income tax and related sections, by contrast, take up more than 2,000 sections and 1,000 pages with thousands of pages of Treasury regulations.[1] The four pages of the Act of 1861, nevertheless, laid the groundwork for an eventual American Gestapo through which the government would abolish every right contained in the Constitution. The full text of the income tax provisions of that Act can be found in Appendix C.

Three Percent Tax Rate

Note that the rate of tax was 3 percent for incomes in excess of $800 though Americans living abroad were taxed at 5 percent while "income" from U.S notes and other securities were to be taxed at 1-1½ percent. To put the tax in its proper perspective, it should be noted that an American earning $1,000 per year (better than average since the per capita annual income in America in 1860 was approximately $150) would owe $6.00 in income taxes. This was, at least, reasonable and close to the levels referred to by Adam Smith. Such a tax rate did not convert taxpayers into slaves or serfs (which rates in excess of 25 percent obviously do). In contrast, income tax rates reached 90 percent from 1944 to 1964. High levels of taxation may be justified in time of war when greater sacrifices from the people can be expected and demanded, so income tax rates reached a height of 3 percent during the Civil War for Americans living in the states.

What Constitutes "Income"?

With the exception of a deduction permitted for taxes, the Act did not provide for any deductions or exemptions. On the face of it, therefore, it should have been an easy tax to figure. The reality was something else. Since no "lists" were required to be completed (either by the assessors or the taxpayers) showing the "income" subject to the tax, how could one determine what type of documentation was used to establish the tax? It would appear from the wording of the law that, initially, it

---

[1] So complicated is this overwhelming mass of regulations that IRS tax collectors are frequently found to be ignorant of its provisions.

was to be based on the assessor's best judgement. In addition, if no deductions were provided for, how was "income" determined?

Were farmers, for example, allowed to deduct the cost of seed, fertilizer, and the wages of hired hands (including the cost of their keep)? Could ranchers deduct the cost of their stock and all the costs of bringing their cattle to market? Could grocers and other merchants deduct the cost of their wares (as well as such costs as advertising, salaries, maintenance of their place of business, etc.) before their "income" was determined? The original Act did not say. It would appear that "income" had to be determined on a purely *arbitrary basis* if only by its vagueness and, as such, the tax *had to be illegal,* regardless of any other consideration. But, to the extent that the tax was arbitrary, it was not unlike today's income tax — because what constitutes "income" today is just as arbitrary (regardless of the 1,000 pages in the current "law") and thus it too has to be illegal.

A Phony "Duty" Is Created!

In order to avoid the apportionment provisions of the Constitution, the Act of 1861 labelled the income tax "an internal duty." This was done so that the tax would fall under Article 1, Section 8 of the Constitution and not under Article 1, Sections 2 and 9 and, therefore, it could be collected as an indirect tax — one *not* subject to apportionment. An income tax is not, by any stretch of the imagination, a "duty" — internal or otherwise. A "duty" is a tax applied to articles as they are imported into a country (though there are sometimes export duties) and is obviously an indirect tax. The tax is added to the price of the product and is passed on to the ultimate consumer who pays the tax indirectly. To the extent that such "duties" are levied internally, they are referred to as excise taxes. An income tax, however, is clearly not a "duty" — it is a dirrect tax, plain and simple. It is not paid *indirectly* by the public — it is paid *directly* by them to the government. It is a direct tax, based not on real estate or slaves, but on "income, " whatever that means. (Moreover, such a term can *never* apply to individuals! See page 222.) How can a tax based on income fall into a different basic category than one based upon wealth? The government could have just as logically called the tax based on real estate an "internal duty" and proceeded to collect it without apportionment, though since Congress had already correctly identified it as a direct tax, Congress could not now change it. But the income tax was a new tax — so Congress felt that it could call it anything it wanted to, and who would be the wiser?

This was a clear case of government levying a direct tax in the guise of an indirect tax in obvious violation of the Constitution. The government got away with it until 1872 when the tax was repealed. But this illegal, war-imposed tax, provided the basis for many other arbitrary and lawless acts to follow. It also laid the foundation for the Gestapo-like IRS we have today.

Act Created a New Federal Agency

Section 50 of the Act states that one principal assessor and one principal collector shall be appointed "in each of the States and Territories of the United States and in the District of Columbia, to assess and collect the internal *duties* or income tax imposed by this act. . . " Section 56 of the Act created a new position in the U.S. Treasury Department: a Commissioner of Taxes whose job it was to superintend "the collection of the direct tax and internal duties of income tax laid by this act." Note that the word "duties" (in connection with income taxes) is used three times in this section. Note also that the Commissioner's salary was to be $3,000 per year and he was authorized to have "the necessary clerks . . . whose aggregate salaries shall not exceed six thousand dollars." In addition, Section 50 further authorized the assessors and collectors to appoint, with the approval of the Secretary of the Treasury, "so many assistants as the public service may require." The salaries of the principal assessors and collectors were to be $2,500 and $1,200 for their assistants — a juicy patronage plum for the President. In addition, the collectors were to be bonded.

First, note that the assessors and collectors (in the case of the income tax) were to be Federal employees, as opposed to the assessors and collectors of the direct tax who were not. Second, the collectors and assessors of the direct tax had to be residents of the collection districts they were in charge of. No such residence requirement was attached to these positions in connection with income taxes. Thus the assessors and collectors of the income tax could be strangers in the community and could be shifted from one state to another. They would be rootless and thus ruthless.

Criminal Penalties Now Created for Taxpayers

There were no criminal penalties that applied to the public in connection with the direct tax but *such penalties were now created in connection with income taxes!* In addition, there was no oath that the assessors or collectors of income taxes had to take that was comparable to the one imposed on those collecting direct taxes, nor did the Act provide for any penalties for income tax collectors if they collected the tax unlawfully or extracted more from the public than the law demanded — as was provided in previous statutes.

Tax Assessments Arbitrary

The most glaring omission regarding income taxes, however, was the absence of any "list" or "tax return" that had to be completed by either the taxpayer or the assessor. How then were the "assessments" provided for in Section 49 to be determined? On what document were they to be based? The Act did not say. It said only that the tax "shall be assessed upon the annual income of the persons hereinafter named. . . " but the Act itself does not give us a clue as to how the assessments were to be determined. At least under the direct tax the assessors were specifically authorized to visit the taxpayer's property to determine its value (if the taxpayer did not provide his own list) but no such direction or authorization is included in connection with income taxes. Were the assessors supposed to visit employers and ask questions concerning the salaries of their employees? Were they authorized to get information from the banks as to the possible interest earnings of the taxpayer? Were employers and banks *required* to give out this information? On all these points the Act was silent. [2]

In fact, Section 51 contains the only provision in the Act wherein citizens could be required to give the government information — and it concerns examining "under oath the person assessed under this act" in connection with discovering where he might have assets that could be seized by the tax collectors to satisfy the taxes owed. But this section has nothing to do with determining the tax itself. Notice, too, that no provisions were included that provided for due process or that indicated under what legal form these "examinations" were to take place. In addition, the section incredibly stated that "in case he refuses to testify, the said several collectors and assistants shall have power *to arrest such person and commit him to prison,* to be held in custody until the same shall be paid, with interest thereon, at the rate of six per centum per annum, from the time when the same was payable as aforesaid, and all fees and charges of such commitment and custody." (Emphasis added.) In short, these provisions scrapped the Bill of Rights and placed the tax collector above the law. The Act provided that individuals could be thrown in jail for refusing to testify against themselves without a trial of any kind. Assessments could be levied with no prescribed documentation at all, with no machinery for appeals. Perhaps, since President Lincoln had suspended *habeas corpus* as a war-time measure, the Congress felt that it could abrocate the rest of the Constitution.

---

[2]No attempt was made in this chapter to comment on the various amendments and changes that were subsequently added to this Act. Eventual amendments provided that citizens had to supply either a "return or a list" and provisions were made for deductions from gross income.

Notice that these "examinations" took place only when tax collectors could not locate enough "visible property" or real estate of taxpayers to seize and sell in order to satisfy alleged tax liabilities. The collectors had to pry out of them where their other assets might be located. If direct taxes are based on the ownership of real estate then the property needed to satisfy the taxes is known and such "examinations" are unnecessary. This raises the question of why direct taxes should be based on only real estate. Why, for example, should a man with $100,000 in cash pay less of a direct tax than one who owns $100,000 in real estate? The answer is, he will not. The individual with $100,000 in cash has to live somewhere. The property where he lives will be taxed and his rent will therefore be higher in order to absorb the tax. In these cases, the direct tax on the landlord converts itself into an indirect tax on the tenant. The problem for society, however, is how to collect taxes equitably while still preserving the public's right to privacy (and all the other rights guaranteed by the Constitution) and how to avoid the abuses referred to by Hamilton on page 27 so that citizens do not end up as the property of the state.

An income tax, apart from being the most economically destructive tax possible, [3] inevitably leads to the loss of almost every constitutional right as illustrated by Section 51 and as demonstrated by the manner in which the IRS collects income taxes today. When taxes are collected on the basis of real estate and on articles of consumption, such tyranny can be avoided. The easiest way, however, for the government to collect taxes is to have them be reasonable so the public will not cheat or try to avoid them, but rather, will regard them as a cheap price to pay for the economic and social benefits that presumably result from a well-run government. Today, runaway taxation is directly responsible for government waste running into billions of dollars. [4]

The avoidance of taxes in America is now a full-time activity, with tax shelters a twenty billion dollar a year industry. Almost every American business decision is now based upon tax implications. Income tax considerations affect such decisions as whether or not to own a home, when a child should be born, when people should be married or if they should *stay* married, as well as the financial terms of a divorce.

[3] See *The Biggest Con: How The Government is Fleecing You* (by Irwin Schiff, Hamden, CT: Freedom Books, 1977), Chapter 7: "U.S. Taxes — How They Have Coverted the American Worker into a Serf" and Chapter 8: "Taxes: The Arsenic in Our System."

[4] J. Peter Grace, head of The Grace Commission, President Reagan's private-sector group formed to survey areas of cost-control inefficiencies within government recently commented, "If you are still paying taxes. . . Hi, sucker." For the complete commentary on this report by the late Jason Tyrell, State Chairman of The Committee To Stop IRS Tax Abuses headquartered in Darien, Connecticut, see *The Schiff Report*, Volume 2, Number 4.

Government Usurps Power To Seize Private Property Unconstitutionally

As explained earlier, the most important constitutional right Americans have (and what probably distinguishes us — theoretically — from citizens of any other country) is contained in the Fifth Amendment which states: "No person shall . . . be deprived of life, liberty, or property, without due process of law." In essence, "due process of law" means a hearing before an impartial judge with all the judicial safeguards provided in the 6th and 7th Amendments. Note, however, in Section 51 that collectors were authorized "to levy [i.e. seize] the same on the visible property of any such person." Collectors were authorized to seize property for the U.S. government without hearings or due process of any kind, in total disregard, and in complete violation of, the 5th Amendment. The IRS seizes property without hearings or court orders of any kind in exactly the same manner as provided for in Section 51 — only the technique *appears to be* a little more legal. The "laws" that apparently allow the IRS to get away with this are more elaborate, ensuring that the public cannot figure them out. [5] But, in essence this aspect of the government's illegal income tax activities has not changed one iota from the obviously illegal nature of the original Act that inspired it.

The Tax Return Is Born

Strange as it may seem, the Tax Act of 1861 created the infamous income tax return, but that document was not for the public to complete, it was to be completed by the tax collectors themselves. The income tax return was born within the confines of Section 50 and authorized the Secretary to "prescribe the forms of *returns* to be made to the department by all assessors and collectors *appointed under the authority of this act*. He shall also prescribe the form of *oath* or obligation to be taken by the several officers authorized or directed to be appointed and commissioned by the President under the act, before a competent magistrate duly authorized to administer the oaths, and the form of *the return* to be made thereon to the Treasury Department." (Emphasis added.) *Returns* were to be prepared by the assessors and collectors and not by the public — why else would they be called "returns"? "Return" means "to go or come back, as to a former place: to revert to a former owner. . . "; and assessors and collectors (working for the government) could "return" the information they collected to the Treasury Department

---

[5] For an in-depth study of how the IRS goes about illegally seizing bank accounts, wages, homes, etc., see *The Schiff Report*, Volume 2, Numbers 4 and 6.

(which obviously was the real owner of all such information), and the documents containing the information were properly called "returns." But when private citizens complete and submit 1040s, are they *returning* anything to the government that belongs to the government? What citizens make out, therefore, are not "returns" at all — they are "confessions."

Citizens submit sworn "confessions" listing their receipts and disbursements (which they have been deceived into believing reflect their "income") and what they believe they owe in taxes; and the government has conned the public into believing that such "confessions" are really "returns." Would the government chance telling the public: "Tax confessions have to be in by April 15th?" [6] However, given the present level of understanding among Americans concerning their constitutional rights, they might at this point even believe they have to submit "confessions" if ordered by the government to do so!

Note also that "oaths" were to be administered (which presumably would be part of the "return") in much the same way as tax returns are signed today under penalty of perjury. But oaths can only be voluntarily given. You cannot be compelled to take an oath. Government employees, on the other hand, could be required to take an oath as a prerequisite to employment. If they objected to the oath, they did not have to work for the government but would still be free to work elsewhere. But private citizens, not on the public payroll, cannot be required to take oaths, which is why the filing of tax returns must be voluntary and why there is no provision in the Internal Revenue Code requiring anyone to file a tax return. True, some people have gone to jail for not filing income tax returns, but that is because Federal judges are willing to subvert the law and their oath to uphold the Constitution in order to extort income taxes from the American public. Because of such judicial perversion the public has been misled into believing that it is required to file income tax returns when such is not the case.

If citizens could be required to file anything, it would be "lists, " not "returns" — and this distinction is still preserved in the law! In Section 6201 (Exhibit 7, page 257) of the Internal Revenue Code, the Secretary of the Treasury is authorized only to "assess all taxes determined by the taxpayer or by the Secretary as to which *returns or lists* are made under this title." (Emphasis added.) The Secretary, therefore, has no authority to assess any income tax unless taxpayers send in either a tax return or a list admitting receipts and expenditures. In this case, the government is authorized to make their assessments based on the in-

---

[6] In *United States vs Kahriger* 345 US 22, Supreme Court Justice Hugo Black observed, "The United States has a system of taxation by confession."

formation they *voluntarily* supplied. Code Section 6201 also clearly establishes that even today income taxes, by law, still have to be assessed before they can be lawfully due and payable. And the "list" (as referred to in the tax statute of 1798) is still preserved in our laws today — except that nobody in America (including the entire legal establishment) has any idea as to what the list referred to in Code Sections 6011 and 6201 actually mean. Now they should know!

The legal community will now know what a "list" is, while *we know* the source and basis of current Federal tax tyranny — it was a war-inspired tax. During a war-time crisis, the Federal government arbitrarily took the power to deprive people of both their liberty and their property (in total violation of the due process clause of the Constitution — to say nothing of a citizen's 5th Amendment right not to be compelled to be a witness against himself) and Federal judges allowed the government to do this — despite their sworn oaths to protect and defend that Constitution.

As far as providing the North with money to fight the War, both taxes were relatively unimportant. The North was forced to raise the bulk of its revenue through borrowing and the printing of paper money — eventually redeemed for gold subsequent to 1878.

The direct tax eventually took in about $17 million while the income tax took in about $347 million over the ten year period it remained in force. By comparison, the North raised approximately $2.683 billion in long-and short-term notes, including the $433 million raised through the issuance of "greenbacks" — unredeemable paper money. The total amount received by the North through all forms of taxation was only $667 million, showing the relative importance of debt creation as compared to taxation in the North's financing of the Civil War. It was this debt creation that was responsible for the Civil War inflation that cut the value of the dollar in half, though sounder money policies subsequently restored its value. In comparison, the inflation generated by the Federal Reserve (since its establishment) has reduced the value of our 1909 "dollar" by 94 percent.

The next time an income tax reared its ugly head was in 1894 when the Congress enacted another income tax statute. This time, however, in one of the greatest — but most ignored — Supreme Court decisions, the Court declared it unconstitutional.

8

The Supreme Court Declares an Income Tax Unconstitutional

In *Pollock vs Farmers' Loan & Trust Co.*, the United States Supreme Court achieved its finest hour.[1] In that momentous 1895 decision the Court declared the income tax act of 1894 unconstitutional and, in the process, corrected and clarified a number of prior Supreme Court decisions. This was, therefore, a rare decision since it took the unusual position of holding that a string of prior decisions were in error or misconstrued. In this case the Court refused to be bound by *stare decisis* (the powerful legal principle which generally binds Federal courts to blindly following and upholding prior court decisions). In this instance the Court maintained that it would be bound by a higher legal principle — fidelity to the U.S. Constitution. For such fidelity the Court received much harsh criticism which depicted it as a lackey of the rich.

In holding the income tax unconstitutional, the Supreme Court did an exhaustive review of:

1. the taxing provisions of the Constitution;
2. their historic underpinnings; and
3. a number of prior Court decisions.

Chief Justice Fuller wrote the opinion and his comments and research in these areas (together with a concurring opinion by Justice Stephen J. Field) provide an excellent background of the history and philosophy of American taxation.

The *Pollock* decision represents the most important weapon in the arsenal of those seeking a return to limited, republican government in America and it must, therefore, be resurrected from the judicial graveyard to which it has been consigned by both the Federal government and

[1]There were two decisions in this case: 1) 157 US 429 was decided on April 8, 1895, and 2) 158 US 601 was a rehearing that was decided on May 20, 1895. Most of these excerpts were taken from the former case.

the American legal establishment. For ninety years this decision has been misrepresented, distorted and maligned by the entire legal establishment. Even the honesty and integrity of the judges who decided the case have been impugned.[2] The *Pollock* decision offers concrete proof that the Supreme Court has been systematically subverting the U.S. Constitution.

Bear in mind that this landmark case has never been reversed. The legal principles expressed in it still hold and can be cited as valid legal precedent even today. Federal judges simply ignore the case (as if it never existed) since they can cite nothing to refute it. In addition, American law schools teach their students that the case was actually overturned by the 16th Amendment *which is not true at all.*

A thorough knowledge of this decision will provide a better understanding of the lawful basis of taxation in America than now exists among 99 percent of all practicing lawyers and the professors who "teach" them. Before turning to the decision itself, it should be noted that Pollock was represented by two outstanding attorneys — Joseph Choate of New York, one of the most renowned lawyers of his time, and George Edmunds, a former Senator from Vermont. Choate ended his remarks at the first hearing with the following statements:

> I do not believe that any member of this court ever has sat or ever will sit to hear and decide a case *the consequences of which will be so far-reaching as this* — not even the venerable member who survives from the early days of the civil war, and has sat upon every question of reconstruction, of national destiny, of state destiny that has come up during the last thirty years. No member of this court will live long enough to hear a case which will involve a question of more importance than this, *the preservation of the fundamental rights of private property* and equality before the law, and *the ability of the people of these United States to rely upon the guaranties of the Constitution.* If it be true, as my friend said in closing, that the passions of the people are aroused on this subject, if it be true that *a mighty army of sixty million citizens is likely to be incensed by this decision,* it is the more vital to the future welfare of this country that *this court* again resolutely and courageously declare, as Marshall did, that it *has the power to set aside an act of Congress violative of the Constitution,* and that it will not hesitate in executing that power, no matter what the threatened consequences of popular or populistic wrath may be. With the deepest earnestness and confidence we submit that all patriotic Americans must pray that our views shall prevail. We could not magnify the scope of your decision, whatever it may be. No mortal could rise above "the height of this great argument." (Emphasis added)

[2]"The question arises, how far a court is entitled to indulge in bad history and bad logic without having its good faith challenged." *Court Over Constitution* (Princeton: 1938), page 188, by E. S. Corwin.

Income Tax Violated Apportionment Provisions

The Supreme Court declared the income tax of 1894 unconstitutional on the grounds that it was essentially a direct tax — one not apportioned and, therefore, unconstitutional. In a separate opinion (not adopted by the Court) Justice Field also argued that the tax was unconstitutional even if levied as an indirect tax, since its discriminatory features rendered it void of any uniformity.

Chief Justice Fuller first explained the Court's judicial duty in upholding the Constitution as follows:

> Since the opinion in *Marbury v. Madison,* 1 Cranch, 137, 177, was delivered, it has not been doubted that it is within judicial competency, by express provisions of the Constitution or by necessary inference and implication, to determine whether a given law of the United States is or is not made in pursuance of the Constitution, and to hold it valid or void accordingly. "If, " said Chief Justice Marshall, "both the law and the Constitution apply to a particular case, so that the court must either decide that case conformably to the law, disregarding the Constitution; or conformably to the Constitution, disregarding the law; the court must determine which of these conflicting rules governs the case. This is of the very essence of judicial duty." And the Chief Justice added that the doctrine *"that courts must close their eyes on the Constitution, and see only the law, . . . would subvert the very foundation of all written constitutions."* Necessarily the power to declare a law unconstitutional is always exercised with reluctance; but the duty to do so, in a proper case, cannot be declined, and must be discharged in accordance with the deliberate judgement of the tribual in which the validity of the enactment is directly drawn in question.[3] (Emphasis added)

Then he went on to explain in detail the reasons for apportionment:

> The men who framed and adopted that instrument had just emerged from the struggle for independence whose rallying cry had been that *"taxation and representation go together."*
>
> The mother country had taught the colonists, in the contests waged to establish that taxes could not be imposed by the sovereign except as they were granted by the representatives of the realm, that self-taxation constituted the main security against oppression. As Burke declared, in his speech on Conciliation with America, the defenders of the excellence of the English constitution "took infinite pains to inculcate, as a fundamental principle, that, in all monarchies, the people must, in effect, themselves, mediately or immediately, possess the power of granting their own money, or no shadow of liberty could subsist." The principle was that the

[3]*Pollock vs Farmers' Loan* 157 US 429, page 554.

consent of those who were expected to pay it was essential to the validity of any tax.

The States were about, for all national purposes embraced in the Constitution, to become one, united under the same sovereign authority, and governed by the same laws. But as they still retained their jurisdiction over all persons and things within their territorial limits, except where surrendered to the general government or restrained by the *Constitution, they were careful to see to it that taxation and representation should go together, so that the sovereignty reserved should not be impaired, and that when Congress, and especially the House of Representatives, where it was specifically provided that all revenue bills must originate, voted a tax upon property, it should be with the consciousness, and under the responsibility, that in so doing the tax so voted would proportionately fall upon the immediate constituents for those who imposed it.*

More than this, by the Constitution the States not only gave to the Nation the concurrent power to tax persons and property directly, but they surrendered their own power to levy taxes·on imports and to regulate commerce. All the thirteen were seaboard States, but they varied in maritime importance, and differences existed between them in population, in wealth, in the character of property and of business interests. Moreover, they looked forward to the coming of new States from the great West into the vast empire of their anticipations. *So when the wealthier States as between themselves and their less favored associates, and all as between themselves and those who were to come, gave up for the common good the great sources of revenue derived through commerce, they did so in reliance on the protection afforded by restrictions on the grant of power.*[4]

Fuller then examined and reviewed the two great classes of taxation that were established in the Constitution:

Thus, in the matter of taxation, the Constitution recognizes the two great classes of direct and indirect taxes, and lays down two rules by which their imposition must be governed, namely: The rule of apportionment as to direct taxes, and the rule of uniformity as to duties, imposts and excises.

The rule of uniformity was not prescribed to the exercise of the power granted by the first paragraph of section eight, to lay and collect taxes, because the rule of apportionment as to taxes had already been laid down in the third paragraph of the second section.

And this view was expressed by Mr. Chief Justice Chase in *The License Tax Cases,* 5 Wall. 462, 471, when he said: *"It is true that the*

[4]Ibid., pages 556, 557.

power of Congress to tax is a very extensive power. It is given in the Constitution, with only one exception and only two qualifications. Congress cannot tax exports, and it must impose direct taxes by the rule of apportionment, and indirect taxes by the rule of uniformity. Thus limited, and thus only, it reaches every subject, and may be exercised at discretion."

And although there have been from time to time intimations that there might be some tax which was not a direct tax nor included under the words "duties, imposts and excises," such a tax for more than one hundred years of national existence has as yet remained undiscovered. . .[5]

In the above excerpt, Fuller reiterates the fact that there can be no lawful tax that does not fall into one class or the other.[6] It should be noted that even in the following quotation Fuller did not hit the nail precisely on the head when explaining the differences between direct and indirect taxes, though he came close to it, and also conscientiously pointed out that "the Constitution may bear a different meaning (which) must be recognized." Instead of explaining that indirect taxes are simply taxes paid indirectly to the government on consumable items as opposed to taxes paid directly to the government based on various criteria, he chose to explain the differences in this manner:

Ordinarily, all taxes paid primarily by persons who can shift the burden upon someone else, or who are under no legal compulsion to pay then, are considered indirect taxes; but a tax whether real or personal, or of the income yielded by such estates, upon property holders in respect of their estates, and the payment of which cannot be avoided, are direct taxes.[7]

This was, of course, a good definition of direct versus indirect taxes and was, by far, the best definition to have appeared in any court case either before or since. Prior distinctions made by other courts were entirely incorrect. To say, as Fuller did, that an indirect tax is one where the payer can shift the burden of the tax to someone else is to state what happens when taxes are placed on articles of consumption. His definition does describe what actually happens when taxes are levied on articles of consumption, but it still unnecessarily complicates the distinction and fails to explain that the purpose of all such taxes is to tax the public *indirectly* rather than attempting to tax them directly.

[5]Ibid., page 557.

[6]Since the current income tax is levied neither as an excise tax nor as an apportioned, direct tax, it falls into neither of these "two great classes" and, therefore, cannot be a lawful tax as the Court explains.

[7]*Pollock vs Farmers' Loan, supra,* page 558.

Fuller then pointed out that "a tax upon property holders in respect of their estates, whether real or personal or of the income yielded by such estates and the payment of which cannot be avoided are direct taxes." This definition (which was ultimately adopted by the Court) again falls short of defining what a direct tax actually is, since it could be interpreted as limiting the tax to accumulated, *tangible property,* both real and personal. Thus some could argue that this definition excludes taxes based on wages or earnings from self-employment. But if one understands that an individual's labor is also personal property[8] this (coupled with Fuller's recognition that a direct tax is one "which cannot be avoided") clearly establishes that taxes based on wages or the net earnings from self-employment must also fall into this category and, therefore, they too must qualify as direct taxes. Fuller's *seemingly* narrower definition, however, is understandable since by this time Federal courts had totally distorted the meaning and distinctions between the two classes of taxes. His definition, however, is certainly good enough to demonstrate that the government's present enforcement of the income tax (as well as gift and estate taxes) is totally illegal.[9]

Court Rules That an Income Tax is a Direct Tax

The important thing to note in this decision is that this Court ultimately ruled that a tax on income from real estate or personal property (such as dividends and interest) is, *without question, a direct tax and, therefore, illegal if not apportioned.* This principle is as valid today as it was then. The Court did not rule on whether a tax based on wages or self-employment income was also a direct tax because *neither item was an issue in this case.*

The case was initiated by Charles Pollock, a stockholder in Farm-

---

[8]In *Butchers' Union vs Cresent* 111 US 746 (1884), Justice Field (quoting from Adam Smith's *The Wealth of Nations*) said, "The property which every man has in his own labor, as it is the original foundation of all other property, so it is the most sacred and inviolable. The patrimony of the poor man lies in the strength and dexterity of his own hands, and to hinder his employing this strength and dexterity in what manner he thinks proper, without injury to his neighbor, is a plain violation of this most sacred property."

[9]Notice I said the "enforcement" of the tax was illegal. The tax itself is not illegal since there is nothing in the Internal Revenue Code that *requires* anyone or any business to pay it or to provide the government with any information with respect to any aspect of it. The government is able to enforce it illegally — and thoroughly deceive the public — because of the cooperation it gets from the Federal judiciary, the U.S. "Justice" Department and all the rest of America's lawyers. For a fuller explanation of the voluntary nature of the income tax (as provided by law), see *How Anyone Can Stop Paying Income Taxes* (Schiff), and Chapter 15 of this book.

ers' Loan & Trust Company (a New York corporation). He brought the action on behalf of himself and all other stockholders to restrain the company from paying the tax. The suit, therefore, was not a frontal attack on the act itself but came to the Court in the nature of a restraining order that had been denied by a lower court (see page 399). Pollock claimed "that voluntary compliance[10] with the income tax provisions would expose the company to a multiplicity of suits not only by and on behalf of its numerous shareholders, but by and on behalf of numerous minors and others for whom it acts in a fiduciary capacity." The trust company's assets were invested exclusively in real estate, municipal bonds, and common stocks and it was Pollock's contention that a Federal tax on these items was unconstitutional if not apportioned. The question of the taxability of wages and self-employment earnings, not being at issue in this case, was not ruled on. But the Court's analysis and decision relating to these other forms of income makes it clear that a tax on wages and self-employment earnings must also (employing the same logic) qualify as a direct tax (see page 121).

Getting Around Prior Case Law

In reaching this decision, Fuller had to dispose of a number of prior Supreme Court decisions which had obviously been made in error. This undoubtedly took a good deal of judicial courage and conscientiousness. After examining several earlier, erroneous Court decisions, Fuller explained why the Court would not be bound by the doctrine of *stare decisis:*

> We proceed then to examine certain decisions of this court under the acts of 1861 and following years, in which it is claimed that this court has heretofore adjudicated that taxes like those under consideration are not direct taxes and subject to the rule of apportionment, and that we are bound to accept the rulings thus asserted to have been made as conclusive in the premises. Is this contention well founded as respects the question now under examination? Doubtless the doctrine of *stare decisis* is a salutary one, and to be adhered to on all proper occasions, but it only arises in respect of decisions directly upon the points in issue.[11]

The Court's Embarrassment

After quoting Chief Justice John Marshall and other authorities as a basis for not having to be bound by precedent, the Court, in a rare expression of its embarrassing predicament, explained:

---

[10]Note the admission here of the "voluntary" nature of the income tax. See also *The Schiff Report,* Volume 2, Number 5.

[11]*Pollock vs Farmers' Loan, supra,* page 574.

. . . It is the decision in the case of *The Thomas Jefferson which mainly embarrasses the court* in the present inquiry. We are sensible of the great weight to which it is entitled. But at the same time we are convinced that, *if we follow it, we follow an erroneous decision* into which the court fell, when the great importance of the question as it now presents itself could not be foreseen; and the subject did not therefore receive that deliberate consideration which at this time would have been given to it by the eminent men who presided here when that case was decided.

. . . Manifestly, as this court is clothed with the power, and entrusted with the duty, to maintain the fundamental law of the Constitution, the discharge of that duty requires it not to extend any decision upon a constitutional question if it is convinced that error in principle might supervene.[12] (Emphasis added)

Let us now examine some of the earlier Supreme Court decisions that the *Pollock* Court examined and temporarily corrected.

The 1794 Carriage Tax

It did not take long for the Supreme Court to begin its assault on the Constitution. The faulty 1796 *Hylton* decision could have resulted from simple error rather than from design. It involved an insignificant carriage tax passed by Congress in 1794. Though the tax remained in force for only two years, it was to directly and erroneously affect every tax law and decision that followed. So, in essence, the American public has been victimized for two hundred years by a 1794 tax on carriages, chariots, phaetons, and coaches. In reviewing the Supreme Court decision which upheld this carriage tax as an *excise* tax, the *Pollock* Court referred to the debates that took place in Congress in connection with its passage. For example, the Court quoted a House member as saying that

". . . a capitation tax, and taxes on land and on property and income generally, were direct charges, as well in the immediate as ultimate sources of contribution. He had considered those, and those only, as direct taxes in their operation and effects. On the other hand, a tax imposed on a specific article of personal property, and particularly if objects of luxury, as in the case under consideration, he had never supposed had been considered a direct tax, within the meaning of the Constitution."[13]

The Court then provided additional statements made by other Congressmen, all of which indicate a surprising misunderstanding on their

[12]Ibid., pages 575, 576.
[13]Ibid., page 568.

part of the specific nature of an indirect tax. Fuller continued with his analysis of the passage of the bill as follows:

> At a subsequent day of the debate, Mr. Madison objected to the tax on carriages as *"an unconstitutional tax,"* but Fisher Ames declared that he had satisfied himself that it was not a direct tax, as *"the duty falls not on the possession but on the use. . ."*
>
> Mr. Madison wrote to Jefferson on May 11, 1794: "And the tax on carriages succeeded, in spite of the Constitution, *by a majority of twenty,* the advocates for the principle being reinforced by *the adversaries to luxuries. . .* Some of the motives which they decoyed to their support ought to premonish them of the danger. By breaking down the barriers of the Constitution, and giving sanction to the idea of sumptuary regulations, wealth may find a precarious defence in the shield of justice. If luxury, *as such,* is to be taxed, the greatest of àll luxuries, says Paine, is a great estate. . ."[14] (Emphasis added)

We see, then, that Madison was of the opinion that the tax was unconstitutional and said that it was passed by men who were "adversaries to luxuries."

When Fisher Ames suggests that the "tax falls not on the possession but on the use" we can begin to see the type of confusion that politicians inject into the field of taxation. To suggest that the tax did not fall "on the possession" but on the "use" is sheer casuistry. If someone happens to own a carriage but does not "use" it, will he be excused from the tax? Conversely, if someone "uses" a carriage but does not own it, will he be taxed? The tax obviously fell on those individuals who owned carriages and they were expected to pay a new tax based on that ownership — and "use" had nothing to do with it. As cited in *Pollock,* the Act provided:

> ". . . that there shall be levied, collected, and paid upon all carriages for the conveyance of persons, which shall be kept by or for any person for his or her own use, or to be let out to hire or for the conveyance of passengers, the several duties and rates following, " and then followed a fixed yearly rate on every coach; chariot; phaeton and coachee; every four-wheel and every two-wheel top carriage; and upon every other two-wheel carriage; varying according to the vehicle."[15]

Elements of Two Taxes in One

The real problem with the carriage tax is that it actually combined, in one act, both an indirect and a direct tax. But since the ma-

[14]Ibid., page 569.
[15]Ibid., page 570.

jority of the members of Congress evidently did not care to see the distinction, they wandered off into legislative error. If Congress had simply taxed all carriages used for hire, such a tax would be indirect since it would be passed on to the public in the form of higher rental fees. The tax thus imposed could be handled by stamp, with the stamp displayed on all carriages used for hire. But when the tax is applied to carriages not for hire, such a tax is obviously not *indirect* at all. It is not a tax on the "use" of carriages but a direct tax based on their ownership and, as such, can neither be passed on nor avoided. It is no different than a tax based on the ownership of real estate or slaves — the only difference is in the nature of the property upon which the tax is imposed. But the Congress (for its own reasons) proclaimed that such a tax, allegedly being indirect, did not require apportionment. Such a determination and conclusion by Congress was obviously incorrect.

The *Hylton* Case — A Monstrous Supreme Court Error

Before refuting the fundamental error in this decision (i.e., that the carriage tax was an indirect, excise tax), Fuller sought to establish that the framers of the Constitution knew full well the differences between both classes of taxes and fully expected that each would be levied according to its own constitutional restrictions. To help dispel the myth that the Founding Fathers were unsure of the meaning of both direct and indirect taxes, the *Pollock* Court cited numerous historical references to establish that these terms meant exactly what *we know* them to mean, and that those who wrote the Constitution *knew it too!* No less than twenty-six excerpts from The Elliot Debates (see Appendix B) were included along with numerous quotes from *The Federalist Papers,* Adam Smith and other sources. This is the only place where the Supreme Court ever presented a comprehensive study of the meaning of these terms and the historical and constitutional setting in which they evolved. Despite all this, law book references to *Pollock* simply disregard the wealth of evidence the decision presents and disparage the decision out of hand. For example, in *The American Constitution, Its Origins and Development,*[16] the authors claimed, with respect to Chief Justice Fuller, that:

> His appeal to history did not bear out his contention. If his evidence proved anything, it was merely that the term "direct taxes" had as of 1787 no certain and fixed meaning at all. . .
>
> It is difficult to escape the conclusion that the two Pollock cases con-

[16]Fifth Edition, (NORTON: New York), by Alfred H. Kelly and Winfred A. Harbison, pages 535 and 538-539.

stituted exceedingly unsound and unwise decisions on the part of the Court. The opinions disregarded one hundred years of decisions by the Court itself in which the meaning of a direct tax had been narrowly and definitely established. . .

The speciousness of Chief Justice Fuller's historical argument hardly needs further comment. He could not, in fact, show that in 1787 there was any general understanding about direct taxes.

Such contentions by the authors in this influential text are, of course, sheer nonsense since the evidence is overwhelming that the Court was right.

Fuller then discoursed on the development of the two taxing classes and the constitutional distinction between Federal and state governments. This sort of understanding is completely foreign to the thinking of most Americans today, though it is vital to this nation's welfare that the American public rediscover these distinctions and press for their enforcement.

Congress under the articles of confederation *had no actual operative power of taxation.* It could call upon the States for their respective contributions or quotas as previously determined on; but in ease of the failure or omission of the States to furnish such contribution, there were no means of compulsion, as Congress had no power whatever to lay any tax upon individuals. This imperatively demanded a remedy; but the opposition to granting the power of direct taxation in addition to the substantially exclusive power of laying imposts and duties was so strong that it required the convention, in securing effective powers of taxation to the Federal government, to use the utmost care and skill to so harmonize conflicting interests that the ratification of the instrument could be obtained.

The situation and the result are thus described by Mr. Chief Justice Chase in *Lane County* v. *Oregon,* 7 Wall. 71, 76: "The people of the United States constitute one nation, under one government, and this government, within the scope of the powers with which it is invested, is supreme. On the other hand, the people of each State compose a State, having its own government, and endowed with all the functions essential to separate and independent existence. The States disunited might continue to exist. WIthout the States in union there could be no such political body as the United States. Both the States and the United States existed before the Constitution. *The people, through that instrument, established a more perfect union by substituting a national government, acting, with ample power, directly upon the citizens, instead of the confederate government, which acted with powers, greatly restricted, only upon the States. But in many articles of the Constitution the necessary existence of the States, and within their proper spheres, the independent authority of the*

States, is distinctly recognized. To them nearly the whole charge of interior regulation is committed or left; *to them and to the people all powers not expressly delegated to the national government are reserved.* The general condition was well stated by Mr. Madison in the Federalist, thus: 'The Federal and state governments are in fact but different agents and trustees of the people, constituted with different powers and designated for different purposes.' Now, to the existence of the States, themselves necessary to the existence of the United States, the power of taxation is indispensable. It is an essential function of government. It was exercised by the colonies; and when the colonies became States, both before and after the formation of the confederation, it was exercised by the new governments. Under the Articles of Confederation the government of the United States was limited in the exercise of this power to requisitions upon the States, while the whole power of direct and indirect taxation of persons and property, whether by taxes on polls; or duties on imports, or duties on internal production, manufacture, or use, *was acknowledged to belong exclusively to the States, without any other limitation than that of non-interference with certain treaties made by Congress.* The Constitution, it is true, greatly changed this condition of things. It gave the power *to tax, both directly and indirectly, to the national government, and, subject to the one-prohibition of any tax upon exports* and to the conditions *of uniformity in respect to indirect and of proportion in respect to direct taxes, the power was given without any express reservation.* On the other hand, no power to tax exports, or imports except for a single purpose and to an insignificant extent, or to lay any duty on tonnage, was permitted to the States. In respect, however, to property, business, and persons, within their respective limits, their power of taxation remained and remains entire. It is indeed a concurrent power, and in the case of a tax on the same subject by both governments, the claim of the United States, as the supreme authority, must be preferred; but with this qualification it is absolute. The extent to which it shall be exercised, the subjects upon which it shall be exercised, and the mode in which it shall be exercised, are all equally within the discretion of the legislatures to which the States commit the exercise of the power. *That discretion is restrained only by the will of the people expressed in the state constitutions or through elections, and by the condition that it must not be so used as to burden or embarrass the operations of the national government. There is nothing in the Constitution which contemplates or authorizes any direct abridgment of this power by national legislation.* To the extent just indicated it is as complete in the States as the like power, *within the limits of the Constitution,* is complete in Congress.[17] (Emphasis added)

Fuller further explained the "great" constitutional compromise that resulted in the development of the two classes of taxation and the fear that still existed among the states even after the classes and the

[17]*Pollock vs Farmers' Loan, supra,* pages 559–562.

restrictions were established. No Supreme Court (either before or since the *Pollock* case) ever explored these constitutional considerations with greater thoroughness.

Thus was accomplished one of the great compromises of the Constitution, resting on the doctrine that the right of representation ought to be conceded to every community on which a tax is to be imposed, but crystallizing it in such form as to allay jealousies in respect of the future balance of power; to reconcile conflicting views in respect of the enumeration of slaves; and to remove the objection that, in adjusting a system of representation between the States, *regard should be had to their relative wealth, since those who were to be most heavily taxed ought to have a proportionate influence in the government.*

The compromise, in embracing the power of direct taxation, consisted not simply in including part of the slaves in the enumeration of population, but in providing that as between State and State such taxation should be proportioned to representation. The establishment of the same rule for the apportionment of taxes as for regulating the proportion of representatives, observed Mr. Madison in No. 54 of the Federalist, was by no means founded on the same principle, for as to the former it had reference to the proportion of wealth, and although in respect of that it was in ordinary cases a very unfit measure, it "had too recently obtained the general sanction of America, not to have found a ready preference with the convention, " while the opposite interests of the States, balancing each other, would produce impartiality in enumeration. By prescribing this rule, Hamilton wrote (Federalist, No. 36) that the door was shut *"to partiality or oppression," and "the abuse of this power of taxation to have been provided against with guarded circumspection;"* and obviously the operation of direct taxation on every State tended to prevent resort to that mode of supply except under pressure of necessity and to promote prudence and economy in expenditure.

We repeat that the right of the Federal government to directly assess and collect its own taxes, at least until after requisitions upon the States had been made and failed, **was one of the chief points of conflict, and Massachusetts, in ratifying, recommended the adoption of an amendment in these words: "That Congress do not lay direct taxes but when the moneys arising from the impost and excise are insufficient for the public exigencies, nor then until Congress shall have first made a requisition upon the States to assess, levy, and pay, their respective proportions of such requisition, agreeably to the census fixed in the said Constitution,** in such way and manner as the legislatures of the States shall think best." 1 Elliot, 322. And in this South Carolina, New York, New Hampshire, and Rhode Island concurred.[18] (Emphasis added)

[18]Ibid., pages 563-564.

So the Court thoroughly established the constitutional differences between direct and indirect taxes (and why and how they were to be levied) and then turned to the *Hylton* case. Apparently there were six judges then sitting on the Supreme Court and Fuller noted that "Chief Justice Ellsworth and Mr. Justice Cushing took no part in the decision, and Mr. Justice Wilson gave no reasons." The other three Justices in the case wrote, as was then the practice, their own, separate opinions.

The Opinion of Justice Chase

The Court commented on Justice Chase's opinion as follows:

> In *Hylton* v. *United States,* 3 Dall. 171, decided in March, 1796, this court held the act to be constitutional, because not laying a direct tax. Chief Justice Ellsworth and Mr. Justice Cushing took no part in the decision, and Mr. Justice Wilson gave no reasons.
>
> Mr. Justice Chase said that he was inclined to think, but of this he did not "give a judicial opinion," that *"the direct taxes contemplated by the Constitution, are only two, to wit, a capitation, or poll tax, simply, without regard to property, profession, or any other circumstance; and a tax on land;"* and that he doubted "whether a tax, by a general assessment of personal property, within the United States, is included within the term direct tax." But he thought that "an annual tax on carriages for the conveyance of persons, may be considered as within the power granted to Congress to lay duties. The term duty, is the most comprehensive next to the generical term tax; and practically in Great Britain, (whence we take our general ideas of taxes, duties, imposts, excises, customs, etc.,) embraces taxes on stamps, tolls for passage, etc., and is not confined to taxes on importation only. It seems to me, that a tax on expense is an indirect tax; and I think, an annual tax on a carriage for the conveyance of persons, is of that kind; because a carriage is a consumable commodity; and such annual tax on it, is on the expense of the owner."[19] (Emphasis added)

Fuller made no further specific comment on Chase's opinion but it is obvious that Chase was, indeed, confused. He believed that direct taxes only encompassed capitation taxes (personal taxes levied without regard to "property, profession, or any other circumstance"). If this were so, Article I, Section 9, Clause 4 of the Constitution would have read "No capitation or taxes on land shall be laid unless. . ." But the clause reads "No capitation or *other direct taxes* shall be laid unless. . ." This clearly signifies that capitations were merely one of many forms of taxes that might fall within that clause. Thus the framers of the Constitution

[19] Ibid., pages 570–571.

were obviously talking about a class, a power of taxation, and not limiting the government's taxing power to specific items of taxation. His confusion resulted, no doubt, from the fact that "land" was the most common type of property used to levy a direct tax based on wealth. But direct taxes are not limited to one form of wealth.[20] If land is property, would a tax measured by one kind of property fall into a different tax class (given only two classes) than a tax measured by another type of property? What also could have confused Chase was the fact that England apparently placed an excise tax on the sale of carriages and such a tax would indeed, be indirect. What he missed was that while a tax on the purchase of a carriage is an indirect tax (since the tax is paid to *the seller*), a tax paid *directly* to the government (based upon the ownership of a carriage) is obviously a direct tax. Such distinctions, however, were apparently lost on Chase who appears to have been hopelessly confused on this whole subject.

Justice Paterson's Opinion

Concerning this opinion Fuller wrote:

> Mr. Justice Paterson said that, the Constitution declares, that a capitation tax is a direct tax; and, both in theory and practice, a tax on land is deemed to be a direct tax. . . *It is not necessary to determine, whether a tax on the product of land be a direct or indirect tax.* Perhaps, the immediate product of land, in its original and crude state, ought to be considered as the land itself; it makes part of it; or else the provision made against taxing exports would be easily eluded. Land, independently of its produce is of no value . . . Whether direct taxes, in the sense of the Constitution, comprehend any other tax than a capitation tax, and taxes on land, is a questionable point. . . But as it is not before the court, it would be improper to give any decisive opinion upon it." And he concluded: *"All taxes on expenses or consumption are indirect taxes. A tax on carriages is of this kind, and of course is not a direct tax."* This conclusion he fortified by reading extracts from Adam Smith on the taxation of consumable commodities."[21] (Emphasis added)

It is obvious from the above that Paterson was just as confused as Chase. He also fails to understand that a tax on "expenses or consumption" is indirect because it is paid to the seller of the taxed product and the government would not even know who the actual payer of the tax was.

[20]The fact that slaves were included as taxable property in the direct tax acts of 1796, 1813, and 1815 is proof that Congress certainly did not believe that direct taxes were limited only to land.

[21]*Pollock vs Farmers' Loan, supra,* page 571.

A tax paid *directly* to government by an individual based on any type of property (consumable or otherwise) is, by definition, a *direct* tax. It should also be noted that all property (with the possible exception of land) is, in essence, "consumable." Homes get "consumed" as they age and deteriorate and money gets "consumed" as it is spent. It is obvious, therefore, that despite Paterson's apparent familiarity with Adam Smith's work (a work that he obviously misread) he, too, remained as confused as Chase.

The Opinion of Justice Iredell

Fuller wrote the following about Justice Iredell's opinion:

> Mr. Justice Iredell said: "There is no necessity, or propriety, in determining what is or is not, a direct, or indirect, tax in all cases. Some difficulties may occur which we do not at present foresee. Perhaps a direct tax, in the sense of the Constitution, can mean nothing but a tax on something inseparably annexed to the soil; something capable of apportionment under all such circumstances. A land or a poll tax may be considered of this description. . . In regard to other articles, there may possibly be considerable doubt. It is sufficient, on the present occasion, for the court to be satisfied, that this is not a direct tax contemplated by the Constitution, in order to affirm the present judgement."[22]

Iredell's comments are so vague and inconclusive that it is obvious he did not have the faintest idea of what he was talking about either and was basically flying by the seat of his pants.

So here we have a Supreme Court decision based on the opinions of three Justices — none of whom obviously had the foggiest idea of what they were talking about. And, based upon such a totally erroneous decision, numerous, far-reaching Supreme Court decisions rest.

Fuller, out of obvious kindness to his former colleagues (and in order to preserve the dignity of the Court), avoids making specific comments concerning any of these separate opinions, and only summarizes the totality of these opinions in one short and restrained paragraph.

> It will be perceived that each of the justices, while suggesting doubt whether anything but a capitation or a land tax was a direct tax within the meaning of the Constitution, distinctly avoided expressing an opinion upon that question or laying down a comprehensive definition, but confined his opinion to the case before the court.[23]

[22]Ibid.
[23]Ibid., pages 571, 572.

Hamilton's Inconsistency

An interesting aspect of the *Hylton* discussion was the part played by Alexander Hamilton (who prepared the government's case). After stating that Hamilton's brief "obviously influenced" the Court, Fuller quotes from that brief as follows:

> . . . he [Hamilton] said: "The following are presumed to be the only direct taxes: Capitation or poll taxes, taxes on lands and buildings, *general assessments,* whether on the *whole* property of individuals, or on their *whole* real or personal estate. All else must of necessity be considered as indirect taxes."[24] (Emphasis added)

While Hamilton's definition of what constitutes a direct tax is certainly broader than those of the three Justices (since his definition also includes "general assessments" and taxes upon personal property), he suddenly introduces the word "whole" as a significant criterion in determining whether a tax is direct or indirect. Presumably since the carriage tax did not attempt to tax the "whole (of a) personal estate" its status changed from direct to indirect. Such a distinction by Hamilton was, of course, absurd and can be found nowhere in his clear exposition of both forms of taxes as shown on pages 25–27. In any case, now that he was a part of the government, Hamilton enjoyed the fruits of power; while — when he wrote *The Federalist Papers* — he had none, save that which comes from an ability to logically and forcefully present the truth. Thus the corrupting influence of government service can be seen working even on an Alexander Hamilton.

Commenting further, Fuller noted that Hamilton stated in his brief that

> If the meaning of the word "excise" is to be sought in a British statute, it will be found to include the duty on carriages, which is there considered as an "excise". . .[25]

and further,

> that if "so important a distinction in the Constitution is to be realized" its meaning should be sought in terms of "the statutory language of that country from which our jurisprudence is derived."[26]

First of all, why examine the statutory language of British law regarding the meaning of excises when Hamilton had explained them so

---

[24]Ibid., page 572.
[25]Ibid.
[26]Ibid.

well in *Federalist Papers 12 and 21* (see pages 25 and 27)? In any case, why should an *obscure tax* on one item in the British economy settle a *major American constitutional question?* Since, however, Hamilton's observation did have a particular bearing on the income tax then under consideration, the *Pollock* Court was moved to observe:

> If the question had related to an income tax, the reference would have been fatal, as such taxes have been always classed by the law of Great Britain as direct taxes.[27]

Court Reviews Tax Acts

Having disposed of any legal restraints imposed by the *Hylton* decision, Fuller next turned to briefly reviewing *all* the direct tax acts covered in Chapter six. Following that, the Court arrived at the Income Tax Act of 1861 which obviously presented the Court with a tax entirely similar to the one it was now considering. If the income tax before the Court was unconstitutional, so too was the income tax of 1861. Yet taxes under that Act had been collected for ten years! Had the government then extracted millions in taxes illegally? This obviously presented the Court with a terrible dilemma. Swallowing hard, the Court sought to distinguish the two income tax acts in the following manner:

> The differences between the latter acts and that of August 15, 1894, call for no remark in this connection. *These acts grew out of the war of the rebellion,* and were, to use the language of Mr. Justice Miller, "part of the system of taxing incomes, earnings, and profits adopted during the late war, and abandoned as soon after that war was ended as it could be done safely." *Railroad Company v. Collector,* 100 U.S. 595, 598. . . . The act of that date *was passed in a time of profound peace,* and if we assume that *no special exigency called for unusual legislation,* and that resort to this mode of taxation *is to become an ordinary and usual means of supply, that fact furnishes an additional reason for circumspection and care in disposing of the case.*[28] (Emphasis added)

Court Distinguishes Between War and Peace

In contrast to these prior income tax acts (imposed in time of war), the Court pointed out that the Tax Act of 1894 was different in that it was imposed "in time of profound peace."

---

[27]Ibid.

[28]Ibid., pages 573, 574.

Before discussing a number of Court cases upon which the constitutionality of the Income Tax Act of 1861 relied, Fuller firmly explained that, based upon all the direct taxing acts that had been passed, and all other things considered

> 1. That the distinction between direct and indirect taxation was well understood by the framers of the Constitution and those who adopted it. 2. That under the state systems of taxation all taxes on real estate or personal property or the rents or income thereof were regarded as direct taxes. 3. That the rules of apportionment and of uniformity were adopted in view of that distinction and those systems. 4. That whether the tax on carriages was direct or indirect was disputed, but the tax was sustained as a tax on the use and an excise. 5. That the original expectation was that the power of direct taxation would be exercised only in extraordinary exigencies, and down to August 15, 1894, this expectation has been realized.[29]

Three Important Cases

Of other Supreme Court decisions examined, three were most important: *Insurance Co. vs Soule* 7 Wall 433, *Veazie Bank vs Fenno* 8 Wall 533, and *Springer vs U.S.* 102 US 586.

Insurance Co. vs Soule

Fuller pointed out that in this 1869 decision

> . . . the validity of a tax which was described as upon the business of an insurance company was sustained on the ground that it was "a duty or excise," and came within the decision in *Hylton's* Case.[30]

In checking the *Soule* case itself, however, we discover that that Court was for more enamored of the *Hylton* decision than the brief quote from *Pollock* suggests. I think it might be instructive to quote directly from the *Soule* decision.

> What are *direct taxes,* was elaborately argued and considered by this court in *Hylton v. United States.* . .[31] (Emphasis not added)

I suggest that that statement is not true, but then the Court added:

[29]Ibid., page 574.
[30]Ibid.
[31]*Insurance Co. vs Soule* 7 Wall 433, page 444.

If a tax upon carriages, kept for its own use by the owner, is not a direct tax, we can see no ground upon which a tax upon the business of an insurance company can be held to belong to that class of revenue charges.[32]

Thus, we see how judicial error becomes compounded and codified into "law." Despite the fact that the insurance company's brief explained the historic differences between direct and indirect taxes, the government was able to overcome all valid arguments solely because of the *Hylton* decision. The government merely claimed that:

The tax on incomes is not a "direct tax" within the meaning of the Constitution and is not subject to the rule of apportionment prescribed by Article 1, section 2, of the Constitution.

The case of *Hylton v. U.S.* 3 Dall, 171 seems conclusive on the point here raised.[33]

End of argument. The government apparently based its whole case on the totally erroneous *Hylton* decision and the *Soule* Court went along with it. Such is the power of prior Court decisions. In rendering its decision, the Court (in *Soule*) elaborated as follows:

The consequences which would follow the apportionment of the tax in question among the States and Territories of the Union, in the manner prescribed by the Constitution, must not be overlooked. They are very obvious. Where such corporations are numerous and rich, it might be light; where none exist, it could not be collected; where they are few and poor, it would fall upon them with such weight as to involve annihilation. It cannot be supposed that the framers of the Constitution intended that any tax should be apportioned, the collection of which on that principle would be attended with such results. The consequences are fatal to the proposition.[34]

This objection, while missing from the *Pollock* decision itself, was none-the-less decisively answered by that Court in the following manner:

Nothing can be clearer than that what the Constitution intended to guard against was the exercise by the general government of the power of directly taxing persons and property within any *State through a majority made up from the other States*. It is true that the effect of requiring direct

[32]Ibid., page 446.
[33]Ibid., page 439.
[34]Ibid., page 446.

The Supreme Court Declares an Income Tax Unconstitutional

taxes to be apportioned among the States in proportion to their population is necessarily that the amount of taxes on the individual taxpayer in a State having the taxable subject matter to a larger extent in proportion to its population than another State has, would be less than in such other State, *but this inequality must be held to have been contemplated,* and was manifestly *designed to operate to restrain the exercise of the power of direct taxation to extraordinary emergencies,* and to prevent *an attack upon accumulated property by mere force of numbers.*[35] (Emphasis added)

In commenting directly on the *Soule* case the *Pollock* Court stated:

The arguments for the insurance company were elaborate and took a wide range, but the decision rested on narrow ground, and turned on the distinction between an excise duty and a tax strictly so termed, regarding the former *a charge for a privilege, or on the transaction of business,* without any necessary reference to the amount of property belonging to those on whom the charge might fall, although it might be increased or diminished by the extent to which *the privilege* was exercised or the business done. This was in accordance with *Society for Savings v. Coite,* 6 Wall. 594; *Provident Institution v. Massachusetts,* 6 Wall. 611; and *Hamilton Company v. Massachusetts,* 6 Wall. 632; in which cases there was a difference of opinion on the question whether the tax under consideration was a tax on the property and not upon the franchise or privilege.[36] (Emphasis added)

A "privilege" tax is another fallacious issue (as explained fully on pages 141–143) that was created by Federal courts and apparently helped the government in this case. At least a tax on insurance premiums (as levied by many states) is indirect, since it is passed on to insurance buyers in the form of higher premiums. But how can there be any such thing as a "privilege" in connection with insurance? Those who buy insurance merely attempt to (collectively) protect themselves from a hazard of life, risks everyone faces. Insurance is not something that anyone really *wants* — it's a cost that responsible people absorb for the protection of themselves, their families, and society. By electing to pay (and thus allow for the pooling of risks), those who insure are less likely to become (or leave spouses and/or children to become) public charges because of death, disability or any of the other hazards one insures against. The pool of money formed by "insurance" is not created from the sale of any product or desired consumable service. It merely constitutes a common pool out of which the losses suffered by those in the pool can be paid. The building up of such a pool naturally creates many

[35]*Pollock vs Farmers' Loan, supra,* page 583.
[36]Ibid., page 576.

other expenses (in addition to the raw, actuarial cost of the risk itself) which also have to be absorbed by those insured. Any artificial increases in these expenses (such as taxes placed on insurance) only increases the cost to the public of insuring against life's hazards. All governmental taxes on insurance do is simply increase the price society has to pay to protect itself against tragedy. Is this a "product" that any sane and responsible government should consider taxing? In addition, of course, many of the social programs urged upon us by government and its supporters are responsibly handled by people through insurance. So government, by artificially increasing the cost of insurance by taxing it, diminishes its use and increases government's ability to propose its own wasteful alternatives.

A tax (allegedly on the profit of an insurance company) is, however, another matter and is a direct tax on the company itself (but related to profit rather than to the ownership of real estate, for instance). It can, by no stretch of the imagination, be said to be indirect. In addition, to suggest that it is a "duty" on the "privilege" of operating an insurance company is sheer judicial nonsense.[37]

Veazie Bank vs Fenno

In this decision, the Supreme Court upheld as legal a Federal tax laid on the circulation of state banknotes. In reaching its decision in this case, the *Veazie* Court again relied heavily on the *Hylton* case. The Court also said that the tax was a "duty" that fell within the same category of tax as that in the *Soule* case. Commenting on this decision the *Pollock* Court observed:

> In *Bank v. Fenno,* 8 Wall. 533, a tax was laid on the circulation of state banks or national banks paying out the notes of individuals or state banks, and it was held that it might well be classed under the head of duties, and as falling within the same category as *Soule's* Case 7 Wall. 433.

---

[37]No corporation (or any other business) should pay any form of direct tax — including property taxes. As explained earlier, in the final analysis *only people pay taxes*. It is important, therefore, that they realize exactly how much taxes they do pay. All business taxes are ultimately passed on to the public either in the form of higher prices, lower wages, lower dividends, or a combination of all three. Tax money that the government extracts from business must, eventually, come from all the people that these businesses serve — either their stockholders, employees or the consuming public. The public, however, never fully realizes that they actually pay all those Federal taxes ostensibly paid by "business." So in taxing "business", the politicians are able to hide the actual amount of taxes the public pays. If people were taxed directly (rather than indirectly through taxes on "business") they would realize how much in taxes they really pay and would never allow politicians to spend so much of their money. For more on this, see Irwin Schiff's *How Anyone Can Stop Paying Income Taxes.*

It was declared to be of the same nature as excise taxation on freight receipts, bills of lading, and passenger tickets issued by a railroad company. *Referring to the discussions in the convention which framed the constitution, Mr. Chief Justice Chase observed that what was said there "doubtless shows uncertainly as to the true meaning of the term 'direct tax',* but it indicates also an understanding that direct taxes were such as may be levied by capitation and on land and appurtenances, or perhaps by valuation and assessment of personal property upon general lists; for these were the subjects from which the states at that time usually raised their principal supplies." And in respect of the opinions in *Hylton's* Case the chief justice said: "It may further be taken as established upon the testimony of Paterson that the words 'direct taxes', as used in the constitution, comprehended only capitation taxes and taxes on land, and perhaps taxes on personal property by general valuation and assessment of the various descriptions possessed within the several states." [38] (Emphasis added)

This decision was, therefore, based on *two* erroneous prior Supreme Court decisions and also on the fallacy that those who wrote the Constitution did not know what they were writing about. While the *Pollock* Court cites little else from this decision, digressing from the *Pollock* decision and covering the *Veazie* case in far more detail is relevant here since it was an extremely important, though totally erroneous, decision. Substantially (and illegally) it increased the Federal government's power in two vital areas: 1) its ability to create paper money; and 2) its ability to levy taxes illegally. Therefore, it represents one of the most important decisions to ever come before the Court — yet the extent of the deception involved in this case has never been fully explored. *The case vividly demonstrates how the Supreme Court can throw both fact and law to the winds when it wants to contrive a decision favorable to the government.*

It must be noted that this decision was written by Chief Justice Samuel Chase who was Lincoln's Secretary of the Treasury when these taxing statutes were adopted. Since he was largely responsible for designing these measures, he was not exactly an impartial judge. In all fairness to him, though, it must also be said that he did not let such considerations influence his decisions in the legal rendering of such cases as *Hepburn vs. Griswold* 8 Wall. 513 and *Knox vs. Lee* 12 Wall. 281 which are totally irreconsilable to his opinion here. In *Hepburn* he wrote the majority opinion which held that U.S. notes issued during the Civil War were not legal tender for debts contracted prior to the War. In *Knox* (which reversed *Hepburn*) he wrote the minority opinion. His opinions in both cases are excellent and certainly deserve reading.

[38]*Pollock vs Farmers' Loan, supra,* page 577.

In *Hepburn* it was assumed that Chase would be on the other side since he was instrumental in creating the notes in question. Chase, however, provided an unusually forthright explanation when he wrote in *Hepburn:*

> It is not surprising that amid the tumult of the late Civil War, and under the influence of apprehensions for the safety of the Republic almost universal, different views, never before entertained by American statesmen or jurists, were adopted by many. *The time was not favorable to considerate reflection upon the constitutional limits of legislative or executive authority.* If power was assumed from patriotic motives the assumption found ready justification in patriotic hearts. *Many who doubted yielded their doubts;* many who did not doubt were silent. Some who were strongly averse to making government notes a legal tender felt themselves constrained to acquiesce in the views of the advocates of the measure. *Not a few* who then insisted upon its necessity, or acquiesced in that view, *have, since the return of peace,* and under the influence of calmer time, *reconsidered their conclusions.*[39] (Emphasis added)

Tax on State Banknotes

The case actually involved a tax that was passed just before the Civil War ended. On March 3, 1865 Congress placed a "duty" of 10 percent on notes issued by state banks, though no comparable duty was imposed on notes issued by the newly created Federal banks. In addition, a 5 percent "duty" was placed on dividends paid out, a monthly "duty" of 1/24 of one percent was placed on all deposits, and the same monthly "duty" was levied on the capital of each state bank. The North was, admittedly, hardpressed for money with which to fight the War. One of the devices used early in the War to raise money was the establishment (by the Federal government) of a system of federally chartered "national" banks. These banks were required (under the Act of February 25, 1863) to invest a percentage of their paid-in capital in government bonds and to maintain a reserve of Federal bonds as backing for a new type of "national banknote" that was also created under the Act. (These new, national banknotes were in addition to the federally issued "greenbacks" that were also a product of the Civil War.)

A new post, "controller of the currency" was also created to supervise the issuance of these banknotes. This new "national" currency and the adoption of a system of "national" banks were created solely to help the North finance the War. There is no question that if there had been no Civil War the need for a "national" currency or a new system of "na-

---

[39]*Hepburn vs. Griswold* 75 US 603 (1869), page 625.

tional" banks would never have been proposed or adopted. No national currency or system of federally chartered banks had ever before been considered (although the Federal government did, at one time, run its own bank) since neither were authorized by or suggested in the Constitution. It is, of course, one thing for the government to adopt certain procedures as emergency, war-time measures (dismantling them as soon as the emergency is over), and even to justify them on that basis alone. It is quite another thing, however, for the Supreme Court to attempt to legitimatize unusual war-time usurpations as being authorized by and in harmony with the U.S. Constitution (when they obviously are not) because the principles developed in such decisions are adopted by other courts in order to justify other unlawful, Federal acts. When this happens, error is piled on error and the government's illegal powers grow. This is precisely the type of influence the *Veazie* case had.

The case itself was based upon prior Court error which the *Veazie* Court proceeded to enlarge. The government's action in laying a 10 percent tax on state banknotes was patently unconstitutional and could only be justified as a necessary and desperate war-time expedient. The Supreme Court, however (instead of simply treating it as such) tried to justify the tax as a constitutionally authorized tax and, in so doing, had to stand both logic and law on their heads — making it a whole lot easier for future Supreme Courts to do the same thing.

Civil War Changes The Monetary System

The *Veazie* decision started out as follows:

> The necessity of adequate provision *for the financial exigencies created by the late rebellion,* suggested to the administrative and legislative departments of the government *important changes in the systems of currency and taxation which had hitherto prevailed.* These changes, more or less distinctly shown in administrative recommendations, took form and substance in legislative acts. We have now to consider, within a limited range, those which relate to circulating notes and the taxation of circulation.
>
> At the beginning of the rebellion the circulating medium *consisted almost entirely of bank notes issued by numerous independent corporations* variously organized under State legislation, of various degrees of credit, and very unequal resources, administered often with great, and not unfrequently, with little skill, prudence, and integrity. The acts of Congress, then in force, *prohibiting the receipt or disbursement, in the transactions of the National government, of anything except gold and silver,* and the laws of the States requiring the redemption of bank notes in coin on demand, prevented the disappearance of gold and silver from circulation. *There was, then, no National currency except coin;* there was no general regu-

lation of any other by National legislation; and *no National taxation was imposed in any form on the State bank circulation.*[40] (Emphasis added)

By the Court's own admission it was obvious that:

1. changes in the nation's "system of currency" were necessitated by the "financial exigencies" created by the Civil War;
2. until that time there was no national currency;
3. only gold and silver coin circulated as lawful money;
4. notes (promises to pay lawful money, i.e. gold and silver coin) were issued by state banks as well as private citizens;
5. Federal law prohibited the Federal government from receiving or disbursing anything but gold and silver; and
6. state laws required the redemption of banknotes in either gold or silver coin, on demand.

Not one of these conditions exists today, though they did exist during the first eighty years of our nation's history! Why? Because until the Civil War the Constitution was generally obeyed. Due to decisions such as *Veazie*, however, the Federal establishment has since been able to practically scrap the entire document and institute Federal programs entirely foreign to it.

Next, the *Veazie* Court briefly reviewed the development of paper currency in the United States, including the suspension of specie payments (gold and silver coin) by the state banks on December 31, 1861. (It was the issuance of non-redeemable currency by the Federal government that caused a run on the banks that eventually culminated in the suspension of specie payments.) After reviewing the development of Federal note-currency that occurred subsequent to 1861, the Court stated:

> This currency, issued directly by the government for the disbursement of the war and other expenditures, could not, obviously, be a proper object of taxation.[41]

Just why Federal currency could not be "a proper object of taxation" is not explained. The Court then reviewed the development of the tax on state banknotes as follows:

> But on the 25th of February, 1863 [in connection with the national banking act] . . . Congress recognized the expediency and duty of imposing a tax upon currency. . .[42]

[40]*Veazie vs Fenno* 75 US 533, pages 536, 537.
[41]Ibid., page 538.
[42]Ibid.

Federal Government Taxes Capital

Under this Act the Federal government admittedly also taxed capital as an excise tax. The Court blandly admitted that:

> Both acts also imposed taxes on *capital* and *deposits,* which need not be noticed here.[43] (Emphasis added)

The Court then reviewed the succession of increases in these levies and explained the issues before it as follows:

> The general question now before us is, whether or not the tax of ten per cent, imposed on State banks or national banks paying out the notes of individuals or State banks used for circulation, is repugnant to the Constitution of the United States.[44]

Note also how the *Veazie* Court (in the following excerpt) misrepresented the government's taxing power by: 1) misstating the taxing clauses in the Constitution by suggesting that it is difficult to define "with accuracy the terms used in the Constitution" with respect to those powers; and 2) suggesting that because (under the Articles of Confederation) the "General Government . . . had been reduced to impotency" the Constitution obviously sought to convey "comprehensive" taxing powers — supposedly not limited by either apportionment or uniformity.

> In support of the position that the act of Congress, so far as it provides for the levy and collection of this tax, is repugnant to the Constitution, two propositions have been argued with much force and earnestness.
>
> The first is that the tax in question is a direct tax, and has not been apportioned among the States agreeably to the Constitution.
>
> The second is that the act imposing the tax impairs a franchise granted by the State, and that Congress has no power to pass any law with that intent or effect.
>
> The first of these propositions will be first examined.
>
> *The difficulty of defining with accuracy the terms used in the clause of the Constitution which confers the power of taxation upon Congress, was felt in the Convention which framed that instrument,* and has always been experienced by courts when called upon to determine their meaning.
>
> The general intent of the Constitution, however, seems plain. The General Government, administered by the *Congress of the Confederation,*

---

[43]Ibid.
[44]Ibid., pages 539, 540.

had been reduced to the verge of impotency by the necessity of relying for revenue upon requisitions on the States, and it was a leading object in the adoption of the Constitution to relieve the government, to be organized under it, from this necessity, *and confer upon it ample power to provide revenue by the taxation* of persons and property. And nothing is clearer, from the discussions in the Convention and the discussions which preceded final ratification by the necessary number of States, than the purpose to give this power to Congress, as to the taxation of everything except exports, in its fullest extent.

This purpose is apparent, also, from the terms in which the taxing power is granted. The power is "to lay and collect taxes, duties, imposts, and excises, to pay the debt and provide for the common defence and general welfare of the United States." *More comprehensive words could not have been used.* Exports only are by another provision excluded from its application.[45] (Emphasis added)

The Court began to address the first of these two questions in the following eight paragraphs in which Chase attempted to add confusion to a very simple issue. He erected numerous straw men to argue against it. And, while there are references to apportionment and uniformity, their meaning is not explained. Indeed, such limitations would appear to be meaningless since Chase went on to note an alleged "absence of any attempt by members of the Convention to define . . . the terms of the grant."

There are, indeed, certain virtual limitations, arising from the principles of the Constitution itself. It would undoubtedly be an abuse of the power if so exercised as to impair the separate existence and independent self-government of the States, or if exercised for ends inconsistent with the limited grants of power in the Constitution.

And there are directions as to the mode of exercising the power. If Congress sees fit to impose a capitation, or other direct tax, it must be laid in proportion to the census; if Congress determines to impose duties, imposts, and excises, they must be uniform throughout the United States. These are not strictly limitations of power. They are rules prescribing the mode in which it shall be exercised. It still extends to every object of taxation, except exports, and may be applied to every object of taxation, to which it extends, in such measure as Congress may determine.

The comprehensiveness of the power, thus given to Congress, may serve to explain, at least, *the absence of any attempt by members of the Convention to define, even in debate, the terms of the grant.* The words used

---

[45]Ibid., page 540.

certainly describe the *whole power,* and it was the intention of the *Convention that the whole power should be conferred.* **The definition of particular words, therefore, became unimportant.**

It may be said, indeed, that this observation, however just in its application to the general grant of power, cannot be applied to the rules by which different descriptions of taxes are directed to be laid and collected.

Direct taxes must be laid and collected by the rule of apportionment; duties, imposts, and excises must be laid and collected under the rule of uniformity.

Much diversity of opinion has always prevailed upon the question, what are direct taxes? Attempts to answer it by reference to the definitions of political economists have been frequently made, but without satisfactory results. The enumeration of the different kinds of taxes which Congress was authorized to impose was probably made with very little reference to their speculations. **The great work of Adam Smith, the first comprehensive treatise on political economy in the English language, had then been recently published; but in this work, though there are passages which refer to the characteristic difference between direct and indirect taxation, there is nothing which affords any valuable light on the use of the words "direct taxes" in the Constitution.**[46] (Emphasis added)

For Chase to suggest that "the definition of particular words, [i.e., direct versus indirect taxation], therefore, became unimportant" has no justification. It is "unimportant" if one does not want to face the obvious differences in these terms — which is what Chase obviously did not want to do. In addition, his assertion that in the "great work of Adam Smith . . . there is nothing which affords any valuable light on the use of the words 'direct taxes' in the Constitution" is flagrantly untrue. The Court concluded its examination of the subject and completely fudged on the subject of direct versus indirect taxes by stating:

It may be safely assumed, therefore, as the unanimous judgment of the court, that a tax on carriages is not a direct tax. And it may further be taken as established upon the testimony of Paterson, that the words direct taxes, as used in the Constitution, *comprehended only capitation taxes, and taxes on land, and perhaps taxes on personal property* by general valuation and assessment of the various descriptions possessed within the several States.

It follows necessarily that the power to tax without apportionment extends to all other objects. Taxes on other objects are included under the heads of taxes not direct, duties, imposts, and excises, and must be laid

[46]Ibid., pages 541, 542.

and collected by the rule of uniformity. The tax under consideration is a tax on bank circulation, and may very well be classed under the head of duties. Certainly it is not, in the sense of the Constitution, a direct tax. It may be said to come within the same category of taxation as the tax on incomes of insurance companies, which this court, at the last term, in the case of *Pacific Insurance Company v. Soule* held not to be a direct tax. [47]

The Court then asked:

Is it, then, a tax on a franchise granted by a State, which Congress, upon any principle exempting the reserved powers of the States from impairment by taxation, must be held to have no authority to lay and collect?[48]

Tax on Banknotes Compared to Taxes on Railroad Tickets

Next, the Court equated a tax on *debt* (banknotes) with a tax on a consumable service — railroad tickets. This, of course, demonstrates a complete lack of knowledge concerning the principles of taxation.

We do not say that there may not be such a tax. It may be admitted that the reserved rights of the States, such as the right to pass laws, to give effect to laws through executive action, to administer justice through the courts, and to employ all necessary agencies for legitimate purposes of State government, are not proper subjects of the taxing power of Congress. **But it cannot be admitted that franchises granted by a State are necessarily exempt from taxation;** for franchises are property, often very valuable and productive property; and when not conferred for the purpose of giving effect to some reserved power of a State, seem to be *as properly objects of taxation as any other property.*

But in the case before us the object of taxation is not the franchise of the bank, but property created, or contracts made and issued under the franchise, or power to issue bank bills. *A railroad company, in the exercise of its corporate franchises, issues freight receipts, bills of lading, and passenger tickets;* and it cannot be doubted that the organization of railroads is quite as important to the State as the organization of banks. But it will hardly be questioned that these contracts of the company are objects of taxation within the powers of Congress, and not exempted by any relation to the State which granted the charter of the railroad. *And it seems difficult to distinguish the taxation of notes issued for circulation from the taxation of these railroad contracts.* Both descriptions of contracts are means of profit to the corporations which issue them; and both, as we think may properly be made contributory to the public revenue.[49] (Emphasis added)

[47]Ibid., pages 546, 547.
[48]Ibid., page 547.
[49]Ibid, page 547, 548.

Note here how the Court talked about a "tax on a franchise" as being "as properly objects of taxation as any other property." First, the Court (as do all courts) became involved in the fallacy that property gets taxed when, in reality, it is always *people* who get taxed. In addition, to compare a Federal tax on railroad tickets to a Federal tax on capital stock or banknotes was totally devoid of logic, mainly because a tax on a railroad ticket was an obvious excise tax. The tax was levied *on those* who could afford this mode of transportation, with the price of tickets raised accordingly. Such taxes were legitimately levied in order to raise revenue (not to discourage the use of railroads), which was not the purpose of the 10 percent tax on state banknotes. The tax on state banknotes was not levied to raise revenue (for any of the purposes shown on page 31) but to penalize state banks in order to create a strong incentive for banks to join the newly created Federal banking system — where no such punitive tax applied.

Further, the taxes levied as a monthly "duty" on bank deposits and capital were apparently not an issue in this case. It was not an indirect "duty" but a direct tax imposed on each bank, based upon its deposits and capital stock. Such taxes cannot be avoided or passed on like taxes on railroad tickets can because they are taxes based on the accumulation of wealth or property and, therefore, no different than taxes related to other forms of wealth such as real estate. But a tax on banknotes is another type of tax altogether — it is a tax based on debt rather than on wealth! The fallacy of such a tax will be covered in excerpts from the dissenting opinion. But to say that a tax on a debt instrument is comparable, *in any way,* to a tax based on wealth (or on the purchase of consumable goods or services such as a railroad ticket) escapes understanding.

Tax Blatantly Discriminatory

What the Court also failed to take into consideration in this matter was that the tax on banknotes was not uniform because it did not apply to notes issued by *all* banks. The tax was, admittedly, discriminatory and designed to speed up applications for Federal bank charters, which it did. It was, therefore, flagrantly unconstitutional (for the reasons covered in Field's opinion, see page 118) on this one issue alone.

The tax represented an attempt by Congress to interfere and curtail (through the abuse of Federal taxing powers) legitimate state functions. Since the Federal government could not pass a law directly outlawing state-chartered banks, it sought to kill them off through this tax in order to sell government bonds to Federal banks to finance the War. But the Supreme Court (trying to legally justify such a war-time expediency) resorted to creating absurd and high-handed legal doctrine that could and did serve as legal precedent for generations to come.

Misstating the Law on Money

The *Veazie* Court went even further in making its own amendments to the Constitution:

> It cannot be doubted that under the Constitution the power to provide a circulation of coin is given to Congress. And it is settled by the uniform practice of the government and by repeated decisions, that Congress may constitutionally authorize the emission of bills of credit.[50]

While there is no argument that the Constitution gave Congress the power to provide for "a circulation of coin, " there is absolutely nothing in it that authorizes "the emission of bills of credit." (How such "emission" was deliberately denied was explained on page 53.) Note, too, how the Court cleverly twisted phrases in order to create the illusion that the Constitution authorized such an "emission." In the first sentence Chase clearly stated that the Constitution provided for a "circulation of coin." But when talking about the "emission of bills of credit, " he switched to such phraseology as "the uniform practice of the government" and "repeated decisions." He could not say, "under the Constitution the power to provide for a circulation of currency (paper money) was also given to Congress" because he knew that no such power was given to Congress "under the Constitution, " and he also knew that few would recognize the linguistic subterfuge he used to create that false impression. If, as tacitly admitted by Chase, the Federal government did not get its power to emit bills of credit from the Constitution, where did it get the power? It usurped it — on the basis of those "uniform practices" and "repeated decisions" to which he referred.

The reason the Federal government only circulated silver and gold coin up until the time of the Civil War was because it was the *only* form of money the Constitution authorized. Further on we find this statement in connection with this very issue:

> These powers [the alleged power to issue note currency] until recently, were only partially and occasionally exercised. Lately, however, they have been called into full activity, and congress has undertaken to supply a currency for the entire country.[51]

The Constitution has absolutely no provisions authorizing Congress to supply any form of paper currency whatsoever. Had there been any such provision, Congress certainly would have "undertaken" to supply it long before 1861.

[50]Ibid., page 548.
[51]Ibid.

The Dissenting Opinion

Two justices of that Court evidently felt a greater responsibility to uphold both law and reason in connection with this case as is obvious from the following excerpts taken from their excellent dissenting opinion.

Since the adoption of the Constitution, down to the present act of Congress, and the case now before us, the question in Congress and in the courts has been, not whether the State banks were constitutional institutions, but whether Congress had the power conferred on it by the States, to establish a National bank. As we have said, that question was closed by the judgment of this court in *McCulloch* v. *The State of Maryland*. At the time of the adoption of the Constitution, there were four State banks in existence and in operation — one in each of the States of Pennsylvania, New York, Massachusetts, and Maryland. The one in Philadelphia had been originally chartered by the Confederation, but subsequently took a charter under the State of Pennsylvania. *The framers of the Constitution were, therefore, familiar with these State banks, and the circulation of their paper as money;* and were also *familiar with the practice of the States, that was so common, to issue* bills of credit, which *were* bills *issued by the State,* exclusively on its own credit, and intended to circulate as currency, redeemable at a future day. *They guarded the people against the evils of this practice of the State governments by the provision in the tenth section of the first article, "that no State shall" "emit bills of credit," and, in the same section, guard against any abuse of paper money of the State banks in the following words:* **"nor make anything but gold and silver coin a tender in payment of debts."** *As bills of credit were thus entirely abolished, the paper money of the State banks was the only currency or circulating medium to which this prohibition could have had any application, and was the only currency, except gold and silver, left to the States.* **The prohibition took from this paper all coercive circulation, and left it to stand alone upon the credit of the banks.**

It was no longer an irredeemable currency, as the banks were under obligation, including, frequently, that of its stockholders, to redeem their paper in circulation, in gold or silver, at the counter. *The State banks were left in this condition by the Constitution, untouched by any other provision.* As a consequence, they were gradually established in most or all of the States, and had not been encroached upon or legislated against, or in any other way interfered with, by acts of Congress, for more than three-quarters of a century — from 1787 to 1864. . . .

The constitutional power of the States, being thus established by incontrovertible authority, to create State banking institutions, the next question is, *whether or not the tax in question can be upheld, consistently with the enjoyment of this power.*

The act of Congress, July 13th, 1866, declares, that the State banks shall pay ten per centum on the amount of their notes, or the notes of any person, or other State bank, used for circulation, and paid out by them after the 1st of August, 1866. In addition to this tax, there is also a tax of *five per centum per annum, upon all dividends to stockholders,* besides a duty of one twenty-fourth of one per centum, monthly, upon all deposits, and the same monthly duty upon the capital of the bank. This makes an aggregate of *some sixteen per cent, imposed annually upon these banks.* It will be observed, the tax of ten per centum upon the bills in circulation is not a tax on the property of the institutions. *The bills in circulation are not the property, but the debts of the bank,* and, *in their account of debits and credits, are placed to the debit side. Certainly, no government has yet made the discovery of taxing both sides of this account, debit and credit, as the property of a taxable person or corporation. If both these items could be made available for this purpose, a heavy* National debt *need not create any very great alarm,* neither as it respects its pressure on the industry of the country, for the time being, or of its possible duration. ***There is nothing in the debts of a bank to distinguish them in this respect from the debts of individuals or persons.*** The discounted paper received for the notes in circulation is the property of the bank, and is taxed as such, as is the property of individuals received for their notes that may be outstanding.

The imposition upon the banks cannot be upheld as *a tax upon property;* neither could it have been so intended. ***It is, simply, a mode by which the powers or faculties of the States, to incorporate banks, are subjected to taxation, and, which, if maintainable, may annihilate those powers...***

It is true, that the present decision strikes only at the power to create banks, *but no person can fail to see that the principle involved affects the power to create any other description of corporations, such as railroads, turnpikes, manufacturing companies, and others.*

This taxation of the powers and faculties of the State governments, which are essential to their sovereignty, and to the efficient and independent management and administration of their internal affairs, is, for the first time, advanced as an attribute of Federal authority. It finds no support or countenance in the early history of the government, or in the opinions of the illustrious statesmen who founded it. These statesmen scrupulously abstained from any encroachment upon the reserved rights of the States; and, within these limits, sustained and supported them as sovereign States.

We say nothing, as to the purpose of this heavy tax of some sixteen per centum upon the banks, ten of which we cannot but regard as imposed upon the power of the States to create them. ***Indeed, the purpose is scarcely concealed, in the opinion of the court, namely, to encourage the National banks.*** It is sufficient to add, that the burden of the tax, while it has encouraged these banks, ***has proved fatal to those of the States;*** and, if we are at liberty to judge of the purpose of an act, from the consequences that have followed, it is not, perhaps, going too far to say, that these consequences were intended.[52] (Emphasis added)

There can be no doubt that the minority opinion clearly exposes the majority opinion in this case to be a fraud and a hoax.

Springer vs. U.S. 102 US 586

The *Pollock* Court next discussed the *Springer* case (closely related to the issue under consideration) which, it noted, was "urged upon us as decisive." The *Springer* case involved an individual who claimed (correctly) that the seizure of his property in payment of income taxes was illegal because the tax, being direct, was not apportioned. The *Springer* Court, however, had disagreed. In connection with that decision the *Pollock* Court stated:

> The statement of the case in the report shows that Springer returned a certain amount as his net income for the particular year, but does not give the details of what his income, gains, and profits consisted in.
>
> The original record discloses that the income was not derived in any degree from real estate but was in part professional as attorney-at-law and the rest interest on United States bonds. It would seem probable that the court did not feel called upon to advert to the distinction between the latter and the former source of income, as the validity of the tax as to either would sustain the action.
>
> The opinion thus concludes: "Our conclusions are, that *direct taxes*, within the meaning of the constitution, are only capitation taxes, as expressed in that instrument, and taxes on real estate; and that the tax of which the plaintiff in error complains is within the category of an excise or duty."[53] (Emphasis added)

The *Springer* case cut close to the issue raised in this case, but the *Pollock* Court escaped it in the following manner:

> While this language is broad enough to cover the interest as well as the professional earnings, the case would have been more significant as a precedent if the distinction had been brought out in the report and commented on in arriving at judgement, for a tax on professional receipts might be treated as an excise or duty, and therefore indirect, when a tax on the income of personalty might be held to be direct.[54]

---

[52]Ibid., pages 551-556.
[53]*Pollock vs Farmers' Loan, supra,* pages 578, 579.
[54]Ibid., page 579.

Income From Professional Earnings Not Relevant

The Court refused to be bound by *Springer* because it felt Springer's income came largely from professional earnings while (in the case at hand) the issue involved income not from professional earnings but income from real estate, stocks and bonds. In distinguishing both cases, the Court observed "that a tax on professional receipts might be treated as an excise or duty, and therefore indirect, when a tax on the income of personalty might be held to be direct." The subtleties involved in this statement indicate that the *Pollock* court had a good grasp of the differences between both types of taxes.

Note that the Court speaks of an excise tax on "professional *receipts,* " not professional *"income."* This is distinguished from "income of personalty" which was used to describe a direct tax. The indirect tax would, therefore, apply to *gross receipts* from a profession while the direct tax would apply to the *net receipts* from personal property. What the Court was getting at was that a tax on "professional receipts" implied a form of sales tax that conceivably could be tacked onto the price of the professional service — and, therefore, was a tax that could be passed on to those receiving that service. But a tax "on the income of personalty" (since it could not be passed on) would have to be direct. Such a distinction allowed the Court to differentiate this case from *Springer,* though lesser Courts would have undoubtedly found the issues in both cases practically identical.

Taxes on Land and Rent — Direct Taxes

Having thus disposed of a variety of prior tax cases (all of which were decided incorrectly), Chief Justice Fuller warmed up to the issue at hand by first establishing the following:

> Be this as it may, it is conceded in all these cases, from that of Hylton to that of Springer, that taxes on land are direct taxes and in none of them is it determined that taxes on rents or income derived from land are not taxes on land.[55]

Having clearly established that taxes *on* land were always regarded as direct, the Court then established that taxes "on" rents must also be direct and logically so the income from personal property — dividends and interest from stocks and bonds.

> We admit that it may not unreasonably be said that logically, if taxes on the rents, issues, and profits of real estate *are equivalent to taxes on*

55Ibid, page 580.

real estate, and are therefore direct taxes, taxes on the income of personal property as such are equivalent to taxes on such property, and therefore direct taxes. But we are considering the rule *stare decisis,* and we must decline to hold ourselves bound to extend the scope of decisions — none of which discussed the question whether a tax on the income from personalty is equivalent to a tax on that personalty, but all of which held real estate liable to direct taxation only — so as to sustain a tax on the income of realty on the ground of being an excise of duty.

As no capitation or other direct tax was to be laid otherwise than in proportion to the population, some other direct tax than a capitation tax (and, it might well enough be argued, some other tax of the same kind as a capitation tax) must be referred to, and it has always been considered that a tax upon real estate co nomine, or upon its owners in respect thereof, is a direct tax, within the meaning of the constitution. *But is there any distinction between the real estate itself or its owners in respect of it and the rents or income of the real estate coming to the owners as the natural and ordinary incident of their ownership?*

If the constitution had provided that congress should not levy any tax upon the real estate of any citizen of any state, could it be contended that congress could put an annual tax for five or any other number of years upon the rent or income of the real estate? And if, as the constitution now reads, no unapportioned tax can be imposed upon real estate, *can congress without apportionment nevertheless impose taxes upon such real estate under the guise of an annual tax upon its rents or income?...*

The requirement of the constitution is that no direct tax shall be laid otherwise than by apportionment. The prohibition is not against direct taxes on land, from which the implication is sought to be drawn that indirect taxes on land would be constitutional, but it is against all direct taxes; and it is admitted that a tax on real estate is a direct tax. *Unless, therefore, a tax upon rents or income issuing out of lands is intrinsically so different from a tax on the land itself that it belongs to a wholly different class of taxes, such taxes must be regarded as falling within the same category as a tax on real estate co nomine. The name of the tax is unimportant.* The real question is, is there any basis upon which to rest the contention that real estate belongs to one of the two great classes of taxes, and the rent or income which is the incident of its ownership belongs to the other? *We are unable to perceive any ground for the alleged distinction.* An annual tax upon the annual value or annual user of real estate appears to us the same in substance as an annual tax on the real estate, which would be paid out of the rent or income. This law taxes the income received from land and the growth or produce of the land. Mr. Justice Paterson observed in Hylton's Case, "land, independently of its produce, is of no value, " and certainly had no thought that direct taxes were confined to unproductive land.

If it be true that by varying the form the substance may be changed, it is not easy to see *that anything would remain of the limitations of the constitution, or of the rule of taxation and representation,* so carefully recognized and guarded in favor of the citizens of each state. *But constitutional provisions cannot be thus evaded. It is the substance, and not the form, which controls,* as has indeed been established by repeated decisions of this court. Thus in Brown v. Maryland, 12 Wheat. 419, 444, it was held that the tax on the occupation of an importer was the same as a tax on imports, and therefore void. And Chief Justice Marshall said: *"It is impossible to conceal from ourselves that this is varying the form without varying the substance.* It is treating a prohibition which is general as if it were confined to a particular mode of doing the forbidden thing. All must perceive that a tax on the sale of an article imported only for sale is a tax on the article itself."[56] (Emphasis added)

Field's Thunderous Opinion

The following quotations are taken from Justice Field's concurring opinion. His remarks throw needed light on the whole subject of taxation and the legality of current income tax "law, " as well as the legitimacy of all its "loopholes, " "incentives, " "exclusions, " and "deductions."

Development of Tax Classes Reviewed

The subject of taxation in the new government which was to be established created *great interest in the convention which framed the Constitution, and was the cause of much difference of opinion among its members and earnest contention between the States. The great source of weakness of the confederation was its inability to levy taxes of any kind for the support of its government.* **To raise revenue it was obliged to make requisitions upon the States, which were respected or disregarded at their pleasure.** Great embarrassments followed the consequent inability to obtain the necessary funds to carry on the government. One of the principal objects of the proposed new government was to obviate this defect of the confederacy by conferring authority upon the new government by which taxes could be directly laid whenever desired. *Great difficulty in accomplishing this object was found to exist.* The States bordering on the ocean were unwilling to give up their right to lay duties upon imports which were their chief source of revenue. The other States, on the other hand, were unwilling to make any agreement for the levying of taxes directly upon real and personal property, the smaller States fearing that they would be overborne by unequal burdens forced upon them by the action of the larger States. In this condition of things great em-

[56]Ibid., pages 580, 581.

barrassment was felt by the members of the convention. It was feared at times that the effort to form a new government would fail. *But happily a compromise was effected by an agreement that direct taxes should be laid by Congress by apportioning them among the States according to their representation.* In return for this *concession* by some of the States, the other States bordering on navigable waters consented to *relinquish* to the new government the control of *duties, imposts,* and *excises,* and the regulation of commerce, with the condition that the duties, imposts, and excises should be *uniform throughout the United States. So that, on the one hand, anything like oppression or undue advantage of any one State over the others would be* **prevented by the apportionment of the direct taxes among the States according to their representation,** and, on the other hand, anything like oppression or hardship in the levying of duties, imposts, and excises would be avoided by the provision that they should be uniform throughout the United States. This compromise was essential to the continued union and harmony of the States. It protected every State from being controlled in its taxation by the superior numbers of one or more other States.

The Constitution accordingly, when completed, *divided the taxes which might be levied under the authority of Congress into those which were* **direct** *and those which were* **indirect.** *Direct taxes, in a general and large sense, may be described as taxes derived immediately from the person, or from real or personal property, without any recourse therefrom to other sources for reinbursement.* In a more restricted sense, they have sometimes been confined to taxes *on real property, including the rents and income derived therefrom.* Such taxes are conceded to be direct taxes, however taxes on other property are designated, and they are to be apportioned among the States of the Union according to their respective numbers. The second section of article I of the Constitution declares that representatives and direct taxes shall be thus apportioned. *It had been a favorite doctrine in England and in the colonies, before the adoption of the Constitution, that taxation and representation should go together.* The Constitution prescribes such apportionment among the several States according to their respective numbers, to be determined by adding to the whole number of free persons, including those bound to service for a term of years, and excluding Indians not taxed, three-fifths of all other persons.

Some decisions of this court have qualified or thrown doubts upon the exact meaning of the words "direct taxes." Thus in *Springer v. United States,* 102 U.S. 586, it was held that a tax upon gains, profits, and income was an excise or duty and not a direct tax within the meaning of the Constitution, and that its imposition was not therefore unconstitutional. And in *Pacific Insurance Co. v. Soule,* 7 Wall. 433, it was held that an income tax or duty upon the amounts insured, renewed or continued by insurance companies, upon the gross amounts of premiums received by them and upon assessments made by them, and upon dividends and undistributed sums, was not a direct tax but a duty or excise.

In the discussions on the subject of direct taxes in the British Parliament *an income tax has been generally designated as a direct tax,* differing in that respect from the decision of this court in *Springer v. United States.* But whether the latter can be accepted as correct or otherwise, it does not affect the tax upon real property and its rents and income as a direct tax. *Such a tax is by universal consent recognized to be a direct tax.*

As stated, the rents and income of real property are included in the designation of direct taxes as part of the real property. Such has been the law in England for centuries, and in this country from the early settlement of the colonies; and it is strange that any member of the legal profession should, at this day, *question a doctrine which has always been thus accepted by common-law lawyers. . .*[57] (Emphasis added)

Field: Law Violated Principle of Uniformity

Historically, the courts had always defined the uniformity provision of the Constitution solely to mean *geographic* uniformity, but Field further broadened the concept of uniformity which made far more sense. He packed his analysis with good sense, historical references and sound republican principles.

But the law is not invalid merely in its disregard of the rule of apportionment of the direct tax levied. There is another and an equally cogent objection to it. In taxing incomes other than rents and profits of real estate it disregards the rule of uniformity which is prescirbed in such cases by the Constitution. The eighth section of the first article of the Constitution declares that "the Congress shall have power to lay and collect taxes, duties, imposts, and excises, to pay the debts and provide for the common defence and general welfare of the United States; *but all duties, imposts, and excises shall be uniform throughout the United States."* **Excises are a species of tax consisting generally of duties laid upon the manufacture, sale, or consumption of commodities within the country, or upon certain callings or occupations, often taking the form of exactions for licenses to pursue them.** The taxes created by the law under consideration as applied to savings banks, insurance companies, whether of fire, life, or marine, to building or other associations, or to the conduct of any other kind of business, are excise taxes, and fall within the requirement, so far as they are laid by Congress, that they must be uniform throughout the United States.

The uniformity thus required is the uniformity throughout the United States of the duty, impost, and excise levied. That is, the tax levied cannot be one sum upon an article at one place and a different sum upon the same article at another place. The duty received must be the same at all places throughout the United States, proportioned to the quantity of

[57]Ibid., pages 587-589.

the article disposed of or the extent of the business done. If, for instance, one kind of wine or grain or produce has a certain duty laid upon it proportioned to its quantity in New York, it must have a like duty proportioned to its quantity when imported at Charleston or San Francisco, or if a tax be laid upon a certain kind of business proportioned to its extent at one place, it must be a like tax on the same kind of business proportioned to its extent at another place. In that sense the duty must be uniform throughout the United States.

It is contended by the government that the Constitution only requires an uniformity geographical in its character. That position would be satisfied if the same duty were laid in all the States, however variant it might be in different places of the same State. But it could not be sustained in the latter case without defeating the equality, which is an essential element of the uniformity required, so far as the same is practicable.

In *United States v. Singer,* 15 Wall. 111, 121, a tax was imposed upon a distiller, in the nature of an excise, and the question arose whether in its imposition upon different distillers the uniformity of the tax was preserved, and the court said: "The law is not in our judgment subject to any constitutional objection.. The tax imposed upon the distiller is in the nature of an excise, and the only limitation upon the power of Congress in the imposition of taxes of this character is that they shall be 'uniform throughout the United States.' The tax here is uniform in its operation; *that is, it is assessed equally upon all manufacturers of spirits wherever they are. The law does not establish one rule for one distiller and a different rule for another, but the same rule for all should be alike."*

. . . One of the learned counsel puts it very clearly when he says that the correct meaning of the provisions requiring duties, imposts, and excises to be "uniform throughout the United States" is, that the law imposing them should "have an equal *and* uniform application in every part of the Union."

If, there were any doubt as to the intention of the States to make the grant of the right to impose indirect taxes subject to the condition that such taxes shall be in all respects uniform and impartial, that doubt, as said by counsel, should be resolved in the interest of justice, in favor of the taxpayer.

Exemptions from the operation of a tax always create inequalities. Those not exempted must, in the end, bear an additional burden or pay more than their share. A law containing arbitrary exemptions can in no just sense be termed uniform. . .

Where property is exempt from taxation, the exemption, as has been justly stated, must be supported by some consideration that the public, and not private interests will be advanced by it. Private corporations and private enterprises cannot be aided under the pretence that it is the exercise of the discretion of the legislature to exempt them.[58] (Emphasis added)

Exemptions in Tax Laws Capricious and Illegally Discriminatory

Cooley, in his treatise on taxation (2d Ed. 215) justly observes that: "It is difficult to conceive of a justifiable exemption law which should select single individuals or corporations, or single articles of property, and, taking them out of the class to which they belong, make them the subject of capricious legislative favor. Such favoritism could make no pretence to equality; it would lack the semblance of legitimate tax legislation."

The income tax law under consideration is marked by discriminating features which affect the whole law. *It discriminates between those who receive an income of four thousand dollars and those who do not. It thus vitiates, in my judgment, by this arbitrary discrimination, the whole legislation. Hamilton says in one of his papers, (the Continentalist,) "the genius of liberty reprobates everything arbitrary or discretionary in taxation. It exacts that every man, by a definite and general rule, should know what proportion of his property the State demands; whatever liberty we may boast of in theory, it cannot exist in fact while [arbitrary] assessments continue."* 1 Hamilton's Works, ed. 1885, 270. The legislation, in the discrimination it makes, is class legislation. Whenever a distinction is made in the burdens a law imposes or in the benefits it confers on any citizens by reason of their birth, or wealth, or religion, *it is class legislation, and leads inevitably to oppression and abuses, and to general unrest and disturbance in society.* It was hoped and believed that the great amendments to the Constitution which followed the late civil war had rendered such legislation impossible for all future time. But the objectionable legislation reappears in the act under consideration. *It is the same in essential character as that of the English income statute of 1691, which taxed Protestants at a certain rate, Catholics, as a class, at double the rate of Protestants, and Jews at another and separate rate. Under wise and constitutional legislation every citizen should contribute his proportion, however small the sum, to the support of the government, and it is no kindness to urge any of our citizens to escape from that obligation. If he contributes the smallest mite of his earnings to that purpose he will have a greater regard for the government and more self-respect for himself feeling that though he is poor in fact, he is not a pauper of his government. And it is to be hoped that, whatever woes and embarrassments may betide our people, they may never lose their manliness and self-respect.* Those qualities preserved, they will ultimately triumph over all reverses of fortune.

[58]Ibid., pages 593–595.

There is nothing in the nature of the corporations or associations exempted in the present act, or in their method of doing business, which can be claimed to be of a public or benevolent nature. They differ in no essential characteristic in their business from "all other corporations, companies, or associations doing business for profit in the United States."

As stated by counsel: "There is no such thing in the theory of our national government as unlimited power of taxation in Congress. There are limitations," as he justly observes, "of its powers arising out of the essential nature of all free governments; there are reservations of individual rights, without which society could not exist, and which are respected by every government. The right of taxation is subject to these limitations." *Loan Association v. Topeka,* 20 Wall. 655, and *Parkersburg v. Brown,* 106 U.S. 487.

The inherent and fundamental nature and character of a tax is that of a contribution to the support of the government, levied upon the principle of equal and uniform apportionment among the persons taxed, and any other exaction does not come within the legal definition of a tax.

This inherent limitation upon the taxing power *forbids the imposition of taxes which are unequal in their operation upon similar kinds of property, and necessarily strikes down the gross and arbitrary distinctions in the income law as passed by Congress.* The law, as we have seen, distinguishes in the taxation between corporations by exempting the property of some of them from taxation and levying the tax on the property of others when the corporations do not materially differ from one another in the character of their business or in the protection required by the government. *Trifling differences in their modes of business, but not in their results, are made the ground and occasion of the greatest possible differences in the amount of taxes levied upon their income, showing that the action of the legislative power upon them has been arbitrary and capricious and sometimes merely fanciful. . .*

Here I close my opinion. I could not say less in view of questions of such gravity that go down to the very foundation of the government. **If the provisions of the Constitution can be set aside by an act of Congress, where is the course of usurpation to end? The present assault upon capital is but the beginning. It will be but the stepping-stone to others, larger and more sweeping, till our political contests will become a war of the poor against the rich; a war constantly growing in intensity and bitterness.**

"If the court sanctions the power of discriminating taxation, and nullifies the uniformity mandate of the Constitution," as said by one who has been all his life a student of our institutions, *"it will mark the hour when the sure decadence of our present government will commence."* If the purely arbitrary limitation of $4000 in the present law can be sustained, none having less than that amount of income being assessed or taxed for the support of the government, the limitation of future Congresses may be fixed at a much larger sum, at five or ten or twenty thousand dollars, parties possessing an income of that amount alone being bound to bear the burdens of government; or the limitation may be designated at such an amount as a board of "walking delegates" may deem necesary. There is no safety in allowing the limitation to be adjusted except in strict compliance with the mandates of the Constitution which require its taxation, if imposed by direct taxes, to be apportioned among the States according to their representation, and if imposed by indirect taxes, to be uniform in operation and, so far as practicable, in proportion to their property, equal upon all citizens. *Unless the rule of the Constitution governs, a majority may fix the limitations at such rate as will not include any of their own number.*

I am of opinion that the whole law of 1894 should be declared void and without any binding force — that part which relates to the tax on the rents, profits or income from real estate, that is, so much as constitutes part of the direct tax, because, not imposed by the rule of apportionment according to the representation of the states, as prescribed by the constitution; and that part which imposes a tax upon the bonds and securities of the several states, and upon the bonds and securities of their municipal bodies, and upon the salaries of judges of the courts of the United States, as being beyond the power of congress; and that part which lays duties, imposts, and excises, as void in not providing for the uniformity required by the constitution in such cases.[59] (Emphasis added)

Two Decisions Necessary

Despite the above, however, the first *Pollock* decision was inconclusive. Only eight Justices took part (Justice Jackson being absent) and the only majority positions reached were:

1. the unconstitutionality of the provisions that sought to tax municipal bonds; and
2. that income from real estate was a direct tax, requiring apportionment (though two justices dissented).

But since the Court was equally divided (four to four) on all the other issues and couldn't decide whether its opinion on muncipal bonds and real estate income rendered the entire Act unconstitutional, a rehearing of the case was requested.

It was assumed that Justice Jackson's early return would give the full Court an opportunity to rule on the issues. The case was re-argued on May 6, 7, and 8 and a second opinion was handed down on May 20. This time the *Pollock* forces — and the forces of constitutional govern-

---

[59]Ibid., pages 596–608.

ment — gained a complete victory. In a five to four[60] decision the Court struck down all the income tax provisions of the Wilson-Gorman Tariff Act as unconstitutional. In this second opinion (apart from holding that the government could not tax the interest of municipal bonds and that the income from real estate was a direct tax) *the Court also held that taxes on personal property (and on the income from personal property) were direct and had to be apportioned.* This latter holding was crucial and established that all Federal taxes on wages (the personal property of wage earners), as well as taxes on dividends and interest, were only lawful if levied by the rule of apportionment. The Court expressed it this way:

> *First.* We adhere to the opinion already announced, that, taxes on real estate being indisputably direct taxes, taxes on the rents or income of real estate are equally direct taxes.
> *Second.* We are of opinion that *taxes on personal property, or on the income of personal property, are likewise direct taxes.*
> *Third.* The tax imposed by sections twenty-seven to thirty-seven, inclusive, of the act of 1894, so far as it falls on the *income* of real estate and *of personal property, being a direct tax* within the meaning of the Constitution, and, therefore, unconstitutional and void *because not apportioned* according to representation, all those sections, constituting one entire scheme of taxation, are necessarily invalid.
> *The decrees hereinbefore entered in this court will be vacated; the decrees below will be reversed, and the cases remanded, with instructions to grant the relief prayed.*[61] (Emphasis added)

Thus the *Pollock* decision clearly established that all Federal taxes on wages (the personal property of the laborer), as well as all taxes on interest and dividends, are lawful only if apportioned. This decision has never been challenged, let alone reversed or overturned, and proves the total illegality of the Federal government's entire income tax collecting activities and its contention that it can lawfully tax such income without apportionment.

The Federal government has been able to illegally extract income taxes from the American public by promoting the fiction that the 16th Amendment voided the *Pollock* decision. This is not true. **The *Pollock* decision is the law of the land (untouched by the 16th Amendment) and, therefore, clearly establishes that the enforcement of the current income tax (i.e., by directly taxing wages, dividends, rents, alimony, etc.) is illegal!**

[60]When Justice Jackson returned he voted with the minority so one of the other Justices switched his vote. Which one did remains a mystery.
[61]*Pollock vs Farmers' Loan,* 158 US 601, page 637.

9

The Agitation For The Income Tax: 1895–1909

Public agitation regarding an income tax really began with the *Pollock* decision which polarized public attitudes toward the tax as noted by both Choate and the U.S. Attorney General (see page 78). In contrast to the income tax of 1894, the Civil War income tax had been generally accepted as an emergency war-time measure and it was considered unpatriotic to even question the validity of it. In any event, its importance had dwindled to the point where it produced less than $5 million in revenue in 1873, whereas it had raised $72 million in 1866.

The determined opposition to the tax (in and out of Congress) prior to its becoming law; the violent opposition to it after it became law; plus the decision itself (and Choate's characterization of the tax) all combined to set off a minor class struggle on its behalf. This struggle generally pitted the less affluent against the more affluent — those whose swollen fortunes (proponents of the income tax contended) should bear a greater burden of the cost of government.

Such an argument struck responsive chords in various segments of society (especially agragarian interests and the laboring class) because of the way the Federal government raised its revenue — generally through internal excises on products such as tobacco and spirits as well as a system of protective tariffs.[1] Therefore, agitation regarding an income tax developed largely because of a growing public feeling that Americans were being cheated by the rich, Eastern industrial class whose fortunes they believed were generated and protected by such tariffs. The consensus was that not only were the rich not paying their fair share of taxes but that they were actually growing richer at the expense of the working and consuming public. It is important to note that the

---

[1] Though they insulated American goods from the full impact of foreign competition, protective tariffs also raised consumer prices.

public at large did not equate protective tariffs (now referred to as import duties and quotas) with job protection as is the vogue today. Such protective tariffs were perceived as a means of protecting industrial profits and the fortunes of the rich at the expense (and to the detriment) of the consuming public. They were right — protective tariffs and import quotas do exactly that. They penalize the public and compel them to pay higher prices in order to support the activities of non-competitive producers.

America's protective tariffs, however, were erected during a period when America was still a debtor nation. (America only became a creditor nation around the time of World War I.) These tariffs originally sought to protect America's fledgling industrial businesses from competing with their older, more established European counterparts. This tariff protection gave U.S. industries time to accumulate the necessary capital and expertise to eventually become truly competitive on a world-wide basis. In addition, these tariffs were applied during a period of continually falling domestic prices (not increasing prices as is the case today). This was mainly because domestic competition (both labor and industrial), coupled with a far better monetary system and a far better economic climate (primarily due to the absence of government and its fiscal policies), combined to produce low interest rates and expanded employment opportunities — even for the millions of penniless immigrants that streamed to our shores. Though such arguments might have been academically correct, the absence of income taxes (and government interference in general) created a climate that allowed consumer prices to fall for the ultimate benefit of the consuming public. To the extent that tariff policies did (to any extent) swell the fortunes of the Eastern establishment, these fortunes were used to increase America's industrial power and to finance the nation's economic expansion (see Chapter Addendum, page 130).

Although America's working consumers felt exploited by this system of protective tariffs, such abuse was mostly an illusion. For example, in 1900 the gross revenue of the Federal government was $567 million of which $233 million (or 41 percent) came from tariffs (including tonnage taxes). America's population in 1900 was 76 million which means that, on the average, each American only paid $3.00 in tariff taxes as his/her contribution to government. If these consumers felt exploited by such a rate of tax then, how should consumers feel today when the average American works at least four months to support the Federal government and its myriad activities? Under what system were America's working consumers better off — paying taxes through tariffs or being subjected to an income tax?

Typical of the initial press reaction to the *Pollock* decision was an editorial that appeared in the *New York World* which called the decision "the triumph of selfishness over patriotism." In another editorial the newspaper suggested, "If the Constitution really prevents equal and just taxation, the people can amend their Constitution. And they will!" Other newspapers such as the *New York Tribune*, however, echoed the sentiments of Choate: that the decision preserved the Constitution against communistic assault. In any case, the lines were drawn.[2]

Many people saw an income tax as simply a tax on wealth — the wealth of the rich who, the public believed, were escaping their fair share of taxes. They believed an income tax would remedy that, but in light of the *Pollock* decision they now also viewed the Supreme Court as the protector of the rich.

Strangely enough, the income tax of 1894 was adopted without any social pressure for it. Neither of the two major political parties had called for such a tax in their 1892 party platforms (although the need for such a tax, especially in time of war, had been discussed). The tax was first mentioned by President Cleveland in his message to Congress on December 4, 1893.[3] He alluded to the action of the "Committee" in recommending a "small tax upon incomes derived from certain corporate investments." On January 24, the House Committee on Ways and Means recommended an income tax modelled after the Civil War acts. This was subsequently incorporated into the general revenue measure and passed on February 1, 1894. The income tax had been resurrected to help the government close the sudden deficit that developed because of the Panic of 1893. The Panic produced the first Federal deficit in *twenty-eight years* and was, itself, caused by the government, irresponsibly increasing silver coinage pursuant to the Bland-Allison and Sherman Silver Purchase Acts of 1878 and 1890.[4]

It is apparent that Congress conceived of an income tax as a tax on wealth itself. For example, in the final debate on the income tax bill in the House of Representatives, Congressman Crisp, speaking for the majority party, said:

---

[2] *PUBLIC OPINION — A COMPREHENSIVE SUMMARY OF THE PRESS THROUGHOUT THE WORLD ON ALL IMPORTANT CURRENT TOPICS*, Volume XVIII, January, 1895 — June, 1895 (The Public Opinion Co., New York).

[3] 26 Cong. Rec., Part 1, 53rd Congress, 2nd Session, pages 2, 9.

[4] Under the Bland-Allison Act the Treasury had to purchase $2 million worth of silver each month thereby inflating the money supply to that extent. Up until 1873 only 8 million silver dollars had been coined, so under the Bland-Allison Act one year's coinage amounted to three times as many silver dollars as had been coined up until that time. Under the Sherman Act the mandatory purchases (and, therefore, the rate of inflation) was doubled. This inflationary lunacy was finally stopped in 1893 with the repeal of the Sherman Act but the damage (which culminated in the Panic of 1893) had already been done.

We propose in this new system simply to put part of the burden of the support of this Government upon wealth, and to take off a portion of the burden from consumption.[5]

Along the same lines Congressman Lane stated:

We are confronted with a deficit of revenue, and the question is presented whether it is best to put a light income tax on the rich man's income or to tax the poor man's sugar.[6]

And Congressman Bretz considered it as a means to

. . . emancipate the people of this country from an unjust system of taxation . . . (and hailed) with welcome the demand of the American people that the accumulated wealth of the land shall be taxed.[7]

Congressman Hudson of Kansas said:

This method [the income tax] lays the burdens on those possessing the ability to pay, and compels those who reap the largest harvests . . . to give more of that harvest for the common good. I know that many wealthy men are generous and charitable . . . On the other hand, the majority of the very wealthy are haughty, overbearing, autocratic, mean, and it is that class in particular that the income tax is designed to reach.[8]

There can, therefore, be no doubt that the income tax was sold to the nation as a "tax the rich" scheme and, since it represented an admitted attempt to tax wealth (i.e. relate taxes to wealth) by taxing income, it should be obvious that the tax was basically dishonest and unconstitutional. If Congress wanted to "tax" wealth it had the power to do so; but that, obviously, would have required apportionment. In order to avoid the republican principle of apportionment and the restraints it imposed, Congress sought to tax wealth by the democratic (but unprincipled) method of taxing "income" in its stead. In so doing, it concocted a tax never conceived by those who wrote and ratified the U.S. Constitution.

[5] 26 Cong. Rec., Part 2, 53rd Congress, 2nd Session, page 1791.

[6] Ibid., page 1753.
[7] Ibid., page 1709.
[8] 26 Cong. Rec., Part 9, 53rd Congress, 2nd Session, page 1714.

[9] *Official Proceedings of the Democratic Convention* (1896), pages 252–253.

Public agitation for an income tax did not begin in earnest until the tax was held to be unconstitutional. From *Pollock* up until the 16th Amendment, advocates of an income tax believed that the *Pollock* decision could be reversed.

The Presidential Campaign of 1896

The first time the income tax played a role in a Presidential campaign was in 1896. That year the Democratic Party became the first major political party to endorse the tax. Its 1896 platform stated that:

> It is the duty of Congress to use all the Constitutional power which remains after that (the *Pollock*) decision, or which may come from its reversal by the court as it may hereafter be constituted, so that burdens of taxation may be equally and impartially laid, to the end that wealth may bear its due proportion of the expense of Government.[9]

The Populist party platform of 1896 also demanded a graduated income tax "to the end that aggregated wealth shall bear its just proportion of taxation";[10] and middle-of-the-road Populists called for a graduated income tax and "a constitutional amendment to secure the same, if necessary";[11] while that year's platform for the Farmers' Alliance and Industrial Union also called for an income tax and pledged its support to candidates to be nominated by the Democrats.[12]

The Socialist Labor Party asked for an income tax that year at its Ninth Annual Convention, as did the Silver Republicans, who also declared in favor of a graduated income tax and a constitutional amendment, if needed[13] and in his campaign for the Presidency, William Jennings Bryan also called for the adoption of an income tax.[14]

The demand for an income tax was generally advocated by those seeking basic socio-economic changes in the American economic and social scenes. This involved a shift away from trust in a *laissez faire* environment (an environment that had built up the country in a relatively

---

[10] *A History of the Presidency From 1897 to 1909* (1912), by Edward Stanwood, pages 32–33.

[11] Ibid., page 43.

[12] Ibid., pages 32–33.

[13] *Proceedings of the Ninth Annual Convention,* Resolution 8, page 65.

[14] Charles Beard, author of *Contemporary American History,* published in 1914 (page 194) wrote: "Some of Mr. Bryan's utterances, particularly on the income tax, frightened the rich into believing or pretending to believe, that his election would be the beginning of a wholesale confiscation."

short time) to greater trust in government and government interference in the economy, supposedly done in the public's interest.[15]

Charles and Mary Beard said:[16]

> . . . It was no accident therefore that in the movement toward social democracy a deliberate and overt attempt was made to shift a part of the burden of sustaining the federal government from the consuming masses to the possessors of great fortunes. It is true that the Supreme Court had declared the income tax law of 1894 unconstitutional and that citizens who enjoyed large revenues from enterprises and investments imagined themselves securely wrapped in the strong mantle of protective legality. But Bryan and his legions were still active in the field, vociferously demonstrating to farmers and wage earners the justice of a levy on the incomes of the prosperous. In fact at the turn of the century, discontent with established practices in taxation — that is, collecting federal revenues from the masses by indirection — was spreading like a virus through the left wings of both political parties, especially in the regions where great estates were few in number.

In the 1900 campaign the platforms of both major parties were silent on the issue of income taxes. Theodore Roosevelt, however, raised it himself between 1904 and 1908. In his message to Congress in 1906 he said that the income tax was, in essence, a "question of the proper adjustments of burdens to benefits," although he recognized the problems presented by the *Pollock* decision.[17] In 1907 he again urged "a graduated income tax of the proper type" and expressed the hope that an income tax might be devised that the Supreme Court would uphold.[18]

---

[15] The tragic consequences in this shift should be painfully apparent in America's failing economy as evidenced by the squalor of American cities (urban blight), the growing inability of America to manufacture goods at competitive prices (our huge trade deficit), and the growing number of women forced by economic need to join the work force.

[16] *The Rise of American Civilization*, Volume II, (The MacMillan Company, New Edition, 1935), pages 580–581.

[17] 41 Cong. Rec., Part 1, 59th Congress, 2nd Session, pages 27–28.

[18] See *Taxation of Government Bondholders and Employees*, U.S. Department of Justice, J1.2:T19/939, pages 131–132, which will provide numerous other references on this subject. Throughout this chapter I have freely quoted from this source.

The 1908 Presidential Campaign

The 1908 Democratic platform again called for

a constitutional amendment specifically authorizing Congress to levy and collect a tax upon individual and corporate incomes, to the end that wealth may bear its proportionate share of the burdens of government.[19]

This statement was indicative of Bryan's return to Party leadership. Calls for an income tax now also came from the Prohibition Party while the Socialists called for an income tax as "an opportunity of using the power of taxation for the purposes of social control." No mention of an income tax was included in the Republican platform. Taft, however (in accepting the nomination), gave a limited endorsement to an income tax if it could be written in a manner that would be constitutional.

We can see that public demand for an income tax came first from agrarian and radical Populist groups who had strong ties to causes such as cheap money, redistribution of wealth, and other views generally compatible with socialism. This idea found increasing acceptance among a coalition of western and southern congressmen — its chief advocates in Congress — who were opposed to apportionment *for the very reason that it was included in the Constitution.* The political appeal for an income tax (a tax on the rich) proved overwhelming, and increasing numbers of eastern politicians (both Republican and Democrat) jumped on the income tax bandwagon.

The Final Push For The Income Tax

Congress was convened on March 15, 1909 for a special session to revise tariffs. On the first day of the session Cordell Hull of Tennessee offered an income tax bill as an amendment to the tariff bill but the bill was returned by the Committee on Ways and Means without Hull's amendment. The House bill that was laid before the Senate on April 10, 1909 did not contain an income tax amendment. Between April 15 and April 21, two Senators (Bailey of Texas and Cummins of Iowa) introduced in the Senate amendments to the tariff bill calling for an income tax. These two men would lead the Senate drive (spearheaded mainly by other Western and Southern Senators) for the income tax which they believed a changed Supreme Court would now find constitutional.

While Congress was in session, wrestling with the tariff bill and on the verge of passing such a measure, Taft sent his June 15 message calling for 1) a constitutional amendment authorizing a general income

---

[19] Ibid., page 132.

tax; and 2) a corporate income tax (under the guise of an excise tax on corporate profit) that could, he suggested, be passed immediately.

It is obvious that Taft's recommendation for an income tax amendment to the Constitution was done to derail what looked like certain passage of some type of income tax measure in Congress which would appear as a political victory for the Democrats (who had been pushing for such a tax). Favorable passage of the amendment (as recommended by a Republican President) would deny the Democrats any such political advantage. Speculation has it that Taft was persuaded that such an amendment would not be ratified by three-quarters of the States and congressional approval of such an amendment, therefore, would not necessarily produce an income tax.

In any case, the Senate voted for the amendment 77 to 0 and it passed the House 318 to 14.[20] In this way Congress sought to amend the Constitution in order to add a tax called for by the Second plank in Karl Marx's *Communist Manifesto*. In that endeavor, however, they failed — but that failure has been the best kept secret of the 20th Century.

Chapter Addendum

Current import restrictions (such as those imposed on Japanese automobiles, for example, and as are suggested for steel and certain other products) are not like the protective tariffs erected to protect American industry in the 19th Century. For one thing, current import protection is asked for in the name of large, well-established American industries that, at one time, were larger than the combined industries of the rest of the world. The pervasive business attitude of "its deductible" literally promotes wasteful and unnecessary business expenditures which result in higher consumer prices. In addition, excessive American wage demands (not tied to increased productivity), brought about by unrealistic union pressure (encouraged and protected by government), has also played a significant role in pricing American goods out of markets they once dominated.

[20] 44 Cong. Rec., Part 4, 61st Congress, 1st Session, page 4121.

10

The Corporation Excise Tax of 1909

In 1909 the U.S. Congress once again sought to impose an unapportioned income tax on the nation. That attempt failed. In order to really understand current income tax "law" and how it came about, it is necessary to be familiar with another income tax that no longer exists — the corporation income tax of 1909, which was deceptively called the *Corporation Excise Tax of 1909*. This corporate income tax is closely related to the current income tax for a number of reasons.

President Taft Recommends An "Excise" Tax and The 16th Amendment

As noted previously, on June 15, 1909 President Taft sent a message to Congress about the tariff bill then under consideration. In his message he advised Congress that a "rapidly increasing deficit" imposed an "obligation" on Congress to arrange the new tariff bill "so as to secure an adequate income (and) that it was not possible to do so by import duties, (and that) new kinds of taxation must be adopted." Taft recommended, therefore, that Congress pass legislation establishing 1) a graduated inheritance tax; 2) a general income tax; and 3) a new corporate income tax.

Since Taft recognized that the *Pollock* decision actually prevented the government from establishing a general income tax, he recommended that:

> both Houses by a two thirds vote, shall propose an amendment to the Constitution conferring the power to levy an income tax upon the National Government without apportionment among the States in proportion to population.

Though the President stated he was "convinced that a great majority of the people of this country are in favor of investing the National

Government with power to levy an income tax, " he still conceded that the time needed to ratify such an amendment would prevent money from being brought "into the Treasury to meet the present deficiency." Actually, there really was no deficiency problem since Congress could have increased both tariffs and legitimate internal excises in order to raise the necessary revenue. A tax levied on "big business" and on the "rich, " however, was infinitely better politically so Taft proposed:

> an amendment to the tariff bill imposing upon all corporations and joint stock companies for profit, except national banks (otherwise taxed), savings banks, and loan associations, an excise tax measured by 2 per cent on the net income of such corporations. This (would be) an excise tax upon the privilege of doing business as an artificial entity and of freedom from a general partnership liability enjoyed by those who own the stock.

Taft believed that Congress could pass such an income tax on corporations (under the guise of an alleged excise tax on corporate "privileges") on the basis of a 1904 Supreme Court decision. He explained that the *Spreckles Sugar Refining* case[1] seemed:

> clearly to establish the principle that such a tax as this (an income tax) is an excise upon privilege and not a direct tax on property and is within the federal power without apportionment according to population". He then added, "the tax on net income is preferable to one proportionate to a percentage of the gross receipts, because it is a tax upon *success* and not failure . . . Another merit of this tax is the federal supervision which must be exercised in order to make the law effective over the annual accounts and business transactions of all corporations.

Taft then went on to explain:

> While the facility of assuming a corporate form has been of the utmost utility in the business world, it is also true that substantially all of the abuses and all of the evils which have aroused the public to the necessity of reform were made possible by the use of this very faculty. If now, by a perfectly legitimate and effective system of taxation, we are incidentally able to possess the Government and the stockholders and the public of the knowledge of the real business transactions and the gains and profits of every corporation in the country, we have made a long step toward supervisory control of corporations which may prevent a further abuse of power.

---

[1] *Spreckles Sugar Refining Co. vs McClain* 192 US 397, decided February 23, 1904.

Income Taxes Urged for "Control"

So, in addition to providing revenue for the government (for the purposes listed on page 31), the corporate income tax of 1909 was admittedly imposed to gain "supervisory control of corporations." Where in the Constitution is the Federal government empowered to have such "supervisory" control? And where in Article 1, Section 8, clause 1 is the government authorized to impose taxes for these purposes? Taxes imposed for such purposes violate the spirit and clear intent of the Constitution! And if a corporate income tax can give the Federal government control over corporations because it gives the government access to the "annual accounts and business transactions of all corporations," does not a *personal* income tax give the government the same power and control over *individuals?* More importantly, who is more likely to abuse its power — government or business? Because there are so many companies competing for business, few businesses can *force* the consumer to buy their products. But if the government decides to provide a service, the taxpayer is forced to pay for it through taxation regardless of how costly and overpriced.

The story of mankind is a tale of the constant struggle against the tyranny of government and its abuse of power. As Woodrow Wilson stated, "the struggle for liberty is the struggle to contain government power." And, as President Taft tacitly admitted, another reason for an income tax was to give the Federal government illegal control and power over American business, and individuals as well.

Profit — Not Income — To Be Taxed

It is obvious from Taft's remarks that this so-called *excise* tax was not to be based on corporate *income* but on corporate *profit* and, in reality, would be a *profits* tax not an *income* tax. This is easy to see by Taft's own statement that the tax was to be determined by *net income* rather than *gross receipts*.[2] This is further substantiated by Taft's assertion that the tax was to be "upon success and not failure." Today's alleged *income* tax is actually a *profits* tax and because individuals do not generate "profits" they cannot be subject to it. Individuals are not subject to this tax for a variety of other reasons, but this one is basic.

---

[2] Net corporate *income* is actually a corporation's *profit* since *net receipts* (as used by Taft) represent receipts (income) less disbursements (outgo). So to refer to a corporations "net income" really means to talk about a corporation's *profit*.

The *Spreckles* Case

As a result of the Spanish-American War, Congress passed the War Revenue Act of 1898 which levied an excise tax of one-quarter of one percent on the gross annual receipts in excess of $250,000 of any corporation or company refining sugar. In challenging the tax before the Supreme Court, the Spreckles Company had raised two issues: 1) the tax was unconstitutional on the basis that it was direct and not apportioned; and 2) if it were constitutional, the tax could not apply to income from stocks and dividends. The Supreme Court found in favor of Spreckles on the stock and dividend issue but ruled that the tax (overall) was a valid excise tax.

In declaring the tax an "excise," the Court cited the *Soule* case (see pages 95–98) in which that Court held that a tax on gross premiums "was not a direct tax, but an excise duty or tax within the meaning of the Constitution." It also cited the *Veazie* decision (see page 98–111) and said:

> . . . in *Nicol v. Ames*, 173 U.S. 509, that the tax imposed (30 Stat. 448) upon each sale or agreement to sell any products or merchandise at an exchange, or board of trade, or other similar place, either for present or future delivery, was not in the constitutional sense a direct tax upon the business itself, but in effect *"a duty or excise law upon the privilege, opportunity or facility offered at boards of trade or exchanges for the transaction of the business mentioned in the act," which was "separate and apart from the business itself;" in Knowlton v. Moore, 178 U.S. 41, 81, that an inheritance or succession tax was not a direct tax on property, as ordinarily understood, but an excise levied on the transmission or receipt of property occasioned by death;* and, in *Patton v. Brady,* 184 U.S. 608, that the tax imposed by the act of June 13, 1898, upon tobacco, however prepared, manufactured and sold, for consumption or sale, was not a direct tax, but an excise tax which Congress could impose; that it was not "a tax upon property as such but upon *certain kinds of property, having reference to their origin and intended use."*
>
> In view of these and other decided cases, we cannot hold that the tax imposed on the plaintiff expressly with reference to its "carrying on or doing the business of . . . refining sugar," and which was to be measured by its gross annual receipts in excess of a named sum, is other than is described in the act of Congress, *a special excise tax, and not a direct one to be apportioned among the States according to their respective numbers.* This conclusion is inevitable from the judgements in prior cases, in which the court has dealt with the distinctions, **often very difficult to be expressed in words, between taxes that are direct and those which are to be regarded simply as excises.** The grounds upon which those judgements were rested need not be restated or reexamined. It would subserve no useful purpose to do so. It must suffice now to say that they clearly

negative the idea that the tax here involved is a direct one, to be apportioned among the States according to numbers.

It is said that if regard be had to the decision in the *Income Tax Cases*, a different conclusion from that just stated must be reached. On the contrary, the precise question here was not intended to be decided in those cases. For, in the opinion on the rehearing of the *Income Tax Cases* the Chief Justice said: "We have considered the act only in respect of the tax on income derived from real estate, and from invested personal property, and have not commented on so much of it as bears on gains or profits from business, privileges or employments . . ."[3] (Emphasis added)

We are being told here that taxes are not levied on people directly, or indirectly through the products they buy, but levied on "privileges," "opportunities," "facilities offered at boards," and on "exchanges for the transaction of business," which we are supposed to believe are "separate and apart from" the business itself. In addition, the *Knowlton* decision is cited (another monumental Supreme Court swindle) wherein the Court ruled that the Federal estate tax (passed because of the Spanish-American War) was not "a direct tax on property, as ordinarily understood, but an excise tax on the transmission or receipt of property occasioned by death." To top it off, we are also told that excise taxes can apply to property (not because of its ownership) but because of its "origin" (whatever that means) or its "intended" use!

All of this is pure, legalistic mumbo-jumbo. If the Constitution contained an *absolute bar* against taxing the public directly, the U.S. government (with the aid of its "judges") would have gotten around it by taxing the public on the basis of their "use" of certain objects or by taxing "privileges" such as breathing (the "use" of one's lungs), walking (the "use" of one's legs and feet), talking (the "use" of one's brain and speech organs), on writing letters (the "use" of one's arms, hands and fingers), or even on the "privilege" of being born or reaching a certain age! Such is the ingenuity employed by government lawyers (masquerading as Federal judges) to concoct taxes (and laws) to help the government avoid the restraints imposed by the Constitution.

Notice also how the Court claims that distinctions between direct and indirect taxes are "often very difficult to express in words" — true only if the honorable Court did not know the difference, or if it did, did not want to explain it. Generally, all taxes paid directly to government are *direct* and all taxes paid indirectly are *indirect* — how much simpler can it be?

The Court next stated that it was suggested that based upon "the income taxes cases (*Pollock*) a different conclusion" would have to be

---

[3] *Spreckles vs McClain, supra,* pages 412–413.

reached. This suggestion is resisted by the *Spreckles* Court on the grounds that the *Pollock* Court decision only applied to income "derived from real estate, and from invested personal property, " and that it did not comment on the "gains or profits from business, privileges or employments." The reason the *Pollock* Court did not comment on these items is that none of them applied in that case (see page 83). In any case, *Pollock* did not apply here because that case involved a profits tax (a tax on *net* income) and *Spreckles* involved a tax on gross receipts (or *gross* income). Since the economic consequences of each tax are fundamentally different, different considerations would apply in any analysis of whether one or the other was either direct or indirect. If the *Spreckles* Court wanted to avoid the *Pollock* case, it had ample grounds to do so — but not those used.

In holding for Spreckles on the dividends and interest issue, the Court interestingly enough relied on the dissenting opinion in the lower court case that had initially upheld the tax — which the Court would now strike down. Citing that dissenting opinion the Court said:

> Keeping in mind the well settled rule, that the citizen is exempt from taxation, unless the same is imposed by clear and unequivocal language, and that where the construction of a tax is doubtful, the doubt is to be resolved in favor of those upon whom the tax is sought to be laid.[4]

It was this decision that persuaded Taft that the government could legally tax corporate income (despite the *Pollock* decision) on the grounds that it could levy the tax *not* on corporate income directly but *on the privilege* of operating as a corporation and that the tax could be *measured* by the income (actually profit) earned. The *Spreckles* case, however, involved an excise tax on *gross* receipts and not on *profits* (as Taft now viewed the corporate tax). The *Spreckles* decision, therefore, provided no legal basis whatsoever for an excise tax on profits. Based upon his misconception of the *Spreckles* decision, Taft nevertheless used it as the basis for recommending the Corporation Excise Tax of 1909 and Congress passed it presumably as an excise tax on the privilege of operating as a corporation (though non-corporate entities such as joint stock companies and associations were also taxed, while various other businesses that also fell into this category were excluded).

The Act provided for:

> A special excise tax with respect to the carrying on or doing business by such corporation, joint stock company or association, or insurance com-

---

[4] Ibid., page 416. *This principle alone brands the income tax "law" illegal!*

pany, equivalent to one per centum upon the entire net income over and above five thousand dollars received by it from all sources during such year, exclusive of amounts received by it as dividends upon stock of other corporations, joint stock companies, subject to the tax hereby imposed.

The Act further provided

that when determining "such net income, " corporations could deduct "all the ordinary and necessary expenses actually paid within the year out of income in the maintenance and operation of its business and properties." It then enumerated the types of expenditures that could be deducted including "all amounts received by it within the year as dividends upon stock of other corporations . . . subject to the tax hereby imposed."

This dividend deduction is not authorized today (see page 190) with the result that many corporations and individuals pay taxes on the receipt of corporate dividends upon which Federal taxes have already been paid! In small, family-owned corporations this double taxation of corporate profits is brutal. The same situation occurs in public corporations whose profit (as far as public stockholders are concerned) is also taxed twice. And such profits could theoretically be taxed three or four times — depending on the number of corporations through which such profits might flow before reaching the final, individual taxpayer. Such outrageous taxing policies have enabled the Federal government to *nationalize* all of America's major corporations — and the public is not even aware that such a *de facto* nationalization has occurred![5]

In addition, the Act omitted the following types of corporations from the tax: labor, agricultural or horticultural organizations, fraternal beneficiary societies, orders or associations operating under the lodge system, domestic building and loan associations, corporations and associations organized and operated for religious, charitable, or educational purposes.

The hypocrisy of the Act is revealed in the following coloquiy that took place in the U.S. Senate:

Mr. HUGHES. It is apparent that the business or occupation of the corporation is not the object sought to be reached by this law as was attempted to be done by the peculiar and guarded language of that act which the court construed in sustaining the validity of that particular act. I do not believe that anyone who studies this amendment believes that it is the business conducted which is sought to be taxed; but the incomes of these

[5] For an in-depth explanation and irrefutable proof that the government has, in fact, nationalized all major U.S. businesses, see pages 137–139 of *The Biggest Con: How The Government is Fleecing You,* by Irwin Schiff.

corporations are in fact sought to be subjected to the tax, while the language of the act is —

Mr. RAYNER. Mr. President —

Mr. HUGHES. That is what was said in the President's message; that is what he said in his speech of acceptance; that is what he told his Attorney-General to do — to draw an income-tax law that would be consistent with the construction of the Constitution; and that is what this is in its essence, in my judgement — an income tax, a tax upon all Incomes from all sources of the corporations enumerated.[6]

Senator Cummins (one of the two leaders in the Senate pushing for an income tax) had this to say about the corporate excise tax:

Congress cannot make an income tax a special excise tax by so denominating it. It cannot make an excise tax a direct tax by so nominating it. We must look further into the subject than the language used by the committee.

Congress cannot justly levy a tax on business unless it includes all those who are engaged in that business. I deny the right, in fairness, of Congress to levy a tax upon John Smith because he is engaged in the dry goods business, if John Jones is next to him and is doing the same dry goods business without being taxed. That is not an excise tax.[7]

In the House, Congressman Pickett raised some of the same issues. Pickett, however, also noted that only "four hours had been set aside for discussion" of the corporation tax and that the tax did not originate in the House but "came before us for the first time as an amendment to (a) Senate Bill." The revenue measure, therefore, did not originate in the House as called for by the Constitution. Commenting on the short time allowed the House for discussing the tax, Pickett said:

I venture to say that such action on a measure of so vast importance, so comprehensive in character, is without a precedent or a parallel in the history of parliamentary procedure.[8]

He then commented on the corporate excise tax as follows:

I realize that the corporation tax comes before us with the recommendation of the President, for whom, and for whose judgement, I have the profoundest respect. The recommendation should be treated with a consideration commensurate with his high office and great ability. I can not, however, either forget or ignore the wisdom of our forefathers in the

[6] 44 Cong. Rec., 61st Congress, 1st Session, page 4043.

[7] Ibid., page 3976.

[8] Ibid., page 4395.

distribution of the powers of government. As a part of the legislative branch, we are expected to , and ought to, be guided by our own best thought and convictions — otherwise our form of government would cease, except in name. I am quite sure the President, with his exalted and patriotic conception of duty wherever vested, would not wish us to do otherwise.

Time does not permit more than a pointed reference to the merits of the tax. It is urged in justification of it that it is a tax on the privilege of doing business as an artificial entity and of freedom from general partnership liability. I concede that corporations should pay for that privilege, but it does not follow that the Federal Government should charge for it, at least in respect to certain classes of corporations. The privilege is granted by the state and should be taxed by the State.

The right of the Federal Government to tax a privilege granted by a State can not be justified upon any reasoning other than the power to do so.

Taxation is one of the gravest problems of government. History is replete with illustrations which establish the rule of governmental action, that all doubt as to the justice or equity of a tax should be resolved against it. There is a vital distinction, from a legislative point of view, between the power to impose a tax and the justice of doing so.

I do not affirm that this tax would not be sustained by the courts on the reasoning which controlled the decision in the inheritance tax case of *Knowlton v. Moore.* My objection goes to the equity of the tax and the unlimited powers given the Federal Government over matters which seem to me to be purely within the jurisdiction of the States.

There are many corporations organized for and engaged in business of a purely local character. They derive no special privilege from the Federal Government as distinguished from individuals. To illustrate: in the city where I live, on opposite corners are two office buildings of the same general character. One of these buildings is owned by a corporation, the other by an individual. The corporation will come within the operation of the proposed tax. I can not reconcile the collection of a tax by the Federal Government on one, for that is what it amounts to, and not on the other. Numerous illustrations of the same character might be urged as between competitors in every community.[9]

Taxes On Privileges

In this tax we again see how important the issue of a tax on a "privilege" is to the government. Let us examine this issue in greater detail since it represents a totally false and judicially contrived "tax" that few Americans are hardly aware of.

[9] Ibid.

There can be no such thing in America as a tax on a privilege. Taxes, as you already know, are always levied on individuals since it is only individuals who pay taxes (either directly or indirectly). So a so-called tax on a "privilege" is really a tax on an individual (or business) based upon their receiving or enjoying some alleged special "privilege."

A number of U.S. taxes are based on the public's alleged receipt of a "privilege." Apart from the Corporation Excise Tax, Federal estate and gift taxes were held to be excises placed upon the "privilege" of bequeathing property at death or giving away property during life.

The Corporation Excise Tax of 1909 was being based on the alleged "privilege" of operating as a corporation with the amount of the tax measured by the corporation's profit in exercising this "privilege." So this tax was not levied *on profits* themselves (as Congress and the courts said), but supposedly *on* the "privilege" of *operating* as a corporation. Why was the tax allegedly levied *on* the "privilege" and not *on* the profits themselves? The latter would generate the same revenue for the government as the former and a "profits" tax would be more descriptive and accurate than a "privilege" tax. The reason was that the *Pollock* Court had already ruled that a tax levied on income was direct and, therefore, had to be apportioned; while taxes levied on supposed privileges had been "interpreted" by some courts as being indirect and, therefore, did not have to be apportioned. In this way the government (with the help of its "courts") could get at the income (really profits) of corporations by claiming that it was not taxing their *income* but merely taxing their privilege of "doing business in a corporate capacity"; while measuring the amount of the tax by the *income* generated by the exercise of this "privilege" — a shameless semantic swindle!

The government operates the same scam in connection with Federal estate and gift taxes. You now know that such Federal taxes are not levied on the property bequeathed at death or gifted during life, but, rather, are "excise" taxes levied on the "privilege" of *making* such bequests and gifts. The tax levied on these "privileges, " however, is measured by *the value* of the property left or given so the government receives the same amount it would if the taxes were levied directly on the property itself rather than on any "privilege." Why then did Federal judges and politicians insist on creating "privileges" to tax rather than taxing profits, bequests and gifts directly? Because they needed to create *fictitious excise taxes in order to avoid the apportionment provisions of the Constitution.*

Taxing Real Estate as a Privilege

Look, for example, at the Federal estate tax and how it works. If a man left his heirs $1,000,000 worth of real estate could the Federal government impose an "estate tax" on this real estate without apportioning it? It could not since Federal taxes "on" real estate have been, *in every case,* held to be direct. How then could the Federal government "tax" such real estate without apportioning it? It simply levied the tax on the real estate but *claimed* that what was actually being taxed was a *privilege.* Then they taxed the *privilege (based on the value of the real estate)* and *violá,* the real estate was "taxed" and the government claimed it only really "taxed" a privilege! This is how the Federal government had been able to avoid apportioning direct taxes "on" real estate — despite the fact that every Federal court (including the *Hylton* Court) has agreed that a tax "on" real estate is a direct tax requiring apportionment.

Americans Receive "Privileges"?

The whole concept of taxing Americans on the basis of their receiving certain "privileges" is vicious nonsense. There are no such things as "privileges" in America. Under a monarchy, the nobility might enjoy certain privileges that commoners do not share. In America, however, Article 1, Section 9 of the Constitution bars the granting of nobility — that is the granting of privileges. Where in the Constitution, for example, is the Federal government authorized to grant privileges? Americans either have a right to do something or they do not. Even if the activity requires a license or a certificate of incorporation, getting that license or certificate does not constitute a privilege since anyone who meets the requirements and pays the license or certificate fee has a right to them. A citizen's right to the license or certificate is established by law and is not granted on the basis of any arbitrary decision made by a king or a bureaucrat as to who should be granted the "privilege" of such license or certificate. A king, of course, can arbitrarily confer knighthood or elevate someone in the peerage (to which certain privileges might attend). But no such system of "privileges" can exist in America and, therefore, neither can taxes be levied on the basis of the receipt of such fictitious "privileges."

Government Illegally Taxes Rights

What the government has been taxing are rights, not privileges. But rights cannot be taxed since, if they could, they would not be "unalienable" as established in the Declaration of Independence. Chief Justice John Marshall correctly pointed out that "the power to tax involves the power to destroy." If the U.S. government had the lawful power to tax rights, it would have the lawful power to abolish them — which it obviously does not have. If the individual owns property, a right recognized by the Constitution, does he not possess the right to use it, consume it, or give it away? If he does not have the right to give it away (if it is a "privilege" that can be taxed — as in the case of gift taxes), then by extension, he should not have the right to use or consume it either except with the government's permission. And if he does not have these rights, then obviously the government, not he, owns the property. Based upon the government's enforcement of the income, estate, and gift tax "laws" (and the public's docile acceptance of them), today's taxes are a veiled but real declaration that the government owns everything — and that what we possess we do so only with government's sufferance. In effect, the government (through taxation) has abolished private ownership of practically all property.

Corporate "Privileges"

Organizing a corporation in America does not involve the receipt of any "privilege." It is a right Americans enjoy as long as they conform to the laws which govern such organizations. In essence, this is no different than an American's right to life, which may be forfeited only if he feloniously takes another's life. The Federal government did not create corporate "privileges" since corporations existed as early as the Middle Ages. In fact, by the 15th Century, English courts had already established the principle of limited corporate liability — "*Si quid universitas debetur, singulis non debetur, nec quod debet universitas, singuli*" (If something is owed to the group, it is not owed to the individuals nor do the individuals owe what the group owes). Therefore, the issue of limited liability referred to by Taft was no privilege created or conferred by government but, instead, was established in the common law long before our government was formed. In addition, limited liability is merely one of many attributes characteristic of a corporate entity. In reality, a corporation is an artificial person created by law — it can own property in its own name; it can sue and be sued; it has perpetuity, since it cannot die, though it can be disolved; and it confers a limited liability on its owners (the stockholders) who can lose their initial investment but no more. This limited liability that according to Taft made corporations subject to an excise, is a two-edged sword since corporate owners (stockholders) have no direct ownership of any of the assets they theoretically "own." All of these attributes (or "privileges" as our courts refer to them) are simply the economic and legal characteristics of any corporate entity and the things that give almost instant liquidity to corporate stock (as demonstrated by our numerous regional and national stock exchanges). This gives corporations the unique ability (as opposed to other forms of business organization) to be able to generate large pools of capital from a multitude of investors. It also permits corporations to launch large scale, economic and social projects for the ultimate economic benefit of society. Without such limited liability, large pools of capital could not be quickly or easily raised and would be detrimental to the economy and society as a whole as we have seen when there is little capital accumulation. America would not have had its railroads, its utilities, its steel and auto industries (and in many cases even its hospitals or churches) without the limited liability inherent in corporate organization and stock ownership. Indeed, Japan's miraculous post-war economic boom is largely attributable to the introduction of American-style corporations during the American occupation after World War II and the breaking up of Japanese *zaibatsu* (family-owned and controlled holding companies) which had totally dominated the pre-war Japanese economy. To suggest that such limited liability is a "privilege" conferred by government to stockholders for their exclusive benefit is absurd, and typical of the type of economic nonsense that usually emanates from the nation's politicians.

In addition, corporate charters are actually granted only by state governments, so any Federal claim of "privilege" is a violation of the 9th and 10th Amendments and constitutionally repugnant. It is, as has been demonstrated, a "legal" sleight of hand trick to allow the Federal government to contrive an unapportioned "excise" tax. Even a tax on an alleged "privilege" is nothing but a direct tax based upon that "privilege".

The Corporation Excise Tax was passed as recommended by Taft and was incorporated into the Payne-Aldrich Tariff Act — the constitutionality of which ultimately reached the Supreme Court in March, 1911.

Flint vs Stone Tracy 220 US 107

A number of individual cases challenging the Act's constitutionality on a variety of grounds were consolidated and brought before the Court in the above referenced case. Some of the issues raised included:

1. that the Act was unconstitutional because it singled out businesses created by the states and therefore invaded state sovereignty;
2. that no opportunity for a hearing was given to the corporations by any committee of the Senate or House, nor was any revenue measure ever passed by Congress with less scrutiny;
3. that the Act was arbitrary and discriminatory since individuals and co-partnerships (though carrying on the same type of business) were exempt from the tax; and
4. that requiring a corporation to make a return constituted a "search" within the language of the 4th Amendment.

Throwing both law and logic to the winds, the Supreme Court found in favor of the government in all instances. Among other things the Court held:

1. that the corporate tax was not a direct tax but an excise on the privilege of doing business in a corporate capacity:

2. that the corporate tax provisions of the Tariff Act of 1909 were not unconstitutional, although they were a revenue measure not originated in the House;

3. that joint stock companies and associations (while differing somewhat from corporations) have many of the same attributes and enjoy many of the same privileges and are therefore properly classified with corporations in a tax measure such as the Corporation Tax;

4. that while the legislature cannot (by declaration) change the real nature of a tax it imposes, its declaration is entitled to weigh when construing the statute;

5. that excises are taxes laid upon the manufacture, sale or consumption of commodities within the country, upon licenses to pursue certain occupations, and upon corporate privileges. The requirement to pay such taxes involves the exercise of the privilege and, if business is not done in the manner prescribed, no tax is payable;

6. that Congress's power to raise revenue is essential to national existence and cannot be impaired or limited by individuals incorporating and acting under state authority. The mere fact business is transacted pursuant to state authority creating private corporations, does not exempt it from the power of Congress to levy excise laws upon the privilege of so doing;

7. that there are distinct advantages to carrying on business in the manner specified in the Corporation Tax Law (as opposed to carrying it on as a partnership or individual) and it is this privilege that is the subject of the tax — not the mere buying, selling or handling of goods;

8. that it is not part of the essential government function of a state to provide means of transportation or to supply artificial light, water and the like. Although the people of the state may derive a benefit therefrom, the public service companies carrying on such enterprises are private and therefore subject to the same legitimate Federal taxation (such as the Corporation Tax) as are other corporations;

9. that the unreasonable search and seizure provisions of the 4th Amendment do not prevent the Federal government from re-

quiring ordinary and reasonable tax returns (such as those required by the Corporation Tax Law);

10. that the Court would not pass on questions of constitutionality
of the statute until they arose and no questions was presented
concerning the provisions of the Corporation Tax Law that
might offend the self-incrimination provisions of the 5th
Amendment or whether the penalties for non-compliance were
so high as to violate the Constitution. The penalty provisions
of the Act were separable and their constitutionality could be
determined if a proper case arose.

The self-serving hypocrisy of the Supreme Court was clearly evident from this decision since the Act could have been held unconstitutional on any one of a variety of grounds. Though these grounds will not
be analyzed in detail, some comment on them is in order. (The following
observations are numbered to correspond to the previous findings of the
Court.)

1. By no stretch of the imagination could anyone (with an understanding of the U.S. Constitution and the subject of taxation)
hold this tax to be an "excise." The following excerpt from *Pollock* exposes the illegality of the Act:
    The substance, and not the shadow, determines the validity
    of the exercise of the power.[10]

2. A minor matter in view of everything else, but a possible violation of the Constitution, nevertheless.

3. Joint stock companies and associations are not corporations
and if they could be taxed under this Act, why should it not apply to partnerships and sole proprietors? Field's commentaries
on taxation (see page 118) are very appropriate here and expose
the repugnancy of the Court's holding, in this area, to the
Constitution.

4. That is, however, exactly what Congress did — change, by declaration, the real nature of the tax. The Court saw it but conveniently turned its head.

5. The Court tailored its definition to fit the tax. The Court
should have ended its definition after the second phrase since
excises have nothing to do either with "licenses" or "privileges." Any tax connected with either of the latter are paid directly by those taxed. It might be argued that (in certain
cases) a uniform franchise tax unrelated to income might be

[10]*Pollock vs Farmers' Loan* 157 US 429, page 582.

regarded as an indirect tax to the extent that it is passed on
to consumers in terms of higher prices for the products or services sold. However, any such tax related to income or wealth is
obviously a tax "on" income or wealth and not on any "franchise" or "privilege." Adding to the definition the provision
that "if business is not done in this manner described no tax is
payable" was, of course, done to legally justify all those unin-
corporated businesses that had been discriminatorily left out
of a tax "on doing business." Here we have the Federal government's own "Court" tailor making a definition to fit the law.

6. This, again, is a perfect example of either the bias or ignorance
   of the Court. When individuals incorporate, "the power of Congress to raise revenue" is in no way "impaired or limited" as
   claimed by the Court. Congress still has *all the power it ever
   had* to directly tax citizens according to their wealth, their income, or on any other criteria — as long as the tax is apportioned — while still possessing the power to tax them
   indirectly through taxes on consumable products. Congress, of
   course, was never given *carte blanche* to tax on any basis it
   wished — and that was by design. Its ability to "raise revenue"
   is not "impaired" or "limited" by how people conduct their
   business affairs, but by the Constitution itself. The Constitution was deliberately written to deny the Federal government
   the power to "raise revenue" in any way it wished. This was
   done to prevent Federal politicians from passing class and regional legislation (especially in connection with taxes — as
   represented by the Corporation Excise Tax). It is obvious the
   government simply wanted to avoid the restraints imposed upon
   it by the apportionment provisions of the Constitution. In addition, if the Court thought the power of Congress to "raise revenue" was "essential, " what about constitutional rights and
   safeguards? The latter are far more "essential" than the former because the purpose of the Federal government is not to
   arbitrarily raise revenue merely to support and perpetuate itself, but to preserve and protect the rights of the people. It is
   "essential" to preserve a republican form of government and to
   keep government in check to avoid bureaucratic tyranny (two
   considerations which obviously held no interest for this Court
   and which obviously hold little interest for Federal courts in
   general — the *Pollock* case being a rare exception).

7. More judicial double talk reflecting the Court's willingness to
   uphold a tax which is clearly arbitrary in applications and obviously illegal on this one issue alone.

8. Since the tax was allegedly levied on "privilege," some utility companies argued that their services (such as public transportation, light and water) were "essential" to the public. How, then, could it be claimed that in delivering such "essential" services they were themselves receiving a "privilege"? If the tax had been honestly levied on the basis of profit or capital or even if it applied to *all* businesses this argument could not have been made, but the tax (it was claimed) was being levied on their supposed exercise of a "privilege!" In addition, of course, public utilities are, indeed, subject "to legitimate Federal taxes" but not illegitimate ones.

9. Such a consideration certainly does violate the 4th Amendment. If a business is required to provide a return then it is required to allow an inspection (search and seizure) of its books and records in order to *substantiate* the deductions claimed or risk losing them. Therefore, its books and records become open to government scrutiny and to actual seizure — as happened to the author.

10. The inquisitorial nature of a tax (requiring that information be supplied under penalty of perjury — and upon which further inquisitorial audits can be based) has to be repugnant (and *is*) to the 4th and 5th Amendments to the Constitution as even current IRS audit manuals admit!

In upholding the legality of this Act, the *Stone Tracy* Court threw out both the apportionment and uniformity provisions of the Constitution, the 4th Amendment, the equal protection clause, as well as various 5th Amendment guarantees — all in a day's work for the Supreme Court!

11

The Sixteenth Amendment

The 16th Amendment did not amend or change the U.S. Constitution. This, however, is not what American law schools teach nor what is conveyed to the public in many current "readings" of the Constitution. The fact that *the 16th Amendment did not change one word or phrase of the Constitution has, for years, been the U.S. government's best kept secret.* If the government had a choice, it would undoubtedly prefer that the Russians get all our military secrets rather than that the American public get the truth about that Amendment.

As finally adopted the Sixteenth Amendment states:

> The Congress shall have power to lay and collect taxes on incomes, from whatever source derived, without apportionment among the several States, and without regard to any census or enumeration.

It *appears* to have changed the apportionment provisions of the Constitution (at least with respect to an income tax) and to give the Federal government a new taxing power. However, those assumptions are incorrect. When the Amendment and income tax law were passed, Congress

1. believed it was amending the Constitution (which turned out not to be the case);
2. admittedly did not even know what "income" was, but taxed it anyway;
3. stated that its purpose was to shift the tax burden to the rich while lowering taxes for everyone else; and
4. justified the Amendment as necessary in the event of war.

Prior to receiving President Taft's message of June 15, 1909, the Senate was already deeply engrossed in considering an income tax amendment to the revised Dingley Tariff Bill. Senator Bailey's amendment had been submitted on April 15 and was almost exactly like the one passed in 1894 except that it:

1. excluded from taxation interest received on state and municipal bonds;
2. raised the initial exemption from $4,000 to $5,000; and
3. increased the rate of tax from 2 to 3 percent.[1]

A week later, Senator Cummins introduced another amendment which contained some rather interesting departures from both Bailey's Amendment and the Act of 1894. Cummins, an attorney, demonstrated that he had a considerable understanding of the economics of a tax on income and even the inherent problem of *trying* to tax it but, nonetheless, he favored an unapportioned income tax.[2] The income tax bill ultimately adopted by Congress was almost exactly the bill he submitted — including his suggestion of graduating the tax. Surprisingly, Cummins' amendment also *excused all corporations from the tax* and the income tax finally adopted by Congress did not tax corporations! It is true that between the time Cummin's amendment was submitted and the income tax was actually adopted the corporation (excise) tax previously discussed went into effect, but it was not for that reason that corporations were excluded. They were excluded because of Cummin's forceful explanation (still valid today) as to why corporations should not be subject to an income tax. Not one Senator could refute Cummin's arguments, as is illustrated by the following dialogue from the *Congressional Record:*

> The second important particular in which this amendment differs from the amendment already before the Senate is that it is confined to individual incomes; that is to say, the duty is not imposed upon corporate incomes. The reasons that moved me in preparing the amendment in this wise are that the policy of an income law, the policy indeed in almost every kind of law, is to exempt those who are least able to bear the burden from the burden. An income duty imposed upon the aggregate income of a corporation rests with equal weight upon those persons who derive some income from a corporation and yet have an aggregate income below the minimum fixed by the statute and those large incomes upon which it is the policy of the Government to attach a duty.
>
> Further than that, I regard a graduated income duty as impossible if levied upon the incomes of corporations. The reason is obvious. This

---

[1] The interest on state and municipal bonds was excluded because the *Pollock* Court had unanimously agreed that such taxes were unconstitutional, while Bailey believed that increasing both the initial exemption and the rate of tax would raise more revenue and also, I suggest, make the tax more appealing as a "tax the rich" scheme.

[2] It is also apparent that Cummins was misinformed concerning the economic and legal distinctions between direct and indirect taxes and the valid political reasons that made these distinctions necessary.

amendment, for instance, imposes a duty of 2 per cent in the case of an income not exceeding $10,000 upon that part of such income exceeding $5,000. It imposes a duty of 6 per cent upon all incomes in excess of $100,000.

I will take the instance which is in every mind the very moment a corporation is mentioned, namely, the United States Steel Corporation. It had last year, according to its report, an income, not deducting the rewards upon its capital, of $91,000,000. Under any logical or scientific system of graduated tax this income would bear the highest rate, and yet, as we know, there are twenty-five or thirty million dollars of the stock of the United States Steel Corporation held by employees of the corporation whose incomes will average less than $1,200 per year. Therefore, if a graduated tax be accepted and the duty is imposed upon the aggregate income of corporations, the stockholders whose incomes are below the minimum fixed by the amendment would bear the highest rate of duty attached to the largest income. In my opinion, such a result would not only be unjust, but it would destroy the essential and fundamental principle that underlies an income duty.

There is another reason of a legal character which led me to attach these duties to individual incomes only. The very moment that you include a corporation within the scope of an income tax, that moment you must begin a classification of corporations. The law of 1894 excluded from its operation a great number of corporations, and properly excluded them. But this classification had a tendency, in the opinion of the Supreme Court, both of its majority members and its minority members, to destroy the uniformity which the Constitution requires shall inhere in an indirect tax.

I do not suggest, Mr. President, that the amendment I have presented removes all the objections found to such a law in the decision of the Supreme Court in the Pollock case. I recognize that it challenges that opinion in one particular, but I believe that it removes all the points of collision save one. That is this: Is a tax levied upon an income derived from an investment in either real or personal property a direct tax? That question is one so broad and fundamental, that, in my opinion, was utterly impossible to frame any income-tax law that will not run counter to the opinion expressed by a majority of the members of the Supreme Court. If that opinion is to stand in its full scope and with its full vigor, then the United States must abandon for all time, or until the Constitution be amended, the exercise of a power and authority which had been recognized for a hundred years before the opinion was announced.

Therefore, in these two particulars, or, broadly speaking, in this one particular, the amendment I have presented challenges the opinion of the Supreme Court in just the same manner that the amendment offered by the Senator from Texas does.

. . . Mr. RAYNER. Then you have an amendment providing for an income tax which practically exempts every corporation in the United States from paying an income tax? That is the point.

Mr. CUMMINS. Just exactly as the law of 1894 did. The law of 1894 provided that the income derived by the individual from a corporation that had paid an income tax should be deducted from his individual income, and this amendment reaches precisely the same result in, I think, a much more satisfactory and equitable way.

Mr. RAYNER. This amendment, in my judgment, does not at all reach the same practical result. What I want to get at is this: Under the law of 1894, corporations paid taxes on their incomes, while under the Senator's amendment no corporation in the United States would pay a dollar to the Government of the United States except in a roundabout way in which the Senator figures it out that it comes out of the pockets of individuals who get dividends from corporations.

Mr. CUMMINS. The Senator from Maryland is too good a lawyer and is too intelligent a man, I am sure, to put a misconstruction upon this amendment. I ask him again to recur to the point. The steel corporation —

Mr. RAYNER. What I want to ask the Senator is this: When you are imposing an income tax — I am not arguing the income tax at all — why not put the income tax on corporations and exempt whatever corporations you think are proper from the operation of the income tax, provided it is a geographically uniform tax? Why not put a tax on corporations? Why do you exclude corporations from the tax? We have not read the amendment; and I should like to hear some reason for such a provision.

Mr. CUMMINS. I will answer the Senator with pleasure.

Mr. RAYNER. We are after the corporations also, and I thought you were, too.

Mr. CUMMINS. I am after justice; I am not after the coporations.

Mr. RAYNER. No: I am after equal justice, but you are letting the corporations out.

Mr. CUMMINS. I favor an amendment which will accomplish justice throughout the United States. I answer the Senator from Maryland further in this way: The amendment which I have offered provides that the tax shall be levied upon all the dividends received from corporations. It is to be levied not only upon all the dividends received from corporations, but it is to be levied upon all undivided surplus or undivided profits of corporations. In that way it reaches every penny that is accumulated by a corporation in the way of net income.

Now, mark you, the reason that I prefer to reach the individual directly rather than the corporation is the one I have so repeatedly expressed. If you tax the corporation alone, or if you tax the corporation upon its entire net income, suppose that I were receiving from that corporation and from other sources an income of $100,000 — a most impossible hypothesis, but I nevertheless assume it for the moment — and the Senator from Maryland was receiving an income from all sources, partially from the dividends of corporations, of $5,000 —

Mr. RAYNER. That is impossible.

Mr. CUMMINS. Which is no impossible hypothesis —

Mr. RAYNER. It is impossible to myself in the same sense that it is as to the Senator.

Mr. CUMMINS. But do you not see the immediate injustice of it? The Senator would pay an income tax of 6 per cent on the income that he received from that corporation, although his entire income was less than the taxable amount, and I would be taxed also 6 per cent, being in the enjoyment of an income taxed at the highest rate. I am sure that if you once indorse a graduated income tax you must agree that it should be levied in the way that I have suggested, because in the end, I repeat, the income tax reaches the earnings of every corporation in the land and at the same time it does absolute justice among individuals.

Mr. SMITH of Michigan. Mr. President —

The VICE-PRESIDENT. Does the Senator from Iowa yield to the Senator from Michigan?

Mr. CUMMINS. With pleasure.

Mr. SMITH of Michigan. I should like to ask the Senator from Iowa just how he proposes to reach this net income — whether in the form of surplus or undivided profits, where the advantage to the stockholder is in the book value of his stock, or in a suspense account that may not even take the form of surplus? Does the Senator propose to reach that value by some inquisitorial means?

Mr. CUMMINS. Mr. President, it will be necessary for the Senator from Michigan to define what he means by the word "inquisitorial." In a sense every taxing process is inquisitorial.[3]

This discussion also shows that Cummins believed an income tax was an indirect tax. He wanted to make sure his proposed income tax would be *uniform* and explained why this uniformity might be impaired if some corporations were included and others were not. He did not want his proposed tax to be held unconstitutional on this ground.

It was feared that exempting corporations would enable some to evade the tax by employing foreign holding companies. Cummins addressed these concerns as follows:

[3]44 Cong. Reg., 61st Congress, 1st Session, pages 1421 — 1423. The Senator is not at all forthright in this statement. An income tax must be "inquisitorial" by its very nature while taxes on articles of consumption certainly are not. When one pays gasoline, liquor, tobacco and import taxes, for example, no government agent investigates you with respect to the payment of those taxes. Have you ever been "audited" in connection with your payment of those taxes? Regarding income taxes, however, taxpayers are *forced* to submit to IRS inquisitions (or lose deductions) which is why enforcement of such a tax *cannot* be compatible with constitutional rights. Proof of this can be found in the fact that Federal "judges" now disregard every constitutional right in enforcing this tax.

. . . It provides that every corporation shall make a report showing its gross income and its net income, showing the amounts that it has paid in the way of interest, in the way of dividends, showing what the amount of the undivided profits of the year are, and also showing the distributive share of each stockholder in the undivided profits, and that is added to the income of the individual precisely as the income that he has actually received in money.

. . . Mr. SMITH of Michigan. But I do not hesitate one moment to say that there is a large part of the stock and securities of prosperous American corporations held abroad in the leading financial centers of the world. I do not understand why these corporations should be relieved of this additional burden or the exactions by the Government, unless it is as a favor to them and not as a right.

Mr. CUMMINS. Mr. President, with the general sentiment expressed by the Senator from Michigan I am in entire accord, and I think that he does not mean to be understood as accusing me of any desire to favor corporations.

Mr. SMITH of Michigan. No.

Mr. CUMMINS. There is a history behind every man which either approves or condemns his course in any such respect as that; and I have a history which, I think, relieves me of any such imputation.

Mr. SMITH of Michigan. Mr. President —

The VICE-PRESIDENT. Does the Senator from Iowa yield to the Senator from Michigan?

Mr. CUMMINS. I do.

Mr. SMITH of Michigan. With that history I am very familiar. I am well aware of the consistent record of the Senator from Iowa in his desire to have all property, whether corporate or personal, bear its just proportion of the expenses of the Government. I have no criticism to make upon him; in fact, I have nothing but praise for him, and I am listening to what he has to say with a great deal of interest. I regret very much that he seems by force of circumstances to be obliged to speak so briefly this morning, for I had hoped to hear him more at length, and shall examine his amendment with a great deal of care. My respect for the Senator from Iowa is such that I acquit him promptly of any desire to furnish immunity to corporations.

Mr. CUMMINS. Mr. President, I did not believe for a moment that the Senator from Michigan entertained a thought of that character. I said what I did only to prevent the possibility of misapprehension on the part of others. In this amendment I have used all the ingenuity I possess to reach the very persons to whom he has referred. If I have failed in that respect, I can not doubt that before the discussion has gone far in a tribunal of this character that defect will be remedied.

Mr. SUTHERLAND. Mr. President —

The VICE-PRESIDENT. Does the Senator from Iowa yield to the Senator from Utah?

Mr. CUMMINS. Certainly.

Mr. SUTHERLAND. If I will not disturb the Senator from Iowa, I should like to ask him a question for my own information. I did not have the opportunity of hearing the amendment read.

Mr. CUMMINS. It has not been read.

Mr. SUTHERLAND. But if I understand what the Senator has said, his amendment proposes to tax the incomes of individuals only; it makes an exemption of incomes under $5,000, and entirely relieves the incomes of corporations from the tax, provided it has been paid in the shape of dividends. Am I correct about that, I will ask the Senator?

Mr. CUMMINS. The Senator is correct.

Mr. SUTHERLAND. Let me ask the Senator this question: Suppose we have a corporation which distributes dividends amounting to $100,000. It has 50 shareholders, and we will assume that each shareholder has an equal amount of stock, so that each shareholder would receive $2,000 in dividends. Under the Senator's proposed amendment none of those shareholders would pay any tax at all, as I understand.

Mr. CUMMINS. I have not so said.

Mr. SUTHERLAND. Well, then, the Senator did not —

Mr. CUMMINS. If the Senator will permit me, I will correct him just at that point.

Mr. SUTHERLAND. I will be glad to have the Senator do so.

Mr. CUMMINS. In the case that he has imagined, if the $2,000 received as dividends on stock in the corporation constitutes the only income received by the shareholders, then that income would be exempt. If, on the other hand, the income from other sources raises the income of the individual to $5,000 or more, then this tax would fall upon him.

Mr. SUTHERLAND. Mr. President, I did not misunderstand the amendment, only I did not put my supposition quite far enough. We will suppose, then, that the 50 shareholders receive an equal amount of the dividend, $2,000 each and that no one of them has an income from any other source, so that the $2,000 represents the entire income. In that case not one of those shareholders would pay a cent of tax. That is correct, is it not?

Mr. CUMMINS. That is true.

Mr. SUTHERLAND. And, notwithstanding the fact that the corporation had an income of $100,000, the corporation would pay no tax?

Mr. CUMMINS. That is true — no income tax.

Mr. SUTHERLAND. So that there is an income of $100,000 of the corporation upon which no tax at all is paid? Is that the result?

Mr. CUMMINS. That would be the result in the particular instance the Senator has given. But, Mr. President, I am not to be terrified by any such result. I do not believe that an individual with an income of $2,000 derived from a corporation should be taxed any more than an individual receiving $2,000 by way of a salary. I am attempting to reach the aggregate, the ultimate, the final result. *The corporation is simply the instrumentality for the enrichment of its stockholders, and if that instrumentality results in conferring upon its stockholders an income above the minimum fixed by the amendment, then it should be taxed; but if that income is below the minimum, there is no more reason for imposing a tax upon it than there would be if it were derived as a salary or as profit in a real estate transaction or as the profits of a farm.* [4]

Mr. RAYNER. Mr. President —

The VICE-PRESIDENT. Does the Senator from Iowa yield to the Senator from Maryland?

Mr. CUMMINS. Certainly.

Mr. RAYNER. We have not had an opportunity to look at the Senator's amendment. I should like to give the Senator a concrete, but at the same time a supposititious, case. Let us take the case, for instance, of Mr. Carnegie. That merely exemplifies hundreds of cases, because there are hundreds of people living abroad who draw their income and dividends from domestic corporations. There is no doubt about that. Now, suppose that Mr. Carnegie to-day was getting an income of $500,000 a year in the way of dividends from the Bethlehem Steel Company. The Senator's amendment does not touch the steel company, and there is no way on the face of the earth to collect an income tax from him unless he has property in the United States that you can distrain on.

Mr. CUMMINS. The Senator has not read the amendment.

Mr. RAYNER. You can not make an amendment to cover that case.

Mr. CUMMINS. Very well.

Mr. RAYNER. If the man has no property, how will you collect an income tax if he lives abroad?

Mr. CUMMINS. It is evident the Senator does not desire to ask me a question, and I will yield at the proper time to any argument that he may desire to make.

Mr. RAYNER. I ask the Senator how he would get that tax?

Mr. CUMMINS. The Senator says it can not be done.

Mr. RAYNER. If I may be permitted to ask a question. How does the Senator propose to collect an income tax in such a case as I have given?

Mr. CUMMINS. I propose that the corporation shall pay that tax.

Mr. RAYNER. Does the amendment of the Senator say that the corporation shall pay it?

---

[4] Who can find fault with this logic? It clearly explained why corporations should not pay any "income" taxes at all yet today such earnings are taxed at least twice and even more.

Mr. CUMMINS. As I understand, the duty could be collected from the corporation, but I will strengthen it in that particular.

. . . Mr. CUMMINS. I again congratulate the Senator.

Mr. President, I am sure the Senate will acquit me of any original intent to delay the regular order of the Senate by such an extended discussion. I am not at all blamable, I think. I rose simply to make some observations with regard to an income tax generally. The details of the amendment I have offered will be better understood and more intelligently debated after the amendment shall have been printed and after Senators shall have carefully considered it.

But I was rather entertained this morning in reading a newspaper containing the suggestion that it was the purpose of Republican Senators who favor an income-tax law to invade in some way the system of protection — that it was an insidious attack upon this fundamental principle of the Republican organization. I desire to disclaim any such purpose upon my part. There is no Senator who yields allegiance to the Republican party who is more firmly wedded to the doctrine of protection than I. I understand that I came into the Senate with some suspicion respecting my soundness upon the policy of protection. I frankly admit, if I am to be measured by the test imposed by that association of selfishness and slander known as the "Protective League," that I am not sound upon the doctrine of protection; but if I may be measured by Republican platforms, by the utterances of McKinley and of Garfield and of Allison and of Blaine, then I am as sound as any Senator who marches under the political banner to which I yield my loyalty.

I am not in favor of an income tax for the purpose of destroying the efficiency of the system of protection, and if it be true that an import-duty law can not be adjusted so as to afford ample and adequate protection to American industry without foreclosing the opportunity for the operation of an income-tax law, then I abandon the income-tax provision, for I have no desire to invade by a hair's breadth the established and long continued policy of the party to which I belong of giving full and ample protection to the American as against every other man on the face of the earth.

I have heard it said — and I think it was first said by a very distinguished Democrat — that an income tax was a Populistic doctrine. If it be Populistic, if it be the emanation of that party that we know as the Populist party, then we owe that party a deep and abiding obligation.[5]

First Income Tax Amendment Submitted

On April 27, Senator Brown of Nebraska (believing that any income tax measure passed by Congress could be struck down by the Supreme Court) introduced a joint resolution calling for a constitutional amend-

[5]44 Cong. Rec., 61st Congress, 1st Session, pages 1423–1425.

ment. His proposed amendment included provisions for an inheritance tax as well and read:

> The Congress shall have power to lay and collect taxes on incomes and inheritances.

The *Hylton* Case Comes Up

The Senate discussions concerning the income tax were largely dominated by those favoring the tax. One of the few exceptions came from Senator Sutherland of Utah (who later became a Supreme Court Justice). He was obviously more knowledgeable than anyone in the Senate regarding the apportionment provisions of the Constitution, the distinction between direct and indirect taxes, why such distinctions were made, and the legal decisions upon which American tax law was based. If others agreed with Sutherland's views on the *Pollock* case they did not more than make unsubstantiated comments. For example, Senator Borah of Idaho said:

> I am aware, Mr. President, that there are those who believe that the framers of the Constitution did not know the meaning of the language that they were using in the great charter which they were making. . . I am not of that faith.[6]

Sutherland, on the other hand, went to great lengths to analyze the *Hylton* decision (as well as others bearing on taxes) and correctly pointed out:

> . . . *inasmuch as the Hylton case is the foundation for the decision of the Supreme Court in every one of the cases which followed, I think a somewhat careful analysis of that case should be made first, because if that case, which was the foundation case upon which the other cases rest, is incorrect, they all fall.* If you put in a foundation which is insecure, it makes no difference how high the superstructure may be. When you tear out the foundation, the superstructure comes with it. And *if the Hylton case is bad law,* necessarily *the cases which follow it* and depend upon it *must be equally bad.* When I say the cases which follow, I mean the dictum in the various cases upon that subject of direct taxation.[7] (Emphasis added)

Sutherland dissected the *Hylton* case and explained in detail why it could not possibly have been correct and told the Senate:

[6]Ibid., page 2094.

[7]Ibid., page 2093.

Clearly in the opinion of Adam Smith, which the Supreme Court in this earliest case cited with approval, a direct tax is upon the revenue of the taxpayer, while an indirect tax is a tax upon his expense.[8] (Emphasis added)

Sutherland further defended the *Pollock* decision when he said:

Mr. SUTHERLAND. . . The Senator invokes the rule of *stare decisis*. I do not. *Stare decisis* is an adviser, not a dictator. *Stare decisis* operates by way of persuasion, not by way of compulsion. I submit that there is as much virtue in *setting aside a wrong precedent as there is in following a right precedent.*

It has been said that this decision in the *Pollock* case is entitled to little weight because it overrules former decisions; but, on the contrary, it may be entitled to more than ordinary weight, for the very reason that it does overrule the former opinions, if it does so.

The Supreme Court of the United States is the greatest court this world has ever seen. In the year 1895, when the *Pollock* case was decided, its members were as magnificently equipped in learning and ability as any who have sat in that August tribunal before or since. *It is apparent from the reading of this case and the opinion upon the rehearing, that they gave to the question more careful consideration by far than was ever given to it in any preceding case.* If the effect of their decision is to set aside the prior decisions of the court for a hundred years, we may be sure that those judges did not do that for light or trivial reasons. The rule of *stare decisis* was invoked there; indeed it was made the basis of at least one dissenting opinion, that of Mr. Justice Brown; but even if we concede its application, the reasons for a contrary judgement were so imperious and controlling that a majority of the court refused to be governed by the rule. The majority decision in the *Pollock* case is condemned on the ground that it is a dangerous infraction of the rule of *stare decisis*, and yet those who make this complaint in the same breath take the astounding position that the Pollock case which is now *stare decisis* upon that question in its turn shall be reviewed, discredited, and reversed.[9] (Emphasis added)

Unlike Sutherland, however, almost every Senator believed the *Pollock* Court had been in error.

On that same day, Senator Depew of New York (one of the few voices in the Senate against the income tax) commented on those Senators who inveighed against the *Pollock* decision and said that apparently the only remedy "left for defeated attorneys. . . was to go down to the tavern and curse the court, " and additionally pointed out:

[8]Ibid.

[9]Ibid., page 2096.

No one has been able to refute the conclusions of the Finance Committee that the bill under discussion will yield several millions in excess of expenditures. It is claimed that the income tax will produce between sixty and eighty millions of dollars annually. This would create a dangerous surplus and impose a burden for no other purpose than to establish a theory. A theory which will cost the taxpayers of the country, and, in the analysis of distribution, all the people, $80,000,000 which the Government does not need and for which it has no use, is the most expensive educational propaganda ever exploited.

. . . The Constitution was a compromise between the large and populous and the small and sparsely populated States. The small States demanded that in some way they should be protected. The device to protect them was that, regardless of their population, each State should have in the Senate practically two ambassadors with equal vote and equal power. There was as great disparity then as there is now between the States of large population and those of smaller population. *The taxing power and its destructive possibilities were thoroughly understood, and the great States of New York, Pennsylvania, Virginia, and Georgia never intended that they should be outvoted and made to bear undue burdens because of the votes in the Senate of the smaller States.* **There are 15 States with 30 Senators in this body whose aggregate population differs only a few thousand from that of the single State of New York with two Senators. New York has one-seventh of the property of the country. It has one-twelfth of the population. Yet, under an income tax, it would pay 33 per cent of the burdens of the Government.** It is absurd to suppose that with the States rights views that existed among the statesmen of the formative period and in the Constitutional Convention they ever intended that any system should prevail which would distribute so unequally the burdens of the Government among the various States. [10] (Emphasis added)

Passage of the Income Tax Assured

By June 11, Cummins and Bailey had ironed out their differences and Cummins offered their compromise measure to the Senate. Now united, the Senate forces favoring an income tax were confident they could pass it as an amendment to the Tariff Bill. At this time Senator Aldrich (a Rhode Island Republican) succeeded in postponing consideration of the amendment until June 18.[11]

[10]Ibid., page 2103.

[11]Around June 10 a meeting was held between President Taft and the Republican Senate leadership. This unquestionably led to Taft's June 15 message that was apparently designed to head off certain passage of the income tax amendment and with it the appearance of Democratic success and vindication.

The Sixteenth Amendment Introduced

Early on June 17 (following Senate receipt of President Taft's June 15 message) Senator Brown introduced his second joint resolution calling for a constitutional amendment. This differed[12] from the one he previously submitted and read as follows:

> The Congress shall have power to lay and collect direct taxes on incomes without apportionment among the several States according to population.[13]

On June 28 Senator Aldrich reported that the Committee on Finances proposed an amendment to the Constitution which he urged be "disposed of without debate." It read as follows:

> Article XVI. The Congress shall have power to lay and collect taxes on incomes, from whatever source derived, without apportionment among the several States and without regard to any census or enumeration.[14]

Aldrich's amendment differed from Brown's in two significant ways:

1. Brown's amendment called for a tax "on incomes" — Aldrich's called for a tax "on incomes, from whatever source derived." The difference is tremendous. See page 191.
2. Brown's amendment would have labelled the tax on income a "direct" tax while Aldrich's omits such classification.

Although both amendments were obviously *different* — and the Senate *rejected* Brown's and *adopted* Aldrich's — the historic irony is that the income tax is actually enforced on the basis of Brown's amendment not Aldrich's (see page 265).

Congress Not Sure What "Income" Is

Although the amendment was passed and an income tax law was written (supposedly based on that amendment); and although approximately 96,000,000 Americans pay taxes on "income" each year, few Americans realize that the Congress admitted that it did not even know

---

[12]This second proposal eliminated the reference to inheritance taxes and also added the word "direct" to the proposed tax on income.

[13]44 Cong. Rec., 61st Congress, 1st Session, page 3377.

[14]Ibid., page 3900.

(nor had the authority to determine) what "income" was when it decided to tax it. Few Americans realize that Congress has never defined "income" and *no such definition can be found anywhere in the Internal Revenue Code*.[15] According to the Supreme Court, therefore, no American can be subject to such a tax since the "law" neither defines nor identifies what is being taxed! Ironically, it is the very Supreme Court case[16] that paved the way for the income tax that clearly explains why this is so (see page 136).

No Law Can Tax What It Does Not Define

It is this "well settled rule" referred to in the *Spreckles* case that is now being totally ignored by our "courts" when they deal with "income" taxes. This also clearly explains why no American can be legally liable for an income tax and why no such "liability" appears anywhere in the Code. As explained in Chapter 13, "income" is an abstract concept so relating taxes to "income" is not like relating taxes to the value of a house, or placing a tax on wine, or cigarettes, or imported products. Congress not only realized it did not know *what* it was taxing when it taxed "income" — it even admitted it! This is easily seen by examining the Senate discussions that took place prior to the passage of the "law" itself. The following excerpts clearly reveal that the Senate did not understand how "income" was to be determined.

> Mr. WILLIAMS. The Senator seems to attach to the word "income" a meaning that is not attachable to it in this connection. "Income" means the *net gains or profits.* He seems to think that the word "income" is a broader word than "gains, or profits derived from any source whatever."
>
> Mr. CUMMINS. What is it used for?
>
> Mr. WILLIAMS. A man's taxable income means his *gains and profits during the year.* Those *gains* and *profits* or *income derived from any business* of any description are taxed. If a man is engaged in dealing in horses, if he buys horses and sells horses and *makes a profit* or an income out of that dealing, he must pay tax upon the income.
>
> I do not know that I exactly catch the Senator's point. But if I do catch it, *he seems to have in mind the idea that the word "income"* means receipts of every sort. The income *within the contemplation of a tax law does not mean that.* It means net income, and is so defined in the bill. *That means profits or gains.*
>
> Mr. CUMMINS. The Senator from Mississippi must certainly understand what I am trying to say. If applied to a general business, in

---

[15] "The general term 'income' is not defined in the Internal Revenue Code." *U.S. vs Ballard* 535 F2d 400, 404.

[16] *Spreckles Sugar Refining Co. vs McClain* 192 US 397.

which purchases and sales take place and gains and profits are reckoned. I can very well understand that the Senator from Mississippi is right, under the language of this bill. But suppose 10 years ago I had bought a horse for $900, and this year I had sold him for $1,000, what would I do in the way of making a return?

Mr. WILLIAMS. I will tell the Senator precisely what he would do.

Mr. CUMMINS. I mean, what would other men do?

Mr. WILLIAMS. I know; but what I mean is precisely what the Senator would do, or precisely what he ought to do. He bought the horse 10 years ago and sold him this year for a thousand dollars. That thousand dollars, and being a part of his receipts, that much will go in as part of his receipts, and from it would be deducted his disbursements and his exemptions and various other things.

Mr. CUMMINS. *Would the price I paid for the horse originally be deducted?*

Mr. WILLIAMS. **No, because it was not a part of the transactions in that year; but if the Senator turned around and bought another horse that year it would be deducted.**

Mr. CUMMINS. Mr. President, the answer of the Senator from Mississippi has disclosed very clearly the weakness that I have been attempting to point out. This provision, in the form in which it appears, is utterly unworkable. It would involve chaos among the people of this country if returns were attempted to be made in the way suggested by the Senator from Mississippi.

I have no amendment that will meet the emergency, because I did not dream that we would enter upon the consideration of the income-tax provision to-day. I only have to suggest that the sort of thing involved in the homely illustration of the purchase and sale of a horse — an instance which might not occur very often — would occur thousand of times every day in the sale of other kinds of property.

Mr. GALLINGER. Particularly real estate.

Mr. CUMMINS. Yes; by men who are not engaged in what is known generally as a vocation, but who do have occasion to buy and sell property from time to time.

Mr. BRISTOW. Mr. President. I desire to ask a question, and see if I have this matter clear in my mind. As I understood the question of the Senator from Iowa, it was, if he bought a horse 10 years ago for $100 —

Mr. CUMMINS. Nine hundred dollars.

Mr. BRISTOW. And sold it this year for a thousand dollars, whether or not that thousand dollars would be counted as a part of his income for this year, regardless of what he paid for the horse 10 years ago. Is that correct?

Mr. WILLIAMS. No; I did not say that. It would be a part of his gross receipts for the year, of course, but it may not necessarily be a part of his net receipts, and therefore not a part of his income that is taxable.

Mr. CUMMINS. But I asked the Senator from Mississippi specifically whether, in the case I put, the price that was originally paid for the horse could be deducted from the price received.

Mr. WILLIAMS. *The price paid 10 years ago? No: of course not. How could it?* When a man puts in his return for his income of the previous year in order to be taxed he puts down everything he has received and everything he has paid out, subject to the exemptions and limitations otherwise provided in the bill. Necessarily that is so. To answer the Senator, I want to read the precise language of the provision.[17]

Senator Williams (a member of the Senate Finance Committee) specifically admitted that "income" did not mean "receipts of every sort" but only contemplated "profits or gains." To further demonstrate the confusion that existed in Congress concerning even the way income was to be calculated, look at the problem they encountered when they tried to determine the income generated by the sale of a mere horse. Williams was under the impression that its original cost had nothing to do with any "income" derived from its sale, while if another horse was purchased its cost could be deducted from "income." Does the IRS and Federal Tax Court go along with such reasoning today?

A group of men who were totally confused about what constituted "income" on the sale of a simple $1,000 horse could hardly be expected to know what "income" was in a variety of other situations far more complicated than this. And if Congress could not figure out what "income" was, how could they write legislation to tax it and how can anyone else figure out what it is? *They cannot*, which is why no such "liability" with respect to an "income" tax appears anywhere in the Code! (See page 254.)

Senator Cummins (the most influential man trying to shape this legislation in the Senate) explained why Congress could not even define "income, " as shown in the following exchange.

Mr. CUMMINS. It will be observed that here is an attempt, Mr. President, to define the meaning of the word "income, " to describe its scope, to determine its effect. I reiterate that the attempt will be ineffective and may be exceedingly dangerous.

Great Britain might employ such words as these in modification or explanation or enlargement of the word "income, " because Great Britain has no constitutional restriction upon her Parliament. A State might use these words with perfect propriety, because a State has a right to include whatever she likes within the meaning of the word "income"; but the Con-

[17] 50 Cong. Rec., 63rd Congress, 1st Session, pages 3775, 3776.

gress has no right to employ them, because the Congress can not affect the meaning of the word "income" by any legislation whatsoever. The people have granted us the power to levy a tax on incomes, and *it will always be a judicial question as to whether a particular thing is **income** or whether it is **principal.***

Mr. LEWIS. Mr. President, knowing the Senator from Iowa to be an excellent lawyer, will he give me his views on this point: Does the Senator contend that the word "income," therefore, as stated in the Constitution, must be construed to mean what it meant and was understood to mean at the date of its adoption as part of the Constitution?

Mr. CUMMINS. I do not so say. What I have said is, however, that it is not for Congress to interpret what it means; it is for the courts of the country to say, either at this time or at any other time, what it means. *If it were within the power of Congress to enlarge the meaning of the word "income," it could, as I suggested a moment ago, **obliterate all difference between income and principal,*** and obviously the people of this country did not intend to give to Congress the power to levy a direct tax upon all the property of this country without apportionment.[18]

Mr. LEWIS. Then, assuming that the matter would have to be determined finally by the court, which concession we all must make, would the Senator's legal mind revert to the theory that the court, then, would have a right to define the word "income" to mean whatever was understood judicially by "income" at the date of the adoption of this act?

Mr. CUMMINS. I do not accept that at all, because it is entirely beyond the domain of Congress. In 1789, I believe, the people of this country gave Congress the power to regulate commerce among the States. It is not within the power of Congress to say what commerce is. "Commerce" may mean a very different thing now as compared with what it meant in 1789; it has broadened with the times; the instrumentalities have changed with the course of years; but Congress can not make a thing commerce. The court must declare whether a particular regulation is a regulation of commerce, and in so declaring it defines for the time being what commerce is.

Why, Mr. President, should Congress attempt to do more than is declared in the first section of the proposed bill? It is right; it is comprehensible; it embraces everything — no, I will withdraw that; it does not embrace the full power of Congress, because Congress can levy a tax upon gross incomes if it likes, it may diminish the extent of its taxing power or not exercise it all; it may exclude certain things from the taxing power that it might include; but it can not change the character of the taxation; and when it is declared in the first lines of this bill that a tax is levied upon the entire net income of all the citizens of this country, we have exercised all the power we have. If we desire to limit ourselves to net income, we can not define "net income"; we can not say what shall be in-

[18] This, however, is precisely how the Federal government now uses the income tax!

cluded in income and what shall not be included in income. We are only preparing ourselves for delay, for disappointment, and possible defeat if we endeavor to interpret the meaning of the word "income."

Mr. SHIVELY. Mr. President

The PRESIDING OFFICER (Mr. Chilton in the chair). Does the Senator from Iowa yield to the Senator from Indiana?

Mr. CUMMINS. I do.

Mr. SHIVELY. I can readily agree with the Senator that the courts will finally give a definition of "income"; but that does not prevent Congress from limiting the application of the word in legislation.

Mr. CUMMINS. Not at all. I have so said.

Mr. SHIVELY. If the Senator will observe the words "except as hereinafter provided" in the first subdivision of this section —

Mr. CUMMINS. I have not sought to strike out any part of the limitations save the gift, devise, bequest, or descent, and I do not think there is any man in America, were it not for what precedes those words, who would contend or could contend that a gift or devise or bequest of property or property coming to one by descent is income. I never heard of it being so construed; and it is not possible that it could be so construed. It would not have been put in there were it not for the attempted enlargement of the word "income" contained in the previous part of the paragraph.[19]

Mr. WILLIAMS. How does the Senator think that is an attempt to enlarge it? Tell us specifically to what words the Senator refers.

Mr. CUMMINS. Mr. President, if it has not that effect, or attempted effect, it can have none. It is certainly not an attempt to limit or to restrict the meaning of the word "income"; and if it has not the effect or if it is not thought or if it was not in the mind of the person who drew it to enlarge the meaning of the word "income, " then the draftsman of the bill has offended against the first principles of legislation by incorporating language that is absolutely meaningless.

Mr. WILLIAMS. Now, if the Senator will pardon me a moment —

The PRESIDING OFFICER. Does the Senator from Iowa yield to the Senator from Mississippi?

Mr. CUMMINS. I do.

Mr. WILLIAMS. It was not the intent there to enlarge or to stretch the meaning of the words "net income, " which is the income referred to here, and not gross income at all.

Mr. CUMMINS. I have not said it was gross income.

Mr. WILLIAMS. The Congress in undertaking to specify what it proposes to tax does undertake neither to enlarge nor to restrict the meaning of the words "net income, " but to define their meaning for the

---

[19] The Senate had originally sought to tax gifts and bequests as "income" but, through Cummins' initiative, this was struck out.

purposes of this bill, for the purposes of this taxation. It may be that a court might come to the conclusion that Congress had wrongfully defined the term. If so, the court will correct the definition, and if the court corrects the definition, then this bill will be to that extent altered or changed; but the contention is that this is a correct definition of the articles which, under a bill seeking to tax net incomes, will be taxed. The question I asked the Senator was in what respect he thinks that this definition enlarges the meaning of the words "net income" or restricts them, either?

Mr. CUMMINS. Mr. President, as I remarked before, if these words qualifying, modifying, and explanatory are not intended either to enlarge or to restrict, they are entirely useless. I think, however, with deference —

Mr. WILLIAMS. *Does the Senator think it is useless in a tax bill to try to define the thing you propose to tax?*

Mr. CUMMINS. *Mr. President, I do think in this instance that it is worse than useless; I think it is dangerous, and I will proceed to show why.*

Mr. SIMMONS. Mr. President —

The VICE PRESIDENT. Does the Senator from Iowa yield to the Senator from North Carolina?

Mr. CUMMINS. I do.

Mr. SIMMONS. I readily agree with the Senator in his contention that we have no authority to tax anything except income, and I readily agree with him that, in the last analysis, *the court must decide what is income and what is not income;* but before the court can get jurisdiction of that question, there must be a levy; *there must be an assessment;* there must be an attempt to collect. I can see no other way in which the court could possibly acquire jurisdiction. *So that before the matter can ever reach the court there must be some one who will decide the question of what is "income."* [20] (Emphasis added)

Note that Cummins stated it would be "exceedingly dangerous" to define the meaning of "income."

Then, not even challenging Cummins, Senator Williams asked, "Does the Senator think that it is useless in a tax bill to try to define the thing you propose to tax?"

And Cummins replied, "Worse than useless; I think it is dangerous."[21]

Senator Simmons concurred and said that in the "last analysis the court must decide what is income and what is not income."

[20] 50 Cong. Rec., 63rd Congress, 1st Session, page 3844.

[21] How can it be "useless" and "dangerous" for a government to define something it proposes to tax?

American Public Does Not Know What "Income" Is

The point is, I do not think the American public understands that when Congress passed the income tax, it did not even know what it was taxing and it *still does not know it to this day!* The Supreme Court, which under the Constitution has no legislative authority, ultimately had to legislate the meaning of "income" precisely as Cummins predicted — and its definition conformed loosely to Senator William's description of income as meaning "profits or gains." Finally, Americans today are totally unaware that neither the IRS nor the courts use or conform to the definition of "income" that was originally "adopted" by the Supreme Court! For the purposes of this chapter, however, it is only important to understand that Congress never knew or had the vaguest knowledge of what it was taxing when it sought to tax "income"; and that to this day no definition of "income" exists in the law. On this basis alone (see the Supreme Court's clear statement in *Spreckles*) how can any judge claim that the payment of such a tax can be *mandatory*?

Income Tax Sold To The Public As A "Tax The Rich" Scheme

The Federal government sold an income tax to the pubic based on the myth that such a tax would be a tax *on wealth* (which only the wealthy would pay) as opposed to tariffs (taxes on consumption) which presumably fell on everyone, rich and poor alike. If the public had not believed this, Congress could never have enacted such a tax! In 1909 the people would never have amended the Constitution in order to give the Federal government *power to levy a new tax on them*. People voted for the Amendment because they believed an income tax would not affect them and that an income tax levied on the rich would enable Congress to lower tariffs thus actually *reducing* their other taxes.

Today's Income Tax Falls on the People

The people's misconception of how an "income" tax would actually work was based on the claims made for it by its early proponents and on the initially proposed bills themselves which were written to tax only the wealthy. Today, however (contrary to the claims made for it), the tax falls hardest not on the rich but on the general public [22] — the very people it was supposed to avoid taxing. The rich have numerous ways to es-

---

[22] Not that the rich (considering everything else) do not pay enough taxes, they do. But what they pay merely intrudes on their comforts or luxuries (and sometimes not even on these) while what the general public pays intrudes on their necessities.

cape the punitive affects of the tax. They can, for example, use their businesses to funnel non-taxable benefits to themselves, or pocket cash receipts as well as deduct the cost of cars, travel, dinners, or theater tickets as "business" expenses which, of course, ordinary wage earners cannot do.

Several years ago *60 Minutes* did a segment about two California "farmers" who (because they had poor credit and could not get local bank loans) received millions of dollars in low interest loans from the Department of Agriculture. A number of area farmers objected to these loans and complained that because they were efficient farmers and qualified for local bank loans they had to pay much higher interest rates than the inefficient farmers who qualified for government loans. They argued that not only were they being penalized for being efficient but that if the inefficient farmers did not get the low cost, taxpayer-subsidized government loans, they would have to sell their land to more efficient farmers. Government loans, therefore, merely kept thousands of acres of California farm land out of the hands of efficient producers and in the hands of inefficient ones at a substantial cost to taxpayers.

When the two farmers who had received the government loans were interviewed it was evident that they both lived in luxurious homes. One bred and raised horses as a sideline while the other conducted tennis clinics on the tennis courts situated on his property; and both drove expensive cars. When asked how much they had each paid in income taxes the previous year, both said they had paid nothing. Obviously, both "farmers" were living high on the hog and enjoying a standard of living far exceeding anything the average office or factory worker could even dream of — yet such workers not only pay far more in income taxes than those "farmers, " but they are actually taxed to subsidize them.

Today, of course, there is a multi-billion dollar tax shelter industry devoted entirely to structuring and marketing investments to lower taxes. In addition, tax lawyers get upwards of $100.00 an hour to figure out ways to lower their clients' taxes. Do factory and office workers go into tax shelters or can they afford the services of high priced tax lawyers? The point is that the real burden of income taxes falls directly on the backs of working, middle class Americans — the very people Congress claimed would not be affected by the tax when it was sold to the public.

To illustrate this further, here are some additional excerpts from the Congressional debates. When Senator Bailey offered his income tax proposal to the Senate he said:

> But knowing as we all do know, that it is necessary for the Government to raise a vast sum of money to support its administration, my judge-

ment is that a large part of that money ought to be raised from the abundant incomes of *prosperous people* rather than from the backs and appetites of people who, when doing their best, do none too well. [23] (Emphasis added)

According to Bailey, such a tax would not only *not fall* on the "backs" of those who do "none too well, " it would not even be burdensome to the rich as explained in the following passage:

> The people who have incomes subject to tax under this amendment can not complain that we undully burden them. The exemption of $5,000 (more than enough to buy a good size house) leaves the man with an income of $10,000 to contribute under the provisions of this amendment only $150 to support the General Government; and surely a man *whose abounding prosperity nets him an income of $10,000 a year may be fairly asked to contribute the moderate sum of $150. . .*[24] *(Emphasis added)*

In addition, Bailey said the income tax bill will enable Congress to make

> **the duties lower, [and]. . . lift from the backs and appetites of the toiling millions of the Republic and lay a large part of the burden of government upon the incomes of those who could pay the tax without the subtraction of a single comfort from their homes.** [25] (Emphasis added)

When he introduced his first constitutional amendment Senator Brown of Nebraska stated:

> I want to appeal first to those of us who believe in passing a law which shall reach the *luxurious* incomes of this country and ask them to help pass this resolution that the Constitution may have in it a section that can not be misunderstood.[26] (Emphasis added)

On April 28 Senator Rayner from Maryland said:

> It is the theory of the friends of the income-tax proposition that *property should be taxed and not individuals.*[27] (Emphasis added)

---

[23] 44 Cong. Rec., 61st Congress, 1st Session, page 1351.

[24] Ibid., page 2455. As finally adopted, the bill actually made the tax on this individual $60.00 if married or $70 if single.

[25] Ibid. I wonder how many Americans who pay income taxes today do so without the subtraction "of a single comfort from their homes"?

[26] Ibid., page 1569.

[27] Ibid., page 1570.

Today, however, many pay a considerable amount of income tax even though they have *no property at all*! There are numerous Americans living in furnished rooms, for example, who just get by and who have no property to speak of at all. Yet income taxes alone[28] will take better than 15 percent of their wages (not including other state and city taxes) while the other 7 percent in Social Security taxes paid by their employers must also really be paid by them (as it is paid by all American workers) either in terms of lower wages or higher consumer prices or both.

Meanwhile, in the House of Representatives, the rhetoric concerning how an income tax would soak the rich reached poetic heights. Representative Adir of Indiana stated:

> It is a shame and a disgrace, Mr. Speaker that under our system of taxation *the poor laboring man* and his wife and four and five children to support, *contributes more* toward the expenses of the Government *than does the millionaire* who is too proud to raise a family and has no one to clothe and feed except a wife and a poodle dog.[29] (Emphasis added)

Representative Rucker of Missouri:

> I heartily endorse and support the income-tax proposition. I would make a graduated income tax, and I would adjust the rates as *to compel the millionaires of this country,* who have been immune from taxation, *to pay a just and liberal part* of the revenues required for the support of government.[30] (Emphasis added)

Representative Clark of Missouri:

> It is monstrous to say that the *accumulated wealth* of this country shall not bear its just proportion of the public burdens.[31] (Emphasis added)

Congressman Henry of Texas:

> . . . there should be some method by which the untold *wealth and riches* of this Republic may be compelled to bear their just burdens of government and contribute an equitable share of their incomes to supply the treasury with needed taxes.[32] (Emphasis added)

[28] Including Social Security taxes which, in reality, are just another income tax. For further details, see *The Social Security Swindle — How Anyone Can Drop Out* (FREEDOM BOOKS, 1984) by Irwin Schiff.

[29] 44 Cong. Rec., 61st Congress, 1st Session, page 4434.
[30] Ibid., page 4426.

[31] Ibid., page 4392.
[32] Ibid., page 4414.

The point repeatedly made in both the Senate and the House was that is was "wealth and riches" that were to be reached by an "income" tax, something to be remembered by low and middle income people the next time they pay their income taxes.

Income Tax Not To Interfere With Basic Standard of Living

In line with Congress's purpose to tax "wealth and riches," it also maintained that an income tax would not apply to income needed to give an American family a "reasonable" amount to live on and a "proper standard of living" including the cost of educating his children.

Senator Cummins said:

> My desire is to relieve the incomes of men to the extent necessary to maintain their families, *to support and educate their children,* because I believe that they *owe a higher duty to their families than they owe to the government.*[33] (Emphasis added)

Senator Borah added these comments:

> After a man pays the tax which he must pay *on consumption,* then give him a chance *to clothe and educate his family* and meet the obligations of citizenship and preparation of those dependent upon him for citizenship *before you add any additional tax that is the basis of this exemption* and it is fair and just to all and toward all.[34] (Emphasis added)

And Senator Williams stated:

> The House framed its bill upon the theory that $4,000 was a reasonable amount, in its opinion, *for an American family to live upon, with a proper standard of living,* and that *a sum below that ought not to be taxed.*[35] (Emphasis added)

So "men owe a higher duty to their families than they owe to the government" — what kind of strange political heresy is this? Try telling that to Federal politicians bent on relieving you of thirty to forty percent of your income for the benefit of lobbyists, pressure groups, and subsidy-seeking factions of all kinds. Can you even conceive of anyone rising in the Senate today to proclaim such a weird doctrine? I have seen an ac-

---

[33] Ibid., page 3975.

[34] 50 Cong. Rec., 63rd Congress, 1st Session, page 3841.
[35] Ibid., page 3851.

tual instance where a working wife's net salary (after taxes) was lower than the taxes taken from her husband's wages. She was working full-time just to help pay *a portion* of her husband's taxes which, in reality, means that one spouse was working full-time (without pay) just for the government. How could such a situation occur if indeed a husband or wife owes a higher duty to his/her family than to government?

It should also be clearly noted that Congress sold an income tax to the nation on the basis that the tax would not interfere with what a family needed to maintain a "proper standard of living" and that amounts below that would not be touched by an income tax. That was the specific reason given for the $4,000 initial family deduction and is clearly substantiated by the following:

> The protective system will remain, but it will be supplemented for revenue purposes by federal taxation upon inheritances and incomes. It is not a socialistic scheme for the redistribution of wealth. It is a plan for an equitable distribution of burdens. There are 7,000,000 families of wage-earners in the United States living upon a *medium wage of $436 a year* and 5,000,000 farmers whose *average income is about $350 a year.* The *vast majority* of American families *live on $500 or less per year.* In the great iron and steel industries, in *1900,* the income of the family was about $540 a year, and in 1905, $580 per year. The *cost of living has increased from $74.31 in 1896 to $107.26 in 1906*[36]*; coal increased* in price *$1 per ton; manufactured commodities* advanced *32 per cent.* Under these circumstances, it seems to me that where competition has been destroyed and *the market price of a commodity is maintained at a high price by a trust*[37] the tariff on that commodity should be materially reduced, if not entirely removed, and that the large incomes, both of individuals and of corporations, should be required by an income tax to bear a larger share of the burden of federal taxation than they do now.
>
> *A graduated income tax exempting all incomes of less than $3,000 a year would place upon the wealth of the country a share of the burden of maintaining the Federal Government, which it ought to bear and bear gladly and willingly.*[38] (Emphasis added)

Since the vast majority of American families lived on "$500 or less" in 1909 and the tax for married individuals started at $4,000, a family

---

[36] Consider the extent to which the Federal government has illegally debased U.S. money! Many Americans now get a higher electric bill for one month than what many Americans lived on for a whole year around the turn of the Century. This is what Washington politicians call "economic growth."

[37] Today, "the market price of a commodity is maintained at a high price" not by trusts but by the Federal government through such Federal programs as agricultural subsidies and import restrictions.

[38] 44 Cong. Rec., 61st Congress, 1st Session, page 1962.

living on *eight times the national average would have paid no income taxes.*

What is the situation today? A married couple with a combined[39] taxable income exceeding $24,600 is in the 29 percent tax bracket. However, when you add in the Social Security tax the effective income tax rate becomes 36 percent for employees and 43 percent for the self-employed. On the other hand, a single individual with the same taxable income could find himself in a 42 percent to 49 percent bracket. And assuming an additional $10,000 in taxable income, these brackets could climb as high as 58 percent — and this still does not include state income taxes.

Since we have only a six cent dollar (as compared to a $1.00 dollar in 1913 when gold was officially valued at $20.00 per ounce[40]), both married and single taxpayers would need to have, by comparison, at least $60,000 and $45,000 (respectively) of taxable income today before being subject to the tax. This means that present day Americans, whose comparative 1913 incomes would not even have subjected them to any income tax at all, could, today, find themselves in the 40 percent to 50 percent tax brackets!

When the 16th Amendment was passed and the tax adopted in 1913, would Congress have dared propose such outrageous brackets even for the Carnegies, Astors, Vanderbilts and Rockefellers? Since the tax was only 1 percent on incomes from $4,000 to $20,000, a tax that was initially installed to tax the super rich (at a maximum rate of 7 percent) now subjects families that are just getting by to rates of from 30 percent to better than 50 percent.

Typical of the type of fabrication used by those favoring the income tax are the following remarks made by Senator Borah:

> . . . I am not willing, Mr. President, for one, to concede that the policy which fixes the burdens of government upon property and wealth is not a Republican principle. I am *not willing to concede,* above all things, *that there has been engrafted upon our constitutional power that which is an absolute exemption of property and wealth from the burdens of government.* I am not willing to have it admitted that the Constitution, as made and framed by the fathers, was such as to *exempt the great property interests of this country from the taxing power of the Government* even in the hour when the very exigencies of government may involve the life of the Government

---

[39] "Combined" because both spouses would probably be working as opposed to conditions in 1909 where undoubtedly only one family member was required to be employed to support the family unit.

[40] Today the price is approximately $350 an ounce reflecting a 94 percent devaluation.

itself. Yet I say to you that if the *Pollock* case be the correct interpretation of the law, there is no exigency by which this Government can call upon the great property and wealth of this Nation to meet a portion of its burdens, even if it involves the very life of the Nation itself.[41] (Emphasis added)

Apart from admitting (as did all Senators) that the real purpose of an income tax was to *tax wealth* and *not income,* Borah's suggestion that he was "not willing to concede. . . that there has been engrafted upon our constitutional power that which is an absolute exemption of property and wealth from the burdens of government" and that the Constitution exempted "the great property interests of this country from the taxing power of the Government" was pure rhetorical hogwash. Such wealth and property has always been subject to the Federal government's direct taxing powers as long as such taxes are apportioned. It was *the principle of apportionment* and *not any lack of taxing power* that Borah was inveighing against. These Congressional hypocrites merely objected to the restraints intelligently imposed on their taxing power by men who understood how such power could and would be abused. The politicians did abuse it — precisely as forseen by our Founding Fathers and despite the limitations placed in the Constitution to prevent it from happening.

The Income Tax As A Necessary, Wartime Power

Another major reason advanced to justify the income tax amendment was the necessity of being able to raise revenue in the event of war. While there might be some basis to the argument that the Federal government needs the power to levy an unapportioned income tax in time of war, I suggest that at such times an emergency national sales tax combined with a gross receipts tax (and/or an apportioned, direct tax on property) could be used to raise as much revenue as an income tax. Such taxes could be equitably levied at less cost and repression than an income tax. More importantly, this could be done without violating constitutional rights and thoroughly *corrupting* Federal courts — which the income tax has done.

In addition, any war-related tax must include an absolute bar against its continuance during peacetime. American history is replete with proof that U.S. politicians simply cannot be trusted with "emergency" wartime powers in peacetime. Overlooking completely the special problems that a compulsory income tax must create (such as being violative of numerous constitutional rights), the war argument was

---

[41] 44 Cong. Rec., 61st Congress, 1st Session, page 1682.

used to justify the establishment of an income tax in peacetime. For example, on April 21 Senator Cummins said:

> It is true that we are not in the midst of war; but there is no Senator so keen in his prophecies as to attempt to declare the moment in which we may become involved in war, and then, at least, there will be the same imperious necessity for invoking this authority that there was in 1861.[42]

And on July 12 Congressman Keifer said:

> It is said that this amendment proposed is to be useful in time of war. If there ever is any necessity for an income tax of course it is when the Nation is at war.[43]

So another reason working Americans pay high income taxes today (in times of peace) is because Congress claimed it needed an income tax in time of war. How high would income tax rates really have to go if we ever needed the tax to fund, for example, another World War II?

Perhaps the best commentary on how a Federal income tax would operate occurred in the House when Congressman Hill of Connecticut spoke against it and said:

> Mr. HILL. Mr. President and gentlemen of the House of Representatives. I shall vote against this amendment for the following reasons: In the first place, I do not believe that this extra session of Congress was called to completely change and revolutionize the taxation system of the United States. I think that a question of such magnitude should be submitted to the people and discussed in a campaign preparatory to the presentation of so important a matter as an amendment to the Constitution of the United States. This proposition was found in the Democratic platform and not in the Republican platform on which the presidential campaign of 1908 was won. My understanding is that Congress was called together for the sole purpose of revising the Dingley tariff law on the basis of the difference in the cost of production at home and abroad, and, so far as the House is concerned, an honest attempt has been made to do that. I voted in the Ways and Means Committee for a supplement to that revision in the shape of an inheritance tax. My judgment was then and is now that it was not necessary. I am a firm believer that in times of peace the revenues of this country should be derived from customs duties and internal-revenue taxes, and that if these are not sufficient, as prudent people we ought to reduce our expenses to a point where they will be covered by such revenues; and yet, under all the circumstances, and realizing that the in-

---

[42] *Ibid., page 1422.*
[43] *Ibid., page 4399.*

heritance tax would bear hardly upon the people of my State, I voted for an inheritance tax.

I do not know how but that I may ultimately vote for a corporation tax. My mind is not yet made up on that question. I shall not vote for an income tax. I agree with the chairman of the Ways and Means Committee [Mr. Payne], who made the opening remarks in this discussion, that we ought to have the power to lay an *income tax in time of war, but I am not in favor of giving this Government the power to lay an income tax in time of peace.* With an amendment limiting it to time of war or other extraordinary emergencies, I would gladly vote for it; yes, I would vote to take every dollar of the property of every citizen of the United States, if need be, to defend the honor, dignity, or life of this Nation in the stress of war; *but when it comes to a question of current expenses in time of peace, I would cut the expenses of the Government so as to keep them within our natural income.*

We are a Nation of 90,000,000 of the most extravagant people on the face of the earth, and yet we are now pleading that the system of taxation which the fathers of the Republic provided and which for more than a century has met all expenditures and furnished a surplus besides, from which we have reduced our national debt incurred in war time faster than any nation on earth ever reduced its debt, that such a system is not sufficient to meet our ordinary peace expenses.

Stop a moment and *consider what we are doing in voting to give this Government the power to lay an income tax in time of peace.* I know of no better measure of the way in which this burden would fall on the various States in the Union than to judge of it by the inheritance tax laid to meet the expenses of the Spanish-American war, for the last income tax that was collected from our people was back in the civil-war period, and conditions have mightily changed since then; but we did have an inheritance tax in *1900 to 1909.*

The last full year of that tax showed as follows: The State of New York paid $1,608,000 of it; the collection district of Connecticut and Rhode Island $660,000; the State of Pennsylvania, $641,000; the State of Massachusetts, $559,000; the State of Illinois, Mr. Speaker, paid $325,000; making all told in those five collection districts $3,795,000 that was raised out of a total of $4,842,000 in the last full year of this tax, *so that of the entire amount collected from the inheritance tax in the whole Union* **six states paid three-fourths of it.**

Let me give you a more startling illustration than that. Take the collection district which I have the honor to represent in part, the revenue office being located at Hartford and the collection district including Connecticut and Rhode Island. That district paid $660,753 of that inheritance tax in the year ending June 30, 1902. **How many other States did it take to equal that amount?** Permit me to name them to you; they are as follows: Alabama, Arkansas, Colorado, Wyoming, Florida, Georgia, Territory of Hawaii, Indiana, Kansas, Oklahoma, Indian Territory, Kentucky, Louisiana, Mississippi, Michigan, Minnesota, Nebraska, New Mexico, Arizona, North Carolina, South Carolina, North Dakota, South Dakota, Oregon, Washington, Tennessee, Texas, Virginia, West Virginia, Wisconsin, California, Nevada, Missouri, New Jersey, and Ohio. *All told, 35 States paid $31,000 less than the little States of Connecticut and Rhode Island,* and yet you come and ask me in time of peace and to pay the ordinary current expenses of this Government to vote now for a constitutional amendment which will enable these 35 States to impose a far greater tax upon my people. But it is claimed that the property in these Eastern States escapes taxation. That is not true. In the State of Connecticut more than 80 per cent of all the expenses of our state government is now paid by corporations, and during the past ten years no state tax has been laid upon our people, but the whole amount has been met by corporation, inheritance, and other forms of direct taxation imposed by the State. Every corporation in the State is taxed; every legacy under the inheritance tax law, which we have, pays its fair share.

For more than two centuries our people, by rigid economy and great industry, in the face of conditions which would have discouraged almost any other people in the world, have built up a prosperous community and developed a State, and have done this at their own expense. To-day we are spending millions of dollars for good roads and other public improvements. *We have never asked the General Government to share with us in the cost of these things.*

To-day the State of New York is spending $100,000,000 in the construction of a canal to connect the Lakes with the ocean and another $100,000,000 in the improvement of its highways, and **doing it at its own cost, without asking for any contribution on the part of the General Government.**

I believe that such a work as the Panama Canal, costing as it probably will $500,000,000, is a fair and proper call upon all of the people of this country for contributions, through a general income tax, to meet such expenditure; but you and I know that there are projects now pending by which the Federal Treasury will be called upon for at least $500,000,000 for the canalization of the Mississippi River and other inland waterways, largely local in their character; that a demand is being made for an annual contribution from the Federal Treasury of $50,000,000 for the irrigation of the arid lands of the West, which means five hundred millions more in the next decade; and that the project of the improvement of the highways of the whole country, through the aid of the National Treasury, has only been held back during recent years by the most strenuous exertions on the part of the leaders in Congress. *How much of an obligation upon the National Treasury such a movement would involve no living man can even estimate, but certainly a thousand millions of dollars would be but a drop in the bucket; and the project once entered upon, the maintenance would be more costly for all time to come than even the original construction.*

Is it fair now, after two hundred years of expenditure on our part, that you should come and ask us to vote to tax ourselves in time of peace for a duplication of these things in all of the new and undeveloped States of the Union? It is not because our people desire to avoid taxation, and as I have shown you, the accumulation of wealth in these Eastern States does not escape a fair and just charge upon it. We are ready to vote for an income tax to meet any emergencies which may arise in this Union and to stand by the Government in time of war; but do not ask us, at least without consultation with our people at home, to put this burden on them in addition to one already severe because of local expenditures, made necessary by our geographical position, but cheerfully assumed for the general good.[44]

Hill's comments clearly explained the danger of acceding to the belief that any allegedly necessary, wartime taxing power should be made available to politicians in peacetime too. In addition, the government's total abuse of its taxing powers clearly demonstrate's that those who wrote the apportionment restrictions into the Constitution were indeed right in doing so.

It was the abandonment of these restrictions that allowed Washington politicians to spend money like drunken sailors while encouraging many states to abandon their own governmental responsibilities and barter away their own inherent sovereignty for Federal handouts (persuading the Federal government to tax others on their behalf). As Congressman Hill pointed out, at one time some states actually *did conduct themselves responsibly* — which is no longer the case today. Confiscatory taxes at the Federal level, combined with a system where states vie for Federal subsidies and grants, have made control of public expenditures at all levels of government virtually impossible.

As finally passed, the first income tax law was contained in only fourteen pages. Today it rambles through more than one thousand pages which no single person can possibly understand.[45] The original law levied a delicate tax of 1 percent, graduated as follows:

2 percent on $20,000 — $50,000
3 percent on $50,000 — $75,000
4 percent on $75,000 — $100,000
5 percent on $100,000 — $250,000
6 percent on $250,000 — $500,000
7 percent thereafter.

---

[44] Ibid., pages 4393, 4394.

[45] This renders it *void as law* on this issue alone. Can anything that nobody can understand be "law"? Even Tax Court finds in favor of taxpayers 20 percent of the time (which means it is wrong *at least* 80 percent of the time) which proves that even the IRS, using its own cockeyed version of the law, does not really know what is taxable under it.

As explained earlier, the personal exemption of $3,000 eliminated practically all Americans from the tax. In 1916, for example, only 362,970 Americans out of a population of 102 million paid any income taxes — or less than four-tenths of one percent. Would the public have voted for the Amendment if it believed it would *increase* their own taxes and subject them to IRS harassment as the law is enforced today? Obviously not.

The 16th Amendment, therefore, was ratified and an income tax established

1. on something the U.S. Congress could not define;
2. that was to apply only to the rich and prosperous (and only modestly on them);
3. that would *lower* taxes for the general public; and
4. that would provide necessary wartime revenue.

In reality, the Amendment did none of these. The Amendment was not used by the U.S. government to either impose a modest tax on the rich or to lower taxes for the general public or to merely finance wars. It was, in fact, used (especially after World War II) to substantially increase Federal taxes across the board in order to finance (in peacetime) all manner of unconstitutional Federal schemes while burdening the general public with tax rates that far exceeded anything that would have been attempted by King George III or any medieval tyrant. However, the supreme irony is that all of this was accomplished by the Federal government while it completely ignored the 16th Amendment itself!

12

Surprise — An Income Tax Is An Excise Tax: The **Brushaber** Decision

There is not one graduate of an American law school who does not believe that the 16th Amendment:

1. amended the U.S. Constitution;
2. overturned the *Pollock* decision; and
3. gave the Federal government a new taxing power.

For example, at my "trial" in 1980 (for allegedly failing to file tax returns for the years 1974 and 1975 — I did file returns for those years, see page 279) when I raised the *Pollock* case, Chief Judge T. Emmet Clarie (who also turned out to be the government's *chief prosecutor*) asked, "What was the date of that case?"

"1895 your Honor," I replied from the witness stand.

"That was *before* the Sixteenth Amendment," Claire admonished me (in a voice tinged with authority and incredulity), reflecting his belief that the 16th Amendment overturned *Pollock*.

Correcting him I said, "You are right, but that case is still holding, your Honor."

And Clairie meekly replied, "All right."

In line with Clairie's misconception, note the following excerpt from *Mertin's* (the definitive income tax commentary used by accountants, tax lawyers and even the courts themselves) we find this entry in Chapter 4, page 11:

> The Sixteenth Amendment, however, where it is applicable, *obliterates* any previously existing distinction between income taxes as direct and indirect, putting on the same basis *all* income "from whatever source derived." (Emphasis added)

The irony of that statement is that while it contains a germ of truth, it conveys a meaning totally opposite to the affect of the Amendment. Since the typical lawyer or accountant does not have the vaguest idea of what the Supreme Court said in connection with the 16th Amendment, he would completely misconstrue this misleading reference in *Mertin's*. Such misleading inferences help explain how the Federal government has been able to hide the truth about the 16th Amendment for so long.

The truth of the matter, however, is that the 16th Amendment did none of the things suggested in my opening paragraph or as suggested by *Mertin's*. In the *Brushaber*[1] decision (the decision that held the income tax of 1913 constitutional), the Supreme Court ruled that the legal effect of the Amendment was merely to establish an income tax as an indirect, excise tax so it would not require apportionment — the basis upon which it was held unconstitutional by the *Pollock* Court. In other words, it is the very issue of whether a tax on income is imposed as a *direct* or *indirect* tax that establishes its legality. The *Brushaber* Court, though, said that in order to impose an income tax as an indirect tax, income had to be separated from its "sources" since "the whole purpose of the Amendment was to relieve all income taxes when imposed from apportionment from a consideration of the source whence the income was derived" (see page 197). I doubt if five years ago there were twenty people in the U.S. who knew what those last twenty words mean yet, without such an understanding, no comprehension of Federal income taxes is possible. This chapter is devoted to establishing such a comprehension.

The *Brushaber* Decision

It is the *Brushaber* decision to which the Federal government turns whenever the constitutionality of the income tax is challenged. "The income tax is constitutional, " says the government, because "the *Brushaber* decision says so." That is true but what the government fails to add is that it does not collect Federal income taxes *in accordance with that decision*! In other words, the *Brushaber* decision and the 16th Amendment have absolutely nothing to do with how the Federal government goes about collecting income taxes. Both the decision and the Amendment only serve as a smokescreen behind which the government can hide its illegal enforcement of the Federal income tax. Simply put, while the *Brushaber* Court held an income tax (based on the 16th Amendment) constitutional, the government enforces the income tax *contrary to both the Amendment and the decision!*

[1]*Brushaber vs Union Pacific RR* 240 US 1, decided January 24, 1916.

Brushaber Practically Impossible to Penetrate

Compared to the *Pollock* decision (which is written in clear and logical prose), the *Brushaber* decision is written in a style that practically defies understanding. I am convinced that almost nobody can read and understand it. It is also my belief that it was probably written that way intentionally! My understanding of the case only came about because I read it repeatedly and used highlighting pens to color code related concepts. In addition, if I did not have an accounting background or had not done considerable related study, I doubt if, even then, I could have understood it. Here, for example, is a *two hundred and fifteen word* sentence taken from that decision.

> We say this because it is to be observed that although from the date of the *Hylton* case because the statements made in the opinions in that case it had come to be accepted that direct taxes in the constitutional sense were confined to taxes levied directly on real estate because of its ownership, *the Amendment contains nothing repudiating or challenging the ruling in the Pollock case* that the word direct had a broader significance since it embraced also taxes levied on personal property because of its ownership, the Amendment contains nothing repudiating or challenging the ruling in the Pollock case that the word direct had a broader significance since it embraced also taxes levied on personal property because of its ownership, and therefore the Amendment at least impliedly makes such wider significance a part of the Constitution — a condition which clearly demonstrates that *the purpose was not to change the existing interpretation* except to the extent necessary to accomplish the result intended, that is, *the prevention of the resort to the sources* from which a taxed income was derived in order to cause a direct tax on the income to be a direct tax on the *source* itself and thereby *to take an income out of the class of excises, duties, imposts and place it in the class of direct taxes.*[2] (Emphasis added)

When I first read that sentence I was surprised to discover that the Amendment *did not challenge or repudiate* the *Pollock* case — but what else did it say? Hopefully by the time you finish this chapter you will know.

Pollock Decision Not Overturned By The 16th Amendment

The first fact to be learned from the *Brushaber* case is that (contrary to what Judge Clarie believed) the 16th Amendment did not overturn or change anything in the *Pollock* decision. This is stated in that

[2]Ibid., page 19.

two hundred fifteen word sentence but it deserves repeating. "The Amendment," said the Court, "contains nothing repudiating or challenging the ruling in the *Pollock* case." Here the *Brushaber* Court confirmed that everything in *Pollock* (including its holding that direct taxes "embraced also taxes levied on personal property") still held true — despite the 16th Amendment. So if the Congress thought it was doing away with the *Pollock* decision, it was mistaken. The *Brushaber* Court acknowledged that in upholding the income tax it was not "repudiating or challenging the ruling in the *Pollock* case," so when the *Pollock* Court ruled that taxes on dividends, interest, rents and personal property (and the income from personal property) were *direct taxes that had to be apportioned, that holding still stands today and was not changed one wit by the 16th Amendment or the Brushaber decision!* Yet the government taxes such items today *without apportionment,* in violation of the *Pollock* decision, under the guise of taxing "income" but, by definition, it does not. The government (and its "courts") ignore the legal definition of "income" in enforcing the "income" tax.

The 16th Amendment Did Not Amend The Constitution

Another fallacy promoted by the government and the legal establishment is that the 16th Amendment amended the Constitution. The *Brushaber* Court, however, clearly explained that, in reality, the 16th Amendment did not alter the taxing clauses of the Constitution:

> But it clearly results that the proposition and the contentions under it, if acceded to, would cause *one provision of the Constitution to destroy another;* that is, they would result in bringing the provisions of the Amendment exempting a direct tax from apportionment into *irreconsilable conflict with the general requirement that all direct taxes be apportioned.* Moreover, the tax authorized by the Amendment, being direct, would not come under the rule of uniformity applicable under the Constitution to other than direct taxes, and thus it would come to pass that the Amendment would be to authorize a particular direct tax not subject either to apportionment or to the rule of geographical uniformity, thus giving power to impose a different tax in one state or states than was levied in another state or states. This result instead of simplifying the situation and making clear the limitations on the taxing power, *which obviously the Amendment must have been intended to accomplish would create radical and destructive changes in our constitutional system and multiply confusion.*[3] (Emphasis added)

[3]Ibid., pages 11,12

Here the Court pointed out that any belief that the 16th Amendment gave the government a new, direct taxing power (not limited by either apportionment or the rule of uniformity) would "cause one provision of the Constitution to destroy another", and "if acceded to . . . would create radical and destructive changes in our constitutional system." But that is precisely the assumption that current Federal courts and the entire U.S. legal establishment now make. How could such a false belief have developed when the *Brushaber* Court (at least here) clearly stated that it was acceding to no such belief! As a matter of fact, the *Brushaber* Court reaffirmed and reinforced the *Pollock* decision.

Pollock Case Reaffirmed

In the following excerpt, the *Brushaber* Court refers to *Pollock* in its discussion of the "two great classes" of taxes:

> In fact, the *two great subdivisions* embracing the complete and perfect delegation of the power to tax and the two correlated limitations as to such power were thus aptly stated by Mr. Chief Justice Fuller in *Pollock v. Farmers' Loan & Trust Company,* supra; at page 557. "In the matter of taxation, the Constitution recognizes the *two great classes of direct and indirect taxes,* and lays down two rules by which their *imposition must be governed,* namely: *The rule of apportionment as to direct taxes, and the rule of uniformity as to duties, imposts and excises."* It is to be observed, however, as long ago pointed out in *Veazie Bank v. Fenno,* 8 Wal. 533, 541, that the *requirement of apportionment as to one of the great classes* and of *uniformity* to the other class were not so much a *limitation* upon the *complete and all embracing authority to tax,* but in their essence were simply regulations concerning the *mode* in which the plenary powwer *was to be exerted.* In the whole history of the Government down to the time of the adoption of the Sixteenth Amendment, leaving aside some conjectures expressed of the possibility of *a tax lying intermediate between the two great classes and embraced by neither,* no question has been anywhere made as to the *correctness of these propositions.*[4] (Emphasis added)

The Court affirmed that there were only "two great classes" of taxes and that while there might be a tax "lying intermediate between the two great classes and embraced by neither, " such a proposition had nowhere been sustained. What the Court was getting at, of course, was that if it had sustained the right of the government to levy an income tax in the form of a direct tax without apportionment, it would be creating a tax *not limited either by the rule of uniformity or apportionment, creating a new kind of Federal* tax "lying" between the "two great classes" recognized by the Constitution — and the *Brushaber* Court said *it would not do that*!

[4]Ibid., pages 13, 14

The Income Tax Is An Excise Tax

In essense, the *Brushaber* Court ruled that the 16th Amendment *(while not amending the Constitution* and thus establishing a new type of tax restricted neither by uniformity nor apportionment) established the income tax as an excise. Simply put, the Court said:

1. The 16th Amendment states that taxes on income do not have to be apportioned;
2. under the Constitution, Federal taxes that do not have to be apportioned fall into Article 1, Section 8, Clause 1;
3. ergo, a tax on income *must fall into that section too,* in order to fall into *one* of the taxing classes *recognized* in the Constitution.

What the Supreme Court, in essence, said is that the 16th Amendment gave the government the right to tax income without apportionment if it imposed the tax as an *excise tax*. It cannot, however, be an excise *in name only — it must be levied as one*. Therefor, if an income. *tax is levied as a direct tax, it does not fall within the 16th Amendment and is illegal for want of apportionment*. The affect of the Amendment was *not* to amend or change the Constitution but, rather, to throw an income tax into the section that provided for excise and other indirect taxes. The problem was that the Court stated this proposition in such an obtuse way that hardly anyone realized what the Court had actually said.

This begins to explain that two hundred fifteen word sentence. Instead of simply saying that an income tax was an excise tax, the Court said that the purpose of the Amendment was to *prevent* the courts from taking such a tax "out of the class of excises, duties, imposts" and placing it in "the class of direct taxes" which is what the *Pollock* Court had already done. That was the Court's roundabout way of saying that the purpose of the 16th Amendment was to establish a tax on "income" as a form of excises as opposed to its being a direct tax.[5] It would appear that a few influential congressmen must have realized that this is what the Court would do. It would also account for the elimination of the word "direct" from the proposed 16th Amendment (see page 161). The specific inclusion of the word "direct" would, I suspect, have prevented the Supreme Court from reaching the decision it did and would have presented the Court with an unsolvable dilemma — could it then rule that an income tax was "indirect" when the Amendment itself called it "direct" or that Congress could legally create a tax not limited by any constitu-

---

[5]To see how Federal courts now completely and illegally reverse this, see page 265.

tional restraints whatsoever? The *Brushaber* Court, however, in order to hold an income tax indirect and not be in conflict with the *Pollock* decision — which held that taxes on income from stock, bonds, and real estate were direct taxes and had to be apportioned — had to come up with a different meaning for the word "income." The meaning it adopted differed from that used by the *Pollock* Court and from what the public understands income to mean. It did this (once again in a confusing manner) by *separating* income from its *sources*.

Separating Income From Its Source

The only way that income can be taxed as an indirect, excise tax is to separate it from its source. A tax levied directly on any "source" of income becomes a direct tax *on the source itself*, and (according to both *Pollock* and *Brushaber*) *requires apportionment*. Therefore, a tax on rent is tantamount to a tax on real estate, the "source" that produced it; a tax on dividends is tantamount to a tax on stocks, the "source" that produced it; a tax on interest is tantamount to a tax on the money, the "source" that produced it; and a tax on wages is tantamount to a tax on labor, the "source" that produced it. Thus all such taxes are not taxes on "income" but are *property taxes,* levied on real estate, stocks, bank accounts, and labor. For over seventy years the U.S. government has been collecting *property taxes* (without apportionment) under the guise of taxing "income" — and it has been getting away with it! If it was the *Brushaber* Court's intention to help the government fool the public, it certainly succeeded.

How and where is income separated from its "sources?" It should prove helpful to realize that the *Pollock* and *Brushaber* Courts did not use the word "income" in the same manner, and that is the crux of the confusion. The *Brushaber* Court must have realized it was using the word "income" in a different way than the *Pollock* Court did, but that was the only way the Court could arrive at a decision upholding the income tax while harmonizing the new tax with the 16th Amendment, the *Pollock* decision, prior income tax statutes and, most importantly, the taxing provisions of the Constitution. In order to do all this the Court had to come up with a new definition for income. The Court, however, did it in such a confusing manner that nobody would understand what it had done — and those who could figure it out would not say anything because *it was in their best interest to keep silent*. In essence, what the Court did was to define income to mean "profit" so, in reality, the 16th Amendment established not an income tax but a "profits" tax.

Back To The Corporation Excise Tax

The *Brushaber* decision, in effect, brought the income tax back to the Corporation Excise Tax of 1909 since an unapportioned income tax can only apply to corporate profits and individuals can never be subject to such an income or *profits* tax. Corporations might be subject to it if it were properly imposed; but even U.S. corporations are not subject to the current income tax because it is *not* being imposed as an *excise* tax on their profits. To understand all this you simply have to understand what the *Brushaber* Court meant when it said that when taxing income the "source" cannot be taxed.

The Court actually made the word income a misnomer since the only way income can be viewed without "a consideration of the sources from which the taxed income may be derived" is if all (so-called) income (actually receipts) are funnelled through a corporate profit and loss statement. When this is done, income (what comes in less what goes out) becomes profit — and it is this "profit" (not income) that is separated from the "source."

Exhibit 1 is an example of a corporate profit and loss statement. Note that the corporation had income from real estate commissions, rents, fees, dividends and interest, and that the total income from these "sources" was $395,000. Now, would *Ajax* have to pay any income taxes on its income? No, despite all its income *Ajax* does not have to pay a dime in income taxes. Why not? Because, even though it had all that income, the company did not have a profit. And, because it did not have a profit, it had no "income" and, therefore, no "income" tax liability.[6]

If the Corporation did not have a $1,000 loss carry-forward, it would have had a $1,000 profit and would have paid an "income" tax on that profit. So even though the corporation had $395,000 in income, it had no profit and, therefore, paid no taxes. This, of course, proves that the so-called income tax is really a profits tax and not an income tax at all.

Corporate Profit — Not Traceable to Source

If the *Ajax Company* had no loss carry-forward it would have paid a tax on its $1,000 of "income." But could it be determined exactly how much of that tax applied to its income from commissions, rents, dividends, or to any of the other sources of income listed? No, it could not. No matter how good a firm's accounting, it still could not trace (with precision) exactly how much of its profit came from any one particular *source* of "income." A tax on its profit, therefore, would not be a tax on any of the *sources* that contributed to it — and only on this basis can

[6]Actually, it would not have had a tax liability even if it *showed a profit,* for the reasons explained on page 254.

any of the sources that contributed to it — and only on this basis can a tax be classified as an "income" tax under the 16th Amendment. The key to the income tax puzzle is the word "from" and it is overlooked by the public and *illegally ignored* by the government.

The Significance of "From"

The 16th Amendment and the law itself (Section 61, Exhibit 2) only gives the government authority to tax "income *from* whatever source derived." These four words actually describe the government's only legal income taxing authority.

EXHIBIT 1

Ajax Real Estate & Investment Company, Inc.
Profit and Loss Statement
January 1 - December 31, 1983

Total Income:

Commissions on sales	$200,000	
Rental income	100,000	
Consulting Fees	15,000	
Dividends from stock	50,000	
Bond interest	20,000	
Interest on bank deposits	10,000	
Total Income		$395,000

Less All Expenses:

Rent	$ 40,000	
Salaries	175,000	
Advertising	30,000	
Postage	4,000	
Utilities	15,000	
Depreciation	40,000	
Automobile and insurance	25,000	
Travel and Entertainment	65,000	
Total Expenses		$394,000
Gross Profit (or Gross "Income")		1,000
Loss Carry Over		1,000
Net Profit (or Net "Income")		—0—
Taxable "Income"		—0—

EXHIBIT 2

Sec. 61.   Gross income defined.

(a) General definition.

Except as otherwise provided in this subtitle, gross income means all income from whatever source derived, including (but not limited to) the following items:

(1) Compensation for services, including fees, commissions, fringe benefits, and similar items

(2) Gross income derived from business;

(3) Gains derived from dealings in property;

(4) Interest;

(5) Rents;

(6) Royalties;

(7) Dividends;

(8) Alimony and separate maintenance payments;

(9) Annuities;

(10) Income from life insurance and endowment contracts;

(11) Pensions;

(12) Income from discharge of indebtedness;

(13) Distributive share of partnership gross income;

(14) Income in respect of a decedent; and

(15) Income from an interest in an estate or trust.

*Note that Section (a) does not include either "wages" or "salaries" as a component of "Gross Income." This omission was *not accidental*. The government, however, has succeeded in tricking the public into believing that "wages" and "salaries" are "similar items" to "compensation for services," "fees," and "commissions." They are not. A corporation, for example, can receive "compensation for services" as well as "fees" and "commissions," but it cannot receive "wages" or a salary. So wages and salaries *are not* similar to the items listed in (a) (1) and thus they can not be legally included in "gross income" or any other kind of "income."

Section 61: Gross Income Defined

Section 61 of the Internal Revenue Code (Exhibit 2) contains the "law" concerning what the government can theoretically tax. A lay person reading that section would believe that the section authorizes taxes on fees, commissions, rents, dividends, alimony, and all of those listed (and unlisted) items — and that is exactly what the Federal government wants the public to believe. Section 61, however, does not say this at all. If the Code intended to tax these items it would have said, "There is hereby imposed a tax *on* any and all sources of income including, but not limited to, the following: commissions, wages, rent, dividends, alimony, etc." But it says no such thing. What it says is that the tax is levied on income *derived* "from" these *sources* (*"from* whatever source derived") not "on" the sources themselves. The key word is "from." Income derived "from" rent is not the same thing as rent itself. Income derived "from" commissions is not the same thing as commissions themselves.

This becomes clear when you examine a corporate profit and loss statement. But when individuals pay income taxes *on* wages, rents, dividends, etc., they are paying a tax *on* these items (sources), and not a tax on the "income" *from* these sources. All such "income" taxes paid on such items are, therefore, imposed and extracted illegally.

Under the 16th Amendment the government was only authorized to tax "income" — not commissions, not interest, not wages, not rents, not dividends — but income *"from* whatever source derived." And "income" (as used in this context, as defined in *Brushaber* and numerous other decisions — see Chapter 11, and as written into the "law") can only, by definition, be a corporate profit.

Wages Not Taxable On *Any* Basis

When wage earners pay income taxes on their wages they are not paying a tax on "income" derived "from" wages, they are paying a tax *on wages themselves*. Nowhere in the Internal Revenue Code does it state that wages are even a component of "income." As a matter of fact, Section 61 does not even mention the words "wages" or "salary." The confusion again comes about because of the way Section 61 is worded. In its title it purports to define "Gross income" but does not since "income" is used in the "definition" and — as any eighth grader knows — a word cannot be used to define itself. The definition should have been worded as follows: "Except as provided in this subtitle, gross income means all *profit* from whatever source derived. . . ."⁷ Such wording would have made clear exactly what "income" is and what could be lawfully taxed. An understanding of what "income" actually means and what it had to mean to the *Brushaber* Court will make it much easier to understand the actual language used in the decision.

We have already seen one reference to the income tax being an excise tax in the citation shown on page 183. Here are additional references from the *Brushaber* decision having the same theme.

At the very beginning, however, there arose differences of opinion concerning the criteria to be applied in determining *in which of the two great subdivisions a tax would fall.* Without pausing to state at length the basis of these differences and the consequences which arose from them, *as the whole subject was elaborately reviewed in Pollock v. Farmers' Loan & Trust Company,* 157 U.S. 429; 158 U.S. 601, we make a condensed statement which is in substance taken from what was said in that case. Early the differences were manifested in pressing of an act levying a tax without apportionment on carriages "for the conveyance of persons, " and when such a tax was enacted the question of its repugnancy to the Constitution soon came to this court for determination. *(Hylton v. United States,* 3 Dall. 171.) *It was held that the tax came within the class of excises, duties and imposts and therefore did not require apportionment,* and while this conclusion was agreed to by all the members of the court who took part in the decision of the case, there was not an exact coincidence in the reasoning by which the conclusion was sustained. Without stating the minor differences, it may be said with substantial accuracy that the divergent reasoning was this: On the one hand, that the tax was not in the class of direct taxes requiring apportionment because it was not levied *directly on property because of its ownership but rather on its use and was therefore an excise,* duty or impost; and on the other, that in any event the class of *direct taxes included only taxes directly levied on real estate because of its ownership.* Putting out of view the difference of reasoning which led to the concurrent conclusion in the *Hylton Case,* it is undoubted that it came to pass in legislative practice that the line of demarcation between *the two great classes of direct taxes on the one hand and excises, duties and imposts* on the other which was exemplified by the ruling in that case, was accepted and acted upon. In the first place this is shown by the fact that *wherever* (and there were a number of cases of that kind) *a tax was levied directly on real estate or slaves because of ownership,* it was treated as coming within the direct class and apportionment was provided for, *while no instance of apportionment as to any other kind of tax is afforded.* Again the situation is aptly illustrated by the various acts taxing incomes derived from property of

---

⁷ This lack of definition is recognized by the courts. "The Internal Revenue Code does not define income." *US vs Ballard* 535 F.2d 400. For an in-depth analysis of this and other phony "income" definitions, see *The Social Security Swindle — How Anyone Can Drop Out* by Irwin Schiff, pages 31–36 and 54–60.

every kind and nature which were enacted beginning in 1861 and lasting during what may be termed the Civil War period. *It is not disputable that these latter taxing laws* **were classed under the head of excises,** *duties and imposts because it was assumed that they were of that character inasmuch, as although putting a tax burden on income of every kind, including that derived from property real or personal, they were not taxes directly on property because of its ownership.* And this practical construction came in theory to be the accepted one since it was adopted without dissent by the most eminent of the textwriters.[8]

. . . Upon the lapsing of a considerable period *after the repeal of the income tax laws* referred to, in 1894 an act was passed laying a tax on incomes from all classes of property and other sources of revenue which was not apportioned, and which therefore *was of course assumed* to come within the classification of excises, duties and imposts which were subject to the rule of uniformity but not to the rule of apportionment. The constitutional validity of this law was challenged on the ground that it did not fall within the class of excises, duties and imposts, but was direct in the constitutional sense and was therefore void for want of apportionment, and that question came to this court and was passed upon in *Pollock v. Farmers' Loan & Trust Co.,* 157 U.S. 429, 158 U.S. 601. The court, fully recognizing in the passage which we have previously quoted the all-embracing character of the two great classifications including, on the one hand, direct taxes subject to apportionment, and on the other, excises, duties and imposts subject to uniformity, held the law to be unconstitutional in substance for these reasons: *Concluding that the classification of direct was adopted for the purpose of rendering it impossible to burden by taxation* **accumulations of property, real or personal, except subject to the regulation of apportionment,**[9] *it was held that the duty existed to fix what was a direct tax in the constitutional sense so as to accomplish this purpose contemplated by the Constitution. (157 U.S. 581.) Coming to consider the validity of the tax from this point of view, while not questioning at all that in common understanding it was direct merely on income and only indirect on property, it was held that considering the substance of things it was direct on property in a constitutional sense since to burden an income by a tax was from the point of substance to burden the property from which the income was derived and thus accomplish the very thing which the provision as to apportionment of direct taxes was adopted to prevent. As this conclusion but enforced a regulation as to the mode of exercising power under particular circumstances, it did not in any way dispute the all-embracing taxing authority possessed by Congress, including necessarily therein the power to impose income taxes if only they conformed to the constitutional regulations which were applicable to them. Moreover in addition the conclusions reached*

---

[8]*Brushaber vs Union Pacific, supra,* page 14, 15.

[9] This proves that estate and gift taxes are direct taxes (and not indirect as illegally viewed) and must be apportioned.

in the Pollock Case did not in any degree *involve holding that income taxes generically and necessarily came within the class of direct taxes on property, but on the contrary recognized the fact that taxation **on income was in its nature an excise entitled to be enforced as such*** unless and until it was concluded that to enforce it would amount to accomplishing the result which the requirement as to apportionment of direct taxation was adopted to prevent, in which case the duty would arise to disregard form and consider substance alone and hence subject the tax to the regulation as to apportionment which otherwise as an excise would not apply to it. Nothing could serve to make this clearer than to recall that in the *Pollock Case* in so far as the law taxed incomes from other classes of property than real estate and invested personal property, that is, income from "professions, trades, employments, or vocations" (158 U.S. 637), its validity was recognized; indeed it was expressly declared that no dispute was made upon that subject and attention was called to the fact *that taxes on such income had been sustained as excise taxes in the past. Id.,* p. 635. The whole law was however declared unconstitutional on the ground that to permit it to thus operate would relieve real estate and invested personal property from taxation and "would leave the burden of the tax to be borne by professions, trades, employments, or vocations; and in that way what was intended as a tax on capital would remain, in substance, a tax on occupations and labor, " *(Id.,* p. 637) a result which it was held could not have been contemplated by Congress. [10]

At the beginning of this excerpt, the *Brushaber* Court stated that from "the very beginning" the only question was into which "of the two great subdivisions a tax would fall." The Court pointed out that the *Hylton* Court ("putting out of view the. . . reasons") held that the tax came "within the class of excises, duties and imposts, " and that "wherever a tax was levied directly on real estate or slaves because of ownership, it was treated as" a direct tax and apportioned. The Court then began laying the deceptive groundwork upon which to make its decision in favor of the income tax by saying that "no instance of apportionment as to any other kind of tax is afforded."

The Court expected us to believe that because of this, "real estate and slaves" represent the only two items upon which a direct tax can be based. While it is true these were the only items that were ever honestly used to determine a direct Federal tax, they were, by no means, the only items to which such a tax could apply. The Court's inference that only taxes on "real estate and slaves" could be the objects of a direct tax was totally fallacious.[11]

[10]*Brushaber vs Union Pacific, supra,* page 16, 17.

[11] Chief Justice White dissented in the *Pollock* decision so he can hardly be expected to objectively (or enthusiastically) present the majority opinion of that case as he attempts to do here.

The Court continued building its specious argument by further pointing out that "beginning in 1861 an lasting during what may be termed the Civil War" various acts "taxing incomes derived from property of every kind. . . were classed under the heads of excises." The Court now tried to establish that because the Civil War income tax was classed as an excise tax *it was upheld for that reason*. What the Court did not say was that the tax was improperly classified and was not held to be unconstitutional simply because no court was honest enough to treat the tax correctly.[12] In explaining why such taxes "were classed under the head of excises, " the Court stated that it was

> because it was assumed that they were of that character inasmuch as although putting a tax burden on income of every kind, including that derived from property real and personal, they were not taxed directly on property because of its ownership.[13]

This is an example of the type of legal gibberish with which Supreme Court decisions are filled and affords an understanding of the reason why the power of judges (to illegally create law through such legalistic mumbo-jumbo) must be drastically curtailed.

First of all, the tax referred to did not place "a tax *burden* on income." The *burden* was obviously placed right on those individuals expected to pay the tax. How could the Court conclude that the "burden" lay elsewhere?

In addition, no tax "is on property, " as the Court suggests, but on the individuals who own the property. And when the Court says that income taxes "were not taxes on property because of ownership, " it implies that a tax on property can exist because of a *different* criteria than ownership (such as its "use"). The Civil War income tax was labelled an excise for no other reason than expediency (and to give the Federal government an excuse for not having to contend with the problems of apportionment). Thus Congress arbitrarily and illegally labelled an obviously direct tax an indirect "duty"; and because it was not effectively challenged on that basis, the *Brushaber* Court said, "See, when income taxes are 'classed' as duties [excises] they are constitutional!" It then inferred that it was because the 1894 income tax was *not* so classed that it was held to be direct *and* therefore unconstitutional. To further shore up its contrived decision, the Court then stated that the *Pollock* decision did not.

---

[12] And if the *Pollock* Court had done so, the door would have been opened for a rash of lawsuits against the government as a result of this war-inspired tax.

[13] *Brushaber vs Union Pacific, supra,* pages 14, 15.

involve holding that income taxes generically and necessarilly came within the class of direct taxes on property, but on the contrary, recognized the fact that taxation on income was in its nature an excise entitled to be enforced as such.[14]

Here, again, it tried to strengthen its contention that the 16th Amendment established an excise tax because income taxes "had been sustained as excise taxes in the past."

Courts Cannot Change The Nature of a Tax by Decree

It can be successfully argued that the *Pollock* Court never claimed that an income tax was "in its nature an excise tax." But even if the *Pollock* Court did, that still would not make an income tax "in its nature an excise" for the simple reason that an income tax is, "in its nature," a direct tax and no court (Supreme or otherwise) can, by decree, contravene fact. A court might just as well decree that the moon is green cheese or that two plus two is five. Income taxes *are* direct taxes based on *income* just as property taxes *are* direct taxes based on *property* — and no Supreme Court decision, or string of decisions, can change that. It is clear, however, that what the *Brushaber* Court was doing was trying to build a legal case for holding an income tax (under the 16th Amendment) to be an excise tax and desperately looking for some legal support. So, although the *Brushaber* Court held the income tax (based on the 16th Amendment) to be an excise tax, *this does not make it so,* except in the *Alice-in-Wonderland* world of Supreme Court decisions.

An income tax based on *gross* income (i.e., a sales tax as in the *Spreckles* case) *might* be an excise since such an income tax could be passed on. But a tax levied on net income (i.e. profit) cannot be passed on and is obviously direct. All businesses operate to maximize profits and once a profit has been made, a tax on that profit cannot be avoided or passed on. So a tax on those profits is a direct tax and must be apportioned.[15] The *Brushaber* Court, however, had to know that its basic premise (that the income tax was an excise tax) was *nonsense* simply because *the tax was not levied as one.* It was not levied *on* a product or even *on* a contrived privilege as defined in the *Spreckles* and *Flint Stone Tracy* decisions (see pages 134 and 144). So if *the law itself did not claim it was an excise tax,* and if *the tax was not levied as an excise tax,* how could the Court claim it was one?

---

[14] Ibid., page 16, 17.

[15] I suppose that such a direct tax on corporations could be apportioned on the basis of the number of corporations domiciled in each state.

The following quote from the decision will officially tie together practically all of the points so far covered.

This is the text of the Amendment:

"The Congress shall have power to lay and collect taxes on incomes, from whatever source derived, without apportionment among the several States, and without regard to any census or enumeration."

It is clear on the face of this text that it does not purport to confer power to levy income taxes in a generic sense — an authority already possessed and never questioned — or to limit and distinguish between one kind of income taxes and another, but that *the whole purpose of the Amendment was to relieve all income taxes when imposed from apportionment from a consideration of the* **source** *whence the income was derived.* Indeed in the light of the history which we have given and of the decision in the *Pollock Case* and the ground upon which the ruling in that case was based, there is no escape from the conclusion that the Amendment was drawn for the purpose of doing away for the future with the principle upon which the *Pollock Case* was decided, that is, of determining whether a tax on income was direct not by a consideration of the burden placed on the taxed income upon which it directly operated, but by taking into view the burden which resulted on the property from which the income was derived, since in express terms the Amendment provides that income taxes, *from whatever* **source** the income may be derived, shall not be subject to the regulation of apportionment. From this in substance it indisputably arises, first, that all the contentions which we have previously noticed concerning the assumed limitations to be implied from the language of the Amendment as to the nature and character of the income taxes which it authorizes find no support in the text and are in irreconcilable conflict with the very purpose which the Amendment was adopted to accomplish. *Second, that the contention that the Amendment treats a tax on income as a direct tax although it is relieved from apportionment and is necessarily therefore not subject to the rule of uniformity as such rule only applies to taxes which are not direct,* **thus destroying the two great classifications which have been recognized and enforced from the beginning, is also wholly without foundation** since the command of the Amendment that all income taxes shall not be subject to apportionment *by a consideration of the* **sources** from which the taxed income may be derived, forbids the application to such taxes of the rule applied in the *Pollock Case* by which alone *such taxes were removed from the great class of excises, duties and imposts subject to the rule of uniformity and were placed under the other or direct class.* This must be unless it can be said that although the Constitution as a result of the Amendment in express terms excludes the criterion of **source** *of income,* that criterion yet remains for the purpose of *destroying* the classifications of the Constitution *by taking an excise out of the class to which it belongs* and transferring it to a class in which it cannot be placed consistently with the requirements of the Constitution. Indeed, from another point of view, the Amendment demonstrates that **no such** *purpose was intended* and *on the contrary shows that it was drawn with the object of* **maintaining the limitations** *of the Constitution and* **harmonizing** *their operation.*[16]

It is obvious from the above that the Court admitted that the 16th Amendment gave the government no new taxing power. It did not "confer power to levy income taxes in a generic sense — an authority already possessed and never questioned." But if it gave the government no power it did not already have, what did the Amendment do? Restating the purpose of the Amendment the Court said that:

> the whole purpose of the Amendment was to relieve all income taxes when imposed from apportionment *from a consideration of the source* whence the income was derived.[17]

This merely confirms what we already know. In addition, the Court reaffirmed that any contention that the Amendment "treats a tax on income as a direct tax although it is relieved from apportionment" is also "wholly without foundation" and that such a contention would destroy "the two great classifications" or taxes in the Constitution and that only by not taxing *the sources* from which "the taxed income may be derived, " can we escape "the application of the rule applied in the *Pollock* case" which caused that Court to take an income tax out of the category of an indirect tax and place it in the category of those taxes that are direct. This, the *Brushaber* Court says (again in a totally obscure manner), is what the Amendment prevents.

The Court said the Amendment "excludes the criterion of source of income" in order to prevent the tax from being transferred "to a class in which it cannot be placed consistent with the requirements of the Constitution." An finally, the Court states (if anyone still has any doubt that the amendment did not change or amend the Constitution) that the Amendment "was drawn" not to change or amend the Constitution but with "the object of maintaining the limitations of the Constitution and harmonizing their operation." This merely reaffirms all we have learned about the 16th Amendment:

1. it gave the government no new taxing power;
2. it did not amend the Constitution;
3. it supposedly established the income tax as an excise tax; and
4. it forbids the levying of income taxes on sources of income without apportionment.

[16] Ibid., pages 17, 18, 19.

[17] Ibid., page 17.

There were other issues raised in this case that should have been resolved against the government but were not. For example, the requirement that corporations collect taxes from interest and mortgage payments created administrative costs that, in essence, deprived them of property without due process of law; and other exemptions written into the law robbed the Act of uniformity. Both of these objections were valid, but these and other objections were summarily denied, some on the basis that they were "hypocritical contentions. . . based upon an assumed violation of the uniformity clause."

If there was *anything* hypocritical connected with the decision, it lay with Chief Justice White who wrote it. He acknowledged that individuals, as well as corporations, were subject to the tax. But the case itself involved a corporation, so individual income taxes were not an issue and were not dealt with. If individual taxes had been the subject of the case, on what basis could the Court have proponded its *excise* tax theory? How could individuals be expected to *separate* their income from its sources? And on what *privilege* would such an *excise* fall? On the privilege of breathing? Remember that Chief Justice White dissented in the *Pollock* decision and if Chief Justice Fuller's arguments and Fields' masterful presentation did not persuade him then, what more could be expected now?

Proof That The Federal Government Knowingly Breaks The Law

If you have any doubts that the Federal government is knowingly breaking the law, prepare to shed them now. THe following quotations were taken *verbatim* from a 1939 study made by the Department of Justice under the direction of Homer Cummings, then the Attorney General.

> Further, it was strongly indicated that *an income tax under the Amendment is an* **indirect tax.** Thus, the Chief Justice said —
> that the contention that the Amendment treats a tax on income as a direct tax although it is relieved from apportionment and is necessarily therefore not subject to the rule of uniformity as such rule only applies to taxes which are not direct, thus destroying the two great classifications which have been recognized and enforced from the beginning, is also wholly without foundation since the command of the Amendment that all income taxes shall not be subject to approtionment by a consideration of the sources from which the taxed income may be derived, forbids the application to such taxes of the rule applied in the *Pollock* Case by which alone such taxes were removed from

the great class of excises, duties, and imposts subject to the rule of uniformity and were placed under the other or direct class.

Continuing, Mr. Chief Justice White emphasized that *an income tax, in his view, was an excise* by saying that —

This must be unless it can be said that although the Constitution as a result of the Amendment is express terms excludes the criterion of source of income, that criterion yet remains for the purpose of destroying the classifications of the constitution by taking an excise out of the class to which it belongs and transferring it to a class in which it cannot be placed consistently with the requirements of the Constitution. Indeed, from another point of view, the Amendment demonstrates that no such purpose was intended and on the contrary shows that it was drawn with the object of maintaining the limitations of the constitution and harmonizing their operation.[18] (Emphasis added)

This report admitted that the income tax "is an indirect tax."

The following, from this same report, should be of additional interest since it confirms and reveals how the legal profession (especially government lawyers) misstate the *Brushaber* decision.

The case of *Stanton v. Baltic Mining Co.* was a suit by a stockholder to enjoin his corporation, a mining company, from *voluntarily paying the tax* assessed against it under the income tax provisions of the Act of October 3, 1913. The basis of the attack was very similar to that in the *Brushaber* case with the addition that the stockholder contended that the depletion allowance was so small as to make the tax in part a direct tax on the property of the mining company. Mr. Chief Justice White, speaking for a unanimous Court, again made it clear that under the Amendment an income tax *is an indirect tax* and that the source from whence such income is derived is unimportant. In this connection he said:

"But aside from the obvious error of the proposition intrinsically considered, it manifestly disregards the fact that by the previous ruling it was settled that *the provisions of the Sixteenth Amendment conferred no new power of taxation* but simply prohibited the previous complete and plenary power of income taxation possessed by Congress from the beginning from being taken out of the category of indirect taxation to which it inherently belonged and being placed in the category of direct taxation subject to apportionment by a consideration of *the sources from which the income was derived,* that is by testing the tax not by what it was — a tax on income, but by a mistaken theory deduced from the origin or source of the income taxed."

---

[18] *Taxation of Government Bondholders and Employees,* United States Department of Justice, 1939, page 205.

The statement that the "Amendment conferred no new power" must be carefully considered in its context. *The Chief Justice was very obviously inferring that he considered the Pollock decision to be erroneous in treating an income tax as a direct tax, and that therefore the Amendment restored a power rather than granted a new one.*[19] *(Emphasis added)*

As we know, Chief Justice White never for a moment contended that the *Pollock* decision was "erroneous" or that the amendment, in any way, either "restored a power" or "granted a new one" as this government report erroneously suggests.

In addition, on February 20, 1980, I received a report prepared by Howard M. Zaritsky (Legislative Attorney, American Law Division) of the Library of Congress. In that report Zaritsky wrote:

The Court noted that *the inherent character of an income tax was that of an* **indirect** tax, stating:

Moreover in addition the conclusion reached in the *Pollock Case* did not in any degree involve the holding that income taxes generically and necessarily came within the class of direct taxes on property, but on the contrary recognized the fact that taxation on income tax in the nature an excise entitled to be enforced as such unless and until it was concluded that to enforce it would amount to accomplishing the result which the requirement as to apportionment of direct taxes was adopted to prevent, in which case the duty would arise to disregard from the consider substance alone and hence subject the tax to the regulation as to apportionment which otherwise as an excise would not apply to it. 240 U.S. at 16–17.

The language of the Sixteenth Amendment, the Court found in *Brushaber,* was solely intended to eliminate:

the principle upon which the *Pollock Case* was decided, that is, of determining whether a tax on income was direct not by a consideration of the burden placed on the taxed income upon which it directly operated, but by taking into view the burden which resulted on the property from which the income was derived, since in express terms the Amendment provides that income taxes, from whatever source derived, shall not be subject to the regulation of apportionment. 240 U.S. at 18.[20] (Emphasis added)

---

[19] Ibid., pages 206, 207.

[20] *SOME CONSTITUTIONAL QUESTIONS REGARDING THE FEDERAL INCOME TAX LAWS,* Report No. 80–19 A 723/275, May 25, 1979, Updated January 17, 1980, by Howard M. Zaritsky, pages CRS–5, 6.

Here Zaritsky admitted that the income tax's "inherent character" is "that of an indirect tax" while also using one of the more confusing passages from *Brushaber* which attempts to distinguish an income tax from the "burden" placed on the source.

Zaritsky, however, must have known that the inquiry to which he was responding was somehow related to the increasing pressure being created by so-called "tax protestors" who were increasingly raising the issue that wages cannot be taxed as income under the 16th Amendment at trials in District Courts and in hearings in Tax Court. Realizing how this report might be used, Zaritzky also wrote:

> Types of Taxable Income
>
> In recent years it has been argued unsuccessfully by some taxpayers that, because *the income tax is an **excise** tax by definition*, it cannot be imposed on income from wages or certain other designated forms of income. *See e.g., Cardinalli v. Commissioner,* T.C. Memo. 1979–462 (1979); and *Kindred v. Commissioner,* T. C. Memo. 1979–457 (1979). It is clear from the history of the judicial interpretation of the income tax that, *while the income tax is an excise tax,* it may be imposed on wages, salaries, and virtually all other forms of income.[21] (Emphasis added)

Zaritsky's opinion that an excise tax can be levied on the wages of labor is obviously erroneous and was made simply to support the government's illegal enforcement of the tax.

Proof That The Current Enforcement Of The Income Tax Is Illegal

It is universally agreed that the income tax is, by law, an excise tax, yet look at Exhibit 3, page 204. It is an excerpt from the IRS's Handbook for Special Agents[22] in which the Treasury admits that income taxes and excise taxes are *different* and even defines and distinguishes their *differences.* Also note that the handbook states that "Income taxes are based on net income or net profits." Do we have an income tax or a profits tax? It cannot be both. This is an official admission that the income tax is, in reality, a *profits* tax.

In addition, in *Helvering vs Davis*[23] (the totally fallacious and in-

---

[21] Ibid., pages CRS–7, 8.

[22] Internal Revenue Manual, MT 9900–26 (1-29-75).

[23] *Helvering vs Davis* 301 US 619 (1937). For a thorough analysis of this absurd Supreme Court Decision see Chapter 5 of *The Social Security Swindle — How Anyone Can Drop Out,* "The Supreme Court — Playing Games with the Law," by Irwin Schiff.

credible Supreme Court decision that upheld the constitutionality of Social Security), Justice Cardozo (explaining the differences between the employers' and employees' portion of Social Security taxes) wrote as follows:

> Title VIII, as we have said, lays two different types of tax, an "income tax on employees, " and "an excise tax on employers."

Apart from admitting that employee Social Security taxes are really income taxes, the Supreme Court admits that the government imposes the income tax not as an excise but as a direct tax without apportionment. **Thus we have an official admission by the Supreme Court that income taxes are being levied in violation of both the *Brushaber* and *Pollock* decisions!**

Now you have it all. What can be simpler than understanding that the Federal government is *flagrantly breaking the law* in connection with income taxes? It is clearly admitted by every government authority that income taxes are excise taxes and, therefore, *can only be lawful if they are levied as excise taxes.* It is further acknowledged by the highest government sources that the tax is not being levied as such but, rather, is being levied as a direct tax without apportionment *in clear violation of the 16th Amendment and the taxing clauses of the Constitution.* Today the government throws people in jail and confiscates property in open and flagrant violation of its own laws and the Constitution. On the basis of such evidence, how can anyone argue the fact that an outlaw government has installed itself in our nation's capital?

EXHIBIT 3

340
Excise Taxes

341 Definition and Purposes

(1) *Definition* — An excise tax is a duty or impost levied upon the manufacture, sale, or consumption of commodities within the country, and upon certain occupations.

(2) *Purposes* — A few excise taxes are merely regulatory and some are imposed for both regulatory and revenue purposes. Most excise taxes, however, are levied exclusively for the purpose of revenue.

342
Excise and Income Taxes Distinguished

342.1
Base

Income taxes are based on net income or net profits, and are graduated. Excise taxes are not graduated, and they can be based upon any of the following factors: selling price of merchandise or facilities; services sold or used; number, weight, or volume of units sold; and nature of occupation.

Internal Revenue Manual, MT 9900-26 (1-29-75)

13

"Income" — What Is It?

This chapter will explore:

1. the difficulty experienced by the Supreme Court in arriving at a definition of "income"; and
2. the policy of illegally ignoring the definition of income ultimately decided upon by the Supreme Court by all Federal courts (past and present) and the IRS.

The basic problem in dealing with the subject of "income" is a semantic one. The word "income" (for income tax purposes) *simply does not mean what the public thinks it means.*

Not too long ago a Federal district judge in Texas ruled that "income was everything that came in." He made this ruling in rejecting a claim that wages were not income. *Income* might mean "everything that comes in, " but such *income* might also be called "gross receipts, " or "gross earnings, " or even (as the government calls it) "gross income" — but such receipts, earnings or income is not at all what is meant by "income" under the 16th Amendment and as defined by the Supreme Court.

A Problem Of Semantics

The root of this semantic problem starts with the Amendment itself. It authorizes a tax on income "from whatever source derived." It does not say that the government can tax wages, dividends, interest, prize money, alimony, and all those other things the public thinks are income. The 16th Amendment only authorizes a tax *on* income *derived from* these sources and not a tax *on* such sources. How do we arrive at a definition for the *thing* that is "derived from" these sources and taxable under the 16th Amendment as "income?" The answer is not as simple as what that Texas judge would have the public believe.

First, the Senate itself did not know what income was when it decided to tax it. Senator Cummins (one of the most knowledgable members on the subject in the Senate) admitted that Congress could not define it and that it would be "worse than useless" even "dangerous" to attempt to do so. If that Texas judge was correct, why did Congress have trouble defining it? Why could Congress not say that "income is everything that comes in?" Because of that semantic problem I referred to earlier. If they had written the law correctly (by stating that they were taxing *profits,* not income), or if the 16th Amendment used the word "profit" and not "income, " Congress would have had no problem defining what it sought to tax.

Senator Cummins Spots The Problem

Senator Cummins put his finger on the problem when he said, "Great Britain might employ" words to modify or enlarge "income" because its Parliament was not bound by any *constitutional restrictions.* He also pointed out that a state "has a right to include whatever she likes within the meaning of the word 'income' but the Congress has no [such] right." Cummins (correctly) explained the reason for this when he said, "The people have granted us the power to levy a tax on incomes, it will always be a judicial question as to whether a particular thing is income or *whether it is principal."* Here *Cummins admits that a return of principal is not "income" in any form — either "gross" or "net."*

Developing this theme further, he then went on to point out that Congress was not given the power to "obliterate all differences between income and principal" since "the people of this country did not intend to give Congress the power to levy a direct tax upon all the property of this country without apportionment." As Cummins saw so well, this was the heart of the problem for the government. The reason England (and even state governments) can define income any way they choose is because they are not bound by the rule of apportionment. So if their definition of income happens to include a return of capital, it would present no legal problem since such governments have the power *to tax capital without apportionment anyway — but the Federal government has no such comparable power.* The Federal government can only tax "income, " not capital (i.e. property), without apportionment, so a return of capital cannot fall within the legal definition of "income" on any basis! The fact that Cummins spotted this problem shows that he had a good deal of accounting as well as legal insight. What Cummins was referring to can best be illustrated by the following example.

Returns Of Capital Are Not "Income," Either "Gross" or "Net"

Suppose Johnny Appleseed purchased $20,000 worth of apples and sold them for $50,000. Could the government (under the 16th Amendment) tax the entire $50,000 received on this sale as income? The answer is no, but only because of the principle of apportionment as the following example illustrates.

Suppose Johnny had the $20,000 in the bank prior to purchasing the apples. Could the government lay an income tax on that $20,000? The answer is obviously no. Suppose Johnny took the $20,000 out of the bank and bought a load of apples, has he changed his asset position? Again the answer is no. He simply has his wealth in apples rather than in a bank credit. If he then sold his apples for $50,000 and put the proceeds back in the bank, he only has $30,000 more than he had before. If the government claims it can tax the entire $50,000 received from the sale as "income," Johnny would obviously be paying a tax on his original $20,000 worth of capital.

Carry this one step further.

Suppose Johnny also took $5,000 out of the bank to advertise the fact that he had apples for sale and another $10,000 to pay an individual to handle their actual sale and delivery. Johnny would have taken a total of $35,000 out of the bank in order to buy, advertise and sell his apples so that $35,000 received from their sale would merely represent a "return of capital." Such a return of capital cannot, again, constitute "income" in any way, shape or form — either "gross" or "net." Why then should any such information be supplied on any document asking for information on "gross" or "net" income? If it could be said that Appleseed had any "gross income" at all it could only have been the $15,000 worth of "profit" he realized from the sale, since everything else was merely a return of capital.

As Cummins admitted, returns of capital *form no component of "income,"* so why should such receipts be reported as receipts of "income"? It should be obvious that an "income" tax can only apply to "profits" and not transactions involving capital or property since such items *do not even fall within any category of "income."* For Johnny to report that he had $50,000 "gross income" from the sale of apples is totally incorrect.

An "income" tax can only tax (and inquire about) "profits" while the Federal government must still tax all returns of capital on the basis of apportionment. Can you begin to see the dimensions of the problem? How can income be defined so as to 1) eliminate from such a definition all returns of capital that might flow back as income, and 2) separate all income from those sources that produced it? The government, by way of the Internal Revenue Code, attempts to get around this problem by trying to restrict the meaning of "income" without *actually defining it!* The Internal Revenue Code speaks of such things as "gross income," "net income," and "taxable income, " but never defines "income" itself.[1] But it is only "income" itself — not *net* income or *taxable* income — that the 16th Amendment presumably allows the government to tax. The Amendment does not qualify "income" by referring either to "gross" or "net" or "taxable" income and it is the unadorned and unqualified concept of "income" that the government must define if "income" is to be taxed on *any* basis. The problem of definition would not arise if the government honestly sought to tax "profit" derived from income.[2]

Profit could be defined very easily, but "income" derived from various sources (and separated from those sources) is impossible to define unless one defines it as "profit." But then wages and salaries would be excluded from the tax which is what the government wants desperately to avoid and that is essentially what created the problem that Cummins forsaw. The government's illegal ability to tax wages as "income" (forgetting all about the other erroneous forms of "income" taxes) *absolutely hinges on its ability to hide the real definition of "income" from the public!*

Cummins Misleads Congress

Having said all that (and even given Cummins's insight into the problem) it must now be obvious that he misled the Senate (though I am not saying he did it deliberately) when he said:

> Congress can levy a tax upon gross incomes if it likes, it may diminish the extent of its taxing powers or not exercise it at all; it may exclude certain things from the taxing power that it might include. . .

[1] "The general term 'income' is not defined in the Internal Revenue Code." *US vs Ballard* 535 F2d 400.

[2] A and B, for example, have the same "net income" but one makes alimony payments and has three more dependents than the other. He would, therefore, pay far less taxes, despite the fact that they *both have the same "net income."* How can that be? If A and B both have the same "net income" they both should pay the same tax. The fact that one has more children and makes alimony payments is only indicative of how he chooses to spend his income. Does the 16th Amendment say that "Congress shall have the power to lay and collect taxes on incomes less personal expenditures?" All corporations with the same profit pay the same income tax so how can individuals with the same income *legally* pay *different taxes?*

Cummins was dead wrong when he suggested that Congress could tax "gross income" for the very reasons he, himself, stated and as illustrated by the Johnny Appleseed example. Could Congress levy an income tax on the entire $50,000 in the Appleseed sale (as Cummins suggested) by calling it "gross income?" Cummins himself would have been the first to deny it if he were confronted with that example. What could Cummins have possibly meant since he obviously understood that Congress could not tax "gross income?" He was obviously talking about "gross profits, " not "gross income, " and once that is understood everything else Cummins said begins to make some sense.

Whether he realized it or not, Cummins was thinking about "profit" but was calling it *income* since Congress might, indeed, tax "gross profits" but limit the tax to something less than this. He had to be thinking this because only "gross profit" excludes all returns of capital (which Cummins had to know because he also knew that capital had to be scrupulously eliminated from "income" in order for "income" to be taxed without apportionment). His apparent confusion obviously resulted from the fact that he could not get himself to talk in terms of a "profits" tax when he was pushing for an "income" tax. He probably felt that only a tax patterned after previous "income" tax measures would be acceptable to Congress and to the public.

Once this is understood, Cummins's remarks and seeming confusion, as well as the rest of what he said, begin to make some sense especially since he went on to say:

> If we desire we (can) limit ourselves to net income (but) we cannot define net income; we cannot say what shall be included in income and what shall not be included in income.

His suggestion that it is up to Congress to limit the tax to "net income" again makes no sense if he was not referring to "profit" because, as we already saw, *it is not up to Congress* at all and Cummins had to know it. This also explains why he said that Congress could not define "income." If it tried to come up with a definition it would end up with a definition for *"profit"* and not a definition for *income* — which is *exactly* what happened when the Supreme Court tried to define "income."

The Supreme Court Defines Income

The search to find a definition for "income" basically began when British-owned Stratton's Independence, Ltd. (a company that carried out mining operations in Colorado) challenged the Corporation Excise Tax before the Supreme Court. The company argued that since it was a mining Company it was essentially in the business of selling land and maintained that land could only be taxed on the basis of apportionment. The Court stated the company's position as follows:

> That the provisions of [the act] do not fit the conditions of a mining corporation; that such corporations are not in truth engaged in carrying on business within the meaning of the Act; that the application of the Act to them results in a tax upon capital, while as applied to other corporations it does not result in such a tax, the result being an inequality of operation that is inherently unjust; that the proceeds of mining operations do not represent values created by or incident to business activities of such a corporation and therefore cannot be a bona fide measure of a tax levied at such corporate business activities; that the proceeds of mining operations result from a conversion of the capital represented by real estate into capital represented by cash, and are in no true sense income; and that to measure the tax by the excess of the receipts for one marketed over the cost of mining, extracting and marketing the same, is equivalent to a direct tax upon property and hence unconstitutional.[3]

This was an interesting argument and exactly fits the situation when the government taxes wages as "income." (Simply substitute the word "labor" and "wages" for "capital, " "property, " and "real estate" where such words appear in that paragraph). How did the Court answer this? Before answering, the Court said a few other things that bear repeating since they verify and strengthen a few other matters we have already covered.

Continuing Authority of **Pollock** Shown

Now let us examine another interesting excerpt from *Stratton's*:

> As has been repeatedly remarked, the Corporation Tax Act of 1909 was not intended to be and is not in any proper sense an income tax law. This court had decided in the *Pollock Case* that the income tax law of 1894 amounted in effect to a direct tax upon property, and was invalid because not apportioned according to population as prescribed by the Constitution. The act of 1909 avoided this difficulty by imposing not an income tax, but an excise tax upon the conduct of business in a corporate capacity, measuring, however, the amount of tax by the income of the corporation, with certain qualifications prescribed by the Act itself. [4]

Aside from providing official, capsulized proof of the Corporation Excise Tax swindle (the act did not "impose an income tax" — ha!) the

---

[3] *Stratton's Independence vs Howbert* 231 US 406, pages 409–413.
[4] Ibid., page 414.

above excerpt demonstrates the continuing authority of *Pollock*. Getting back to the question raised by *Stratton's*, the Court answered it in the following manner; and, in so doing, laid the foundation for the definition of income that all future Supreme Courts would follow.

> The sale outright of a mining property might be fairly described as a mere conversion of the capital from land into money. But when a company is digging pits, sinking shafts, tunneling, drifting, stopping, drilling, blasting, and hoisting ores, *it is employing capital and labor in transmuting a part of the realty into personalty, and putting it into marketable form.* The very process of mining is, in a sense, equivalent in its results to a manufacturing process. And, however the operation shall be described, the transaction is indubitably "business" within the fair meaning of the act of 1909; and the gains derived from it are properly and strictly the income from that business; for "income" *may be defined as the gain derived from capital, from labor, or from both combined*, and here we have combined operations of capital and labor.[5] (Emphasis added)

Thus the Court said that "income" may be defined as the *gain derived from capital, from labor or from both combined.*" Here we have the definition of "income" that every Supreme Court — with one minor addition — has used ever since!

Note that "income" is not "everything that comes in" but by the Supreme Court's definition is a "gain." The Court might have also used the word "profit" since (in this sense) they both mean the same thing. Note also that the "gain" came about (was derived from) the employment of both capital and labor (*from which the company derived a gain or a profit.* The Court basically said, "True, you are in the business of selling land, but when you dug pits, blasted, drilled, etc., you used capital and labor to transform that realty into personalty and to get the land into marketable and profitable form." The Court concluded that on that basis the sale of that land (now transformed from land to personalty) could be taxed as "income."

Now you can see how labor comes into the income tax picture. The Court pointed out that Stratton's derived gain from the *employment of* labor and, therefore, had income "derived" from that labor. In this case the tax was not applied *on* labor, but was applied to the *gain derived from its use* (or employment). What is the meaning of "income, derived from labor?" It means the *gain* or *profit* achieved through the hiring or employing of the labor of *others* — it does not mean the money (or goods) received from the sale or exchange of one's own labor. Here the Court treated **labor and capital as economic equals** (as they both are,

[5] Ibid., pages 414, 415.

since both represent two of the three basic factors of production,[6] the third being land). But since the government cannot tax capital (in the guise of a tax on "income"), **neither can it tax labor under the same guise.** The *Stratton's* Court's explanation and definition of "income" clearly demonstrates that "income derived from labor" is not wages or salary at all but *profit derived from their employment.* In short, the government cannot place a tax *on your labor* whether its value is received through wages or through self-employment in the guise of an "income" or "profits" tax.

Charlie's Chair

A simple illustration of this might be the following.

> Suppose I hired Charlie to make a chair for me out of wood I had found (which cost me nothing), which I believed I could sell for $50.00. I agreed to pay Charlie $25.00 to make the chair and he applied his labor to the task and turned out a magnificent chair in 8 hours. I sold the chair, not for $50,00 but for $100.00! Now, when I sold the chair for $100.00, did I make a gain or a profit derived from Charlie's labor? I apparently made a gain — the question is how much?

It is only in this context that anyone can have "income derived from labor" — but it would appear I *gained from Charlie's labor, not my own.* Did Charlie have a gain from his labor? No, he merely exchanged the value of his labor for the money I gave him which we had both determined was a fair price for that labor. But, as it turned out, I probably underpaid Charlie, since he worked 8 hours in the hot sun and made me a far better chair than I ever expected. And since I only expected to sell his chair for $50.00, I probably paid him less than the actual value of his labor. It is obvious from this angle, too, that Charlie lost on the deal. In any case, I made a $75.00 profit on Charlie's labor — or did I? It could be argued that I got that much for the chair, not because of Charlie's labor, but my own; that my ability to get $100.00 for it was largely due to my own skill and hard work in selling the chair and finding a buyer who would pay that much, to say nothing about the time and effort I put into finding the wood. The problem now becomes one of determining how much of my alleged $75.00 gain "derived from Charlie's labor" was actually due to my own labor. Depending on how much labor I had to expend to find the wood and sell the chair, I also might not have had any gain "derived from" Charlie's labor or my own for that matter.

---

[6] The Court spoke of "operations of capital and labor" so both factors of production must stand *equally* before the law for tax purposes.

Income Is Not "Income"

The 1918 case of *Doyle vs Mitchell*[7] involved the appreciation of assets acquired prior to the income tax taking effect and their subsequent sale. The assets involved trees purchased in 1903 for approximately $20.00 an acre. After the passage of the Corporation Excise Tax Act the company revalued the timber to reflect its appreciated 1909 value of $40.00 an acre and paid taxes for the years 1909 – 1912 on that basis. The Commissioner of Internal Revenue allowed the deduction based on the 1903 cost but disallowed a deduction based upon the 1909 appreciated value. Mitchell Brothers paid the tax in protest and sued for a refund, which they won in both district and appellate courts. The government, however, appealed to the Supreme Court which upheld the lower courts and found against the government. In reaching the decision in this case the Court said:

> Starting from this point, the learned Solicitor General has submitted an elaborate argument in behalf of the Government, based in part upon theoretical definitions of "capital, " "income, " "profits, " etc., and in part upon expressions quoted from our opinions in *Flint v. Stone Tracy Co.,* 220 U.S. 107, 147, and *Anderson v. Forty-two Broadway,* 239 U.S. 69, 72, with the object of showing that *a conversion of capital into money always produces income, and that for the purposes of the present case the words "gross income" are equivalent to "gross receipts,"* the insistence being that the entire proceeds of a conversion of capital assets should be treated as gross income, and that by deducting the mere cost of such assets we arrive at net income.[8] (Emphasis added)

Note how the government tried to claim "that a conversion of capital into money always produces income" and that the "words 'gross income' are equivalent to 'gross receipts'." In both cases the Court said they were not. This distinction should still hold true today, except that Federal "courts" illegally refuse to see such differences. The government's attempt to tax as "income" gains that occurred *prior to the law's passage,* was too blatant even for the Supreme Court!

In deciding the issue the *Mitchell* Court also said:

> Yet it is plain, we think, that by the true intent and meaning of the Act the entire proceeds of *a mere conversion of capital assets were not to be treated as income. Whatever difficulty there may be about a precise and sci-*

---

[7] *Emanuel J. Doyle vs Mitchell Brothers Company* 247 US 179, decided May 20, 1918.

[8] *Doyle vs Mitchell,* 247 US 179, pages 183, 184.

entific definition of "income" it imports, as used here, something entirely distinct from principal or capital either as a subject of taxation or as a measure of the tax; conveying rather the idea of *gain or increase arising from corporate activities.* As was said in *Stratton's Independence v. Howbert,* 231 U.S. 399, 415: "Income may be defined as the gain derived from capital, from labor, or from both combined."[9] (Emphasis added)

The Court's words must be summarized as follows:

1. Conversions of capital assets "were not to be treated as income" — either gross or net.
2. There is difficulty in arriving at a precise definition for "income."
3. Whatever difficulty there may be in (2) above, the word "income" conveys "the idea of gain arising from corporate activity" (i.e. corporate profit).

Apart from the fact that the Court established that the income tax must be "void for vagueness" and for the reason given by the *Spreckles* Court (see page 136), it also established that wages cannot be taxes as "income" since wages are nothing more than a "conversion" of a capital asset, (labor into cash). Notice, too, the development of the idea that "income" is, in reality, a corporate profit.

Income Requires Economic Gain

Another early Supreme Court decision that sheds additional light on the concept of income was the 1918 case of *Towne vs Eisner*.[10] In this case Towne challenged the "income" tax on the basis that the stock dividend he received was not "income." The collector of taxes, Mark Eisner of New York, claimed otherwise so Towne paid the tax under duress and sued for a refund. He lost in the lower courts and appealed to the Supreme Court. In this instance the lower courts' rulings were reversed and the Supreme Court ruled that a stock dividend was not "income."

In writing the short opinion in this case, Oliver Wendell Holmes (quoting *Billings vs United States* 232 US 261) said:

"A stock dividend really takes nothing from the property of the corporation, and adds nothing to the interest of the shareholders. Its property is not diminished and their interests are not increased. . ."[11]

[9] Ibid., pages 184,185.

[10] *Henry R. Towne vs Mark Eisner* 245 US 418, decided January 7, 1918.

[11] Ibid., page 426.

What Holmes was pointing out was that since there was no "gain" to the recipient of the stock dividend, there was no "income."

The Supreme Court: Income Is Not "What Comes In"

The next significant case involving the meaning of "income" was *Southern Pacific vs Lowe*.[12] It involved a distribution to Southern Pacific of profits acquired by a subsidiary prior to the income tax becoming law. The Collector of Internal Revenue in New York, John Lowe Jr., said that the distribution was taxable income, so Southern Pacific paid the tax under duress and sued for a refund. Lowe was upheld in the lower courts and Southern Pacific appealed to the Supreme Court. The Court found in favor of Southern Pacific and again reversed the lower courts' decisions.

In finding in favor of *Southern Pacific* the Court said:

> We must reject in this case, as we have rejected in cases arising under the Corporation Excise Tax Act of 1909 (*Doyle v. Mitchell Brothers Co., ante,* 179, and *Hays v. Gauley Mountain Coal Co., ante,* 189) the broad contention submitted in behalf of the Government that *all receipts — everything that comes in — are income within the proper definition of the term "gross income,"* and that the entire proceeds of a conversion of capital assets, in whatever form and under whatever circumstances accomplished, should be treated as gross income. *Certainly the term "income" has no broader meaning in the 1913 Act than in that of 1909 (see Stratton's Independence v. Howbert, 231 U.S. 399, 416, 417), and for the present purpose we assume there is no difference in its meaning as used in the two acts.*[13] (Emphasis added)

The Supreme Court (unlike that Texas judge) rejected the idea that "everything that comes in" is "income" and demonstrates how lower Federal courts today ignore early Supreme Court decisions bearing on the meaning of "income." Note further the Court's upholding of the meaning of "income" as expressed in *Stratton's*. Another significant point is the Court's observation that "the term 'income' has no broader meaning in the 1913 Act than in that of 1909. . . and for the present purpose we assume that there is no difference in its meaning as used in the two Acts." This is, of course, official proof (more will follow) that "income" really means "profit" since what was taxable as "income" in the Act of 1909 *was simply corporate profit.*

[12] *Southern Pacific Company vs John Z. Lowe, Jr.* 247 US 330, decided June 3, 1918.

[13] Ibid., page 335.

Eisner vs Macomber — Closing The Ring

The *Eisner*[14] case (along with *Pollock* and *Brushaber*) completes the triumverate of the most important Supreme Court cases dealing with Federal income taxes. Whereas *Pollock* established that taxes "on" property and "on" the income (using income in its ordinary, non-tax sense) from property were direct and had to be apportioned; and whereas *Brushaber* established that income (separated from its source) could be taxed indirectly as an excise, the *Eisner* Court focused (more than any other Court) on the definition of "income" and came up with the definition that is considered the official, legal definition of income. No other definition supercedes it and no other Supreme Court has attempted to change it.

In arriving at its definition, however, the *Eisner* Court had a number of interesting things to say about the "income" tax and the 16th Amendment. Because of the weight and authority of this case they bear repeating.

Case Involved Stock Dividends

Like *Towne* this case involved a stock dividend which had been received by Myrtle Macomber. The tax collector ruled that it was "income." Ms. Macomber paid the tax under protest and sued for a refund. This time she won in the lower courts (that based their decisions on the *Towne* case (see page 214). The government, nevertheless, appealed to the Supreme Court. The *Eisner* Court easily sustained the lower courts on the basis of the *Towne* decision and then used the issue presented as a springboard into other related issues.

Sixteenth Amendment Did Not Amend Constitution

Reaffirming that the 16th Amendment did not amend the Constitution, the Court said:

> The Sixteenth Amendment must be construed in connection with the taxing clauses of the original Constitution and the effect attributed to them before the Amendment was adopted.[15]

This was the Court's way of saying, "Forget the 16th Amendment — it didn't change a thing as far as the taxing clauses of the Constitution are concerned." The *Brushaber* Court had said as much in 1915, but the

---

[14] *Mark Eisner vs Myrtle H. Macomber* 252 US 189, decided March 8, 1920.
[15] Ibid., page 205

Supreme Court repeated it in 1920. Apparently the executive branch of government (which operates the IRS) refused to get the message — and even today it still pretends it knows nothing about it. The public thinks the 16th Amendment amended the Constitution and each year thousands of graduating law students believe it too, though the two most important Supreme Court cases that deal with the matter emphatically state otherwise. How is this possible?

Eisner Court Relies on *Pollock*

Notice how the *Eisner* Court relied on the *Pollock* decision in the following excerpts:

> In *Pollock v. Farmers' Loan & Trust,* it was held that *taxes upon rents* and profits of real estate and upon *returns from investments of personal property were in effect direct taxes* upon the property from which such *income* arose, imposed by reason of ownership; and that Congress *could not impose such taxes without apportioning them* among the States according to population, as required by Art. 1, Sect. 2, Cl. 3, and Sect. 9, C1. 4, of the original Constitution.[16]

So again, as late as 1920 (11 years after the 16th Amendment was passed by Congress), the Supreme Court still quoted *Pollock* and affirmed that taxes on rents and income from investments of personal property (such as bank accounts, stocks and bonds) were direct taxes that required apportionment.[17]

Restating the 16th Amendment the Court then said:

> As repeatedly held, this [the 16th Amendment] did not extend the taxing power to new subjects, but merely removed the necessity which otherwise might exist for an apportionment among the states of taxes laid on income [cases cited]. [18]

When the Court used the word "income" it was referring to "profits" or "gains" separated from their sources, not income in the ordinary sense of the word (meaning money that *comes in*).

---

[16] Ibid.

[17] Remember that T. Emmet Clarie, the Chief Judge for the Connecticut District, at my "trial" tried to tell the jury that the 16th Amendment reversed *Pollock*.

[18]*Eisner vs Macomber, supra,* page 206.

Sixteenth Amendment Should Not Be Extended By "Loose Construction"

The Court next cautioned that the 16th Amendment should not be extended by "loose construction" to repeal the taxing clauses of the Constitution. That is, of course, precisely what the Federal government (with the help of *every* Federal "court" in the land) has been doing. At least here (perhaps to atone for all its prior lax decisions) the Supreme Court appears to have been trying to make amends in order to stop what it perceived to be the headlong drive of the government (now supposedly armed with the 16th Amendment) to tax everything in sight as "income." Today every Federal "court" totally disregards *Eisner* on this issue, but read the Court's words:

> A proper regard for its genesis, as well as its very clear language, requires also that this Amendment *shall not be extended by loose construction, so as to repeal or modify, except as applied to income, those provisions of the Constitution that require an apportionment* according to population for direct taxes upon property real and personal. This limitation *still* has an appropriate and important function, and *is not* to be overridden by Congress or *disregarded* by the courts.[19]

The Federal courts now do exactly what the *Eisner* Court said they could not do:

1. allow the U.S. Congress to override the taxing clauses of the Constitution; and
2. disregard these same taxing clauses themselves.

The Meaning Of Income

The Court then turned to the meaning of income and stated:

> In order, therefore, that the clauses cited from Article I of the Constitution may have proper force and effect, save only as modified by the Amendment, and that the latter also may have proper effect, it becomes essential to *distinguish* between what is and what is not "income," as the term is there used; and to apply the distinction, as cases arise, according to truth and substance, without regard to form. *Congress cannot by any definition it may adopt conclude the matter, since **it cannot by legislation alter the Constitution,** from which alone it derives its *power* to legislate, and within whose *limitations* alone that power can be *lawfully* exercised.[20] (Emphasis added)

[19] Ibid.

[20] Ibid.

The Court also stated that Congress cannot by "any definition" it chooses decide what income is. This is, of course, precisely the problem that Cummins forsaw, but it only developed because the word "income" was inaccurate (because it did not automatically exclude *returns of capital*, nor did it separate income from its source). This meant that the Courts had to develop a constitutional definition so "income" could be taxed without apportionment. If the law had been written as a tax on "profit" no such problem of definition would have developed because "profit" excludes returns of capital and automatically separates "income" from its source(s).

The Official Definition Of "Income"

The Court then turned its attention to defining and describing "income" and stated:

> After examining dictionaries in common use (Bouv. L.D.; Standard Dict.; Webster's Internat. Dict.; Century Dict.), we find little to add to the succinct definition adopted in two cases arising under the Corporation Tax Act of 1909 *(Stratton's Independence v. Howbert,* 231 U.S. 399,415; *Doyle v. Mitchell Bros. Co,* 247 U.S. 179,185) — "Income may be defined as the gain derived from capital, from labor, or from both combined, " provided it be understood to include profit gained through a sale or conversion of capital assets, to which it was applied in the *Doyle Case* (pp. 183, 185).
>
> Brief as it is, this indicates the characteristic and distinguishing attribute of income essential to a correct solution of the present controversy. The government (though basing its argument on the definition as quoted) placed chief emphasis upon the word "gain" (extended to include a variety of meanings) while the significance of "gain derived from capital" was either overlooked or misconceived. "Derived-from-capital"; — "the gain-derived-from-capital, " etc. Here we have the essential matter — *not* a gain *accruing to* capital, not a *growth* or *increment* of value *in* the investment; but a gain, a profit, something of exchangeable value *proceeding from* the property, *severed from* the capital however invested or employed, and *coming in,* being *"derived,"* that is *received* or *drawn by* the recipient (the taxpayer) for his *separate* use, benefit and disposal; — *that* is income derived from property. Nothing else answers the description.
>
> The same fundamental conception is clearly set forth in the Sixteenth Amendment — "income, *from* whatever *source derived"* — the essential thought being expressed with a conciseness and lucidity entirely in harmony with the form and style of the Constitution.[21] (Emphasis *not* added)

[21] Ibid., pages 207, 208.

Note how the *Eisner* Court accepted the definition of income exactly as it was stated in *Stratton's* (see page 211) with the provision that it also include "profit gained through a sale or conversion of capital assets."

Based on all this material, "income" was officially defined as follows:

Income is the gain derived from capital, from labor, or from both combined including the profit gained through a sale or conversion of capital assets.

The Court stressed that in trying to tax a stock dividend as "income" (because the stock dividend "came in") even the government emphasized that it was a "gain." The Court said that even if we have a "gain" this gain must be "severed from the capital however invested or employed." Assuming that an asset appreciated in value (a home, for instance), no taxable "gain" is realized until the asset is sold so that the "gain" can be severed from the capital" received and used by the taxpayer "for his separate use, benefit and disposal." Or in simpler terms, a stock dividend was still a part of the original investment and until it was sold for cash there could be no realized taxable gain — no "income."

Eisner *Decision Applies Equally to Labor*

The principle expressed in *Eisner* and its definition of "income" has to apply to all forms of property, not merely to stocks. Gain-derived-from-labor must, therefore, be given the same meaning as "gain-derived-from-capital, etc." As *Stratton's* pointed out (see page 211) capital and labor are equals in the income tax equation and taxing principles that apply to one must also apply to the other. So when the Court says that "income" is "the gain-derived-from-capital, etc." it also must apply to labor.

Therefore, "income" as applied to labor means "the gain-derived-from labor" which is *not* the same thing as wages or salary (which represents the exchange of labor — an asset — for money).

Coming Full Circle — The *Smietanka* Case

Finally, in March of 1921, the Supreme Court explicitly admitted (as it did in the *Southern Pacific* case) that "income" could only mean a corporate profit. This case[22] involved the appreciation of stock in an estate and its final distribution by the trustees. Julius F. Smietanka, the

[22]*Merchant's Loan & Trust Company vs Smietanka* 255 US 509, decided March 28, 1921.

tax collector in Illinois, said that the distribution was taxable as income to the recipients. The trustee, Merchant's Loan & Trust Company, said the appreciation was not income within the meaning of the 16th Amendment. So the taxes were paid in protest and the Merchant's Loan & Trust sued to recover the amount paid. The Supreme Court upheld the tax and said:

> . . . it was the purpose of Congress to tax gains, derived from such a sale as we have here [and that] it is the purpose of that act. . . to treat such a trustee as we have as a "taxable person". . . precisely as if the beneficiaries had received it in person.[23]

In arriving at its decision, the Court felt it had to say something about the meaning of "income" and, therefore, gave what is the most complete and all-inclusive definition of "income" that appears in any Supreme Court case and qualifies as the definitive Supreme Court definition of "income":

> It is obvious that these decisions in principle rule the case at bar if the word "income" has the same meaning in the Income Tax Act of 1913 that it had in the Corporation Excise Tax Act of 1909, and that it has the same scope of meaning was in effect decided in *Southern Pacific Co. v. Lowe*, 247 U.S. 330, 335, where it was assumed for the purposes of decision that there was no difference in its meaning as used in the Act of 1909 and in the Income Tax Act of 1913. There can be no doubt that the word must be given the same meaning and content in the Income Tax Acts of 1916 and 1917 that it had in the Act of 1913. When to this we add that in *Eisner v. Macomber,* supra, a case arising under the same Income Tax Act of 1916 which is here involved, the definition of "income" which was applied was adopted from *Stratton's Independence v. Howbert,* supra, arising under the Corporation Excise Tax Act of 1909, with the addition that it should include "profit gained through a sale or conversion of capital assets, " there would seem to be no room to doubt that the word must be given the same meaning in all of the Income Tax Acts of Congress *that was given to it in the Corporation Excise Tax Act and that what that meaning is has now become definitely settled by decisions of this court.*[24] (Emphasis added)

Thus the *Smietanka* Court said that the "meaning" of "income" had become *final* and was now "definitely settled by decisions of this court" and that "income" had the same "meaning. . . that was given to it in

---

[23] Ibid., page 516.

[24] Ibid., pages 518, 519.

[25] *Burnet vs. Harmel* 287 US 103 (1932). Additional cases are cited in the motion in Appendix D.

the Corporation Excise Tax Act of 1909." What *was* the "meaning" of "income" as used in the Corporation Excise Tax Act? A corporate profit! Therefore, if you do not have a corporate profit you cannot have any income subject to an "income" tax!

Since the recipients of the distributions in this case were not corporations (and did not show a "profit") how could anything they received be classified as "income, " including the trust distributions the *Smietanka* Court ruled were "income"? I will return to this anomoly later, but what should be noted now is that this Court finally concluded that the search for a legal definition of "income" was *over* and that "income" meant *a corporate profit*. Therefore, nothing but a corporate profit can fit the definition of what "income" *has to mean* in order for it to be taxable as an *indirect excise tax* according to the *Brushaber* Court's interpretation of the 16th Amendment and by all of the Supreme Court cases just discussed.

Courts Affirm *Eisner* and *Smietanka*

The following excerpts from *Burnet vs. Harmel*[25] (decided some nineteen years and numerous Court cases after the income tax was passed) provides further legal confirmation of the meaning of "income" as we just established — that it is a corporate profit; and that this meaning has been accepted by every Supreme Court that ever considered the meaning of "income":

> . . . before the 1921 Act this Court had indicated (see *Eisner v. Macomber,* 252 U.S. 189, 207, 64 L.ed. 521, 9 A.L.R. 1570, 40 S. Ct. 189), what it later held, that "income, " as used in the revenue acts taxing income, adopted since the 16th Amendment, *has the same meaning that it had in the Act of 1909. Merchants; Loan & T. Co. v. Smietanka,* 255 U.S. 509, 519, 65 L.ed. 751, 755, 15 A.L.R. 1305, 41 S. Ct. 386; see *Southern Pacific Co. v. Lowe.* 247 U.S. 330, 335, 62 L.ed. 114, 1147, 38 S. Ct. 540.[26] (Emphasis added)

> *Stated simply this says that if you do not have a corporate profit you cannot have any "income" subject to an income tax!*

[26] Ibid., page 108.

14

Why No One Can Have Taxable Income

It should now be obvious that no individual can have taxable income for the following reasons:

1. Since an unapportioned income tax is, by law, an excise tax (which otherwise requires apportionment), it must be *levied as an excise to be legally mandatory*. Since the current income tax is not levied as an excise tax (either on individuals or corporations) it cannot be legally mandatory on any basis! In enforcing the income taxes, the government simply disregards both the 16th Amendment and the taxing clauses of the Constitution, which (under both *Brushaber* and *Eisner*) it cannot do. [1]
2. Since the Courts have ruled that "income" (for "income" tax purposes) means "a corporate profit" and since private citizens do not generate "profit" (nor could they be made to keep books from which a contrived "profit" could even be estimated), they can have no "income" that is subject to an "income" tax. [2]

The point is that these two facts alone establish why nothing in connection with Federal individual "income" taxes can be legally compelling or required: Not filing, not withholding, not IRS examining of any books and records, not the reporting by banks, other financial institutions, and employers of interest and wages paid, not tax "court" decisions, and certainly not "trials" for failing to file tax returns or for tax evasion, but because the crimes of the Federal government are so vast in connection with this tax and because the numbers of people in the private sector (lawyers, accountants, bank trust departments — which

---

[1] For the legal definition of an excise, see Justice Field's opinion, page 116 and the *Flint Stone* opinion, page 144.

[2] There are, of course, a number of other reasons (see page 240, 241) why an "income" tax cannot be mandatory, but we need not concern ourselves with them here.

can be sued for having paid taxes on trust income that was really not taxable at all) who are involved in the hoax is so huge, overkill is probably necessary to slay the income tax dragon.

Individuals Generate No "Profits" So They Can Have No "Income"

Since the Courts have ruled that income must be separated from its sources, it should now be clear that private individuals cannot have "income" because it is impossible for individuals to separate personal income from its sources.[3] You already know that the 16th Amendment did not overturn the *Pollock* decision which ruled that a tax on the income from real estate, bonds and bank deposits is a tax on those sources and must be apportioned. So, when the government tries to tax income directly (based on *Pollock*) it is equivalent to a direct tax on the capital sources themselves and thus constitutes a tax *on* property not a tax on "income" (again realizing that what is really being taxed in both cases is neither income nor property but *the individual, measured by* his property or income).[4]

This taxing principle, as has been carefully demonstrated, was extensively discussed and decided by the *Pollock* Court and was not overturned by the 16th Amendment *nor has it been overturned or subsequently challenged* by any other Supreme Court. So this principle laid down in *Pollock* stands as fundamental tax law and is not to be "disregarded by the courts" (see the *Eisner* case, page 218).

Since the *Pollock* decision did not directly concern wages or income from self-employment, the Court rendered no decision on these items. Can these sources of income be taxed as "income" under current tax law or under the 16th Amendment? The question itself supplies its own answer.

Wages and Self Employment Earnings Are Not "Income" and Cannot Be Taxed As Such

There are many reasons why wages cannot be taxed under the Internal Revenue Code — though the fact that the tax is *not being imposed as an excise tax* would make it illegal (if mandatory) regardless of any other consideration.

---

[3]Individuals do not prepare profit and loss statements comparable to the one shown in Exhibit 1, page 189.

[4]When I put quotes around the word "income" I am using it in its strict, 16th Amendment (taxable) sense to mean *income separated from both capital and its source*. When I omit the quotes around it I am using it in its ordinary sense which can include returns of capital or when it is related to its *source*.

A significant clue to the reason why wages and salaries are not "income" is furnished by Section 61 itself (Exhibit 2). Wages or salaries are not even listed there as a *source* of income, so how can they be "income" on any basis? The Mamelukes (Federal "judges," U.S. Attorneys, and the IRS) insist that salaries and wages fall into the category of "compensation for service" and are "similar" to "fees and commissions" which is simply not true for a variety of reasons.

First, if Section 61 intended to include "wages" why did it not say so? If it could specifically include "commissions," why could it not have included "wages"? Was it omitted accidentally? Of course not. "Income" must be given the same meaning as it had in the Corporation Excise Tax Act of 1909 and "wages" and "salaries" can never be a component of corporate "gross income." For example, a real estate corporation can manage property, sell property, and give advice. For such services it can receive either management or service fees, commissions on sales, or "similar items" of compensation. But can such a corporation receive *wages*? No, proving that wages are not similar to "compensation for services" and that wages and salary are not provided for in Section 61. Therefore, "wages" and "salary" *cannot be taxable* as "income" according to the Code itself.

Payment For Labor Is Not "Income"

Even overlooking the *Stratton* case which orders that payments for labor (wages) are not "income," we now know that "income" can only mean a "gain" or "profit" and does not mean mere receipt of income. But payments for labor (usually referred to as wages or salary) are not "gains" or "profits." They represent *exchanges*, with labor (an asset) being exchanged for its dollar equivalent *which, in many cases, represents a sale by an individual of the only asset he has — his labor.*

For example, take an employer and one of his own employees, say an electrical contractor and one of his electricians such as attended one of my recent tax seminars. I asked the employee, "Does he (pointing to his employer seated next to him) pay you wages?"

"Yes he does," replied the electrician.

"Are you worth what he pays you?" I asked.

"I'm worth more." His answer — the standard one — evoked laughter from the audience.

I then turned to his employer and said, "Is he really worth more than what you pay him?"

Now the employer appeared perplexed since, if he said yes, he might be hit for an immediate raise. But finally he good naturedly replied, "Yes, he is." The audience responded with more laughter.

Carrying this admission further, I asked, "In other words, Mr. Employer, your employee *is* worth a good deal more than what you are paying him, is that right?"

Once again the employer said yes and drew more laughter from the audience and a good natured reaction from his (admittedly) underpaid employee. I decided to take the pressure off the employer and said to the audience, "Of course his employee is worth more than he pays him. What would be the point of hiring him if he weren't?" And, looking at the employee, I said, "You better hope you're worth more than he's paying you. If you're not then he's overpaying you and his other employees, and he'll soon be broke and out of business and you'll be out of a job!"

Essentially companies are in business to make a profit by paying their employees less (collectively) than what they can sell their work-product for. If they cannot do that they will go out of business and their employees will be out of jobs.

Driving my point further I said to the employer, "In other words, Mr. Employer, you might bill a customer $40.00 an hour for your employee's time but pay the employee only $20.00 an hour, isn't that right?"

"Yes, " he replied.

"Now, " I continued, "I realize that some of that differential is to cover your overhead, but you still make a direct profit on his labor don't you?"

"Yes, " he said, "I do."

"So, he gives you his labor, and you give him money which we'll call wages, is that correct?"

"Yes, " he answered.

"You receive his labor and he receives your money — but, in any case, the labor you get from him is worth more than the money he gets from you. Is that correct?"

"Yes, " he replied.

"Now, " I asked the employee, "did you pay income taxes last year on the money he gave you?"

"Yes, " answered the employee. Obviously this was his first seminar.

Turning once again to the employer I said, "Did you pay income taxes last year?"

"Yes, " he answered. Obviously it was *his* first seminar, too.

"In the tax return you filed, did you include the value of the labor you received from him?"

With his eyes riveted to mine and a puzzled look on his face the employer replied, "I'm not sure I understand you."

"Look, " I said, "you just admitted that your employee gave you his labor. Did you add the value of that labor — as indicated by his wages — to the income you reported for tax purposes?"

He hesitated before replying, "No."

"Then how did you show the value of the labor you received from him on your tax return?" I asked.

"Well, I took his wages as a tax deduction, " he said.

"So, not only didn't you pay a penny of taxes on the labor you received from him but you actually reduced your own taxes by the amount of that labor, correct?"

"That's right, " he said.

Turning back to the employee I said, "Did you hear what your employer just said? He said that not only didn't he pay taxes on what you gave him — your labor — but he actually paid *less* taxes because of it. You, however, told me a short while ago that *you paid taxes* on what *he gave you*. Now we find out that what he got from you actually *reduced* his taxes. Does that make sense to you?"

"No, it doesn't, " he replied.

"Well, it doesn't make sense to me either. So why don't you do what he does? If he deducts from his income taxes the labor you give him, why don't you deduct from your income tax the money he gives you? In other words, since he deducts the value of your labor from his income, why don't you deduct the value of his money from your income and treat his wages the way he treats your labor. Then you won't have any income taxes to pay. Doesn't that make more sense than what you're doing now?"

"It certainly does, " he replied. [5]

Can you see why the electrician had no "income"? He had no "income" because he had no *gain* on his labor. His employer admitted he paid him less for his labor than it was worth. As a matter of fact, not only did the electrician not have a "gain" on the transaction, he actually lost on the exchange!

Illogical Situations

There are numerous illogical and inexplicable situations that occur because of the government's erroneous attempt to tax labor (property) as "income" (a profit). Here are several examples.

---

[5]At these seminars, of course, I never analyzed the reason why "income" taxes had to be levied as an excise tax nor why "income" (for tax purposes) really means a "profit." Such an explanation would have required more time than I had in a three hour lecture in which I also had to cover other practical subjects such as how to stop employers from taking taxes out of your pay, how to overcome IRS audits and summonses, and how to handle IRS agents (their calls and letters).

Now You See It, Now You Don't Income

In order to reduce taxes many people resort to barter and, as a result, large bartering exchanges have developed all over the country. The IRS, however, takes the position that barter arrangements create taxable income that must be reported. It is, of course, difficult for the IRS to discover these transactions because, in many cases, they do not appear "on the books." Let us take a simple barter arrangement between a physician and a dentist wherein each provides his services to the other in lieu of exchanging money. If the IRS discovered this arrangement, and could prove it, it would impute additional taxable income to each doctor and the IRS would seek to assess the fair market value of the services received and attempt to collect additional taxes.

With this in mind, consider the following example between the same dentist and Mary, his dental hygenist. They also have a "barter" arrangement, but in this case the dentist gives her $10,000 per year for her services rather than exchanging his own dental services for her services as a hygenist. In this instance the IRS would never call Mary's services "income" that the dentist would have to report. As a matter of fact, he can even take a deduction for the $10,000 he pays her. With the physician, the dentist exchanged service for service and the IRS claimed he received taxable "income." With Mary, however, since he exchanged money for service (and not service for service) not only did he not receive any taxable "income" in return (according to the IRS), he even got to lower his taxable "income." This makes no sense at all.

Now assume that Mary has a very large family and that the whole family needs dental care. Mary estimates this care will cost more than the $10,000 a year she earns so, to save on her own income taxes, she proposes the following arrangement to her employer: She will work for him for nothing in exchange for his services to her and her family (just like the barter deal he has with the physician). Assume further that Mary has this arrangement for at least one year and that the following year she and her husband find themselves audited by the IRS. The IRS agent notices that their combined income dropped by $10,000 (and thus they paid less taxes) for the year Mary bartered her services. When he asks why, Mary tells him that she accepted dental services from her employer in lieu of wages.

"Those dental services are taxable income to you!" the IRS agent would exclaim. "You must include the fair market value of the services you received with your other income for that year and recompute your taxes." [6]

---

[6] I do not see where Mary had any "gain," but every Federal "court" would agree with the agent.

"Are you going to tell Dr. Smith to include my services in his income, too?" Mary asks.

"You better believe I am, " replies the agent, licking his chops at his good fortune at having uncovered a devious plot to cheat the government out of tax revenue. "I'm going to his office as soon as I finish here. He'll have to include the value of your services in his taxable income, too."

"Why, " Mary inquires, "didn't he have to include the value of my services *before,* since he's been getting them for years — whether he pays for them in *services* or in *cash?*"

When Returns of Capital Aren't

Suppose Herbert Jones died leaving $50,000 to each of his two sons, Lester and Fred. Suppose Lester, being an adventurous sort (and one who didn't like to work), invests his $50,000 in a piece of land which he hopes will increase in value. Being more conscientious and not wanting to gamble, Fred decides to invest his money in his own education and spends his entire inheritance for tuition and related expenses at college studying architecture. Five years later, as Fred graduates from college, Lester's gamble pays off and he sells his land for $100,000. What are the tax consequences?

First, Lester gets back his $50,000 tax free (since it represents a return of capital) and only has to pay taxes on 40 percent of his gain. [7] Since (for reasons that will be explained shortly) this is the only income Lester reports, his income tax would amount to about $3,000 leaving him with $97,000 to either spend or invest.

Fred, on the other hand, leaves college dead broke but with a diploma for which he invested five years of his life and $50,000. Suppose Fred (being a top student who conscientiously put in long hours of study) is immediately able to get a job paying $20,000 a year. After working one year and paying all his living expenses he is able to put $492 in the bank. Has he recovered his capital yet? How about that $50,000 investment (not to mention his investment in time and effort in getting his degree), how does he recover that? The IRS would insist that his entire first year's salary of $20,000 was taxable. If Fred were single his personal income tax would amount to approximately $3,000 plus $1,400 in Social Security taxes giving him a total tax bill of $4,400. Though Fred married Thelma just prior to entering college and also has a child, his married status and two additional dependents still give him a tax due of around $3,000 (including Social Security taxes of $1,400).

[7]Because this is treated as a "capital gain" he not only gets his capital back — tax free — he also receives 60 percent of his gain tax free and only pays taxes on 40 percent (or $20,000) of it.

Therefore, Fred's income tax on his $20,000 worth of wages is approximately the same as Lester's income tax on the $50,000 he gained on the sale of his property. But Lester put in no time or effort on his $50,000 gain while Fred invested not ony time and effort but used $50,000 of his own money in order to acquire his $20,000 salary. The irony, of course, is that Lester's $50,000 gain on the sale of his property falls (to a far greater extent) within the Supreme Court's definition of "income" than does Fred's $20,000 salary. Yet, by comparision, Lester will pay far less in taxes on that gain than Fred will pay on his salary.

But what about Fred's investment in his education? When will he get that back? Unfortunately he will not get it back at all because the government will contend that it was a "personal" expense. Such a contention, however, is ludicrous. [8] How can the government claim that such expenditures are personal rather than business related? Would Fred have received a $20,000 salary from that architectural firm if he had no degree in architecture? How then can the government claim that Fred's costs in acquiring that expertise had nothing to do with the salary he received? With equal logic the government could claim that the $50,000 Lester spent for his property had nothing to do with the $100,000 he received from its sale! The government has been able to get away with such arbitrary and idiotic distinctions between investments in capital and investments in labor because the working public apparently is prepared to accept everything and anything the Mamelukes tell them about "income" taxes. Of course, the Mamelukes do get a lot of help from all the incompetents in the private sector who are involved in the preparation of income tax returns.

Suppose Fred died a year after graduation. His wife, Thelma, would only have $492 in the bank and is out $49,508 ($50,000 minus $492). When does she recover that? According to the IRS and the "courts" — never.

Meanwhile, Lester took the $97,000 he received (after taxes) from the sale of his first piece of property and invested it in another. One year later (around the time of Fred's death) he sold it for $200,000. But suppose now that Lester dies too, what happens? His estate will recover the $97,000 (tax free) and will only have to pay taxes on 40 percent of the gain (or $41,000) — a tax of about $10,000. For the sake of our illustration also suppose that while Lester was waiting for his first land pur-

---

[8]This claim *might* have some validity if Fred took a general college course in Philosophy or Comparative Literature; but individuals who major in architecture, medicine, engineering, accounting, dentistry, etc. obviously do so because they expect to make money through the application of their studies — money that otherwise could not possibly be earned.

chase to appreciate in value (and while Fred was slaving away in college) Lester went to a tropical island where he spent five years loafing and met and married Tamara. When Lester died Tamara received the after tax proceeds from his second sale ($190,000) and returned to her island paradise and bought the biggest hut available, living in luxury for the rest of her life. After paying the income taxes on Fred's last annual salary ($3,000 including the $1,400 in Social Security taxes), Thelma was forced to apply for welfare.

Who Really Is Penalized By Income Taxes?

While containing some of the elements of the previous example, the following illustration introduces another facet of the income tax hoax. Suppose Mr. I. M. Rich dies leaving $200,000 worth of stock to his son, Dudley. Each year Dudley liquidates $20,000 from that stock portfolio and uses the money to buy food, clothing, and shelter. Assuming that the value of the stock neither increases or decreases in value, Dudley will not have to pay any income taxes when he converts (sells) his capital (the stock) to buy food, clothing and shelter in order to maintain himself. [9]

I. M. Poor, on the other hand, has no wealth to leave his son, Hyman, so he has taught him (prior to his own death) a trade. Each year Hyman is able to convert the skill his father gave him into $10,000 which he also converts into the food, clothing, and shelter he needs in order to maintain himself.

The IRS would tell Hyman that he has two "income" taxes to pay on his alleged $10,000 "income": 1) regular "income" taxes, and 2) another "income" tax erroneously called a "self-employment" tax, presumably to fund his Social Security benefits. [10] The combination of both of these taxes will take more than $2,000 from Hyman (assuming a standard deduction), *or more than 20 percent of what he earns through the sale of his labor.*

And what does the IRS take from Dudley? *Nothing.* Though Hyman is a poor man he is compelled to give the government 20 percent of what he gets for his labor, while Dudley (wealthier by far than Hyman and living on more than twice the income) is required to pay nothing! How can the government justify taxing Hyman $2,000 a year while Dudley

---

[9] For the purpose of illustration we will forget any interest he earns or could earn on his capital, since this would only complicate the example without changing the principle involved.

[10] For proof that all Social Security taxes are nothing but "income" taxes, see *The Social Security Swindle — How Anyone Can Drop Out* by Irwin Schiff.

escapes taxes altogether? Under these circumstances, any society that taxes Hyman and not Dudley must be sick.

What Is a Kidney Worth?

Not too long ago someone advertised to sell a kidney for $10,000. This presented an interesting income tax question. Suppose the individual sold his kidney for $10,000, how would the IRS treat the sale? The IRS would claim that the $10,000 was taxable as "income." Would the IRS allow the seller a cost basis [11] for his kidney and if so, how would the cost basis be determined? The point is, would the sale of a kidney constitute "income" within the definition arrived at by the Supreme Court? Would there be any "gain" or "profit" to the seller in connection with the sale? If so, how much? Would *you* sell your kidney for $10,000? How about $100,000 or $1,000,000? Many people would claim that a kidney is priceless since if the remaining one were to become impaired one's very life could be in danger. Most people would consider a functioning kidney to be worth a whole lot more (though certainly at least as much) as the $10,000 paid for it in this example. Under these circumstances there could be no "gain" or "profit" from its sale. The sale of one's labor (energy, sweat, physical appearance, brain power, etc.), however, contains all the same elements and problems inherent in the sale of one's kidney. So if the sale of a kidney cannot produce "income, " neither can the sale of one's labor.

Because of all the nonsense regarding income taxes (as illustrated by these examples) it is important for us to analyze more fully why individuals cannot have "income" as defined by the courts. Since the courts have already ruled that income from real estate and personal property (i.e. rent, dividends, and interest) are direct taxes (equivalent to a direct tax on the "source" — the underlying property), and that direct taxes must be apportioned, such income cannot be taxed as "income" to individuals on any basis. For such income to be taxed it must be separated from its source(s) and this only occurs on corporate profit and loss statements where *all* expenses are deducted from *all* income to arrive at a profit (the excess of income over outgo). It is only this gain, this profit, this "income" that can be taxable under the 16th Amendment. The only way individuals can even begin to determine whether or not they have "income" is if they treat all their income and all their expenditures in a similar manner.

The Federal government has completely brainwashed American workers (and most professionals, too) convincing them that, for tax purposes, they are completely different from corporations and businesses in

---

[11]"Cost basis" is the accounting procedure for determining the cost of producing an item (materials, labor, marketing, etc.) in order to arrive at an amount that is not subject to tax.

general. The average American worker incurs significant expenses directly related to his ability to sell his labor, as well as significant indirect (but related) costs, all of which he is fraudulently told are "personal" expenditures and not deductible.

Mary Brown, Receptionist

Mary Brown is a receptionist for the *Sunshine Advertising Company*. If I were to ask Mary if she was in business for herself she would say, "No, I work for *Sunshine Advertising.*" *All* employees make the same mistake.

My response is usually, "Oh, you're not in business for yourself? Who are you in business for?"

This usually generates some surprise and repartee in which all employees finally say, "Yes, I guess I am in business for myself."

Every wage earner is in the business of earning money just as IBM, General Motors or any sole proprietorship is except that the mechanics of how it is done are different. The first thing all American workers must realize is that they are in business just like any corporation; the single difference is that they sell their product (their labor) to one buyer rather than to many.

Do you think *Sunshine Advertising* would allow Mary to come to work naked or in a bathrobe? No, she has to come to work dressed properly because, as a receptionist, she is *expected* to look neat and crisp. Not only does she have to be appropriately dressed, she has to look good, too. This means she has to spend money on makeup, hair dressers, dry cleaning and a variety of other things related to her appearance. In addition, she also has to get to work which means using cab, subway or bus, or the cost of operating a car — insurance, taxes, maintenance, a garage (if she lives in the city), and perhaps parking. It also means higher food costs because Mary simply does not have the time or energy to shop and prepare her own meals after putting in a full day's work. All these expenditures are directly related to Mary's job and her ability to sell her labor to *Sunshine Advertising* and these business-related expenses could easily come to $50.00 per week or 20 percent of her gross wages of $250.00 (and a far larger percentage of her *net*, after-tax wages), yet the IRS tells her that these expenditures are *not deductible* because they are "personal, " not business, expenditures.

Mary also has many other expenses that are business-related which, if not incurred, could prevent her from selling her labor. Since she cannot sell substandard or sick labor, she must be in good health. To be in good health she must eat properly, have a place to live, get regular medical and dental care, and pay utility bills, among other things. The IRS, however, also maintains (backed up by the "courts") that these expenditures are not deductible. If, however, we use the Supreme Court's definition of income, they most certainly are!

Under the "income" tax law "income" must be given the same meaning it was given in the Corporation Excise Act of 1909. What did that Act say was deductible from income (which it called gross income)? It said (see page 137) that a corporation could deduct "all the *ordinary* and *necessary* expenses actually *paid* within the year out of income in the maintanance and operation of its business and properties." For the purpose of figuring Mary's "income" she is the "business" and the "property" and should, therefore, be allowed to deduct all the "ordinary and necessary" expenses paid out "in the maintenance and operation" of her business which is the selling of her own labor. How can the law treat her any differently than it treats any other business? How can she have less rights than an artificial entity created by law? Since she is in business (just like any corporate entity) she has the right to deduct the same expenditures in order to keep her business (in this case herself) running. Regardless of what the government *now* says, if the IRS and/ or the courts claim differently they are *breaking the law.* And if they are breaking the law with respect to her "income" taxes, why should Mary (or anyone else for that matter) cooperate with them in any way?

The Supreme Court ruled that "income" is the equivalent of a corporate profit and "Congress (or the IRS) cannot by any definition it may adopt" change it. Does a corporation deduct *rent* when converting income to "income"? Certainly it does, and so can Mary. Is the paying of rent a "necessary" and "ordinary" expense of Mary's business? Of course. Could she sell her labor to *Sunshine Advertising* if she lived on a bench in the park? [12] Where would she shower, put on her makeup, fix her hair, and get dressed so she could come to work looking neat and crisp as is expected? Would she even have been hired if she had written on her job application that her address was "on a bench in the park"? Paying rent (thus establishing an address) is "necessary" to her busi-

---

[12]Recently Public Television aired a report on the homeless in Philadelphia in which one man (once the head of a Teamster's local) explained how he lived on the Philadelphia streets often sleeping in public shelters. He also told of his attempts to get a job and said, "You can't get hired in Philadelphia unless you have a permanent address." This proves that *a permanent address is a necessary business expense.*

[13]Actually she should deduct the $50.00 income received as dividends on the stock given to her by her grandfather because in the definition of "income" used in the Corporation Tax Act such income was to be deducted before arriving at taxable "income" (see page 137). Since that is still the official definition of "income," such dividends can still be deducted until the Supreme Court changes its definition. This also proves that the government's taxing of corporate dividends today — which have already been taxed to the corporation — has been illegal for all these years.

ness as is proper food and sleep and taking care of her health. In order
for Mary to have "income" from her business she, like any corporation,
should complete a profit and loss statement similar to the one in
Exhibit 4.

Mary's profit and loss statement shows that her income of $13,080
came from four sources [13] and does not reflect the recovery of any educational or technical training investment she might have made. [14] It
also does not take into account items such as vacations or gifts.

Mary's profit and loss statement shows a negative cash flow (after
taxes) which was covered by a $1,000 cash grant from her grandfather,
without whose help she could not even maintain herself even on this
modest scale. Also note that despite what government tax tables claim,
Mary's "gross income" of $13,000 does not put her in a 19 or even a 50
percent tax bracket, but in a 100 percent tax bracket!

I personally witnessed this outrageous situation a number of years
ago. My sister was then living in a New York suburb and worked in New
York City's garment center as a bookkeeper with some additional show-
room duties. This meant she had to pay the cost of commuting as well
as a variety of other business-related expenses since she was expected
to be well-dressed and professional looking in this highly competitive
environment. While her husband was alive there were two salaries to
share expenses and two people to share common chores. When he died
the full burden of maintaining herself fell on her shoulders. Between her
rent (which was modest), commuting, clothing, hairdressers, lunches,
and three income taxes (Federal, state, and city) she was left with less
than nothing from her wages. She complained that she had to withdraw
savings every month just to meet her ordinary living expenses even
though she lived very modestly! I could not help but be struck by the injustice of her plight. She was struggling and barely getting by and the
government was taxing her in order to provide subsidies and grants to
many who were *far wealthier than she*. She was being taxed to provide
"rent supplements" for others when paying her own rent had now become a burden. She was also being taxed (though she could hardly support herself) to provide "aid" for foreign governments and foreign
nationals through a variety of government programs and banking
commitments.

In any case, by definition, did she have a "gain" from her labor? No,
she had a *loss* which she had to make up each month with withdrawals

---

[14]Profit and loss statements made out by individuals must reflect returns of capital expended for college or vocational (barber, beautician, bartender, welder, etc.) training,
all of which the IRS now claims are not deductible and are not recoverable. Such expenses can, however, be capitalized and recovered under the *Supreme Court's definition of "income."*

from her savings account. Yet the income tax was created, we were told, *to tax the wealth of the rich!*

Is The Value Of Your Labor Really Worth Nothing?

If a business sells a chair for $250.00, must it report the entire $250.00 as "income"? No, it is allowed to deduct all the costs of getting and marketing the chair. If those costs came to $200.00 the business would deduct that amount and pay a tax on $50.00. But when Mary Brown sells her labor for $250.00 per week the government tells her that *all of it is "income"* and she is not entitled to any deductions that might reflect a "cost" or value for that labor. Essentially they tell her that her labor is worth *nothing,* though it is obviously worth at least $250.00 or her employer would not have given her that much for it. Why, then, can't Mary deduct the costs incurred in producing that labor just as other businesses deduct the costs incurred in producing the products/ services they sell?

Labor Includes Putting In Time

The value of labor is obviously worth something based on the time, talent, ability, and sweat that goes into it. Apart from the *obvious costs* the government says *are not* recoverable (such as education, transportation, rent, food, etc.) there is also the time, effort, and often sheer drudgery that must be put into it — time that could otherwise be spent in other pursuits or in relaxation and self-indulgence. What is the raw dollar value of eight hours spent in a coal mine as opposed to eight hours spent on a beach? A miner should be able to deduct that cost factor from the money he gets for being in a coal mine rather than not being on the beach. But the government says these costs, efforts, and time *have absolutely no dollar value* and cannot be recovered from the sale of labor by individuals while, at the same time, allowing business and industry to recover *all* their costs from the sale of their products and services. Such a claim by the government (besides making no economic sense), violates tax law as well as the equal protection clause of the Constitution.

The Final Insult — Capital Gains

As if the government's refusal to recognize the sweat, effort, and costs that go into producing labor value is not bad enough, look at how the government taxes gains on capital. As explained earlier, when Lester sold his property for $100,000 he had $50,000 of pure gain that he did absolutely nothing to produce. Yet on this $50,000 gain he would only have had to report and pay a tax on 40 percent or $20,000 of that gain. A single coal miner, however, earning $50,000 by the sweat of his brow would have had to pay approximately $16,000 in income taxes (including Social Security taxes) on $50,000 received from the sale of his labor. In addition, a $50,000 capital gain is obviously "a gain derived from capital" and certainly fulfills the legal definition of "income" far more than the wages received by a coal miner. Why, therefore, should anyone with a comparable $50,000 capital gain pay less in taxes than a coal miner earning $50,000 in wages?

In many cases, however, capital gains are illusions since these "gains" are calculated in dollars of ever-decreasing purchasing power. For example, if one purchased a home twenty-five years ago for $25,000 and sold it today for $50,000 the government would claim he had a $25,000 capital "gain." Such a claim, however, would be nonsense because $50,000 today is actually worth less in real purchasing power than $25,000 was twenty-five years ago. The homeowner would, in reality, suffer an economic loss but the IRS would say that he must pay taxes on his "gain."[15]

So, while an income tax was supposedly installed as a modest, almost "delicate" tax on the wealth of the rich, it ended up as a heavy tax on the labor of the wage earner. As for regressive taxation — there can be no more vicious example than one that places a tax on a worker's gross wages while taxing the *appreciation* of capital at far lower rates and taxing capital itself not at all.

---

[15]For a satirical account of this fraudulent phenomenon, see *The Kingdom of Moltz, About Inflation and Where it Comes From,* by Irwin Schiff (FREEDOM BOOKS, 1980).

EXHIBIT 4

Profit and Loss Statement of

Mary Brown
555 Maple Avenue
Smallville, New York 00001

INCOME:

Wages — @ $250.00 per week	$13,000.00
Interest on $239.00 in Savings Account — @ (6%)	14.00
Dividend on 10 Shares of Stock given to me by my grandfather — @ $5.00 per share	50.00
Winnings in office football pool (less losses)	16.00
TOTAL INCOME	$13,080.00

EXPENSES:

Rent — @ $250 per month	$ 3,000.00
Food — @ $50 per week	2,600.00
Utilities — @ 60 per month	720.00
Clothing	1,000.00
Medical & Dental	450.00
Cosmetics & Hair Dresser	350.00
Miscellaneous	500.00
Automobile:	
Upkeep, gas, oil, maintenance	520.00
Insurance — @ $15.00 per week	780.00
Depreciation	1,000.00
LESS TOTAL EXPENSES	$10,920.00
Profit ("Income") from Income	$ 2,160.00
Income taxes paid (including Social Security taxes)	2,200.00
NET LOSS	($ 40.00)

15

Income Tax "Laws" And How The IRS Disregards Them

"*Law*" (as it applies to income taxes) is in quotes because there really are no *laws* in connection with income taxes. Laws are *mandatory* and have penalties attached to them for non-compliance. Income taxes, however, are based on voluntary — *not mandatory* — compliance so there can be no legal penalties for non-compliance. The only law that can apply to income taxes relates to employers that *elect* to withhold taxes from their employees. They are not *required* to do so, though the IRS says they are. It is legally mandatory that they account for that money to the Federal government. Apart from this there is nothing in the Internal Revenue Code (with respect to income taxes) that *requires* anyone or any corporation to:

1. file tax returns;
2. pay such taxes or have them withheld from wages, commissions, dividends or interest;
3. file or pay estimated taxes;
4. submit to IRS audits or turn over books and/or records in connection with an IRS summons;
5. report to the IRS wages, dividends, or commissions paid;
6. provide the IRS with any records or information with respect to income taxes for either yourself, your employees, or anyone you do business with; and
7. surrender property solely on the strength of IRS liens or levy notices.

In other words, there is simply *nothing* in the Internal Revenue Code or Federal law that *requires* anyone or any corporation to do *anything at all* with respect to Federal income taxes. If this is so, how can the Federal government confiscate billions in taxes, throw people in jail for not filing, and intimidate 98 million Americans into believing that they are required to file income tax returns and pay federal income taxes when such is not the case? Americans must face the disquieting fact that we have *largely criminals* — not judges — *presiding over Federal courts*. The criminal culpability of the Federal judiciary is patently obvious and is the main reason the government has managed to intimidate the public into filing and paying income taxes.

There are two other factors that explain how the "income" tax hoax was successfully carried out for so long:

1. the general incompetence and mendacious nature of the American legal profession; and
2. the Pravda-like mentality of much of the American press when confronted with the IRS's illegal activities.

Income Tax Laws Would Be Unconstitutional If Mandatory

The reason the income tax "law" is voluntary is simple — if it were not it would be unconstitutional. The government contends that those of us who oppose the tax claim it is unconstitutional. This is nonsense. We maintain (and the government admits) that the tax is voluntary and anything inherently voluntary cannot be unconstitutional. The tax, however, is *enforced* unconstitutionally. The IRS claims that the income tax was upheld as being constitutional. This is true, but neither the IRS nor the "courts" enforce the tax in the manner that it was upheld or in the manner the "law" is written — and this is the crux of the problem.

The income tax was held to be an excise tax but the government does not impose it as such (see pages 203, 204). If the government does not impose the income tax as an indirect, excise tax, and if the government does not apportion it as a direct tax, then the tax does not fall into either of the taxing clauses of the Constitution. And if the income tax does not fall into either of the taxing clauses of the Constitution, it cannot be mandatory and nothing in connection with it can be mandatory: not filing, not withholding, not paying, not the supplying of records, and not the confiscation of property. In addition, all such IRS activities violate a number of *other* constitutional rights. [1]

By law, all the information on a tax return can be turned over to the Department of Justice, numerous other Federal and state agencies, and foreign governments. All of these government agencies are free to use the information against the taxpayer in any way they choose, including criminal prosecution. Any "law" that compels individuals to

---

[1] The mere requirement to file income tax returns, as we have seen, violates the Fourth, Fifth, Ninth and Thirteenth Amendments *at the very least*.

turn over such information to the government is repugnant to the Fifth Amendment and, therefore, is unconstitutional on this ground alone. This is why there can be no provision in the "law" that requires the filing of income tax returns. Anyone who files such returns does so (whether he knows it or not) voluntarily, which is why they can be used against him. In all income tax evasion trials, the defendant's tax return is introduced and used against him. Since the Fifth Amendment bars the use of *compelled* testimony against individuals in criminal trials, if tax returns were required (i.e. compelled) the information contained in them could not be used against alleged tax evaders and income tax "evasion" could never be prosecuted. In addition, verification of individual tax returns requires that taxpayers produce their personal books and records (or forfeit claimed deductions) so any such "requirement" also violates the Fourth Amendment.

Tax Returns Violate Right to Privacy

The requirement to submit *all* the *personal* and *financial* data requested on a tax return also violates an individual's right to privacy "retained" under the Ninth Amendment. The Nixon Administration's use of such information *and* IRS audits against those on its "enemies list" was widely reported. Senator Eagleton, for example, was forced to drop out of the vice-presidential race because of publicized disclosures that he had undergone psychiatric treatment. The Nixon people lifted this information from his tax returns (where the treatments were listed to get medical deductions) and leaked it to the media — obviously political blackmail. In addition, being required to keep records (giving the government all sorts of tax information) or being forced to collect taxes (such as employee withholding) without compensation, all violate the 13th Amendment which abolished *involuntary servitude* along with slavery.

The point is that a compulsory income tax encompassing all of its myriad procedures not only violates the taxing clauses of the Constitution but a number of other constitutional clauses as well. Some of these issues were raised in connection with the *Stone Tracy* decision (see page 147) and were resolved in favor of the government. But that case involved corporations, entities which do not have certain 5th Amendment rights. In addition, corporations keep records anyway since (legally) they have to report to stockholders and these reports are a matter of public record. But individuals do not have to report to anybody nor do they have to keep records and they cannot be compelled, by law, to keep records solely to accommodate the government. [2]

[2]Manufacturers of products subject to excise taxes can be required to keep records and perform certain acts with respect to their products, but that is a far cry from requiring private citizens to keep all kinds of records and to produce them for government inspection.

Voluntary Compliance

In the first chapter of *How Anyone Can Stop Paying Income Taxes* ("Surprise: The Income Tax Is Voluntary") I provided numerous excerpts from government documents that attested to the voluntary nature of the income tax. For example, the Appendix of *How Anyone. . .* contains the entire introductory statement (over the signature of IRS Commissioner, Jerome Kurtz) that appeared in the 1979 *Annual Report of the Commissioner of Internal Revenue* wherein he said no less than *six times* that complying with income tax "laws" is "voluntary." Kurtz said,

> To put these figures in context, [comparing statistics on non-filers] in the same year individuals *voluntarily* reported nearly $1.1 trillion in income tax and paid a total of $142 billion in income taxes.

Why would Kurtz say that individuals *voluntarily* file tax returns if they are *required* to do so?

But other IRS Commissioners have admitted the same thing. For example, in the 1975 *IRS Audit Manual* Commissioner Mortimer Caplan said, "Our tax system is based on individual self-assessment and voluntary compliance." Even the Supreme Court has admitted that the payment of income taxes is voluntary:

> Our tax system [income] is based upon voluntary assessment and payment, not upon distraint [force]. [3]

The Mission of the Internal Revenue Service

The *Federal Register* defined the mission of the IRS as follows:

> The mission of the Service is to encourage and achieve the highest possible degree of *voluntary* compliance. . . [4]

Once individuals discover that the income tax system is indeed voluntary, the IRS tries to confuse them regarding the meaning of "voluntary compliance." The IRS claims that because it does not have the personnel to make everyone file that — only in this sense — income taxes are *voluntary*. But it is the way the law is written that compels compliance and not the supervisory ability of IRS personnel. "Voluntary compliance" pertains to *everything* connected with income taxes *including* the *paying* of the tax, the *furnishing* of records, and even wage

---

[3]*Flora vs U.S.* 362 US 145, page 176.
[4] Volume 39, No. 62, Friday, March 29, 1974.

withholding. If the filing, paying and reporting of income taxes were *mandatory* why would the government say that anything to do with it is "voluntary?"

Voluntary vs Mandatory Price Controls

Under the Nixon Administration price controls were initially voluntary. When prices continued to rise, however, controls were (unconstitutionally) declared mandatory. The difference between voluntary and mandatory price controls is not very complicated. When controls are made mandatory it does not mean that swarms of government agents suddenly descend like locusts on all businesses, making sure their current posted prices do not exceed their prior posted prices. It only means that penalties for violating the controls are now included in the law. When they are based on "voluntary compliance" no penlaties are provided by law. The same is true for the income tax — nowhere in the Internal Revenue Code are there any penalties for not filing income tax returns, nor are there any requirements or penalties with respect to any aspect of the income tax "law" because compliance is "voluntary."

Distinctions between voluntary and compulsory compliance can be found in other government pamphlets, too. A four page booklet containing information for aliens [5] states:

> 7. *US Federal Tax Information.* Because the American tax system is based on *voluntary compliance* and self assessment, each year taxpayers make their own determination of their tax liability and file returns reporting the correct tax. (Emphasis added)

In this pamphlet aliens are also informed:

> 2. *Notification of your Address.* You must report your address to the Immigration and Naturalization Service. . . no later than ten days after the change on Form AR-11.

They are not similiarly informed, however, that such reporting is based on "voluntary compliance" because it is not.

IRS Regulations Also Admit Income Tax "Laws" Are Voluntary

Additional proof of the voluntary nature of income taxes can be found in the IRS's own regulations. For example, under Section 601.601 dealing with "Objectives and Standards for Publication" we find this admission:

[5]*WELCOME to the United States of America,* Form 1-357 Re. 7-19-80, the United States Department of Justice, Immigration and Naturalization Service.

The purpose of publishing revenue rulings and revenue procedures in the Internal Revenue Bulletin is to promote correct and uniform applications of the tax laws by the Internal Revenue Service employees and to assist taxpayers in attaining maximum *voluntary compliance. . .* (Emphasis added)

Section 601.602 dealing with "Tax Forms and Instructions" states:

The tax system is based on voluntary compliance, and the taxpayers complete and return forms with payment of the tax *owed.* (Emphasis added)

And on July 8, 1981 a report [6] issued by the Controller General of the United States claimed that illegal tax protesters threaten our tax system because

. . . they represent a threat to our nation's *voluntary* tax system. (Emphasis added)

How many official government documents does it take to convince the public that the Federal income tax is, *by law*, voluntary?

Making "Voluntary Compliance" Compulsory

The primary technique used by the government to illegally compel compliance to "income tax laws" is the use of enforcement provisions of the Internal Revenue Code that *do not apply to income taxes at all* but, rather, that relate to other taxes that are compulsory such as liquor and tobacco. In short, the Federal government seizes and confiscates property, throws people in jail, and destroys lives because of income taxes when there is absolutely nothing in the law that allows them to do it. The government has been able to get away with such outrageous behavior because of a totally corrupt or incompetent Federal judiciary, a KGB-like Department of Justice, and a Congress that goes along.

Criminal Conduct Of The IRS

The April 12th, 1981 issue of *Parade Magazine* (a Sunday newspaper supplement) carried a feature story detailing various criminal actions of the IRS which the public was led to believe were legal. Entitled "Fear The IRS, " it described an armed raid on the home of Dwight Snyder and began (on the cover)

[6]*Illegal Tax Protesters Threaten Tax System,* GGD-81-83.

**A HEAVILY ARMED FORCE FROM THE IRS VISITED CABI-
NETMAKER DWIGHT SNYDER AND HIS FAMILY. THEY TOOK
HIS VEHICLES, HIS MACHINERY, HIS TOOLS — EVERYTHING
DOWN TO SOAP DISHES & TOOTHBRUSHES. . .**

According to the article, the IRS admitted that at least "two dozen" men
participated in the raid while Snyder claimed there were at least forty.
In any case, the raiding party included

> U.S. marshalls, state patrolmen, IRS revenue officers and IRS special
> agents — some brandishing M-16 automatic rifles, shotguns and
> sidearms. . . [and] all of his vehicles, his machinery, tools and stock were
> seized-from a pickup truck and tractor down to towel holders, soap dishes,
> sink strainers, toothbrush holders and a half-empty box of staples.

Another incident described in the article took place in Fairbanks,
Alaska and involved an IRS seizure of an automobile belonging to Stephen and Mona Oliver. The IRS claimed that the Oliver's owed the government $4,700 and had, accordingly, filed a levy against Mr. Oliver's
wages. The Olivers disagreed with the assessment and tried to get a
court hearing whereupon the IRS

> decided to teach them a lesson by grabbing their 1970 Volkswagen while
> it was parked in downtown Fairbanks. The Olivers, however, locked them-
> selves in the car and refused to hand over the keys, whereupon IRS agents
> smashed the windows, dragged Mona Oliver out of the car and across a
> sidewalk littered with broken glass and towed their car away — in full
> view of astonished bystanders and a local newspaper photographer.

The story of Dr. Eugene Brasseur was also reported. He was an op-
thalmologist and father of six from Richland, Washington, who also ran
an optical shop and laboratory. According to the article "a tough economy" caused Brasseur to hold off paying withholding taxes on his thirteen employees. Legally he may have been wrong, but under the
circumstances the article pointed out, "Dr. Brasseur felt that his position was morally defensible. The IRS did not."

The IRS refused to allow the doctor to pay his $11,000 debt in in-
stallments and proceeded to clean out his bank account. As a result, his
ability to get credit vanished and he was forced to close his optical business and fire his employees. The IRS then hit him with an additional
$15,000 lien for back personal taxes (including interest and penalties)
and seized his car. The article said that agents

> broke into this opthalmology offices, changed the lock, padlocked the doors
> and put up warning signs ordering him and his patients to stay out.

According to the Doctor,

> I had patients who needed help, but the IRS wouldn't let me back into the office for three months. My practice was dead in two weeks. I had no way of seeing patients and no way to make a living. And no way to pay the IRS.

Further, to satisfy his IRS lien he made a crash sale of his house and, as a result, only realized $20,000. After paying off state taxes and attorneys he was left with nothing. So, the article continued, with

> no home, no money (and with his credit and reputation ruined) and no immediate way to make a living, the Brasseurs farmed out their children with families from their church and moved in temporarily with friends.

All these actions were *totally* illegal and the IRS agents involved could and should have been arrested on the spot. Not only did they violate the Internal Revenue Code itself, they also violated Sections 241 and 242 of the U.S. Criminal Code (Exhibit 11, page 294) as well as the instructions contained in their own *Legal Reference Guide for Revenue Officers*. IRS goons such as these routinely and illegally confiscate property and terrorize private citizens all across the country because they know the courts and the Department of Justice will back them up.

Proof That All The IRS Seizures Described Were Illegal

IRC Section 7608 (Exhibit 5) is entitled "Authority of internal revenue enforcement officers." The first paragraph of that section relates to the enforcement "provisions of subtitle E" and says that the authority of revenue officers to "carry firearms" is specifically limited to the collection of taxes covered in that subtitle. The taxes covered in Subtitle E are "Alcohol, Tobacco, and Certain other excises." The subtitle deals with these and other excise taxes related to machine guns and certain other firearms. Income taxes fall into Subtitle A of the Code and IRS agents are *not permitted* to carry firearms to collect Subtitle A taxes. Therefore, if any IRS revenue officers in the Snyder raiding party mentioned above carried guns to enforce the payment of income taxes, such enforcement was *not authorized by law.* Anyone in that raiding party who took Snyder's possessions at gun point could and should have been arrested and prosecuted for violating both state and Federal law. But since the government knows that revenue agents are not authorized to carry guns in connection with the collection of income taxes (while private individuals can carry guns to protect themselves against unlawful seizures of their property), the IRS (for its own protection) tries to con local law enforcement people into accompanying them on these illegal siezures, which makes it appear that such seizures are really lawful.

EXHIBIT 5

Sec. 7608. Authority of internal revenue enforcement officers.

(a) Enforcement of subtitle E and other laws pertaining to liquor, tobacco, and firearms.

Any investigator, agent, or other internal revenue officer by whatever term designated, whom the Secretary charges with the duty of enforcing any of the criminal, seizure, or forfeiture provisions of subtitle E or of any other law of the United States pertaining to the commodities subject to tax under such subtitle for the enforcement of which the Secretary is responsible may—

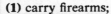 **(1)** carry firearms;

(2) execute and serve search warrants and arrest warrants, and serve subpoenas and summonses issued under authority of the United States;

(3) in respect to the performance of such duty, make arrests without warrant for any offense against the United States committed in his presence, or for any felony cognizable under the laws of the United States if he has reasonable grounds to believe that the person to be arrested has committed, or is committing, such felony; and

(4) in respect to the performance of such duty, make seizures of property subject to forfeiture to the United States.

(b) Enforcement of laws relating to internal revenue other than subtitle E.

(1) Any criminal investigator of the Intelligence Division or of the Internal Security Division of the Internal Revenue Service whom the Secretary charges with the duty of enforcing any of the criminal provisions of the internal revenue laws or any other criminal provisions of law relating to internal revenue for the enforcement of which the Secretary is responsible is, in the performance of his duties, authorized to perform the functions described in paragraph (2).

*Note: Income taxes do not fall into Subtitle E but into Subtitle A, so the use of firearms is not authorized for the collection of income taxes.

The IRS's *Legal Reference Guide For Revenue Officers* (MT 58 [10][0]-14) says:

332 *(10-29-79)*   58(10)0
Constitutional Limitations

(1) During the course of administratively collecting a tax, an occasion may arise where service of a levy or notice of levy is not adequate to seize property of the taxpayer. However, it cannot be emphasized too strongly that constitutional guarantees and individual rights must not be violated. Property should not be forceably removed from the person of a taxpayer. Such conduct may expose a revenue officer to an action in trespass, assault and battery, conversion, etc. *Larson v. Domestic and Foreign Commerce Corp.,* 337 U.S. 682 (1949), *rehearing denied,* 337 U.S. 682 (1949). *Maule Industries v. Tomlinson,* 224 F. 2d 897, (5th Cir. 1949). If there is reason to suspect a failure to honor a notice of levy or an interference with a levy, the matter should be referred for proper legal action against the offending party. Remedies available to the Government, as contained in the Code and other statutes, are more than adequate to cope with the problem.

(2) The Supreme Court in *G.M. Leasing Corp. v. United States*, 429 U.S. 336 (1977) held that warrantless entries into the private premises of a person by the Internal Revenue Service for the purpose of seizing property to satisfy a tax liability is a violation of that person's reasonable expectation of privacy under the Fourth Amendment to the Constitution. Before levies or seizures of property located on private premises are made, permission of the occupant of the premises on which the seizure is to take place must be obtained. If the occupant refuses to permit the entry, the matter should be referred to District Counsel so that a court order authorizing the entry may be obtained.

334.2 *(10-29-79)*   58(10)0
Final Demand

Where a notice of levy is served upon a third party and there is no response within ten days, it is followed by service of a Final Demand (Form 668-C). IRC 6332(a) states that except as otherwise provided in subsection (b), (which contains a special rule for life insurance and endownment contracts) a person in possession of property or rights to property upon which levy has been made shall, upon demand, surrender such property. The demand is contained in the Notice of Levy (Form 668-A). A Notice of Final Demand (Form 668-C) is not required to be served under the Code, although use of the form as an administrative tool is generally uniform. In the event the Final Demand is not responded to, a suit will ordinarily be required to reach the property. ◄——— ❗

334.3*(10-29-79)*   58(10)0
Seizure

(2) As previously indicated, force should not be used in seizing property of a taxpayer. The same reasoning applies where property has been levied upon and seized and, at some later date, it is sought to remove the levied property to another location or to sell such property. Local or other law enforcement authorities may be contacted to assist the revenue officer in performing his/her duties. Also, resort can be had to the courts to restrain the taxpayer or third party from interfering with such removal or sale. (Emphasis added)

(Emphasis added)

Under Sections 332 and 334.3 revenue officers are *specifically* instructed that "force should not be used in seizing property of a taxpayer [and that] such conduct may expose a revenue officer to an action in trespass, assault and battery, conversion, etc." Did the revenue officers in Mona Oliver's case have her "permission" to smash "the [car] windows [and drag her] out of the car and across a sidewalk littered with broken glass" as provided for in Section 332 of their own *Legal Reference Guide.* . . ?

It also states that before seizures of property located on "private premises are made, permission of the occupant. . . must be obtained." And "If the occupant refuses to permit entry" a court order has to be obtained. Snyder's raiding party did not have his permission to burst into his home and confiscate all of his goods. Neither did it have a court order. But the raiding party got away with these unlawful acts because the criminals who preside over our Federal courts permit, and even encourage, this sort of illegal behavior.

In another case the government prosecuted and convicted an individual of willfully resisting, opposing, impeding, and interfering with Federal officers in the exercise of their official duties when he placed himself in a doorway and refused to allow IRS revenue officers to enter his property and confiscate assets for non-payment of quarterly corporate taxes. Apparently a scuffle took place as this private citizen sought to protect his property from a threatened illegal seizure by IRS storm troopers [7] who sought to confiscate it without a court order — in payment of a tax for which no liability could exist and for which no forcible seizure is provided for by law. These agents used procedures that violated their own legal reference manual (as well as other laws as previously mentioned) and, therefore, were acting like common criminals. Yet the private citizen — who was legally within his rights — was prosecuted instead of the revenue "officers."

Another example of Gestapo-type justice in America involved an individual who was prosecuted because he appeared in his doorway "in either his pajamas or underwear" with a double-barrelled shotgun as Internal Revenue agents were backing his truck out of his driveway. The agents had no court order, were trespassing on private property, and were actually in the process of *stealing his truck!* Yet there is no law that could have authorized the forcible seizure of his truck by the IRS in payment of taxes [8] but the individual was prosecuted for protecting his property from this illegal government seizure.

These kinds of prosecutions are part of another technique used by the government to intimidate and fool the public — calling IRS agents revenue "officers." The public is led to believe that such "officers" are comparable to police "officers, " FBI agents, or Secret Service personnel.

With respect to income taxes they are no more "officers" than you or I are. These "officers" have no official, lawful duties other than to request that individuals *voluntarily* pay whatever it is the government claims is owed. Once they are told to "get lost" they have no further "lawful duties." IRS revenue "officers, " however, are encouraged to break the law and exceed their "lawful duties" by engaging in a type of extortion in order to *compel* "voluntary compliance." When their intended victims legally resist (even in a modest manner) the Federal Mafia sees to it that these innocent citizens are prosecuted for "interfering with the duties of an IRS revenue officer." At their trials these victims do not understand that they could not have interfered with the agent's "duties" since agents do not have any lawful "duties" so they never put up a proper defense and have, invariably, been convicted. The

---

[7]*U.S. vs Johnson C.A.N.J.* 462 F2nd 423 (1972), certiary denied 410 US 937.
[8]*U.S. vs Rybicki C. A. Mich.* 403 F2nd 599 (1968).

presiding "judge" cooperates with the prosecuting attorney to erroneously convey to the jury that revenue "officers" are comparable to FBI agents or Secret Service officers who, in reality, do have lawful "duties" that can be interfered with.

IRS "Notices of Levy" — A Total Fraud

Section 334.2 of the *Legal Reference Guide for Revenue Officers* (see page 248) states that if a Notice of Levy and a Final Demand are not responded to, a suit (court order) will be "required to reach the property." In addition, the law itself (Section 6331) provides that such Notices of Levy can only apply to the *accrued salaries of Federal employees* yet the government uses these notices to extort billions of dollars from private citizens. [9] Lawyers for banks, insurance companies and businesses in general routinely turn over money to the IRS that belongs to private citizens solely on the basis of these "notices" and "demands." Any business that turns over a taxpayer's money to the IRS without a court order (on the basis of these "notices" and/or "demands") should be sued and disbarment proceedings would be instituted against their attorneys.

Confusing The Public

The *Legal Reference Guide*. . . also tells revenue "officers" to seek the help of "local or other law enforcement authorities." They are told to do this because when an IRS revenue "officer" shows up with a local policeman the taxpayer (and the media) are conned into thinking that their actions are *legal*. In reality, it is the law enforcement officer's authority, presence, and power that intimidates and he is the one who does the seizing, not the revenue "officer" who has no legal power or authority to forcibly seize property on his own.

The local police do not realize they are being used to protect the criminal acts of the IRS revenue "officer" since taxpayers would be perfectly within their rights to use whatever force necessary to prevent IRS revenue "officers" from taking their property (in payment of "income" taxes) by force as is verified by the *Legal Reference Guide*. . . of the IRS itself.

All three paragraphs admit that if taxpayers or third parties disregard and/or resist IRS seizure attempts the IRS has to go to court. The Olivers resisted but the IRS did not take them to court (which is where the Olivers wanted to go) — because the IRS never takes anyone

---

[9] A detailed account of how the government specifically uses this section to illegally sieze property (including bank accounts) and how you can protect yourself is contained in *The Schiff Report,* Volume 2, Numbers 4 and 6.

to court to enforce the collection of income taxes since they know they would lose even in our corrupt courts if they ever initiated such legal procedures (see pages 303, 304).

When that agent "dragged Mona Oliver out of her car and across a sidewalk littered with broken glass, " she would have been within her rights if she had scratched out the agent's eyes or kicked him in the groin. Her husband would have been within his rights to do anything he would have done to any common thug whom he saw dragging his wife out of their car and across a sidewalk.

Dr. Brasseur would also have been within his rights if he used whatever force necessary to throw IRS trespassers out of his office. In addition, when they padlocked his door he should have cut the chaiin, removed the padlock and gone back in. Any "warning" signs that IRS agents put up should have been torn down.

Intimidating and Misleading The Public

The *Parade* article began by stating:

> The Tax Man. He doesn't wear a uniform, but the has more authority than a policeman. He would never be addressed as "Your Honor, " but he can exercise more control over your life than a judge. In pursuit of his goals, he can pester you, your family, your friends and business associates, pry into your private affairs and harass you in a dozen different ways — all of them legal. [10]

It further stated:

> He can empty your bank account, tow away your car, seize your home and some of the things in it, sell them and keep the money.
>
> He can take all the equipment, furniture, machinery, tools and stock from your place of business. He can scoop the last cent from your cash register, padlock your doors and throw your employees onto the street.
>
> Under his Orwellian system, you are presumed guilty until you can prove your innocence. He can lien, levy, summons and seize your money, property and assets — all without the due process of law guaranteed even to common criminals under the U.S. Constitution.

While *Parade Magazine* was trying to provide a public service by accurately and dramatically depicting the Gestapo-like actions of the IRS (as opposed to many publications that fear IRS retribution and shy away from such exposés), it actually played right into the IRS's hands.

---

[10]*This is not true at all. All of the mentioned actions are, by law, illegal.*

Though the IRS has no real power when it comes to enforcing the payment of income taxes, the article helped create the illusion that it has.
Parade readers could not be expected to know that all of the reported
behavior was illegal and should have resulted in the arrest of the IRS
agents. Even the article's title, "Fear the IRS," is one more weapon in
the IRS's arsenal that helps enforce "voluntary compliance."

The *reason* the reporter believed that the IRS could legally do
everything he described is because Federal judges *allow* the IRS to
break the law and the reporter *assumed* that if these actions were sanc-
tioned by the courts, they had to be legal. Unfortunately, the public gets
precisely the same impression. This is what enables the courts and the
IRS to intimidate and terrorize the country into believing that our voluntary system is *mandatory*! Readers of that article could never realize
that anyone who catches an IRS agent forcibly seizing his property
(in connection with income taxes) could legally tie the culprit to a tree
and call the police to have him arrested for attempted theft and trespassing; or that the public can *legally* throw all IRS requests, letters,
summonses, and notices of levy into the nearest trash can.

The Internal Revenue Code — A Masterpiece Of Deception

Before turning to specific Code sections that reveal why (under the
law) all the acts described in the *Parade* article were illegal, let us look
at the Code itself. Those who wrote it knew that any Code provision that
mandated (with respect to income taxes) filing, paying, producing records, confiscating property without court orders, etc. would render the
Code unconstitutional. Therefore, the Code was cleverly written so it
would not contain *any compulsory provisions* regarding income taxes
and the "law" could not be held unconstitutional on these grounds. The
Code was slyly and deliberately written to make it *appear* that those
sections that applied to income taxes were *mandatory* when in fact *they
were not.*

One technique used by the government was the use of "shall" to imply "required." Legally speaking, the word "required" is mandatory
while the word "shall" can also mean "may." So when the Code says
something (in connection with income taxes) "shall be" done, legally it
means "may be done" but the public does not understand this. [11]

In *How Anyone Can Stop Paying Income Taxes* I wrote the following
about this aspect of the Code:

[11]For an in-depth analysis of this legal principle (including Code sections and excerpts
from court opinions), *see How Anyone Can Stop Paying Income Taxes,* Chapter 3: "The
Internal Revenue Code — A Masterpiece of Deception."

The Internal Revenue Code is a thorough fraud. It was deliberately written to mislead the American public concerning federal income taxes. To do this, hundreds of sections had to be written and pieced together in such a way that, while no section technically misstates the law, the sections do, *individually* and *collectively,* convey a meaning that is not actually contained in the law itself.

To repeat:

1. No "liability" for income tax nor any requirement that such taxes be paid appears anywhere in the Code.
2. No authority is contained in the Code that allows the government to assess income taxes against those who refuse to do so on their own.
3. No civil or criminal penalties are provided in the Code for not filing or paying income taxes.

The Internal Revenue Code itself provides proof that the payment of income taxes is voluntary and that all IRS enforcement procedures are illegal because it does not contain any provision for a "liability" with respect to "income" taxes nor does it provide that such a tax is "required" to be paid or "shall" be paid. [12]

Where Tax Liabilities Occur

Three sections of the Code that refer to a Federal tax "liability" are 5703, 5005, and 4401 (see Exhibit 6) which deal with tobacco products, distilled spirits, and wagering respectively. Section 4401, for example, states that a tax is "imposed on any wager, " while Section 4401(c) contains the statement (in connection with such wagering taxes) that

Each person who is engaged in the business of accepting wagers shall be liable for and shall pay the tax under this subchapter. . .

The Code, however, contains no comparable entry dealing with a liability for "income" taxes, i.e., "Individuals or corporations having income shall be liable for the taxes imposed by Section 1."

True, Section 1 of the Internal Revenue Code "imposes" a tax on "taxable income" [13] but it does not make anyone "liable" for the tax so "imposed." In the sections cited previously certain persons are made "liable" for the taxes "imposed." So even though taxes on income are "im-

[12]The Code does, however, use such language in connection with a variety of other Federal taxes!

[13]But the Code does not define "taxable income" so how can it "impose" a tax on it?

EXHIBIT 6

Sec. 4401. Imposition of tax.

(a) Wagers.

(c) Persons liable for tax.

Each person who is engaged in the business of accepting wagers <u>shall be liable for and shall pay the tax</u> under this subchapter on all wagers placed with him. Each person who conducts any wagering pool or lottery <u>shall be liable for and shall pay the tax under this subchapter</u> on all wagers placed in such pool or lottery. Any person required to register under section 4412 who receives wagers for or on behalf of another person without having registered under section 4412 the name and place of residence of such other person <u>shall be liable for and shall pay the tax under this subchapter</u> on all such wagers received by him.

Sec. 5005. Persons liable for tax.

(a) General.

The distiller or importer of distilled spirits <u>shall be liable for the taxes imposed</u> thereon by section 5001(a)(1).

Sec. 5703. Liability for tax and method of payment.

(a) Liability for tax.

(1) Original liability. The manufacturer or importer of tobacco products and cigarette papers and tubes <u>shall be liable for the taxes imposed thereon by section 5701</u>.

(2) Transfer of liability. When tobacco products and cigarette papers and tubes are transferred, without payment of tax, pursuant to section 5704, <u>the liability for tax shall be transferred</u> in accordance with the provisions of this paragraph. When tobacco products and cigarette papers and tubes are transferred between the bonded premises of manufacturers and export warehouse proprietors, the transferee shall <u>become liable</u> for the tax upon receipt by him of such articles, and the transferor shall thereupon be relieved of his <u>liability</u> for such tax. When tobacco products and cigarette papers and tubes are released in bond from customs custody for transfer to the bonded premises of a manufacturer of tobacco products or cigarette papers and tubes, the transferee shall <u>become liable</u> for the tax on such articles upon release from customs custody, and the importer shall thereupon be relieved of his liability for such tax. All provisions of this chapter applicable to tobacco products and cigarette papers and tubes in bond shall be applicable to such articles returned to bond upon withdrawal from the market or returned to bond after previous removal for a tax-exempt purpose.

posed" they cannot apply to any individual since no one is "made liable" for the tax nor does it state that anyone is "required" (or "shall") pay them.

The fact that the Code does not contain any provision establishing an income tax *liability* is proof that everything the IRS does to compel the payment of income taxes is *illegal.*

Though All Federal Taxes Must Be Assessed, The IRS Cannot Assess Income Taxes.

All Federal taxes must be assessed before they can be owed and the current Internal Revenue Code does provide for such assessments [14] except that the Federal government was given *no independent authority to assess "income" taxes.* The Code sections that deal with the assessment and payment of Federal taxes are Sections 6201, 6203, and 6303 (Exhibit 7). Code Section 6201 gives the Secretary of the Treasury the authority to assess "all taxes. . which have not been duly paid by stamp at the time and in the manner provided by law." On his own the Secretary can assess taxes such as alcohol, tobacco, and other taxes that are paid by stamp. Subparagraph (1), however, places limitations on his assessment authority and provides that in cases *other than taxes paid by stamp,* the Secretary is only authorized to assess taxes "as to which *returns or lists are made* under this title." So if a "return" (a 1040 form) is not filed or if a "list" of "income" and expenses is not voluntarily supplied pursuant to Section 6014, the Secretary has *no authority to assess the tax!* [15]

This is what "self-assessment" is all about. The reason for self-assessment is obvious: since an "income" tax does not fall into either of the two classes of taxes provided for in the Constitution the government cannot legally assess such an illegal tax; therefore, individuals have to be conned into assessing themselves because the government has no constitutional authority to do so. And suppose an individual or corporation refuses to assess itself? In that case the government has no statutory authority to assess any "income" tax and, *by law,* no "income" tax can possibly be due. [16]

---

[14]"Once the [income] tax is assessed the taxpayer will owe the sovereign the amount. . . *"Bull vs U.S.* 295 US 247 (see Exhibit 10).

[15]Section 6014 provides that taxpayers can send in a list of their income and expenses and ask the Secretary to determine the tax due.

[16]Legally it would not be "due" even if one *did assess himself,* but that involves other legal considerations.

EXHIBIT 7

Sec. 6201.   Assessment authority.

(a) Authority of Secretary.

The Secretary is authorized and required to make the inquiries, determinations, and assessments of all taxes (including interest, additional amounts, additions to the tax, and assessable penalties) imposed by this title, or accruing under any former internal revenue law, which have not been duly paid by stamp at the time and in the manner provided by law. Such authority shall extend to and include the following:

(1) Taxes shown on return. The Secretary shall assess all taxes determined by the taxpayer or by the Secretary as to which returns or lists are made under this title.

(2) Unpaid taxes payable by stamp.

(A) Omitted stamps. Whenever any article upon which a tax is required to be paid by means of a stamp is sold or removed for sale or use by the manufacturer thereof or whenever any transaction or act upon which a tax is required to be paid by means of a stamp occurs without the use of the proper stamp, it shall be the duty of the Secretary, upon such information as he can obtain, to estimate the amount of tax which has been omitted to be paid and to make assessment therefor upon the person or persons the Secretary determines to be liable for such tax.

Sec. 6203.   Method of assessment.

The assessment shall be made by recording the liability of the taxpayer in the office of the Secretary in accordance with rules or regulations prescribed by the Secretary. Upon request of the taxpayer, the Secretary shall furnish the taxpayer a copy of the record of the assessment.

Sec. 6303.   Notice and demand for tax.

(a) General rule.

Where it is not otherwise provided by this title, the Secretary shall, as soon as practicable, and within 60 days, after the making of an assessment of a tax pursuant to section 6203, give notice to each person liable for the unpaid tax, stating the amount and demanding payment thereof. Such notice shall be left at the dwelling or usual place of business of such person, or shall be sent by mail to such person's last known address.

Further corroboration can be found in Section 6201(a)(2) (Exhibit 7) wherein the Secretary is specifically authorized to *"estimate* the amount of [any] tax which has been omitted to be paid." This only applies to taxes "required to be paid by means of a stamp, " however. Since income taxes are not paid by *stamp*, the Secretary is not permitted to "estimate" such taxes and nowhere in Chapter 63 of the Code (the Chapter dealing with assessments) is the Secretary or the IRS authorized to "estimate" any "income" taxes **when a return or list is not submitted.**

The law does make provisions for taxpayers who submit returns or lists on their own (and *swear* they owe the tax or had "income"). The Secretary is then authorized to assess the taxes "determined by the taxpayer" (as shown on his return) or "determined" by the Secretary on the basis of the "list" the taxpayer voluntarily provides. The whole purpose of the IRS is to deceive the public into providing it with sworn statements (i.e., tax returns or lists) or **the government is barred by law from assessing income taxes!**

Government Barred By Law From Assessing "Income" Taxes

Only after a tax is assessed can the "liability" of the taxpayer be established. This is accomplished by recording the "liability of the taxpayer in the office of the Secretary" pursuant to Section 6203. Once that has been done the Secretary (pursuant to Section 6303) has to "give notice to each person *liable* for the unpaid tax, stating the amount and demanding payment thereof." Therefore, not only are Americans tricked into assessing themselves for a tax they cannot possibly be liable for, they also get conned into paying the tax either by authorizing withholding from their wages or paying an estimated tax — all without being made "liable" for the tax or billed for it pursuant to Sections 6201, 6203, and 6303.

Proof That The IRS Has No Legal Authority To Seize Property In Payment Of Income Taxes

Section 7401 states:

No civil action for the collection or recovery of taxes, or of any fine, penalty, or forfeiture, shall be commenced unless the Secretary authorizes or sanctions the proceedings and the Attorney General or his delegate directs that the action be commenced.

This means that the IRS can only *recommend* that the U.S. Attorney bring an action in court to collect, *by court order,* any taxes allegedly owed. Section 7402(e) states:

The United States district courts shall have jurisdiction of any action brought by the United States to quiet title to property if the title claimed by the United States to such property was derived from enforcement of a lien under this title.

In other words, the Federal government (under the Code) is supposed to take an individual to court (per the 5th Amendment) before forcibly taking his property in payment of income taxes.

Two other sections of the Code shed additional light on this aspect of the limited legal authority of the IRS: Section 6651 (Exhibit 8) — "Failure to file tax return or to pay tax" — and Section 7203 (Exhibit 9) — "Willful failure to file return, supply information, or pay tax." Section 6651 provides *civil* penalties for failure to pay a variety of taxes such as those on distilled spirits, wines, beer, cigarettes, cigars, etc., but *there are no penalties listed* for failure to *file income tax returns* or *pay income taxes*. While Section 6651 covers civil fines, Section 7203 is the section used to prosecute so-called "tax protesters." Unlike Section 6651, no specific taxes are mentioned in Section 7203, nor does it say exactly who is "required" to pay the taxes or "make a return" under that section. In essence, Code section 7203 is fallacious because it does not establish exactly who is "required" to do anything, nor does it refer to any other Code section where such requirements are to be found. In legal language, Section 7203 does not allege an offense and gives no Federal judge subject matter jurisdiction to prosecute anyone for any of the "crimes" allegedly contained in it.

EXHIBIT 8

Sec. 6651.   Failure to file tax return or to pay tax.

(a) Addition to the tax.

In case of failure—

(1) to file any return required under authority of subchapter A of chapter 61 (other than part III thereof), subchapter A of chapter 51 (relating to distilled spirits, wines, and beer), or of subchapter A of chapter 52 (relating to tobacco, cigars, cigarettes, and cigarette papers and tubes), or of subchapter A of chapter 53 (relating to machine guns and certain other firearms), on the date prescribed therefor (determined with regard to any extension of time for filing), unless it is shown that such failure is due to reasonable cause and not due to willful neglect, there shall be added to the amount required to be shown as tax on such return 5 percent of the amount of such tax if the failure is for not more than 1 month, with an additional 5 percent for each additional month or fraction thereof during which such failure continues, not exceeding 25 percent of the aggregate;

EXHIBIT 9

**Sec. 7203.   Willful failure to file return, supply infor-
mation, or pay tax.**

Any person required under this title to pay any
estimated tax or tax, or required by this title or by
regulations made under authority thereof to make a
return, keep any records, or supply any information,
who willfully fails to pay such estimated tax or tax,
make such return, keep such records, or supply such
information, at the time or times required by law or
regulations, shall, in addition to other penalties provided by law, be guilty of a misdemeanor and, upon
conviction thereof, shall be fined not more than $25,000
($100,000 in the case of a corporation) or imprisoned
not more than 1 year, or both, together with the costs
of prosecution. In the case of any person with respect to
whom there is a failure to pay any estimated tax, this
section shall not apply to such person with respect to
such failure if there is no addition to tax under section
6654 or 6655 with respect to such failure.

*Note: Where does it say anything about an income tax re-
turn? The "returns" referred to are obviously the same returns referred to in Section 6651, Exhibit 8.

Jurisdiction of Federal Courts

Section 7401(f) states:

> For general jurisdiction of the district courts of the United States in *civil*
> actions involving internal revenue, see section 1340 of title 28 of the
> United States Code. (Emphasis added)

Clearly, Federal courts only have civil, *not criminal*, jurisdiction in tax
matters. There is no section in the Internal Revenue Code that gives
Federal courts *criminal* jurisdiction in tax matters, nor are there any
provisions in the U.S. Criminal Code that establish any income tax
"crimes." [17] Only civil fines and forfeitures can apply in Federal tax
matters, proving again that all criminal trials in connection with Federal income taxes *have been* illegal.

As explained earlier, the Code is cleverly but diabolically written so
that it does not contain any provision that could render it unconstitu-

---

[17]This is exactly like the first direct taxing statutes that contained only civil penalties
for not filing "lists" or for filing ones. See page 62.

tional, and if it contained any criminal penalties with respect to Federal income tax it would be. [18]

Right now there are probably fifty people in jail who allegedly violated Section 7203. *They are all political prisoners.* Many more are probably incarcerated for income tax evasion (they filed tax returns), though they could have been prosecuted (somewhat less illegally) under Section 1001 of the U.S. Criminal Code which makes giving false information to the government a crime. [19] But no one can be lawfully prosecuted for income tax evasion because no such crime is listed in Title 18 of the U.S. Criminal Code. This means that all prosecutions for income tax evasion (felonies) as well as criminal trials for failing to file income tax returns or for submitting allegedly false withholding statements (both misdemeaners) have all been illegal. The only reason that such prosecutions can and do take place is because of the "judges" and lawyers who make a living from these illegal litigations, both criminal and civil. All lawyers, lawyer-judges, and lawyer-prosecutors have a huge financial stake in keeping the American public ignorant of the real meaning of "voluntary compliance."

In conclusion, the enforced collection of Federal income taxes is carried out illegally, contrary to both the Internal Revenue Code and the Constitution. Let us, therefore, examine in greater detail just how those black-robed criminals who masquerade as Federal judges operate.

---

[18]Since the only Federal crimes listed in the Constitution are counterfeiting, treason, piracy, and felonies committed on the high seas, it requires a constitutional amendment to make anything else a *Federal crime*. True, a number of other crimes (i.e., kidnapping and mail fraud) have been made Federal "crimes" but this is only one more example of how the Federal government usurps jurisdiction.

[19]I always thought that Section 1001 of the U.S. Criminal Code was both ironic and illegal since if it can be a crime for private citizens to give false information to the government, it should also be a crime for government officials (in matters other than of national security) to give false information to the public. If that were a crime, of course, no information whatsoever would ever come out of Washington.

EXHIBIT 10
Bull vs U.S. 295 US 247

[4] A tax is an exaction by the sovereign, and necessarily the sovereign has an enforceable claim against every one within the taxable class for the amount lawfully due from him. The statute prescribes the rule of taxation. Some machinery must be provided for applying the rule to the facts in each taxpayer's case, in order to ascertain the amount due. The chosen instrumentality for the purpose is an administrative agency whose action is called an assessment. The assessment may be a valuation of property subject to taxation, which valuation is to be multiplied by the statutory rate to ascertain the amount of tax. Or it may include the calculation and fix the amount of tax payable, and assessments of federal estate and income taxes are of this type. Once the tax is assessed, the ◀ | taxpayer will owe the sovereign the amount when the date fixed by law for payment arrives.

*Note: Apart from everything else, no "income" tax can be "due" until the correct amount is "assessed."

16

The Federal "Judiciary"

In its enforcement of the income tax the Federal judiciary has managed to throw out the entire Constitution. That the Federal judiciary was able to accomplish this feat is no small tribute to the massive incompetence (or culpability) of America's legal community and the ignorance of the media.

The Federal courts have deceived the public about Federal taxation. Proof of this can be drawn directly from the controversy that surrounded the inclusion of direct taxes in the Constitution. What happened to one of the two "great classes" of taxes established in the Constitution, and why were our Founding Fathers so concerned with giving the Federal government a direct taxing power? Apparently the government can function quite well without such a power, even in time of war. Since the Federal government does not apportion any taxes, it presumably levies no direct taxes at all. Is this assumption realistic? Has our government really been able to fight our numerous wars and today collect in excess of $900 billion per year in taxes *without* utilizing the power of direct taxation? Of course not. The Federal government has obviously been collecting *direct* taxes (income, estate, and gift taxes) all along under the guise of collecting *indirect* taxes. The Federal courts have simply deceived the public regarding the legal nature of those taxes — just as the Federal judiciary has deceived the public concerning the legal nature of U.S. coin and currency, [1] the Federal government's lawful monetary and regulatory powers, and the protection (from the government) afforded the people by the Fourth and Fifth Amendments. In short, the Federal judiciary has effectively dismantled just about every safeguard the Founding Fathers built into the Constitution to protect the American public from the stupidity, greed, and/or tyranny of government.

When the Federal judiciary wants to disregard the Constitution and increase Federal power, it does so by simply proclaiming that it is "interpreting" the Constitution "broadly." The Supreme Court created the fallacious notion that there is a legitimate distinction between

[1]See Appendix E.

"strict" and "loose" constitutional "construction," and the public docilely accepted this absurdity. The Constitution is the "supreme law of the land" but we never hear about "strict" or "loose" construction of other laws that affect the public such as motor vehicle laws and the laws covering murder, rape, or extortion. Isn't it strange that the only laws subject to "loose" or "strict" construction are those that affect government power?

The public is fooled into thinking that the judiciary is seriously concerned about enforcing the Constitution and upholding constitutional rights because the courts make such a fuss when they uphold the constitutional "rights" of criminals.[2] In all cases where Federal courts really protect constitutional rights, the interest of the Federal government is never threatened. For example, if a murderer goes free because the police did not afford him his full constitutional rights, he only represents a threat to other Americans and not a threat to the government itself. In these instances Federal courts will be very protective and generous with constitutional rights, but let these same rights clash with the illegal exercise of Federal power (or with the legal profession's monopoly of our courts) and constitutional rights go out the window without so much as a by-your-leave.

Open Admission That The Courts Disregard The Nature Of Income When Allegedly Taxing It

In discussing the legal definition of "income" (for tax purposes), *Mertin's* (see page 181) was forced to use the *Eisner* definition:

> in the early case of *Eisner v. Macomber* the Supreme Court defined income as the "gain derived from capital, from [the] labor [of others], or from both combined, provided it be understood to include profit gained through sale or conversion of capital assets" (paragraph 5.02, Chapter 5, page 3).

In the next paragraph (entitled "'Income' as a Changing Concept"), however, *Mertin's* states that while in *Eisner* the Supreme Court

> attempted a definition of income — shortly thereafter, however, it was prophesized that the scope of the Sixteenth Amendment would not forever be limited by this judicial definition and that taxable income would be judicially found, although outside the precise scope of the Supreme Court's def-

[2]The "courts" also make a big display of protecting the constitutional rights of women and other "minorities" (generally in their relationship to others), but when it comes to the enforced collection of Federal income taxes these same women and minorities have no constitutional rights at all.

inition. The fulfillment of that prophesy is shown by the many departures from the *Macomber* case and by the gradual growth of the income tax law.

Thus this definitive work on income taxes admits that the government openly breaks the law by "looking. . . outside the Supreme Court's definition" of income when taxing it. *Mertin's* does not even attempt to supply any legal definition of "income" other than the *Eisner* definition *which it admits the courts do not now follow.* In enforcing the income tax "outside" of the law, Federal judges have become outlaws as the above reference makes clear and as is further confirmed by the following examples.

Standing The Law on Its Head

On February 27, 1980 the Court of Appeals for the Eighth Circuit affirmed the conviction of Harold L. Francisco on three counts of failure to file income tax returns (pursuant to Code Section 7203) for the years 1972, 1973, and 1974. Francisco had been indicted in March of 1979, had waived a jury trial, was tried and convicted before District Judge Donald E. O'Brien on all three counts, and was sentenced to a one year confinement on each count (to be served concurrently).

In upholding Francisco's conviction, the Appelate court stated:

Francisco's challenge is premised upon two theories: (1) the income tax is an indirect tax; and (2) income received in exchange for labor or services is not income within the meaning of the Sixteenth Amendment.[3]

The court further clarified Francisco's reasons for not reporting his wages on the tax returns he filed and for not paying any income taxes as follows:

1. the income tax was, by law, an indirect tax and since it was not levied as one he could not legally be subject to it; and
2. payment for his labor was "not income within the meaning of the Sixteenth Amendment."

In other words, Harold L. Francisco knew exactly what he was talking about and demonstrated that he was 100 percent right on the law. This august panel of Circuit court judges thought otherwise and said:

(8) the cases cited by Francisco clearly establish that the income tax is a direct tax, thus refuting the argument based upon his first theory. See

[3]*U.S. vs Francisco* 614 F.2d 617 (1980), page 619.

Brushaber v. Union Pacific Railroad Co., 240 U.S. 1, 19, 36. . . (1916) (the purpose of the Sixteenth Amendment was to take the income tax "out of the class of excises, duties and imposts and place it in the class of direct taxes").[4]

The panel of "judges" in this case included Floyd R. Gibson, the Chief Judge of the Eighth Circuit, and Judges McMillan and Lay who wrote the opinion. All three of them believed that the income tax was held to be a direct tax and that "the purpose of the 16th Amendment" was to take the income tax "out of the class of excises, duties and imposts and place it in the class of direct taxes." It would be impossible for any panel of judges chosen to hear a case to be more wrong on the law. Clearly, this "court" turned the law and the *Brushaber* decision on their heads (see pages 194 and 202).

The mere fact that the "court" believed it *had* to rule that the income tax *was not an excise tax* is *proof* that it knew no one is subject to this tax. Obviously the "court" believed it *had* to rule this way or else Francisco would be *innocent* and *not subject to the tax*. But the "court" had to know that the income tax *is an excise tax* and its convoluted position on this issue is, in itself, proof that it knew no one is subject to it.

Court Admits Francisco Filed

Francisco elected a trial before a judge because he believed no judge would convict him. He felt a jury could be misled by a prosecutor and might find him guilty simply because it resented the fact that he did not pay taxes (which should not be an issue in this type of "crime" though trial judges and prosecutors usually inject it to prejudice juries by inferring that since members of the jury pay taxes should not let someone off who does not.[5]

In his opinion Lay wrote:

> Because his returns contain 'some information,' Francisco urges that filing requirements were satisfied. However, his returns contain no information from which tax liability can be calculated. Hence, they do not satisfy filing requirements.[6]

[4]Ibid.
[5]At my sentencing Judge Clarie said, "Is this fair, that everyone else pays taxes?"
I replied, "Pardon?"
Clarie said, "Is it fair. . . that you shouldn't pay income taxes, but is it all right if everyone else does?"
I answered, "The issue is not whether I pay taxes at all."
And Clarie replied, "I understand, but I'm asking the question."
[6]*U.S. vs Francisco, supra*, page 618.

The appellate panel specifically stated that Francisco's "returns contain no income information from which tax liability can be calculated." The court, therefore, admitted that Francisco filed returns but that "his returns" contained no "income information." The court said *he filed returns,* though he was indicted and prosecuted for *not* filing returns? Section 7203 also says (theoretically) that it is a "crime" not to "supply any information." Why then was Francisco not charged with that crime instead of the "crime" of not filing (when the "court" admitted that he did)? In addition to being innocent of the "crime" alleged, he was also charged with the wrong "crime."

Francisco filed a return as defined in Internal Revenue Code Section 6103, which specifically distinguishes between a "return" and "return information." If Francisco did, in fact, do anything wrong, it was that he did not supply any information, not that he did not file a return. He was not charged with that "crime" because the Mamelukes, for some reason, never make that charge. The court stated that he did not supply information from which his "tax liability can be calculated, " but there is no section of the Code that provides for any such "liability." They also refer to "filing requirements" when there are no "filing requirements" with respect to income taxes in the Code.

In *Garner vs U.S.* 424 US 648, the Supreme Court ruled that:

> The information revealed in the preparation and filing of an income tax return is, for Fifth Amendment analysis, the testimony of a "witness" as that term is used herein.

If the testimony on a 1040 (which the preparer *swears* is true) is "the testimony of a witness, " how can anybody be "required" to give it? Such a "requirement" would render the law unconstitutional — which is why no such requirement appears in the Code and why *income* tax returns are not even mentioned in either Section 6651 or Section 7203 (see pages 259, 260).

Court Rules Francisco's Views Are Beyond Rational Belief

In order to illegally prosecute and convict Francisco (and others), the government has to prove that any alleged failure to file is also "willfull, " in that he did not file and also *believed* he had a *legal duty* to file something *other* than what he filed, and that, *without cause,* he refused to do so. According to the two most definitive Supreme Court cases on this subject, to act "willfully" means that one acts

> . . . with a bad purpose [citations omitted]; without justifiable excuse [citations omitted]; stubbornly, obstinately, perversely [citations omitted]. The word is also employed to characterize a thing done without ground for

believing it is lawful [citations omitted], or conduct marked by careless disregard whether or not one has the right so to act [citations omitted]. [7]

In addition, in *U.S. vs Bishop* (while referring to *Murdock*) the Supreme Court stated:

> The requirement of an offense committed "willfully" is not met, therefore, if a taxpayer has relied in good faith on a prior decision of this court [citations omitted]. . . [8]

Since the trial Judge found Francisco guilty of "willfulness" (and the Appellate judges upheld the conviction), he had to believe (beyond a *reasonable doubt*) that 1) Francisco was wrong on the law, and 2) Francisco could not possibly have believed that the income tax was indirect and wages were not income. In other words, the court had to be convinced that Francisco's *legal beliefs* were so weird that they were *actually beyond rational belief*. And, at the same time, the "judges" had to believe (even if Francisco's interpretation was wrong) that Francisco could not, in good faith, have relied on such "prior decisions" of the Supreme Court as *Pollock, Eisner, Smietanka, Flint vs Stone Tracy,* and others which he explained had formed the basis of his beliefs. If ever there was an innocent man it was Harold Francisco; and if ever there were judicial rogues and charlatans it was the "judges" who tried and affirmed his conviction.[9] It is also important to note that this case not only completely reversed the law but has and is being used by the "courts" as legal precedent with which to find others guilty.

Justice in Alaska

On April 20, 1983 Mr. and Mrs. John Hett appeared before James M. Fitzgerald, a District Court Judge in Anchorage, Alaska to explain why they had not given any tax information to the IRS pursuant to a Section 7602 summons that had been served upon them. Since compliance with income tax laws is voluntary, the IRS does not have any legal

---

[7] *U.S. vs Murdock* 290 US 389, pages 394, 395.

[8] *U.S. vs Bishop* 412 US 346, page 361. In the opinion that found Francisco guilty, Judge Lay cited both of these cases so he cannot claim he was unfamiliar with them. He either did not understand them or simply chose to ignore them along with everything else he did not understand or chose to ignore.

[9] They are actually worse than "rogues and charlatans" since they are all guilty (along with the U.S. Attorney who prosecuted Francisco) of violating Sections 241 and 242 of the U.S. Criminal Code. Their guilt could easily be established by any objective Federal grand jury looking into Francisco's illegal prosecution and conviction.

authority to compel any testimony or the production of any material in connection with such summonses. With the help of the legal establishment and the Federal judiciary the IRS has, however, succeeded in deceiving the public with these fraudulent summonses for years.

First, Section 7602 states that summonses issued under it can only apply to persons "liable for a tax or required to perform [some] act" or to third parties in possession of records of persons *so liable* or *so required.* Such summonses *cannot*, therefore, apply to *income* taxes since no person can be *liable* for income taxes nor be *required* to perform any act with respect to such taxes. [10]

Mr. Hett was sworn in and on the witness stand when "Judge" Fitzgerald asked him why he had not complied with the summons. Hett responded as follows:

> Well, your Honor, we feel we have complied with the summons by actually appearing at the place indicated and we have answered questions in this regard. We have imposed our Fifth Amendment privilege as to the fact that our answers might tend to incriminate us.[11]

Hett's answer should have been enough to terminate the hearing. What followed, however, was a total perversion of the entire American legal system and of the protection of the Fifth Amendment.

Instead of terminating the hearing, Fitzgerald told Mr. Hett that he could not impose a blanket Fifth Amendment claim "as to the documents or parts of them. . . you may state what the basis of your claim is." Fitzgerald further informed Hett that he [Fitzgerald] ". . . was required to make an examination, and you may testify under oath relating to the basis of your examination. I am required to make the determination as to whether or not your claim is, in fact, valid. You have to relate it to some specific offense which you believe disclosure of doc-

---

[10]For complete details on how to handle and defeat these phony 7602 summonses, see *The Schiff Report,* Volume 1, Numbers 3, 4, 5, and 6.

[11]Recorded on page 5 of the hearing transcript. Actually, Hett was in error. He should not have raised the issue of *self-incrimination,* but the more fundamental issue of not wanting to be a witness against oneself and the judge knew that this was Hett's intent. Hett was under no legal obligation to testify regardless of whether the information sought from him was incriminating or not, nor did he have to make any such determination. For a fuller explanation of how Federal courts knowingly confuse and pervert this distinction in tax cases, see *How Anyone Can Stop Paying Income Taxes,* pages 15–22. In all other cases, including those of espionage and subversion, the courts have repeatedly ruled that a plea of self-incrimination cannot be challenged nor can the grounds for belief that testimony might be incriminatory be questioned by the court. To compel a witness to explain the basis for his belief would nullify the Fifth Amendment protection. The witness can only be compelled to explain why testimony would be self-incriminatory if he is granted immunity. To compel such testimony without the grant of immunity is reversible error.

uments will expose to [sic] or will tend to incriminate you in connection with, but I may not accept a blanket claim of Fifth Amendment privilege." [12]

Fitzgerald, however, kept raising the same theme each time Hett expressed bewilderment at the court's insistence that he testify against himself. For example:

. . . the burden is on you to establish that you do have a valid Fifth Amendment claim [Hett had no such burden]. . . I may not accept a claim to produce those documents violates a Fifth Amendment right. You have to establish in what way the Fifth Amendment right — that you will be exposed to a criminal prosecution. The purpose of allowing you to testify [the judge now infers that by "allowing" Hett to testify he is actually doing him a favor] is to establish that so that a determination can be made by me as to whether or not your claims are frivolous or your claims are real. [13]

Based upon Fitzgerald's insistance that he [Hett] testify about matters he believed could be used against him, Hett asked, "Can you grant us any kind of immunity that will clear us from any kind of prosecution?"[14]

And Judge Fitzgerald replied, "I have no authority to grant immunity. That may be done only under the statute which places the responsibility for granting immunity with the Attorney General of the United States."[15]

It is perfectly obvious why Hett's testimony could incriminate him and why the U.S. Attorney wanted it: the government was pressing for information about his bank accounts. If Hett had filed no tax returns for the years in question, deposits to such accounts could furnish the Justice Department with a basis for building a case that Hett had a legal duty to file,[16] or if he *had* filed without reporting bank interest, he could be prosecuted for tax evasion and /or giving false information to the government. According to Judge Fitzgerald, however, the only way Hett *could keep from testifying against himself was to testify against himself and explain why he believed his testimony might incriminate him!* Fitzgerald was attempting to extract *a confession* from Hett *in*

[12]Fitzgerald had to know that such a pronouncement was in total error. Once Hett invoked his constitutional right not to supply information that he believed could be used against him, that should have, legally, ended the matter. "Judge" Fitzgerald had no further judicial duties to perform in this case (as is clearly pointed out in the IRS's own handbook). See *How Anyone Can Stop Paying Income Taxes*, page 81–90.

[13]From the hearing transcript, page 7, 8.

[14]Ibid., page 18.

[15]Ibid.

[16]At both my trials the government used a bank employee as a witness to introduce my cancelled checks as evidence in my illegal prosecution.

open court. He wanted Hett to admit that he either did not file a return (regarded as a crime by the government) or that he had filed but supplied false information on his return and, therefore, was either guilty of tax evasion and/or of supplying false information to the government.

In the absence of immunity, Hett's testimony could expose him to criminal prosecution in at least three areas, but Fitzgerald kept pressing for his testimony (in open court and before the U.S. Attorney). Immunity, however, should have been a moot point because Fitzgerald was constitutionally barred from demanding such testimony from Hett in the first place. And while the judge was technically correct (in that he could not grant him immunity), he could have asked the U.S. Attorney if the government was prepared to give the witness (now ordered to testify against himself) immunity in exchange for his testimony. If the government said no, Hett should have been excused on this basis. But the government would not give Hett immunity because it specifically *wanted* his testimony to use *against him* — either to press criminal charges or to determine civil fines or penalites.

A Mafia informant would have received immunity *immediately* because nothing could *compel* him to reveal any information, nor would he have been required to prove to the "court" why he believed his testimony would incriminate him. Common criminals, of course, have their constitutional rights scrupulously protected but Hett — an ordinary working American who was trying to protect his person and property from illegal prosecution and confiscation by the government — apparently had no rights at all in Fitzgeralds's courtroom. [17]

Hett also informed the "court" that he had heard former IRS Assistant Regional Counsel, John Lynch, say that "innocent people are as likely to be prosecuted as the guilty." Because of this comment Hett testified that he did not "know what to say." Since Hett believed that the Fifth Amendment is supposed to protect the innocent as well as the guilty (and that the government prosecutes innocent people), he did not want to give the government any information that could give it any basis on which to prosecute him.

Hett next asked, "Well, if I answer this question, can it ever be used against me?"[18]

Fitzgerald answered, "I can't say it wouldn't because I don't know what you are concerned about. You have to establish what it is. You assert the Fifth Amendment claim, and you have to set out the basis for it. This is what I must determine as either sound or unsound." [19]

---

[17]Perhaps Federal judges zealously protect the rights of criminals as a *professional* courtesy!

[18]From the hearing transcript, page 19.

[19]Ibid., pages 19, 20.

Again Hett asked, "Can you explain to me how I can answer that question without the possiblity of incriminating myself?"[20]

Earlier in the hearing Hett had asked Fitzgerald if he was not being asked to testify "against myself" and the Judge answered, "Well, you are not testifying against yourself [*who then would he be testifying against?*]. You are testifying to establish your claim. . . if you refuse to testify to establish your claim, then I must find that the claim was without merit and order the documents to be turned over."[21]

Toward the end of this inquisition Hett asked, "Aren't you asking me to be a witness against myself?"

Completely avoiding Hett's question, the court responded, "I will tell you again, to answer the question."

And Hett said, "I don't understand how I can forfeit my Fifth Amendment rights."

"All right, I am telling you to answer it," Fitzgerald said. "If you shall not answer it, I will order that you be held in custody until you purge yourself of civil contempt. . ."[22]

According to the transcript Fitzgerald turned Hett over to the U.S. Marshalls at 10:30 a.m. who hauled him away and threw him in a cell[23] — just because he did not want to testify against himself!

Then, at 4:45,[24] Hett was brought back before the Judge, apparently prepared to answer the court's questions and the hearing continued. The transcript records the following:

John Hett having been previously sworn on oath testified as follows:

Continued direct examination by Mr. Ridner:
Q. Mr. Hett, since 1975 do you or have you any bank accounts either savings or checking?
A. Yes.
Q. Where are those accounts? Which banks do you have those accounts in?
A. Well, I feel at this time that the First National Bank is the only place.
Q. First National Bank of where, what branch?
A. Oh, Palmer.
Q. You said at this time you feel. Since 1976, have there been other bank accounts. . .?[25]

The point is, both Fitzgerald and Ridner illegally contrived to de-

[20]Ibid., page 19.
[21]Ibid., pages 6, 7.
[22]Ibid., pages 21, 22.
[23]Ibid., page 24.
[24]Ibid.
[25]Ibid., page 27.

prive Hett of his constitutional rights and illegally deprived him of his liberty. Their guilt is open and shut and already recorded by a court reporter so a trial is not even necessary. The question remains — what will the people in Alaska do about such blatant law breakers?

Hett's Way Out

In *The Schiff Report*, Volume 1, Number 3, I first reported this "hearing" and reproduced about 7½ pages of the hearing transcipt. In that *Report* I suggested that Mr. Hett should have responded as follows when first asked about his bank accounts:

> *The answer I am about to give is not being given voluntarily but is being forced from my lips under threat of imprisonment in flagrant violation of my 5th Amendment right not to be compelled to be a witness against myself: NO, I DO NOT NOW HAVE, NOR HAVE I EVER HAD, CHECKING OR SAVINGS ACCOUNTS!"*

Even if the above answer is false, how can Mr. Hett be convicted of perjury? How can they use the statement against him?. . .

Federal Railroad Stations — How They Operate

In December, 1981, John Babtist Kotmire, Jr. (a 47 year old, 6'3" builder from Westminster, Maryland) was indicted for failing to file income tax returns for the years 1975 and 1976. Like Francisco, Kotmire had filed tax returns for those years, but had filed "Fifth Amendment" returns in accordance with the instructions laid down by Oliver Wendell Holmes in the *Sullivan* decision.[26]

In that case, Holmes (recognizing that all information on a tax return can be used against a filer) ruled that individuals could invoke their Fifth Amendment right with respect to any question on a return, so Kotmire did. A deeply religious, moral and proud man, Kotmire quit the Baltimore police force after eight years because he could not stand the corruption he witnessed. As a student of American history and the Constitution, he had spent many hours studying our income tax laws and the court cases bearing on them and was deeply committed to the free-enterprise system he, like numerous other Americans, felt was being undermined (along with the Constitution) by Federal income taxes. He was very active in the effort to expose the illegality of the income tax's enforcement and provided strong and knowledgeable leadership in the tax resistance movement in the Baltimore area.

---

[26]This decision has been misstated and misrepresented by every Federal Court (including the Supreme Court in *Garner vs U.S.* 424 US 648) since it was rendered in 1927. A full account of it is provided in *How Anyone Can Stop Paying Income Taxes,* pages 144–150.

Because of this the Mamelukes decided to *get* him and illegally indicted him for violating Section 7203 of the Internal Revenue Code. At this point Kotmire contacted me to ask if I would represent him as his attorney or "counsel" (as provided for in the Sixth Amendment) at his arraignment. I agreed, telling him I could present arguments to the court that had never been raised before and which, I believed, would enable us to abort the arraignment and intended illegal prosecution. Only months before I had discovered that Federal courts had no criminal jurisdiction to prosecute anyone for not filing income tax returns, and if anybody *could* be prosecuted for such a "crime" it could only be the Secretary of the Treasury since he is charged under Section 6020 of the Code with the responsibility of filing returns for those who do not voluntarily do so on their own.[27]

We did some further checking and found Fourth Circuit rules of procedure and case law that affirmed and supported his right to have me act as both attorney and counsel for him. After many hours of research regarding the legal aspects of the arraignment, I went to Baltimore the day before it was scheduled in order to go over everything we planned to do. We agreed that, under no circumstances, would he plead "not guilty" thus giving subject-matter jurisdiction to a court which had none at all.

With Kotmire's power-of-attorney in my pocket I took my seat at the counsel table in the courtroom of District Court Judge James Miller just before 2:00 p.m. on January 5, 1981. Kotmire and his wife, Nancy, seated themselves in the gallery amidst some seventy or eighty of his supporters. While waiting for the judge to appear, I filled out a form giving my name and stating that I was appearing as the defendant's attorney.

The Assistant U.S. Attorney did not recognize me as being a local and asked where I "practiced." I told him that "I do not practice, I do this for real, but not in any particular location." When he realized that I was not a licensed lawyer he hurredly left the counsel table and the courtroom, apparently to report this to the court. I suspect this was the reason Judge Miller was fifteen minutes late making his appearance. After Miller finally arrived and court was convened, the U.S. Attorney moved to amend the indictment which he claimed contained a clerical error. I immediately objected on the grounds that the whole indictment was in error because it indicted the wrong man. At this point Judge Miller asked me if I was an attorney. "Yes, " I replied. "I have Mr. Kot-

[27]This section specifically states that if an individual does not "consent" to file a return, "the Secretary shall make such return from his own knowledge. . . " So, if the government did not receive John Kotmire's return, it was because the Secretary of the Treasury had obviously "failed to file" one (not Kotmire) and he should have been prosecuted instead.

mire's power-of-attorney right here, " holding it up so he could see it.

"But you are not a member of any bar?" Miller questioned.

"No, your honor, " I replied. "I am only an attorney-in-fact not an attorney-at-law and I am here merely to explain to the court why it has no subject matter jurisdiction over Mr. Kotmire in this matter and that if indeed a crime has been committed the government has indicted the wrong man."

Judge Miller explained that only members of the bar could represent individuals in his court. I told him that I had rules of procedure and case law from his own Circuit (which I offered to show him) that clearly established Kotmire's right to have me represent him, but Judge Miller refused even to look at, much less discuss, that evidence and insisted that I immediately remove myself from the counsel table. I pointed out that it was Kotmire's intention to challenge the jurisdiction of the court and it would be pointless for him to have an officer of that court (which is what all bar lawyers are) defend his contention that the court had no jurisdiction in the case. Such representation, I added, could not be effective. I further pointed out that it would only take me ten minutes to prove that the court was without subject-matter jurisdiction over Mr. Kotmire. Without responding to, or commenting on, anything I said, Miller again ordered me to leave the counsel table.

"But your honor, " I persisted, "how will justice not be served by your allowing me to show you why you don't have jurisdiction in this matter?" Judge Miller was unmoved and again insisted that I leave the counsel table.

Nevertheless, I continued, "But your honor, I spent six hours just getting here by train to present these arguments to you, how will justice not be served by your hearing them?"

Judge Miller would have none of it and finally warned me that if I said another word he would hold me in contempt. I saw the marshalls moving in my direction and, believing I could do no more, gathered up my material and squeezed into the gallery.

Kotmire had appeared before Judge Miller numerous times and when he spotted him seated among the spectators he said, "Mr. Kotmire would you please come up here."

Kotmire, however, said that his attorney was in court to challenge the jurisdiction of the court and since he was not persuaded that the court had any jurisdiction over him he would decline Miller's request to come forward.

Miller asked him again to come forward and again Kotmire declined, whereupon Miller turned to the marshalls and said, "Arrest that man, " as a gasp of disbelief arose from the spectators in the gallery.

Two marshalls forcibly proceeded to take Kotmire to the bench as he shouted, "Let the record show that the defendant is being dragged before the bar."

And Miller interjected, "You're not being dragged, you're being escorted."

Because of the audience's reaction to the arrest Miller ordered the courtroom cleared, allowing only five people (including Kotmire's wife) to stay leaving twelve marshalls and five spectators in the courtroom.

At this point, Miller asked Kotmire (who usually represented himself in court) if he wished to represent himself. Kotmire replied that he had his attorney there to represent him and that he wished to be represented by me. Miller explained that according to the rules of the court I could not represent him. Kotmire stated that this was not true and that his attorney was prepared to present evidence to the contrary. He further pointed out that under the Constitution he had a right to have counsel of his own choice.

Miller kept pressing Kotmire to agree to represent himself and to make a plea but Kotmire would not relent, insisting that he did not understand the charges and was being denied counsel of his choice by the court. Miller finally realized he could not proceed because court rules provide that a defendant has the right to counsel at *each stage* of his prosecution. The court had denied Kotmire that counsel and Kotmire claimed he did not understand the charges or what Miller was saying so, legally, the judge could not continue.

Neither Kotmire nor I thought that Miller would totally deny my ability to act as John's counsel, a right clearly provided for in the Sixth Amendment. While we realized that the court might illegally and arbitrarily deny my right to speak for him as his attorney, we assumed that I would at least be allowed to confer with and counsel him. But Miller would not allow me to confer with Kotmire or allow me to pass him written notes. Such a blatant denial of a constitutional right was outrageous. In any case, Miller realized what he had stepped into and ordered the clerk to get the Public Defender to act as Kotmire's counsel. Because Miller realized it would be reversible error to conduct an arraignment while denying a defendant counsel, he decided to *force* ineffective counsel on Kotmire — not for Kotmire's protection, but for his own. We waited some twenty minutes for the public defender to arrive and when he entered the courtroom Kotmire turned to the Judge and said, "That man can't represent me, he's already told me that I'm going to jail." Kotmire knew the public defender who had already assured him that he would be convicted and sent to jail. He believed Kotmire to be guilty of the offense charged and did not have the slightest understanding of the legal issues involved in the case. As far as he was concerned,

Kotmire should have pleaded guilty right then and there, so Kotmire strongly objected to being represented by him on any basis.[28] Making it appear as if he had complied with the law, Miller proceeded with the arraignment. He persisted in trying to get Kotmire to plead not guilty, but Kotmire refused, insisting on his right to consult with me. Miller continued to deny this request. I even tried passing John a note suggesting that he offer to plead "guilty," saving himself and the state the expense of a trial, if the court could prove that it had jurisdiction. The court, however, would not allow me to pass him *any* messages. Finally, Miller said he would enter a plea of not guilty for Kotmire if he refused to enter a plea himself.

A Doctored Transcript

The transcript records Kotmire stating the following:

> I am entering a plea of not guilty. I am challenging the jurisdiction of this court. I am here under duress and I am here without counsel.

Kotmire said no such thing. He never would have pleaded not guilty to the charge while saying that he was challenging the jurisdiction of the court because by pleading "not guilty" he would be acceding to the court's jurisdiction which would have defeated everything we had planned. Kotmire has affidavits from at least five people attesting to the fact that he said no such thing. His transcript was doctored.

Kotmire testified at great length in his four-week trial concerning the cases he relied on (*Brushaber, Sullivan, Eisner,* etc.), so he could not have acted "willfully." He was convicted only because both the judge and the U.S. Attorney deceived the grand and petit juries regarding applicable law.

Kotmire was subsequently convicted and given the maximum sentence of two years by Judge Miller. He served the full time (less time off for good behavior) of 17 months and 5 days at the Federal Prison Camp at Maxwell Air Force Base, Montgomery, Alabama.[29]

---

[28]For the court to appoint a "counsel" who had not spent five minutes on the issues of a case — while denying the defendant the counsel of someone who had spent hundreds of hours on those issues — was a farce and a fraud perpetrated by the court, designed merely to protect the court and not the defendant. The rule that an American is entitled to counsel means *effective counsel,* not just any yo-yo with a bar license who happens to pass by. Under these circumstances, how could Miller assume that the public defender could supply John Kotmire with more effective counsel than I?

[29]John Kotmire now runs *S.A.P.* ("Save A Patriot"), P.O. Box 91, Westminster, Maryland 21157. By a pooling of risks, members of S.A.P. seek to provide protection for themselves against the illegal confiscation of their property as well as offer financial help to the family of an individual if he is illegally convicted of failure to file income taxes.

In any case, this incident explodes the myth that our "courts" have set up bar requirements to ensure that individuals get the best legal representation possible. Such a policy merely forces the public to accept incompetent and frequently overpriced lawyers when far more competent and cheaper "counsel" might be available. This is done to maintain the illegal court monopoly lawyers and judges (lawyers themselves) have established.

If it were the court's intention to help an accused get the best possible counsel, Miller would have tried to determine what I really knew. I was well-dressed, courteous, and had a number of documents laid out in front of me on the counsel table, including the Internal Revenue Code. Why did he not question me to determine my competence or lack thereof? If he discovered I was incompetent, he could have told Kotmire that he would be better advised to get a licensed lawyer rather than be represented by someone who did not know what he was talking about. That would have made sense and would have demonstrated that the court was really concerned about protecting the accused's interests. The court, however, made no attempt to establish my competence but, instead, took the position that a licensed lawyer — who already had told the accused he would go to jail, who may never have looked into the Internal Revenue Code in his life[30], and who was certainly not prepared to challenge the court's jurisdiction — would provide him with more effective counsel than someone who was familiar with the Code and all the important Supreme Court cases bearing on it and who could conduct a competent and informed defense.

The most hypocritical aspect of this case was that though Judge Miller sentenced Kotmire to two years in jail for an offense he could not possibly have been guilty of (either on the basis of law or fact), only a few months before he had *dismissed indictments* against Thomas J. Whohlemuth Jr. Whohlemuth was an attorney (serving as the counsel for the Anne Arundel County School Board and the Community college of Anne Arundel County) who was indicted for failure to file income tax returns for the years 1975 and 1976 on earnings in excess of $68,000 per year. On the basis of testimony from one psychologist and two psychiatrists who stated that Wohlemuth was "incapable of understanding the criminality of not filing tax returns," Judge Miller dismissed the indictments against him. Because Kotmire so fervently believed in the lawfullness of his position he could not possibly have seen the "criminalty of not filing tax returns" either, but he was imprisoned for seventeen months while Wohlemuth (who pleaded "no contest" to the charges) went scott free.

---

[30]Most lawyers who are not tax lawyers are usually not familiar with the Code.

The United States vs Schiff

I was also prosecuted for failure to file tax returns, for the years 1974 and 1975, even though I had (like Kotmire) filed Fifth Amendment returns for those years. My illegal prosecution began when the then U.S. Attorney, Richard Blumenthal, filed a false "Information" against me on April 17, 1978 — five days after my second appearance in one month on *NBC*'s nationally televised "Tomorrow" show with Tom Snyder. A trial and conviction followed, though this conviction (my first) was subsequently reversed by the Second Circuit Court of Appeals on the grounds that the trial Judge, T.F. Gilroy Daly, erred in allowing an hour-long tape of one of those broadcasts to be introduced at trial.[31]

In reversing that conviction, though, the Appellate court still said

> The defense did not seriously contend that the conglomeration of papers filed along with the almost blank 1040 form constituted the tax return required by law.

There are three bold-faced lies in that one short statement. First, I did "seriously contend" at my trial that what I had filed was, as I read the statute, a lawful return. Second, my return was far from blank. On the face of it (besides "taking the Fifth") I included, among other things:

1. citings from the *Sullivan* case;
2. excerpts from the *Miranda* decision in which the Court ruled that the Fifth Amendment is available *"outside of* court proceedings and serves to protect persons in all settings in which their freedom of action is curtailed" and that an individual is "guaranteed the right to remain silent unless he chooses to speak in unfettered exercise of his own will" (emphasis added); and
3. a request for immunity in exchange for the information presumably "required" on the tax return.

Because the government's chief witness had testified that my return was "blank, " the Second Circuit sought to give judicial credence, legitimacy, and support to what was (in view of all of the above) an obviously false contention. Third, there is no income tax return "required by law, "[32] which at the time I filed my Fifth Amendment returns I did not even realize.

---

[31]*U.S. vs Schiff* 612 F2d 73. For a more detailed account of these illegal prosecutions and convictions, see *How Anyone Can Stop Paying Income Taxes,* pages 121–126 and 133–169.

[32]While I do not wish to analyze all the misleading material in this decision, it is important to note that the Second Circuit Court of Appeals held that individuals are required to file returns that at least show "the amount, if not the source, of their income."

In order to prove "willfulness" at both my trials, the government introduced (*and used against me*) my last traditionally filed return (1973). It is also of great importance to note that even in reversing my conviction the Second Circuit ruled:

> The [trial] court specifically stated, "The law applicable to this case is that a taxpayer can comply with tax laws and exercise his Fifth Amendment rights by listing *the amount, not the source*, of his income from *illegal* sources. . . " That charge was correct.[33] (Emphasis added)

The tremendous importance of this holding by the court — and how it can be devastatingly used against the government will be fully explained in Chapter 18, but a comment on the strange doctrine suggested there (that I could exercise my Fifth Amendment right only as it related to the "sources" not the "amount" of my income) is in order.

Apart from the doctrine constituting an open admission that the government is indeed illegally taxing "sources" of "income" as "income" itself, it was propounded because the government also contends that even illegally acquired income is "required" to be reported on a 1040. To get around the obvious repugnancy to the Fifth Amendment of any such "requirement, " lower courts concocted the absured doctrine that as long as the *amount* but not the *source* of the income is revealed, the filer is not supplying incriminating information. The total absurdity of such a doctrine is made clear by the following example. Assume that Joe Smith, a bank teller, embezzled $100,000 from the bank where he is employed. Further assume that he only receives $15,000 per year in salary but to be within the tax "law" he reports the entire $115,000 as "income" on his 1040 and omits identifying the "sources" of his "income." Would anyone with an ounce of intelligence suggest (as our Federal "courts" now do) that because he did not identify the "sources" of his "income" (listing only the "amount") that *he had not incriminated himself?* My 1973 tax return (a perfectly benign return) was used against me at my trial, demonstrating that non-incriminatory information can also be used against a taxpayer. Obviously, then, the "source" argument is one more legal absurdity that Federal "judges" have concocted to help rationalize how tax returns can be "required."

In reversing my conviction the Second Circuit also stated, "But the Fifth Amendment privilege does not immunize all witnesses from testifying." [34] It certainly does if they are asked to *testify against themselves* as the Second Circuit "judges" had to know. In addition, I had

[33]*U.S. vs Schiff, supra,* page 83.

[34]Ibid., page 83.

raised (on appeal) the fact that I never had an "evidentiary hearing" with respect to my claim of Fifth Amendment protection and the Appellate Court ruled that the trial court was not in error for refusing me an evidentiary hearing "on the question of Schiff's assertion of his Fifth Amendment privilege." In its decision the court continually referred to my "Fifth Amendment *privilege*" while only *once* referring to my Fifth Amendment *right*. In denying me that hearing the court relied on *U.S. vs Jordan* 508 F.2d 750, a non-binding lower court opinion and completely ignored a *binding* Supreme Court opinion *which clearly called for such a hearing*.

Garner vs U.S.

The Supreme Court's decision in the *Garner* case[35] represents one of the most contrived snake-in-the-grass opinions ever concocted by that Court. Fraud and deceipt litterly ooze from every line.

In this case Garner was convicted of violating Federal gambling laws. The Justice Department used information taken from his own tax return to assist in that conviction. Garner, therefore, appealed his conviction to the Ninth Circuit on the grounds that this violated his Fifth Amendment right against self-incrimination. The Ninth Circuit agreed with Garner[36] and reversed the conviction in a two-to-one opinion. The government then requested a rehearing "en banc" (before all the judges in the Circuit). This time an "en banc" court (in a seven-to-five decision) affirmed Garner's conviction.[37] The dissent in this case was so intense and formidable (the five judge minority literally chastizing the seven judge majority in language that was virtually vituperative) that Garner adopted the dissent and used it as his own appeal to the Supreme Court.

It is perfectly obvious that the Supreme Court (in affirming Garner's conviction) *wanted to* reach the decision it did regardless of either law or fact. It worked backward, twisting and misstating both fact and law as it went along, and then topped it all off with one of the most preposterous assumptions ever made by any American court. Had the Court reversed Garner's conviction, it would have signalled the income tax's death warrant.[38] Instead it chose to slay law and reason to keep the income tax alive. If the Court ruled that the government could not legally use information from Garner's tax return to convict him of violating Federal gambling laws, it would have to follow that the govern-

---

[35]*Garner vs U.S.* 424 US 648.

[36]*Garner vs U.S.* 501 F.2d. 228.

[37]*Garner vs U.S.* 501 F.2d. 236.

[38]Which, from a purely constitutional sense, was its only valid, legal choice.

ment also could not use such information to convict citizens of violating Federal tax laws, thus barring tax evasion trials. And if citizens could not be prosecuted for tax evasion (supplying allegedly false information on a return), they would not be fearful of filing totally fraudulent returns and the government's ability to collect income taxes would fly right out the window.[39] So the Court's problem was *how to justify Garner's conviction (with information taken from his own tax return) while still maintaining the legal fiction that citizens were still "required," by law, to furnish such information.* Let us see how the court attempted to reconcile such a legal impossibility.

First, the Supreme Court affirmed his conviction on the grounds that Garner supplied the incriminating information on his tax return "voluntarily" since he could have withheld the information by claiming the Fifth. Against the contention that had Garner done so he could have been prosecuted (as I and others have been), the Court argued that his constitutional rights were not impaired since a "valid claim of privilege [the Fifth] cannot be the basis for a Sec. 7203 conviction"; while even a "good faith erroneous claim of privilege entitles a taxpayer to acquittal under Sec. 7203." How could either the Supreme Court or Garner have known that if he had claimed the Fifth he could have been certain of acquittal on *either basis* as suggested by the Court? Indeed, how could the Supreme Court under this new doctrine be certain that all future judges and juries would refuse to convict defendants based on these two Pollyanna principles. Certainly both Mr. Kotmire (see page 273) and I were "entitled" to "acquittal" based on this doctrine, so why were we not acquited? Can we sue the Supreme Court justices that misled us into believing we would get such "acquittals"?

Note that the Court specifically said that even "erroneous [though] good faith" beliefs entitle those who take the Fifth to "acquittals." What does someone do if he is confronted by a judge like Clarie (and an Appeals Court like the Second Circuit) who instructs juries that "good faith" beliefs are not a defense against Section 7203 prosecutions?

The colossal hypocrisy, however, is how the Court could even *suggest* that a *valid* claim of the Fifth could *subject an American to prosecution!* At the very least the Court should have said that a *valid* claim of the Fifth is *a bar to prosecution,* not a bar to conviction. Stating that American citizens who make *valid assertions* of their Fifth Amendment *rights* can be *prosecuted* because of it is to say that Americans who validly assert constitutional rights can be punished for doing so. Since

---

[39]It is going there anyway — see Chapter 18.

[40]In this instance, however, New York state law was correct and did not interfere with a citizen's basic Fifth Amendment protection.

when do *constitutional rights* have these kinds of strings attached to them?

In effect, the Court said that *even though* it might cost a citizen $5,000 to claim his Fifth Amendment right (as a defense) the right itself *has not been diminished*. This makes no legal sense whatsoever! The Supreme Court, of course, is normally quick to strike down any state law that casts even a tiny shadow over the Fifth Amendment — as when the Court struck down the New York state law that allowed it to discharge, but not otherwise punish, state employees who took the Fifth before grand juries investigating the operation of state government. "Such a law," the Supreme Court thundered, "punishes the individual for claiming the Fifth, so that New York law must go." And it did.[40] State employment, however, is not a matter of right and taxpayers (represented by elected officials) can set standards for public employees. If these employees do not like the standards they can work elsewhere, but to suggest that a state *has to* continue employing a policeman who takes the Fifth before a grand jury investigating police corruption, for example, is totally unreasonable and a distortion of the purpose behind the Fifth Amendment. By maintaining that this New York state law diminished Fifth Amendment protection but Federal law (allowing citizens to be prosecuted, albeit not convicted for validly asserting this same right) did not diminish the right, has to set a new standard for judicial hypocrisy.

In any case, the following claim of the *Garner* Court *presupposes* an evidentiary hearing before a judge prior to any trials for the "crime" of asserting the Fifth Amendment on a tax return can take place.[41]

> . . . a *valid* claim of privilege cannot be the basis for a Sec. 7203 conviction. . . [42] [and that] "Only because a good faith *erroneous* claim of privilege *entitles a taxpayer to acquittal* under Sec. 7203 can I conclude that petitioner's disclosures are admissible against him."[43] (Emphasis added in both quotes.)

"Validity" a Matter of Law

What constitutes a "valid" or "erroneous" claim of one's Fifth Amendment right is a question of *law* that obviously must be decided (based on *Garner*) by a judge before an accused can ever find himself before a jury can attempt to judge his "good faith." At such an eviden-

---

[41]To simply see through the absurdity of the *Garner* doctrine, ask yourself, "Since when did Congress make it a *crime* to claim the Fifth Amendment on a tax return *in any case?*"

[42]*Garner vs U.S., supra,* page 663.

[43]Ibid., page 668 from Justice Marshall's concurring opinion, Justice Brennan joining.

tiary hearing, if a judge decides that the right was *validly* claimed, the accused must be set free. If, on the other hand, the judge concludes that the claim was "erroneous," the accused can still be found not guilty by a jury that believed he acted in "good faith."[44] Once the case is *before* the jury the jury *must assume* that the defendant's Fifth Amendment claim was both *legally invalid and erroneous* or why would he be on trial?

Neither I nor others ever got the evidentiary hearings that the *Garner* doctrine calls for. Such hearings are never held because no judge (even the Mamelukes we are forced to deal with) could rule that Fifth Amendment claims on tax returns are "invalid" or "erroneous" when all the information on them (even that which could be considered benign) can be used against those who give it to determine either *civil* or *criminal* liability.

In addition, how could the *Garner* Court even question the validity of a Fifth Amendment claim when it also stated *(in the very same decision)*:

> The information revealed in the preparation and filing of an income tax return, is for the purpose of Fifth Amendment analysis, the testimony of a "witness" as that term is used herein.[45]

Obviously if the filer of a tax return is being *involuntarily made to be a witness against himself,* he has a constitutional right to claim the Fifth with respect to any question he is being compelled to answer whether it is incriminatory on its face or not.[46] In every case all such claims to Fifth Amendment protection would have to be judged legally "valid" and, even under *Garner,* no one could theoretically be prosecuted (let alone convicted) for claiming the Fifth on a tax return. For this reason the *Garner* doctrine was not meant to be implemented (which is also why it is totally ignored by lower "courts") but was merely advanced as a specious device to extract the Court from the dilemma presented by the *Garner* case.

---

[44]This, of course, presupposes that one also gets a *fair trial* before a *fair and honest* "judge" which rarely happens. Even against such odds, however, some Fifth Amendment filers have been found not guilty: Charles Riley of Mesa, Arizona (1979) and Warren Eilertson of Ft. Washington, Maryland (1983). Even though these and other Fifth Amendment filers were found not guilty, a better approach is to file no tax returns at all. Ray Garland of Sycamore, Illinois (1983) and Jack Pierce of Ilion, New York (1983), as well as others, have been found not guilty on this basis.

[45]*Garner vs U.S.* 424 US 648, page 656.

[46]This had already been established by the Supreme Court in the 1927 decision in *U.S. vs Sullivan* 274 US 259, 264, but this case was cleverly distorted by the *Garner* Court so it could arrive at its own absurd decision.

My Second "Trial"

At my second trial (where I represented myself because "Judge" Clarie denied me the assistance of counsel) I objected to the use of my 1973 return on the grounds that when I filed it I believed it was required and, therefore, the government could not use such "compelled" testimony against me. In what has to be one of the most obviously illegal rulings ever recorded in the annals of American jurisprudence, Judge Clarie overruled my objection saying that since I filed my 1973 return "voluntarily" it could be used against me to prove that I understood I was "required" to file tax returns for the years 1974 and 1975! And this brilliant ruling came, not from any run-of-the-mill Federal judge, but from a *Chief* Judge.

Clarie's ruling on this one issue should give you some idea of what his charge to the jury was like. That forty-five minute piece of legal gibberish was full of lies, half-truths, and misleading inferences. Among the many lies Clarie told the jury were these:

1. persons are required to file income tax returns;
2. the government is not required to assess individuals in connection with income taxes; and
3. my good faith belief that the income tax was not being constitutionally enforced was not a defense to the charge.

Judge Clarie instructed the jury that I was wrong — as a matter of law — and that my good faith beliefs did not constitute a defense, leaving the jury with absolutely no basis whatsoever to find me innocent.[47] The Appeal's Court affirmed my conviction *orally* since there was no other way the Second Circuit[48] could affirm this legal abortion in writing without compromising itself. The court further ruled that its oral decision "shall not be reported, cited. . . or used in unrelated cases before this or any other court." It was then ordered that I be incarcerated immediately — *on a first offense misdemeanor* — even though I had far from exhausted my appeal remedies. Word that the Supreme Court had declined to hear my appeal came *five months after I had completed my jail sentence*. Convicted felons are routinely allowed to remain free on bond for years until they have exhausted their appeal remedies because their crimes do not involve the government or income taxes.

[47]On July 11, 1984, the Fifth Circuit Court *reversed* a conviction (*U.S. vs T. Burton* [5th Cir., No. 83-2579, 1984]) when a lower court gave *this very same instruction to the jury.* In my case, however, the "judges" on the Second Circuit thought it an entirely acceptable one so they sent me to jail immediately!

[48]Judges Ellsworth A. VanGraafeiland, J. Edward Lombard, and Amalya L. Kearse heard the appeal and rendered the oral decision.

During my second trial I presented more law to the jury than, I suspect, any jury ever saw in the history of American jurisprudence. I now recognize that this was a mistake but the government did not attempt to cross-examine me on one word of it and Clarie later ruled that the bulk of my testimony was "not a defense." If this was true, why did he allow me to testify at all on these issues and submit more case law than is even covered in this book? I also introduced the Internal Revenue code, which the Assistant U.S. Attorney, Michael Hartmere, objected to. In one of the few times the government was overruled, the court allowed it to be introduced into evidence; but this has to be the only time in the history of American criminal justice that *a defendant introduced the law over the government's objection.*[49]

All these cases give you some idea of the lawlessness and treachery with which the Federal judiciary operates (to say nothing of the Justice Department itself). They only represent the tip of the iceburg. This lawlessness now involves practically every sitting Federal judge, every Appellate Court and the Supreme Court itself. By comparison, it makes *Watergate* look like a cub scout outing. Before leaving this subject, however, I would like to briefly touch on a few other cases, some of which I was personally involved in.

Americans For Constitutional Taxation

On a Saturday morning early in 1979 I did a three-hour call-in phone interview with radio station WXYZ in Detroit. Two auto workers, Dean Hazel and Jim Lott (known in the Detroit area as "No Tax Jim") heard the show and contacted me. From this humble beginning and much hard work, dedication, and the dynamic leadership of Hazel and others, came A.C.T. — *Americans For Constitutional Taxation.* Within three years thousands of Michigan auto workers were dropping out of the tax system by claiming "exempt" on their employee withholding forms and were no longer filing tax returns. This received so much national publicity in February, March, and April of 1981 that the government felt it had to do something or risk being overwhelmed by tax drop-outs throughout the auto industry and (because of all the publicity) eventually being owerwhelmed by tax drop-outs throughout the

[49]In addition to detailing the cases mentioned in this book I had submitted (at both trials) motions to dismiss the charges, supported by the brief in Appendix D. It was denied by both judges (though the government did not even attempt to answer it with a written response) and neither judge allowed me the oral argument I requested. As a matter of fact, neither judge allowed me oral argument on any of the issues of law I raised.

country. Therefore, the government indicted Lott and Hazel for filing false and fraudulent withholding certificates (W-4s).

Hazel worked in a plant in Pontiac and after absorbing all of the material in my "Freedom Kit" he immersed himself in further study of the income tax and related subjects. He studied constitutional law and familiarized himself with all the cases covered in this book. He practically memorized the writings of Washington, Jefferson, and Hamilton and would, matter-of-factly, interject excerpts of what they said in conversation. He truly became a student of the "Constitutional Era." He knew that the income tax was an excise that could not apply to his wages. He also knew that he was legally exempt from withholding until he was officially "assessed" and, therefore, could claim "exempt" (pursuant to Code Section 3402(n) on his W-4.[50]

At his trial Hazel proved to be an excellent witness. He explained in detail why his wages (based upon the definition of income as developed by the Supreme Court) could not constitute income and why he could, therefore, lawfully claim exempt on his W-4. Based upon his testimony (even if it were wrong) no legitimate judge could possibly have concluded that he was "willful" or that his actions were tainted, to any degree, by criminal intent.

Part of his testimony dealt with the fact that I had advised him to claim exempt. When I took the stand I confirmed this. So if Hazel was guilty of any "crime, " I had to be (at the very least) an accessory, guilty of violating Code Section 6701 which says that "Any person — who aids or assists. . . or advises [any person in] the preparation of any document. . . arising under the internal revenue laws. . . in an understatement of the liability for tax. . . shall pay a penalty with respect to each such document. . ."

In his charge to the jury, Presiding "Judge" Churchill made it a point to emphasize and mislead it into believing that wages *were* "income." He said that Hazel must have known this since he had attended my trial (where I was convicted) and should have realized that not only were my views wrong, but that I was a law-breaker to boot. In the final analysis, my testimony actually hurt Hazel, who otherwise might have been found not guilty. Though I did not attend Lott's trial (he was also found guilty), I must say that I never met a man more inbued with the spirit of the *Federalist Papers* than he. And these are the kind of citizens the Federal government jails as "illegal tax protesters?"

---

[50]The media carried the erroneous account (fed to them by the government) that those auto workers were "inflating" their allowances" which made it sound as if they were lying. However, the vast majority of them — and certainly those associated with A.C.T. — were not increasing the number of their allowances but were merely claiming "exempt" from withholding pursuant to Code Section 3402(n). They *were* legally exempt from withholding for all the reasons covered in this book.

The Carlson Case

Though all the cases mentioned illustrate the criminal nature of our "courts," this court actually admitted (then sought to justify) its criminal behavior in *U.S. vs Carlson* 617 F.2d 518.

Carlson, a factory worker, claimed 99 withholding allowances in 1974 and 1975. While he had filed and paid taxes in previous years, he filed Fifth Amendment returns for 1974 and 1975. At his trial he stated that had he filed "traditional" returns (for 1974 and 1975) he would have exposed himself to criminal prosecution for allegedly filing false W-4s (claiming 99 exemptions which the Appellate court admitted was absolutely true). As the Appellate panel admitted, had Carlson filed a tax return (even if he only showed the amount, and not the source, of his income) it would have exposed him to criminal prosecution; and under the Constitution he was legally protected from having to do so. But the Ninth Circuit Court of Appeals upheld his conviction.[51] In his opinion Judge Wallace acknowledged that

> An examination of the facts of the case reveals that Carlson did assert the privilege. . . while facing a real and appreciable hazard of prosecution for having previously filed false withholding forms. In addition, there is little doubt that a truthfully completed tax return, stating his gross income, the lack of federal income taxes actually withheld and the true number of available deductions would have provided "a lead or clue to evidence having a tendency to incriminate . . ." The government concedes that Carlson could have been prosecuted under 26 U.S.C., Sec. 7205 for filing a false withholding form. . . [and that the] privilege is asserted to avoid incrimination for past tax crimes.[52]

Overlooking the sanctimonious and self-serving case law cited by the court (including the *Garner* case under which Carlson was absolutely barred from conviction), its decision boiled down to this:

> If Carlson's assertion of the privilege were valid, it would license a form of conduct that would undermine the entire system of personal income tax collection. . . We are thus confronted with the collusion of two critical interests: the privilege against self-incrimination, and the need for public revenue collection by a process necessarily reliant on self-

---

[51]He was prosecuted in the U.S. District Court for the Northern District of California before Samuel J. Conti. His conviction was affirmed by Appellate Court Judges Wallace and Kennedy with Earl R. Larson, a District Court judge from Minnesota "sitting by designation." Wallace wrote the opinion.

[52]*U.S. vs Carlson, supra,* page 520.

reporting[53]. . . [and that] the character and urgency of the public interest in raising revenue through self-reporting weighs heavily against affording the privilege to Carlson[54]. . . [and that since the government's power] to raise revenue is its life blood. . . [if other taxpayers were] permitted to employ Carlson's scheme. . . [this would] seriously impair the government's ability to determine tax liability. . . [and the government's ability to collect income taxes would be] *inordinately burdensome if not impossible.* . . [and that since] The record clearly discloses that Carlson was a tax protestor. . . *Carlson failed to assert the privilege in good faith.*[55] (Emphasis added)

It is obvious, therefore, that this court (along with other Federal courts) thought nothing of re-writing the Constitution. The court openly admitted that if Carlson filed a traditional return he could have been criminally prosecuted for doing so, but that he still, nevertheless, was legally required to file! The Fifth Amendment clearly states that "No person. . . shall be compelled. . . to be a witness against himself." So how could the Appellate court conclude that the Fifth Amendment was not available to Carlson because he was a tax protester? Does the Fifth Amendment say that "No person. . . shall be compelled. . . to be a witness against himself *except in tax cases?"*

The Fifth Amendment is law that the government *must* obey — in all circumstances, even those dealing with taxes. If the government's ability to collect a tax collides with a constitutional right, then the method of collecting the tax must yield, not the constitutional right. The public has a right to expect that the Constitution and the Bill of Rights will be enforced as written, *especially* in situations "burdensome" to the government because that is precisely why these rights were written into the Constitution in the first place. Our Founding Fathers were smart enough to know that — sooner or later — all governments come to regard individual rights and individual liberties as "burdensome."

In effect, the Carlson court ruled that while individuals may be required to obey the law, the government is not. It proves that the Mamelukes believe that they are free to openly admit they can disregard the Constitution whenever it serves their purposes.

---

[53] Wrong. The collusion was between his constitutional right of not being compelled to be a witness against himself and the government's insatiable appetite for more money to waste.

[54] Note here how the judiciary converted the Bill of Rights into the *Bill of Privileges.*

[55] *U.S. vs Carlson, supra,* pages 520–524.

290 The Great Income Tax Hoax

Signs That The Mamelukes Are Panicky

In case you think the Mamelukes are only content with doing away with the Fifth Amendment, on November 2, 1984 in Kansas City, Missouri, they did away with the First Amendment, too. On that date U.S. District Court of the Western District of Missouri issued a gag order prohibiting John Oaks (of Denver, Colorado) from "promoting the theory that income from wages and salaries is not taxable." On that same date the Justice Department filed suit in U.S. District Court of the Western District of Oklahoma seeking to get a similar gag order against James Turner of Oklahoma City. Sensing that the end is in sight, the Mamelukes are trying desperately to silence the truth with gag orders. In addition to gag orders, the Mamelukes also seek to suppress the truth with arbitrary and punitive court rulings. Recently the Second Circuit Court of Appeals doubled the fine and added a $500 penalty because Joseph W. Hennessey, Jr. (an accountant from Troy, New York) appealed his three-year sentence for failing to file on the grounds that his wages were not income.

Charles Keller

In early October, 1984 Charles Keller (a 37-year old bread salesman from Salem, Oregon) was prosecuted in Portland, Oregon before U.S. District Court "Judge" James M. Burns. Keller was indicted on a two count felony charge for tax fraud (pursuant to Code Section 7206) in connection with a Subchapter "S" return he filed in 1977; and three misdemeanor counts for allegedly failing to file personal income tax returns for 1978, 1979, and 1980 (pursuant to Code Section 7203). What sets his prosecution apart is that it demonstrates the totally arbitrary and capricious manner with which the government can enforce and criminally prosecute anyone under our present income tax "laws."

His alleged criminal tax fraud stemmed from contested business deductions of $3,967.05 and the alleged miscalculation of the capital gains tax on the sale of a $7,000 delivery truck (which Special Agent Philip Hopkins admitted would only have netted the government an additional $168 if calculated their way). Overlooking entirely the fact that these items were vigorously defended by Keller at trial, and overlooking completely the court's conduct (which at times found "Judge" Burns objecting for the government and admonishing the government's attorney for not doing so on his own), to charge a citizen with criminal fraud over such amounts is a measure of legal vindictiveness.

Countless Americans have business and personal deductions disallowed that amount to hundreds of times the amounts dealt with in

Keller's case and they receive no more than a civil penalty. Even Vice President Bush (in a highly publicized story during the last election) reduced his taxes by an erroneous capital gains calculation many times greater than Keller's, but he was not charged with criminal tax fraud because of it. Criminal fraud charges are traditionally reserved for those who fail to report *substantial* amounts of alleged income to the government. To brand a citizen a *felon* and send an otherwise productive and law-abiding American to prison because of disallowed buisness deductions (that would not have netted the government $1,000) is another example of the government's ruthless, corrupt, and arbitrary exercise of its taxing powers and demonstrates why such powers must be stripped from them.

The reason Keller was prosecuted in this way is because the IRS regards him as a tax protestor — someone exercising his First Amendment right of free speech to educate and arouse a sleeping public concerning the government's illegal enforcement of the income tax. Because of the government's arbitrary and ruthless criminal prosecution of Keller (for something generally given only a civil penalty) the government has made a sham and a mockery of the American principle of equal justice under the law. But what is one more mockery to a Federal judiciary that constantly mocks the entire Constitution?

On November 19, 1984, Charles Keller received a three year sentence (with two years suspended) and five years probation on the criminal fraud charges, and a suspended sentence with probation on the failure to file charge. He was immediately ordered incarcerated at his sentencing.[56] In this case, for example, where the defendant is no more guilty of the "crimes" for which he was convicted than Mother Hubbard[57], and where court error (in order to get the conviction) would have to be a mile high and a mile wide, Burns held that Keller had no legitimate basis for an appeal and immediately ordered him locked up!

How does this differ from the legal procedures manual of the Soviet Union? Yet these are the kinds of "trials" that now take place in America. They reveal the danger of filing — the risk of exposing oneself to felony charges even over *minor* disputed deductions! In essence, Keller

[56]Under a new law that went into effect on October 12, 1984 judges (even if informed of a defendant's intent to appeal) can nevertheless order them immediately imprisoned if *they believe* that an appeal is groundless and/or instituted merely for delay, which only demonstrates the inherent danger of giving additional arbitrary powers to Federal "judges."

[57]The real law-breakers in this affair are the "judge" who sentenced him and Arthur Davis, the Justice Department torpedo who flew in from Washington, D.C. to prosecute him.

was prosecuted and jailed because he openly espoused and promoted the perfectly correct legal belief that filing and paying income taxes are voluntary. So he, like many other Americans, was locked up **as a political prisoner:** Yes, we do have them in America, too!

"Lee" Mele

On February 10, 1982 Armond "Lee" Mele, a retired newspaper publisher from Franklin Lakes, New Jersey, was *invited* to testify before a grand jury that was to consider indicting him for failure to file income tax returns pursuant to Section 7203. A Section 7203 violation is a misdemeanor, not a felony, so the government normally initiates prosecutions (as it did in my case) by way of an "information, " a document filed by a U.S. Attorney stating that he has *information* that the accused committed the alleged "crime" without any probable cause having to be otherwise established.[58] In Mele's case, however, the government (for some strange reason) decided to proceed legally and seek an indictment. Most criminal lawyers advise targets of grand jury investigations *not* to testify since, in such circumstances, they are not permitted assistance of counsel and the government's attorney can spring any kind of question on them and confront them with all sorts of documents. In addition, *everything* they say can be used against them at a regular trial if the investigation results in an indictment. Despite all of this Mele wanted to testify anyway.

Fortunately for him, my book, *How Anyone Can Stop Paying Income Taxes*, had just been published and a copy was immediately dispatched to him right from the printer. In a letter to me on February 12, 1982, he said:

> The information I derived from your latest book "How Anyone Can Stop Paying Income Taxes" was responsible for the Grand Jury to return a verdict in my favor. The thirteen hours I spent reading and absorbing all the pertinent information in your book enabled me to overcome anything the U.S. Attorneys presented to the jury.

This was confirmed in a letter Mele received from W. Hunt Dumont, U.S. Attorney for the District of New Jersey, in which he stated:

> The purpose of this letter is to advise you that the Tax Division of the Department of Justice has declined prosecution in connection with your non-filing of federal income tax returns for the years 1977 and 1978.

[58]Omitting an analysis of why such "Informations" (even in these cases) are illegal, it is easy to see how "Informations" can be used by the government to prosecute as "criminals" those who are merely attempting to expose its illegal, taxing activities while hoodwinking the public into thinking that traditional American concepts of justice are being observed.

So even though he admittedly filed no income tax returns for the years in question, the U.S. Attorney informed him that the grand jury refused to indict him. (Both of these letters were reproduced in *The Schiff Report*, Volume 2, Number 6.)

Had the government elected to prosecute Mele by way of an "Information, " he could have found himself (as I did) prosecuted and imprisoned for a "crime" for which a grand jury (given the same facts) would have refused to indict. How do we account for this strange situation? When Mele was before the grand jury he did not have to contend with a Federal "judge" running and controlling the proceedings. Free from such overbearing, judicial tyranny, Mele was easily able to beat two seasoned government lawyers who were sent to "get" him — proof that the government has been getting Section 7203 *convictions* not because of the ability of its prosecutors, but because of the assistance of its prosecuting "judges."

Mele's experience proves that all Section 7203 prosecutions (as well as all "tax protest" prosecutions) initiated either by way of an "Information" or an indictment had to have been illegal and fraudulently obtained. If individuals can be legally prosecuted and convicted for such "crimes, " why could not two U.S. Attorneys get a simple indictment against Mele? The difference is that Mele showed the grand jury the law (proving he could legally do what he had done) and he also pointed out the government's responsibility under that law — and two U.S. Attorneys could not refute his testimony *because they did not have a Federal "judge" to help them confuse the jury!* "Lee" Mele, apprehensive private citizen — who had never been in such a setting — was able to successfully rout two U.S. Attorneys, armed only with my book!

Why Federal "Judges" Believe They Can Break The Law

Immediately after leaving the Federal Correctional Institute in Lexington, Kentucky in July, 1981, I wrote letters to the three Federal Grand Juries sitting in New Haven, Connecticut. I informed them that I had evidence that would establish the criminal culpability of the Federal judges and U.S. Attorneys who had taken part in my two trials and that their actions violated Sections 241 and 242 of the U.S. Criminal Code (see Exhibit 11). I was never called to testify despite the fact that I had reached the foreman of one of the juries by phone.[59]

When I did not hear from the grand jury for more than five months, I went to the New Haven office of District Court Judge, Ellen Burns to

---

[59]I have since written to other grand juries with the same results. At one point I notified the U.S. Attorney's office that I wished to appear but I still have not been called to testify, but I have evidence that the U.S. Attorney's office actually influenced the grand jury *not* to call me!

complain.[60] I was not able to speak to Judge Burns but her law clerk consented to see me. I explained my problem to him (my belief that I had sufficient evidence to get Judge Clarie and others involved in my illegal prosecutions indicted) and said I wanted to present this evidence to a grand jury but none of them would call me to testify. He then bluntly asked, "Suppose you did get the indictments, who would you get to prosecute?"

I answered, "Just let me get the indictments, I'm not concerned with their prosecution."

His implication, however, was clear and explains why Federal "judges"feel free to break the law: They are positive they will never be indicted or prosecuted for ciminally breaking laws in favor of the government. This we are determined to change!

EXHIBIT 11

§ 241. Conspiracy against rights of citizens

If two or more persons conspire to injure, oppress, threaten, or intimidate any citizen in the free exercise or enjoyment of any right or privilege secured to him by the Constitution or laws of the United States, or because of his having so exercised the same; or

If two or more persons go in disguise on the highway, or on the premises of another, with intent to prevent or hinder his free exercise or enjoyment of any right or privilege so secured—

They shall be fined not more than $10,000 or imprisoned not more than ten years, or both; and if death results, they shall be subject to imprisonment for any term of years or for life.

§ 242. Deprivation of rights under color of law

Whoever, under color of any law, statute, ordinance, regulation, or custom, willfully subjects any inhabitant of any State, Territory, or District to the deprivation of any rights, privileges, or immunities secured or protected by the Constitution or laws of the United States, or to different punishments, pains, or penalties, on account of such inhabitant being an alien, or by reason of his color, or race, than are prescribed for the punishment of citizens, shall be fined not more than $1,000 or imprisoned not more than one year, or both; and if death results shall be subject to imprisonment for any term of years or for life.

---

[60]Since grand juries fall within the judicial branch of government and are specifically charged with investigating crimes brought to their attention, I assumed it was a responsibility of the district judge who empanelled them to remind them of that duty.

17

Tax "Court" and Other Tax-Related Scams

The income tax scam involves hoaxes within hoaxes, the greatest being "Tax Court." First, such "courts" are not constitutional. Federal courts are provided for in Article III of the Constitution which begins "The judicial power of the United States shall be vested. . . " Tax Court, on the other hand, is established under Article I which deals with the *powers of Congress* (hence the term "Article I courts"). "Article I courts" were first established by Congress in the territories before they achieved statehood. Not being a formal part of the Union, these territories could not have a legal system that was integrated with the nation's regular system, so to keep law and order Congress established (under its own authority) these "courts." Congress, however, is not granted any power in Article I to establish courts *of any kind* in the United States. "Tax Court," therefore, is really a "territorial court" and that is precisely how it is run. In fact, most tax "court" decisions sound as if they were written by "judges" who just spent half their day carousing in a frontier saloon.

Tax court "judges" are, by definition, not even judges though the Federal government deceives the public into believing otherwise. Legitimate Federal judges are established under Article I, Section 1 of the Constitution which states, that "judges, both of the Supreme and *inferior* courts, shall hold their offices during good behavior. . . " In other words, they are appointed for life. Tax court "judges," on the other hand, are appointed for a fifteen year period and, therefore (by definition), cannot be lawful Federal judges in America. Tax "Courts," moreover, violate the "separation of powers" principle since they are creatures of the Executive branch of government and not of an independent and co-equal judiciary. Yet the rulings of these "courts," which have no more judicial standing than the opinion of a bureaucrat are treated by the Federal judiciary as if they had the color of law.

Tax "Court" differs in other ways from regular courts. Taxpayers have to petition Tax "Court" to hear their cases or the "court" cannot get jurisdiction. For example, the IRS makes a determination that a taxpayer owes a "deficiency" on his taxes and the taxpayer then has to take the government (IRS) to Tax "Court" *to prove that he does not owe it*. This is the exact opposite of the usual condition which places the burden of proof on the party claiming the money. Individuals are conned into petitioning Tax "Court" because they receive a "Notice of Deficiency" (commonly called a 90 Day Letter, see Appendix F) from the IRS which they believe is a *demand* for payment. They are further tricked into believing that if they do not petition Tax "Court" and challenge the phony demand, the government can lawfully collect the amount allegedly owed by force and, therefore, they petition Tax "Court" for a "hearing."

An important element that enables Tax "Court" to perpetuate the income tax scam (and to protect itself) is its refusal to allow petitioners to have as counsel anyone who the "court" has not approved beforehand. Naturally the "court" will only approve individuals who basically accept the "court's" perversion of the entire income tax "law" (that individuals are *required* to file and to pay income taxes; that sources of income are taxable; and all the other standard garbage that lawyers, accountants, and the IRS have been feeding the American public for years). On September 14, 1984, for example, Chief Tax "Court" Judge Howard Dawson suspended Denver Attorney Cecil A. Hartman from practicing before that "court" because, Dawson said, Hartman was arguing "that wages are not income, and such arguments can only be characterized as frivolous." This makes it a waste of time to go before a Tax "Court" — and anyone who is "approved" to practice in that "court" either does not know the law or, if he does, is barred from applying it.

To show just how fearful Tax "Court" is of someone with any legal skill who raises this issue, Hartman never even argued this issue before that "court!" His suspension involved four cases (he initiated the petitions in only two of them) that he never was allowed to argue. Hartman is currently appealing the suspension — but that is how Tax "Court" operates. Nobody who appears in Tax "Court" can possibly get effective counsel so he must either represent himself (a difficult task at best) or use the "court's" own lackey. In short, Tax "Court" is nothing more than a drumhead court martial.

Irwin Schiff In Tax "Court"

In February, 1982 I received a 90 Day Letter (dated January 29, 1982) under the *typed* name of Roscoe Egger, Commissioner of Internal Revenue. It alleged that I had been assessed a tax "deficiency" of $19,632 for the years 1974 and 1975 and listed interest penalties in the amount of $664.00 plus $9,800 in *fraud* penalties. Before explaining the total illegality of this "notice, " I must recount another incident that has a bearing on the fraudulent nature of the "notice" and also establishes the blatant illegality of all IRS seizure activities.

On July 16, 1981 (immediately upon my release from Federal detention) I filed a complaint in Federal District Court against the United States government, U.S. Attorney Richard Blumenthal, and Assistant U.S. Attorney Michael Hartmere. I was seeking declaratory relief (a restraining order) to enjoin the defendants from prosecuting me for not filing income tax returns for the years 1976 through 1980 on the grounds that since I had been illegally prosecuted once I faced the danger of being illegally prosecuted again for the years for which I openly admitted not filing.[1]

On September 16 the government filed a motion (and brief) asking for dismissal of my suit and $468.75 to cover the cost of responding to it. Despite refuting the government's arguments in my reply brief, and besting them in oral argument, the District Court nevertheless granted the government's motion to dismiss and, parroting its claim of "contumacy indicative of bad faith, " awarded the government attorney's fees of $468.75.[2]

When "Judge" Ellen Burns ordered me to pay this amount, I filed a motion "to correct an ambiguous and therefore illegal fine" in which I explained that since the government no longer provided lawful dollars and since the only kind of ersatz money I had was Federal Reserve Notes (no longer redeemable for lawful dollars) and tokens (coined to look like lawful dollars), I could not legally pay the fine ordered by the "court." On December 8, 1981 "Judge" Burns (relying solely on an immaterial lower court case — *United States vs Daly* 481 F.2d 28 [8th Circuit]) held my claim "wholly without merit" and ordered me to pay "FOUR HUNDRED SIXTY-EIGHT DOLLARS AND SEVENTY-FIVE CENTS (468.75), payable in legal tender, namely, federal reserve notes." On December 24, 1981 I moved for relief of that judgement pursuant to Rule 60(b) on the following grounds:

1. that since a note is a promise to pay, and currently issued Fed-

---

[1]This was tantamount to someone who was convicted of robbing one bank, walking into court admitting to robbing other banks but now asking the court's protection from additional prosecution. In my case, however, my motion *proved* I was illegally prosecuted and why I had a right to the restraining order. But if not filing income tax returns is *really* a "crime, " why did the government not immediately prosecute me for all the years I openly admitted to not filing?

[2]See Appendix E for the full text of my answer to the government's Motion to Dismiss my suit.

eral reserve "notes" contained no such promise, I could not pay
the fine in "notes" as ordered by the "court";

2. that the *Daly* decision had to do with the taxability of such
   "notes" and was not relevant to the issues I raised; and

3. that pursuant to a number of Supreme Court cases the "court"
   had no authority to order me to pay a fine in the bogus notes of
   a private banking syndicate and "unless the Plaintiff can secure bonafide Federal Reserve notes that are redeemable in lawful dollars, the judgement of this court as contained in its order
   of December 8, 1981 is clearly void and contrary to law."

On December 28, 1981 Judge Burns denied my motion without comment. I was preparing to appeal her unlawful order to the Second Circuit Court of Appeals, but before I could, something happened that
sheds a tremendous amount of light on the illegal seizure activities of
the IRS.

In early May, 1982 a United States marshall served my bank with
a court order for the $468.75 fine. My bank informed me of this imme-
diately and said that the amount would be frozen pending a final disposition of the matter since I had the right to complete an affidavit
certifying I did not owe the amount claimed, which I did. Connecticut
banking regulations apparently provide that if a bank depositor certi-
fies he does not owe the amount claimed by a judgement creditor, the
judgement creditor has thirty days to go back into court to resolve the
matter. The following month (much to my surprise) I received a copy of
a motion in which the government asked the District Court to set aside
this regulation because it had allowed the thirty days to elapse and,
therefore, the bank removed the lien and cleared my funds. I responded
by pointing out to the "court" that it had no authority to set aside Connecticut banking regulations. The "court" agreed and denied the motion on June 24, 1982. So, even with a court order and a U.S. marshall,
the Federal government was unable to get my funds out of my bank.[3]
Next I filed an appeal of Judge Burns' unlawful order with the Second
Circuit Court of Appeals.[4]

Getting back to the "Notice of Deficiency" I had received (alleging
more than $19,000 in taxes due *plus* interest *and* fraud penalties), the
government had already sent me to jail for not filing tax returns for the

---

[3]Contrast this with how easily an IRS agent was able to remove my funds from the same
bank without a court order of any kind and without the bank even notifying me that
my funds were leaving the bank! (See page 366.)

[4]Both of my appeal briefs and the government's brief (together with the "decision" of the
Appeals Court on this issue) are shown in Appendix E.

years they now claimed I owed a tax. Under the law (Section 6201) the IRS had absolutely *no authority* to even *estimate* a tax (let alone assess one) since I had neither sent in a "return" nor a "list" for either year. To understand the full extent of the corruption, lawlessness, and tyranny with which the entire Federal income tax is run, one has to understand how this totally unauthorized "estimate" of my "tax deficiency" and penalties were arrived at.

In 1974 I was living in Ft. Lauderdale, Florida working full-time writing my first book, *The Biggest Con: How The Government is Fleecing You.* I drew a $300.00 a week salary from my Connecticut corporation and supplemented it by occasionally selling precious metals. Using illegally subpoenaed bank records to "estimate" my 1974 "income, " the IRS listed as "income" the following items:

1. my $15,000 salary (which they termed "compensation" to illegally place it within the provisions of Section 61);
2. a $1,000 initial royalty advance from my book;
3. some $4,000 in other "commissions and dividends"; and
4. a lone $38,000 bank deposit which reflected funds given to me in my capacity as a broker for the purchase of some silver and gold coin.

The IRS was not only seeking to tax sources of "income" as "income" itself, but in seeking to tax a lone $38,000 bank deposit as "income" (without making any attempt to determine its source), it was arbitrarily and outrageously seeking to tax pure conjecture as "income." It must be clearly understood that there is absolutely nothing in the law that even comes close to allowing this.

In addition, the $9,800 "fraud" penalty was imposed allegedly pursuant to Section 6653(b). But this section only provides that

If *any part* of any *underpayment* (as defined in subsection (c)) of tax *required* to be shown on a return *is due to fraud,* there shall be added to the tax an amount equal to 50 percent of the underpayment. (Emphasis added)

Subsection (c) defines underpayment as "the tax shown on a return." This section can, therefore, only apply to

1. someone who *files a return*; and/or
2. someone who *makes fraudulent statements; and/or payments* (under penalty of perjury) in connection with returns that are "required" to be filed.

Fraud penalties under Section 6653(b), therefore, could not apply to me on any basis because:

1. I made no payment of any tax for either year so it was impossible that "any part of any underpayment" could be due to fraud for the simple reason that there was no "part" to which "fraud" could apply — because no "part" of any payment was ever made so there was no "part" for the government to consider; and
2. there was no "tax shown on a return" for either year so this also ruled out any possibility that Code Section 6653(b) could apply to me.

Any semi-literate Federal bureaucrat should have been able to figure out that no *fraud* penalties (pursuant to Section 6653(b) could have applied to me. The IRS's total disregard of the obvious provisions of that section of the Code, is so indisputably clear that it permits almost instant evaluation of the entire Federal income tax operation.

1. If the IRS can impose substantial "fraud" penalties under a Code provision that *clearly does not apply;*
2. if such obviously illegal penalties can be staunchly defended and affirmed by both Tax "Court" and a Federal Appellate court; and
3. if such an obvious and total disregard of Code provisions can still provide the basis for IRS seizures of property without a court order

then *it must be obvious* that when you deal with the Federal government you are dealing with the *real crime syndicate* in America.

Apart from all of the above there is another reason why Section 6653(b) could not apply to me — or to *anyone else* for that matter — even if false statements were made on a tax return. Recognizing and understanding this subtrefuge helps explain how the government is able to *forcibly* collect income taxes and related penalties even though *no such forced exactions are authorized anywhere in the Code.*

Note that Section 6653(b) does not *merely* state that penalties under that section apply to "any underpayment of tax shown on a return, " but only to underpayments *"required* to be shown on a return." Therefore, the section cannot apply to income taxes[5] because "income" taxes are not one of the Federal taxes *"required* to be shown on a return, " so all the billions of dollars in "fraud" penalties (with respect to income

---

[5]Note there is no mention of "income" taxes anywhere in Section 6653(b).

taxes) extracted from the public under this statute were *never owed or even provided for by it!* So, in collecting these fictitious "fraud" penalties, the Federal government itself has been engaged in massive criminal fraud involving major governmental institutions — the Department of the Treasury, the Justice Department, and the *entire* Federal judiciary.

Interest Penalties

In addition to the fraud penalties assessed, the IRS added $664.00 in interest penalties pursuant to Section 6654. This section provides that "In the case of any *underpayment* of estimated tax by an individual. . .[that]. . . the amount of the installment which would be *required* to be paid if the estimated tax were equal to 80 percent. . ." This section also could not apply to me — nor to anyone else with respect to income taxes — for all the same reasons discussed in connection with Code Section 6653(b) and specifically because I made no "underpayment of [an] estimated tax."

On top of all this, a few months after receiving my "Notice of Deficiency" I wrote to the Secretary of the Treasury asking (pursuant to Section 6203) for a copy of the record of my assessment. In a letter received from the IRS Service Center in Andover, Massachusetts dated June 23, 1982 (see Exhibit 12), I was informed that as of that date "there is no record of a tax assessment for [you] for the years 1974 and 1975 at the present time." **Five months after I was notified by the Commissioner of Internal Revenue that I owed the government some $31,000 in back taxes and penalties his department informed me that I did not owe the government a dime!** And since I had not been assessed any taxes as of June 23, 1982, how could I have possibly been assessed as of January 22, 1982 — the date of the "Notice of Deficiency — or owe any interest on taxes that were never assessed (and thus were not "due") or committed "fraud" with respect to taxes never assessed?

The Fraudulent "Notice Of Deficiency"

One of the most blatantly illegal ploys used by the government in its income tax operations[6] is its use of the "Notice Of Deficiency" which

---

[6]The government collects income taxes on the basis that it makes no difference how many Code sections it violates. Thus, given the public's total unfamiliarity with the law (and the duplicity of lawyers) as well as its naive belief in the honesty of the Federal judiciary, it can get away with *anything. And it does!*

EXHIBIT 12

Internal Revenue Service

Department of the Treasury

P. O. Box 1500
Andover, MA 01810

Date:

JUN 2 3 1982

In reply refer to:
0858O535

Person to Contact:
Richard J. DeLotto

Telephone Number:
617-681-9793

Irwin A. Schiff
Freedom Books
P. O. Box 5303
Hamden, Connecticut 06518

Dear Mr. Schiff:

This is in response to your inquiry to Mr. Donald T. Regan, Secretary of the Treasury, which has been forwarded to us for response.

In accordance with Internal Revenue Code Section 6203, there is no record of a tax assessment for the tax years 1974 and 1975 at the present time.

If you have any further question regarding this matter you may call Mr. DeLotto of my staff at the telephone number shown above. Since this is not a toll-free number, you may prefer to write to him at the address in the heading of this letter.

Sincerely yours,

JOSEPH H. CLOONAN
Director

deceives the public into conferring jurisdiction over non-existent tax liabilities to "courts" that have no interest whatsoever in their legitimacy. When taxpayers petition Tax "Court," the rules of the "court" (which the public never understands) say that in so petitioning, petitioners have accepted the basic legality of both the deficiency and the penalties, and are only requesting a "redetermination" of the amount(s) due. Petitioners never discover this diabolical trap (if they ever do) until *after they go to Tax "Court"* which, by then, is too late.

Individuals who receive these "notices" are misled into believing that they represent *final demands* for payment of the amount(s) shown and that they basically have four choices:[7]

1. petition Tax "Court" within ninety days for a "redetermination"of the amount(s) shown:
2. pay the amount(s) shown and then (if they wish) sue for a refund in District court, thereby conferring jurisdiction to a Federal "court";
3. negotiate a settlement; or
4. do nothing and see all their assets systematically and illegally confiscated by the government (without court orders of any kind).[8]

The government has very cleverly arranged this process so that no matter what option an individual chooses it is *the citizen who must initiate the court action* — either as the petitioner in Tax "Court" or as the plaintiff in District court. The government did this because there is nothing in the law that says anyone has to pay income taxes so the government could never get into court on its own. It would be a simple matter (not even requiring the help of a high-priced or even tax-knowledgeable lawyer) for any citizen to get such government-inititated lawsuits dismissed (even from its own crooked courts) on any one of a number of grounds, one of which is that no liability for such a tax is found anywhere in the law. The government could not refute a defense

---

[7]Until now these were realistically the only choices available to the public, but Chapter 18 of this book presents a fifth choice.

[8]In many instances "deficiency assessments" and penalties are set so arbitrarily high that they can bankrupt individuals or leave them without the necessary funds to effectively fight the government in District courts. This is also a part of the government's well-thought-out scam to prevent the illegality of its acts from being successfully challenged. Another problem facing taxpayers is the impossibility of finding knowledgeable and effective legal counsel. Most lawyers simply to not know the law and those few who do and might press it will be intimidated, fined, and otherwise disciplined by the "courts." (See page 296.)

as simple as this if it were made in a defendant's motion to dismiss so any such government lawsuit *would have to be thrown out even by a partisan judiciary.*[9] *By forcing citizens to initiate court action, the government avoids having to establish the legal legitimacy of its tax claim!* In addition, this shifts the burden of proof to the public under conditions that render it *impossible for them to carry their burden.* The Mamelukes have not overlooked a thing!

What "Deficiencies" Are and How They Are Illegally Created

Section 6211 of the Internal Revenue Code defines a "deficiency assessment" as

> the amount by which the [deficiency]. . . exceeds the excess of-
> (1) The sum of
> (A) the amount *shown as the tax by the taxpayer upon his return,* if a return was made by the taxpayer and an amount was shown as the tax by the taxpayer thereon, plus
> (B) the amounts *previously assessed* (or collected without assessment as a deficiency. . .) (Emphasis added)

It is obvious from the above that no "deficiency assessment" can exist unless the taxpayer files a return and shows a tax due. Since income taxes are based on "self-assessment" the government has no statutory authority to assess income taxes on its own. It, therefore, uses the following ploy: once an individual foolishly files a return and swears on it (under "penalty of perjury") that he has "income" and owes an "income" tax, the government takes him at his word. Once this is done, the government is authorized to assess the taxes shown on the return and then has a *statutory basis* for *increasing* this assessment by a "deficiency" based upon all the *false* assumptions made by the taxpayer on his return (i.e., that he had *gross* and *taxable* "income"). If the individual did not voluntarily agree to assess himself by sending in either a "return or a list," the government has no *statutory authority to make either an assessment or a "deficiency assessment."* Even the latter term admits there must have been an initial *assessment* before there can logically be a subsequent "deficiency." This is confirmed by the following court cases. In *Lydon & Company vs U.S.* 158 F. Supp. 951, the court stated:

> When one files a return showing a tax due, he has presumably assessed himself and is content to become liable for the tax and to pay it either when it is due according to the statute or when he can get the money together.

[9]I assume that there are limits beyond which even Federal "judges" can contrive decisions.

In *Uncasville Mfg. Company vs Commissioner of IRS* 55 F.2d. 893, the court held:

> A deficiency is an amount by which the tax exceeds [the] sum of [the] amount shown by [a] return and [the] amount previously assessed as [a] deficiency "held to mean deficiency conceded by [the] taxpayer."

Therefore, if the taxpayer has *conceded* no amount due (by not filing a tax return) there can be no "deficiency assessment."

In *Lisner vs McCanless* 356 F. Supp. 398, the court clarified the above positions by stating:

> Ordinarily, the procedure for collection of income tax would be for the taxpayer to file an annual return and to pay the amount due. At this point an "ordinary assessment" is made by entering on the rolls the tax reported and crediting the amount paid (*Flora vs U.S.* [see page 242], other citings omitted]. Thus section 6201(a) does provide assessment authority; that authority is limited on its face however.[7] As a general matter, taxes beyond those admitted by the taxpayer cannot be assessed except as a deficiency.

In a lengthy footnote (7 in above quote) the court stated in relevant part:

> Whether or not certain procedural rights attach therefore depends on the underlying nature of the assessment; "ordinary, " deficiency, or jeopardy. The cases do not always maintain this important semantic distinction. "Stated simply, a 'deficiency' is the excess of the amount of the tax (determined due the IRS) over the amount of tax reported by the taxpayer. . . "

As is obvious from these court explanations, there can be no "deficiency assessment" unless a taxpayer 1) first concedes that he owes a tax on a return, and 2) that there is a difference between an "ordinary" assessment and a "deficiency assessment" which the government conveniently overlooks so it can swindle the public.

Since I *never* conceded a tax on a return or had an "ordinary" assessment, by law I could not possibly have had a "deficiency." In other words, the entire "Notice of Deficiency" I received (including the fraud and interest penalties) was illegal and Roscoe Egger and all the other government officials who had a hand in preparing and sending it are candidates (under various Federal statutes — including mail fraud) for incarceration.

Prior to receiving the 90 Day Letter I received a 30 Day Letter suggesting that I owed these same amounts. It asked for my signature indicating my acceptance of these determinations. I acknowledged the letter and in rejecting the government's claims as absurd, I reminded the government that the income tax is based on self-assessment and voluntary compliance, and since it falls into none of the taxing clauses of the Constitution, I could not possibly "owe" what the government contended. I also explained that under the *Pollock, Brushaber,* and *Smietanka* decisions I had no taxable income. The IRS did not respond to the issues raised in my letter and simply disregarded it as if it had been sent to the KGB.[10]

I was not really familiar with Tax "Court" and wanted to find out how it operated so I submitted my petition. Since I was travelling at this time (promoting my book and conducting seminars) and knew nothing about Tax "Court" procedures, I relied on a paralegal who presumably did know. Unfortunately, this paralegal dropped the ball completely and filed nothing in a timely manner. As a result, I was forced to fly in from Portland, Oregon on Sunday March 27, 1983 for a Tax "Court" hearing in Hartford, Connecticut the next day.

Among other things, I submitted the following documents to the "Court":

1. Copies of letters sent to the government (pursuant to Section 6203) asking for the record of my assessment for the years in question (which I had done no less than *four* times).

2. The IRS's letter of June 23, 1982 stating that as of that date no income tax assessments had been made against me — proving that my "deficiency assessment" of December 29, 1982 (and all related penalties) were contrary to law and nothing but legal fabrications.

3. Numerous government documents attesting to the voluntary and self-assessment natures of the income tax including the Controller General's Report (see page 244) and excerpts from the Congressional Record (see page 242).

4. Excerpts from the following Supreme Court cases that corroborated my testimony: *Flora vs U.S., Brushaber vs Union Pacific Railroad, Eisner vs Macomber, Merchants' Loan vs Smietanka, Garner vs U.S., U.S. vs Ballard,* and the Zaretsky report (see page 201). All this material specifically attested to the fact that the income tax was an excise tax and, therefore, had to be levied

---

[10]In this respect the government has also done away with an individual's First Amendment *Right of Petition* which has also gone the way of the dodo bird.

as one in order for it to be legally mandatory and that payment of income taxes was voluntary and, therefore, I could not be *liable* for any of the taxes and penalties claimed.

In addition, I testified under oath regarding the following:

1. that I had no "income" for the years 1974 and 1975 but, rather, had only miscellaneous non-taxable receipts and that none of the penalty provisions (for all of the reasons stated) could apply to me;
2. that since tax returns under Section 6103 of the code are "open to inspection" by the Justice Department and can be used against taxpayers in all types of "civil or criminal" procedures, any *mandatory* "requirement" for providing such information would render the law unconstitutional on its very face. (I specifically testified that the income tax — so as not to be unconstitutional — contained no mandatory provisions and that for a variety of reasons the law would be unconstitutional if it were otherwise, and all penalties levied against me for not filing were, therefore, violative of the law.);
3. that Judge Clarie specifically ruled at my trial that tax returns are filed voluntarily;
4. that if the government's attorney, Robert Percy, Esq., could produce any official government document stating that income taxes were based on "compulsory compliance" (contrary to the evidence I had presented attesting that compliance was voluntary), I would immediately pay all alleged taxes due as well as all fines and penalties;
5. that the Supreme Court had clearly ruled that the government could not tax sources of income without apportioning the tax, and that the government (by simply listing alleged *sources* of my income — the bank deposit not even being a source) sought to tax such sources directly, in flagrant violation of both the *Brushaber* and *Pollock* decisions:
6. that I would pay Mr. Percy $100,000 if he would point out any Section of the Internal Revenue Code that "required the filing of tax returns";
7. that though my "deficiency assessment" specifically referred several times to "your [my] tax liability, " no code section establishing such a "liability" was ever cited in the notice;
8. that my main reason for not filing tax returns was based on the fact that the law did not require it; but, if anything, the issue involved was one of not wanting to be a witness against myself

and had nothing to do with the issue of self-incrimination;
9. and, finally, I asked the government (or the court) to clarify if the tax it sought to extract from me was an indirect tax and into which taxing clause of the Constitution the tax fell.

The government did not attempt to refute (either by cross-examination or through its own witnesses) anything I testified to, nor did Mr. Percy make any attempt to claim the $100,000 by producing the Code section that "required" the filing of income tax returns. He also did not cite the Code section that established the "liability" referred to in the contested notice.

Since the government was also claiming "fraud" penalites, it had the burden of *proving* fraud. But the hearing transcript will show that the government did not produce any evidence or cross-examine me with respect to any document allegedly reflecting a false or fraudulent statement. Neither did the government call any witnesses who would testify regarding the fraudulent character of any document. The government's entire "fraud" case was based on its naked assertion — believe it or not — that (based on my *college grades* that Mr. Percy introduced a transcript of) *I must have known I was acting fraudulently!* Similarly, Mr. Percy introduced my books, *The Biggest Con. . .* and *How Anyone. . .* , which also had nothing to do with any "fraud" I might have committed with respect to income taxes.

A sampling of Mr. Percy's questions follows:

PERCY: You received a Bachelor of Science degree from the School of Business Administration?
SCHIFF: That's irrelevant. I will stipulate to the fact that I was educated.
THE COURT: Well, you know —
SCHIFF: What has that got to do with whether or not I had income?

My objection was overruled and my college grades were entered into the trial and used against me by the "court." Next, the government introduced my book, *The Biggest Con. . .* , and the questioning continued:

PERCY: Chapter seven is entitled, *U.S. Taxes: How They Have Converted the American Worker Into a Serf.*
SCHIFF: No question about it. The average person, you Honor, now pays 40 percent of his productivity in taxes.[11]
THE COURT: Just answer the question.
PERCY: Chapter eight says taxes are the arsenic in our system.

---

[11]This was before I saw the Federal Reserve report shown in Appendix A.

SCHIFF: That is correct.
PERCY: And, the subtitle under that is *Let's have a tax revolt?*
SCHIFF: That's correct.
PERCY: And these were your beliefs at the time?

Here the government (which has the burden of proving "fraud" on a return) was trying to prove tax fraud based upon books and documents having absolutely nothing to do with any tax return or with Section 6653(b) upon which fraud penalties are based. The point is, the government had no basis for tax fraud whatsoever and was simply trying to build a case on the basis of a book I wrote that received over eighty excellent reviews, sold over 90,000 copies, and has been used as a college and high school text. How more blatantly illegal can the government's case have been?

Next, the government introduced my book, *How Anyone Can Stop Paying Income Taxes,* and questioned me as follows:

PERCY: In your book on page 85 you advocate telephoning the IRS agent on the day before the scheduled audit, preferably late in the afternoon, and simply break the appointment?
SCHIFF: Thats is correct.
PERCY: You also advocate -
SCHIFF: Your Honor, this has nothing to do with whether I had taxable income in '74 and '75.
THE COURT: He is getting to the issue.
SCHIFF: If that is illegal why doesn't the government arrest me for advocating breaking appointments with the IRS? Your Honor, all this is irrelevant. My testimony dealt with —
THE COURT: We understand what your — you made an objection to the relevancy of this.
SCHIFF: That is irrelevant.
THE COURT: All right, sir. We will take that under consideration.
PERCY: You also advocate that the IRS agents should be asked to put everything in writing.
SCHIFF: No question about it. It is my experience with IRS agents that they don't understand the law. So, therefore, get it in writing.

So, while the government's attorney sought here to establish "fraud" on the basis of my book, *How Anyone. . . ,* the government itself never attempted to refute one word of it![12]

[12]When media people contact IRS public relations offices to get background material on me they get lengthy dissertations about my convictions, the confiscation of my money, and a general misstatement of my views. But, despite the fact that this book has been in circulation for three years — certainly a thorn in the government's side — to this day neither the IRS nor anyone else has attempted to specifically refute one line of it.

Mr. Percy next went over the items shown on my "Notice of Deficiency." I pointed out that none of these items constituted income but were merely "sources" of "income." As far as Percy was concerned, though, I might have been talking to the wall.

The Government's Case

The government's sole witness was a Mr. Richard Hammond, identified as an IRS agent with five years of service. He testified that he "was detailed to district counsel two weeks ago to assist in the preparation of the trial." His testimony took up 5 1/2 pages of the hearing transcript and in cross-examination he disclosed that his sole duty and knowlege of the taxes and penalties shown on my deficiency notice was that he "verified the calculations." The judge would not allow me to cross-examine him regarding any matter of substance in connection with the taxes or penalties shown on the notice so I said the following to the court:

> SCHIFF: I am frustrated. Let me tell you why. I testified under oath that I am willing to be cross-examined on my belief that I don't owe a tax, that income tax is voluntary. I expect the government to put on the stand an expert witness to dispute my testimony. It is not fair that Mr. Hammond testify on matters of which he has no knowledge. . .

It is part of the government's tax strategy never to put on the witness stand a qualified government expert (such as an IRS attorney) since they could be cross-examined on the law. At all "trials" and "hearings" the government makes sure that only non-lawyers testify (for the government) so that "judges" can step in to prevent any in-depth legal cross-examination of witnesses on the grounds that because such witnesses are not lawyers they are not "experts in the law." Tax Court "judges," therefore, sustain all government objections to questions asked of government witnesses that involve issues of law. In cross-examining Mr. Hammond I said:

> SCHIFF: Does the code provide for an income tax on these items [wages, commissions, and bank deposits]?
> PERCY: I object.
> SCHIFF: I'm going to give you [Hammond] Section 61 and you show me where in Section 61 —
> PERCY: I object.
> THE COURT: Sustained.
> SCHIFF: Your Honor, Section 61 did not lay a tax on these specific items.

> THE COURT: Well, if that is your position — the court understands that.
> It is his position that it does and it is also the position of the
> IRS that it does.
>
> SCHIFF: Is it the court's position?
>
> THE COURT: [in an attempt to evade the issue] You people are at issue on
> that.
>
> SCHIFF: Is it the court's position that Section 61 provides a direct tax on
> these items?
>
> THE COURT: I am not going to answer that here, because you know that
> it is.
>
> SCHIFF: It is?
>
> THE COURT: Certainly it is.
>
> SCHIFF: Is it the court's position that Section 61 provides a tax on inter-
> est, rents and royalties?
>
> THE COURT: Yes, sir.

Here Hamblen openly admitted that the government was not taxing "income" but was directly taxing *property* without apportionment
— *in open and flagrant violation of the apportionment provisions of the
Constitution, the 16th Amendment, the Brushaber decision and the Internal Revenue Code itself!* How much more evidence is needed to prove that
the government's entire income tax operation is based upon fraud and
coercion — and these Mamelukes know it.

I continued to question Mr. Hammond as follows:

> SCHIFF: Are you going to testify under oath, sir, that I committed fraud
> with respect to my '74 and '75 returns, is that your testimony?
>
> PERCY: I object, your Honor. I would say, he is not.
>
> SCHIFF: Oh, he is not. Well, then who is?
>
> THE COURT: Would you again relate to Mr. Schiff what your purpose is
> in connection with the exhibit that you testified about.
>
> HAMMOND: Yes, sir. I looked at the copy of the Statutory Notice of Defi-
> ciency, made through the calculations, looked over the case
> file and verified the calculations apart from the typograph-
> ical error which was mentioned previously in the recapitu-
> lation of items. And that is what I did.

Because the government put no one on the stand who would *swear*
to the accuracy of lawfullness of any of the items on the deficiency notice, I could not cross-examine anyone who actually had a hand in determining (or who was qualified to discuss) my alleged taxes or the
penalties assessed. While I (under oath) testified (*swore*) that all such
items were false and contrary to law and the government made no attempt to refute my sworn testimony. Any *legitimate* court would have accepted my *sworn testimony* as true since the government made no effort

to *challenge* it either by cross-examining me or through the direct testimony of any qualified witnesses of its own. *How, then, could any legitimate court find me guilty of anything?*

At the end of Mr. Percy's brief cross-examination of me I addressed the "court" as follows:

> SCHIFF: Let me point out your Honor, that the government did not cross-examine me with respect to my claim that income taxes are indeed voluntary. The government did not cross-examine me with respect to my contention that the income tax is based upon self-assessment. The government did not deny any of this — the government merely cross-examined with respect to my college grades, with respect to my Freedom Kit, with the fact that I wrote some books, and, all of the government's questioning had nothing to do with whether I had a tax liability. Again all of this is immaterial as to whether I owed any taxes or whether or not I committed fraud in connection with any document I submitted to the government. . . Nor did the government produce any document or Code Section that said filing was mandatory [though I produced government documents that said it was not] nor did Percy attempt to claim his $100,000 reward. Though the issue of *fraud* has to be proved by the government *it did not offer one document* on which it was alleged that a false or fraudulent statement had been made.[13] (Emphasis added)

"Judge" Hamblen's Decision

A reading of "Judge" Lapsley W. Hamblen Jr.'s Tax "Court" decision[14] reveals why tax court "judges" are indeed judges in name only. It is apparent that Hamblen did not have the slightest interest in either the facts or the law in this case. In arguments made before the "court" and in briefs filed with the "court" I basically presented all the material and arguments contained in this book — but it made no difference to that "court" or to "Judge" Hamblen. I could not have fared any worse if a Soviet judge had been flown in from Moscow to sit in for Hamblen.

From the following excerpt from "Judge" Hamblen's decision one would assume that he never even attended my "hearing":

> Petitioner argues that the Fifth Amendment privilege against self-incrimination relieves him of the obligation to file returns and pay taxes.[15]

---

[13]In essence, the government found me guilty of tax fraud because it took exception to some books I wrote. So, apart from violating all tax law, the "court" also violated my First Amendment right of free speech (i.e., my right to write and publish).

[14]*Irwin A. Schiff vs Commissioner* T.C. Memo 1984-223.

[15]Ibid., page 1707.

The transcript proves I "argued" no such thing. I even *denied* raising this very issue:

> SCHIFF: Section 6020 [Exhibit 13] says that if I consent to give information to the government they will prepare my tax return. And, if I don't consent they will prepare those returns on their own. And, there is no penalty in Section 6020 for not electing to voluntarily self-assess yourself. . . [16]
>
> I am swearing under penalty of perjury that there is no section of the code requiring anybody to file a tax return. And, if the government's attorney would point to any such section while he is under oath, in addition to paying all the taxes that he alleges, I will give him a hundred thousand dollars. . . [17]
>
> . . . the Fifth Amendment says nothing about self-incrimination. I am saying that the issue of self-incrimination has gotten into the tax issue because the original person who raised the issue, Sullivan, raised the lesser issue of self-incrimination when he should have raised the issue of not wanting to be a witness against himself. . . [18]
>
> The Constitution says that I cannot be compelled to be a witness against myself. Now if the government is going to maintain that the Internal Revenue Code can compel me to be a witness [against myself] under threat of prosecution, then the Internal Revenue Code would be unconstitutional. . . [19]

Does that sound as if I "argued" that it was the issue of "self-incrimination" that relieved me of my "obligation" to file tax returns as "Judge" Hamblen fraudulently contended? He simply fabricated my alleged "argument" just as he fabricated the rest of his decision. He further wrote:

> At trial, petitioner did not refute the correctness of respondents determination of tax liability. Instead petitioner offered various constitutional and other arguments as to his obligations to file returns and pay taxes.[20]

But look at what the trial transcript records as my sworn testimony:

[16]Trial transcript, pages 21, 22
[17]Ibid., page 22.
[18]Ibid., page 27.
[19]Ibid., pages 28, 29.
[20]*Schiff vs Commissioner, supra,* page 1707.

EXHIBIT 13

Sec. 6020.   Returns prepared for or executed by Secretary.

(a) Preparation of return by Secretary.

If any person shall fail to make a return required by this title or by regulations prescribed thereunder, but <u>shall consent</u> to disclose all information necessary for the preparation thereof, then, and in that case, the <u>Secretary may prepare such return, which, being signed</u> <u>by such person, may be received by the Secretary as the</u> <u>return of such person.</u>

(b) Execution of return by Secretary.

(1) Authority of Secretary to execute return. If any person <u>fails to make any return</u> required by an internal revenue law or regulation made thereunder at the time prescribed therefor, or makes, willfully or otherwise, a false or fraudulent return, <u>the Secretary</u> <u>shall make such return from his own knowledge and</u> <u>from such information as he can obtain through</u> <u>testimony or otherwise.</u>

SCHIFF: Your Honor, you have my word. The minute the government sends me an assessment under Section 6303, making me liable for the tax, I will send them a check. And, if they make me liable under Section 6303 and if I do send them a check, I would never have filed a return.[21] The reason I haven't paid any income tax is that I haven't been made liable for any tax. So for the government to contend that I am liable for a tax that has never been assessed, is fraud. . . Section 6020 of the code, imposes no obligation on anyone to file a tax return. . . There is no such liability. So, I haven't refused to file returns. The law imposes no such liability on me. . . [22]

I offered Code Section 6020 to the "court" as proof that I had no "obligation" to file so Hamblen's suggestion that I only offered "constitutional arguments" to relieve me of my "obligations to file returns and

---

[21]This explains why returns are not legally necessary even if payment of income taxes were compulsory. See pages 32–34 *How Anyone Can Stop Paying Income Taxes,* by Irwin Schiff.

[22]Trial transcript, pages 72, 73.

pay taxes" was *a boldfaced lie!* In addition, not only did I refute the "correctness" of the tax "liability," I offered evidence proving that, under the law — and not by way of any constitutional argument — that *no such "liability" could exist.* My testimony on this was not even disputed or challenged by the government as the following shows:

> SCHIFF:. . . The general term income is not defined in the Internal Revenue Code [submitting an excerpt from *U.S. vs Ballard, supra,* as legal substantiation for this claim] and if the government is going to claim that I had income, it is going to have to define it. And, tell me where they got its definition. [Needless to say, they did not define it.]. . . Sources of income are cash receipts, bank deposits are capital and are not subject to a tax on income. . . [23]
>
> [citing *Merchants Loan & Trust Co. vs Smietanka, supra,* I stated that this decision supplied the] clearest definition of income [and that it had never] been reversed or overturned. [Reading directly from the decision] The word income must be given the same meaning in all of the income tax acts of Congress that was given to it in the Corporation Excise Tax Act of 1909. And that meaning has now become a definite decision of this court. . . [24]
>
> Now, I have before me the Corporation Excise Tax Act of 1909. And, there is nothing in the Act that says bank deposits are taxable. There is nothing in that Act even using the word wages, your Honor. The government now seeks to tax my wages, but the word wages or salaries does not even appear in Section 61 as even being a component of income. Wages, therefore, cannot even be a source of income, let alone income itself — and, the reason why wages is not included in Section 61 is that the word wages does not appear in the Corporation Excise Tax Act of 1909. . . [25]

Does that sound as if I did not refute the correctness of the government's determination of a "tax liability" or that I merely attempted to refute it on "various constitutional grounds"? I refuted it on the basis of what is contained in the law itself — the definition of income as decided by the Supreme Court — and the government did not challenge it.

Quoting further from both the *Brushaber* and *Eisner* cases I testified:

[23]Ibid., page 35.
[24]Ibid., page 36.
[25]Ibid., pages 36, 37.

SCHIFF: . . . The Sixteenth Amendment must be construed in connection with the taxing clauses of the original Constitution. And the effects attributed to them before the Amendment was adopted: "The Sixteenth Amendment gave the government no new taxing power.". . . [quoting from *Eisner*] "The Sixteenth Amendment shall not be extended by loose construction so as to repeal or modify, except as applied to income, those provisions of the Constitution that require an apportionment according to population for taxes upon property real and personal."[26]

. . . So, the Supreme Court said that taxes on property real and personal must be apportioned. Now, a tax on my labor [wages] is a tax on my property and the government cannot tax my property without apportioning it. The government said that my dividends are to be taxed. Dividends are property, sir. Also, the government seeks to tax undisclosed bank deposits. Now, bank deposits, of course, are property and a tax on property has to be apportioned. . . If the government wants to tax my income, it has to do so as an excise tax with income severed from the sources that produced it.[27]

. . . It is very clear that in *Eisner vs Macomber* [supra], the court stated that the Sixteenth Amendment does not allow the Federal government to tax property real and personal as income. Dividends are my property. My labor is my property. And, the government is not going to get away with attempting to con me into believing that property is taxable under the Sixteenth Amendment.[28]

Does any of this sound as if I did not "refute the correctness of the respondent's determination of tax liability?" I proved that no such "liability" even existed and the government (at trial) and Hamblen (in his opinion) simply ignored the law as written and accused me of raising "constitutional" arguments. Hamblen apparently felt that as a "tax court judge" he had a license to lie about everything. The sum and substance of his opinion can be gleaned from the following excerpt:

With regard to petitioner's argument that the Federal Income tax laws are unconstitutional as an indirect tax, the courts have found on numerous occasions that since the ratification of the 16th Amendment it is immaterial

[26]Ibid., pages 38, 39.
[27]Ibid., pages 39, 40.
[28]Ibid., page 41.

whether the tax is a direct or indirect tax. *Brushaber v. Union Pacific RR* 240 US 1 (1916); *Hayward v. Day* 619 F.2d 716 (8th Cir. 1980).[29]

That statement capsulized both the spuriousness and speciousness of Hamblen's entire opinion. First, I never claimed (as he incorrectly stated) that the income tax laws themselves were unconstitutional. I carefully explained that *since the tax was voluntary, the "law" itself was not unconstitutional*. If, however, it were enforced the way "Judge" Hamblen sought to enforce it, then *its enforcement was certainly unconstitutional*. And he still did not answer my question by identifying into what taxing clause the income tax (as it is currently extracted) falls!

His further reference to *Brushaber* both misstates and makes a mockery of that citing.[30] Though he cites *Brushaber,* he totally disregards the substance of that decision, which was that in taxing income the government must separate income from its source(s) — precisely what I testified that the government was not doing in my case. He even allowed the government to tax a "bank deposit" as *income*. So Hamblen admitted doing precisely what the *Brushaber* Court said he could not do.

Hamblen also incredibly stated that it is "immaterial" whether the government levies an income tax as a "direct or indirect tax." Such a consideration *is material* or there never would have been a 16th Amendment. I purposely went into this at great length and even quoted the *Eisner* Court as specifically stating, "The Sixteenth Amendment must be construed in connection with the taxing clauses of the original Constitution." So if the government levied a tax on the source(s) of my income (as Hamblen admitted the government had done in my case), the law (according to the Supreme Court) states that such a tax must be apportioned in order for it to be binding. How, then, could Hamblen say that the way the tax is levied is "immaterial?" On the basis of such an admittedly fallacious statement by a "Tax Court judge" (on whose decision other decisions will be based), who could dare claim that Federal taxes are collected according to law? And on the basis of the "court's" admitted ignorance, "Judge" Hamblen determined that I owed the government some $30,000 in taxes — including $10,000 in *fraud* penalties.

Hamblen further stated:

Petitioner's "taxation on source" argument is spurious; the tax is imposed on the money petitioner receives for his services, not on the performance of

[29]*Schiff vs Commissioner, supra,* page 1708.

[30]His additional reference to an 8th Circuit Appellate opinion is characteristic of what Federal "courts" do — especially in tax cases. They attempt to give legal weight to their opinions by citing other lower court decisions which are just as lawless as their own.

those services. Section 61 (a) specifically includes "wages" in its definition of gross income.[31]

Can you believe the fraud and deceipt Hamblen managed to pack into just two lines?[32] His claim that "Section 61(a) specifically includes 'wages'" is an outright lie which can be verified by looking at the section itself (Exhibit 2, page 190). Look also at how he twisted my explanation of the government's attempt to tax sources of "income" as 'income' itself. He pretended (again for the benefit of other "judges" who may also want to disregard the "source" issue and cite his decision) that I claimed that the government was taxing my "performance" as opposed to taxing my "money." His absurd perversion of the entire *source* issue establishes that either he was guilty of outright judicial perjury or is simply someone who cannot understand simple English when he hears it. A review of the transcript shows that I did not even remotely suggest any such thing, as this brief excerpt from my lengthy explanation of the "source" issue clearly demonstrates:

> SCHIFF: So, when the government said that I had sources of income, I don't deny that I had sources. But sources of income are not taxable. Only income is taxable. And the government has yet to tell me what income is.[33]

Does that sound as if I raised the "source" issue as a matter related to job "performance" as Hamblen contended?

Continuing with Hamblen's decision:

> Petitioner placed great emphasis upon various statements culled from cases [here he means *court* cases such as the Supreme Court case of *Flora vs U.S., supra*, which he did not even try to refute], Treasury Department publications, and other writings to the effect that the income tax is based upon "voluntary compliance," and he announces that he does not volunteer to comply. As we have previously noted, this argument "is nothing but arrogant sophistry." Implicit in the statements relied upon by the petitioner is the fact that the effectiveness of the tax system depends upon the taxpayer's voluntary obedience to the law.[34]

[31]*Schiff vs Commissioner, supra*, page 1708.

[32]It is important to understand that Hamblen was writing to provide quotes and legal prescedents so that other "judges" (in both tax and regular "courts") could cite from his opinion. The government has already widely circulated this decision and is using Hamblen's garbage as "case law" against others.

[33]Trial transcript, page 58.

[34]*Schiff vs Commissioner, supra* page 1708. Note Hamblen's attempt to distort the meaning of "voluntary compliance" as described on page 243.

Overlooking my testimony on the *Flora* case (page 23 of the trial transcript) as well as the fact that Judge Clarie had ruled at my trial that I filed my 1973 return "voluntarily" (so that it could be used against me, see page 285), Hamblen suggested that those who wrote "voluntary" into all the government documents I submitted really meant to write "compulsory." In addition, the thrust of my testimony was that since it was voluntary I did not choose to "volunteer, " not that I did not "volunteer to comply." He attempted to twist my testimony so that it appeared I simply "announced" an arbitrary refusal "to comply" — overlooking entirely that what I really said was that I did not choose to "volunteer, " and compliance had nothing to do with it at all. And he had the nerve to accuse *me* of "arrogant sophistry"!

Hamblen's Finding Of "Fraud"

Hamblen's finding of "fraud" was widely reported in the press. It was the headline story in the May 3, 1984 issue of the *Staten Island Advance* (see *The Schiff Report,* Volume 2, Number 2) and appeared in newspapers across the country even making the front page of the *London Daily Mail.* The story originated as an IRS press release which sought to brand both me and my book as "frauds." Apart from getting my books mixed up, the story revealed how the Federal government manipulates a gullible press in order to keep the public buffaloed. The issues in my "trial" and what occurred were completely distorted in the story, but because a conviction for fraud can be so personally damaging, I believe the public should be aware of how our government actually goes about stigmatizing people in this manner when it has absolutely no basis for the charge, while exacting substantial monetary penalties in the process.

The following is a detailed breakdown of Hamblen's opinion and the elements upon which he based his fraud finding. It provides a clearer understanding of those who work as "judges" in Tax "Court." First, he stated:

> In this case there is no question that petitioner's purpose in failing to file returns was to avoid payment of taxes that he claims he was not obligated to pay. As indicated above his claim that he did not receive income is frivolous.[35]

This statement entirely overlooks my testimony (not challenged or disputed at trial) that

---

[35]Ibid., pages 1709, 1710.

1. there is no Code section that requires anyone to file and that *without an assessment* I owed no tax;
2. even if these beliefs were legally wrong, my reliance on them did not constitute fraud;
3. nowhere does the "court" attempt to cite any Code section which "obligates [me] to pay" the taxes the "court" claimed I sought to avoid; and
4. how could the introduction of numerous Supreme Court cases showing that a) income cannot be taxed (except by apportionment) if not separated from its sources, and b) that "income" has been defined by the courts as a corporate profit, be termed "frivolous?"[36]

Next Hamblen stated:

Although petitioner complains that respondent did not cooperate with him by attempting to deal with all of the attacks petitioner made on the income tax system, petitioner admits he never provided any financial information to respondent's agents. His refusal to cooperate in the attempt to determine his correct liability is, in the context of this record, further indicia of fraud.[37]

The "attacks" I allegedly made on the "income tax system" that the "respondent did not cooperate with" involved my numerous letters to IRS officials asking them to explain to me how I could fill out a tax return without waiving any of my constitutional rights. They refused to tell me and advised me to seek such information from private attorneys (see Appendix F). But when I checked with private attorneys they all told me that they knew of no way I could fill out a tax return without waiving constitutional rights. How could such inquiries be considered an "attack" on the "income tax system?" And if neither the government nor any private attorney could tell me how to file a tax return without waiving constitutional rights, am I required to file one anyway just to accommodate the government?

As far as my "refusal to cooperate" in an attempt "to determine [my] correct [tax] liability" is concerned, Hamblen referred to my refusal to turn over books and records to the IRS for audit purposes. However, the IRS's own audit manuals state that citizens who do so waive

---

[36]"Frivolous" is a term Federal "judges" use whenever they are confronted with issues of law they cannot refute. As can be imagined, they use the term repeatedly in so-called "tax protester" cases.

[37]*Schiff vs Commissioner, supra,* page 1710.

their Fourth and Fifth Amendment rights and that individuals are free to raise these rights when refusing to do so. Is it an "indicia of fraud" to refuse to turn over books and records in accordance with the IRS's own manuals? The IRS agent who was sent to audit me specifically told me that if I gave him any information it could be used against me and, as a consequence, I was not legally required to give him such information.[38]

More importantly, Section 6020 of the Internal Revenue Code (Exhibit 13) states that if I do not "consent to disclose" the information "necessary for the preparation" of my tax return, the government is required to "make such returns from [its] own knowledge. . . " In addition, if one declines to give such information to the government, there are no *fraud* penalties indicated in that, or any other, Code section. At my "hearing" I testified at great length regarding this section and pointed out that there is nothing in it, or in any other section, that states I am *required* to help the government determine my "correct [income tax] liability." When did Congress establish fraud penalties for citizens who refuse to "cooperate" with the IRS? How can there be "fraud" if citizens simply refuse to supply the government with information that can be used against them? Where is the statute that requires individuals to assist the IRS in its determination of their "correct liability?" How can it be "fraud" if one simply tells the IRS, "Figure out my tax liability and tell me what I owe, " when that is precisely what the Code, the Constitution and the 16th Amendment say the government has to do?[39] Where is the "fraud" in any of these actions?

The real fraud was committed by Hamblen in his use of the word "liability" in connection with income taxes. There is no Code section that establishes any such "liability" and Hamblen had to know it. This makes him guilty of judicial perjury and a candidate for criminal prosecution under Sections 1001 and 1018 of the U.S. Criminal Code which deals with the making of false and fraudulent statements.[40]

Continuing with Hamblen's finding of "fraud":

Petitioner omitted all items of "income" from his purported 1974 and 1975

---

[38]This "audit" interview was witnessed by some six people in the media and a newspaper account of it was reproduced on page 78 of *How Anyone Can Stop Paying Income Taxes* by Irwin Schiff.

[39]The 16th Amendment states that "The Congress shall have power to *lay* and *collect* taxes. . . " Therefore, it must "lay" the tax before it can collect the tax. Nowhere does the Amendment — or the Code — say that citizens are "required" to help the government "lay" the tax.

[40]As soon as I complete this book I will swear out a criminal Complaint against Hamblen and others pursuant to Rule 3 of the U.S. Criminal Code (see page 385) charging him with these and other offenses.

> returns. He attempted to obtain refunds of his taxes paid in earlier years. Petitioner took these actions despite his knowledge of required reporting procedures, as evidenced by his earlier proper returns and his concurrent proper filing of correct returns for his business. While arguing the wages received by him from his corporation were not taxable to him, petitioner directed his corporation to deduct this compensation from its income. We see these actions to be a further indicia of fraud.[41]

In addition, Hamblen mentioned my "1974 and 1975 returns," but the government jailed me for not filing those returns. How then could Hamblen even raise the issue of those returns — "purported" or otherwise?[42] In addition, I explained at my criminal trial that 1) I had no income to report and 2) if I had reported it without a grant of immunity (which I had asked for on the return), the information could be used against me. And the fact that I applied for refunds for taxes paid in earlier years does not constitute fraud for 1974 and 1975.[43] Indeed, when I discovered I had been fraudulently induced to pay taxes for a number of years prior to 1974 (when I never really owed them) I filed a claim for a refund for those years. If anything, this does not constitute fraud but exactly the reverse — it shows a consistency in my honest belief that I could never have "owed" the government any income taxes at all.

Note also that the "court" attempts to establish "fraud" on the basis that I filed returns during the years when I was ignorant of our income tax "laws." Hamblen thus laid down an interesting legal doctrine with respect to income taxes: Citizens are not permitted to rise above their former tax ignorance. In addition, the fact that I had filed corporate returns for 1974 and 1975 had nothing to do with whether I committed "fraud" with respect to my *personal* taxes for those years. I voluntarily filed corporate returns because others beside myself were involved in the corporation and I did not want to involve them in the course I was prepared to take. More importantly, this demonstrates once again how even benign tax returns can be used against you (the benign corporate returns I filed were being used against me to estab-

---

[41]*Schiff vs Commissioner, supra*, page 1710.

[42]Had the government prosecuted me for not "supplying any information" on my 1974 and 1975 returns pursuant to Section 7203 or for filing false information pursuant to Section 7206, Hamblen might have used those returns as a basis for his opinion. But since the government chose to jail me for allegedly *not filing any returns at all for 1974 and 1975* ("purported" or otherwise), how could any legitmate court raise the issue of my "1974 and 1975 returns" on any basis?

[43]If this claim for tax refunds constituted "fraud," why did the government not charge me with making fraudulent claims against the government pursuant to Code Section 7206?

lish "fraud" in connection with personal returns).

Continuing on the same vein, Hamblen stated:

> We note that petitioner's education and obvious intelligence are relevant to our determination of fraud. We are convinced that petitioner was familiar with relevant law and was aware of his obligation to file proper returns and to pay taxes. Petitioner did extensive research in an attempt to legitimize his position [none of which the government or the "court" could refute]. During the years in issue, petitioner wrote a book [*The Biggest Con: How The Government Is Fleecing You*] advocating tax revolt [is that "fraud?"], clearly indicating that at that time petitioner was well aware of his obligations to file returns and pay taxes [the reverse is true since the book — based upon extensive research — clearly showed why Americans, both economically and legally, should immediately stop paying income taxes]. By his own admission, petitioner believed taxes to be "compulsory." We are convinced that he knew that the tactics he employed were not legitimate tax avoidance.[44]

Here Hamblen sought to establish "fraud" on the basis of my "education. . . intelligence. . . [because I was] familiar with relevant law. . . extensive research. . . [and the fact that I] wrote a book"[45] while leaving out the most significant element of all — the document on which the alleged "fraud" was based!

In addition, Hamblen actually sought to use against me a lone statement I made regarding a *false impression I once had* (from 1974 to 1977) as if that statement, in and of itself, were factually correct while he totally disregarded numerous other statements I made which corrected it! True, in 1974 I believed filing was compulsory which is why I filed returns. At the same time I also believed that the payment of income taxes was "compulsory" if the tax was first "laid" upon you by the government, since the 16th Amendment said the government shall "lay and collect taxes on incomes. . . " So though I once thought that income

---

[44]*Schiff vs Commissioner, supra*, page 1710.

[45]If there was "fraud" in this book the critics certainly did not think so as evidenced by the following remarks: "An important well researched compendium. . . logical and virtually irrefutable." [Allen C. Brownfeld, author and Washington columnist]; "A blockbuster. . . brilliant. . . hilarious." [John Chamberlain, author and syndicated columnist]; "A superb job of exposing the evils of paper money." [Elgin Groseclose, Ph.D., Institute for Monetary Research in Washington, D.C.]; "The single most important book on the status of this nation I have ever read." [Howard Ruff, author and editor of *The Ruff Times*]; "His analysis is hard to refute." [*The Wall Street Journal*]; "Forceful indeed. . ." [*Publisher's Weekly*]; "A stirring treatise. . ." [*Parade of Books*]; "Your blood pressure rises and the body juices boil. . . an indictment of all forms of collectivism. . ." [*The New Guard*]; and "Should be required reading." [*The Jewish Press*].

taxes might be "compulsory," " I also believed that it was not incumbent upon me to pay them before they were "laid" on me.

It was not until much later that I discovered I was right and that the Code indeed provided that taxes had to be first assessed by the government before they were due and that citizens were not required to file income tax returns at all — which is why I stopped filing Fifth Amendment returns altogether. Even later I discovered that (for all the reasons stated in this book) I was not even under any obligation to pay income taxes on any basis — either under the Code or the Constitution. But Hamblen attempted to base his decision on an "admission" of mine regarding an earlier misconception I had as if I still held that same false belief. But my earlier behavior (based upon my misconception) was not "fraudulent" either since I filed Fifth Amendment returns when I thought I had to file and stopped filing completely when I discovered the truth. Hamblen asserted (as if it were proven fact) that my admission of a false earlier belief (now thoroughly refuted by me in all of my unchallenged written and oral testimony) must be my *current* belief and it was "fraud" for me to suggest otherwise![46]

The Appeal Process

I appealed Hamblen's decision to the Second Circuit Court of Appeals in what I believed would probably be a useless expenditure of both time and money but I wished to exhaust all legal remedies. Since I was devoting all my time to writing this book and could not take the time to handle the details of it myself, I engaged an attorney and, with the exception of the material on fraud, I explained all the legal arugments I wanted to raise. Though his fifteen page brief was a bit skimpier than what I would have preferred, all the major points of law were there.

1. Based upon *Pollock, Eisner, Brushaber, Smietanka* and several other Supreme Court cases, I demonstrated that under the law I had no "income" that was subject to the income tax.
2. Under the specific provisions of Code Section 6201 (since I submitted no "return or list" as provided for), the Federal government was without any statutory authority to estimate, let alone assess, any income taxes against me; and based upon that section and Section 6219(a), no "deficiency" was possible. And,
3. under every legal test for tax fraud no such fraud could possibly exist.

[46]Naturally, Hamblen attempted to buttress his totally contrived decision with references to other decisions while disregarding the statutes completely. To the extent that any of the cited decisions actually supported his decision, this simply meant that those decisions were no more legally valid than Hamblen's own fraudulent one.

In the appeal I showed that there was no "underpayment" or falsification of any tax return(s) and, therefore, there could not be any tax "fraud." Cited were numerous cases that clearly establish that for tax fraud to exist three elements have to be present:

1. a conscious falsification of a return;
2. an intent to evade; and
3. some part of an "underpayment" for each year was due to fraud.

For example,

> The language of Section 6653(b). . . *presupposes the existence of an underpayment. Absent an underpayment, there is nothing to which the fraud addition may attach.*[47] (Emphasis added)

That fraud envisioned under Section 6653(b) involved:

> . . . knowing falsification of a material item in the return. . . which can be related to the intent to evade [if that is proved]. . . [48]

Based upon these cases alone it is obvious that there could have been no "fraud" in my case.

In addition, Exhibit 10 is an excerpt from the Supreme Court case of *Bull vs U.S.* 295 US 247 in which the Court clearly ruled that no income tax is "owed" until an assessment is made. And since I was officially informed by the government that as of the date of my "Notice of Deficiency" no assessment had as yet been made against me, by law no deficiency, interest, or fraud could possibly have existed. Coupled with the fact that the government presented no evidence of tax "fraud" at my trial, the Second Circuit Court of Appeals could not legitimately sustain a finding of "fraud" (or anything else for that matter) on any basis.

The appeal was argued in New York City on November 27, 1984 before Appellate Court "Judges" Timbers, Van Graafeiland, and Pierce, while my written appeal was submitted some sixty days beforehand. "Judge" Timbers revealed the mentality of the "court" when he asked my attorney, "How could a New Haven lawyer put his name on such an appeal?"[49] Based upon this remark, it was apparent that these judicial

---

[47]*Hebrank vs Commissioner* 81 T.C. 640 (1983); *Ellison vs Phillips* 47 T.C.M. 1289 (1984).

[48]*Considine vs U.S.* 683 F.2d 1285, 1286 (1982).

[49]Actually, I wanted to argue my own case before the Appeals Court since I knew the law and the facts in the case better than the attorney who prepared the written appeal. But based upon his claim that since he initiated and signed the appeal as my attorney he would find himself in trouble with the "court" if I did that, I agreed to let him argue it against my better judgement. However, based on "Judge" Timber's remark, this was obviously a mistake. But once again this demonstrates how "court" rules and procedures force private citizens to use licensed lawyers even when they are not necessary.

Mamelukes were not prepared to take any notice of the law at all. Unfortunately, my attorney felt obliged to respond to this attempted intimidation and explained why I was entitled to legal representation which consumed about two minutes of the little time he had to argue the appeal, which was only *ten minutes* to begin with!

On January 3, 1985 (while writing this chapter) I received word that the Second Circuit Court of Appeals sustained the Tax "Court" *on all counts* and added $2,400 in additional penalties.[50] The decision was handed down by "Judges" William H. Timbers, Ellsworth A. Van Graafeiland, and Lawrence W. Pierce, which indicates that these "judges" have about as much interest in Federal tax law and in upholding the Constitution as does the Ayatollah Khomeini.

How The Government Steals Property On A Massive Scale

The Federal government now routinely steals billions of dollars in private property each year on a scale I doubt is even attempted in countries dominated by Soviet- or Nazi-like regimes. Yet the overwhelming majority of Americans are totally unaware of this despite the fact that in order to do it, the government had to dispose of the entire Bill of Rights.

For example, in early December, 1982 I received another "Notice Of Deficiency" (Exhibit 14) dated December 2, 1982 over the typed and ersatz written signature of Roscoe L. Egger, Jr., the Commissioner of Internal Revenue, and James E. Quinn, the Connecticut District Director. This time the government claimed I owed it, as of that date, $91,000 in tax deficiencies, $45,500 in fraud penalties, and $3,078 in interest penalties, for a grand total of $139,775 for the years 1976, 1977, and 1978.[51]

In response to this "Notice of Deficiency" I sent a letter (Exhibit 15) to Secretary of the Treasury, Donald T. Regan (since as Egger's boss he is the one ultimately responsible for the notices sent out by the IRS). Regan never answered it.

This time I did not bother wasting my time petitioning Tax "Court" but, instead, wrote the government for a copy of my tax assessments for those years pursuant to Section 6201 (Exhibit 7, page 257). In a letter dated January 25, 1983 (Exhibit 16) I was informed by Henry F.

---

[50]See Appendix F for the complete text of this opinion.

[51]The government got the information for its contrived "assessment" by subpoenaing my books and records — without notifying me as required by law — from the Connecticut State Tax Department which had illegally stolen them from me in 1979. My lawsuit against the State of Connecticut for its illegal actions is currently pending in Federal District Court and hopefully will come to trial in the spring of 1985.

EXHIBIT 14

Internal Revenue Service
District Director

CERTIFIED MAIL
No 143,723

Date:
    DEC 0 2 1982

Mr. Irwin A. Schiff
P.O. Box 5303
60 Connolly Parkway
Hamden, CT   06518

Department of the Treasury
135 High Street - Stop 190
Hartford, CT   06103

Social Security ~~xxx~~
~~Employer Identification~~ Number:
047-16-2491

~~Tax Year Ended and Deficiency~~
Additions to the Tax
Internal Revenue Code of 1954

Tax Year Ended	Deficiency	Section 6653(b)	Section 6654
December 31, 1976	$19,006.00	$ 9,503.00	$ 709.00
December 31, 1977	$18,678.00	$ 9,339.00	$ 663.00
December 31, 1978	$53,447.00	$26,724.00	$1,706.00

Person to Contact:
Thomas J. Smith
Contact Telephone Number:
722-3060

CERTIFIED MAIL

Dear Mr. Schiff:

    We have determined that there is a deficiency (increase) in your income tax as shown above. This letter is a <u>NOTICE OF DEFICIENCY</u> sent to you as required by law. The enclosed statement shows how we figured the deficiency.

    If you want to contest this deficiency in court before making any payment, you have 90 days from the above mailing date of this letter (150 days if addressed to you outside of the United States) to file a petition with the United States Tax Court for a redetermination of the deficiency. The petition should be filed with the United States Tax Court, 400 Second Street NW., Washington, D.C. 20217, and the copy of this letter should be attached to the petition. The time in which you must file a petition with the Court (90 or 150 days as the case may be) is fixed by law and <u>the Court cannot consider your case if your petition is filed late</u>. If this letter is addressed to both a husband and wife, and both want to petition the Tax Court, <u>both</u> must sign the petition or each must file a separate, signed petition. You can get a copy of the rules for filing a petition by writing to the Clerk of the Tax Court at the Court's Washington, D.C. address shown above.

    If you decide not to file a petition with the Tax Court, we would appreciate it if you would sign and return the enclosed waiver form. This will permit us to charge your account quickly and will limit the accumulation of interest. The enclosed addressed envelope is for your convenience. If you decide not to sign and return the statement and you do not timely petition the Tax Court, the law requires us to bill you after 90 days from the above mailing date of this letter (150 days if this letter is addressed to you outside the United States).

    If you have any questions, please contact the person whose name and telephone number are shown above.

          Sincerely yours,

          Roscoe L. Egger, Jr.
          Commissioner
          By *James E. Quinn* pm

Enclosures:
Copy of this letter
Waiver
Envelope
  paf
District Director, Hartford District

          District Director   Letter 892(DO) (Rev. 3–79)

EXHIBIT 15

 Freedom Books

P.O. BOX 5303   HAMDEN, CONNECTICUT 06518   PHONE (203) 281-6791

If a nation values anything more than freedom, it will lose its freedom; and the
irony of it is that if it is comfort or money that it values more, it will lose that too.—Somerset Maugham

December 7, 1982

Donald T. Regan, Secretary of the Treasury
Department of the Treasury
Main Treasury Building
15th Street & Pennsylvania Avenue, NW
Washington, D.C. 20220

Dear Mr. Secretary:

I received the attached notice from Roscoe L. Egger, Jr., Commissioner of the Internal Revenue Service, who acts under your
authority.

I am writing directly to you to determine whether you are aware
that your agents - Commissioner Egger and Connecticut District
Director, James E. Quinn - are assessing taxes and fraud and interest penalties contrary to law and whether they are violating
these laws with your knowledge and approval.

I would, therefore, like your answers to the following questions
with respect to the attached "Notice of Deficiency."

  1.   Is the assessment of taxes shown on this document le-
       vied pursuant to Section 6303 of the Internal Revenue
       Code?
  2.   Has the liability of $91,131.00 shown as a "deficiency"
       been recorded in your office pursuant to Section 6203
       of the Internal Revenue Code?
  3.   Has there been any tax liability recorded in your of-
       fice with respect to any taxes due from me for the
       years 1976, 1977, and 1978?
  4.   If not taxes have been assessed against me and record-
       ed in your office, can I have a "deficiency assess-
       ment?"
  5.   Am I to understand that this 90 Day Letter makes me li-
       able for $91,131.00 in taxes?
  6.   Are you authorized, by law, to determine a tax defi-
       ciency before you have even determined a tax liability,
       as provided for in Section 6201?
  7.   What section of the Internal Revenue Code authorizes
       you, as Secretary, to determine a tax deficiency before
       you even determine a tax, record the liability, and no-
       tify the taxpayer as provided for in Sections 6201,
       6203, and 6303?
  8.   Am I to assume that you have authorized Mr. Egger to
       assess fraud and interest penalties against individuals

(continued next page)

EXHIBIT 15 (Continued)

who refuse to voluntarily disclose tax information to the government in accordance with Section 6020(a) of the Internal Revenue Code?

9. Was my tax liability as calculated by Mr. Egger determined in accordance with Section 6020(b) of the Internal Revenue Code?

10. Does Section 6020(b) provide that fraud and interest penalties apply if "the Secretary makes a return from his own knowledge?"

11. I note that Section 6020(a) states that a taxpayer can "consent to disclose information necessary for the preparation of [the return]," but nowhere in Section 6020 does it state that there are penalties if a taxpayer does not consent to disclose information. Have you, therefore, authorized the Commissioner to assess fraud and interest penalties against those who elect to follow the law as contained in Section 6020(a) of the Internal Revenue Code?

12. Has Section 6020(a) of the Internal Revenue Code been revoked? Is there a new section that provides for fraud and interest penalties if a taxpayer does not consent to disclose information necessary for the preparation of his return?

13. Can you provide me with any section of the law that says that there are interest and fraud penalties if a taxpayer does not consent to give the Internal Revenue Service information from which a tax can be computed?

14. Is compliance with IRS rules and regulations voluntary or mandatory? If it is your view that compliance is compulsory please provide me with any published IRS material that confirms this.

15. Were you, as Secretary of the Treasury, given any authority by Congress other than to encourage voluntary compliance with Internal Revenue laws and regulations?

I would further like to remind you that Section 6214(a)(1) & (2) makes it a crime for you to knowingly demand of me a sum which is greater than authorized by law. The question is, does the Internal Revenue Code authorize you to demand of me - through your agents, Mr. Egger and Mr. Quinn - $91,131.00 as a tax deficiency; $45,566.00 in fraud penalties; and $3,078.00 in interest penalties as a result of my not having filed tax returns for the years 1976, 1977, and 1978 as provided for in Section 6020(a) of the Internal Revenue Code?

Respectfully,

Irwin A. Schiff

Camacho, IRS Disclosure Officer for the Northeast Region, that "a search was made of the Individual Master File and our records show that as of this date, January 25th, there is no record of assessments for these periods (1976, 1977 & 1978)." But Egger and Quinn had notified me that as of December 2, 1982 I "owed" the government some $91,000 in taxes and $3,000 in interest penalties (forgetting completely about the $45,500 in fraud penalties) for the same years. Camacho told me that as of *some 54 days later* I had never even been assessed for the years in question! By law, therefore, I could not have possibly "owed" the

---

EXHIBIT 16

Internal Revenue Service   Department of the Treasury

Internal Revenue   North-Atlantic Region   310 Lowell St., Andover, Mass.   01812
Service Center

Mr. Irwin A. Schiff   **Person to Contact:**
P. O. Box 5303   Disclosure Office
Hamden, CT 06518   **Telephone Number:**
                                            617-681-5618
                                            Refer Reply to:
                                            83D009
                                            Date:
                                            January 25, 1983

Dear Mr. Schiff:

In response to your request dated 12/21/82 for a record of assessment
of your individual income taxes for 1976, 1977 and 1978, <u>a search was
made of the Individual Master File</u> and our records show that as of
this date, January 25th, there is no record of assessments for
these periods (1976, 1977 & 1978).

This information is furnished to you in accordance with Internal
Revenue Code Section 6203.

                        Sincerely yours,

                        [signature]

                        HENRY F. CAMACHO
                        Disclosure Officer

---

government any taxes or interest penalties as of December 2, 1982 (as
shown in Code Sections 6203 and 6303, Exhibit 7, page 257) and
according to the Supreme Court itself as stated in the *Bull* decision (see
Exhibit 10, page 262) — *even if we overlook every other legal
consideration!*[52] It is clear then that the "Notice of Deficiency" from
Egger and Quinn was out and out fraud, constituting nothing more
than a government tax shakedown. It is important to note that the IRS
always claims that so-called "tax protesters" (like myself) always raise

---

[52]Few Americans would know when receiving similar "Notices of Deficiency" that they
were fraudulent and not based on any assessments as required by law, because they
would never write the government to ask for a copy of their assessment as provided by
Section 6201.

"constitutional arguments" when attacking the enforcement of the income tax and the public and the press generally buy it. In this instance, however, "constitutional arguments" had absolutely nothing to do with this illegal attempt to extort $139,775 from me. The executive branch of the government (as represented by the Treasury Department — which includes the IRS) simply disregarded the actual tax laws as passed by Congress and as they appear in the Internal Revenue Code itself. The facts speak for themselves:

1. The IRS was attempting to collect taxes that had never been legally assessed pursuant to law (further confirmed on April 7, 1983 when I received three separate "Tax Due" notices (Exhibit 17) now "billing" me for the taxes and penalties shown in the "Notice of Deficiency" of December 2, 1982).

2. The "assessment date" shown on these notices is "04-01-83" which means that these taxes could only have been "assessed" *four days* prior to their preparation and only days before being sent to me. And if the taxes for the three years in question were admittedly not "assessed" until April 1, 1983, how could Eggar and Quinn have claimed that I "owed" them (*plus interest and fraud penalties*) as early as December 2, 1982 — some **four months** before they were actually "assessed?"

3. Note further that these *new* notices contained another item not shown in the original "Notice of Deficiency" — some $52,069 in *additional interest charges*, bringing the amount I allegedly "owed" the Federal government to $181,844! This meant that for taxes admittedly only assessed on April 1, 1983 I had incurred *$52,069 in interest penalties on a "bill" that was only four days old!*

4. Technically, this was the *first* notice I ever received from the government that even remotely conformed with the law as contained in Section 6303 (Exhibit 7, page 257) which requires the government to notify persons "liable" for the tax "after the making of an assessment."

5. The government's claim to $52,069 in interest — covering a period of time *prior* to its having made the assessment required by law — is out and out fraud and *a clear violation of the tax statutes themselves*.

Apart from all of the above, the "notices" are fraught with fraud for a variety of other reasons. First, the documents are not signed. No Federal employee takes responsibility for the lawfulness and/or the accuracy of the items shown. These documents *seem* to tell me that I owe

EXHIBIT 17

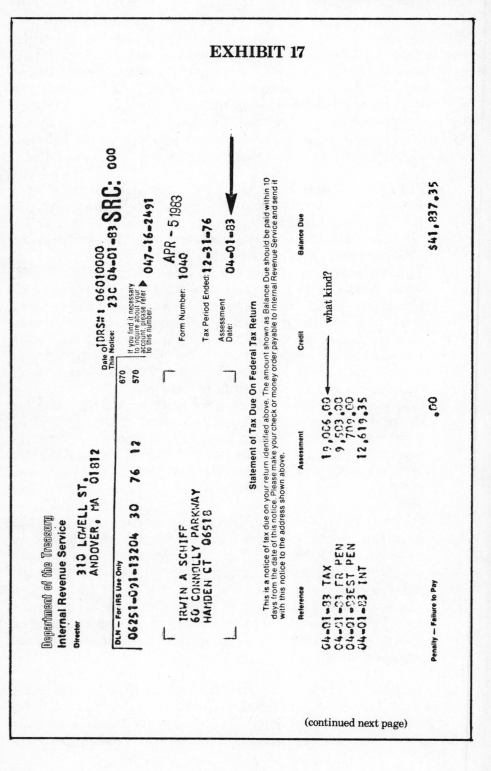

Department of the Treasury
Internal Revenue Service

Director   310 LOWELL ST.
              ANDOVER, MA 01812

Date of   IDRS#: 06010000
This Notice: 23C 04-01-83 SRC: 000

                                   670
                                   570

If you find it necessary
to inquire about your   ▶ 047-16-2491
account, please refer
to this number.

Form Number: 1040   APR - 5 1983

Tax Period Ended: 12-31-76

Assessment
Date: 04-01-83

DLN — For IRS Use Only
06251-091-13204 30   76 12

IRWIN A SCHIFF
60 CONNOLLY PARKWAY
HAMDEN CT 06518

Statement of Tax Due On Federal Tax Return

This is a notice of tax due on your return identified above. The amount shown as Balance Due should be paid within 10 days from the date of this notice. Please make your check or money order payable to Internal Revenue Service and send it with this notice to the address shown above.

Reference	Assessment	Credit	Balance Due
04-01-83 TAX	19,006.00	*what kind?*	
04-01-83 FR PEN	9,503.00		
04-01-83 EST PEN	709.00		
04-01-83 INT	12,619.35		
Penalty — Failure to Pay	.00		$41,837.35

(continued next page)

EXHIBIT 17 (continued)

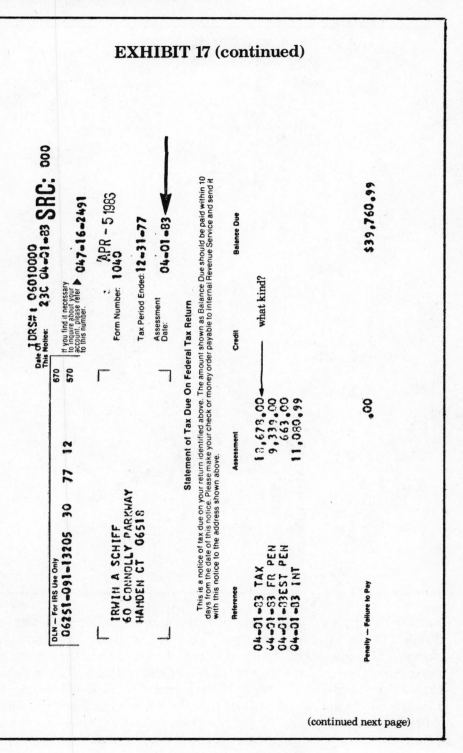

DLN — For IRS Use Only
06251-091-13205   30   77   12

Date of
This Notice: 23C 04-01-83 **SRC:** 000

IRS# ‡ 0601000

670
570

If you find it necessary
to inquire about your
account, please refer ▶ 047-16-2491
to this number.

IRWIN A SCHIFF
60 CONNOLLY PARKWAY
HAMDEN CT 06518

Form Number: 1040   APR – 5 1983

Tax Period Ended: 12-31-77

Assessment
Date: 04-01-83

Statement of Tax Due On Federal Tax Return

This is a notice of tax due on your return identified above. The amount shown as Balance Due should be paid within 10 days from the date of this notice. Please make your check or money order payable to Internal Revenue Service and send it with this notice to the address shown above.

Reference	Assessment	Credit	Balance Due
04-01-83 TAX	18,678.00	*what kind?*	
04-01-83 FR PEN	9,339.00		
04-01-83 EST PEN	663.00		
04-01-83 INT	11,080.99		
Penalty — Failure to Pay		.00	$39,760.99

(continued next page)

EXHIBIT 17 (continued)

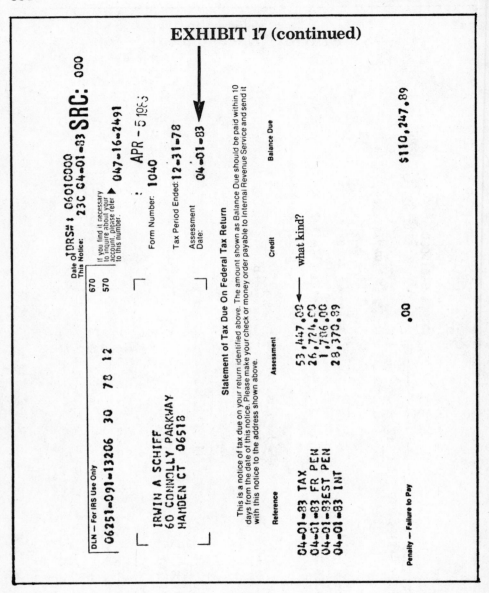

$91,131 in "income" taxes, $48,644 in fraud and other penalties, and
$52,071.23 in interest penalties. But *the documents make no actual
demand for payment of the items listed.* The fact that each document
states that the amounts shown "should be paid within 10 days" *is not a
demand for payment.* The word "should" *is not a "demand" for payment.*
Most people would also not notice that the documents themselves make
no reference to any specific Code section that authorizes the tax and
penalties. *This is not an accidental omission.* The reason that there are

no Code sections listed is because *there are no Code sections that mandate the payment of such taxes and penalties!*

In addition, the form simply refers to a "tax" and a "notice of tax due," but makes no specific mention of an "income" tax due. Since the government collects a variety of taxes, one would asume that the specific type of tax due would be clearly identified on the "bill." The subterfuge being attempted here is obvious — the IRS relies on the fact that individuals automatically assume (since they do not owe taxes on alcohol, cigarettes, gasoline, etc.) that the tax they presumably "owe" — and the one the bill indicates "should be paid" — is a tax on "income." *But the documents themselves say nothing about owing a tax on "income" because no one can "owe" or be "liable" for a tax on "income."*

The Federal government gets away with succh subterfuge because a thoroughly intimidated and uninformed public blindly accepts as fact that amounts shown on such government documents are legitimate, if not always accurate. Because of its total lack of understanding of the Internal Revenue Code and relevant Supreme Court decisions, and because of its faith in the integrity of Federal "courts," the public automatically assumes that the billions of dollars collected by the IRS on the basis of such documents *must be* legitimate. And, based upon such a false assumption and misguided faith, billions of dollars in "income" taxes are routinely extracted from the American public every year.

Before proceeding with an explanation of how the government actually confiscated my money (with the help and cooperation of the Federal "courts"), it is important to understand the fraudulent and illegal character of the $181,844 claim against me.

1. The government's claim for interest penalties — prior to an assessment being made and a tax "liability" being established as required by law — is blatantly fraudulent for the reasons discussed on page 256.
2. These "notices" sought to "bill" me for $45,500 in *fraud penalties* though no court (not even tax "court") ever proved that I had committed tax fraud with respect to the years 1976, 1977, and 1978.[53]
3. No basic "assessment" could have been made in the first place since I had never sent in either a "return or list" which, by law

---

[53]In tax fraud claims the burden of proof is on the government, see page 365. There is no Federal tax statute that authorizes any employee of the United States Treasury Department to take it upon himself to determine that a citizen has committed civil "fraud" and then to arbitrarily "bill" him and demand payment of such "fraud penalties."

(Section 6201(a)(1), Exhibit 7, page 257) the government must have before any income tax "assessment" can be made.[54]

Therefore, the unsigned "notices" I received from the government in the beginning of April, 1983 — claiming that I owed $181,844 in taxes, interest, and fraud penalties — *were not supported by any tax statutes* whatsoever but were merely based upon fraud themselves.

The next "notice" I received from the government was a "Final Notice" dated April 18, 1983 (Exhibit 18) which was loaded with as much fraud as the other three notices I received only a few weeks before. This "notice" stated that "notices and demands" had been made upon me for the payment of "your Federal taxes." No such "demand" had ever been made upon me. The only "notices" that I received prior to this "Final Notice" were the "Notice Of Deficiency" and the three "Tax Due" notices, and none of them contained a "demand" for the payment of anything.

For example, the "Notice Of Deficiency" said that it was "sent to [me] as required by law." This statement is a lie, designed to create a false air of legal compulsion.[55] It then stated that "if [I] want to contest this deficiency in court before making any payment" I can and even told me how to go about doing it. Next it informed me that if I "decide not to file a petition" that the Commissioner "would appreciate it" if I would "sign and return the enclosed waiver forms" [and if I] "decide not to sign and return the statement" [that the] law required us to bill you after 90 days. . ."[56] The point is, this "notice" is cleverly designed to trick people.

The biggest deception in the "Final Notice" (which I am sure is never noticed by those who receive it) is that there is no mention anywhere in it of the *specific* Federal tax that the "notice" claims is owed or the Code Section that establishes the "liability" referred to in it. Was the $181,844 in taxes, interest, and fraud penalties being "demanded"

---

[54]Actually, these "notices" were designed to be used in connection with Code Section 6014 (Exhibit 19) which provides that when a taxpayer "elects" to have the government compute his tax he sends in a "list" of the items upon which such a calculation can be based. This section also provides that "the tax shall be computed by the Secretary [of the Treasury] who shall mail to the taxpayer a notice stating the amount determined to be payable." So, legally, these "notices" could not, under any circumstances, apply to me since I had not sent in a "return or list."

[55]In Section 6212 the "law" says that the "Secretary. . . is authorized to send a notice of deficiency to the taxpayer. . ." An "authorization" to do something is not the same thing as a "requirement" to do something.

[56]Also a lie since no such "requirement" is contained in the law or Egger would have identified the Code section that authorized such a "requirement."

EXHIBIT 18

Internal Revenue Service
District Director

Department of the Treasury
150 Court Street Room 205
New Haven, Connecticut 06510

Date: April 18, 1983

Social Security or
Employer Identification Number:

047-16-2491
Person to Contact:

J Holmberg
Contact Telephone Number:

773-2053

Irwin A. Schiff
60 Connolly Parkway
Hamden, Connecticut 06518

FINAL NOTICE

Reply Within 10 Days to Avoid Enforcement
Action and Additional Penalties

Dear Mr. Schiff:

Although notices and demands have been made for payment of your Federal taxes shown on the back of this letter, we have no record of receiving the amount due. This is your final notice before we proceed with enforcement action.

To prevent such action, send us, within 10 days from the date of this letter, your check or money order for the total amount due, payable to the Internal Revenue Service. Show your taxpayer identifying number (social security or employer identification number) on it and enclose this letter to assure prompt and accurate credit. An envelope is enclosed for your convenience. The copy of this letter is for your records.

If you have recently paid the amount due but your payment has not been credited to your account, or if you cannot pay this amount in full, contact the person whose name and telephone number are shown above within 10 days from the date of this letter.

If we do not receive your payment or if you do not contact our office, enforcement action may be taken at any time after 10 days from the date of this letter without any further notice to you. Salary or wages due you may be levied upon, as provided by section 6331 of the Internal Revenue Code, by serving a notice of levy on your employer. Bank accounts, receivables, commissions, or any other kind of income you have are also subject to levy. Property or rights to property, such as automobiles, may also be seized and sold

(continued next page)

for liquor taxes I had neglected to pay? Or for estate, gift, or tobacco taxes that were due? I have no way of knowing from this "notice." It is like getting billed $300 from a department store but never being told what the bill is for. The government, of course, hopes that those who receive such "notices" will not catch this omission and merely assume that the "demand" is for income taxes. But the "bill" itself does not say so since there is no law that allows the government to "demand" payment of such a tax.

All the "notice" mentions is a "Form Number 1040." Why "Form Number 1040" instead of a clear identification of the type of tax alleg-

EXHIBIT 18 (Continued)

Sincerely yours,

District Director

to satisfy your tax liability.

Enclosures:
Envelope
Copy of this letter

Form Number	Tax Period	Tax Balance	Accumulated Penalty	Accumulated Interest	Amount Due
1040	12-31-76	Tax Assessed	19,006.00		
		Fraud penalty	9,503.00		
		Estimated Tax Penalty	709.00		
		Interest	13,117.35		
		Total this period			42,335.35
1040	12-31-77	Tax Assessed	18,678.00		
		Fraud penalty	9,339.00		
		Estimated Tax Penalty	663.00		
		Interest	11,554.28		
		Total this period			40,234.28
1040	12-31-78	Tax Assessed	53,447.00		
		Fraud penalty	26,724.00		
		Estimated Tax Penalty	1,706.00		
		Interest	29,683.20		
		Total this period			111,560.20
		Total 1976 through 1978			194,129.83

Above totals computed to April 25, 1983. Interest continues to accrue at 1% annually.

James Holmberg

edly owed? Because if an individual sends in a "1040" and claims he owes a tax on that *form,* he has supposedly established that he owes a Federal tax pursuant to that form. But under the Code, no one can "owe" an income tax so the "Form [on which the taxpayer himself has admitted to owing a Federal tax] Number" *is shown instead.* But *I never sent in* a "Form Number 1040" so such a "form" (or any tax associated with it) *could not apply to me.*

In addition, the only Code section mentioned in the entire "Final Notice" is Section 6331 which Quinn cited as his alleged *authority* for seizing my property "to satisfy [my] tax liability." If the "notice" could cite a Code section authorizing the seizure of my property, why could it not also cite the Code section that established the "liability?" If any such section existed *it would have been mentioned* but because it was not, it is obvious that it does not exist.

So the "Final Notice" I received represents nothing more than an illegal shakedown attempt and falls into precisely the same category as a ransom note received from a kidnapper or a demand for payment from a blackmailer or extortionist — which is exactly what Egger and Quinn are![57]

When I received the "Final Notice" I sent Quinn a sixteen page letter[58] explaining why I could not possibly owe the amounts demanded in this "notice" and (among other things) asked and reminded him of the following:

1. No court had ever established that I owed any of the amounts shown in the "Final Notice." And since the Fifth Amendment bars the government from taking property without "due process of law, " I reminded him of his oath to "uphold the Constitution, " and asked him how (in view of that oath) he could legally seize my property without my ever having had a hearing that established whether I legally owed these amounts.

2. I asked him to specifically cite the section of the Code that established the "tax liability" referred to in the "notice." (Why should I accept a mere letter as proof that such a "liability" exists in the law?)

3. I reminded him of the Supreme Court case of *Flora vs U.S.* 362 US 145, in which the Court declared that the payment of income taxes was voluntary and not based upon "distraint." In view of this, I asked how he could legally take my property by "distraint" in payment of income taxes. I identified Code Section 5006(c) (Exhibit 20) which authorized him to collect taxes owed on distilled spirits "by distraint" and asked him to identify any Code section that authorizied him to collect "income taxes by distraint."

4. I identified numerous other Code sections that specifically established a "liability" with respect to various Federal taxes (such as those shown in Exhibit 6, page 255) and that also established *requirements* that "such taxes shall be paid on the

---

[57]Unlike run-of-the-mill extortionists, Egger and Quinn knew they could count on the U.S. "Justice" Department and the Federal "judiciary" to protect them.

[58]The full text of this letter is reproduced in *The Schiff Report*, Volume 2, Numbers 2 and 3.

EXHIBIT 19

Sec. 6014.   Income tax return—tax not computed by taxpayer.

(a) Election by taxpayer.

An individual who does not itemize his deductions and who does not have an unused zero bracket amount (determined under section 63(e)), whose gross income is less than $10,000 and includes no income other than remuneration for services performed by him as an employee, dividends or interest, and whose gross income other than wages, as defined in section 3401(a), does not exceed $100, <u>shall at his election</u> not be required to show on the return the tax imposed by section 1. <u>Such election shall</u> be made by using the form prescribed for purposes of this section. <u>In such case the tax shall be computed by the Secretary who shall mail to the taxpayer a notice stating the amount determined as payable.</u>

---

basis of a return" (as does Section 5703 regarding tobacco taxes). I asked him to identify any similar section in the law that states that "income" taxes shall be paid on the basis of a return."

5. I explained why no deficiency assessment was possible in my case (see page 304) and included the Court cases and excerpts referred to.

6. I pointed out that "Since I did not supply information on a 1040," nor did I give the government a "list" as provided for in Section 6014 (which was the basis of the notices of April 5), the purported "assessments" were fallacious and any attempt by the Secretary to make an "assessment" upon me by implying that I filed either a tax return or a list "constitutes nothing less than criminal fraud."[59]

7. Since his "notice" sought to tax my income, I asked him to provide me with the definition of "income" and to identify the source of said definition.

8. I notified him that nowhere does the Internal Revenue Code "authorize the IRS to demand fraud penalties which have not been determined by any court of law," and asked him on what basis he could demand or seize property based on such unproven charges.

---

[59]Remember that without either a "return or a list" the Federal government has no statutory authority to even assess an income tax (see page 256).

9. I pointed out why (for all the reasons covered in this book) "fraud" penalties could not apply to me.

10. I reminded him that it was his own office that refused to explain to me how I could complete a tax return without waiving any of my constitutional rights and that his office had advised me to consult with private legal counsel for the answer. I explained that private counsel told me that there was no way I could file a tax return without waiving constitutional rights and asked how I could now be assessed *penalties* for not filing when neither his office nor any private legal counsel could tell me how to safeguard my constitutional rights and file such a return, too.

11. I cited *U.S. Bank of Commerce vs D.C. Tennessee* 32 Fed. Supp. 942 (1940), in which the court held

> The date when the Commissioner signs an assessment list in each case must be considered as the date of his official action in making the assessment.

12. In view of this ruling, I asked how I could owe interest penalties prior to the date of the "assessment" which, admittedly, was not (albeit fraudulently) until April 1, 1983.

13. I asked him to identify whether the tax he was attempting to collect from me was a direct or an indirect tax and into which of the three taxing clauses of the Constitution it fell. (Obviously if it fell into none of these clauses I could not be compelled to pay it.)

Mr. Quinn's response to this letter and a much shorter follow-up letter (in which I simply ask him to identify the Code section that establishes the "liability" for the tax being "demanded") is shown in Exhibit 21. In his reply Quinn did not answer any of the questions raised in either letter. He said I raised "numerous contentions concerning the legality of the actions taken or proposed by this office," which is not true. I merely asked him to cite the Code section(s) that established the tax "liability" he stated I owed and the Code section(s) that authorized the threatened seizure of my property since such citations were omitted from his "notice." [60] In any case, is it illegal or wrong for a private citizen to ask his government these questions? If the government is indeed legally authorized to assess such taxes, why will it not state the type of

---

[60] The Code Section cited, 6331, only authorizes the IRS to seize property "If any person *liable* to pay any tax neglects or refuses to pay the same. . ." But this section could not apply to me since no "liability" for an income tax was cited. And I certainly could not have been "liable" for "fraud" penalties which had never been proven.

EXHIBIT 20

Sec. 5006.   Determination of tax.

(c) Distilled spirits not bonded.
  (1) General. <u>The tax on any distilled spirits,</u> removed
  <u>from the place where they were distilled</u> and (except
  as otherwise provided by law) not deposited in stor-
  age on bonded premises of a distilled spirits plant,
  shall, at any time within the period of limitation
  provided in section 6501, <u>when knowledge of such
  fact is obtained</u> by the Secretary, <u>be assessed on the
  distiller of such distilled spirits (or other person liable
  for the tax)</u> and payment of such tax immediately
  demanded and, on the neglect or refusal of payment,
  <u>the Secretary shall proceed to collect the same by
  distraint.</u> This paragraph shall not exclude any other
  remedy or proceeding provided by law.

---

tax it is demanding and the section of the law that makes the individual
"liable" for paying it? How can these simple questions be dismissed as
merely raising "numerous contentions?"

And as far as the $45,500 in "fraud" penalties is concerned, it must
be remembered that I went into Federal "court" in July, 1981 and not
only openly proclaimed that I had not filed tax returns for 1976, 1977,
and 1978, but also demanded court protection from illegal prosecution
because of it! Based on this, how could anyone claim I committed
"fraud" with respect to tax returns for those years? If it can be said that
no one in this country could have committed "fraud" with respect to
their income tax returns it would be me.

To this day the government has yet to answer either of these two
questions for me with respect to my alleged 1976, 1977, and 1978 tax
"liability" though they have confiscated my property, to the tune of
more than $180,000, in payment of "taxes and penalties" for those years.

Initially, even though I wrote that long letter to Quinn, I really did
not take his threat to seize my property seriously. While I was certainly
aware that the government had seized the property of others in payment
of income taxes, I believed my case was different. I assumed that other
individuals in somewhat similar situations had filed returns — swearing that they had income — and, therefore, "deficiency" and other assessments had been made pursuant to Section 6203. In addition, the
"Final Notice" contained "penalties" for "fraud" which had never been

---

EXHIBIT 21

Internal Revenue Service   Department of the Treasury

District   P.O. Box 959, Hartford, Conn.   06101
Director

MAY 11 1983

Mr. Irwin A. Schiff
Post Office Box 5303
Hamden, Connecticut   06518

Dear Mr. Schiff:

Reference is made to your correspondence to this office dated
April 12, 1983 and April 23, 1983, wherein <u>you raise numerous
contentions concerning the legality of the actions</u> taken or
proposed by this office.

In response thereto, it is the position of this office that all
actions taken to date have been done in compliance with the provisions of Title 26 of the United States Code and the regulations
promulgated thereunder. Further, all future actions will be taken
in compliance with said law.

Sincerely yours,

Ronald J. Lambert
for   JAMES E. QUINN
                        District Director

Freedom Books

P.O. BOX 5303   HAMDEN, CONNECTICUT 06518   PHONE (203) 281-6791

*If a nation values anything more than freedom, it will lose its freedom; and the
irony of it is that if it is comfort or money that it values more, it will lose that too.—Somerset Maugham*

May 25, 1983

James R. Quinn
District Director
P.O. Box 959
Hartford, CT   06101

Dear Director Quinn:

Your letter of May 11, 1983 states (regarding my letters of Ap-

(continued next page)

EXHIBIT 21 (Continued)

ril 12 and 23) that "I raised numerous contentions concerning
the legality of the actions taken or proposed by this office."

I not only made some contentions I also asked you some important
questions which were designed to reveal whether or not I indeed
had a Federal tax liability as contended in your "Final Notice"
of April 18, 1983. Your reply that "all future actions will be
taken in compliance with said law" was totally unresponsive to
the specific questions I raised and in no way established whether I indeed had a tax liability and/or if your notice was pursuant to any Federal law and the United States Constitution.
Therefore, I respectfully request that you answer the following
two simple questions regarding your "Final Notice" since this
information was missing on it:

1. What kind of a Federal tax do you allege I am liable
   for (i.e., alcohol, tobacco, estate, gift, income,
   etc.)? It certainly is not unreasonable for a citizen
   to be told the specific nature of the Federal taxes
   that he allegedly is liable for.
2. In addition, since Section 6333 only authorizes siezure
   of property if a "person liable to pay any tax neglects
   or refuses" to do so, please tell me the specific section of the Internal Revenue Code that makes me "liable" for the type of Federal tax you claim I owe.

Very truly yours,

Irwin A. Schiff

---

adjudicated in a court of law[61] so, under no circumstances, could I have
had any legal liability with respect to such penalties. Given all this,
plus the fact that I had put Quinn on notice that any IRS seizures were
illegal as a matter of law (which I also believed that others in my situation had not done), I felt he would not even *attempt* to seize any of my
property using the Gestapo-lilke tactics the IRS is famous for. I sincerely believed that he would proceed by taking me to court, as provided
in Section 7401 (Exhibit 22). I was sure that I could get such a court proceeding dismissed for the reasons explained on page 303. This shows how
naive I was even as late as the Spring of 1983 regarding the willingness
of IRS officials to break the law. I was confident of my position and even
said to those around me who were concerned about the government's
threatened seizure that the Fifth Amendment was clear: "The government cannot take my property without due process of law," I insisted. I
just must have a hearing, especially since a portion of the monies demanded are for fraud penalties which even the law admits must be

[61]How could Quinn believe he was legally authorized to seize property for the payment
of unproven civil fraud charges?

EXHIBIT 22

Sec. 7401.   Authorization.

No civil action for the collection or recovery of taxes, or of any fine, penalty, or forfeiture, shall be commenced unless <u>the Secretary</u> authorizes or sanctions the proceedings and <u>the Attorney General or his delegate directs that the action be commenced.</u>

---

proven." As I have already pointed out, I also had the notice from the government stating that no taxes for the years in question had ever been assessed. How then could any of my property be seized?

An attorney warned me, however, that despite all my legal arguments the IRS could begin seizing my property. He said they might padlock my business and my home, only allowing me to remove approximately $2,500 worth of personal possessions. I asked him, "How can they legally do that when no court has ever either determined I owed the government any money nor ordered me to pay anything to the government?"

"They can do it," he said, "and whether or not it is legal they do it, and the courts let them get away with it."

I was further advised that if I resisted the illegal confiscation of my property I could really be in trouble since then the government could charge me criminally under statutes that provided stiff penalties for such resistance. [62] Suddenly the situation seemed far more serious than I had imagined. The IRS apparently had the power and the guns and being "right" would do me absolutely no good if the Mamelukes could padlock my business and eject me from my home. Even if I was wrong, did I not have the same right to due process as a mugger or a subversive?

How could I fight back? The only things I had going for me were the truth (the law obviously does not count for much in Federal "courts") and my ability to spread that truth to others through my newsletter, tapes, and books. But I needed my office in order to keep fighting (and ultimately win as I knew I would), and I needed my home which contained my library and all of my research material. I realized that such confiscation — no matter how illegal — would seriously disrupt my

---

[62]This is what the law seems to suggest. However, after doing additional research, I found that this legal advice was incorrect. Citizens can indeed resist the taking of their property by the IRS in payment of income taxes, and there is no section in the law which prevents them from doing so. In such instances, however, since private citizens will be dealing with rattlesnakes (including Federal "judges," see page 250), they must know exactly *what* to do and *how* to do it (see page 381, 382).

work and hamper my ability to expose the government's actions so I immediately took steps (which I had never done previously) to protect myself. In addition, I filed a lawsuit in Federal "court" asking for a restraining order against Quinn's threatened seizures and a hearing to determine whether or not I legally owed the government the sums demanded.

The Joke of Federal "Courts"

I was unable to get a hearing, even in the face of Quinn's threatened seizure of all of my property — a violation of not only all existing Federal law but an obvious violation of the whole concept of American government, demonstrating that the entire Federal "court" system had become one tragic joke. If Federal "courts" have any function at all it is to protect the rights and property of private citizens, especially against the awesome power of the Federal government. If our "courts" will not protect citizens in such cases, then they are worth nothing. It is only the zealous protection by the courts of the rights of the individual that separates America from communist and fascist governments. But since Federal "courts" today refuse to provide such protection — and actually help government tyranny — the only difference between government in America and government in the Soviet Union is the overt *degree* of oppression that exists.

Before analyzing how and why Judge Burns turned down my request for a hearing on the legal merits of my case, I need to familiarize you with another unconstitutional and insidious "legal" device that the Mamelukes have installed, the Anti-Injunction Act. This device is hidden in Section 7421 of the Internal Revenue Code (Exhibit 23) and gives them a way to illegally strip citizens of their property while providing Federal "judges" with a convenient excuse for ignoring it.

What this statute seems to say (forget the "exceptions") is that no Federal court has the authority to hear suits in which citizens seek to restrain the assessment or the collection of Federal taxes. This section is continually misrepresented and misused by Federal "judges," but why is such a provision in the law in the first place? Why should a private citizen not have the legal right to restrain the government from seizing property for the payment of taxes that he does not owe? This provision was put into the law during the Civil War. The rationalization for the statute was that the government needed tax money quickly and could not afford to be tied up in litigation before getting it. But at least then there was a war going on. There is no such excuse today.

The Mamelukes argued that constitutional due process was maintained because individuals could pay the tax and then sue for a re-

---

EXHIBIT 23

Sec. 7421. Prohibition of suits to restrain assessment or collection.

(a) Tax.

Except as provided in sections 6212(a) and (c), 6213(a), and 7426(a) and (b)(1), and 7429(b), no suit for the purpose of restraining the assessment or collection of any tax shall be maintained in any court by any person, whether or not such person is the person against whom such tax was assessed.

(b) Liability of transferee or fiduciary.

No suit shall be maintained in any court for the purpose of restraining the assessment or collection (pursuant to the provisions of chapter 71) of—

(1) the amount of the liability, <u>at law or in equity,</u> of a transferee of property of a taxpayer in respect of any internal revenue tax, or

(2) the amount of the liability of a fiduciary under section 3713(b) of title 31, United States Code in respect of any such tax.

---

fund.[63] This, of course, overlooks the obvious hardship imposed on those who *really do not owe the tax* but are forced to pay it anyway. If the tax demanded is obviously illegal (as in my case) and set arbitrarily (and vindictively) high, paying such a tax could literally destroy some taxpayers and prevent them from effectively suing for a refund. In some cases (as shown in Chapter 13) taxpayers have had to go as high as the Supreme Court to get their refunds.[64] But suppose the taxpayer lacks the funds to make such an expensive legal trip?[65]

---

[63]This is why all the taxpayers referred to in the cases in Chapter 13 first paid the tax and then sued for a refund, even though in some cases (as in the *Eisner* case, see page 216) case law was already firmly established in the taxpayer's favor..

[64]In most cases the Mamelukes know that taxpayers cannot and will not sue for a refund. If the government illegally seeks $2,500 from a typical wage earner how can he realistically pay this amount and also sue for a refund? Most taxpayers will neither have the *time* nor the *expertise* to go up against experienced U.S. Attorneys alone and the typical incompetent attorneys still demand at least $2,500 to bring suit (which, in all probability, the taxpayer would not have after paying the tax nor would wish to risk).

[65]This first direct taxing acts provided specific legal protection to the public against tax collectors who "shall demand other or greater sums than shall be authorized by law." Today, *the people have no comparable protection!* Why then do the people permit such a statute to remain on the books?

The statute covering this presumes that tax collectors will not *arbitrarily* seek to collect taxes not legally owed while, at the same time, private citizens will try to restrain the collection of taxes they really owe merely for delay. It is easy to see how such thinking might have developed during a precarious war, but today such reasoning cannot be seriously sustained. The Mamelukes have established the legal principle that the government's interest in tax revenue takes precedence over the people's interest in the preservation of constitutional rights.

It is clear that a significant factor in the Mameluke's success in illegally collecting taxes is due to the protection they get from the Anti-Injuction Act and the way the "courts" use it. For example, if the IRS sends you an unsigned and uncertified tax "bill" for $1,000,000 (without either identifying the tax or the Code section that makes you *liable* for it) the "courts" can rule that you still have to pay the "bill" even if it takes *all of your assets*.[66]

By reading the statute itself it is clear that it refers specifically to the *"assessment* or *collection* of any *tax"* and therefore cannot apply to penalties levied in connection with such taxes and certainly not to civil fraud penalties. In addition, even the "courts" have recognized that the statute could not (on constitutional grounds) serve as an *absolute bar to injunctive relief,* so they carved out exceptions to the Act under which they could take jurisdiction. The problem is that Federal "judges" are free to arbitrarily disregard those exceptions and fraudulently hide behind the statute, as Judge Burns did in my case.[67]

For example, Judge Burns cites two such exceptions:

1. If the levying of the tax will cause irreparable injury; and
2. the plaintiff can expect "certainty of success on the merits."

These exceptions, however, are by no means the *only* exceptions. She conveniently forgot to mention at least two others:

1. Suit may be maintained to enjoin collection of illegal tax under "special and extraordinary circumstances." [68]
2. Federal Courts can take equity jurisdiction in the absence of any remedy at law.

---

[66]Section 7421 obviously cannot be tolerated a moment longer and Americans must *immediately* begin applying political pressure to get it repealed. If representatives do not favorably respond to this, we should immediately seek to remove them from office — *regardless of their stand on any other issue.*

[67]"Judge" Burns' decision appears in Appendix F.

[68]*Miller vs Standard Nut Margarine Co. of Florida* 284 US 498 (four other cases were also cited).

Tax "Court" and Other Tax-Related Scams

The latter reference to a Federal court's *equity* power requires some explanation. All Federal courts are courts of equity in addition to being courts of law. Equity refers to the principle of fairness and applies when there is no apparent legal remedy available in a given situation. In this instance the courts can become courts of equity (as opposed to courts of law) and apply this equity power to redressing or correcting an obvious wrong that has been brought to their attention.[69]

The *Pollock* case, as we have seen, was an action to *restrain* Farmers' Loan from voluntarily paying the income tax (and the Supreme Court heard that case *sitting as a court of equity)*; while in the *Brushaber* case (which was also an action to restrain the Union Pacific Railroad from voluntarily paying the income tax) the government also raised the Anti-Injunction Act as a bar to a Federal "court" hearing, and the lower "court" actually denied relief to Brushaber on that basis. The Supreme Court, however, reversed the lower court and stated:

> To put out of the way a question of jurisdiction, we at once say that in view of these averments and the ruling in *Pollock v. Farmers' Loan and Trust Co.,* 157 U.S. 429 sustaining the right of a stockholder to sue to restrain a corporation unconstitutional on the ground that to permit such a suit did not violate the prohibitions of Section 3224, Rev. Stat., against enjoining the enforcement of taxes, we are of the opinion that the contention here made that there was no jurisdiction of the cause since to entertain it would violate the provisions of the Revised Statutes referred is without merit."

Note that Section 7421(b)(1) (when referring to the liability of a "transferee of property") specifically states both "at law or in equity." So if Section 7421(a) bars a remedy "at law," it certainly does not bar a remedy "in equity."

Anticipating that "Judge" Burns would use Section 7421 as an excuse not to hear my case, my suit was designed to show her why it fell into all of the exceptions recognized in the law while, at the same time, pointing out why the court could also take jurisdiction simply as a court of equity.

There were a number of "special and extraordinary circumstances" involved in my cases which we set out for the court:

1. Over a protracted period of time I had written extensively to the government for clarification and guidance regarding Fed-

---

[69]A famous example of an equity remedy is King Solomon's decree regarding the child claimed by two women. Since there was no "remedy at law" he provided an *equity* remedy.

eral income taxes but it continually refused to give me any
help, telling me instead to seek the advice of private counsel.
Therefore, my actions were based upon the advice of the government itself, so how could I be fined (or be guilty of fraud) for
taking the government's advice?[70]

2. The books and records used by the government "in determining [my alleged] income tax deficiency" were themselves seized
from me by agents of the Special Investigative Section of the
Connecticut Tax Department "under questionable authority. . . the legality of [which] is currently being litigated." In
addition, the government subpoenaed these records from the
Connecticut Tax Department without sending me a copy of the
subpoena, which is a violation of law.[71]

3. The 90 Day Notice of Deficiency I received stated in its final
sentence that if I had "any questions, " I should contact the
"above referenced person." When I did, neither that person nor
any other IRS representative would answer any of my
questions.[72]

4. On January 25, 1983 (33 days after receipt of my 90 Day Deficiency Notice) I received another notice from the IRS informing me that as "of that date no assessment against [me] had
been filed." Therefore, I notified the court, that "as of that
point, Plaintiff naturally assumed the matter concluded."

5. On April 5, 1983, I received a "Statement of Tax Due on Federal Tax Return" which, in addition to the alleged deficiencies
and penalties, "now purported to impose a substantial and un-
justified interest charge totalling over $50,000. . . which for
various reasons [as explained at length] could not refer to
plaintiff, " and that my inquiries concerning these notices
went unanswered.

6. As of April 14, "Plaintiff having failed to evoke [any replies]
from defendents relating to his alleged tax liabilities" contacted legal counsel who also "dispatched a letter and as of this
date has not received a reply."

7. Despite all of the above, on April 19 plaintiff received a Final
Notice demanding payment "in full of the alleged income tax,
interest thereon, as well as fraud and estimated tax penalties,
representing a sum of $191,846.23."

8. On April 21 "Plaintiff directed correspondence to Donald T.

---

[70]A portion of the correspondence shown to the court is contained in Appendix F.
[71]The case was being heard by "Judge" Burns so she had to know all about it.
[72]My unanswered letters substantiating this were supplied to the court.

Regan, Secretary of the Department of the Treasury, demanding to be furnished with a copy of any alleged tax 'assessment'" for the years in question and that as of the date of the filing I still did not have a response.

9. On April 23, 1983 plaintiff directed correspondence to Defendant James Quinn, "raising his objections and setting forth the basis of this complaint" but as of the date of the complaint, no response had been received.[73]

10. While fraud is violative of the statute itself, to additonally attempt to collect such penalties when the allegations themselves were never adjudicated is flagrantly illegal.

11. "In this instance, the Plaintiff attests that the Tax Court has no jurisdiction, but to submit to its jurisdiction would prevent him from making his constitutional due process argument."

12. I had acted *in good faith,* relying on the government's Privacy Act Notice and therefore could not be punished for having done so.

13. The sum involved was devastatingly high and exceeded all of my available assets. To be compelled to pay such an enormous sum (which I could not possibly do) and then sue for a refund would represent an intolerable and unreasonable deprivation and was an obvious violation of my constitutional rights.

14. As a writer and publisher on the subject of taxes and economics, to be stigmatized by having to pay "fraud" penalties as a prerequisite to any refund action would obviously destroy my reputation and result in the "ruin of my business and livelihood." And since such penalties appeared to have been imposed for *just such a purpose*, the issue affects "the public interest. . . in First Amendment Rights."

In addition to the above, [74] my attorney's Memorandum of Law set forth at length why my case could be heard, but if that was not the case then:

It has been established that in the absense of an adequate remedy at law to contest the legality of the assessment and the resulting irreparable injury to the taxpayer constitute a ground for exception to the operation of I.R.C. Section 7421(a). Plaintiff clearly falls within the equity jurisdiction

---

[73]This comprehensive sixteen page letter (as covered on page 339) was also furnished to the "court."

[74]No attempt is being made to develop these arguments as fully as they were in my suit or to cite all of the supporting case law. By discussing the extensive material that was brought to "Judge" Burns' attention, readers will have a better understanding of just how Federal "judges" operate.

of this Court, by adequately demonstrating that he would be irreparably
injured and lacks an adequate remedy at law.

There is simply no question that:

1. given all of the above facts;
2. in light of the unproven fraud charges (in the face of all the letters that I had written to the IRS that had gone unanswered);
   and
3. the devastatingly high (and obviously punitive) amounts
   demanded

a hearing on the merits — either at law or equity — was called for. Under such circumstances to suggest that Federal law does not mandate,
or at least provide for, a bonafide court hearing, prior to allowing the
government to confiscate all of an individual's property, is to suggest
that America's entire legal system is a farce and in need of a total
overhauling.

The above issues did not go into the *legal* merits of my case but
merely sought to establish the "extraordinary circumstances" that
qualified the case for injunctive relief despite the Anti-Injunction statute. The following points of law were specifically covered in my memorandum of law:

I. The Imposition of "Fraud" Penalties I.R.C. Section 6653(b) is illegal and contrary to all Legal Authority.

Basically, I went into all the material covered on pages 299–300
which demonstrated that Section 6653(b) could not apply to me at
all. In addition, I pointed out that even if the alleged "fraud" could
fall within this statute, the allegations *still had to be proved,*
which had not been done. I also presented a case (*Raley vs Commissioner of Internal Revenue* 676 F.2d 980 [3rd Cir. 1982]) that
supported this very issue. In this case the only issue before the
court was whether Raley was liable for civil fraud penalties. The
Commissioner (as in my case) had imposed fraud penalties in a
"Notice of Deficiency" which was upheld by Tax Court. In reversing
the Tax Court decision the Third Circuit Court held:

. . . *appellant went out of his way to inform every person involved in the
collection process that he was not going to pay any federal income taxes.* The
letters do not support a claim of fraud; to the contrary, they make it clear
that Raley *intended to call attention to his failure to pay* taxes. *It would be
anomalous to suggest that Raley's numerous attempts to notify the Govern-*

ment are supportive, let alone suggestive, of an intent to defraud. Id. at 983-984. (Emphasis added)

My attorney also pointed out:

Likewise, intent to defraud is absent in the instant case[75] and the imposition of said penalty is not only erroneous, but appears to be an attempt on the part of the Government designed to discredit the plaintiff and devastate plaintiff's business.

In the *Raley* case it could be said that at least Tax "Court" found (however erroneous) that "fraud" had been committed. In my case, however, *no court of any kind* had made such a determination. It was perfectly clear that no law authorizes the IRS to:

1. merely allege *civil fraud;* and
2. *proceed* to seize property based upon its own unproven allegations.

If the government can legally deprive citizens of property based upon *unproven civil fraud allegations*, it could also conceivably deprive them of their *freedom* based upon *unproven criminal fraud allegations*. Since "Judge" Burns ruled that the government could indeed deprive me of my property based upon its unproven allegations, *and that it was legal for it to do so.* Did she also believe that citizens could be deprived of their freedom based upon unproven *criminal fraud* allegations?

II. Plaintiff Sought The Advice and Counsel of the IRS and Relied on that Advice and Counsel

[I pointed out that I sought] clarification of whether or not [I] could file a return without surrendering any of [my] constitutional rights [and that I] was directed to consult an attorney, which [I] did and was advised that [I] could not file a return without forfeiting [my] Fifth Amendment right which guarantees that a person cannot be compelled to be a witness against himself. A "return" must

[75]It is important to point out that this was the very same "judge" before whom I had appeared two years earlier and not only had I admitted to not filing for 1976, 1977, and 1978, I had also demanded that she protect me from further illegal government prosecutions for doing so. If anyone in the country knew that I had "gone out of [my] way to inform every person involved in the collection process that [I] was not going to pay any Federal income taxes," it was "Judge" Burns so how could she believe I had acted fraudulently or tried to deceive the government with respect to my income taxes for those years?

necessarily be voluntary since an individual forfeits his Fifth Amendment right by virtue of filing it, since one must file under "penalties of perjury." If it is not voluntary then it is compulsory and unconstitutional because it strips an individual of a constitutional guarantee.

Based upon this analysis, "Judge" Burns had to clearly understand that filing was indeed voluntary. Suppose someone was being tried in her "court" for income tax evasion. When the government introduced the defendant's tax return and the defendant objected on the grounds that he was required to file the return so it could not be used against him (because it represented compelled testimony), would she sustain the objection and toss the government's entire case right out of the window? No, she would rule that the defendant filed voluntarily so the return could be admitted and used against him.[76] "Judge" Burns knew that *legally* I did not have to file and consequently that all the penalties demanded by the government for not filing were erroneous. My attorney further pointed out that (based upon these legal facts):

> Plaintiff relied on the representations of I.R.S. officials, and in his knowledge and belief, formed the unassailable opinion that the filing of a "return" is voluntary.

III. The Privacy Act Notice Accompanying I.R.S. Form 1040 is Statutorily Defective

I went into an in-depth analysis of the Privacy Act Notice which, by law, is supposed to inform the public whether filing an income tax return is "voluntary or mandatory" and the "affects on him, *if any*, of not providing all or any part of the requested information." I pointed out that the government had

> failed to carry out their statutory duty of informing [me] whether the filing of a return was mandatory or voluntary and whether or not a penalty [such as tax fraud] would be imposed [for not filing and that] the Privacy Act Notice, on its face is vague, ambiguous and cannot adequately inform plaintiff of his duty to disclose such requested information, nor does it adequately appraise him of the penalties imposed for failure to file.

---

[76]Precisely as Judge Clarie did to me, see page 285.

Public Law 93-579 imposes a clear duty on the government to inform the public in this Privacy Act Notice whether filing a tax return is "mandatory or voluntary" and the penalties "if any" for not filing so the public can *rely* on what it says. How, then, can anyone be guilty of a crime if he relies on this Notice? If someone can be penalized for civil fraud (without a hearing) for not filing a tax return, then this information, by law, is supposed to appear in the Privacy Act Notice (Exhibit 25, page 375). But such information does not appear in that Notice and if such penalties are legally possible anyway, then the government itself is breaking the law with respect to that Privacy Act Notice.

In addition, while not stating specifically that filing is mandatory or informing individuals of the penalties for not filing, the Notice actually informs people that they are not *required to file* at all. It does so by stating that "you must file a return or statement with us for any tax you are *liable* for." First, the Notice says nothing about filing an "income" tax return, it merely refers to "any" return for which "you are liable." Presumably, then, this Notice applies to those returns and taxes shown in Exhibit 6 and not to "income" taxes at all. [77] The Privacy Act Notice accompanying a 1040 booklet is not supposed to inform individuals about "any" Federal tax, it is supposed to inform individuals about the *income* tax. Why does it not specifically say that an individual is required to file an "income tax return if you are liable for the tax"? Because there is no such *liability* contained in the law so it deceptively refers to *"any tax."* Talk about fraud!

Second, since there is no section of the Code that makes anyone "liable" for an "income" tax, the Notice actually informs individuals that they are not "required" to file. In any case, even based on the government's own distortion of the law, I could not have been "liable" for the tax until after it was assessed which did not occur until (at the earliest) April 1, 1983. Therefore, I could not possibly have been "liable" for the tax prior to that date, which, in turn, meant that I did not have to file income tax returns for 1976, 1977, and 1978 until *after* April 1, 1983 when I was (illegally) "made liable" for the tax. But *if* I had *paid* the tax at that time on the basis of the government's "assessment, " I would have paid it without ever *filing a return*. Why, then, was a return necessary and why was it "fraud" not to have filed one?

It is also obvious that since the Privacy Act Notice does not list

---

[77] The use of the word "any" in the notice is obviously designed to completely mislead its readers and is a *flagrant violation of the law.*

any penalties for not filing an income tax return and, in fact, informs individuals that there are no penalties for not filing, the government should be barred from extracting such penalties based on this issue alone, which should be apparent to any legitimate court.

IV. Interest Can Be Charged Only From the Date Liability Accrued and Is Therefore Improperly Applied In This Case

Because the government did not even assess me until April 1, 1983, I asked the "court" how I could have (legally) owed more than $50,000 in interest on a bill that was only five days old. I pointed out that I.R.C. Sec. 6601 prescribed:

> If any amount of tax imposed by this title. . . is not paid on or before the last day prescribed for payment, interest on such amount. . . shall be paid." Assuming agreement that plaintiff did incur a tax liability, by virtue of the Final Notice (Exh. "P") the plaintiff understands the "last day prescribed for payment" to be ten (10) days after receipt of said final notice.

How could it be otherwise? If I were only made liable for the tax on April 1, 1983, and the tax was (theoretically) demanded in the Final Notice of April 18, 1983, how could any interest have accrued at all? I also pointed out to the "court":

> If any tax liability is owed, plaintiff is clearly not liable for $50,000 in interest charges. He was never appraised of any tax liability, nor warned of such an outrageous sum purporting to be interest.

V. 16th Amendment Does Not Provide For Direct Taxation of Wages (property)

Eighteen pages of the brief were devoted to this particular argument and contained a capsulized version of all the material contained in this book. It proved that neither the 16th Amendment nor the Code allowed for a direct tax on the sources of my income as the government was attempting to extract. I also showed that for an income tax to be constitutional it had to be levied as an excise tax and, since it was not, I was not "liable" for paying it based upon

1. the law as written;
2. the holdings of the Supreme Court; and
3. the Constitution itself.

I submitted significant passages of law from the *Pollock, Brushaber, Eisner,* and *Smietanka* cases as well as from *Stanton vs Baltic Mining, supra* and others. In effect, the "court" was made fully aware of everything covered in this book so "Judge" Burns had to know that, legally, I did not owe the government a dime.

VI. The Alleged Notice of Deficiency and the Internal Revenue Code in General Does Not Apprise Plaintiff of Any Legal Liability

None of the notices I received from the IRS apprised me "of the statutory basis upon which said alleged liability is determined" and without such legal citing(s) I could have no tax liability nor could there be any amount due. I established an air tight case regarding the fact that:

1. there was absolutely no legal basis for either the tax or the penalties demanded by the government for which they threatened to seize $191,000 of my property; and
2. on this basis alone the "court" had plenty of legal jurisdiction to grant me the temporary restraining order and a hearing on the merits as requested.

In addition to all this — as a demonstration of my good faith — I even told the court that I was:

> . . . ready, willing and able to execute a bond payable to the defendant of the United States of America, or to provide other security in such sum as this court seems proper for such costs and damages, if any, as may be incurred or suffered by any party found to have been wrongfully enjoined or restrained.

A few days prior to my hearing the government produced what the U.S. Attorney claimed was my official assessment for 1976, 1977, and 1978 (Exhibit 24) since I had asked the "court" (in my suit) to:

> . . . compel the Internal Revenue Service. . . to furnish to the plaintiff pursuant to IRC 6203, a copy of the alleged assessment record allegedly entered in the IRS files on April 1, 1983, including the character of the liability assessed, the basis upon which said "assessment" was determined and the name of the "assessment officer" whose signature appears thereon.

The court accepted the fraudulent notice that was introduced by the government (Exhibit 24) as my "record of assessment." Its fraudulent nature is apparent because:

1. My name does not specifically appear on the "assessment" (which actually turned out to be a composite assessment of $1,363,925 reflecting what was apparently put on the books at the Andover Service Center on April 1, 1983).

2. This "assessment certificate" combines all Federal taxes such as Social Security, corporation, excise[78], estate and gift, and even Federal unemployment taxes and there is nothing on it that indicated which, if any, of those taxes applied to me.

3. There was nothing on it that indicated that the assessments were made "pursuant to Code Section 6203."

4. There was nothing on it that indicated who was responsible for determining the amounts assessed.

5. If the "Assessment Certificate" was supposed to apply to me, then it certainly was fraudulent because it did not contain a "certification" made by an assessor. For example, if Bill Smith goes to City Hall to check his property assessment he would discover (on his assessment) that the city assessor certified that he made Bill's assessments pursuant to a given statute (which is identified) and further swore that the assessment was "true and correct." On my "Assessment Certificate," however, the "Assessment officer" (whose name was illegible) stated:

I certify that the taxes, penalties and interest of the above classifications, hereby assessed, are specified in supporting records, subject to such correction as subsequent inquiries and determinations respect thereto may indicate to the proper.

If used to support the assessment of my "taxes, penalties, and interest," this "certification" is a total fraud since the only thing being certified to is that the amounts "are specified in supporting records." In addition, no *statutes* were cited that authorized the taxes assessed, yet the government maintained that this "assessment" conformed to my demand for a copy of my *record of assessment* pursuant to Section 6103 and the "court" agreed.

---

[78]Another admission that the tax is not being legally levied as an excise.

EXHIBIT 24

QUICK

ASSESSMENT CERTIFICATE
SUMMARY RECORD OF ASSESSMENTS

1. SERVICE CENTER	2. DATE	3. PREPARED BY	4. NUMBER
ANDOVER	APRIL 1, 1983	MM	482

CLASS OF TAX	CURRENT ASSESSMENTS		DEFICIENCY AND ADDITIONAL ASSESSMENTS (Resulting From Regular Audit Examination)				TOTAL ASSESSMENTS
	TAX & PENALTY (a)	INTEREST (b)	TAX & PENALTY (c)	INTEREST (d)	NO. OF ITEMS (e)		(f)
WITHHELD INDIVIDUAL INCOME AND FICA	2,425 39						2,425 39
INDIVIDUAL INCOME-OTHER			519,611 69	201,893 51	82		721,505 20
CORPORATION INCOME AND EXCESS PROFITS			375,399 70	193,352 17	11		568,751 87
EXCISE							
ESTATE AND GIFT			58,566 49	12,677 00	1		71,243 49
TAX ON CARRIERS AND THEIR EMPLOYEES							
FEDERAL UNEMPLOYMENT TAX ACT							
TOTAL ASSESSMENTS	2,425 39		953,577 88	407,922 68	94		1,363,925 95

5. JEOPARDY ASSESSMENTS AGAINST PRINCIPAL TAXPAYERS (Included in the assessments above)	6. PREPARED FROM ACCOUNTING ASSESSMENT JOURNALS		
	DATE AND NUMBER	THROUGH	DATE AND NUMBER
	4-1-83	8-1936	4-1-83 8-1940
NUMBER OF PRINCIPAL TAXPAYERS	4-1-83	8-5505	
TOTAL ASSESSED AGAINST PRINCIPAL TAXPAYERS	4-1-83	8-5507	

CERTIFICATION

I certify that the taxes, penalties, and interest of the above classifications, hereby assessed, are specified in supporting records, subject to such correction as subsequent inquiries and determinations in respect thereto may indicate to be proper.

7. DATE	8. SIGNATURE (For Service Center Director of Internal Revenue)
APRIL 1, 1983	_[signature]_

Assessment Officer

U. S. TREASURY DEPARTMENT - INTERNAL REVENUE SERVICE

FORM 23C (REV. 9-67)

When my attorney saw this "assessment" she automatically assumed that it applied to me and automatically assumed (because of the $1.36 million amount shown) that it was in error. I made the same mistake.[79] But when she pointed this out to the "court" (that the assessment could not possibly apply to me because of the amount shown even though there was an accompanying document that said that this was my assessment), the U.S. Attorney openly accused her of "lying" to the court (he presumed she knew it was a composite assessment but was pretending that it was otherwise).

"Judge" Burns realized that without any kind of proof of "assessment" the government had no case at all, and she would therefore have no choice but to grant the temporary restraining order and hearing as requested. She had to have something — *anything* — on which to base her claim that an assessment had been made, which of course did not exist. Proof? To this day, I cannot get a certified copy of my own assessment record for 1976, 1977, and 1978.[80] "Judge" Burns, for whatever reason, had to pretend that it did. Perhaps she needed a remedial reading course.

It is obvious why such documents cannot be supplied. No bureaucrat will take the responsibility for making an "assessment" when the law does not authorize any government official to make one without first having either a "return or list" — which I did not supply for the years in question.[81]

On May 20, 1983 we had a preliminary hearing before "Judge" Burns. This involved oral argument as to whether the "court" had jurisdiction to issue a temporary restraining order pending a hearing on the legal merits of the issues involved. All of the arguments relative to this had already been presented to the "court" in briefs filed earlier and

---

[79]Since the assessment was supplied to us just prior to the hearing (when we did not have much time to examine it along with everything else that had to be done), from a cursory scrutiny it appeared to be totally incorrect. It certainly did not comply, in any way, to my request for a copy of "my record of assessment" as required under Section 6203, though both the government and "Judge" Burns fraudulently claimed that it did.

[80]See Appendix F for irrefutable proof that the "assessment" (as far as it related to me) was a total fraud as was "Judge" Burns' claim that "Plaintiff's request for a copy of the record of assessment, to which he is entitled under 26 U.S.C. Sec. 6203, has been granted."

[81]This fact was not brought out in my preliminary hearing since neither my attorney nor I were aware of this statutory restriction at that time (as explained in *The Schiff Report*, Volume 2, Number 5) and because we both also assumed (for the reasons stated) that the "assessment" was obviously erroneous to begin with. The government's revelation (that it was a "summary record") caught us both off guard.

very little was added in oral argument (with the exception of the controversy already noted that developed over the fraudulent assessment notice). The government was represented by the Mameluke's hit man, Gerald Miller, who was flown in from Washington just for the occasion.

"Judge" Burns' decision to deny me a temporary restraining order pending a hearing on the legal merits of my case is reproduced in full in Appendix F and begins as follows:

> Plaintiff in this action is a zealous tax protestor who claims that the federal tax system is unconstitutional as presently administered.[82]
>
> Plaintiff failed to file federal income tax returns or to pay income tax to the Internal Revenue Service for the taxable years 1976, 1977 and 1978. The Commissioner of Internal Revenue determined he had income sufficient to require him to pay tax for each of those years and notified him, on December 2, 1982 of his tax deficiencies. Plaintiff failed to exercise his statutory right under 26 U.S.C. Sect. 7422 to contest the determination of the deficiencies in the Tax Court. On April 1, 1983 the Internal Revenue Service made an assessment against the plaintiff for the unpaid federal income tax, penalties and interest and on April 18, 1983 sent him a final notice advising him of the delinquent status of his 1976, 1977 and 1978 accounts. Plaintiff filed [his] suit on May 4, 1983.

In this statement "Judge" Burns disregarded *every legal* reason I gave her for doing all of the things she lists, *as if such reasons never existed*. Pages and pages of legal arguments (including statutes and case law) were simply ignored. For example,

1. She argued that I "failed to file income tax returns" but overlooked completely my documented contention that I did not file because I could find no section of the Code that required me to file. In addition, the government admitted in the Privacy Act Notice that I was required to file returns only for taxes for which I was "liable." "Judge" Burns could not identify the Code section that "required" me to file nor the one that made me "liable" for the tax, though I *specifically* raised this issue in my motion.
2. She stated that I did not pay my taxes for the taxable years 1976, 1977, and 1978 while admitting that such taxes *were not even assessed* until April 1, 1983. Why should I have paid them

---

[82]Why am I a tax protester, because I point out the law to the "court" and state I expect the government to obey it? "Judge" Burns simply adopted the technique used by the government against those who know the law — "attaint" us as "tax protesters" — which, she believed, enabled her to avoid addressing the valid legal arguments I raised.

sooner since, under the law, no taxes can be *owed* until they are assessed? She could not address this point so she acted as if it did not exist.

3. "Judge" Burns then stated that the Commissioner notified me that I had "income sufficient to require [me] to pay tax for each of those years" and further notified me on December 2, 1982 of my "deficiencies." Again, she simply recited this chain of events without noting the legal inconsistancies of what she was saying or the legal issues I raised in my brief. She completely shut her eyes to the fact that I was officially notified by the government "that as of January 25th [1983] no assessments" against me for 1976, 1977 and 1978 had been made. Why should I have contested the Commissioner's notice of December 2nd when the notice I received informed me that as of January 25th the December 2 notice was in error? She ignored this entirely as if that second notice had neither been received by me nor pointed out to her.[83] She ignored as well the legal reasons I gave to explain why Tax "Court" was not a viable legal option to me.

4. Here and throughout her decision, "Judge" Burns also never mentioned the illegality of the fraud penalties or that the government had not proved fraud.

5. She also stated that on April 18, I was notified "advising [me] of the delinquent status of my 1976, 1977, and 1978 accounts." But, at the most, they could only have been "delinquent" for eighteen days so how could I be liable for $50,000 in interest "penalties?"

6. "Judge" Burns then said that "Federal courts are courts of limited jurisdiction" and that Congress has "explicitly limited the extent to which courts may intrude upon the assessment or collection of Federal taxes." True, Federal courts are "courts of limited jurisdiction" but "Judge" Burns had more than sufficient jurisdiction to hear this case. And while Congress may have "limited the extent to which courts may intrude upon the assessment or collection of Federal taxes," that "extent" certainly did not extend to my case (which contained all of the elements of which she was aware).

I was not trying to "intrude upon the assessment" of a Federal tax. My contention was that the Commissioner of Inernal Revenue threatened to take my property **without any as-**

---

[83]Burns also had to know that the December 2 notice was erroneous since she admitted that no assessment was made until April 1, 1983.

sessment having been made, which was evident to the "court." In addition, the Anti-Injunction statute certainly does not apply to *unproven* fraud charges nor to interest penalties.

According to this logic, if a citizen received a notice from the government that said unless he paid $200,000 (or any other arbitrary sum) in "Lollipop taxes," he could have his property seized to satisfy the payment of that tax and, as a Federal "judge," she would not have the authority to prevent it. The irony was that though "Judge" Burns had plenty of jurisdiction to hear this case she had no lawful jurisdiction to conduct criminal trials for failing to file income tax returns. In 1974, however, she took jurisdiction in just such a case and sentenced Connecticut resident Wendell Cady to jail for failure to file income tax returns. When "Judge" Burns had no jurisdiction she usurped it, and when she did have jurisdiction she denied it.

7. Next "Judge" Burns stated what she claimed were my only legal and equitable choices:
   a. I could "petition Tax Court to review the assessment"; or
   b. I could pay the tax and "sue for a refund."
8. She stated that the Supreme Court "has repeatedly upheld the Anti-Injunction Act's limit on federal jurisdiction . . . [because of] the 'Government's need to assess and collect taxes. . . , '" which, we are supposed to believe, allows Federal bureaucrats to fabricate and extract tax liabilities which Federal "courts" are powerless to control — despite the Constitution.
9. "Judge" Burns then turned to "An exception to the operation of the statute" which, she claimed, exists only when "irreparable injury [and] certainty of success on the merits are found." Here she overlooked two other factors recognized by the "courts" — the existence of "extraordinary circumstances" and her equity jurisdiction.

How do these two exceptions that she *did* grant apply to me? She said

> Plaintiff has not shown either of the two prerequisites for a judicial exception to the Anti-Injunction Act. For one thing, payment of the assessed taxes imposes a financial burden on plaintiff, but does not rise to the level of irreparable harm.

I had already explained to the "court" that $190,000 exceeded all of the assets available to me at the time. How many people have that kind of money lying around that they can just hand over to the Federal government while they wait to sue it for a refund? On what evi-

dence did "Judge" Burns base that conclusion?[84] Apparently it
made no difference to her whether the amount demanded had been
$500,000 or $1 million — she would have arbitrarily claimed the
same thing.

10. "Judge" Burns then insisted that I had an "adequate remedy
at law." I could either submit to a drum-head Tax "Court"
(which had absolutely no function or jurisdiction in this matter), or I could pay the tax and sue for a refund in district
"court." She wrote:

> In addition, not only is there no certainty that plaintiff will succeed
> on the merits, but there is little likelihood that he will do so.

And she had the nerve to cite her own slip opinion — *Schiff vs
United States* of N-81-316 — as a precedent! Her claim that there
was "little likelihood" that I could succeed on the merits was nothing more than an admission that it is impossible to get a fair hearing in a Federal "court." Moreover, to cite her own slip opinion in a
former case as providing a legal basis for the denial in this one
raises some interesting questions as to the incestuousness of the
Federal "judiciary." "Judge" Burns simply used one of her own prior,
arbitrary dismissals as the legal basis to support the later dismissal of a case containing numerous legal elements totally absent
in the former one.

11. She then addressed the issue of my motion made in the form of
a *mandamus* in which I stated:

> . . . compel said defendants to furnish [me] pursuant to 5 U.S.C.
> Sect. 552(e)(3) (hereinafter Privacy Act) with a clear direction as to
> whether or not filing of a "return" under penalties of perjury is vol-
> untary or mandatory and the resultant effect on him for not volun-
> tarily filing a "return."

In her opinion she admitted to half of what I had asked "in the nature of mandamus." As explained previously, the IRS's Privacy Act
Notice in no way meets the requirements of the law. "Judge" Burns,
however, cited four lower "court" appellate decisions which seem to

---

[84]The government was trying to put me out of business as they had done to so many others. The fact that they did not succeed is not because they did not — with the help of
this "court" — give it the old college try. They failed because of certain unique pecu-
larities in my economic situation and because I was forced to take actions which necessitated substantial economic and personal distortions in my life and in the lives of
my children. For example, my son Peter, who had just been accepted by Berkley Business School with a 3.5 GPA, had to drop out of college in his junior year.

have held otherwise — which were as legally valid as the appellate opinion in *U.S. vs Francisco, supra,* (see page 265) and as "Judge" Burns' decision was in this case. This is easily proved by comparing the Notice with the law. Where in the Notice are individuals informed that "filing an income tax return is mandatory" or what the penalties are if one does not file?[85]

I merely asked the "court" to produce a statement signed by a responsible government official, attesting to the fact that filing an income tax return was "mandatory" and that one risked civil fraud penalties for not filing income tax returns because such information is missing from the Privacy Act Notice where, if indeed true, it is supposed to appear. By hiding behind four appellate court cases, "Judge" Burns refused to get such a statement from a government representative. Why?

12. But "Judge" Burns' final footnote was really revealing. Her claim that as a writer and self-publisher my ability to earn a living after having nearly $200,000 extracted from me and being branded a "fraud" would not be "undermined" pales into insignificance when compared to her final observation:

> Plaintiff, also, claims that the assessment of taxes and fraud penalties against him is totally arbitrary and without any basis. *He has provided no evidence to support his claim.* (Emphasis added)

I did not have to prove my innocence; *the government had to prove my guilt.* That is Anglo-Saxon legal principle. In addition to the *Raley* reference (page 352) I pointed out that:

> "Fraud, " as that term is contemplated within I.R.C. Section 6653 means:
> . . . *intentional wrongdoing on the part of a taxpayer motivated by a specific purpose to evade a tax known or believed [by him] to be owing. (Stolzfus v. United States* 398 F.2d 1002, 1004 [3rd Cir. 1968]), cert. denied 393 US 1020, 89 S. Ct. 627, 21 L.Ed.2d 565 (1969). *The burden of proving fraud under Section 6653 rests upon the government,* 398 F.2d at 1005. *That burden is a heavy one (Agnellino v. Commissioner of Internal Revenue* 302 F.2d 797, 801 [3rd Cir. 1962]). (Emphasis added)

[85]The "criminal prosecution" referred to concerns the providing of "fraudulent information" instead of not filing at all. For example, no where does it tell an individual that he can be guilty of "civil fraud" for not filing. The law says that the notice must tell individuals the "effect. . . if any" of not providing the requested information — and this notice does not. For an in-depth analysis of this fraudulent document, see *How Anyone Can Stop Paying Income Taxes,* pages 41–60 by Irwin Schiff and *The Schiff Report,* Volume 1, Number 1.

Fraud can be established only by *clear and convincing proof* or "something impressively more than a slight preponderance of evidence." *(Cirillo v. Commissioner of Internal Revenue* 314 F.2d 478, 482 [3rd Cir. 1963]; *Valetti v. Commissioner of Internal Revenue* 260 F.2d 185, 188 [3rd Cir. 1958]). There must be some convincing affirmative indication of the specific intent to defraud *(Stolzfus v. Commissioner of Internal Revenue* 398 F.2d 1005; *Cirillo v. Commissioner of Internal Revenue* 314 F.2d 483). *The failure to file tax returns is not enough (Stolzfus v. Commissioner of Internal Revnue* 398 F.2d 1005). A showing by the IRS of a willful failure to file income tax returns *without demonstrating the intent which accompanied that failure is insufficient* to meet the clear and convincing standard upon which a finding of fraud must stand *(Cirillo v. Commissioner of Internal Revenue* 314 F.2d 483; *Raley v. Commissioner of Internal Revenue* 676 F.2d 980 [3rd Cir. 1982]). (Emphasis added)

Despite all this, "Judge" Burns claimed I did not supply any evidence to prove that I had not committed fraud.

And, as long as we are discussing fraud, notice that "Judge" Burns' opinion contained nothing — no comment nor any attempt to refute — all the evidence I did supply that

1. proved the income tax is an excise tax; and
2. proved the government was attempting to tax my property directly without apportionment, in violation of the *Pollock* and *Brushaber* cases, as well as the numerous other cases I presented.

Because of her lack of comment one would never know that these issues occupied *fifteen pages* of my brief. Because of her total disregard of these issues — as well as her handling of the fraud issue — it is clearly evident that "Judge" Burns had about as much regard and interest in upholding Federal law and the Constitution as a Soviet judge.

Bank Extortion

On May 25, 1983 (while awaiting "Judge" Burns decision) I received a letter from the American National Bank of Hamden, Connecticut informing me that the previous day the bank had been served "with a Levy on [my] account [and] accordingly, we have deducted two separate amounts from your accounts" which totalled $10,100. This was the same bank that had refused to turn over $468.75 to the government pursuant to a court order served by a U.S. marshall just a few months before. But, without question or a court order, it turned over $10,100 to James Holmberg, an IRS Revenue "Officer," when he walked into the bank with a piece of paper signed only by himself.[86] Soon thereafter I was notified by Investor's Diversified Services (I.D.S.) that they also had turned over $1,000 of my money to the IRS on the same basis. And another bank informed me it had done the same for an additional $500.

At that time, *Simon & Schuster* was acting as the distributor of my book, *How Anyone. . .* and according to our contract the company had a right to set aside a reserve fund for books returned while crediting my account with only those funds above that reserve. When *Simon & Schuster* received its Notice of Levy there was only approximately $8,000 credit in my account. The company was also holding 25,000 copies of my book. About a month previously I had requested that it ship 15,000 books to us to supplement our stock since we also marketed it. *Simon & Schuster* then informed me it could not ship any books to us though it still continued to sell them and pocket its commissions.

Immediately after I was notified that *Simon & Schuster* had received a Notice of Levy, I wrote a letter to the company explaining that such a notice was not a levy and therefore not binding on them in any way. I also pointed out that the piece of paper the company received was certainly not a court order and, further, that I had no "tax liability" as specified in Section 6331 (upon which the Notice of Levy was allegedly based). The legal department of the company assured me that it would do nothing until the matter was settled by a court.

But I still did not have the books I needed and if *Simon & Schuster* would not send any to us, I would have to print more (an expensive and totally unnecessary operation). Fortunately, I discovered a Code section that provided that if the IRS held perishable goods the taxpayer in question could demand that they be sold *immediately* with the proceeds applied to the outstanding tax liability. I wrote the IRS and explained that a non-fiction book was a "perishable" commodity and demanded that it immediately take possession of the books held by *Simon & Schuster* and sell them, crediting my account accordingly.[87]

---

[86]The reason why banks and other businesses turn over money to the IRS without court orders is because (apart from the ignorance of their own lawyers) they are themselves subject to intimidation — i.e., audits. The IRS intimidates everyone!

[87]I wanted to see just how the IRS would sell a book entitled *How Anyone Can Stop Paying Income Taxes!* In addition, Code Section 7302, entitled "Property used in violation of internal revenue laws," states: "It shall be unlawful to have or possess any property intended for use in violating the provisions of the internal revenue law, or regulations proscribed under such laws, or which has been so used, and no property rights shall exist in such property." Despite this "law" my books were (and are) openly being sold in book stores and sent through the mail — proof that while the books explained how anyone could immediately stop paying income taxes that did not violate any IRS law or regulation. And I wanted to see the IRS sell the book itself.

Based upon this demand, the IRS wrote to *Simon & Schuster* on October 6, 1983 and stated:

> In question at this time is the disposition of a quantity of books written by Mr. Schiff and currently in the possession of Simon & Schuster. It was not the intention of the Service to attach these books and, in fact, a notice of seizure would be required to take possession of these assets. The Service makes no claim against these books and they may be distributed in any way mutually agreeable between Mr. Schiff and Simon & Schuster.

Because the IRS sent this letter I eventually did get all of the books, but had I not found that provision in the law I would have had to print more books at great expense. Why could *Simon & Schuster's* own legal department not have determined (before I did) that the Notice of Levy it received did not apply to my books?

In the same letter Revenue "Officer" Holmberg wrote (with respect to the money being held):

> My understanding is that the funds are being held by Simon & Schuster in this regard and will be held until the question of payment of these funds is *decided by the courts.*

This reflected the assurances I had received from *Simon & Schuster's* legal department and, for the moment, I felt my money was safe. I soon found out how wrong that feeling was.

I should have brought suit immediately so the question could be decided, but since I was rushing to complete a new book, *The Social Security Swindle — How Anyone Can Drop Out,* I unfortunately put the matter on the back burner. Despite Holmberg's letter and *Simon & Schuster's* assurances, I was notified on February 17, 1984 that *Simon & Schuster* had turned over $8,748 of my money to the IRS (without a court order) and it continued to do so until the company had turned over more than $150,000. Because the actions of both the American National Bank and *Simon & Schuster* were violative of my contracts with them, I decided to file suit against the bank first. This suit was summarily dismissed by "Judge" Warren Edgerton on the grounds that since the bank had no legal choice but to turn over the funds to the IRS I therefore had no cause of action.

Between the time of my suit against the bank and the filing of my suit against *Simon & Schuster,* I discovered a great deal more concerning the differences between a Notice of Levy (what both firms had received) and a Levy (what they *thought* they had received). In addition, apart from the IRS's open acknowledgement that the issue was awaiting a court test, there were significant differences between the banks actions and those of *Simon & Schuster.*

I discovered the following with respect to the actions of the IRS:

1. According to Section 6331, a Notice of Levy can only pertain to the "accrued wages and salary of any officer, employee, or elected official of the United States, the District of Columbia, or any agency or instrumentality of the United States or the District of Columbia. . ."

2. Before a "Levy" can take place the property must first be "seized" and a Notice of Seizure given. (Note that reference was made to this in Holmberg's letter to *Simon & Schuster* except that it was misleading. A Notice of Seizure would be required to take possession of either the books or the money).

3. The IRS deliberately confuses the public concerning the differences between a Notice of Levy (IRS Form 668-A) and a Levy (IRS Form 668-B).

4. The IRS's own *Legal Reference Guide.* . . admitted (see Section 332, page 248) that a "notice of levy is not adequate to seize property of the taxpayer." It also stated, (see Section 334.2, page 248), in relevant part, that "Where a notice of levy [or] Final Demand [are] not responded to, a suit will ordinarily be required to reach the property."

In addition to the above, my suit against Simon & Schuster contained an element lacking in my suit against the bank. Section 6331(b) specifically states that a "levy shall extend only to the property possessed and obligations existing at the time thereof." So even if *Simon & Schuster* had been "required" to turn money over, the $8,748 in my account at the time of the purported "levy" should have been all the company turned over. *Simon & Schuster,* however, kept sending money to the government as it came due me (on the basis of that one notice) — which was a violation of law.

All this information was presented to the "court" in my suit against *Simon & Schuster* and proved, absolutely, that it was under no legal obligation to turn over any money (let alone any in excess of the $8,748 it originally gave the government) on the basis of its receipt of a "Notice of Levy" as "Judge" Eginton contended when he dismissed the bank suit.

Regardless of all the material presented, "Judge" Eginton waited months to dismiss the suit (see Appendix F for the text of his dismissal) on the claim that *Simon & Schuster* was *required* to turn over the money, disregarding the relevant statutes and the IRS's own legal manual. I have filed a notice of appeal with the Second Circuit "Court" and can only wait to see what it has to say on the matter.

The IRS also subpoenaed my bank records, which I sought to prevent by filing a Motion to Quash in Federal court pursuant to Section 7609(h) of the Internal Revenue Code. That section was added to the Code (effective January 1, 1983) and provided for a specific procedure whereby taxpayers could quash such subpoenas and also provided Federal courts with specific jurisdiction to hear such suits.[88] This section was added to help the government not the taxpayer. Before, if a bank got such a subpoena the party whose records were about to be subpoenaed could send a letter to the bank threatening to sue if it turned over such records without a court order. This would force the IRS to have the Justice Department file a lawsuit against the bank in which it was asked to show cause why it should not comply with the subpoena. At such hearings the bank would not put up a fight since they would just as soon turn over such records.[89]

Taxpayers, however, could intervene and were developing some powerful techniques to use against the government at these hearings. The Mamelukes decided it was getting too easy for the public (and too rough for them) at these hearings so they changed the rules. The new procedure was diabolical since it was made to appear that individuals were being given greater access to the "courts" (when in reality they actually had less) while, at the same time, the Act substantially increased both the cost to and the burden on individuals in preventing the illegal seizure of their bank records. With this legislation on the books, both the banks and the "courts" could now claim that the banks were legally obligated to turn over records (without a court order) if an individual did not initiate a lawsuit.[90] So instead of merely having to write a letter and having an absolute right to intervene in a government-initiated show-cause hearing, the government:

1. placed a complicated legal burden on individuals;
2. provided "judges" with the opportunity to arbitrarily dismiss such lawsuits; and
3. eliminated the need for the government to initiate lawsuits itself in order to seize bank records.

[88]When the IRS similarly subpoenaed my bank records in 1979 and I filed a Motion to Quash, Federal "Judge" John Newman denied it on the grounds that he did not have jurisdiction to hear it.

[89]American banks are largely bookkeepers and informers for the IRS and individuals should use them as little as possible.

[90]This whole procedure is a sham since banks are still not required to turn over records without a court order and the government cannot force private citizens to initiate litigation.

And, while it appeared as if individuals were being given greater access to the courts, the effect was to give them less access while substantially increasing both their costs and their burdens. Many lawyers were charging $2,500 to handle these usually ineffective motions so I developed an absolutely unassailable do-it-yourself Motion to Quash (see *The Schiff Report*, Volume 1, Number 6) and instructions on how to argue it in "court." Beating any IRS subpoena for income tax-related records with that Motion to Quash would be as easy as shooting fish in a barrel — which is why the government has dropped an Iron Curtain between itself and the people. For example, when I got my copy of the bank subpoena, I immediately had an attorney file this Motion to Quash. Soon after filing it, he received a call from the U.S. Attorney's office in Washington, D.C. threatening him with legal penalties if he did not withdraw my suit. This telephone threat was confirmed by a letter received from Glenn L. Aercher, Jr., Assistant Attorney General, Tax Division, signed by D. Patrick Mullarkey, Chief, Civil Trial Section for the Northern Region, which read in relevant part:

> This is to confirm a telephone conversation between trial attorney Peter Sklarew of this office and yourself. As indicated by Mr. Sklarew, because the petitions to quash in the above-named case raise only defenses that have been squarely and uniformly rejected by numerous courts, the United States will move for attorney's fees against both you and your client. . . if it remains necessary for the United States to file a response. . . If you and your client will concede this case, Mr. Sklarew will draft a stipulation and agreed enforcement order. However, inasmuch as the United States' response is due on June 11, 1984, we request that you call Mr. Sklarew by Wednesday, June 6, and indicate whether or not you plan to press ahead with this case. . . We hope this case can be resolved with a minimum of expense so that it will not be necessary to move for attorney's fees . . . telephone number is 202-724-6560.

These assertions were not true. The "defenses" raised in my petition had never been rejected by "numerous courts" nor could they be. This was shown when the government was forced to file its response and simply disregarded these "defenses" and refused to address them at all.

When my attorney notified me of this phone threat I immediately called Mr. Sklarew at his Washington office and he confirmed that the threat had indeed been made. I told him that I regarded the threat to be a criminal violation of Sections 241 and 242 of the U.S. Criminal Code but that I would make it easy on him. If he would cite the Code sections "that made me liable for an income tax or required me to perform any act with respect to it" (the only two bases upon which such subpoenas can be issued), I would immediately withdraw my motion. When he was unable to find such sections I warned him that he should consider himself put on notice that the IRS subpoena was illegal and if he did not withdraw it I would seek substantial civil damages as well as his criminal prosecution. At this point he told me that the government had a right to seek the records even if I had no tax liability, and I challenged him to make such an assertion on the witness stand where he could be cross-examined.

In any case, my attorney took the threat seriously and prepared an additional and extensive response to it seeking to justify my legal right to pursue the matter and explaining why the government's threat to seek punitive damages from him was uncalled for. Naturally this additional legal expense was added to my bill and I instructed my attorney to sue the government for reimbursement.

I was really anxious to cross-examine Mr. Sklarew regarding the government's scurrilous and illegal threat and to press for payment of my legal expenses. But in order to protect the government's illegal activities from certain exposire, "Judge" Warren Eginton again arbitrarily dismissed my motion without a hearing again and, in addition, awarded damages *to the government!*

More Justice Department Criminals

While all this was going on, the Justice Department was seeking to indict me criminally for some kind of tax "crime." Assistant U.S. Attorney, Michael Hartmere — Connecticut's foremost expert on illegal prosecutions — was put in charge of the campaign. He began contacting people all over the country who I might have done business with or who had sent me any significant amount of money. He even sent one of his winged messengers to contact my children's dentist in California. He also contacted a friend and former business associate who had wired me a few thousand dollars a number of years previously for a reason neither of us could now remember.

Hartmere's agents also fanned out to contact everyone I had ever done business with in the New Haven area. People were asked questions "in connection with a grand jury investigation of Mr. Schiff's affairs." This was obviously being done to discredit me (by insinuating that I was involved in something illegal) and interfere with my ability to conduct my business.[91]

In most cases Hartmere's messengers tried to get the information informally (by intimidation) rather than eliciting the facts before a

---

[91]Some people are still reluctant (despite my otherwise excellent credit reputation) to extend me significant credit for fear that I am in imminent danger of prosecution.

grand jury. Most of the people these messengers approached told the agents they would not give out any information except to a grand jury — and they were largely left alone.

Through all of this, however, Michael Hartmere knew that I was innocent of any crime since I had made him aware (through numerous letters) of the information contained in this book. I even demanded that he present this material to the grand jury but he refused.

I also sent a letter (together with a copy of my letter to Hartmere) to Mr. William F. Smith, the Attorney General of the United States, in which I pointed out:

> The attached letter to Mr. Michael Hartmere. . . clearly indicates that a crime which you have the authority and the obligation to prevent, is taking place. . .
>
> If Mr. Hartmere persists in this matter I will also hold you criminally and civilly accountable.

Both Hartmere and the Attorney General knew I could not be guilty of any tax "crime, " but they, nevertheless, zealously proceeded to try (so far without success) to get me indicted. I had written to Hartmere many times, offering to appear before the grand jury and answer any questions it might have. Hartmere would not call me, however, because he knew that if I ever got him before a grand jury it could easily lead to **his indictment** for violating a number of Federal laws.

On May 30, 1984 I filed a *sixteen* page complaint (together with about *twenty* pages of supporting exhibits) with Alonzo L. Lacey, Jr., the FBI's Special Agent in Charge in New Haven, Connecticut. In it I stated:

> I charge these individuals:
>
> Judge T. Emmet Clarie. . . Michael Hartmere, Esq. . . Judge Lapsley Hamblen. . . James E. Quinn. . . James Holmberg. . . Jerome Donovan, Esq. . . Robert Percy, Esq. . .

1. with violating Sections 241 and 242 of the U.S. Criminal Code, in that they collectively conspired "to injure, oppress, threaten [and] intimidate" me in the free exercise of a number of rights and privileges secured to me by the U.S. Constitution and the laws of the United States;
2. that Hamblen, Quinn, and Holmberg also violated sections of the Internal Revenue Code (including Section 7214(a)(1)(2), which covers "offenses by officers and employees of the United States"; and
3. that through their collective efforts, over $150,000 of my property was extorted from me (plus I had to pay $10,000 to ransom myself from prison) by the fraudulent use of Notice(s) of Levy,

a. which can only apply to the "accrued salary or wages" of Federal employees as specifically covered in Section 6331;

b. without an actual Levy as provided for by Section 6502;

c. without any Notice of Seizure as provided for in Section 6335;

d. without any "liability" being established as provided for in Section 6331; and

e. in violation of the procedures contained in Sections 7401, 7402(e), and 7403(c);

4. and that such organized collective actions also fall within the RICO Act dealing with organized crime and racketeering. All of these government employees combined in an illegal criminal conspiracy to "extort" money from me (and the community at large) as covered by Section 1951(a); "under color of official right," as provided in Section 1951(b)(2); which took place "interstate. . . including the mail," as provided in Section 1951(a); such "extortion. . . is chargeable under state law," as defined in Section 1961(1); and meets the test of a "pattern of racketeering activity" as defined in Section 1961(5).

The FBI told me it had turned my complaint over to the Justice Department. To date it has done nothing with respect to my complaint.

The Government's Procedures

Regardless of my efforts, the "courts" have never allowed me to bring the government before the bar of justice. They have disregarded my ability to prove that government agents acted illegally, in violation of the law and my constitutional rights. In contrast, the government illegally took me to "court" twice and without any jurisdiction whatsoever the "judges" not only allowed it, they proceeded to deceive the juries concerning both the facts and the law in order to get me convicted.[92] The actions of these Federal "judges" have been deliberately calculated to deny me access to the "courts" so that the government could continue to violate the rights of others.[93] My experiences in the "courts" are by no means unique. Such judicial treachery occurs on a daily basis in Federal "courts" throughout the country. There is no doubt that the biggest and

---

[92]The "hearings" I did have were only to get my suits dismissed, not to decide the legal merits of my claims. For the legal propriety of such dismissals, see Chief Justice Warren Burger's observation on page 486.

[93]The culpability of the U.S. Justice Department cannot be ignored. U.S. Attorneys around the country go after alleged "tax protesters" much in the same way as the Polish government has gone after members of Solidarity.

EXHIBIT 25

Privacy Act and Paperwork Reduction Act Notice

The Privacy Act of 1974 and Paperwork Reduction Act of 1980 say that when we ask you for information, we must tell you:

a. Our legal right to ask for the information.

b. What major purposes we have in asking for it, and how it will be used.

c. What could happen if we do not receive it.

d. Whether your response is voluntary, required to obtain a benefit, or mandatory under the law.

For the Internal Revenue Service, the laws include:

• Tax returns and any papers filed with them.

• Any questions we need to ask you so we can:

Complete, correct, or process your return.

Figure your tax.

Collect tax, interest, or penalties.

Our legal right to ask for information is Internal Revenue Code sections 6001 and 6011 and their regulations. They say that you must file a return or statement with us for any tax you are liable for. Your response is mandatory under these sections. Code section 6109 and its regulations say that you must show your social security number on what you file. This is so we know who you are, and can process your return and papers.

You must fill in all parts of the tax form that apply to you. But you do not have to check the boxes for the Presidential Election Campaign Fund.

We ask for tax return information to carry out the Internal Revenue laws of the United States. We need it to figure and collect the right amount of tax.

We may give the information to the Department of Justice and to other Federal agencies, as provided by law. We may also give it to States, the District of Columbia, and U.S. commonwealths or possessions to carry out their tax laws. And we may give it to foreign governments because of tax treaties they have with the United States.

If you do not file a return, do not provide the information we ask for, or provide fraudulent information, the law provides that you may be charged penalties and, in certain cases, you may be subject to criminal prosecution. We may also have to disallow the exemptions, exclusions, credits, deductions, or adjustments shown on the tax return. This could make the tax higher or delay any refund. Interest may also be charged.

Please keep this notice with your records. It may help you if we ask you for other information. If you have questions about the rules for filing and giving information, please call or visit any Internal Revenue Service office.

A: You are required to file only if you wish to "obtain a benefit." If you do not want the "benefit" (whatever it is) you are obviously not "required" to file.

B: What "must" you file — a "return or statement?" To what Federal tax, therefore, does the "any" apply? Does the Notice state *anywhere* that individuals are *required* to file *income* tax returns? Are you required to file returns for taxes you are not *liable* for? The Notice says *no.*

C: Can the Federal government *require* that you give information to all these government agencies so that they can use such information against you?

D: The "criminal prosecution" refers only to giving "fraudulent information." Where does the Notice tell you that you can be charged criminally or be subject to civil fraud penalties for giving *no* information?

most powerful lawbreakers in the nation are the "judges" who sit on the Federal bench. [94]

Lord Acton's observation that "power corrupts and absolute power corrupts absolutely," explains the Federal judiciary since Federal "judges" today have nearly *absolute* power.[95] This "absolute power" is a result of

1. their power to hold anyone in contempt, under which they can put people in prison without a trial;
2. their sure knowledge that they can break the law in favor of the government — without any risk of criminal prosecution.
3. their unchallenged ability to arbitrarily intimidate, discipline, and fine any member of the public or the bar who attempts, in any way, to challenge their conduct in "court";
4. the fact that these "judges" know that they can count on judicial backing — all the way to the Supreme Court; and
5. their knowledge that no matter how outrageous their rulings, they will never come under sharp attack.

How many lawyers, for example, would publically call a Federal "judge" a criminal, even when they witness actual criminal judicial behavior — such as denying defendants the right to be assisted by counsel of their choice? "Judges" know they have nothing to fear from lawyers because caution and legal "ethics" prevent lawyers from publicly criticising the "courts."

How can we deal with these judicial malefactors and the Mameluke empire they protect? How can we topple that empire in order to reestablish constitutional rights and a republican form of government in America? Turn the page.

[94]It is my belief that all candidates for the Federal judiciary are given a test on the Constitution and only those who fail are eligible to be appointed.

[95]The only reason the Mamelukes went after Judge Claiborn of Las Vegas (and convicted him of income tax evasion) is because he was practically the only Federal judge in the country who did not let the IRS get away with murder in his courtroom.

18

How To End The Income Tax Now!

It should be clear by now that we live under a government of men, not the government of law envisioned in the Constitution. The Mamelukes have extensively usurped power, and their closure of the courts to those seeking peaceful and lawful redress has made a shambles of our society. In the face of this some have suggested that armed resistance may become necessary. James Madison's admonition.

> If the federal government should overpass the just bounds of its authority . . . the people must take such measures to redress the injury done to the Constitution as the exigency may suggest and prudence justify [and that] acts of usurpation . . . will deserve to be treated as such

does not rule out armed resistance as a lawful option. The use of armed force against the Mamelukes is totally unnecessary since we can (based upon the following program I have outlined) rid ourselves of the Mamelukes and their income tax in short order without anyone having to fire a shot.

Jury Nullification

We can get rid of the income tax very quickly using jury nullification, i.e., by jurors refusing to convict anyone charged with any income tax "crime." If the Mamelukes cannot convict anyone of breaking their "laws," then the "laws" themselves are automatically nullified — they cease to exist. This is but one example of the ultimate power each American has over Congress and the government itself. The problem is that few Americans realize they have this power.

In order for the government to convict anyone of a crime all twelve jurors have to vote guilty. If only one juror votes not guilty, the jury is "hung" and the defendant either goes free or has to be retried. *If only one juror out of twelve in every criminal income tax trial voted not guilty, the Mamelukes could never convict anyone of such "crimes"* and, in effect, the law would be nullified. This can be done on a community-by-community basis and does not even require the educating of a significant number of people — only approximately 8 percent of the adult population in any particular Federal court district. If only 8 percent of the adult population in any Federal court district understood their *right* to vote "not guilty" (regardless of the facts or what any "judge" might tell them), the government would be unable to get criminal convictions in that district. A mere 8 percent of the people in that district would have wiped out the income tax for the entire district.[1]

American Jurors Can Decide The Law As Well As The Facts

Few American jurors realize that they have a legal right to this prerogative in any criminal case. Along with the fallacy that the Founding Fathers did not know the difference between direct and indirect taxes, the "courts" also promote the fallacy that American jurors only have the right to decide on the facts not the law and that they must accept the trial "judge's" interpretation and instructions. None of this is true. In *criminal* trials any American juror can (if he wishes) legally disregard everything the trial "judge" says and vote his own conscience. He can vote not guilty for any reason he chooses on the basis of the facts, because he does not like the law or the punishment, or for *any* reason that strikes his fancy. A dramatic example of this occurred several years ago when a former congressman was prosecuted for padding his payroll and pocketing the money. The evidence pointed to his guilt and all the jurors but one voted guilty resulting in a hung jury. Because the government decided not to retry him the man went free. When the dissenting juror was asked why he voted not guilty, he said that the former congressman, now in his 70's, was "too old to go to jail." In voting as he did this juror disregarded both the law and the facts and voted "not guilty" for his own reasons. The Supreme Court provides legal support for this principle.

Georgia vs Brailsford 3 Dall 1, 4 (1774)

Initially, the Supreme Court was a court of original jurisdiction be-

---

[1]As word of this spreads, lawyers and other tax preparers would start moving out — leaving room for more creative and productive citizens to move in — and the economic climate of such a judicial district would start to brighten immediately.

fore which jury trials took place as this case illustrates and it affords an opportunity to see how our jury system was meant to operate. In charging the jury, Chief Justice John Jay said:

> It may not be amiss, here, Gentlemen, to remind you of the good old rule, that on questions of fact, it is the province of the jury, on questions of law, it is the province of the court to decide. But it must be observed that by the same law, which recognizes this reasonable distribution of jurisdiction, you have nevertheless a right to take upon yourselves to judge of both, and to determine the law as well as the fact in controversy. On this, and on every other occasion, however, we have no doubt, you will pay that respect, which is due to the opinion of the court: For, as on the one hand, it is presumed, that juries are the best judges of facts; it is, on the other hand, presumable, that the courts are the best judges of law. *But still both objects are lawfully, within you power of decision.* (Emphasis added)

John Jay (not only America's first Chief Justice but a man who presided over sessions of the Constitutional Convention as well as one of the authors of the *Federalist Papers*) told a jury sitting before the Supreme Court that each member had the right to reject the Court's opinion of the law and substitute his own. And if America's first Chief Justice did that, what right do far lesser American "judges" have to tell jurors today that they are unequivocally bound to accept the law as laid down to them?

In criminal cases, jury trials devoid of the right of jurors to decide both the law as well as the facts, if they so wish, are subversive of the entire jury system and the protection against government tyranny that it affords.

The ability to nullify laws is the ultimate protection that the people have over the potential tyranny that government can impose. It protects the public *even if every other element of government falls under despotic control.*

Jury nullification[2] is such a powerful weapon it has even been used to amend the Constitution. An example of this happened in Massachusetts. Article 4, Section 2 of the Constitution provides for the return of runaway slaves but jurors in that state refused to grant extradition requests made under this provision by "owners" seeking the return of their runaway slaves so the provision was effectively nullifed.

In order to get convictions in cases of willful failure to file income

---

[2]For information regarding jury nullification the author is indebted to Godfrey Lehman of San Francisco, California who has done extensive research in this area. For an excellent understanding of the jury system, send $3.00 to FREEDOM BOOKS for *The Rights of Jurors in Criminal Cases* by The Honorable B. F. Thomas (1874).

tax returns, the Mamelukes have various ways of stacking juries — including the checking of tax records of individual jurors to see if they have "not been the subject of any audit or other tax investigation by the Internal Revenue Service."[3] This enables the Justice Department to keep those people off juries who might be biased against the IRS (because of their own experiences) and more sympathetic to the accused. But juries are supposed to reflect a cross section of the community and if 15 percent of the community has a strong bias against the IRS this should be rejected in the jury. To deliberately keep such people off juries in tax cases is tantamount to stacking juries against defendants which must be resisted by the public. I have personally witnessed "judges" asking potential jurors if their own experience with the IRS might affect their impartiality in a tax case. I have then seen those whose hands went up excused when, in reality, they were the *very people* who should have been on the jury.[4]

Because Americans cannot allow the Mamelukes free rein in their attempt to stack juries, individuals should never let a Federal "judge" know that they

1. are aware of jury nullification, or
2. are aware of the criminal nature of the IRS and are therefore biased against it.

To help get rid of the income tax, individuals have to get on juries and vote not guilty in tax cases. More importantly, they should not change their vote regardless of the pressure put on them by other jurors or the "court" when it insists that the jury come up with a conclusive vote — guilty or not guilty. They must also remember that they do not have to justify their not guilty vote to anyone.

Tell Your Friends Now!

Each individual also has to inform all of his friends and family members about jury nullification and explain the reasons why they should vote not guilty in tax cases *before* they get on any jury. If individuals tell someone *after* he gets on a jury the Mamelukes might try to frame them for jury tampering.

---

[3]Internal Revenue Code Section 6103(h)(5).
[4]Many people who serve on juries are automatically prejudiced *against* defendants who do not file regardless of the legal aspects of the case, and *the government and "judges" exploit this kind of impartiality to the fullest.*

Arresting IRS Agents and "Judges"

It should now be obvious that there are no laws that *require* anyone to file income tax returns and pay income taxes, nor any that give Federal prosecutors and "judges" the authority to prosecute income tax "crimes." Therefore, all IRS agents, members of the Justice Department, and Federal "judges" who engage in such activities are operating outside both Federal and state laws which makes them *outlaws*, and they should be treated as such. When such individuals operate *within* Federal law they are usually protected from civil lawsuits and criminal prosecution even if they make serious errors. But when they operate *outside* Federal law they do not have the same protection. *All* Federal employees (including "judges") who seek to compel compliance with respect to income tax "laws" cannot claim protection under Federal law since there are no such laws. By doing this they expose themselves to criminal prosecution under state and Federal laws just like anyone else.

Arresting IRS Personnel Under State Law

The first IRS operatives we should seek to arrest under state law are IRS revenue officers who engage in or threaten to take property by force (either by direct means, through the filing of liens, or by the fraudulent and extortionary use of the "Notice of Levy." In its *Legal Reference Guide* . . . (see page 248) the IRS admits that revenue officers are subject to prosecution for "trespass, assault and battery, conversion, etc." These are all state crimes and an open admission by the IRS itself that IRS personnel who exceed their statutory authority (which is only to encourage voluntary compliance, see page 242) are subject to arrest and prosecution under a variety of state laws.

This is how to do it: All Code sections that authorize seizures and liens also clearly specify that they only apply to taxes for which the individual is "liable." Therefore, anyone threatened with coerceve IRS action should (if possible) immediately confront the person making the threat and demand to be shown the Code section that makes him "liable" for the tax. In the event that an individual received a "Final Notice" threatening the seizure of his property for non-payment of income taxes, he should visit the District Director, his closest aide, or the revenue officer referred to in the notice. Ask the following questions:

1. This notice tells me that I owe $10,000, is that the amount I am *liable* for? When the agent answers yes, say,
2. Since I am a law abiding citizen I want to pay the government every penny I am liable for. I have my checkbook right here [take out your check book and put it on the table] so I can immediately

pay the amount for which I am *liable*. I have one problem, however. Your notice did not say what section of the Code made me "liable" for the tax so could you please give me the section number so I can note it on my check stub?

Though this certainly shows your willingness to be law-abiding and cooperative, the revenue "officer" will generally become defensive at this point. He may say that it is not up to him to show you the section that makes you "liable" for the tax.[5] When the agent refuses to show you the section of the law that provides a "liability" for the tax he alleges you owe, you have to decide just how tough you want to get with him. You have several objectives in this confrontation:

1. To demonstrate your peaceful purpose, good faith, and your willingness to pay any tax for which you are "liable."[6]
2. To prove bad faith on the part of the IRS in that the agent would not identify the Code section that makes you "liable" for the tax.
3. To involve as many IRS personnel in this confrontation as possible so you can get them all on conspiracy charges.[7]
4. To have clear-cut proof that the IRS personnel involved *knew* you were not "liable" for the tax but they knowingly and willfully seized or attempted to seize your property anyway, in violation of the law.
5. To do everything possible to discourage IRS personnel from illegally taking your property.

    You must be particularly forceful in this because if any agent succeeds in taking your property, you will be forced into a time consuming and costly legal battle to get it back. In addition, once the revenue officer reduces any of your property to his "possession and control," you risk criminal penalties if you physically try to take it back. Therefore, if a government agent threatens to seize your property in payment of a tax *that you have offered to pay* — and refuses to show you where in the law you are "liable" for that tax — he must know that such a threatened seizure is illegal.

---

[5]Such a contention has no standing in law. If a government tax collector claims you are "liable" for a tax he should show you the section of the law that specifically establishes that liability.

[6]For these reasons you should have at least one witness with you or a tape recorder to tape the interview if at all possible. If the agent will not allow you to tape the interview this fact should be noted.

[7]When confronting such agents you should ask, "Does your supervisor know about this? Get him in here to confirm what you are telling me."

At this point you would be entirely within your rights to warn anyone involved in such threats that if they attempt to forcibly take any of your property in payment of a tax for which they cannot show you a statutory liability, you will use whatever force is necessary to protect your property from such illegal seizures and that they — and all other IRS employees — *will make such seizures at their peril.* For your own protection, you might want to leave the following statement with the IRS. Ask the agent to sign your copy.

On _____ (date) _____, I, _____ (your name) _____, appeared at the office of the IRS at _____ (street, city, state) _____ and offered to *immediately* pay any Federal tax for which I was liable. I asked _____ (names of Agents) _____

to identify the Code Section that makes me liable for such a Federal tax and he (they) refused to do so. Therefore, I can only conclude that no such Code section exists and that the above named IRS employee(s) know(s) it. I am hereby putting the above named IRS agent(s) on notice that any attempt to take any of my property in payment of a tax for which no law makes me liable, will be resisted by any force necessary and that any IRS agent(s) who attempt(s) such illegal seizures does (do) so at his (their) own peril.

I stand ready, at all times, to immediately pay the IRS any tax for which I am liable if any will identify the section of the law that establishes such a "liability," thereby rendering seizure of my property unnecessary.

This "threat" by you — in writing — was made only *after* you demonstrated your willingness to pay any tax for which you are liable. If an IRS revenue officer refuses to show you where the law says you are liable, he is obviously threatening to seize your property in violation of both Federal and state law and under such circumstances, I believe, you have a perfect right to use whatever force is necessary to protect your property and to warn potential IRS lawbreakers accordingly. Your "threat" is not aimed at any IRS agent engaged in *legal* seizures of property (for taxes for which a liability exists) but only at those making *illegal* seizures which your statement makes perfectly clear. But because of the viciousness of Federal "courts" and the Justice Department, you will have to decide how firm you want the language in your statement to be. The point is, it should reflect:

1. that you appeared and offered to pay any Federal tax for which

the law established a *liability;*

2. the revenue officer refused to produce the Code section that established such a liability;
3. when he refused you informed him that you could not *legally* owe any taxes for which the law did not make you liable;
4. he has no statutory authority to seize any property in payment of any Federal tax for which he refuses to establish a liability; and
5. if he proceeds to seize any of your property based on points 1, 2, 3, and 4, then he is knowingly breaking the law and can expect to receive the same treatment you might afford any other common thief or would-be extortionist.

You might wish to study your state's citizen's arrest statutes since it might be possible to make a citizen's arrest of IRS agents who threaten to illegally seize your property under the color of law.

When arresting IRS agents, in the process of taking your property (as when they go to banks or employers with a "Notice of Levy"), make a citizen's arrest then call the local police. In the presence of the police, demand that the IRS agent point out 1) the code section that makes you liable for the tax he claims you owe, and 2) the Code section that authorizes him to collect income taxes by "distraint." In this connection you could point to section 5006(c) which authorizes the IRS to collect liquor taxes by distraint and demand that he show you a similar section that authorizes him to collect income taxes in the same manner.[8]

If an IRS revenue officer is in the process of trying to seize your car, or attempting to get your bank to turn over your funds on the basis of a "Notice of Levy, "[9] this arrest could be made pursuant to the statutes against attempted larceny, conspiracy to defraud, illegal conversion, or any number of other local statutes.

The Authority of Local Sheriffs

A county sheriff is, or should be, the most powerful law enforcement officer in the county, since he (as opposed to a police chief) is an elected

[8]By way of illustration and comparison you could point out to the police the Code sections shown in Exhibit 6. As you can see, your best weapon against the IRS is the Internal Revenue Code itself. I recommend that you use it in all confrontations with the IRS. A copy can be ordered from FREEDOM BOOKS, see page 557. When you get your copy of the Code you should tab and highlight it for easier and more effective reference.

[9]Remember, the law provides that a "Notice of Levy" can only be used in connection with the accrued wages and salaries of Federal employees so its use in *all* other situations is not authorized by Federal law and in those cases its use would constitute larceny under state law.

law enforcement official specifically charged with protecting the lives and property of those within the county. And this means protecting lives and property against the illegal use of force by Federal outlaws. Under local law a sheriff has plenty of authority to arrest any Federal "judge" or U.S. Attorney who conducts criminal tax trials, especially those involving willful failure to file income tax returns. Any state grand jury that subpoenas Federal "judges" or U.S. Attorneys who have conducted such trials could get indictments against them for violating numerous state laws including deprevation of rights secured by every state constitution.

All that is really required to blow the income tax right out of the water is for *one* local sheriff (or any other local or state police officer) to arrest an IRS agent based upon any or all of the grounds furnished by this book. I can guarantee that the first local law enforcement officer who does so will secure an honored place in American history.

If you anticipate all illegal IRS seizure, contact the sheriff or local police *first* and demand their protection *under local law* against such a seizure. Familiarize them with the relevant material in this book and persuade them to call the IRS directly and ask to be told specifically what Code section makes you liable for the tax being demanded. If IRS employees refuse to specifically identify the section, then the sheriff or police officer should warn them that if they attempt to seize property from individuals within that county — without first furnishing the Code section that establishes the liability for the tax — they will be arrested for illegal conversion under state law. Local police chiefs and sheriffs who will not protect the lives and property of citizens in this manner should be removed from office. **One responsible, informed sheriff could run the IRS right out of his county.**

Filing Criminal Charges On The Federal Level

For the past three years I have attempted to appear before a Federal grand jury (see page 293) to present evidence that every Federal "judge, " Justice Department and IRS attorney, and most IRS employees with whom I have come in contact have been guilty of criminal conduct under Federal law. Not one Federal grand jury has allowed me to testify despite the fact that I have contacted many and complained about it in letters to the district "court." A few months ago, however, I discovered Rule 3 of the *Federal Rules of Criminal Procedure*. It provides that private citizens can initiate Federal prosecutions when they have *personal knowledge* that Federal crimes have been committed. All they need do to start the ball rolling is to swear out a Criminal Complaint.

Neither grand jurors nor U.S. Attorneys have to have *personal knowledge* of crimes when handing down indictments or informations under Rule 6 which is why they need the testimony of others. If, however, a private citizen has *personal knowledge* that a crime has been committed and wants to take the initiative and responsibility of filing a Criminal Complaint under Rule 3 he can. Under the Rule the person the Complaint is filed against must be arrested (or, at the discretion of the "court," issued a summons) and afforded a hearing based on those charges.

Exhibit 11, page 294 contains Sections 241 and 242 of the United States Criminal Code (Title 18). These statutes make it a Federal crime for any Federal employee (under Section 242) or any two or more (under Section 241) to

> injure, oppress, threaten, or intimidate any citizen in the free exercise or enjoyment of any right or privilege secured to him by the Constitution or laws of the United States . . . [or seek to deprive him of] any rights, privileges, or immunities secured or protected by the constitution or laws of the United States.

All American citizens are protected by the Constitution against

1. being compelled to be witnesses against themselves;
2. having property taken from them without due process of law; and
3. being directly taxed except on the basis of apportionment.

So, if any Federal "judge" or Justice Department attorney sought to prosecute a citizen for willful failure to file a tax return, or if any IRS employee attempted to take any of his property by force (without a court order), or tried to interfere with the receipt of his wages by corresponding with his employer, the citizen would have *personal knowledge* of the crime.

In all these cases any individual who has *personal knowledge* of such behavior should seek out the nearest Federal magistrate (as provided for in Rule 3) and swear out Criminal Complaints against such individuals, demanding that they be arrested. In the event that a Federal magistrate refuses to act on such a Complaint as provided by law, a Complaint against him should also be lodged,[10] since he is guilty of misprison — covering up a crime.

---

[10]For more detailed information on this subject, see *The Schiff Report*, Volume 2, Number 7.

How To Stop The IRS From Interfering With Your Legal Right To Stop The Withholding Of Taxes From Your Wages.

Of all the illegal procedures employed by the IRS, none so clearly demonstrates the total duplicity and decadence of America's entire legal establishment than the one used to interfere with a worker's right to claim "exempt" from withholding pursuant to Section 3402(n) of the Internal Revenue Code (Exhibit 26).

This section specifically states

> Not withstanding any other provisions of this section an employer *shall not be required to deduct and withhold any tax under this chapter*. . . if there is in effect a withholding exemption certificate . . . furnished by the employee [that he] incured *no liability* [for income taxes during the proceeding taxable year and that he] anticipates that he will incur *no liability* [for the current taxable year]. (Emphasis added)

Any employee can truthfully swear to this because no one can incur a tax liability for *either* year since no such "liability" exists in the law. Even if an individual paid a tax in the preceeding year, he still did not incur a "liability" since he paid the tax without incurring a "liability," based solely on the government's ability to intimidate him into paying it.[11]

Now, however, the government sends lengthy questionnaires to taxpayers demanding that they justify why they are "exempt," though the law itself imposes no such burden. In addition, the employees "certification" is proof of the truth of the claim because it is his own sworn statement. Presumably, if one cannot prove his sworn statement is true then he has "proved" the reverse — that he perjured himself on the certification. The government cannot "require" individuals to prove they have not committed perjury because a sworn statement establishes its own truthfulness until it is challenged by another sworn statement or disproven in a court of law, which is the whole point of a certification.

In addition to illegally demanding proof that one's sworn statement is correct, the government disregards the valid reasons that are supplied (i.e., the employee has not been assessed pursuant to law, wages are not income, etc.) and the IRS then sends a form letter (Form

---

[11]An employee's W-4 was designed to incorporate these two statements but it skirts the law and substitutes the word "owe" for the word "liability." In *The Schiff Report* (Volume 2, Number 2) readers are provided with a certification that incorporates the actual wording of the law and it is suggested that employees provide such a certification to their employers along with the IRS Form W-4 which does not conform to the law.

EXHIBIT 26

Sec. 3402. Income tax collected at source.

(n) Employees incurring no income tax liability.

Not withstanding any other provision of this section, an employer shall not be required to deduct and withhold any tax under this chapter upon a payment of wages to an employee if there is in effect with respect to such payment a withholding exemption certificate (in such form and containing such other information as the Secretary may prescribe) furnished to the employer by the employee certifying that the employee—

    (1) incurred no liability for income tax imposed under subtitle A for his preceding taxable year, and

    (2) anticipates that he will incur no liability for income tax imposed under subtitle A for his current taxable year.

The Secretary shall by regulations provide for the coordination of the provisions of this subsection with the provisions of subsection (f).

Note: The reference to subsection (f) was added in 1984 in order to provide a contrived basis for the IRS to illegaly interfere with the law as otherwise clearly written. Treasury Department "regulations" cannot "coordinate" the provisions of this section so as to render them inoperative, which is what the IRS seeks to do through its "coordination." Presently, the IRS sends a long form letter to those claiming exempt requesting that they complete a form to establish why they are exempt. The illegallity of such a request is obvious. The law itself imposes no such duty on those claiming exempt and Treasury Department regulations cannot amend the law to establish such a duty.

1385 [SC Rev. 4–82]) telling the employer to disregard the sworn statement given to him by his employee. Such letters tell employers that their employee's W-4 "does not meet the requirements of Internal Revenue Section 3402" and they are "directed" to disregard it and deduct taxes from his pay as if he had claimed one exemption — and most American employers will do just that.

Proof That America's Lawyers Represent The World's Largest Collection Of Parasites

That the Federal government can believe, let alone get away with, the above policy is proof of the uselessness and incompetence of America's entire "legal" establishment providing us with ample reason for smashing the monopoly that the organized bar has over the nation's "courts." All licensed lawyers are "officers of the court" which makes them an extension of the government itself. Such government agents cannot effectively protect the public from the lawlessness of their own principal. The government's ability to confiscate the wages of millions of Americans on the basis of form letters over unchallenged, certified documents to the contrary, constitutes a flagrant violation of basic legal principles, to say nothing of the Fifth Amendment. It makes you wonder whether America, despite all of its law schools, really has anyone out there practicing law.

Do The Wages of American Workers Belong to Them or to The Government?

It is ridiculous for an American writer to have to argue that the wages of American workers belong to them, but the country is now run in a way that suggests that such wages belong to the government. If a worker has absolutely no control over his wages, can he be said to own them? And if workers do not own their wages, who does? The party who controls their disposition and use does. If the government can send out form letters with mimeographed signatures and receive as much of a worker's pay as it wants — *despite the worker's sworn statement that no such amounts are owed* — then it is obviously the government that controls, and thus owns, those wages; and if the government owns a worker's wages (i.e., his productivity) it reduces the worker to the ranks of a slave. There is absolutely no doubt that the Federal government, through the use of illusionary "legal" procedures, has, in reality, transformed American workers into slaves of the "state." Those who wish to dismiss this charge as utter nonsense simply do not understand the nature of slavery because they automatically associate slavery with chains and whips. Based upon such an image my analogy might appear irresponsible and far-fetched, but the basic difference between a slave and a free man is that a free man *owns* his labor and a slave does not. If someone or something has the power to take the fruits of your labor and you are legally powerless to do anything about it, then you are, in effect, being held in object slavery. Many people have been left with literally nothing (even slaves have to be fed, clothed, and housed) after the government "requested" that their employers deduct money from their wages and send it to the government in payment of

1. alleged back taxes due;
2. $500 "fines" (for various "offenses" for which no hearings were ever held and for which no court verdicts were ever rendered); and
3. current taxes (for which it is alleged that false claims were made by the worker).

When an American worker explains that anywhere from one-third to all of his paycheck is going to the government to pay taxes, fines, and penalties[12] that, by law, he could not possibly owe, how can anyone say that such an individual is not a "slave of the state?"

Tax "laws" were written to be constitutional, but the government violates those "laws" while implementing the tax. For example, the W-4 form itself is an acknowledgement that American workers own their wages just as they own the money in their wallets, the food in their lunch pails, or the cars they drive to work.[13] Employers cannot arbitrarily take this property (wages) and send it to a third party (even the Federal government) without permission. An employee gives his employer *permission* by submitting a W-4 form to the employer indicating various withholding allowances which represent the employee's willingness to have an amount withheld from his pay.[14] If an employee chooses not to "allow" such withholding, he has the legal right to do so by claiming "exempt." It is up to the worker to decide his own tax status and what to "allow" the employer to do with *his* money. Without a court order only the worker has the legal right to determine who gets his wages — and *if he does not have this right he does not own his wages.*

In connection with this I have contacted the legal departments of numerous American companies and/or their independent counsels and, in every case, found these lawyers to be openly deceitful and perfectly willing to knowingly violate the rights of workers just to appease the IRS. Typical of these encounters is the experience of Ron Ward, a 35

---

[12]What the public does not realize is that by imposing such arbitrary fines and penalties the government has been able to raise taxes by this ruse. I have seen situations where the government claimed the taxpayer owed $2,500 in taxes and $10,000 in fines, penalties, and interest; and the penalties and interest accumulated faster than the citizen's ability to pay the amounts off.

[13]Could an employer confiscate *these* items and turn them over to the government?

[14]The W-4 is called "Employee's Withholding Allowance Certificate." In other words, the employee is "allowing" his employer to withhold a certain amount from his pay to send to the government on his behalf.

year old maintenance worker with fifteen years experience at the Omaha, Nebraska plant of Continental Can Company. He informed me that his payroll department told him that they were no longer going to honor his "exempt" W-4 and would start deducting taxes on the basis of one exemption as "requested" by the IRS. He had explained to the payroll department why they were not legally authorized to do that but got nowhere. I always advise people to speak to the company's legal department, not with payroll personnel, but in the case of large corporations it can be inconvenient. Ward decided to send Continental Can's legal department in Connecticut a letter with supporting documents to explain why the company had no legal right to confiscate his wages in this manner.[15] Since the executive offices of the company were convenient to me I agreed to call the company to discuss the matter directly with them and also to alert them of the fact that they would be getting Ward's letter. I spoke with Mr. Sheppard, an attorney in the legal department who, I was told, was in charge of such matters.

I informed him that I was representing Mr. Ward in this matter and advised him of the problem he was having with the company. I said that Ward had done everything the law required of him and explained why Continental Can could not confiscate any part of his wages without either his permission or a court order. I discussed the fraudulent nature of the IRS letter and the fact that there would be no legal consequences to the company if it took the IRS's letter and threw it in the trash can where it belonged. I explained to Sheppard something I assumed (at one time) that *all* lawyers learned in law school: that the government cannot deprive an American of property without due process of law and Sheppard said he understood this. I told him that Ward had never had a hearing on his claim of "exempt" so there was no lawful basis upon which Continental Can could summarily disregard his certified statement of exemption and turn his property (wages) over to a third party. It was apparent to me that Sheppard realized (based on elementary principles of law) that Continental Can was under no legal obligation to turn over any of Ward's wages to the government. To solidify matters I told Sheppard I would send him some material that would clarify all of this, which I did.

A few weeks later Ward told me that Continental Can had notified him that they were going to honor the IRS's "request." I called Sheppard and he informed me that he would not discuss the matter with me any

---

[15]It has also been reported to me that workers have received absolutely no help in this area from their unions. Unions could stop these illegal seizures in a minute if they wanted to. The unwillingness of American unions to protect their own members from these illegal seizures (which are in violation of their wage contracts) is but one more example of how American workers are betrayed by their own unions.

further. The last time I spoke to Ron Ward he was in the process of swearing out a Criminal Complaint (pursuant to Rule 3 of the U.S. Criminal Code) against the agent who illegally sent the notice to his employer, interfering with his right to receive his wages.

Mario Pepe, a bus driver for the New Jersey Transit Authority from Cliffside Park, New Jersey, called to tell me that his employer (the State of New Jersey) was disregarding his W-4 and withholding taxes on the basis of one exemption. I called the New Jersey States Attorney General's office and was referred to Kenneth S. Levy, the Deputy Attorney General for the State. I explained that I was representing one of their bus drivers (who I identified) in a matter which I hoped could be resolved amicably so that "we would not be forced to institute a lawsuit for which Pepe and the State of New Jersey would incur needless legal expenses." Levy was very attentive and cordial (obviously under the impression that he was speaking to a licensed lawyer) as I explained the law to him and told him that under both Federal and State law the State of New Jersey was bound to honor Pepe's W-4. After listening to my explanation Levy said he would check the law himself and get back to me. When he called back he said the State had no choice but to honor the IRS's "request." I asked, "On what basis? Do you have a court order?"

"No, " he replied, and then said something that almost all lawyers in this situation have said, "we have to do what the IRS tells us."

I was ready for this answer and asked, "Suppose the IRS told you to shoot him, would you shoot him?"

"That's different, " he said.

"Why is it different?" I asked. "If the IRS can order you to deprive Pepe of his property without a hearing why can't it order you to deprive him of his life without a hearing?"

"Oh, he has not had a hearing on this matter?" Levy queried.

"Of course not, " I replied. "The determination that this W-4 was false was done without any testimony taken from Pepe or anyone else so how could any Federal agency legally determine that his affidavit was false?"

"Well, I was not aware that he did not have a hearing, " Levy said.

"Well, " I replied, "why don't you determine that for yourself before you start taking any of his money away from him? Call Pepe, or the IRS, to determine whether he had a hearing and inquire how the 'false' nature of his W-4 was determined."

"No, " Levy said, "I cannot get into that."

"Why?" I asked, but he would not tell me.

At this point I reminded Levy that Pepe had given him a *sworn* affidavit certifying that he was exempt, and then asked *the New Jersey Deputy Attorney General,* "You mean to tell me that as a lawyer you are going to take the position that an unsworn, mimeographed letter can take precedence over a sworn affidavit?"

Levy declined to answer reiterating that the State of New Jersey would do what the IRS told it to do.[16]

I further reminded Levy that as a state official he had taken an oath to support and defend both the United States and New Jersey Constitutions, both of which included provisions prohibiting the confiscation of property "without due process of law." I asked him if he would openly violate both oaths simply because some faceless IRS employee asked him to do so. When he made no reply it was obvious to me that the Deputy Attorney General of the State of New Jersey was not going to do anything except authorize the confiscation of Pepe's wages. I told him that he was leaving us no choice but to sue to which he replied, "Go ahead."

A few days later, Pepe told me that Levy had called him and said that the State of New Jersey was going to proceed and confiscate such amount from his wages as it was "requested" to do by the IRS. When Pepe asked Levy how the State could do this without a court order Levy said the State had no choice. Pepe then asked him if the IRS "requested" that the State shoot him would the State do that too? Levy replied, "You sound just like your lawyer."

The Federal government will not and cannot do a thing to any employer who disregards these withholding "requests." When an employer asks the IRS what can happen to him if he does so, the IRS sends him a letter designed to both mislead and intimidate him. He is told that those who do not honor these "requests" can be liable for the "amount of the tax *required* to be withheld." Since no amount is "required" to be withheld in the law (especially when an employer receives a sworn affidavit from his employee certifying that he is "exempt"), an employer cannot have any "liability" in either circumstance because he is not "required" to withhold anything.

The Anti-Injunction Statute Surfaces Again

When an employee sues his employer in State court for the wages illegally taken from him, the employer manages to have the suit removed to a Federal "court" where a Federal "judge" is then able to dismiss it on the basis that it is in conflict with the Anti-Injunction Statute. The problem is, taxpayers who try to handle these suits themselves simply do not have the procedural knowledge and skill (and they are usually not familiar with the relevent aspects of the law) to effec-

---

[16]What could the Federal government do to the State of New Jersey, throw it in jail?

tively prosecute such suits; while lawyers who might have these skills are totally ignorant of the applicable law.

These suits should be submitted to State courts in the nature of a Show Cause Order as to why the company is not honoring the individual's W-4 (according to law) *and* his employment contract. The issue involved here is really one of "breach of contract" on the part of the employer and does not become a Federal issue simply because the contract is breached in favor of the Federal government. Actually, both State and Federal laws are being violated so the worker has the choice of where to bring his action. Personally, I would prefer keeping it out of the hands of the Federal Mamelukes and filing suit in State court.

EXHIBIT 27

```
U433224"3 US 30   8112 670 8341   5901              2           12623  22
                       831024
Department of the Treasury
Internal Revenue Service                 If you have any questions, refer to this information:
P.O. BOX 47704                           Date of This Notice: OCT. 24, 1983
DORAVILLE, GA  30362                     Social Security Number:        043-32-2403
                                         Document Locator Number: 07210-260-00248-3
                                         Form 1040A     Tax Year Ended: DEC. 31, 1981

            22                           Call:     354-1760 LOCAL JACKSONVILLE
THOMAS & CHERYL A   MCDZELEWSKI          or        358-5072 LOCAL MIAMI
1322 W LIBBY DR                                    1-800-424-1040 OTHER FLORIDA
WEST PALM BEACH FL    33406              Write:  Chief, Taxpayer Assistance Section
                                                 Internal Revenue Service Center

                                              P.O. BOX 47704
                                              DORAVILLE, GA   30362
                                         If you write, be sure to attach the copy of this notice.
                                         KEEP THIS PART FOR YOUR RECORDS.
```

```
          STATEMENT OF ADJUSTMENT TO YOUR ACCOUNT

BALANCE DUE ON ACCOUNT BEFORE ADJUSTMENT                         $.00

                    ADJUSTMENT COMPUTATION
PENALTY_             SEE EXPLANATION 31              500.00
   NET ADJUSTMENT    CHARGE                                      500.00

          BALANCE DUE                                          $500.00


See codes  16,19,25      on the back of this notice that provide further explanations and instructions.
```

If you have any questions, you may call or write us--see the information in the upper right corner of this notice. To make sure that IRS employees give courteous responses and correct information to taxpayers, a second IRS employee sometimes listens in on telephone calls.   Form 4188B (Rev. 3-83)

An employee bringing suit in Federal court sometimes makes the government a party to that suit. This is a mistake because the issue is strictly between the employer and the employee. The government merely made a "request" of the employer (as could be done by any third party) which the employer was free to accept or reject as he wished. Since the employer was not acting under *orders* of the Federal government nor as its agent, the Federal government is not a party to the suit and must not be included in it.

In any case, when the plaintiff allows the Federal government to become involved, Federal "courts" dismiss the suit either because the government cannot be sued in this manner or on the basis that the Anti-Injunction Statute bars relief. Federal "judge's" use of this statute in these cases irrefutably establishes the reprehensible nature of our Federal "courts" and proves, conclusively, why the Anti-Injunction Statute must go. If the statute has any application at all it can only apply in situations where the government 1) *has alleged that a tax is owed;* and 2) *seeks to collect it from the person taxed.* Neither of these conditions exists with respect to wage withholding. In such cases, no tax was determined (let alone assessed) either by the IRS or the employee, nor is the government seeking to collect a tax it *claims is owed.* Indeed, in such cases *no taxes could have been assessed.* In these cases an independent party (the employer) is merely engaged in confiscating the lawful property of an individual (the employee) — in obvious violation of the tax "laws" themselves, the law of contracts, *and* the Constitution — and *voluntarily* giving it to the government. If, at some future date, the government determines that a tax is owed it will already have the money. Since Federal "judges" are now using the Anti-Injunction Statute[17] in situations where it obviously cannot and does not apply, the entire Federal "judicial" system has become one huge obscene joke.

Another example that indisputably reveals the criminal nature of the Federal government, the incompetence and/or culpability of our lawyers, and the hypocrisy of the American Civil Liberties Union is shown in Exhibit 27. This is only one of the thousands of *unsigned and uncertified* notices that the government uses to "fine" Americans $500 for allegedly violating any one of several Federal tax "laws." No trial, no

---

[17]The Mamelukes (both Federal and State) now use the following Mickey Mouse, lower "court" case "law" for "legal precedent": *Chandler vs Perini* 520 F. Supp. 1152 (1981); *Jules Hairstylists of Maryland, Inc. vs The United States and Irving Machiz* 268 F. Supp. 511 (1967); and *Fernleaf vs Publisher's Paper* OR. App. 657 P. 2d 723 (1983). In the last case the Court of Appeals of the State of Oregon also illegally hid behind 26 U.S.C.A. 7421(a) even though the statute specifically applies to Federal, not State, courts.

hearing, nor an opportunity to cross-examine one's accuser under oath is allowed and the entire Bill of Rights is thrown out in one fell swoop. Why has the ACLU not sought to have this whole Federal procedure declared unconstitutional? Can anything be more violative of an American's constitutional rights and civil liberties? Why would the ACLU even bother with anything else? If the Mamelukes can (using faceless bureaucrats) fine an individual $500 without a trial they could just as logically fine him $5,000 or $50,000, or even hand out a jail sentence without a trial.

In one particular case that I know of, the $500 penalty was for allegedly "making false statements on a Form W-4." However, the person who claimed exempt not only filed a perfectly valid W-4 (which was not honored according to the law) but he was fined (without a hearing) $500 to boot! The Mamelukes try to clothe this operation in legal legitimacy by providing (in Section 6703[3]) that those fined can "pay 15 percent of the amount of such penalty and file a claim for refund. . . ," once again shifting the burden of instituting suit to the public. Anyone fined by a faceless bureaucrat should not have to institute a lawsuit to prove that he has done nothing wrong. In addition, Section 6702(a) specifically provides that in all such suits "the burden of proof with respect to such issue shall be on the Secretary." And if the Secretary (of the Treasury) has the burden of proof, *why is he not required to institute suit?* Why should the fined individual be obliged to pay even 15 percent of the penalty before the Secretary meets any part of his statutory burden?[18]

Realistically, the average worker cannot devote the time necessary to institute such a lawsuit in Federal "court" on his own. In addition, the cost (in time and money) to get a lawyer to do it for him in order to save the $500 would also not be practical. And even if such a suit is instituted, a private citizen has practically no chance of winning against the Mamelukes sitting on the bench. So the only viable choice most workers have is to pay the "juice" since their legal options are nil.[19]

Benefits Of Not Paying

Those employers who are willing to 1) stop paying their own income taxes and 2) stop deducting that of their employees will substantially cut their labor and overhead costs from 30 to 50 percent (to say nothing

[18]The answer is explained on page 303.

[19]The "pay and sue" concept *might* be justified when it comes to taxes, but how can it be justified when it comes to fines? Could individual states get away with such a procedure if they wanted to adapt this to traffic fines? If not, why not?

of the cash saving involved in retaining the money that formerly went for taxes). Such firms could reduce their prices and undersell all of their competitors — companies that still pay and deduct these taxes. They will also have employees who may not mind working overtime now that they will not have half of that overtime pay withheld for taxes. Employees whose employers do not honor their W-4s should consider organizing and going into business against such employers. By eliminating their own income and social security taxes these employees (especially in the construction and repair businesses) should have no trouble competing against former employers.[20]

One small southern painting contractor, so disgusted with taxes and the red tape involved in running his business, was considering closing down when he contacted me. When I explained that he did not have to pay taxes or withhold any from his own employees he became more enthusiastic about staying in business. A year later he called to tell me that since he stopped withholding and paying income taxes he had almost doubled his work force and that doing business was fun again. The only way American products will ever again be competitive in domestic and world markets is if more businessmen do the same thing.

Making Banks and Other American Companies Obey The Law

Today, American banks have largely become informers for the Federal government. They routinely violate their customers' right to privacy by providing the Mamelukes with all sorts of personal and business information and they do it voluntarily — without court orders of any kind! For this reason Americans should use banks as little as possible and, instead, transact business with cash and postal money orders, or recycle checks by endorsing them over to third parties whenever possible.[21]

Another technique you can employ to stop your bank from turning over your money or any information about you to the IRS is to buy stock (one share will do it) in the bank where you deposit your funds. Go to

[20]There are a number of variations on this that can be worked out. For example, not too long ago a telephone installer called to complain that the phone company he worked for would not honor his W-4 or those of the other installers. I told him that he and his co-workers should consider quitting and setting up their own installation company on a subcontracting basis. By eliminating their own income and payroll taxes they should be able to charge the phone company less (while having more spendable income for themselves) than it was costing the company to keep them working as employees.

[21]For information about a commodity bank that backs its depositors' funds with silver coin (and that gives no such information to the government), contact N.C.B.A., 8000 East Girard Avenue, Suite #215, Denver, Colorado 80231.

the next scheduled stockholder's meeting and when appropriate ask the bank's legal counsel, "What is our bank's position with respect to turning over depositor's money to someone without a court order? Do we do this?" If the counsel says yes, then based on all the knowledge you have acquired by reading this book you can ask, "On what legal basis can the bank do such a thing?"

Ask him, "Does the bank turn over money to the IRS pursuant to a "Notice of Levy?" If he says yes ask him, "Don't you know that such notices only apply to *government* employees?" This conversation will undoubtedly stimulate additional comments from the floor so you should be prepared to answer some questions regarding your position. Demand to know what the bank's policy will be in the future. Submit a resolution *on the spot* that states from then on the bank will not turn over any money to the IRS without a court order. If the legal counsel equivocates or seems to be trying to make excuses for the bank's illegal conduct, submit a resolution calling for his resignation.

Even stockholders with only one share of stock can make a significant impact on bank policy if they effectively argue these issues at such meetings. And if you have friends who use the same bank, each one should buy one or more shares and all of you should go to the meeting together to give added support to your challenge. In this way bank depositors can literally force the banks they use to obey the law.

Forcing American Corporations to Obey the Law

In a like manner, employees in large or small companies can force them to honor their W-4s by buying stock in those companies and pressing the issue at a stockholders' meeting.[22] Simply address the corporation's legal counsel as follows:

"What is *our* company's position with respect to *our* employees who claim exempt pursuant to Section 3402(n) of the Internal Revenue Code? Do we honor their exemption certifications?" Let us see if those corporate lawyers who smugly say over the telephone or in the privacy of their own offices that "We have to do what the IRS tells us to do" will they dare make such asinine statements publicly — at a stockholders' meeting before an audience of from 50 to 500 people! Will they say that the company does not obey the law? Frankly, they will not know what to say.

The point is, companies should be made to justify their policy on this issue. And if that policy is not to honor employee W-4s then a stockholders' meeting is the perfect place for stockholders to mercilessly rake

---

[22]This, of course, would not work in companies that are privately owned and that issue no stock for public purchase.

management over the coals for adhering to such an illegal policy. For example, if the company's legal counsel says that they honor IRS form letters over their own employees' certified statements, ask "You mean to tell me that as our lawyer you advise this company to take the word of faceless bureaucrats over the sworn certifications of our own employees?"

Or you could try a different route of questioning. Ask, "If this company were to receive a form letter from the IRS stating that we owed $10,000 would you recommend that on the basis of that letter alone we should immediately send off a check to the IRS?" When he says no (as he probably will) then you ask, "If you would not treat the company's money in that manner what gives you the right to tell the company to do the same thing with our employees' money?"

By taking a copy of the Code with you to the meeting and by knowing the material in this book you should not have a problem forcing any company to take the position, publicly, that it will honor employee W-4s according to the law. A corporate resolution to this effect should also be introduced. All those who normally attend stockholders' meetings should make a point of raising this issue along with those who may buy stock in a company where they work in order to specifically raise it.

Another issue that can be raised at such meetings is why the company is paying income taxes at all when, under the law, it has no liability for the tax. If the corporate counsel thinks that such a liability exists, offer him the Code and challenge him to find the section of the Code that establishes such a liability. When he cannot find it ask, "If the corporation is not liable for such taxes, by what authority are corporate officers paying it to the financial detriment of the stockholders?"

One other thing you can do to stop corporations from voluntarily paying income taxes is to file a restraining order to that effect. If the government attempts (and it will) to raise the Anti-Injunction Statute in order to bar such a suit, you have two powerful legal precedents to refute it: both the *Pollock* and *Brushaber* cases were initiated on this basis and when the government raised this very issue as a bar to injunctive relief the Supreme Court (in both cases) rejected the argument. In the face of such powerful legal precedents, lower "courts" cannot now claim the reverse.

Bank Trust Departments

Those who are the beneficiaries of a trust are aware that trust companies automatically pay trust income taxes thereby reducing the amount available to the trust beneficiary. If you are the beneficiary of a trust you should immediately tell your trustee to stop making these income tax payments on the grounds that the trust is not liable for such taxes and that by paying them the trustee is illegally diminishing your funds. Trustees should be warned that unless they can produce a section of the Code that makes the trust liable for such taxes, the trustee will be sued for any of the trust income that the trustee voluntarily pays over to the government.

Beating The IRS In "Court"

The government prosecutes two different types of tax offenses: tax evasion (a felony) and willful failure to file (a misdemeanor). Tax evaders are prosecuted as criminals because they filed an income tax return while non-filers are prosecuted as criminals because they did not. In order to convict the former, the government contends that filing is *voluntary* so the defendant's own income tax returns can be used against him. In order to convict the latter, the government contends that filing is *not voluntary*. The government cannot have it both ways.

Although there have been cases where some individuals prosecuted for either of the above offenses have been found not guilty, I still believe that *all* such defendants were defended improperly — including myself. When an individual is charged with willful failure to file, a written motion requesting dismissal of all the charges should be filed *immediately* upon being notified of such charges. This motion must be submitted *before the arraignment* so the government is forced to argue the issues raised *before any plea is made*. A written motion requesting dismissal of all the charges (whether by Information or indictment) should be made because the "court" lacks subject matter jurisdiction in both instances. If the defendants in such cases allow the "court" to extract a plea of "not guilty" beforehand, they have turned themselves over (conferred subject matter jurisdiction) to Mameluke "judges" who (at least in willful failure to file cases) will then set out to convict regardless of either law or fact.

Willful Failure To File

In cases involving willful failure to file, individuals charged with this "crime" should file a Motion to Dismiss[23] for lack of subject matter jurisdiction on the following grounds:

1. Section 7203 only applies to returns *required* to be filed by law

---

[23]The exact wording and format of this Motion, together with instructions on how it should be argued, is contained in *The Schiff Report*, Volume 2, Numbers 6 and 7.

so the section cannot apply to income taxes since no section of the Internal Revenue Code *requires* the filing of such returns.

2. Since there is no Section of the Code that establishes a *liability* for income taxes, and since the filing of a return is nothing more than a method of paying such a liability, the accused could not have been *required* to file an income tax return.

3. The "court" is without subject matter jurisdiction because — though the Code specifically confers *civil* jurisdiction on Federal "courts" in tax cases — there is no section that similarly confers *criminal* jurisdiction.

4. Because the income tax is not levied pursuant to any of the taxing clauses of the Constitution the accused could not be *required* to perform *any* act with respect to it. (A brief in support of this point can be found in Appendix F. It only requires minor changes to conform to the specifics of any other case.)

Tax Evasion

If they do not succeed in getting such charges dismissed at the arraignment, individuals charged with income tax evasion should have no trouble aborting the trial *as soon as it gets underway*. The following information should make it *impossible* for the government to prosecute anyone for income tax evasion.

In the past, the only reason these prosecutions have taken place is because lawyers make so much money from them. Individuals charged with tax evasion will undoubtedly make better use of this information since they are usually far more affluent than those charged with failure to file. They will be able to spend more money on their defense and should be better able to present and argue these issues than so-called "tax protesters" who, in many cases, have tried to represent themselves.

Over the last five years we have witnessed several celebrated tax evasion trials that must have cost the defendants at least $100,000 and that much again to appeal. Most of that money would not have been paid to the lawyers involved if those cases had been defended properly. Indeed, once these cases *are* defended properly the legal fraternity will lose these fees forever.

For a proper defense (overlooking entirely the legal challenge that could be mounted on the direct tax issue) the lawyers of those charged with tax evasion should seek to have the charges dismissed at the arraignment by demonstrating that the "court" does not have jurisdiction to criminally try anyone under the Internal Revenue Code. In these cases attorneys should only use the issues listed as points three and four on page 401.[24]

Assuming the government could get by this jurisdictional challenge, the defense still has the ability to knock out the government's case by preventing the introduction of the defendant's income tax returns without which the government *has no case*. The government cannot force a confession and then use it against an individual in a criminal trial, so only information *voluntarily* given can be used against someone. An income tax return is a confession (see page 75) in which the taxpayer "confesses, " under penalty of perjury, to certain facts with respect to his receipts and expenditures. Even crossing out the "under penalty of perjury" endorsement on a Form 1040 does not help — the IRS has fined individuals who have done that and the "courts" have upheld these fines ruling that taxpayers are not free to make such "changes" on the 1040.[25]

Given 1) all of the prosecutions for non- and Fifth Amendment filing, and 2) all the case "law" such prosecutions have generated, I do not see how any district "court" (certainly not one in the Second Circuit) can take the position that filing an income tax return that shows the amount, if not the source (thus providing a basis for calculating the amount of tax allegedly due), is not *required* since so many appellate "courts" have already ruled precisely that in upholding convictions for not filing.

"Courts" throughout the nation have now (regardless of what the statutes themselves say) made filing *mandatory* under threat of statutory punishment, so how can trial "courts" in tax evasion cases claim otherwise? The "courts" cannot even cite the *Garner* case (see page 281) as allegedly providing a realistic option for claiming the Fifth since too many "courts" have since ruled (as in my case) that Fifth Amendment returns are not the returns "required by law" (see pages 279, 280). In addition, attorneys can also take the position that the defendant was led to believe that he was *required* to file a return based on the language

---

[24]Sometimes the government charges alleged tax evaders under Section 1001 (the section that makes it a crime to provide false information to the government) of Title 18 (the U.S. Criminal Code) instead of under Title 26 (the Internal Revenue Code). In that event, none of these jurisdictional challenges would be appropriate at the arraignment and such individuals will have to be content with knocking out the government's case at trial or in pre-trial argument.

[25]This further reveals the total decadence of Federal "courts." Signing a document under "penalty of perjury" is tantamount to taking an oath — and oaths can only be *voluntarily made*. The same "courts" that claim that filing an income tax return is compulsory, by implication, also claim that individuals can be forced to take an oath!

in the Privacy Act Notice which *is* written to convince individuals that they "must file a return."[26]

Based on all the above and the publicity the government has generated regarding the penalties (both criminal and civil) meted out to non-filers, any decent lawyer should have no trouble making an unassailable case that his client believed that filing was mandatory and submitted his income tax return accordingly. This should prevent the government from being able to get the questionable return (without which it has no case) admitted as evidence in the case thereby ending the government's ability to prosecute *anyone* for income tax evasion. If any individual has been prosecuted and convicted for income tax evasion and his attorney *did not seek* to prevent the admission of the questionable return on this basis, he should sue that attorney for malpractice.[27]

True, my 1973 return was admitted over my objection , but I was not well enough prepared (and lacked the courtroom skill and experience) to enable me to knock "Judge" Clarie's preposterous ruling into a cocked hat.[28]

LAWYERS

I never met a lawer who really understood Federal income taxes. The public cannot trust lawyers to give them accurate information when it comes to our income tax laws which creates serious problems if someone has to go to "court." People have told me that when they gave my book, *How Anyone Can Stop Paying Income Taxes,* to their lawyer it was dismissed on various, always *unspecific,* grounds. If a lawyer tells you that you are *required* to file an income tax return and pay income taxes by the April 15 "deadline, " I suggest you have him sign the following statement:

---

[26]In upholding the conviction in *U.S. vs Wilbur* 696 F.2d 79 (1982), the 8th Circuit Court of Appeals denied Wilbur's contention that the Privacy Act Notice failed to notify him of the dangers of not filing and stated, "Wilbur argues that the IRS notice is insufficient because it does not state in the words of the Act that disclosure is mandatory. This argument is patently frivolous. Nothing in the Privacy Act requires agencies to employ the exact language of the statute to give effective notice. *The IRS booklet clearly notifies taxpayers that filing is mandatory.*" (Emphasis added).

[27] The malpractice involved is comparable to a defense lawyer in a murder case allowing the prosecution to introduce and use against the defendant, without objection, an obviously forced confession on the unchallenged premise that it was given voluntarily.

[28]In addition, there is far more case law today supporting the erroneous contention that tax returns are *required* to be filed.

This is to certify that I,_____(Attorney's name)_____ , being an attorney knowlegeable in the law, have advised_____(your name)_____ that under the income tax laws he is:

1. required to file an income tax return with the government in which he gives the government information that can be used against him; and

2. he is required to pay such a tax before it is assessed and before he is made liable for it pursuant to Sections 6201, 6203, and 6303 of the Internal Revenue Code.

If your lawyer believes that you are required to file an income tax return and pay income taxes (without asking for extensions or being subject to other penalties) by April 15, then he will have no objection to signing such a statement. If, however, any lawyer whom you ask to sign such a declaration refuses to sign it, why should you believe you are legally required to do either of the two things listed in the statement? If your lawyer *does sign* the statement, you will have legal proof that you filed a tax return because you were advised by an attorney that it was *required*. Should any "court" rule otherwise — so the return can be used against you — you will have an airtight malpractice suit against the attorney who advised you to file. In addition, you might ask the same attorney for a *written* explanation regarding how you can file a tax return without waiving any of your constitutional rights.

I have had several lawyers contact me and say that they know I am right on the law and would be willing to represent the public on this basis. One man, Richard Viti of Atlanta, Georgia, has actually gone on radio and television to express this point of view. Viti, who taught a popular course at Georgia State University for four years, was no longer allowed to teach when he expressed his opinions on this issue publicly. He had his employment terminated because of his willingness to tell the public the truth about Federal income taxes. Hopefully, I will be able to put together a national network of lawyers who will represent clients on the basis of what the "law" is and not what they would like it to be or what they are told it is by ignorant law professors and prevaricating "judges". Along these lines, I will be forming a legal defense fund where, for a modest annual fee, citizens will be assured of getting proper legal representation should they be charged with failure to file income tax returns or for filing false or fraudulent W-4s.

THE CHOICE IS CLEAR

Many Americans believe that without an income tax the country will collapse. The fact is our economy is in very serious danger of doing that *because of* the income tax![29] We have a current year trade deficit of over $123.3 billion (which is constantly growing[30]) and more than $200 billion Federal deficit. Our politicians simply lack the backbone to make the necessary political decisions because of the pressure that is generated by special interest groups that always resist the real choices that must be made. The only thing we can count on our spineless politicians to do is allow the nation to drift into bankruptcy.

The Federal government, whose real debt is over $10 trillion not the puny $1.3 trillion it fraudulently reports — or more than $50,000 for every American — is already bankrupt and there is nothing anyone can do to make it worse. The government's repudiation of this debt will either come now or later and the sooner it comes the better off the country will ultimately be because the longer it is allowed to grow the worse the situation and its adjustment will be. Current deficits in excess of $200 billion alone will be adding $20 billion in interest charges to the following year's budget. In fact, the total interest on the debt is the largest single item in the Federal budget. The Reagan Administration tells us that America had a prosperous year in 1984. If we cannot even come close to balancing the budget in a prosperous year, what will the deficit be in a bad one? If we do not balance the budget in a good year, does anyone really believe that our politicians are serious about *ever* balancing it?

On February 4, 1985, President Regan unveiled his $973.7 billion budget for 1986. It allocated 29 percent for "National defense" and 5 percent for "All other Federal operations, " plus 41 percent for "Direct benefit payments to individuals" and 10 percent for "Grants to states and other localities." This means that only 34 percent of Federal expenditures for 1986 will be used for *legitimate constitutional purposes* (see page 31), while 51 percent will be allocated for *expenditures not authorized in the Constitution* — making 51 percent of the proposed Federal budget illegal!

These figures, however, only represent 85 percent of Federal spend-

---

[29] A full page ad attesting to this danger appeared in *The New York Times* on May 4, 1984. It was signed by five former Secretarys of the Treasury and about 500 or so other luminaries from government, foundations and mangement consulting firms, as well as economists, investment bankers and corporate executives. An in-depth analysis of it appears in *The Schiff Report,* Volume 2, Number 2.

[30] The trade deficit was $42.7 billion in 1982 and $69.4 billion in 1983. It is growing by leaps and bounds but the Reagan Administration is doing nothing concrete about it.

ing. The remaining 15 percent is allocated *to pay interest on the national debt!* Incredibly, therefore, in 1986 Washington wastrels will spend *three times as much on interest as they plan to spend on running the entire Federal government* [31] (apart from the Defense Department).

Before the Roosevelt Administration, surplus peacetime budgets were the general rule, not the exception. Peacetime surpluses were generated to pay for the deficits produced by wars. The theory sold to the nation by the New Deal theoreticians and economic tinkerers was that they would *deliberately* create budget deficits based on the premise that such irresponsible fiscal behavior would serve to "prime the pump" and lift the nation out of the depression into the sunlight of prosperity.[32] Surplus revenues would then be generated to pay for the depression deficits. Not only was this economic theory a pipe dream but politicians demonstrated that once they could justify (on any basis) a budget deficit they lost their ability to produce surpluses. The government has not produced a real surplus in over thirty years, during times that were supposedly "prosperous" and loaded with "economic growth." The Mamelukes obviously have no intention of *ever* producing a surplus.

Such fiscal policies must inevitably lead to a fiscal if not total economic collapse. The warning signs are all around us and the Washington propagandists attempt to mask then with optimistic political rhetoric. The nation is plagued by interest rates that were once considered usurious, while the inability of American families to afford homes (with-out both spouses working — and in many cases even that will not be enough) and the increasing inability of American industry to be competitive in the world market, all point in this direction.

The fact that neither the politicians nor most of the American people face is that there can be no balanced budget, no reduction of the national debt, and no sound economy until the Congress turns back to the Federal government its constitutional functions and takes away the unconstitutional encroachments on the rights of the states and the people. The Constitution set very rigorous limits on how and where the Federal government could act. Every dollar spent had to be earmarked for such matters as the national defense, the maintenance of law and order, and other specified activities for the general welfare. And general welfare was narrowly defined, excluding subsidies to identified groups in the population such as farmers, businessmen, college professors, or those who believe that the government "owes" them a living.

Multibillions are spent each year on agriculture and agri-business— and the more the government spends, the worse becomes the plight of the farmer. In order to mute the opposition to special-interest

---

[31]This one item alone exceeds the government's *entire* 1967 budget!

[32]Every one of those "temporary" pump priming programs has become permanently imbedded in the budget and continues to contribute to a ballooning Federal debt.

government, the Congress creates tax shelters which aggrandize the rich and impoverish the economy. The government takes from those who produce the sweat of their labors and lavishly bestows it on a small minority. No nation can prosper if it moves down this primrose path, nor can it survive. The way to Hell, we are told, is paved with good intentions — and so is is the way to national extinction. Even the neo-socialist governments of Western Europe are beginning to understand this!

The constitution set even more rigorous limits on the Federal government's power to tax, though that part of our basic law has been forgotten. The Founding Fathers realized that direct taxation, even at its most restrained, is a form of extortion. The Supreme Court, in the days when the justices read the Constitution and not the works of Harvard professors, recognized this. This, of course, was before politicians had adopted the rule of "tax and tax, spend and spend, elect and elect." Except in emergencies, such as those created by wars, the government financed itself by indirect, or excise taxes — which I have shown gave the taxpayer the right of choice. One of the major causes of the War of the Revolution was taxation, and the American people and their political leaders never really forgot this until the New Deal and World War II. Then, to make the rising income tax "less painful" the withholding tax was introduced as unconstitutional a way of extorting money (without either a liability or an assessment) as the country has ever seen.

To impose this form of systematic extortion, the Federal government, the Congress, and the "courts" have had to scrap almost every one of the ten amendments in the Bill of Rights — and this is what this book has been about. Due process, the right not to be compelled to be a witness against one's self, the protection against unlawful searches and seizure, even free speech — as I have amply demonstrated — have been tossed out the window by tax laws and tax regulations capriciously enforced.

And for what? If the Federal government operated within its constitutional restraints, the excise taxes which supported it through most of the nation's history would be sufficient. There would be no need to surrender the government and the nation to the Mamelukes who are interested not in the general welfare but in the preservation of their power. This country grew from a scattering of states along the Eastern seaboard into a superpower without an inquisitorial system of income taxes. Free Americans produced for themselves the highest standard of living in history, and gave the world a haven for the politically and economically oppressed.

Is the American Dream to become a nightmare? Not if the American people realize that the issue is simple: Either we have a Bill of Rights or we have an inquisitorial and self-defeating income tax. We cannot have both. The question for the American people is, "Which will it be?"

APPENDIX A

The Total American Tax Take

The chart in Exhibit 28 (prepared by the Federal Reserve Bank of St. Louis) explains why the average American household is now experiencing a falling standard of living despite increases in technology. Ever increasing amounts of its consumer dollar are spent on air — taxes and interest.

In 1950 the average American could spend approximately 75 percent of what he earned on himself and only had to spend 25 percent on taxes and interest. Look at how the picture changed in only thirty years. By 1980 (it is obviously *worse* today) he could only spend 40 percent of his consumer dollar on real goods while he had to spend 60 percent on taxes and interest. During this period taxes only appeared to take an additional 5.6 percent of the consumer dollar (for a 26 percent increase) but the increased cost of interest went from 3.7 percent of his spendable dollar to more than 33 percent. This increased cost of interest to the consumer exceeded by 26 percent what he could spend *for all other items except food*. This is why it takes the combined salaries of two people today to have the same actual purchasing power one person had in 1950. It is also why wives have to work to keep a family's economic nose above water and why many single individuals simply cannot earn enough to support themselves (resulting in the trend of single people moving back home to live with parents).

While taxes over this period appear to have increased by only 26 percent, they actually increased by approximately 150 percent because the entire increase in the cost of interest was really *an increase in taxes*. For example, if the Federal government were to act responsibly and tax individuals to the same extent as it spends their money, personal income taxes today would have to be increased by about 50 percent to fund current Federal deficits that account for more than $200 billion a year.

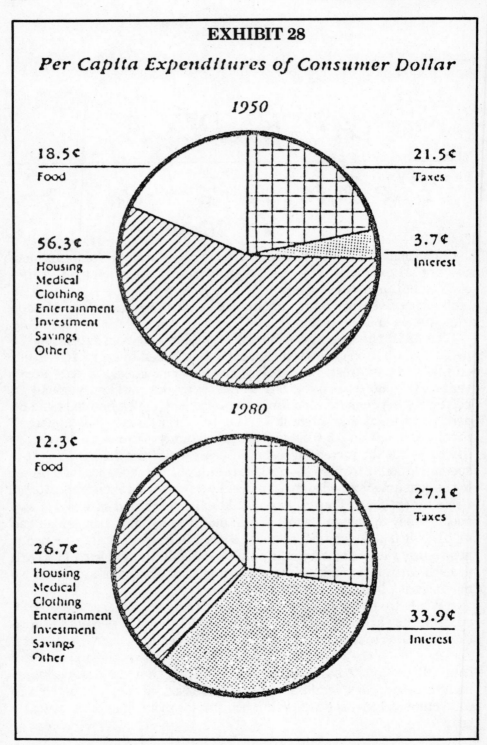

EXHIBIT 28

Per Capita Expenditures of Consumer Dollar

1950

18.5¢
Food

21.5¢
Taxes

56.3¢

Housing
Medical
Clothing
Entertainment
Investment
Savings
Other

3.7¢
Interest

1980

12.3¢
Food

27.1¢
Taxes

26.7¢

Housing
Medical
Clothing
Entertainment
Investment
Savings
Other

33.9¢
Interest

The Federal government has been able to fool the American public regarding its full Federal tax burden by financing its bloated expenditures through debt-creation (which generates higher interest rates) instead of increasing taxes directly. So, by excluding these higher interest costs from the total cost of Federal taxation, the government is able to understate and mislead citizens concerning the true amount of Federal taxes they pay. Such an omission fraudulently distorts and improves the comparisons the government makes (as when it relates Federal taxes to a percentage of the Gross National Product) or when it compares American taxes to those in foreign countries such as Japan. However, persistent government deficits, both past and present (especially during the last fifteen years), have driven interest rates to their highest levels since the Civil War.

In 1950, for example, an American could buy a home for $10,000 (with 10 percent down) and get a 4¼ percent or 4½ percent mortgage. Mortgage payments might have been $65.00 per month of which $55.00 probably would have gone towards interest in the earlier years. Today that same house would sell for about $100,000 and a mortgage (with 20 percent down) would cost about $1,000 per month. This difference to the home-owner of $950.00 per month (for the same home) is a Federal tax[1] that few Americans realize they pay. It is a result of irresponsible deficit financing by the Federal government which has driven up both the prices and interest rates of homes to the point that few young Americans can afford to buy homes as did former generations of Americans.

This is how Federal deficit spending has not only increased prices, but has actually robbed the public of the lower prices that would normally have resulted from extensive advances in technology and production efficiencies. If houses sold for $10,000 in the 1950s they would be selling for a whole lot less today if it were not for the artifical increase in prices that have resulted from government waste and engendered inflation. This is how the Federal government has driven up both the cost of housing and mortgage rates which has now made it almost impossible for most Americans to own their own homes and how it forces a lower standard of living on the nation.

---

[1] I have made no attempt to calculate the specific amount of the tax since the example incorporates a number of variables. But there is no doubt that the Federal tax will add better than $200,000 to the ultimate cost of the home.

APPENDIX B

The Elliot Debates

The following excerpts taken from *The Elliot Debates* [1] should lay to rest *for all time* the absurd contention that those who wrote and ratified the Constitution did not know the difference between direct and indirect taxation or, if anything, considered direct taxes as only applying to land or a uniform poll-tax levied without regard to wealth. In addition, quotes from Luther Martin and George Nicholas provide concrete proof that paper money is completely unconstitutional and that the necessary and proper clause of the Constitution is, in no way, "elastic."

As evidenced by the debates, the Founding Fathers considered direct taxes to be "dangerous and oppressive" [Luther Martin], while they believed indirect taxes to be "safe" because they were "voluntary" [James Wilson]. They knew that indirect taxes were easily collected and they feared the "hosts of tax-gatherers that would swarm throughout the land" to collect direct taxes [James Wilson]. Oliver Ellsworth wrote of the "productive nature of indirect taxes," and Patrick Henry discussed the "evils of direct taxation." Of direct taxes one delegate [Mr. Grayson] wrote, "Giving the right of taxation is giving a right to increase the misery of the people." And it was believed that indirect taxes would "relieve the people from direct taxation" [Mr. Spencer].

Throughout the debates the delegates continously referred to indirect taxes as those that are levied on articles of consumption and referred to direct taxes as those that are levied upon people and personal property. The delegates did not believe that such property was limited to land (as many "judges" have erroneously maintained), but believed it extended to "houses, buildings, windows, fireplaces, cattle, and all kinds of personal property" [Mr. Williams]. In many cases, delegates simply referred to direct taxes as *taxes* because duties, imposts, and excises were not even considered taxes but, rather, were merely thought of as duties, imposts, and excises.

[1] Compiled by Jonathon Elliot in 1836, *The Elliot Debates* are a record of the debates and discussions that took place in the various state conventions that had convened to ratify the Constitution. These views, together with the *Federalist Papers,* constitute the most authoritative sources for understanding the intent of those who wrote and ratified the Constitution.

It is clear that the Founding Fathers understood that direct taxes implied a *class,* a *category,* a *species,* and a *power* of taxation and did not simply refer to a specific item of taxation. They realized that in granting the power of direct taxation they were giving the government a coercive power over each citizen which it would not have otherwise enjoyed. While the thought of giving the Federal government direct taxing power was abhorent to many delegates, they reluctantly agreed on the understanding that such a power was necessary in time of war and would, therefore, be used sparingly. It is obvious from these debates that the delegates believed that direct taxes would never be imposed in peacetime and they relied on the apportionment provision of the Constitution to keep the government from abusing what they believed was to be a temporary, emergency power.

LUTHER MARTIN
(Attorney General and delegate of Maryland)

Volume I, page 365:

As to that part of this section that relates to direct taxation, there was also an objection for the following reasons: It was said that a large sum of money was to be brought into the national treasury by the duties on commerce, which would be almost wholly paid by the commercial states; it would be unequal and unjust that the sum which was necessary to be raised by direct taxation should be apportioned equally upon all the states, obliging the commercial states to pay as large a share of the revenue arising therefrom as the states from whom no revenue had been drawn by imposts; since the wealth and industry of the inhabitants of the commercial states will, in the first place, be severely taxed through their commerce, and afterwards be equally taxed with the industry and wealth of the inhabitants of the other states, who have paid no part of that revenue; so that, by this provision, the inhabitants of the commercial states are, in this system, obliged to bear an unreasonable and disproportionate share in the expenses of the Union, and the payment of that foreign and domestic debt which was incurred not more for the benefit of the commercial than of the other states.

Pages 369, 370:

. . . Many of the members, and myself in the number, thought that states were much better judges of the circumstances of their citizens, and what sum of money could be collected from them by *direct taxation,* and of the manner in which it could be raised with the *greatest ease and convenience to their citizens,* than the general government could be; and that *the general government ought not to have the power of laying direct taxes in any case* but in that of the delinquency of a state. Agreeably to this sentiment, I brought in a proposition on which a vote of the Convention was taken. The proposition was as follows: "And whenever the legislature of the United States shall find it necessary that revenue should be raised *by direct taxation,* having apportioned the same by the above rule, requisitions shall be made of the respective states to pay into the Continental treasury their respective quotas within a time in the said requisition to be specified; and in case of any of the states failing to comply with such requisition, then, and then only, to have power to devise and pass acts directing the mode and authorizing the collection of the same."

Had this proposition been acceded to, *the **dangerous and oppressive power** in the general government of **imposing direct taxes** on the inhabitants,* which it now enjoys in all cases, would have been only vested in it, in case of the non-compliance of a state, as a punishment for its delinquency, and would have ceased the moment that the state complied with the requisition. But the proposition was rejected by a majority, consistent with their aim and desire of increasing the power of the general government as far as possible, and destroying the powers and influence of the states. And though there is a provision that all duties, imposts, and excises, shall be uniform, — that is, to be laid to the same amount on the same articles in each state, — yet this will not prevent Congress from having it in their power to cause them to fall very unequally, and much heavier on some states than on others, because these duties may be laid on articles but little or not at all used in some states, and of absolute necessity for the use and consumption of others; in which case, the first would pay little or no part of the revenue arising therefrom, while the whole, or nearly the whole, of it would be paid by the last, to wit, the states which *use and consume the articles on which the imposts and excises are laid.*

By our original Articles of Confederation, the Congress have power to borrow money and emit bills of credit on the credit of the United States; agreeable to which was the report on this system, as made by the committee of detail. When we came to this part of the report, *a motion was made to strike out the words "to emit bills of credit."* Against the motion we urged, that it would be improper to deprive the Congress of that power; that *it would be a novelty unprecedented to establish a government which should not have such authority;* that it was impossible to look forward into futurity so far as to decide that events might not happen that should *render the exercise of such a power absolutely necessary:* and that we doubted whether, *if a war should take place, it would be possible for this country to defend itself without having recourse to paper credit,* in which case there would be a necessity of becoming a prey to our enemies, or violating the constitution of our government; and that, considering the administration of the government would be principally in the hands of the wealthy, there could be little reason to fear an abuse of the power by an unnecessary or injurious exercise of it. *But, sir, a majority of the Convention, **being wise beyond every event,** and being willing to **risk any political evil rather than admit the idea of a paper emission** in any possible case, refused* *to trust this authority to a government to which they were lavishing the most unlimited powers of taxation, and to the mercy of which they were willing blindly to trust the liberty and property of the citizens of every state in the Union;* **and they erased that clause from the system.**

JUDGE FRANCIS DANA
(Massachusetts)

Volume II, page 42:

Some gentlemen have said, *that Congress may draw their revenue wholly by direct taxes;* but they cannot be induced so to do; it is easier for them to have resort to the *impost and excise*; but as it will not do to over-burden the impost, (because that would promote smuggling, and be dangerous to the revenue,) *therefore Congress should have* **the power of** *applying, in extraordinary cases, to* **direct taxation.** War may take place, in which case it would not be proper to alter those appropriations of impost which may be made for peace establishments. It is inexpedient to divert the public funds; the **power** *of direct taxation* would, *in such circumstances,* be *a very* **necessary power.**

. . . The rule laid down in the paragraph is the best that can be obtained for the apportionment of the *little direct taxes* which Congress will want.

. . . The learned judge began with answering some objections to this paragraph, and urging the necessity of Congress being vested with *power* to levy *direct taxes* on the states, and it was not to be supposed that they would *levy such, unless the impost and excise should be found* **insufficient** *in case of a* **war.**

MR. CHRISTOPHER GORE
(Massachusetts)

Volume II, pages 66, 67

. . . Some have said, that the *impost and excise would be* **sufficient for all** *the purposes of government* **in times of peace:** *and that, in war, requisitions should be made on the several states for sums to supply the deficiencies of this fund.* Those who are best informed supposed this sum inadequate to and none pretend that it can exceed the expenses of a peace establishment. What, then, is to be done? Is America to wait until she is attacked before she attempts a preparation at defence? This would certainly be unwise: it would be courting our enemies to make war upon us. The operations of war are sudden, and call for large sums of money; *collections from states are at all times slow and uncertain*; and, in case of refusal, the non-complying state must be cocreed by arms, which, in its consequences, would involve the innocent with the guilty, and introduce all the horrors of a civil war. But, it is said, we need not fear war; we have no enemies. Let the gentlemen consider the situation of our country; they will find we are circumscribed with enemies from Maine to Georgia. I trust, therefore, that, upon a fair and candid consideration of the subject, it will be found indispensably requisite to peace, dignity, and happiness, *that the proposed government should be vested with all the powers granted by the section under debate.*

MR. THOMAS DAWES
(Massachusetts)

Volume II, page 57:

. . . *The first revenue will be raised from the impost, ιo* **which there is no objection,** *the next from the excise; and if these are not sufficient,* **direct taxes must be laid.** To conclude, sir, if we mean to support an efficient federal government, which, under the old Confederation, can never be the case, the proposed Constitution is, in my opinion, the only one that can be substituted. . .

Pages 59, 60:

. . . The honorable gentleman form Norton, last speaking, says, that, if Congress will have the power of laying and collecting *taxes*, they will use the power of the sword. I hold the reverse to be true. The doctrine of requisitions, or of demands upon a whole state, implies such a power; for surely a whole state, a whole community, can be compelled only by an army; but taxes upon an individual imply only the use of a collector of taxes. *That Congress, however, will not apply to the* **power** *of direct taxation,* **unless in cases of emergency,** *is plain;* because, as thirty thousand inhabitants will elect a representative, eight tenths of which electors perhaps are yeomen, and holders of farms, it will be their own faults if they are not represented by such men as will never permit the land to be injured by unnecessary taxes.

MR. BODMAN
(Massachusetts)

Volume II, page 60:

Mr. BODMAN said, that *the power given to Congress to lay and collect duties, taxes, &c.,* as contained in the section under consideration, *was cercertainly unlimited, and therefore* **dangerous;** *and wished to konw whether it was necessary to give Congress power to* **do harm,** *in order to enable them to do good.* It had been said, that the *sovereignty of the states* remains with them; but if Congress has the power to lay taxes, and, *in cases of negligence or non-compliance, can send a* **power to collect them,** *he thought that the idea of* **sovereignty was destroyed.** This, he said, was an essential point, and ought to be seriously considered. It has been urged that gentlemen were jealous of their rulers. He said, he thought they ought to be so; it was just they should be so; for jealousy was one of the greatest securities of the people in a republic. The power in the 8th section, he said, ought to have been defined; that he was willing to give power to the federal head, but he wished to know what that power was.

MR. THEODORE SEDGWICK
(Massachusetts)

Volume II, pages 60, 61:

Mr. SEDGWICK, in answer to the gentleman last speaking, said, if he believed the adoption of the proposed Constitution would interfere with the state legislatures, he would be the last to vote for it; but he thought all the sources of revenue ought to be put into the hands of government, who were to protect and secure us; and powers to effect this had always been necessarily unlimited. Congress would necessarily take that which was easiest to the people; *the first would be impost, the next excise; and a direct tax will be the last;* for, said the honorable gentleman, *drawing money from the people, by* **direct taxes, being difficult and uncertain** *it would be the* **last source of revenue** *applied to by* **a wise legislature;** and hence, said he, the people may be assured that the delegation of a power to levy them would not be abused. Let us suppose, — and we shall not be thought extravagant in the supposition, — continued Mr. S., that we are attacked by a foreign enemy; *that in this dilemma our treasury was exhausted, our credit gone, our enemy on our borders, and that there was no possible method of raising impost or excise; in this case,* **the only remedy would be a direct tax.** Could, therefore, *this power,* being vested in Congress, lessen the many advantages which may be drawn from it?

MR. PIERCE
(Massachusetts)

Volume II, pages 76, 77:

WEDNESDAY, *January 23.* — Mr. PIERCE rose, he said, to make a few observations on the powers of Congress, in this section.

Gentlemen, he said, in different parts of the house, (Messrs. Dalton, Phillips, and Gore,) had agreed that *Congress will not lay direct taxes, except in cases of war;* for that, to defray the exigencies of peace, the impost and excise would be sufficient; and, as that mode of taxation would be the most expedient and productive, it would undoubtedly be adopted. *But it was necessary Congress should have power to lay direct taxes at all times, although **they will not use it**, because, when our enemies find they have sufficient powers to call forth all the resources of the people, it will **prevent their making war, as they otherwise would.** As the Hon. Mr. Phillips used this proverb, *"A stitch in time will save nine,"* his meaning, *I suppose, was, that we should have war nine times, if Congress **had not such powers**, where we should once if they had such powers.* But these arguments to me are not conclusive; for, if our enemies know they do not use such powers except in a war, although granted to them, what will be the difference if they have the powers *only in the time of war?* But, Mr. President, if Congress have the **powers of direct taxes,** in the manner prescribed in this section, *I fear we shall have that mode of taxation adopted, in preference to imposts and excises;* and the reasons of my fears are these: When the impost was granted to Congress in this state, I, then being a member of court, well remember the gentlemen in trade almost with one consent, agreed that it was an unequal tax bearing hard on them: for, although it *finally was a tax on the consumer* yet in the first instance, it was paid by persons in trade and also that they consumed more than the landed interest of dutied articles; and nothing but necessity induced them to submit to grant said impost as that was the only way Congress could collect money to pay the foreign debt under the *regulations they were then under;* and I fear part of this state's members in Congress, when this Constitution is adopted, will resume their own opinion, when they can lay direct taxes; and, as Rhode Island has always been against an impost, and as they have an equal representation in the Senate, and part of Connecticut will be interested with them, and the Southern States having no manufactures of their own, and consuming much more foreign articles than the Northern, it appears to me, we are not certain of availing ourselves of an impost, *if we give Congress **power** to levy and collect direct taxes in time of peace.*

OLIVER ELSWORTH
(Connecticut)

Volume II, page 190:

JANUARY 7, 1788. [*On the Power of Congress to lay Taxes.*]

OLIVER ELSWORTH. Mr. President, this is a most important clause in the Constitution; and the gentlemen do well to offer all the objections which they have against it. Through the whole of this debate, I have attended to the objections which have been made against this clause; and I think them all to be unfounded. The clause is general; it gives the general legislature "power to lay and collect taxes, duties, imposts, and excises, to pay the debts and provide for the common defence and general welfare of the United States." *There are three objections against this clause — first, that it is too extensive, as it extends to all the objects of taxation; secondly, that it is partial; thirdly, that* **Congress ought not to have power to lay taxes at all.**

Pages 191, 192:

. . . The first is, it is the most fruitful and easy way. All nations have found it to be so. *Direct taxation can go but little way towards raising a revenue. To raise money in this way, people must be provident; they must constantly be laying up money to answer the demands of the collector.* But you cannot make people thus provident. If you would do any thing to the purpose, *you must come in when they are spending, and take a part with them. This does not take away the tools of a man's business, or the necessary utensils of his family: it only comes in when he is taking his pleasure, and feels generous;* when he is laying out a shilling for superfluities, it takes twopence of it for public use, *and the remainder will do him as much good as the whole.* I will instance two facts, which show how easily and insensibly a revenue is raised *by indirect taxation.* I suppose people in general are not sensible that we pay a tax to the state of New York. Yet it is an incontrovertible fact, that we, the people of Connecticut, pay annually into the treasury of New York more than fifty thousand dollars. Another instance I will mention: one of our common river sloops pays in the West Indies a portage bill of £60. This is a tax which foreigners lay upon us, and we pay it; for a duty laid upon our shipping, which transports our produce to foreign markets, sinks the price of our produce, and operates as an effectual tax upon those who till the ground, and bring the fruits of it to market. *All nations have seen the necessity and propriety of raising a revenue by indirect taxation,* **by duties upon articles of consumption.** France raises a revenue of twenty-four millions sterling per annum; and it is chiefly in this way. Fifty millions of livres they raise upon the single article of salt. The Swiss cantons raise almost the whole of their revenue upon salt. Those states purchase all the salt which is to be used in the country: they sell it out to the people at an advanced price; the advance is the revenue of the country. In England, the whole public revenue is about twelve millions sterling per annum. The land tax amounts to about two millions; the window and some other taxes, to about two millions more. The other eight millions are raised upon articles of consumption. *The whole standing army of Great Britain could not enforce the collection of this vast sum by direct taxation.* In Holland, their prodigious taxes, amounting to forty shillings for each inhabitant, are levied chiefly *upon articles of consumption.* They excise every thing, not excepting even their houses of infamy.

The experiments, which have been made in our own country, show **the productive nature of indirect taxes.** The imports into the United States amount to a very large sum. They never will be less, but will continue to increase for centuries to come. As the population of our country increases, the imports will necessarily increase.

MR. WILLIAMS
(New York)

Volume II, pages 330, 331, 332:

Sir, to detail the particulars comprehended in the general terms, *taxes, duties, imposts,* and *excises,* would take up more time than would be proper at present; indeed, it would be a task far beyond my ability, and to which no one can be competent, unless possessed of a mind capable of comprehending every possible source of revenue; for they extend to every possible means of raising money, *whether by direct or indirect taxation. Under this clause may be imposed a poll-tax, a tax on houses and buildings, on windows and fireplaces, on cattle, and on* **all kinds of personal property.** *It extends to duties on all kinds of goods,* to tonnage and poundage of vessels, to duites on written instruments, newspapers, almanacs, &c. *It comprehends an excise on all kinds of liquors, spirits, wine, cider, beer, &c.; indeed, on every* **necessary or convenience of life** whether of foreign or home growth or manufacture. *In short, we can have no conception of any way in which a government can raise money from the people, but what is included in one or the other of these general terms.* Every source of revenue is therefore committed to the hands of the general legislature. Not only these terms are very comprehensive, and extend to a vast number of objects, but *the power to lay and collect has great latitude: it will lead to the passing of* **a vast number of laws,** *which may affect the personal rights of the citizens of the states, and put their lives in jeopardy.* It will open a door to the appointment of a **swarm of revenue and excise officers,** *to prey upon the honest and industrious part of the community.*

. . . I should enlarge on this subject, but as the usual time draws near for an adjournment, *I conclude with this remark, — that I conceive the paragraph gives* **too great a power to Congress;** and in order that the state governments should have some resource of revenue, and the means of support, I beg leave to offer the following resolution; —

"*Resolved,* That no excise shall be imposed on any article of the growth or manufacture of the United States or any part of them; and that Congress do not lay direct taxes, but when moneys arising from the impost and excise are insufficient for the public exigencies; nor then, until Congress shall first have made a requisition upon the states, to assess levy, and pay their respective proportion of such requisition, agreeably to the census fixed in the said Constitution, in such way and manner as the legislatures of the respective states shall judge best; and in such case, if any state shall neglect or refuse to pay its proportion, pursuant to such requisition, then Congress may assess and levy such state's proportion, together with interest thereon, at the rate of six per cent per annum, from the time of payment prescribed in such requisition."

ROBERT R. LIVINGSTON
(New York)

Volume II, pages 341, 342:

The first proposition in the amendment is, that *no excise shall be laid on the manufactures of the United States;* the second, that *a requisition shall precede the imposition of a direct tax.* . .

The second part is of the greatest importance; *its object is to prevent Congress from laying direct taxes in any of the states till they have previously made requisitions.* Let us examine whether this measure will be compatible with sound policy: let us reason from experience. We have seen something of requisitions — enough, one would suppose, to make us exceedingly suspicious of them. We all know how they have hitherto operated. There are no arguments so forcible as those drawn from facts within our own knowledge. We may form as many conjectures and hypotheses as we please, but shall ever recur at last to experience as a sure guide. The gentlemen will, without doubt, allow that the United States will be subject to the same kind of expenses, and will have the same demand for money, as other nations. *There are no governments that have not been obliged to levy direct taxes,* and even procure loans, to answer the public wants; there are no governments which have not, in **certain emergencies, been compelled to call for all the capital resources of the country.** This may be the situation of the United States: we hope not in our day; but we must not presume it will never happen. Indeed, the motion itself is made upon the contemplation of this event. We conclude, therefore, that the gentleman who brought it forward is convinced that *the necessities of government will call for more money than external and indirect taxation can produce.* Our business, then, is to consider the mode recommended by the gentleman, and see whether it can possibly furnish supplies adequate to the **exigencies of government.** . .

Pages 343, 344:

I imagine, sir, that indirect taxes will be generally sufficient in **time of peace.** *But a constitution should be calculated for* **all circumstances —** *for the most critical and dangerous conjunctures.* Let us suppose a sudden emergency, in which the ordinary resources are entirely inadequate to the public wants, and see what difficulties present themselves on the gentleman's plan. First, a requisition is to go out to all the states. . .

. . . Can it be imagined, by any rational man, that the legislature of a state, which has solemnly declared that it will not grant a requisition, will suffer a tax for the same to be immediately levied on its citizens? We are then brought to this dilemma — either the collectors could not be so hardy as to disregard the laws of the states, or an internal war will take place. But, on either of these events, what becomes of the requisition and the tax? Sir, is there a people under heaven, who, countenanced and imboldened by the voice of their state legislatures, will ever pay a farthing of such a tax? They will resist it as they would a foreign tribute, or the invasion of an enemy. Under such circumstances, will Congress be able to borrow? We all know what has been the difficulty of procuring loans: we are sensible that foreign loans could not have been procured at all, had not the lenders been greatly interested in the success of the revolution. Besides, they undoubtedly expected such a change in our government as would enable the United States to provide efficient funds. Now, we are forming a constitution for ages, which will forever preclude the establishment of any certain funds. *What hopes have we of borrowing, unless we have something to pledge for payment. And the* **avails of direct taxes** *are the only positive fund which can be pledged.* I presume the impost and excise will not be more than sufficient to fund the debts we now owe. *If future wars should lead us into extraordinary expenses,* it will be necessary not only *to lay direct taxes,* but *to procure new loans, to support those expenses.*

ALEXANDER HAMILTON
(New York)

Volume II, pages 364, 365:

Sir, it has been said that a poll tax is a **tyrannical tax:** but the legislature of this state can lay it whenever they please. Does then, our Constitution authorize tyranny? *I am as much opposed to capitation as any man. Yet who can deny that there may exist certain circumstances which will render this tax necessary?* In the course of a *war,* it may be necessary to lay hold on every resource: and for a certain period the people may submit to it, *but on removal of the danger or the return of peace, the general sense of the community* **would abolish it.** The United Netherlands were obliged, on an emergency, to give up one twentieth of their property to the government. It has been said that it will be impossible to exercise this power of taxation: if it cannot be exercised, why be alarmed? But the gentlemen say that the difficulty of executing it with moderation will necessarily drive the government into despotic measures. Here, again, they are in the old track of jealousy and conjecture. *Whenever the people feel the hand of despotism, they will not regard forms and parchments.* But the gentlemen's premises are as false as their conclusion. No one reason can be offered why the exercise of the power should be impracticable. No one difficulty can be pointed out which will not apply to our state governments. Congress will have every means of knowledge that any legislature can have. From general observation, and from the revenue systems of the several states, they will derive information as to the most eligible modes of taxation. If a land tax is the object, cannot Congress procure as perfect a valuation as any other assembly? Can they not have all the necessary officers for assessment and collections? Where is the difficulty? Where is the evil? *They never can oppress a particular state by an* **unequal imposition;** *because the Constitution has* **provided a fixed ratio,** *a* **uniform rule,** *by which this must be regulated.* The system will be founded upon the most easy and equal principles — to draw as much as possible from direct taxation; to lay the principal burdens on the wealthy, etc. Even ambitious and unprincipled men will form their system so as to draw forth the resources of the country in the most favorable and gentle methods, because such will be ever the most productive. They never can hope for success by adopting those arbitrary modes which have been used in some of the states.

Pages 368, 369:

. . . One provision in the amendment is that *no direct taxes shall be laid till after the impost and excise shall be found insufficient for the public* **exigencies;** and that no excise shall be laid on articles of the growth or manufacture of the United States.

JAMES WILSON
(Pennsylvania)

Volume II, page 467, 468:

. . . Throughout the Union, direct taxation will be lessened, at least in proportion to the increase of the other objects of revenue. In this Constitution. *a power is given to Congress to collect imposts, which is not given by the present Articles of the Confederation.* A very considerable part of the revenue of the United States will arise from that source; *it is the easiest, most just, and most productive mode of raising revenue;* **and it is a safe one, because it is voluntary.** No man, is obliged to consume more than he pleases, and each buys in proportion only to his consumption. *The price of the commodity is blended with the tax,* and the person is often not sensible of the payment. But would it have been proper to rest the matter there? Suppose this fund should not prove sufficient; *ought the public debts to remain unpaid, or the* **exigencies** *of government be left unprovided for?* should our tranquillity be exposed to the assaults of foreign enemies, or violence among ourselves, because the objects of commerce may not furnish a sufficient revenue to secure them all? *Certainly, Congress should possess the power of raising revenue from their constituents, for the purpose mentioned in the 8th section of the 1st article:* that is "to pay the debts and provide for the common defence and general welfare of the United States." It has been common with the gentlemen, on this subject, to present us with frightful pictures. *We are told of the* **hosts of tax-gatherers** *that will swarm through the land;* and whenever taxes are mentioned, military force seems to be an attending idea. I think I may venture to predict that the taxes of the general government, **if any shall be laid,** *will be more equitable, and much less expensive, than those imposed by state governments.*

JAMES MADISON
(Virginia)

Volume III, pages 95, 96:

. . . If Virginia was separated from all the states, her power and authority would extend to all cases: in like manner, were all powers vested in the general government, it would be a consolidated government; *but the powers of the federal government are enumerated; it can only operate in certain cases; it has legislative powers on* **defined and limited objects,** *beyond which it cannot extend its jurisdiction.*

But the honorable member has satirized, with peculiar acrimony, the powers given to the general government by this Constitution. I conceive that the first question on this subject is, whether these powers be necessary; if they be, we are reduced to the dilemma of either submitting to the inconvenience or losing the Union. Let us consider the most important of these reprobated powers; that of **direct taxation** *is most generally objected to.* With respect to the exigencies of government, there is no question but the most easy mode of providing for them will be adopted. *When, therefore, direct taxes are not necessary, they will not be recurred to. It can be of little advantage to those in power to raise money in a manner* **oppressive to the people.** To consult the conveniences of the people will cost them nothing, and in many respects will be advantageous to them. *Direct taxes will only be recurred to for great purposes.* What has brought on other nations those immense debts, under the pressure of which many of them labor? *Not the expenses of their governments,* **but war.** If this country should be engaged in war, — and I conceive we ought to provide for the possibility of such a case, — how would it be carried on? *By the usual means provided from year to year?* As our imports will be necessary for the expenses of government and other common exigencies, how are we to carry on the means of defence? How is it possible a war could be supported without money or credit? And would it be possible for a government to have credit without having the power of raising money? No; it would be impossible for any government, in such as case, to defend itself. Then, I say, sir, that *it is necessary to establish funds for* **extraordinary exigencies,** *and to give this power to the general government;* for the utter inutility of previous requisitions on the states is too well known. Would it be possible for those countries, whose finances and revenues are carried to the highest perfection, to carry on the operations of government on *great emergencies, such as the maintenance of a war, without an uncontrolled power of raising money?. . .*

*But it is urged that its consolidated nature, joined to **the power of direct taxation**, will give it a tendency to destroy all subordinate authority; that its increasing influence will speedily enable it to absorb the state governments.*

Pages 248, 249:

The subject of direct taxation is perhaps one of the most important that can possibly engage our attention, or that can be involved in the discussion of this question. If it be to be judged by the comments made upon it, by the opposers and favorers of the proposed system, it requires a most clear and critical investigaiton. *The objections against the exercise of **this power** by the general government, as far as I am able to comprehend them, are founded upon the supposition of its being **unnecessary, impracticable, unsafe, and accumulative of expense.*** I shall therefore consider, 1st, how far it may be necessary; 2d, how far it may be practicable; 3d, how far it may be safe, as well with respect to the public liberty at large, as to the state legislatures; and 4th, with respect to economy. First, then, is it necessary? I must acknowledge that I concur in opinion with those gentlemen who told you that this branch of revenue was essential to the salvation of the Union. It appears to me necessary, in order to secure that punctuality which is necessary in revenue matters. Without punctuality, individuals will give it no confidence, without which it cannot get resources. I beg gentlemen to consider the situation of this country; if unhappily the government were to be deprived of this power. Let us suppose, for a moment, that one of those powers which may be unfriendly to us should take advantage of our weakness, which they will be more ready to do when they know the want of this resource in our government. Suppose it should attack us; what forces could we oppose to it? Could we find safety in such forces as we could call out? Could we call forth a sufficient number, either by draughts, or any other way, to repel a powerful enemy? The inability of the government to raise and support regular troops would compel us to depend on militia.

It would be then necessary to give this power to the government, or run the risk of national annihilation. It is my firm belief that, *if a hostile attack were made this moment on the United States,* it would flash conviction on the minds of the citizens of the United States of the necessity of *vesting the government with this **power**, which alone can enable it to protect the community.* I do not wish to frighten the members into a concession of this power, but to bring to their minds those considerations which demonstrate its necessity. *If we were secured from the possibility, or probability, of danger, it might be* **unnecessary.** I shall not review that concourse of dangers which may probably arise at remote periods of futurity, nor all those which we have immediately to apprehend, for this would lead me beyond the bounds which I prescribed myself. But I will mention one single consideration, drawn from fact itself. I hope to have your attention.

Page 251:

Let us consider the alternatives proposed by gentlemen, instead of the power of laying direct taxes. After the states shall have refused to comply, weigh the consequences of the exercise of this power by Congress. *When it comes in the form of a punishment, great clamors will be raised among the people against the government: hatred will be excited against it.* It will be considered as an ignominious stigma on the state. . .

Page 253:

There is another point of view in which this subject affords us instruction. *The imports will decrease in time of war.* The honorable gentleman who spoke yesterday said that *the imposts would be so productive that there would be no occasion of laying* **taxes.** I will submit two observations to him and the committee. First, *in time of war, the imposts will be less;* and as I hope we are considering a government for a perpetual duration, we ought to provide for every future contingency. At present, our importations bear a full proportion to the full amount of our sales, and to the number of our inhabitants; *but when we have inhabitants enough, our imposts will decrease, and as the national demands will increase with our population, our resources will increase as our wants increase.* The other consideration which I will submit on this part of the subject is this: I believe that it will be found, in practice, that those who fix the public burdens will feel a greater degree of responsibility, when they are to impose them on the citizens immediately than if they were to say what sum should be paid by the states. *If they exceed the limits of propriety, universal discontent and clamor will arise.* Let us suppose they were to collet the taxes from the citizens of America; would they not consider their circumstances? Would they not attentively consider what could be done by the citizens at large? Were they to exceed, in their demands, what were reasonable burdens, the people would impute it to the right source, and look on the imposers as odious.

When I consider the nature of the various objections brought against this clause, I should be led to think that the difficulties were such that gentlemen would not be able to get over them and that the power as defined in the plan of the Convention, was impracticable. I shall trouble them with a few observations on that point. . .

Page 255:

. . . *If the general government were tied down to one object, I confess
the objection would have some force in it.* But if this be not the case, it can
have no weight. *If it should have a general power of taxation, they could se-*
lect the *most proper objects, and distribute the taxes in such a manner as
that they should fall in a due degree on every member of the community.*
They will be limited to fix the proportion of each state, and *they must raise
it in the most convenient and satisfactory manner to the public.*

Mr. MADISON. Mr. Chairman: finding, sir, that the clause more immediately under consideration still meets with the disapprobation of the
honorable gentleman over the way, (Mr. Grayson,) and finding that the reasons of the opposition, as further developed, are not satisfactory to myself
and others who are in favor of the clause, I wish that it may meet with the
most thorough and complete investigation. I beg the attention of the committee, in order to obviate what fell from the honorable gentleman. He set
forth that, *by giving up the power of taxation, we should give up every thing,
and still insists on requisitions being made on the states, and then, if they
be not complied with, Congress shall lay* **direct taxes,** *by way of penalty.*
Let us consider the dilemma which arises from this doctrine. Either requisitions will be efficacious, or they will not. If they will be efficacious,
then I say, sir, we give up every thing as much as by direct taxation.

The same amount will be paid by the people as by direct taxes. If they
be not efficacious, where is the advantage of this plan? In what respect will
it relieve us from the inconveniences which we have experienced from requisitions? The power of laying direct taxes by the general government is
supposed by the honorable gentleman to be chimerical and impracticable.
What is the consequence of the alternative he proposes? *We are to rely upon
this power to be ultimately used as a penalty to compel the states to comply.*
If it be chimerical and impracticable in the first instance, it will be
equally so when it will be exercised as a penalty. A reference was made to
concurrent executions as an instance of the possiblity of interference between the two governments. . .

Pages 306, 307:

He compares **resistance of the people to collectors** *to refusal of re-*
quisitions. This goes against all government. It is as much as to urge that
there should be no legislature. The gentlemen who favored us with their
observations on this subject, seemed to reason on a supposition that the
general government was confined, by the paper on your table, to lay general, uniform taxes. Is it necessary that there should be *a tax on any given
article throughout the United States?* It is represented to be oppressive,
that the states which have slaves, and make tobacco, should pay taxes on
these for federal wants, when other states, which have them not, would escape. But does the Constitution on the table admit of this? On the con-

trary, there is a proportion to be laid on each state, *according to its population*. The most proper articles will be selected in each state. If one article, in any state, should be deficient, it will be laid on another article. Our state is secured on this foundation. *Its proportion will* **be commensurate to its population.** *This is a constitutional scale, which is an insuperable* **bar against disproportion,** *and ought to satisfy all resonable minds.*

Page 320:

. . . With respect to requisitions, I beseech gentlemen to consider the importance of the subject. *We, who are for amendments, propose* (as has been frequently mentioned) *that a requisition shall be made for two hundred thousand pounds, for instance, instead of direct taxation, and that, if it be not complied with, then it shall be raised by direct taxes.* We do not wish to have strength, to refuse to pay them, but to possess the power of raising the taxes in the most easy mode for the people. But, says he, you may delay us by this mode. Let us see if there be not sufficient to counterbalance this evil. The oppression arising from taxation is not from the amount, but from the mode: a thorough acquaintance with the condition of the people is necessary to a just distribution of taxes. *The whole wisdom of the science of government, with respect to taxation, consists in selecting that mode of collection which will best accommodate* **the convenience of the people.** . .

GEORGE NICHOLAS
(Virginia)

Volume III, pages 243, 244, 245, 246:

We are next terrified with the thought of excises. In some countries excises are terrible. In others, they are not only harmless, but useful. In our sister states, they are excised without any inconvenience. **They are a kind of tax on manufactures.** Our manufactures are few in proportion to those of other states. We may be assured that Congress will make such regulations as shall *make excises convenient and easy for the people.*

Another argument made use of is, that ours is the largest state, and must pay in proportion to the other states. How does that appear? The proportion **of taxes** *are fixed by the number of inhabitants, and not regulated by the extent of territory, or fertility of soil.* If we be wealthier, in proportion than other states, it will fall lighter upon us than upon poorer states. *They must fix the taxes so that the poorest states can pay; and* **Virginia, being richer, will bear it easier.** . .

Another argument against this disingenuous construction is drawn from that clause which regulates representation, which is conclusive from the words themselves: "Representatives and *direct taxes shall be apportioned among the several states* which may be included within this Union, *according to their respective numbers.*" *Each state will know, from its population, its proportion of any general tax.* As it was justly observed by the gentleman over the way, (Mr. Randolph,) *they cannot possibly exceed that proportion: they are limited and restrained expressly to it.* The state legislatures have no check of this kind. Their power is uncontrolled. This excludes the danger of interference. Each collects its own taxes, and bears its own deficiencies; and officers are accountable to each government for the different collections.

I deny, on my part, what he says with respect to the general welfare. *He tells you that, under pretence of providing for the general welfare, they may lay the most enormous taxes.* **There is nothing in the clause which warrants this suggestion.**

It provides "that Congress shall have the power to lay and collect taxes, duties, imposts, and excises; to pay the debts, and provide for the common defence and general welfare, of the United States." The debts of the Union ought to be paid. Ought not the common defence to be provided for? *Is it not necessary to provide for the general welfare?* It has been fully proved that this power could not be given to another body. The amounts to be raised are confined to these purposes solely. Will oppressive burdens be warranted by this clause? *They are not to raise money for any other purpose.* It is a power which is drawn from his favorite Confederation, the 8th article of which provides "that all charges of war, and all other expenses that shall be incurred by the common defence or general welfare, and allowed by the United States in Congress assembled, shall be defrayed out of a common treasury, which shall be supplied by the several states, in proportion to the value of all lands, within each state, granted to or surveyed for any person, as such land, and the building and improvement thereon, shall be estimated, according to such mode as the United States, in Congress assembled, shall, from time to time, direct and appoint.

"The taxes for paying that proportion shall be laid and levied, by the authority and direction of the legislatures of the several states, within the time agreed upon by the United States, in Congress assembled." Now, sir, by a comparison of this article with the clause in the Constitution, we shall find them to be nearly the same. *The common defence and general welfare are the objects expressly mentioned to be provided for, in both systems.* The power in the Confederation to secure and provide for those objects was constitutionally unlimited. The requisitions of Congress are binding on the states, though, the imbecility of their nature, they cannot be enforced. The same power is intended by the Constitution. *The only difference between them is, that Congress is, by this plan, to impose the taxes on the people, whereas, by the Confederation, they are laid by the states.* The amount to be raised, and the power given to raise it, is the same in principle. The mode of raising only is different, *and this difference is founded on the necessity of giving the government that energy without which it can-*

not exist. The power has not been reprobated in the Confederation. It ought not to be blamed in the proposed plan of government.

The gentleman has adverted to what he calls the *sweeping clause,* &c., and represents it as replete with great dangers. This dreaded clause runs in the following words: "To make all laws which shall be necessary and proper for carrying into execution the foregoing powers, and all other powers vested by this Constitution in the government of the United States, or in any department or officer therof." The committee will perceive that the Constitution had enumerated all the powers which the general government should have, but did not say how they were to be exercised. *Does this give any new power?* **I say not.** Suppose it had been inserted, at the end of every power, that they should have power to make laws to carry that power into execution; *would this have increased their powers? If, therefore, it could not have increased their powers, if placed at the end of each power, it cannot increase them at the end of all. This clause only enables them to carry into execution the* **powers given to them,** *but* **gives them no additional power.**

But it is objected to for want of a bill of rights. It is a principle universally agreed upon, that all powers **not given are retained.** Where, by the Constitution, the general government has general powers for any purpose, *its powers are absolute.* Where it has powers with some exceptions, they are absolute *only as to those exceptions. In either case, the people retain what is not conferred on the general government, as it is* **by their positive grant** *that it has any of its powers.* In England, in all disputes between the king and people, recurrence is had to the enumerated rights of the people, to determine. Are the rights in dispute secured? Are they included in Magna Charta, Bill of Rights, etc.? If not, they are, generally speaking, within the king's prerogative. *In disputes between Congress and the people, the reverse of the proposition holds.* Is the disputed right enumerated? *If not, Congress cannot meddle with it.*

Which is the most safe? The people of America know what they have relinquished for certain purposes. *They also know that they retain every thing else, and have a right to resume what they have given up, if it be perverted from its intended object.*

GEORGE MASON
(Virginia)

Volume III, pages 263, 264, 265:

That unconditional power of taxation which is given to that government cannot but **oppress** *the people. If, instead of this, a conditional power of taxation be given, in case of* **refusal to comply with requisitions,** the same end will be answered with convenience to the people. This will not lessen the power of Congress; we do not want to lessen the power of Congress unnecessarily. This will produce moderation in the demand, and will prevent the ruinous exercise of that power by those who know not our situation. We shall then have that mode of taxation which is the most easy, and least oppressive to the people, because it will be exercised by those who are acquainted with their condition and circumstances. *This, sir, is the great object we wish to secure — that our people should be taxed by those who have a fellow-feeling for them.* I think I can venture to assert that the general government will lay such taxes as are the easiest and the most productive in the collection. This is natural and probable.

For example, they may lay a poll tax. This is simply and easily collected, but *is of all taxes the most grievous.* Why the most grievous? Because it falls light on the rich, and heavy on the poor. *It is most oppressive:* for if the rich man is taxed, he can only retrench his superfluities; but the consequence to the poor man is, that it increases his miseries. *That, they will lay the most simple taxes, and such as are easiest to collect, is highly probable, nay, almost absolutely certain.* I shall take the liberty, on this occasion, to read you a letter, which will show, at least as far as opinion goes, what sort of taxes will be most probably laid on us, if we adopt this Constitution. It was the opinion of a gentleman of information. It will in some degree establish the fallacy of those reports which have been circulated through the country, and which induced a great many poor, ignorant people to believe that the taxes were to be lessened by the adoption of the proposed government.

[Here Mr. Mason read a letter from Mr. Robert Morris, financier of the United States, to Congress, wherein he spoke of the propriety of laying the following taxes for the use of the United States; viz., *six shillings on every hundred acres of land, six shillings per poll, and ninepence per gallon on all spirituous liquors distilled in the country.* Mr. Mason declared that he did not mean to make the smallest reflection on Mr. Morris, but introduced his letter to show what taxes would probably be laid.]

He then continued: This will at least show that such taxes were in agitation, and were strongly advocated by a considerable part of Congress. I have read this letter to show that they will lay taxes most easy to be collected, without any regard to our convenience; so that, instead of amusing ourselves with a diminution of our taxes, we may rest assured that they will be increased. But my principal reason for introducing it was, to show that *taxes would be laid by those who are not acquainted with our situation,* and that the *agents of the collection* may be consulted upon the most productive and simple mode of taxation. The gentleman who wrote this letter had more information on this subject than we have; but this will show gentlemen that we are not to be eased of taxes. Any of those taxes which have been pointed out by this financier as the most eligible, will be ruinous and unequal, and will be particularly oppressive on the poorest part of the people.

As to a poll tax, I have already spoken of its iniquitous operation, and need not say much of it, because it is so generally disliked in this state, that we were obliged to abolish it lastly. *As to a* **land tax,** *it will operate most unequally.* The man who has one hundred acres of the richest land will pay as little as a man who has one hundred acres of the poorest land. Near Philadelphia, or Boston, an acre of land is worth one hundred pounds; yet the possessor of it will pay no more than the man with us whose land is hardly worth twenty shillings an acre. Some landholders in this state will have to pay twenty times as much as will be paid for all the land on which Philadelphia stands; and as to excise, this will carry the exciseman to every farmer's house, who distils a little brandy, where he may search and ransack as he pleases. *These I mention as* **specimens of the kind** *of tax which is to be laid upon us by those who have no information of our situation, and by a government where the wealthy only are represented.*

MR. WILLIAM GRAYSON
(Virginia)

Volume III, page 280:

As to **direct taxation — give up this, and you give up every thing,** *as it is the* **highest act of sovereignty:** *surrender up this inestimable jewel, and you throw away a pearl richer than all your tribe.*

Page 284:

. . . In my opinon, *the states which give up the power of taxation have nothing more to give.* The people of that state which suffers any power but her own immediate government to interfere with the sovereign right of taxation are gone forever. **Giving the right of taxation is giving a right to increase the miseries of the people.** Is it not a politcal absurdity to suppose that there can be two concurrent legislatures, *each possessing the supreme* **power of direct taxation?** If two powers come in contact, must not the one prevail over the other? Must it not strike every man's mind, that two unlimited, coëqual, coördinate authorities, over the same objects, cannot exist together?

Pages 287, 288:

. . . What influence can the state governments be supposed to have, after the loss of their most important rights? Will not the diminuation of their power and influence be an augmentation of those of the general government? Will not the officers of the general government receive higher compensation for their services than those of the state governments? Will not the most influential men be employed by Congress? *I think the state governments will be contemned and despised* **as soon as they give up the power of direct taxation;** *and a state, says Montesquieu, should lose her existence sooner than her importance.*

But, sir, we are told that, if we do not give up this power to Congress, the impost will be stretched to the utmost extent. I do suppose this might follow, if the thing did not correct itself. *But we know that it is the nature of this kind of taxation, that a small duty will bring more real money than a large one.* The experience of the English nation proves the truth of this assertion. There has been much said of the necessity of the five per cent impost. I have been ever of opinion, that two and a half per cent would produce more real money into the treasury. But we need not be alarmed on this account, because, when smugglers will be induced, by heavy imposts, to elude the laws, the general government will find it their interest again to reduce them within reasonable and moderate limits. *But it is suggested that,* **if direct taxation be inflicted by way of punishment,** *it will create great disturbances in the country.* This is an assertion without argument. If man is a reasonable being, he will submit to punishment, and acquiesce in the justice of its infliction, when he knows he deserves it. The states will comply with the requisitions of Congress more readily when they know that *this power* may be ultimately used; and if they do not comply, they will have no reasons to complain of its exercise.

PATRICK HENRY
(Virginia)

Volume III, page 321:

Another valuable thing which it will produce is, that the people will pay the taxes cheerfully. It is supposed that this would occasion a waste of time, and be an injury to public credit. This would only happen if requisitions should not be complied with. In this case the delay would be compensated by the payment of interest, which, with the addition of the credit of the state to that of the general government, would in a great measure obviate this objection. But if it had all the force which it is suppsoed to have, *it would not be adequate to the evils of direct taxation.* But there is every probability that requisitions would be then complied with. Would it not, then, be our interest as well as duty to comply? After non-compliance, there would be a general acquiescence in the exercise of *this power.* We are fond of giving power, at least power which is constitutional. Here is an option to pay according to your own mode or otherwise. If you give probability fair play, you must conclude that they would be complied with. *Would the Assembly of Virginia, by refusal, destroy the country, and plunge the people in misery and distress?* If you give your reasoning faculty fair play, you cannot but know that payment must be made, when *the consequence of a refusal would be an accumulation of inconveniences to the people.* Then they say that, *if requisitions be not complied with, in case of a war, the destruction of the country may be the consequence; that therefore we ought to give the* **power of taxation** *to the government,* **to enable it to protect us.** Would not this be another reason for complying with requisitions, to prevent the country from being destroyed? You tell us that, unless requisitions be complied with, your commerce is gone. The prevention of this, also, will be an additional reason to comply.

He tells us that responsibility is secured by direct taxation. Responsibility instead of being increased, will be lost forever by it. . . .

Pages 455, 456:

. . . Congress, now observed, had power to lay and collect taxes, imposts, and excises. Imposts (or duties) and excises were to be uniform; *but this uniformity* **did not extend to taxes.**

MR. SPENCER
(North Carolina)

Volume IV, pages 75, 76:

MR. SPENCER. Mr. Chairman, *I conceive this power to be too extensive, as it embraces all possible powers of taxation, and gives up to Congress every possible article of taxation that can ever happen.* By means of this, there will be no way for the states of receiving or collecting taxes at all, but what may interfere with the collections of Congress. *Every power is given over our money to those over whom we have no immediate control.* I would give them powers to support the government, but would not agree to annihilate the state governments in an article which is most essential to their existence. I would give them power of laying imposts; and I would give them power to lay and collect excises. *I confess that this is a kind of tax* **so odious to a free people,** *that I should with great reluctance agree to its exercise;* but it is obvious that, unless such excises were admitted, the public burden will be all borne by those parts of the community who do not manufacture for themselves. So manifest an inequality would justify a recurrence to this species of taxes.

How are direct taxes to be laid? By a poll tax, assessments on land **or other property?** Inconvenience and oppression will arise from any of them. I would not be understood that I would not wish to have an efficient government for the United States. I am sensible that laws operating on individuals cannot be carried on against states; because, if they do not comply with the general laws of the Union, there is no way to compel a compliance but force. There must be an army to compel them. Some states may have some excuse for non-compliance. Others will feign excuses. Several states may perhaps be in the same predicament. If force be used to compel them, they will probably call for foreign aid; and the very means of defence will operate to the dissolution of the system, and to the destruction of the states. I would not, therefore, deny that Congress ought to have *the power of taking out of the pockets of the individuals at large,* if the states fail to pay those taxes in a convenient time. If requisitions were to be made on the several states, proportionate to their abilities, the several state legislatures, knowing the circumstances of their constituents, and that they would ultimately be compelled to pay, would lay the tax in a convenient manner, and would be able to pay their quotas at the end of the year. *They are better acquainted with the mode in which taxes can be raised, than the general government can possibly be.*

MR. JAMES IREDELL
(North Carolina)

Volume IV, page 220:

But have we not sufficient security that those powers shall not be abused? *The immediate power of the purse is in the immediate representatives of the people, chosen every two years, who can lay no tax on their constituents* **but what they are subject to at the same time themselves.** The power of taxation must be vested somewhere. Do the committee wish it to be as it has been? Then they must suffer the evils which they have done. Requisitions will be of no avail. No money will be collected but by means of military force. Under the new government, *taxes will probably be much lighter* than they can be under our present one. *The* **impost will af-** *ford vast advantages, and greatly* **relieve the people from direct taxa-** **tion.** *In time of peace, it is supposed by many, the imposts may be alone sufficient; but in the time of* **war,** *it cannot be expected they will.* Our expenses would be much greater, and our ports might be blocked up by the enemy's fleet. Think, then, of the advantage of a national government possessed of energy and credit. *Could government borrow money to any advantage without the* **power of taxation?. . .**

States Seek To Further Limit Government's Direct Taxing Power

The following excerpts (taken directly from the ratification statements of five states) show that the people were so fearful of giving the government any direct taxing power they sought to substantially limit this power even further:

Volume I, page 327:
NEW YORK

That the Congress do not impose any excise on any article (ardent spirits excepted) of the growth, production, or manufacture of the United States, or any of them.

That Congress do not lay direct taxes but when the moneys arising from the impost and excise shall be insufficient for the public exigencies, nor then, until Congress shall first have made a requisition upon the states to assess, levy, and pay, their respective proportions of such requisition, agreeably to the census fixed in the said Constitution, in such way and manner as the legislatures of the respective states shall judge best; and in such case, if any state shall neglect or refuse to pay its proportion, pursuant to such requisition, then Congress may assess and levy such state's proportion, together with interest at the rate of six per centum per annum, from the time of payment prescribed in such requisition.

Page 325:
NEW HAMPSHIRE

IV. *That Congress do not lay direct taxes but when the money arising from impost, excise, and their other resources, are insufficient for the public exigencies, nor then, until Congress shall have first made a requisition upon the states to assess, levy, and pay, their respective proportions of such requisition, agreeably to the census fixed in the said Constitution,* in such way and manner as the legislature of the state shall think best; and in such case, if any state shall neglect, then Congress may assess and levy such state's proportion, together with the interest thereon, at the rate of six per cent per annum, from the time of payment prescribed in such requisition.

Page 322:
MASSACHUSETTS

IV. *That Congress do not lay direct taxes but when the moneys arising from the impost and excise are insufficient for the public exigencies, nor then until Congress shall have first made a requisition upon the states to assess, levy, and pay, their respective proportions of such requisition, agreeably to the census fixed in the said Constitution,* in such way and manner as the legislatures of the states shall think best; and in such case, if any state shall neglect or refuse to pay its proportion, pursuant to such requisition, then Congress may assess and levy such state's proportion, together with interest thereon at the rate of six per cent annum, from the time of payment prescribed in such requisition.

Page 335:
RHODE ISLAND

. . . that the Congress will not lay direct taxes within this state, but when the moneys arising from impost, tonnage, and excise, shall be insufficient for the public exigencies, nor until the Congress shall have first made a requisition upon this state to assess, levy, and pay, the amount of such requisition made agreeable to the census fixed in the said Constitution, in such way and manner as the legislature of this state shall judge best; and that Congress will not lay any capitation or poll tax.

Page 325:
SOUTH CAROLINA

Resolved, *That the general government of the United States ought never to impose direct taxes, but where the moneys arising from the duties, imposts, and excise, are insufficient for the public exigencies, nor then until Congress shall have made a requisition upon the states to assess, levy, and pay, their respective proportions of such requisitions;* and in case any state shall neglect or refuse to pay its proportion, pursuant to such requisition, then Congress may assess and levy such state's proportion, together with interest thereon, at the rate of six per centum per annum, from the time of payment prescribed by such requisition.

(Emphasis added throughout appendix.)

Appendix C

18th and 19th Century Federal Tax Statutes

This Appendix includes:

1. the complete text of the first direct taxing statute enacted by Congress;
2. excerpts from the Direct Tax Act of 1813; and
3. excerpts from the Tax Act of 1861.

FIFTH CONGRESS, Session II, Chapter 77, 1798
(the first direct taxing Statute)

STATUTE II.

CHAP. LXXV.——*An Act to lay and collect a direct tax within the United States.* July 14, 1798.

SECTION 1. *Be it enacted by the Senate and House of Representatives of the United States of America in Congress assembled,* That a direct tax of two millions of dollars shall be, and hereby is laid upon the United States, and apportioned to the states respectively, in the manner following :—

[Obsolete.]
Act of July 9,
1798, ch. 70.
A direct tax
of two millions
laid.
1802, ch. 12.
Apportionment.

To the state of New Hampshire, seventy-seven thousand seven hundred and five dollars, thirty-six cents and two mills.

To the state of Massachusetts, two hundred and sixty thousand four hundred and thirty-five dollars, thirty-one cents and two mills.

To the state of Rhode Island, thirty-seven thousand five hundred and two dollars and eight cents.

To the state of Connecticut, one hundred and twenty-nine thousand seven hundred and sixty-seven dollars, and two mills.

To the state of Vermont, forty-six thousand eight hundred and sixty-four dollars eighteen cents and seven mills.

To the state of New York, one hundred and eighty-one thousand six hundred and eighty dollars, seventy cents and seven mills.

To the state of New Jersey, ninety-eight thousand three hundred and eighty-seven dollars, twenty-five cents, and three mills.

To the state of Pennsylvania, two hundred and thirty-seven thousand one hundred and seventy-seven dollars, seventy-two cents and seven mills.

To the state of Delaware, thirty thousand four hundred and thirty dollars, seventy-nine cents, and two mills.

To the state of Maryland, one hundred and fifty-two thousand five hundred and ninety-nine dollars, ninety-five cents, and four mills.

To the state of Virginia, three hundred and forty-five thousand four hundred and eighty-eight dollars, sixty-six cents, and five mills.

To the state of Kentucky, thirty-seven thousand six hundred and forty-three dollars, ninety-nine cents, and seven mills.

To the state of North Carolina, one hundred and ninety-three thousand six hundred and ninety-seven dollars, ninety-six cents, and five mills.

To the state of Tennessee, eighteen thousand eight hundred and six dollars, thirty-eight cents, and three mills.

To the state of South Carolina, one hundred and twelve thousand nine hundred and ninety-seven dollars, seventy-three cents and nine mills.

And to the state of Georgia, thirty-eight thousand eight hundred and fourteen dollars, eighty-seven cents, and five mills.

How it shall be collected.

SEC. 2. *And be it further enacted*, That the said tax shall be collected by the supervisors, inspectors and collectors of the internal revenues of the United States, under the direction of the Secretary of the Treasury, and pursuant to such regulations as he shall establish; and

It shall be assessed on dwelling houses, lands and slaves; 1798, ch. 70.

shall be assessed upon dwelling-houses, lands and slaves, according to the valuations and enumerations to be made pursuant to the act, intituled "An act to provide for the valuation of lands and dwelling-houses, and the enumeration of slaves within the United States," and in the following manner:

At what rate upon dwelling houses.

Upon every dwelling-house which, with the out-houses appurtenant thereto, and the lot whereon the same are erected, not exceeding two acres in any case, shall be valued in manner aforesaid, at more than one hundred, and not more than five hundred dollars, there shall be assessed in the manner herein provided, a sum equal to two tenths of one per centum on the amount of the valuation: upon every dwelling-house which shall be valued as aforesaid, at more than five hundred, and not more than one thousand dollars, there shall be assessed a sum equal to three tenths of one per centum on the amount of the valuation: upon every dwelling-house which shall be valued as aforesaid, at more than one thousand dollars, and not more than three thousand dollars, there shall be assessed a sum equal to four tenths of one per centum on the amount of the valuation: upon every dwelling-house which shall be valued as aforesaid, at more than three thousand, and not more than six thousand dollars, there shall be assessed a sum equal to one half of one per centum on the amount of the valuation: upon every dwelling-house which shall be valued as aforesaid, at more than six, and not more than ten thousand dollars, there shall be assessed a sum equal to six tenths of one per centum on the amount of the valuation: upon every dwelling-house which shall be valued as aforesaid, at more than ten, and not more than fifteen thousand dollars, there shall be assessed a sum equal to seven tenths of one per centum on the amount of the valuation: upon every dwelling-house which shall be valued as aforesaid, at more than fifteen, and not more than twenty-thousand dollars, there shall be assessed a sum equal to eight tenths of one per centum on the amount of the valuation: upon every dwelling-house which shall be valued as aforesaid, at more than twenty, and not more than thirty thousand dollars, there shall be assessed a sum equal to nine tenths of one per centum on the amount of the valuation; and upon every dwelling-house which shall be valued as aforesaid, at more than thirty thousand dollars, there shall be assessed a sum equal to one per centum on the amount of the valuation.

And upon every slave which shall be enumerated according to the act aforesaid, there shall be assessed fifty cents.

And the whole amount of the sums so to be assessed upon dwelling-houses and slaves within each state respectively, shall be deducted from the sum hereby apportioned to such state, and the remainder of the said sum shall be assessed upon the lands within such state according to the valuations to be made pursuant to the act aforesaid, and at such rate per centum as will be sufficient to produce the said remainder: *Provided,* that no part of said tax shall be assessed upon such lands or dwelling-houses and slaves as at the time of passing this act are especially exempted from taxes by the laws of the states, respectively.

SEC. 3. *And be it further enacted,* That the aforesaid assessments shall be made by the supervisors of the several districts within the United States respectively, and pursuant to instructions from the Secretary of the Treasury; which instructions the said Secretary shall be, and hereby is authorized and required to issue to such supervisors or any of them, so soon as the valuations and enumerations directed to be made by the aforesaid act shall have been completed in the state to which such supervisor belongs. And the said tax shall become due and payable from and after the expiration of three months after the instructions aforesaid shall have been received by the supervisors respectively: *Provided,* that if, on making the assessments as aforesaid, it should appear that the sums so to be assessed on houses and slaves within any state will exceed the sum hereby apportioned to such state, then the supervisor shall be, and hereby is authorized and required to deduct from the sums so to be assessed on houses, such rate per centum as shall be sufficient to reduce the whole amount of the said assessments, to the sum apportioned to such state, as aforesaid.

SEC. 4. *And be it further enacted,* That the said supervisors shall be, and hereby are authorized and required to appoint such and so many suitable persons in each assessment district within their respective districts, as may be necessary for collecting the said tax, and shall assign to them, respectively, their collection districts therein; which persons shall be collectors within their respective collection districts, and shall collect the said tax under the direction of the supervisors respectively, and according to the regulations and provisions contained in this act, or to be established pursuant thereto.

SEC. 5. *And be it further enacted,* That so soon as the aforesaid assessment shall have been completed, the said supervisors shall, by special warrants, under their hands, respectively, cause the surveyors of the revenue within their respective districts, to make out lists containing the sums payable, according to such assessments, for every dwelling-house, tract or lot of land, and slave, within each collection district, respectively; which lists shall contain the name of the proprietor or occupant of each dwelling-house, tract or lot of land and slave, within the collection district, or of the person having the care or superintendence of them, or any of them, where such proprietor, occupant or superintendent is known, and the whole sum payable by each person within the said district, distinguishing what is payable for dwelling-houses, what for slaves, and what for lands. And where there are lands, slaves or dwelling-houses within any collection district, not owned, or occupied by, or under the care or superintendence of any person resident therein, there shall be a separate list of such lands, dwelling-houses and slaves, specify-

At what rate upon slaves:

and the residue of the apportionment shall be assessed upon lands.

Saving of lands and houses exempted by the laws of the states.

Assessments to be made by the supervisors.

When the tax shall become due.

What is to be done, if assessments on houses and slaves exceed the apportionment.

Supervisors shall appoint collectors.

Surveyor of the revenue to make out lists of taxes.

ing the sums payable for each, and the names of the proprietors or superintendents, respectively, where known.

Collectors to be furnished with lists.

SEC. 6. *And be it further enacted,* That each of the collectors, to be appointed as aforesaid, shall be furnished by the surveyor of the revenue for the assessment district within which he shall have been so appointed, with one or more of the said lists, signed and certified by such surveyor. And each collector, on receiving a list as aforesaid, shall subscribe three receipts; one of which shall be given on a full and correct copy of such list, and the other two on aggregate statements thereof, exhibiting the number and valuation of dwelling-houses, the number of slaves, and the amount of the valuation of lands in such collection district, with the amount of the taxes assessed thereon. And the list first mentioned, and receipt, shall remain in the office of the surveyor of the revenue, and shall be opened to the inspection of any person who may apply to inspect the same; and the aggregate statements and receipts aforesaid, shall be transmitted to the inspector of the survey, and one of them shall be by him transmitted to the supervisor of the district.

Collectors to give bond.

SEC. 7. *And be it further enacted,* That each collector, before receiving any list as aforesaid, for collection, shall give bond, with one or more good and sufficient sureties, in at least double the amount of the taxes assessed on the collection district for which he may be appointed; which bond shall be payable to the United States, with condition for the true and faithful discharge of the duties of his office, according to law, and particularly, for the due collection and payment of all monies assessed upon such district.

Tax to be a lien upon the land, &c.

SEC. 8. *And be it further enacted,* That the aforesaid tax shall be, and remain a lien upon all lands, and other real estate, and all slaves, of the individuals who may be assessed for the same, during two years after the time when it shall become due and payable according to this act; and the said lien shall extend to each and every part of all tracts or lots of land, or dwelling-houses, which shall be valued according to the aforesaid act, notwithstanding the same may have been divided or alienated, in part, unless an apportionment of the valuation thereof shall have been made and recorded pursuant to the aforesaid act, prior to the time when the collection lists shall have been stated, in manner herein before prescribed.

How the collectors shall demand and enforce payment.

SEC. 9. *And be it further enacted,* That each of the said collectors shall, immediately after receiving his collection list, advertise, by notifications, to be posted up in at least four public places in each collection district, that the said tax has become due and payable and the times and places at which he will attend to receive the same; and, in respect to persons who shall not attend, according to such notifications, it shall be the duty of each collector to apply once at their respective dwellings, within such district, and there demand the taxes payable by such persons; and if the said taxes shall not be then paid, or within twenty days thereafter, it shall be lawful for such collector to proceed to collect the said taxes, by distress and sale of the goods, chattels or effects of the persons delinquent as aforesaid, with a commission of eight per centum upon the said taxes, to and for the use of such collector : *Provided,* that it shall not be lawful to make distress of the tools or implements of a trade or profession, beasts of the plough necessary for the cultivation of improved lands, arms, or the household utensils, or apparel necessary for a family.

SEC. 10. *And be it further enacted,* That except, as aforesaid, all goods, chattels, and personal effects whatever, being or remaining on lands, subject to the said tax; and all grass, or produce of farms, standing and growing thereon, shall and may be taken and sold for the payment of the said tax, under such regulations as have been or may be made for the sale of goods or effects taken and sold by distress : *Pro-*

vided, that nothing herein contained shall invalidate or impair any contract or agreement between any landlord, tenant, or other person, relative to the payment of taxes.

SEC. 11. *And be it further enacted,* That in respect to lands, dwelling-houses and slaves, which shall not be owned by, or in the occupation, or under the care or superintendence of some person within the collection district where the same shall be situated or found at the time of the assessment aforesaid, the said collectors respectively, upon receiving lists of such lands, dwelling-houses, or slaves, in manner aforesaid, shall transmit copies of such lists, certified under their hands respectively, to the surveyors of the revenue for the assessment districts respectively within which the persons owning, or having the care and superintendence of such dwelling-houses, lands, or slaves, may reside, if such persons be known, together with a statement of the amount of taxes assessed as aforesaid upon such dwelling-houses, lands or slaves, respectively, and a notification to pay, or cause to be paid the said taxes to the said collectors respectively, within thirty days after such notification shall be served as is herein provided; which copies, statements and notifications the surveyors receiving the same respectively shall cause to be personally served on the aforesaid persons respectively, or left at their usual places of abode; and shall cause an affidavit thereof, by the person serving or leaving the same as aforesaid, with the time of such service or leaving, to be immediately transmitted to the aforesaid collector: and if such persons being notified in manner aforesaid, shall not, within sixty days thereafter, pay the said taxes to the collector of the collection district where the said lands, dwelling houses, or slaves, shall be situated, or transmit to him a receipt for the said taxes in the manner herein provided, then the said collector shall proceed to collect the said tax by distress and sale as is herein directed: and if the persons owning or having the care and superintendence of any such lands, dwelling-houses or slaves, shall not be known, then the aforesaid collectors shall cause the said copies, statements and notifications to be published for sixty days in four gazettes of the state, if there be so many; after which publication, if the said taxes shall not be paid, the said collectors shall proceed to collect the same by distress and sale in the manner herein provided.

Provision for the case where lands, &c. are not possessed by a person in the collection district.

SEC. 12. *Provided always, and be it further enacted,* That if any person owning, or having the superintendence or care of any dwelling-houses, lands, or slaves, in a collection district other than that in which he resides, and being served with such copy, statement and notification as is aforesaid, shall, within sixty days thereafter, pay the said taxes to the collector of the collection district within which he resides, and transmit a receipt therefor to the collector sending the said copy, statement and notification, such receipt shall be a discharge to the said last mentioned collector for the said taxes, and he shall thereupon forbear to collect them; and the collector giving such receipt shall become chargeable with the said taxes, and shall account therefor in the final settlement of the accounts of his collection.

Taxes may be paid in the district where the possessor resides.

SEC. 13. *And be it further enacted,* That when any tax assessed on lands or houses, shall have remained unpaid for the term of one year, the collector of the collection district within which such land or houses may be situated, having first advertised the same for two months, in six different public places within the said district, and in two gazettes in the state, if there be so many, one of which shall be the gazette in which the laws of such state shall be published by authority if any such there be, shall proceed to sell at public sale, and under the direction of the inspector of the survey, either the dwelling house, or so much of the tract of land, (as the case may be) as may be necessary to satisfy the taxes due thereon; together with costs and charges, not exceeding at the rate of one per centum, for each and every month the said tax shall have

Lands and houses may be sold for taxes remaining unpaid for one year.

But the owner may redeem within two years.

remained due and unpaid. *Provided,* that in all cases, where any lands or tenements, shall be sold as aforesaid, the owner of the said lands or tenements, his heirs, executors or administrators, shall have liberty to redeem the same at any time within two years, from the time of sale, upon payment, or tender of payment, to the collector for the time being, for the use of the purchaser, his heirs or assignees of the amount of the said taxes, costs and charges, with interest for the same, at the rate of twelve per cent. per annum ; and upon payment or tender of payment as aforesaid such sale shall be void. And no deed shall be given in pursuance of any such sale, until the time of redemption shall have expired.(*a*)

Supervisors to keep accounts of taxes due.

Collectors to account month-ly.

SEC. 14. *And be it further enacted,* That the supervisors of the respective districts, shall keep true and exact accounts of all taxes due and payable in each collection district, and shall charge the amount thereof to the collectors of such districts respectively. And the said collectors shall, at the expiration of every month after they shall, respectively, commence their collections, in manner aforesaid, render to the supervisor of the district, or the inspector of the survey within which the said collections shall, respectively, be made, a full and true account of the collections made by them, respectively, within the month, and pay over to the said supervisor or inspector, the monies by them respectively collected within the said term. And if any such collector shall fail or neglect to account and pay over, as aforesaid, at any of the periods above prescribed, such collector shall forfeit and pay three hundred dollars, to be recovered to the use of the United States, with costs of suit, in any court having competent jurisdiction. And where any monies shall have been paid, as aforesaid, to the inspector of a survey, by any collector, the receipt of such inspector shall be allowed to such collector, in the final settlement of his accounts with the supervisor of the district.

Collectors to complete their duty and pay over the money in one year and one month.

How the payment shall be enforced.

SEC. 15. *And be it further enacted,* That each of the said collectors shall complete the collection of all sums assigned to him, for collection, as aforesaid, and shall account for, and pay over the same to the supervisor of the district, within one year and one month from and after the time when the said tax shall have become due and payable, in manner aforesaid ; and if any collector shall fail so to collect, account and pay over, it shall be the duty of the supervisor of the district, and he is hereby authorized and required to issue a warrant of distress against such delinquent collector and his sureties, directed to the marshal of the district, therein expressing the amount of the taxes imposed on the district of such collector, and the sums, if any, which have been paid ; and the said marshal shall himself, or by his deputy, immediately proceed to levy and collect the sum which may remain due, by distress and sale of the goods and chattels, or any personal effects of the delinquent collector ; and for want of goods, chattels or effects, aforesaid, sufficient to satisfy the said warrant, the same may be levied on the person of the collector, who may be committed to prison, there to remain, until discharged in due course of law. And furthermore, notwithstanding the commitment of the collector to prison, as aforesaid, or if he abscond, and goods, chattels and effects cannot be found, sufficient to satisfy the said warrant, the said marshal, or his deputy, shall and may proceed to levy and collect the sum which may remain due, by distress and sale of the goods and chattels, or any personal effects, of the surety or sureties of the delinquent collector.

Lien upon the real estate of collectors.

SEC. 16. *And be it further enacted,* That the amount of the sums committed to any collector, for collection as aforesaid, shall, and the same are hereby declared to be a lien upon the lands and real estate of such collector, and his sureties, until the same shall be discharged, according to law ; and for want of goods and chattels, or other personal effects of such collector, or his sureties, sufficient to satisfy any warrant of distress issued pursuant to the preceding section of this act, the lands and real estate of such collector, and his sureties, or so much thereof as may be necessary for satisfying the said warrant, after being advertised for at least three weeks, in not less than three public places in the collection district, and in one newspaper printed in the county, if any there be, prior to the proposed time of sale, may and shall be sold by the marshal or his deputy; and for all lands and real estate sold, in pursuance of the authority aforesaid, the conveyances of the marshals, or their deputies, executed in due form of law, shall afford a valid title against all persons claiming under the delinquent collectors, or their sureties, aforesaid; and all monies that may remain of the proceeds of such sale, after satisfying the said warrant of distress, and paying the reasonable costs and charges of sale, shall be returned to the proprietor of the lands or real estate sold as aforesaid.

Sec. 17. *And be it further enacted,* That it shall be lawful for the supervisors of the respective districts, at any time, for good and sufficient cause, to dismiss or discharge each or any collector from office, and to commit the collection of any part of the said tax remaining uncollected, to a new collector; and immediately upon such dismission, and after a notification thereof, in at least two public places in the collection district, by the supervisor, or the surveyor of the revenue for the district, on his behalf, the powers of the collector so dismissed, shall cease and terminate; and if any collector, so dismissed, shall wilfully refuse or neglect to surrender his collection list, and to render a true account of all monies collected, and to pay over the same, according to the directions of the supervisor, each and every such collector shall forfeit and pay a sum not exceeding four thousand dollars, with costs of suit, to be recovered to the use of the United States, in any court having competent jurisdiction: *Provided,* that nothing herein contained shall be construed to impair the responsibility of any collector, or his sureties, arising under the foregoing provisions of this act. *[Collectors may be dismissed by the supervisors.]*

Sec. 18. *And be it further enacted,* That each and every collector, who shall exercise, or be guilty of any extortion or oppression, under colour of this act, or shall demand other or greater sums than shall be authorized by law, shall be liable to pay a sum not exceeding three hundred dollars; to be recovered by and for the use of the party injured, with costs of suit, in any court having competent jurisdiction; and each and every collector shall, if required, give receipts for all sums by them collected and retained, in pursuance of this act. *[Penalty on collectors guilty of extortion, &c. They shall give receipts.]*

Sec. 19. *And be it further enacted,* That for collecting the said tax, there shall be allowed and paid, the following sums, and no more, to be retained by the several officers herein after mentioned, in the final settlement of their accounts, respectively; that is to say:—To each supervisor, one half per centum, on the whole amount of the monies by him received and accounted for, under and by virtue of this act;—to every inspector, one fourth per centum, on the whole amount of the monies to be by him received and accounted for, as aforesaid; and to every collector, five per centum, on the whole amount of the monies by him to be received and accounted for, as aforesaid: *Provided,* that no collector shall receive the said allowance, for, or in respect to any sum for which a warrant of distress shall have been issued by him; and *provided also,* that no collector who shall refuse or neglect to render, according to this act, any monthy account of monies by him received, as aforesaid, or to pay over the same, as is hereby directed, shall be entitled to, or receive the said allowance, upon all or any of the monies by him collected, within the month for which he shall so refuse or neglect to account and pay over, as aforesaid. *[Compensation for collection.]*

Sec. 20. *And be it further enacted,* That there shall be allowed to the surveyors of the revenue, respectively, to be paid by the supervisors, respectively, and exhibited in their accounts, as part of the charge of the said collection, for preparing collection lists, and computing the taxes payable by each individual, at the rate of one dollar for every hundred taxables contained in any such list.

Separate accounts to be kept at the treasury of monies received by virtue of this act.

SEC. 21. *And be it further enacted,* That a separate account shall be kept at the treasury of the United States of all monies to be collected and received by virtue of this act; distinguishing the several amounts received from dwelling-houses, from slaves, and from lands, within each state, and also distinguishing the amount received in each state from each separate description of dwelling-houses, paying the same rate per centum.

APPROVED, July 14, 1798.

The Direct Tax Act of 1813

STATUTE I.

July 22, 1813.

CHAP. XVI.—*An Act for the assessment and collection of direct taxes and internal duties.(a)*

[Repealed.] Act of January 9, 1815, ch. 21, sect. 2.

Be it enacted by the Senate and House of Representatives of the United States of America in Congress assembled, That for the purpose of assessing and collecting direct taxes and internal duties, there shall be, and are hereby designated and established the following collection districts, to wit:

Collection districts. New Hampshire.

The state of New Hampshire shall contain five collection districts, as follow: The first district shall consist of the county of Rockingham; the second of the county of Strafford; the third of the county of Hillsborough; the fourth of the county of Cheshire; and the fifth of the counties of Grafton and Coos.

Massachusetts.

The state of Massachusetts shall contain eighteen collection districts, as follow: The first district shall consist of the county of Washington; the second of the county of Hancock; the third of the county of Lincoln; the fourth of the county of Kennebec; the fifth of the county of Somerset; the sixth of the county of Oxford; the seventh of the county of Cumberland; the eighth of the county of York; the ninth of the county of Essex; the tenth of the county of Middlesex; the eleventh of the county of Suffolk; the twelfth of the county of Norfolk; the thirteenth of the county of Plymouth; the fourteenth of the county of Bristol; the fifteenth of the counties of Barnstable, Dukes, and Nantucket; the sixteenth of the county of Worcester; the seventeenth of the counties of Hampshire, Franklin, and Hampden; and the eighteenth of the county of Berkshire.

Vermont.

The state of Vermont shall contain six collection districts, as follow: The first shall consist of the counties of Bennington and Rutland; the second of the county of Windham; the third of the counties of Windsor and Orange; the fourth of the counties of Addison and Chittenden; the fifth of the counties of Franklin and Grand Isle; and the sixth of the counties of Caledonia, Essex, and Orleans.

The aforesaid counties, comprised in the said districts contained in the state of Vermont, shall be taken to comprehend such territory as was included in the said counties respectively, prior to the formation of the county of Jefferson in said state.

The state of Rhode Island shall contain three collection districts, as follow: The first shall consist of the counties of Newport and Bristol; the second of the county of Providence; and the third of the counties of Washington and Kent.

Rhode Island.

,The state of Connecticut shall contain seven collection districts, as follow: The first shall consist of the county of Litchfield; the second of the county of Fairfield; the third of the county of New Haven; the fourth of the county of Harford; the fifth of the county of New London; the sixth of the county of Middlesex; and the seventh of the counties of Windham and Tolland.

Connecticut.

The state of New York shall contain twenty-eight collection districts, as follow: The first shall consist of the counties of Suffolk, Queens, and Kings; the second of the city and county of New York; the third of the county of Westchester; the fourth of Duchess county; the fifth of the counties of Orange and Rockland; the sixth of the counties of Ulster and Sullivan; the seventh of the county of Schoharie; the eighth of the county of Columbia; the ninth of the county of Rensselaer; the tenth of the county of Washington; the eleventh of the county of Saratoga; the twelfth of the counties of Essex, Clinton, and Franklin; the thirteenth of the counties of Albany and Schenectady; the fourteenth of the county of Montgomery; the fifteenth of the county of Herkimer; the sixteenth of the county of Oneida; the seventeenth of the counties of Lewis, Jefferson, and St. Lawrence; the eighteenth of the county of Otsego; the nineteenth of the county of Chenango; the twentieth of the county of Madison; the twenty-first of the counties of Tioga, Broome, and Steuben; the twenty-second of the counties of Onandago and Cortland; the twenty-third of the counties of Cayuga and Seneca; the twenty-fourth of the county of Ontario; the twenty-fifth of the counties of Gennessee, Niagara, Chautaque, Cataragus, and Allegheny; the twenty-sixth of the county of Richmond; the twenty-seventh of the county of Greene; and the twenty-eighth of the county of Delaware.

New York.

Collection districts.

SEC. 2. *And be it further enacted,* That one collector and one principal assessor shall be appointed for each of the said collection districts, who shall be a respectable freeholder and reside within the same; and if the appointment of the said collectors or any of them, shall not be made during the present session of Congress, the President of the United States shall be, and is hereby empowered to make such appointment during the recess of the Senate, by granting commissions, which shall expire at the end of their next session.

Collector and a principal assessor to be appointed for each.

Qualifications.

SEC. 3. *And be it further enacted,* That each of the principal assessors shall divide his district into a convenient number of assessment districts, within each of which he shall appoint one respectable freeholder to be assistant assessor: *Provided,* That the Secretary of the Treasury shall be, and hereby is authorized to reduce the number of assessment districts in any collection district in any state, if the number shall appear to him to be too great; and each assessor so appointed, and accepting the appointment, shall, before he enters on the duties of his appointment, take and subscribe, before some competent magistrate, or some collector to be appointed by this act (who is hereby empowered to administer the same) the following oath or affirmation, to wit: " I, A. B. do swear or affirm (as the case may be) that I will, to the best of my knowledge, skill, and judgment, diligently and faithfully execute the office and duties of assessor for (naming the assessment district) without favour or partiality, and that I will do equal right and justice, in every

Districts to be divided by the principal assessor.

Proviso, that the Secretary of the Treasury may reduce the number of assessment districts.

Oaths and affirmation of the assessors.

case in which I shall act as assessor." And a certificate of such oath or affirmation shall be delivered to the collector of the district for which such assessor shall be appointed; and every assessor, acting in the said office, without having taken the said oath or affirmation, shall forfeit and pay one hundred dollars, one moiety to the use of the United States, and the other to him who shall first sue for the same, to be recovered with costs of suit, in any court having competent jurisdiction.

Secretary of Treasury to establish necessary regulations.

SEC. 4. *And be it further enacted,* That the Secretary of the Treasury shall establish regulations suitable and necessary for carrying this act into effect; which regulations shall be binding on each assessor in the performance of the duties enjoined by or under this act; and also frame instructions for the said assessors, pursuant to which instructions, and whenever a direct tax shall be laid by the authority of the United States, the said principal assessors shall, respectively, on such day as may be fixed by law laying such a tax, direct and cause the several assistant assessors in the district, to inquire after and concerning all lands, lots of ground with their improvements, dwelling houses and slaves, made liable to taxation, under any direct tax so laid by the authority of the United States, by reference as well to any lists of assessment or collection taken under the laws of the respective states, as to any other records or documents, and by all other lawful ways and means, and to value and enumerate the said objects of taxation in the manner prescribed by this act, and in conformity with the regulations and instructions above mentioned.

Direct taxes to be laid upon the value of lands, &c. &c.

SEC. 5. *And be it further enacted,* That whenever a direct tax shall be laid by the authority of the United States, the same shall be assessed and laid on the value of all lands, lots of ground with their improvements, dwelling houses and slaves, which several articles subject to taxation, shall be enumerated and valued by the respective assessors, at the rate each of them is worth in money: *Provided however,* That all property

Proviso.

of whatever kind, coming within any of the foregoing descriptions, and belonging to the United States or any state, or permanently or specially exempted from taxation by the laws of the state wherein the same may be situated, shall be exempted from the aforesaid enumeration and valuation, and from the direct tax aforesaid.

Lists of taxable property to be delivered to assistant assessors.

SEC. 6. *And be it further enacted,* That the respective assistant assessors shall, immediately after being required as aforesaid by the principal assessors, proceed through every part of their respective districts, and shall require all persons owning, possessing, or having the care or management of any lands, lots of ground, dwelling houses or slaves, lying and being within the collection district where they reside, and liable to the direct tax as aforesaid, to deliver written lists of the same, which lists shall be made in such manner as may be directed by the principal assessor, and as far as practicable, conformably to those which may be required for the same purpose, under the authority of the respective states.

Assessors may write the lists upon the information of the persons to be taxed.

SEC. 7. *And be it further enacted,* That if any person as aforesaid, shall not be prepared to exhibit a written list when required, and shall consent to disclose the particulars of any and all the lands, lots of ground with their improvements, dwelling houses and slaves, taxable as aforesaid, then, and in such case, it shall be the duty of the officer to make such list, which being distinctly read and consented to, shall be received as the list of such person.

Penalties for giving in fraudulent lists.

SEC. 8. *And be it further enacted,* That if any such person shall deliver or disclose to any assessor appointed in pursuance of this act, and requiring a list or lists as aforesaid, any false or fraudulent list, with intent to defeat or evade the valuation or enumeration hereby intended to be made, such person so offending, and being thereof convicted before any court having competent jurisdiction, shall be fined in a sum not exceeding five hundred dollars, nor less than one hundred dollars, at the discretion of the court, and shall pay all costs and charges of prosecution ; and the valuation and enumeration required by this act, shall, in all such cases, be made as aforesaid upon lists according to the form above described, to be made out by the assessors respectively, which lists the said assessors are hereby authorized and required to make, according to the best information they can obtain, and for the purpose of making which they are hereby authorized to enter into and upon all and singular the premises respectively ; and from the valuation and enumeration so made, there shall be no appeal.

SEC. 9. *And be it further enacted,* That in case any person shall be absent from his place of residence, at the time an assessor shall call to receive the list of such person, it shall be the duty of such assessor to leave at the house or place of residence of such person, a written note or memorandum, requiring him to present to such assessor, the list or lists required by this act, within ten days from the date of such note or memorandum.

Absentees to be required in writing to furnish lists.

SEC. 10. *And be it further enacted,* That if any person, on being notified or required as aforesaid, shall refuse or neglect to give such list or lists as aforesaid, within the time required by this act, it shall be the duty of the assessor for the assessment district, within which such person shall reside, and he is hereby authorized and required to enter into, and upon the lands, dwelling houses and premises, if it be necessary, of such person so refusing or neglecting, and to make, according to the best information which he can obtain, and on his own view and information, such lists of the lands, lots of ground with their improvements, dwelling houses and slaves, owned, possessed or under the care or management of such person, as are required by this act; which lists, so made, and subscribed by such assessor, shall be taken and reputed as good and sufficient lists of the persons and property for which such person is to be taxed, for the purposes of this act; and the person so failing or neglecting, unless in case of sickness or absence from home, shall moreover forfeit and pay the sum of one hundred dollars, to be recovered for the use of the United States, with costs of suit, in any court having competent jurisdiction.

Property to be valued by assessors where the parties refuse or neglect to give in lists.

SEC. 11. *And be it further enacted,* That whenever there shall be in any assessment district, any property, lands, lots of ground, dwelling houses or slaves, not owned or possessed by, or under the care or management of any person or persons within such district, and liable to be taxed as aforesaid, and no list of which shall be transmitted to the principal assessor in the manner provided by this act, it shall be the duty of the assessor for such district, and he is hereby authorized and required to enter into and upon the real estate, if it be necessary, and take such view thereof, and of the slaves of such absent persons, of which lists are required, and to make lists of the same according to the form prescribed by this act, which lists, being subscribed by the said assessor, shall be taken and reputed as good and sufficient lists of such property under and for the purposes of this act.

Property of persons not living in the districts may be assessed by assessors.

SEC. 12. *And be it further enacted,* That the owners, possessors, or persons having the care and management of lands, lots of ground, dwelling houses and slaves, not lying or being within the assessment district in which they reside, shall be permitted to make out and deliver the list thereof required by this act, (provided the assessment district in which the said objects of taxation lie or be is therein distinctly stated) at the time and in the manner prescribed to the assessor of the assessment district wherein such persons reside. And it shall be the duty of the assistant assessors in all such cases to transmit such lists at the time and in the manner prescribed for the transmission of the lists of the objects of taxation lying and being within their respective assessment districts to the principal assessor of their collection district, whose duty it shall

Property may be assessed in the districts where the owners reside, though the property is situated in other districts.

be to transmit them to the principal assessor of the collection district wherein the said objects of taxation shall lie or be, immediately after the receipt thereof, and the said lists shall be valid and sufficient for the purposes of this act; and on the delivery of every such list the person making and delivering the same, shall pay to the assistant assessor one dollar, one half whereof he shall retain to his own use, and the other half thereof he shall pay over to the principal assessor of his district for the use of such principal assessor.

Lists to be taken with reference to the day or days fixed by acts of Congress.

SEC. 13. *And be it further enacted,* That the lists aforesaid shall be taken with reference to the day fixed for that purpose by the act or acts of Congress laying the tax or taxes; and the assistant assessors respectively, after collecting the said lists, shall proceed to arrange the same, and to make two general lists, the first of which shall exhibit in alphabetical order, the names of all persons liable to pay a tax under the authority of the United States, residing within the assessment district, together with the value and assessment of the objects liable to taxation within such district for which each such person is liable to pay a direct tax and whenever so required by the principal assessor, the amount of direct tax, payable by each person on such objects under the state laws imposing direct taxes; and the second list shall exhibit in alphabetical order, the names of all persons residing out of the collection district, owners of property within the district, together with the value and assessment thereof, or amount of direct tax due thereon as aforesaid. The forms of the said general lists shall be devised and prescribed by the principal assessor, and lists taken according to such form shall be made out by the assistant assessors, and delivered to the principal assessor within sixty days after the day fixed by the act of Congress requiring lists from individuals. And if any assistant assessors shall fail to perform any duty assigned by this act, within the time prescribed by his precept, warrant, or other legal instructions, not being prevented therefrom by sickness or other unavoidable accident, every such assessor shall be discharged from office, and shall moreover forfeit and pay two hundred dollars, to be recovered for the use of the United States in any court having competent jurisdiction, with costs of suit.

Appeals may be had from the valuations fixed by assessors.

SEC. 14. *And be it further enacted,* That immediately after the valuations and enumerations shall have been completed as aforesaid, the principal assessor in each collection district shall, by advertisement in some public newspaper, if any such there be in such district, and by written notifications to be publicly posted up in at least four of the most public places in each assessment district, advertise all persons concerned of the place where the said lists, valuations, and enumerations may be seen and examined; and that during twenty-five days after the publication of the

Conditions.

notification as aforesaid, appeals will be received and determined by him relative to any erroneous or excessive valuations or enumerations by the assessor. And it shall be the duty of the principal assessor in each collection district, during twenty-five days after the date of public notifi-

Lists to be open for inspection.

cation to be made as aforesaid, to submit the proceedings of the assessors, and the lists by them received or taken as aforesaid, to the inspection of any or all persons who shall apply for that purpose; and the said principal assessors are hereby authorized to receive, hear, and determine, in a summary way, according to law and right, upon any and all appeals which may be exhibited against the proceedings of the said assessors: *Provided always,* That the question to be determined by the principal assessor, on an appeal respecting the valuation of property, shall be, whether the valuation complained of be or be not in a just relation or proportion to other valuations in the same assessment district. And all appeals to the principal assessors as aforesaid, shall be made in writing, and shall specify the particular cause, matter, or thing respecting which a decision is requested; and shall moreover state the ground or principle of inequality or error complained of; and the principal assessor shall have power to re-examine and equalise the valuations as shall appear just and equitable; but no valuation shall be increased without a previous notice of at least five days to the party interested to appear and object to the same, if he judge proper; which notice shall be given by a note in writing, to be left at the dwelling house of the party by such assessor as the principal assessor shall designate for that purpose.

SEC. 15. *And be it further enacted,* That whenever the quotas or portions of direct tax payable by the states respectively, shall be laid and apportioned by law on the counties or state districts, and such county or counties, state, district or districts, shall contain more than one assessment district, then and in that case, the principal assessor shall have power, on examination of the lists rendered by the assistant assessors according to the provisions of this act, to revise, adjust, and equalise the valuations of lands, lots of ground with their improvements, dwelling houses and slaves between such assessment districts, by deducting from or adding to either such a rate per centum as shall appear just and equitable.

SEC. 16. *And be it further enacted,* That immediately after hearing appeals, and adjusting and equalising the valuations according to the provisions of the preceding section, the principal assessors respectively shall make out lists containing the sums payable according to the assessments aforesaid, and according to the provisions of this act, upon every object of taxation within their respective districts, so as to raise upon the county or counties, state, district or districts, contained within the collection districts established by this act, for which they are respectively appointed, the quota of the direct tax laid by the United States, which shall have been imposed on such county or counties, state, district or districts, by the law laying such direct tax; which lists shall contain the name of each person residing within the collection district liable to pay the direct tax, or of the person residing within the said district and having the care or superintendence of property lying within the said district, which is liable to the payment of said tax, where such person or persons are known, together with the sum payable by each such person or persons aforesaid on account of the said direct tax as aforesaid. And where there is any property within any collection district, liable to the payment of the direct tax, not owned or occupied by or under the superintendence of any person resident therein, there shall be a separate list of such property, specifying the sums payable, and the names of the respective proprietors, where known.

SEC. 17. *And be it further enacted,* That each of the collectors to be appointed as aforesaid, shall, within sixty days from the day on which the principal assessors shall have received the lists from the assistant assessors, be furnished by the principal assessors with one or more of the lists prepared in conformity with the preceding sections by the principal assessor, signed and certified by such assessor. And each collector on receiving a list as aforesaid, shall subscribe three receipts, one of which shall be given on a full and correct copy of such list, which list and receipt shall remain with the principal assessor and be open to the inspection of any person who may apply to inspect the same; and the other two receipts shall be given on aggregate statements of the lists aforesaid, exhibiting the gross amount of taxes to be collected in each county or state district contained in the collection district; one of which aggregate statements and receipts shall be transmitted to the Secretary, and the other to the Comptroller of the Treasury.

[Marginal notes: Where counties contain more than one assessment district, then the requisite apportionments may be made. Lists of the property taxed to be made out. Assessors to furnish collectors with taxable lists.]

CHAP. XXXVII.—*An Act to lay and collect a direct tax within the United States.* (b)

Be it enacted by the Senate and House of Representatives of the United States of America in Congress assembled, That a direct tax of three millions of dollars shall be and is hereby laid upon the United States, and apportioned to the states respectively, in the manner following:

To the state of New Hampshire, ninety-six thousand seven hundred ninety-three dollars and thirty-seven cents.

To the state of Massachusetts, three hundred sixteen thousand two hundred seventy dollars and ninety-eight cents.

To the state of Rhode Island, thirty-four thousand seven hundred two dollars and eighteen cents.

To the state of Connecticut, one hundred eighteen thousand one hundred sixty-seven dollars and seventy-one cents.

To the state of Vermont, ninety-eight thousand three hundred forty-three dollars and seventy-one cents.

To the state of New York, four hundred thirty thousand one hundred forty-one dollars and sixty-two cents.

To the state of New Jersey, one hundred eight thousand eight hundred seventy-one dollars and eighty-three cents.

To the state of Pennsylvania, three hundred sixty-five thousand four hundred seventy-nine dollars and sixteen cents.

To the state of Delaware, thirty-two thousand forty-six dollars and twenty-five cents.

To the state of Maryland, one hundred fifty-one thousand six hundred twenty-three dollars and ninety-four cents.

To the state of Virginia, three hundred sixty-nine thousand eighteen dollars and forty-four cents.

To the state of Kentucky, one hundred sixty-eight thousand nine hundred twenty-eight dollars and seventy-six cents.

To the state of Ohio, one hundred four thousand one hundred fifty dollars and fourteen cents.

To the state of North Carolina, two hundred twenty thousand two hundred thirty-eight dollars and twenty-eight cents.

To the state of Tennessee, one hundred ten thousand eighty-six dollars and fifty-five cents.

To the state of South Carolina, one hundred fifty-one thousand nine hundred five dollars and forty-eight cents.

To the state of Georgia, ninety-four thousand nine hundred thirty-six dollars and forty-nine cents.

And to the state of Louisiana, twenty-eight thousand two hundred ninety-five dollars and eleven cents.

SEC. 2. *And be it further enacted,* That the quotas or portions payable by the states respectively shall be laid and apportioned on the several counties and state districts of the said states, as defined with respect to the boundaries of the said counties and state districts by an act, entitled "An act for the assessment and collection of direct taxes and internal duties," in the manner following:

In the State of New Hampshire.—On the county of Rockingham, twenty-five thousand two hundred ninety-eight dollars and eighty-nine cents.

On the county of Strafford, seventeen thousand six hundred ninety-eight dollars and sixty-six cents.

On the county of Hillsborough, twenty thousand two hundred nineteen dollars and sixteen cents.

On the county of Cheshire, nineteen thousand three hundred eighteen dollars and three cents.

On the county of Grafton, eleven thousand nine hundred ten dollars and forty-three cents.

On the county of Coos, two thousand three hundred forty-eight dollars and twenty cents.

In the State of Massachusetts.—On the county of Washington, two thousand six hundred twenty-three dollars and fifty-nine cents.

Massachusetts.

On the county of Hancock, nine thousand one hundred ninety dollars and sixty-five cents.

On the county of Lincoln, thirteen thousand six hundred seventy-two dollars.

On the county of Kennebeck, nine thousand six hundred ninety-six dollars and fifty-two cents.

On the county of Sommerset, three thousand five hundred four dollars and sixty-three cents.

On the county of Oxford, five thousand five hundred fifty-nine dollars and sixty cents.

On the county of Cumberland, fifteen thousand seven hundred eighty-seven dollars and ninety-nine cents.

On the county of York, fourteen thousand one hundred seventy-five dollars and three cents.

On the county of Essex, forty-one thousand six hundred forty-three dollars and one cent.

On the county of Middlesex, twenty-six thousand four hundred thirty-three dollars and forty-five cents.

On the county of Suffolk, forty-three thousand six hundred seventy-six dollars and eighty-three cents.

On the county of Norfolk, fifteen thousand six hundred twenty-nine dollars and eighty-eight cents.

On the county of Plymouth, fourteen thousand four hundred seventy-eight dollars and sixty-seven cents.

On the county of Bristol, fourteen thousand four hundred sixty-nine dollars and sixteen cents.

On the county of Barnstable, six thousand five hundred fifty-three dollars.

On the county of Dukes, one thousand one hundred seventy-three dollars and thirty-three cents.

On the county of Nantucket, four thousand nine hundred twenty-four dollars and thirty-one cents.

Sec. 3. *And be it further enacted,* That the amount of taxes which by virtue of the provisions of the act for the assessment and collection of direct taxes and internal duties, and of this act, should be laid and collected on non-residents' lands, so called, in the states of Kentucky and Ohio shall be ascertained and levied in the same manner and at the same rates respectively, as they were by the laws of those states in the year eighteen hundred and eleven; and lands in that year entered for taxation as non-residents' lands, which since that time may have been sold and transferred to residents, or where the owners of such lands may have become residents, and have had their lands entered for taxation, as residents, the tax on the same shall be collected as the tax on non-residents' lands: *Provided,* In all cases where sales and transfers shall have been made as aforesaid, or where non-residents have become residents, if they reside on the lands formerly entered as non-residents' lands, they shall have notice from the collector, as in other cases of residents. And if the amount thus laid, shall in either of the said states exceed or fall short of the amount fixed by this act as the quota to be laid on non-residents' lands in said states respectively, the difference shall, in the next ensuing direct tax laid by the authority of the United States, be deducted from or added to the quota of such state, as the case may be.

Taxes on lands of non-residents in Kentucky and Ohio.

Residents' lands transferred by non-residents, in certain cases how to be taxed

Proviso.

How the tax-
es are to be as-
sessed and col-
lected.
Act of July 22,
1813, ch. 16.
Additional
collectors in
Ohio.

SEC. 4. *And be it further enacted,* That the said tax shall be assessed and collected in the manner provided, and by the officers to be appointed under and by virtue of the act aforesaid, entitled "An act for the assessment and collection of direct taxes and internal duties:" *Provided,* That there shall be appointed in the state of Ohio six additional collectors, who shall collect the tax due from non-resident proprietors of lands in the said state, shall have the same districts assigned them by the Secretary of the Treasury, reside at the same places which are or may be designated for similar officers under the state authority, and in other respects shall be under the same rules and regulations, be subject to the same penalties and forfeitures as are provided by the above recited act.

Principal as-
sessors to issue
precepts to their
assistants to car-
ry this act into
effect—When.
States to vary,
if they please,
the district and
county appor-
tionments of
tax.

SEC. 5. *And be it further enacted,* That the principal assessors shall issue their precepts to the assistant assessors for the purpose of carrying into effect this act on the first day of February next, and the assessments shall have reference to that day.

SEC. 6. *And be it further enacted,* That each state may vary, by an act of its legislature, the respective quotas imposed by this act on its several counties or districts, so as more equally and equitably to apportion the tax hereby imposed; and the tax laid by this act shall be levied and collected in conformity with such alterations and variations, as if the same made part of this act, provided that an authenticated copy thereof be deposited in the office of the Secretary of the Treasury prior to the first of April next; in which case it shall be the duty of the said Secretary to give notice thereof to the proper principal collectors in such state.

States may pay
their respective
quotas and be
entitled to cer-
tain deductions.
Proviso.

Act of Janu-
ary 17, 1814, ch.
4.

SEC. 7. *And be it further enacted,* That each state may pay its quota into the Treasury of the United States, and thereon shall be entitled to a deduction of fifteen per centum if paid before the tenth day of February next, and of ten per centum if paid before the first day of May, in the same year: *Provided,* That notice of the intention of making such payment be given to the Secretary of the Treasury one month prior to such payment; and in case of payment so made he shall give notice thereof to the principal assessors and collectors of such state; and no further proceedings shall thereafter be had under this act in such state.

The Tax Act of 1861

Massachusetts.
To the State of Massachusetts, eight hundred and twenty-four thousand five hundred and eighty-one and one-third dollars.

Rhode Island
To the State of Rhode Island, one hundred and sixteen thousand nine hundred and sixty-three and two-third dollars.

Connecticut.
To the State of Connecticut, three hundred and eight thousand two hundred and fourteen dollars.

New York.
To the State of New York, two million six hundred and three thousand nine hundred and eighteen and two-third dollars.

New Jersey.
To the State of New Jersey, four hundred and fifty thousand one hundred and thirty-four dollars.

Pennsylvania.
To the State of Pennsylvania, one million nine hundred and forty-six thousand seven hundred nineteen and one-third dollars.

Delaware.
To the State of Delaware, seventy-four thousand six hundred and eighty-three and one-third dollars.

Maryland.
To the State of Maryland, four hundred and thirty-six thousand eight hundred and twenty-three and one-third dollars.

Virginia.
To the State of Virginia, nine hundred and thirty-seven thousand five hundred and fifty and two-third dollars.

North Caroli-
na.
To the State of North Carolina, five hundred and seventy-six thousand one hundred and ninety-four and two-third dollars.

To the State of South Carolina, three hundred and sixty-three thousand five hundred and seventy and two-third dollars.

South Carolina.

To the State of Georgia, five hundred and eighty-four thousand three hundred and sixty-seven and one-third dollars.

Georgia.

To the State of Alabama, five hundred and twenty-nine thousand three hundred and thirteen and one-third dollars.

Alabama.

To the State of Mississippi, four hundred and thirteen thousand eighty-four and two-third dollars.

Mississippi.

SEC. 12. *And be it further enacted,* That the Secretary of the Treasury shall establish regulations suitable and necessary for carrying this act into effect; which regulations shall be binding on each assessor and his assistants in the performance of the duties enjoined by or under this act, and shall also frame instructions for the said assessors and their assistants; pursuant to which instructions the said assessors shall, on the first day of March next, direct and cause the several assistant assessors in the district to inquire after and concerning all lands, lots of ground, with their improvements, buildings, and dwelling-houses, made liable to taxation under this act by reference as well to any lists of assessment or collection taken under the laws of the respective States, as to any other records or documents, and by all other lawful ways and means, and to value and enumerate the said objects of taxation in the manner prescribed by this act, and in conformity with the regulations and instructions above mentioned.

Secretary of Treasury to establish regulations under this act, and frame instructions.

Assessors and assistants to follow them.

SEC. 22. *And be it further enacted,* That immediately after the valuations and enumerations shall have been completed as aforesaid, the assessor in each collection district shall, by advertisement in some public newspaper, if any there be in such district, and by written notifications to be publicly posted up in at least four of the most public places in each collection district, advertise all persons concerned of the place where the said lists, valuations, and enumerations may be seen and examined; and that during twenty-five days after the publication of the notifications, as aforesaid, appeals will be received and determined by him relative to any erroneous or excessive valuations or enumerations by the assessor. And it shall be the duty of the assessor in each collection district, during twenty-five days after the date of publication to be made as aforesaid, to submit the proceedings of the assistant assessors and the list by them received or taken as aforesaid to the inspection of any and all persons who shall apply for that purpose; and the said assessors are hereby authorized to receive, hear, and determine, in a summary way, according to law and right, upon any and all appeals which may be exhibited against the proceedings of the said assessors: *Provided always,* That it shall be the duty of said assessor to advertise and attend, not less than two successive days of the said twenty-five, at the court-house of each county within his collection district, there to receive and determine upon the appeals aforesaid: *And provided also,* That the question to be determined by the assessor, on

Notice to be given when lists, valuations, &c., are completed.

Assessors to submit proceedings of assistants to inspection, &c.

to hear and determine appeals.

an appeal respecting the valuation of property, shall be, whether the valuation complained of be or be not in a just relation or proportion to other valuations in the same collection district. And all appeals to the assessors, as aforesaid, shall be made in writing, and shall specify the particular cause, matter, or thing respecting which a decision is requested; and shall, moreover, state the ground or principle of inequality or error complained of. And the assessor shall have power to re-examine and equalize the valuations as shall appear just and equitable; but no valuation shall be increased without a previous notice, of at least five days, to the party interested, to appear and object to the same, if he judge proper; which notice shall be given by a note in writing, to be left at the dwelling-house of the party by such assessor or an assistant assessor.

How valuations are to be determined.

Appeals to be in writing, what to contain.

Valuations may be re-examined and equalized, not to be increased without notice, &c.

SEC. 30. *And be it further enacted,* That there shall be allowed and paid to the several assessors and assistant assessors, for their services under this act; to each assessor two dollars per day for every day employed in making the necessary arrangements and giving the necessary instructions to the assistant assessors for the valuation, and three dollars per day for every day employed in hearing appeals, revising valuations, and making out lists agreeably to the provisions of this act, and one dollar for every hundred taxable persons contained in the tax list, as delivered by him to said board of assessors; to each assistant assessor two dollars for every day actually employed in collecting lists and making valuations, the number of days necessary for that purpose to be certified by the assessor and approved by the commissioner of taxes, and one dollar for every hundred taxable persons contained in the tax lists, as completed and delivered by him to the assessor; to each of the assessors constituting the board of assessors, as aforesaid, for every day's actual attendance at said board, the sum of three dollars, and for travelling to and from the place designated by the Secretary of the Treasury, ten cents for each mile, by the most direct and usual route; and to each of the clerks of said board two dollars for every day's actual attendance thereon. And the said board of assessors, and said assessors, respectively, shall be allowed their necessary and reasonable charges for stationery and blank books used in the execution of their duties; and the compensation herein specified shall be in full for all expenses not otherwise particularly authorized, and shall be paid at the Treasury, and such amount as shall be required for such payment is hereby appropriated.

Allowed for stationery and blank books.

Penalty for taking false oath or affirmation. SEC. 47. *And be it further enacted,* That any person who shall be convicted of wilfully taking a false oath or affirmation in any of the cases in which an oath or affirmation is required to be taken by this act, shall be liable to the pains and penalties to which persons are liable for wilful and corrupt perjury, and shall, moreover, forfeit the sum of five hundred dollars.

Pay of collectors and deputies.

Commissions. SEC. 48. *And be it further enacted,* That there shall be allowed to the collectors appointed under this act, in full compensation for their services and that of their deputies in carrying this act into effect, a commission of four per centum upon the first hundred thousand dollars, one per centum upon the second one hundred thousand dollars, and one-half of one per centum upon all sums above two hundred thousand dollars; such commissions to be computed upon the amounts by them respectively paid over and accounted for under the instructions of the Treasury Department: *Provided,* That in no case shall such commissions exceed the sum of four thousand dollars for a principal officer and two thousand dollars for an assistant. And there shall be further allowed to each collector their necessary and reasonable charges for stationery and blank books used in the performance of their official duties, which, after being duly examined and certified by the commissioner of taxes, shall be paid out of the Treasury.

Proviso.

Allowance for stationery, blank books, &c.

＊ Income tax.
[Repealed, 1862, ch. 119, § 89. *Post,* p. 473.]

SEC. 49. *And be it further enacted,* That, from and after the first day of January next, there shall be levied, collected, and paid, upon the annual income of every person residing in the United States, whether such income is derived from any kind of property, or from any profession, trade, employment, or vocation carried on in the United States or elsewhere, or from any other source whatever, if such annual income exceeds the sum of eight hundred dollars, a tax of three per centum on the amount of such excess of such income above eight hundred dollars: *Provided,* That upon such portion of said income as shall be derived from interest upon treasury notes or other securities of the United States, there shall be levied, collected, and paid a tax of one and one

Excess over $800.
Proviso.

half per centum. Upon the income, rents, or dividends accruing upon any property, securities, or stocks owned in the United States by any citizen of the United States residing abroad, there shall be levied, collected, and paid a tax of five per centum, excepting that portion of said income derived from interest on treasury notes and other securities of the Government of the United States, which shall pay one and one half per centum. The tax herein provided shall be assessed upon the annual income of the persons hereinafter named for the year next preceding the time for assessing said tax, to wit, the year next preceding the first of January, eighteen hundred and sixty-two; and the said taxes, when so assessed and made public, shall become a lien on the property or other sources of said income for the amount of the same, with the interest and other expenses of collection until paid : *Provided*, That, in estimating said income, all national, state, or local taxes assessed upon the property, from which the income is derived, shall be first deducted.

Of what date to be assessed.

Lien.

Income, how to be estimated.

SEC. 50. *And be it further enacted*, That it shall be the duty of the President of the United States, and he is hereby authorized, by and with the advice and consent of the Senate, to appoint one principal assessor and one principal collector in each of the States and Territories of the United States, and in the District of Columbia, to assess and collect the internal duties or income tax imposed by this act, with authority in each of said officers to appoint so many assistants as the public service may require, to be approved by the Secretary of the Treasury. The said taxes to be assessed and collected under such regulations as the Secretary of the Treasury may prescribe. The said collectors, herein authorized to be appointed, shall give bonds, to the satisfaction of the Secretary of the Treasury, in such sums as he may prescribe, for the faithful performance of their respective duties. And the Secretary of the Treasury shall prescribe such reasonable compensation for the assessment and collection of said internal duties or income tax as may appear to him just and proper ; not, however, to exceed in any case the sum of two thousand five hundred dollars per annum for the principal officers herein referred to, and twelve hundred dollars per annum for an assistant. The assistant collectors herein provided shall give bonds to the satisfaction of the principal collector for the faithful performance of their duties. The Secretary of the Treasury is further authorized to select and appoint one or more depositaries in each State for the deposit and safe-keeping of the moneys arising from the taxes herein imposed when collected, and the receipt of the proper officer of such depository to the collector for the moneys deposited by him shall be the proper voucher for such collector in the settlement of his account at the Treasury Department. And he is further authorized and empowered to make such officer or depositary the disbursing agent of the Treasury for the payment of all interest due to the citizens of such State upon the treasury notes or other government securities issued by authority of law. And he shall also prescribe the forms of returns to be made to the department by all assessors and collectors appointed under the authority of this act. He shall also prescribe the form of oath or obligation to be taken by the several officers authorized or directed to be appointed and commissioned by the President under this act, before a competent magistrate duly authorized to administer oaths, and the form of the return to be made thereon to the Treasury Department.

Mode of assessing and collecting income tax.

[Repealed in part, 1862, ch. 119, § 89. Post, p. 473.]

Collector to give bond.

Pay.

Assistant-Collectors' bond.

Depositaries.

Depositaries to be disbursing agents.

Form of return.

of oath.

SEC. 51. *And be it further enacted*, That the tax herein imposed by the forty-ninth section of this act shall be due and payable on or before the thirtieth day of June, in the year eighteen hundred and sixty-two, and all sums due and unpaid at that day shall draw interest thereafter at the rate of six per centum per annum ; and if any person or persons

When income tax is payable.

[Repealed. 1862, ch. 119, § 89. Post, p. 473.]

Proceedings to enforce payment.

shall neglect or refuse to pay after due notice said tax assessed against him, her, or them, for the space of more than thirty days after the same is due and payable, it shall be lawful for any collector or assistant collector charged with the duty of collecting such tax, and they are hereby authorized, to levy the same on the visible property of any such person, or so much thereof as may be sufficient to pay such tax, with the interest due thereon, and the expenses incident to such levy and sale, first giving thirty days' public notice of the time and place of the sale thereof; and in case of the failure of any person or persons authorized to act as agent or agents for the collection of the rents or other income of any person residing abroad shall neglect or refuse to pay the tax assessed thereon (having had due notice) for more than thirty days after the thirtieth of June, eighteen hundred and sixty-two, the collector or his assistant, for the district where such property is located, or rents or income is payable, shall be and hereby is authorized to levy upon the property itself, and to sell the same, or so much thereof as may be necessary to pay the tax assessed, together with the interest and expenses incident to such levy and sale, first giving thirty days' public notice of the time and place of sale. And in all cases of the sale of property herein authorized, the conveyance by the officer authorized to make the sale, duly executed, shall give a valid title to the purchaser, whether the property sold be real or personal. And the several collectors and assistants appointed under the authority of this act may, if they find no property to satisfy the taxes assessed upon any person by authority of the forty-ninth section of this act, and which such person neglects to pay as hereinbefore provided, shall have power, and it shall be their duty, to examine under oath the person assessed under this act, or any other person, and may sell at public auction, after ten days' notice, any stock, bonds, or choses in action, belonging to said person, or so much thereof as will pay such tax and the expenses of such sale; and in case he refuses to testify, the said several collectors and assistants shall have power to arrest such person and commit him to prison, to be held in custody until the same shall be paid, with interest thereon, at the rate of six per centum per annum, from the time when the same was payable as aforesaid, and all fees and charges of such commitment and custody. And the place of custody shall in all cases be the same provided by law for the custody of persons committed for any cause by the authority of the United States, and the warrant of the collector, stating the cause of commitment, shall be sufficient authority to the proper officer for receiving and keeping such person in custody until the amount of said tax and interest, and all fees and the expense of such custody, shall have been fully paid and discharged; which fees and expenses shall be the same as are chargeable under the laws of the United States in other cases of commitment and custody. And it shall be the duty of such collector to pay the expenses of such custody, and the same, with his fees, shall be allowed on settlement of his accounts. And the person so committed shall have the same right to be discharged from such custody as may be allowed by the laws of the State or Territory, or the District of Columbia, where he is so held in custody, to persons committed under the laws of such State or Territory, or District of Columbia, for the non-payment of taxes, and in the manner provided by such laws; or he may be discharged at any time by order of the Secretary of the Treasury.

Levy.

Sale after notice.

Title under tax sale.

Examinations.

Sales of stocks, &c.

Penalty for refusing to testify.

Custody, place of,

fees and expense of.

Custody, discharge from.

If any State is in rebellion, when this act goes into operation, act to be executed, when, &c.

SEC. 52. *And be it further enacted*, That should any of the people of any of the States or Territories of the United States, or the District of Columbia be in actual rebellion against the authority of the Government of the United States at the time this act goes into operation, so that the laws of the United States cannot be executed therein, it shall be the duty of the President, and he is hereby authorized, to proceed to execute the provisions of this act within the limits of such State or Territory, or District of Columbia, so soon as the authority of the United States therein is re-established, and to collect the sums which would have been due from the persons residing or holding property or stocks therein, with the interest due, at the rate of six per centum per annum thereon until paid in the manner and under the regulations prescribed in the foregoing *in the foregoing* sections of this act.

SEC. 53. *And be it further enacted,* That any State or Territory and the District of Columbia may lawfully assume, assess, collect, and pay into the Treasury of the United States the direct tax, or its quota thereof, imposed by this act upon the State, Territory, or the District of Columbia, in its own way and manner, by and through its own officers, assessors, and collectors ; that it shall be lawful to use for this purpose the last or any subsequent valuation, list, or appraisal made by State or Territorial authority for the purpose of State or Territorial taxation therein, next preceding the date when this act takes effect, to make any laws or regulations for these purposes, to fix or change the compensation to officers, assessors, and collectors ; and any such State, Territory or District, which shall give notice by the Governor, or other proper officer thereof, to the Secretary of the Treasury of the United States, on or before the second Tuesday of February next, and in each succeeding year thereafter, of its intention to assume and pay, or to assess, collect, and pay into the Treasury of the United States, the direct tax imposed by this act, shall be entitled, in lieu of the compensation, pay per diem and per centage herein prescribed and allowed to assessors, assistant assessors, and collectors of the United States, to a deduction of fifteen per centum on the quota of direct tax apportioned to such State, Territory or the District of Columbia levied and collected by said State, Territory, and District of Columbia through its said officers : *Provided, however,* That the deduction shall only be made to apply to such part or parts of the same as shall have been actually paid into the Treasury of the United States on or before the last day of June in the year to which such payment relates, and a deduction of ten per centum to such part or parts of the same as shall have been actually paid into the Treasury of the United States on or before the last day of September in the year to which such payment relates, such year being regarded as commencing on the first day of April : *And provided further,* That whenever notice of the intention to make such payment by the State, or Territory and the District of Columbia shall have been given to the Secretary of the Treasury, in accordance with the foregoing provisions, no assessors, assistant assessors, or collectors, in any State, Territory, or District, so giving notice, shall be appointed, unless said State, Territory, or District shall be in default: *And provided, further,* That the amount of direct tax, apportioned to any State, Territory, or the District of Columbia, shall be liable to be paid and satisfied, in whole or in part, by the release of such State, Territory, or District, duly executed, to the United States, of any liquidated and determined claim of such State, Territory, or District, of equal amount against the United States : *Provided,* That, in case of such release, such State, Territory, or District shall be allowed the same abatement of the amount of such tax as would be allowed in case of payment of the same in money.

SEC. 54. *And be it further enacted,* That it shall be the duty of the collectors aforesaid in their respective districts, and they are hereby authorized, to collect the duties imposed by this act, and to prosecute for the recovery of the same, and for the recovery of any sum or sums which may be forfeited by virtue of this act ; and all fines, penalties, and forfeitures which shall be incurred by force of this act, shall and may be sued for and recovered in the name of the United States or of the collec-

Each State may collect and pay its quota of the direct tax in its own way.

Proceedings in such case.

1862, ch. 66. *Post,* p. 384.

Deduction in such case of 15 per cent.

To what to apply.

No assessors to be appointed in such case.

State may pay its tax by releasing claim against the United States. *Post,* p. 384. Proviso.

Duty of collectors to collect duties imposed by this act.

Fines and penalties, how recovered.

tor within whose district any such fine, penalty, or forfeiture shall have been incurred, by bill, plaint, or information; one moiety thereof to the use of the United States, and the other moiety thereof to the use of such collector.

Debts due from collector to the United States to be a lien on his real estate and that of his sureties.

SEC. 55. *And be it further enacted,* That the amount of all debts due to the United States by any collector, under this act, whether secured by bond or otherwise, shall and are hereby declared to be a lien upon the lands and real estate of such collector, and of his sureties, if he shall have given bond, from the time when suit shall be instituted for recovering the same; and, for want of goods and chattels and other personal effects of such collector or his sureties to satisfy any judgment which shall or may be recovered against them, respectively, such lands and real estate may be sold at public auction, after being advertised for at least three weeks in not less than three public papers within the collection district, and in one newspaper printed in the county, if any there be, at least six weeks prior to the time of sale; and for all lands or real estate sold in pursuance of the authority aforesaid, the conveyances of the marshals or their deputies, executed in due form of law, shall give a valid title against all persons claiming under such collector or his sureties, respectively.

Office of commissioner of taxes created.

SEC. 56. *And be it further enacted,* That, for superintending the collection of the direct tax and internal duties or income tax laid by this act, an officer is hereby authorized in the Treasury Department, to be called "Commissioner of Taxes," who shall be charged, under the direction of the Secretary, with preparing all the forms necessary for the assessment and collection of the tax and duties aforesaid, with preparing, signing, and distributing all such licenses as are required, and with the general superintendence of all the officers employed in assessing and collecting said tax and duties; said commissioner shall be appointed by the President, upon the nomination of the Secretary of the Treasury, and he shall receive an

Authority, duty, salary.

annual salary of three thousand dollars. The Secretary of the Treasury may assign the necessary clerks to the office of said commissioner, whose

Clerks.

aggregate salaries shall not exceed six thousand dollars per annum, and the amount required to pay the salaries of said commissioner and clerks is hereby appropriated.

If a collector is sick, deputy may act, &c.

SEC. 57. *And be it further enacted,* That in case of the sickness or temporary disability of a collector to discharge such of his duties as cannot, under existing laws, be discharged by a deputy, they may be devolved by him upon a deputy: *Provided,* Information thereof be immediately communicated to the Secretary of the Treasury, and shall not be disapproved by him: *And provided,* That the responsibility of the collector or his sureties to the United States shall not be thereby affected or impaired.

If collector dies, resigns, &c., who to act in his place.

SEC. 58. *And be it further enacted,* That in case a collector shall die, resign, or be removed, the deputy of such collector longest in service at the time immediately preceding, who shall have been longest employed by him, may and shall, until a successor shall be appointed, discharge all the duties of said collector, and for whose conduct, in case of the death of the collector, his estate shall be responsible to the United States.

APPROVED, August 5, 1861.

APPENDIX D

Brief Supporting Contention That Wages Are Not Income

The following memorandum was submitted in both of my trials for willful failure to file income tax returns. It was denied by both Judge T. F. Gilroy Daly and Chief Judge T. Emmet Clarie without a governmental answer and without affording me oral arguments as requested so *both* "judges" **had to know I was innocent** on this *one* issue alone, yet both fined me and sentenced me to jail.

IN THE UNITED STATES DISTRICT COURT FOR THE

DISTRICT OF CONNECTICUT

BRIDGEPORT DIVISION

UNITED STATES OF AMERICA
Plaintiff

v.   Criminal Number B 78 - 8

IRWIN A. SCHIFF
Defendant

**MEMORANDUM IN SUPPORT OF MOTION TO DISMISS
BECAUSE DEFENDANT'S WAGES
ARE NOT SUBJECT TO TAX UNDER 16TH AMENDMENT
AND/OR INTERNAL REVENUE CODE**

Comes now the Defendant, Irwin A. Schiff, and in support of his Motion to Dismiss Because Defendant's Wages are not Subject to Tax under 16th Amendment and/or Internal Revenue Code, would respectfully point out the following:

I

PLAINTIFF IS ATTEMPTING TO LEVY A DIRECT TAX ON DEFENDANT'S WAGES

That the Defendant nor any of his personal property is subject to a direct tax under the guise of an "income" tax is amply and irrefutably supported by the following case law:

In *Pollock vs Farmers' Loan & Trust Co.* 157 U S 429 (1894), the Supreme Court held the Income Tax Law of 1894 invalid on the grounds that Congress had, in fact, levied a direct tax on property without apportionment by population as mandated by the Constitution. In its decision, the Court clearly defined the constitutional differences between direct and indirect taxes while citing previous holdings of the Court, on page 557,

"Thus, in the matter of taxation, the Constitution recognizes the two great classes of direct and indirect taxes, and lays down two rules by which their imposition *must be governed,* namely: The rule of *apportionment* as to *direct* taxes, and the rule of *uniformity* as to *duties, imposts,* and *excises.*

The rule of uniformity was not prescribed to the exercise of the power granted by the first paragraph of section eight, to lay and collect taxes, because the rule of apportionment as to taxes had already been laid down in the third paragraph of the second section.

And this view was expressed by Mr. Chief Justice Chase in *The License Tax Cases,* 5 Wall. 462, 471, when he said:

'It is true that the power of Congress to tax is a very extensive power. It is given in the Constitution, with only *one* exception and only *two qualifications.* Congress cannot tax exports, and it must impose direct taxes by the rule of apportionment, and indirect taxes by the rule of uniformity. Thus, limited, and thus only, it reaches every subject, and may be exercised at discretion.'

And although there have been from time to time intimations that there might be some tax which was not a direct tax nor included under the words 'duties, imposts and excises,' *such a tax for more than one hundred years of national existence has as yet remained undiscovered,* not withstanding the stress of particular circumstances has invited thorough investigation into sources of revenue." (Emphasis added)

Thus the Court should take judicial notice of the fact that *direct taxes* must always be levied by *apportionment* by population while *in-*

direct taxes must always be levied on the basis of geographic *uniformity*. For the practical and operational differences between *direct* and *indirect* taxes, the Court in *Pollock* explained, page 558,

> "Ordinarily all taxes paid primarily by persons who can *shift the burden* upon some one else, or who are under *no legal compulsion to pay them*, are considered *indirect* taxes; but a tax upon property holders in respect of their estates, whether real or *personal*, or of the income yielded by such estates, and the payment of which cannot be avoided, are direct taxes." (Emphasis added)

Thus, since the Defendant cannot shift the burden of the tax the Plaintiff is attempting to impose, the tax amounts to *a direct tax on personal property* and since it is not apportioned, it is barred by the Constitution.

In its effort to comprehensively cover the subject of direct versus indirect taxes and how they must legally be treated given their constitutional restrictions, the Court thought it instructive, and the Defendant asks that the Court take judicial notice, to point out, page 572, that Hamilton regarded taxes on *personal property* as being a *direct tax* and further noted that income taxes "have been always classed by the law of Great Britain as direct taxes."

II

POLLOCK CASE NOT OVERTURNED BY THE SIXTEENTH AMENDMENT COURT'S REASONING AND FINDINGS STILL APPLICABLE

Pollock was not overturned by the passage of the Sixteenth Amendment, *Brushaber vs Union Pacific Railroad* 240 US 1 (1915), on page 19,

> ". . . the Amendment [Sixteenth] contains nothing repudiating or challenging the ruling in the *Pollock Case*. . ."

Thus the Court must recognize that in the case at bar the government is attempting to levy what amounts to a *direct tax* (without apportionment) on the *personal property* of the Defendant — this being the alleged 31,200 of "notes" that the Defendant presumably received in exchange for his labor on the specious grounds that such "property," in reality, constitutes "income" within the meaning of the Sixteenth Amendment as interpreted by the courts. Such an attempt is clearly contradictory to the Constitution and the prevailing case law.

In passing it should also be noted that since these "notes" are the non-redeemable, non-interest bearing "notes" of a private banking syndicate fraudulently impressed with a "legal tender" endorsement; they are not taxable on other grounds but these other grounds are immaterial to the point here at issue. In any case, these notes, though being of an indeterminate value and illegal nature, still constitute the personal property belonging to the Defendant and, as such, are not subject to direct taxation.

III

SIXTEENTH AMENDMENT GAVE THE GOVERNMENT NO *NEW* TAXING POWER (SUCH AS THE RIGHT TO LEVY A DIRECT TAX ON PERSONALTY WITHOUT APPORTIONMENT) BUT MERELY REMOVED A TAX, BASED UPON INCOME, FROM THE CLASSIFICATION OF A DIRECT TAX (BY DISREGARDING THE SOURCE) TO THE CLASSIFICATION OF AN INDIRECT TAX OR EXCISE

Contrary to popular belief, the Sixteenth Amendment did not give the Federal government any *new* taxing power, such as the power to levy a *direct tax on personal property without apportionment.* This was clearly stated in *Brushaber vs Union Pacific Railroad, supra,* wherein the court declared, on page 12, that such an erroneous interpretation,

". . . if acceded to, would cause one provision of the Constitution *to destroy another*; that is, they would result in bringing the provisions of the Amendment exempting a direct tax from apportionment into *irreconcilable conflict* with the general requirement that all direct taxes be apportioned." (Emphasis added)

Continuing further, on page 12, the Court observed that such an erroneous interpretation would, in fact, create a new type of tax, one subject to neither *apportionment* nor *uniformity* and,

". . . thus it would come to pass that the result of the Amendment would be to authorize a particular direct tax not subject either to apportionment or to the rule of geographical uniformity, thus giving power to impose a different tax in one State or States than was levied in another State or States."

The Court further attempted to clarify the intent of the Sixteenth Amendment by holding that the Amendment, rather than creating or authorizing a new tax, one subject neither to apportionment nor uniformity, simply clarified that an "income" tax, as defined by the courts, was not a *direct* tax but an *indirect* or *excise tax* whose, on page 19,

". . . purpose was not to change the existing interpretation. . . [but to *prevent* a regard for the *sources* of income to] thereby. . . take an income tax out of the class of excises, duties and imposts and place it in the class of direct taxes."

And further the Court explained, on page 18, that

". . . the command of the Amendment that all income taxes shall not be subject to apportionment by a consideration of the *sources* from which the taxed income may be derived, forbids the application to such taxes of the rule applied in the *Pollock Case* by *which alone such taxes* were removed *from the great class of excises, duties and imposts* subject to the rule of uniformity and were placed under the other or direct class." (Emphasis added)

Also refer to the *Digest of U.S. Supreme Court Reports* (1970), Volume 8, Page 408, Entry F.

In holding the Revenue Act of 1913 to be constitutional and in conformity with the Sixteenth Amendment (since the court held in *Brushaber* that the Revenue Act was an *excise tax,* or indirect tax, and not a direct tax), the Court relied on *Flint v. Stone Tracy Co.* 220 US 108 (1910), page 21. The Court in *Flint v. Stone Tracy Co. supra,* had previously held that the corporation income tax in the Tariff Act of 1909 was not a *direct tax* on income, per se, but an *excise tax* and so it did not fall within the apportionment clause of the Constitution since it was a tax "on the privilege of doing business in a corporate capacity." The Court in this case held that,

"The Corporation Tax is not a direct tax within the enumeration provision of the Constitution, but is an impost or excise which Congress has power to impose under Article I, Section 8, Clause 1, of the Constitution."

To further clarify the nature of an excise tax, the court defined it as follows, on page 110,

"Excises are taxes laid upon the manufacture, sale or consumption of commodities within the country, upon licenses to pursue certain occupations and upon corporate privileges; the requirement to pay such taxes involves the exercise of the privilege and if business is not done in the manner described no tax is payable."

The court in this case pointed out that because the corporation tax was an excise tax, it did not have to be apportioned. The court further held that the tax laid under this statute *was not an income tax* but an *excise tax* levied on the *privilege* of doing business as a corporation with the amount of tax *measured by the income.* The Court emphatically stated that the Corporation "Income Tax" of 1909 was not in any sense an income tax but a true excise tax "levied on a *privilege*" with "income" being only the *measure* in determining the amount of the "privilege tax."

This interpretation was upheld by the Court in *Stratton's Independence Limited vs F. W. Howbert* 231 U.S. 399 (1913), wherein the Court stated, on page 414,

> "As has been repeatedly remarked, the corporation tax act of 1909 was not intended to be and is not, in any proper sense, an income tax law. This court had decided in the *Pollock Case* that the income tax law of 1894 amounted in effect to a *direct tax upon property,* and was invalid because not apportioned according to population as prescribed by the Constitution. The Act of 1909 avoided this difficulty by *imposing not an income tax,* but an excise tax upon the conduct of business in a corporate capacity, measuring, however, the amount of tax by the income of the corporation. . ." (Emphasis added)

The Court's holding in both *Brushaber* and *Stratton's* was consistent with *Stanton vs Baltic Mining Co.* 240 US 103 (1915), wherein the Court held, on page 112,

> ". . . the provisions of the Sixteenth Amendment *conferred no new power of taxation* but simply prohibited the previous complete and plenary power of income taxation possessed by Congress from the beginning from being taken *out* of the category of *indirect taxation* to which it inherently belonged and being placed in the category of *direct taxation* subject to apportionment. . ." (Emphasis added)

IV

GOVERNMENT'S TAXING POWER STILL LIMITED BY RESTRICTIONS OF ORIGINAL CONSTITUTION: AND IT CAN NOT BE EXTENDED BY LOOSE CONSTRUCTION OF SIXTEENTH AMDNEMENT

These fundamental holdings regarding the "income" tax were further delineated and sustained in the authoratative *Eisner vs Macomber* 252 US 189 (1919), wherein the Court held, on page 205,

> "The 16th Amendment must be construed in connection with the taxing clauses of the original Constitution and the effect attributed to them *before the Amendment was adopted.* In Income Tax Cases (*Pollock v. Farmers' Loan and Trust Co.*) 158 U.S. 601, 39 L.ed 1108, 15 Sup. Ct. Rep. 912, under the Act of August 27, 1894 (chap. 349, Section 27, 28 Stat. at L. 509, 553),. . ." (Emphasis added)

And further, on page 206,

> "A proper regard for its genesis, as well as its very clear language, requires also that this Amendment (16th) shall not be *extended by loose construction*, so as to *repeal or modify*, except as applied to income, those provisions of the Constitution that *require an apportionment* according to population for *direct taxes* upon property, real and *personal*. This limitation still has an appropriate and important function, and is not to be overridden by Congress or disregarded by the courts." (Emphasis added)

Also, in *Edwards vs Cuba Railroad Company* 268 US 628 (1925), on page 631,

> "The Sixteenth Amendment, like other laws, authorizing and imposing taxes, is to be taken as written, and is not to be extended beyond the meaning clearly indicated by the language used."

It can thus be seen that the "income" tax is, in reality, an *excise tax* and being an excise tax it can only be levied upon the *manufacture, sale* or *consumption* of a *commodity* or upon a *license* to pursue *certain occupations* or upon *corporate privileges,* with "income" being solely the measure of the excise tax so levied. In this respect it acts precisely like Federal inheritance taxes, wherein the government does not purport to tax the inherited property directly, but rather levies an *excise tax* on the *legatee's privilege* of acceding to the devised property — and measures the *amount* of that tax by the *value of the devised property*.

Therefore, unless the Plaintiff can show why, and on what basis, the Defendant or his property (the alleged 31,200 Federal Reserve "notes") are subject to an excise tax — the Plaintiff's efforts must *fail on this ground alone*.

V

NO BRANCH OF GOVERNMENT SAVE THE JUDICIAL HAS THE POWER TO DETERMINE WHAT CONSTITUTES "INCOME;" AND THE COURT HAS DECLARED THAT DEFENDANT'S "NOTES" DO NOT FALL WITHIN THE MEANING OF "INCOME"

The 31,200 of "notes" allegedly received by the Defendant do not even fall within the meaning of "income" as defined and interpreted by the Supreme Court; and the Defendant respectfully requests this Court to take judicial notice that *neither the legislative or executive branches of government have any power or authority to decide what is, or is not, "income."* That authority rests solely within the power of the Court and that the Supreme Court, in line with that authority, has determined what is "income" and has given to the word "income" a definitive meaning which has been consistently upheld before that court. Therefore, in the case at bar, this Court is not at liberty to give to the word "income" a meaning different from the one already established and sustained in numerous cases before that Court. Nor can this Court arbitrarily classify as "income" that which clearly falls outside the meaning of "income" as established by the Supreme Court.

VI

GOODS OR SERVICES RECEIVED IN EXCHANGE FOR PERSONAL LABOR (WAGES) FALL OUTSIDE THE LEGAL MEANING OF "INCOME;" WHILE "INCOME" IS SOLELY FOR THE PURPOSE OF MEASURING AN EXCISE TAX

It is clear, when one refers to the Congressional debates connected with the Revenue Act of 1913, that Congress did not know, nor did it presume to know, what the word "income" (as used in the Sixteenth Amendment) legally covered. For example, quoting from Page 3844 of Volume L of the Congressional Record, 63rd Congress, First Session, 1913, we note the following dialogue,

Mr. CUMMINS: It will be observed that here is an attempt, Mr. President, to define the meaning of the word "income," to describe its scope, to determine its effect. I reiterate that the attempt will be ineffective and may be exceedingly dangerous.

Great Britain might employ such words as these in modification or explanation or enlargement of the word "income," because Great Britain has no constitutional restriction upon her Parliament. A State might use these words with perfect propriety, because a State has the right to include whatever she likes within the meaning of the word "income"; but the Congress has no right to employ them, because the Congress can not affect the meaning of the word "income" by any legislation whatsoever. The people have granted us the power to levy a tax on incomes, and it will always be a judicial question as to whether a particular thing is income or whether it is principal.

Mr. LEWIS. Mr. President, knowing the Senator from Iowa to be an excellent lawyer, will he give me his views on this point: Does the Senator contend that the word "income," therefore, as stated in the Constitution, must be construed to mean what it meant and was understood to mean at the date of its adoption as part of the constitution?

Mr. CUMMINS. I do not so say. What I have said is, however, that it is not for Congress to interpret what it means; it is for the courts of the country to say, either at this time or at any other time, what it means. If it were within the power of Congress to enlarge the meaning of the word "income," it could, as I suggested a moment ago, obliterate all difference between income and principal, and obviously the people of this country did not intend to give to Congress the power to levy a direct tax upon all the property of this country without apportionment.

Mr. LEWIS. Then, assuming that the matter would have to be determined finally by the court, which concession we all must make, would the Senator's legal mind revert to the theory that the court, then, would have a right to define the word "income" to mean whatever was understood judicially by "income" at the date of the adoption of this act?

Mr. CUMMINS. I do not accept that at all, because it is entirely beyond the domain of Congress. In 1789, I believe, the people of this country gave Congress the power to regulate commerce among the States. It is not within the power of Congress to say what commerce is. "Commerce" may mean a very different thing now as compared with what it meant in 1789; it has broadened with the times; the instrumentalities have changed with the course of years; but Congress can not make a thing commerce. The court must declare whether a particular regulation is a regulation of commerce, and in so declaring it defines for the time being what commerce is.

Why, Mr. President, should Congress attempt to do more than is declared in the first section of the proposed bill? It is right; it is comprehensible; it embraces everything — no, I will withdraw that; it does not embrace the full power of Congress, because Congress can levy a tax upon gross incomes if it likes, it may diminsh the extent of its taxing power or not exercise it all; it may exclude certain things from taxing power that it might include; but it can not change the character of taxation; and when it is declared in the first lines of this bill that a tax is levied upon the entire net income of all the citizens of this country, we have exercised all the power we have. If we desire to limit ourselves to net income, we can not define "net income"; we can not say what shall be included in income and what shall not be included in income. We are only preparing ourselves for delay, for disappointment, and possible defeat if we endeavor to interpret the meaning of the word "income."

Mr. SHIVELY. Mr. President

The PRESIDING OFFICER (Mr. Chilton in the chair). Does the Senator from Iowa yield to the Senator from Indiana?

Mr. CUMMINS. I do.

Mr. SHIVELY. I can readily agree with the Senator that the courts will finally give a definition of "income"; but that does not prevent Congress from limiting the application of the word in legislation.

Mr. CUMMINS. Not at all. I have so said.

Mr. SHIVELY. If the Senator will observe the words "except as hereinafter provided" in the first subdivision of this section —

Mr. CUMMINS. I have not sought to strike out any part of the limitations save the gift, devise, bequest, or descent, and I do not think there is any man in America, were it not for what precedes those words, who would contend or could contend that a gift or devise or bequest of property or property coming to one by descent is income. I never heard of it being so construed; and it is not possible that it could be so construed. It would not have been put in there were it not for the attempted enlargement of the word "income" contained in the previous part of the paragraph.

Mr. WILLIAMS. How does the Senator think that is an attempt to enlarge it? Tell us specifically to what words the Senator refers.

Mr. CUMMINS. Mr. President, if it has not that effect, or attempted effect, it can have none. It is certainly not an attempt to limit or to restrict the meaning of the word "income"; and if it has not the effect or if it is not thought or if it was not in the mind of the person who drew it to enlarge the meaning of the word "income," then the draftsman of the bill has offended against the first principles of legislation by incorporating language that is absolutely meaningless.

Mr. WILLIAMS. Now, if the Senator will pardon me a moment —

The PRESIDING OFFICER. Does the Senator from Iowa yield to the Senator from Mississippi?

Mr. CUMMINS. I do.

Mr. WILLIAMS. It was not the intent there to enlarge or to stretch the meaning of the words "net income," which is the income referred to here, and not gross income at all.

Mr. CUMMINS. I have not said it was gross income.

Mr. WILLIAMS. The Congress in undertaking to specify what it proposes to tax does undertake neither to enlarge nor to restrict the meaning of the words "net income," but to define their meaning for the purposes of this bill, for the purposes of this taxation. It may be that a court might come to the conclusion that Congress had wrongfully defined the term. If so, the court will correct the definition, and if the court corrects the definition, then this bill will be to that extent altered or changed; but the contention is that this is a correct definition of the articles which, under a bill seeking to tax net incomes, will be taxed. The question I asked the Senator was in what respect he thinks that this definition enlarges the meaning of the words "net income" or restricts them, either?

Mr. CUMMINS. Mr. President, as I remarked before, if these words qualifying, modifying, and explanatory are not intended either to enlarge or to restrict, they are entirely useless. I think, however, with deference—

Mr. WILLIAMS. Does the Senator think it is useless in a tax bill to try to define the thing you propose to tax?

Mr. CUMMINS. Mr. President, I do think in this instance that it is worse than useless; I think it is dangerous, and I will proceed to show why.

Mr. SIMMONS. Mr. President —

The VICE PRESIDENT. Does the Senator from Iowa yield to the Senator from North Carolina?

Mr. CUMMINS. I do.

Mr. SIMMONS. I readily agree with the Senator in his contention that we have no authority to tax anything except income, and I readily agree with him that, in the last analysis, the court must decide what is income and what is not income; but before the court can get jurisdiction of that question, there must be a levy; there must be an assessment; there must be and attempt to collect. I can see no other way in which the court could possibly acquire jurisdiction. So that before the matter can ever reach the court there must be some one who will decide the question of what is "income."

VII

SUPREME COURT DEFINES "INCOME DERIVED FROM LABOR"

The supreme Court did determine the legal definition of "income." In *Stratton's Independence Limited vs. F. W. Howbert's, supra,* the plaintiff contended that, as a mining company, it sold only its ore, in essence its capital; and that the "income" tax amounted to a direct tax on capital which is barred by the Constitution. On this basis, the plaintiff argued that it was not subject to the Corporation Income Tax of 1909. In explaining why the Corporation "Income" Tax did apply to the plaintiff's profits from mining, the court explained, on page 415,

". . .when a company is digging pits, sinking shafts, tunneling, drifting, stoping, drilling, blasting, and hoisting ores, it is employing capital and *labor* in transmitting a part of the realty into personalty, and putting it into marketable form." (Emphasis added)

So the court held that such gains and profits were indeed taxable as "income" since the court defined "income" on page 415, as follows,

"'income' may be defined as the *gain derived from capital,* from *labor,* or from *both combined,* and here we have combined operations of capital and *labor*." (Emphasis added)

It is clear from this example that the court viewed *income derived from labor* as the gain or profit derived by the indirect *sale of labor* — which is not the same thing as property (wages) directly received in *exchange for one's own labor*— such as the 31,200 of bogus notes that the Plaintiff alleges the Defendant received in exchange for his personal labor.

In the definitive case of *Eisner vs Macomber supra,* the Supreme Court went to great lengths to clarify and codify this meaning of "income" and also to clarify the significance of the Sixteenth Amendment as it applied to the "income" tax statutes then being passed subsequent to its adoption. For example, on pages 206, 207, and 208,

> [206] "For the present purpose we require only a clear definition of the term "income," [207] as used in common speech, in order to determine its meaning in the Amendment; and, having formed also a correct judgment as to the nature of a stock dividend, we shall find it easy to decide the matter at issue.
>
> After examining dictionaries in common use (Bouvier's Law Dict.; Standard Dict.; Webster's Int. Dict.; Century Dict.;), we find little to add to the succinct definition adopted in two cases arising under the Corporation Tax Act of August 5, 1909 (36 Stat. at L. 11, chap. 6), (*Stratton's Independence v. Howbert*, 231 U.S. 399, 415, 58 L. ed. 285, 292, 34 Sup. Ct. Rep. 136; *Doyle v. Mitchell Bros. Co.* 247 U.S 179, 185, 621. ed. 1054, 1059, 38 Sup. Ct. Rep. 467): 'Income may be defined as the gain derived from capital, from labor, or from both combined,' provided it be understood to include profit gained through a sale or conversion of capital assets, to which it was applied in the Doyle Case (pp. 183, 185).
>
> Brief as it is, it indicated the characteristic and distinguishing attribute of income, essential for a correct solution of the present controversy. The government, although basing its argument upon the definition as quoted, placed chief emphasis upon the word "gain," which was extended to include a variety of meanings: while the significance of the next three words was either overlooked or misconceived, — 'derived-from-capital;' — 'the gain-derived-from-capital,' etc. Here we have the essential matter: not a gain accruing to capital, not a growth or increment of value in the investment; but a gain, a profit, something of exchangeable value proceeding from the property, severed from the capital, however invested or employed, and coming in, being 'derived,' that is, received or drawn by the recipient (the taxpayer) for his separate use, benefit, and disposal; that is income derived from property. Nothing else answers the description.
>
> The same fundamental conception is clearly set forth in the 16th Amendment — 'incomes, from whatever source derived,' — the essential thought being expressed [208] with a conciseness and lucidity entirely in harmony with the form and style of the Constitution."

Thus "gain-derived-from-labor" must be given the same meaning as "gain-derived-from-capital" and cannot be viewed differently — as if the words were to mean "the value of labor." "Income" attributed to labor is in every instance a "gain-derived-from-labor" — which is obviously not the same thing as the *mere exchange* of one's labor for a comparable amount of goods and services. Any "income" that the Plaintiff alleges was received by the Defendant as a result of labor must be "gain-derived-from-labor" and must fall within the meaning of *Stratton's, supra,* and *Eisner, supra,* and in the wording of *Eisner* it must be

". . . a gain, a *profit*, something of exchangeable value proceeding from the (labor), something *severed* from the (labor). . . That is income *derived* from (labor). . . Nothing else answers the description." (Emphasis added)

Since a "gain-from-labor" can only result when one sells the labor of others (clearly illustrated in *Stratton's, supra*) — or when one profitably invests the fruits of one's own labor (since such a gain can be "severed" from the value of the initial labor[1]) — and since no such condition is alleged to exist relative to the erzats notes the Defendant is alleged to have received, *no "income" can exist*. In short, what the Plaintiff is attempting to do is to impose a naked, direct tax on the person of the Defendant, on the unsupportable pretext that some bogus notes the Defendant allegedly received was a "profit-derived-from-labor" while, in reality, any dubious value these "notes" possess was received by the Defendant through an exchange of labor, without *gain* or *profit*. Thus the Plaintiff exhibits a flagrant contempt for the findings of the Supreme Court (and the rights of the Defendant) as evidenced by *Stratton's* and *Eisner,* and a host of cases (some previously cited and others I will cite).

The aforementioned meaning of "income-derived-from-labor" is the only meaning that can apply to an "income" tax on "labor" if such a "tax" is to be lawfully and logically reconciled with the restrictions placed in the Constitution relevant to direct and indirect taxes, as well as being reconciled with the interpretation given to the Sixteenth Amendment by the bedrock cases already cited. It should be judicially noted that these decisions (as well as others to be cited) were handed down by the court at a time when all of these Constitutional elements were legally and semantically clearer than they are today — since they were hammered out when the laws themselves were being passed.

It should also be judicially noted that with the passage of time and especially given the apparant blurring of Constitutional vision surrounding World War II, the import of these decisions was either overlooked or not understood. Thus the Federal government succeeded in changing the popular understanding of the word "income" so that property which could never be regarded as "income, " as initially defined by the Court, is today automatically assumed to be "income." This has enabled the Federal government to usurp taxing power in order to accommodate the gargantuan appetites of politicians who, in the words of Harry Hopkins, seek to "tax tax, spend spend, elect elect" as they sap the nation's economic and social vitality to gain public office and access to the public purse.

[1] I was in error here — such an "investment" is still not a "gain" from one's own labor as I mistakenly viewed it in 1978.

VIII

DEFENDANT'S WAGES NOT "INCOME" AS DEFINED BY SUPREME COURT

Numerous Supreme Court cases will substantiate that the Defendant had no "income" as defined by the Supreme Court. For example, *Merchants' Loan & Trust Company vs. Smietanka* 255 US 509 (1920), wherein the Court declared, on page 517,

> "The question is one of definition and the answer to it may be found in recent decisions of this court.
>
> The Corporation Excise Tax Act of August 5, 1909, c. 6, 36 Stat. 11, 112, was not an income tax law, but a definition of the word "income" was so necessary in its administration that in an early case it was formulated as 'the gain derived from capital, from labor, or from both combined'. *Stratton's Independence v. Howbert,* 231 U.S. 399, 415.
>
> This definition, frequently approved by this court, received an addition, in its latest income tax decision, which is especially significant in its application to such a case as we have here, so that it now reads: 'Income may be defined as the gain derived from capital, from labor, or from both combined,' provided it be understood to include profit through a sale or conversion of capital assets." *Eisner v. Macomber,* 252 U.S. 189, 207.

Pages 518 and 519:

> "It is obvious that these decisions in principle rule the case at bar if the word 'income' *has the same meaning in the Income Tax Act of 1913 that it had in the Corporation Excise Act of 1909,* and that it has the same scope of meaning was in effect decided in *Southern Pacific Co. v. Lowe,* 247 U.S. 330, 335, where it was assumed for the purposes of decision that there was no difference in its meaning as used in the Act of 1909 and in the Income Tax Act of 1913. *There can be no doubt that the word must be given the same meaning and content in the Income Tax Acts of 1916 and 1917 that it had in the Act of 1913.* When to this we add that in *Eisner v. Macomber, supra,* a case arising under the same Income Tax Act of 1916 which is here involved, the definition of 'income' which was applied was adopted from *Stratton's Independence v. Howbert, supra,* arising under the Corporation Excise Tax Act of 1909, with the addition that it should include 'profit gained through a sale or conversion of capital assets,' there would seem to be no room to doubt that the word must be given the *same meaning in all of the Income Tax Acts of Congress that was given to it in the Corporation Excise Tax Act* and that what *that meaning is has now become definitely settled by decisions of this court.*" (Emphasis added)

Thus again this Court must give to the word "income," in the instant case, the same meaning that it had in the Corporation Excise Tax

Act of 1909 — and since "income" in the Corporation Excise Tax Act of 1909 did not include property received in exchange-for-personal labor, wages, this Court cannot include property received in exchange for personal labor, wages, as coming within the constitutional meaning of "income." This again only substantiates the Defendant's prior contention regarding the meaning of "income."

Burnet vs Harmel, 287 US 103 (1932), on page 108,

". . . and before the 1921 Act this Court had indicated (see *Eisner v. Macomber,* 252 U.S. 189, 207, 64 L.ed. 521, 9 A.L.R. 1570, 40 S. Ct. 189), what it later held, that 'income,' as used in the revenue acts taxing income, adopted since the 16th Amendment, *has the same meaning that it had in the Act of 1909. Merchants' Loan & T. Co. v. Smietanka,* 255 U.S. 509, 519, 65 L.ed. 751, 755, 15 A.L.R. 1305, 41 S. Ct. 386; see *Southern Pacific Co. v. Loew.* 247 U.S. 330, 335, 62 L.ed. 114, 1147, 38 S. Ct. 540." (Emphasis added)

Bowers vs Kerbaugh-Empire Company, 271 US 887 (1926), on page 174,

"'Income' has been taken to mean the *same thing as used in the Corporation Excise Tax Act of (August 5), 1909* (36 Stat. at L. 11, Chap. 6), in the 16th Amendment and in the various revenue acts subsequently passed. *Southern P. Co. v. Lowe.* 247 U.S. 330, 335, 62 L.ed. 1142, 1147, 38 Sup. Ct. Rep. 540;" (Emphasis added)

In addition to the cases cited above, the following also support and affirm this definition of "income": *Southern Pacific Co. v. Lowe* 247 US 330; *Doyle v. Mitchell Bros. Co.* 247 US 179; *Goodrich v. Edwards* 255 US 527; *United States v. Supplee-Biddle Hardware Co.* 265 US 189; *United States v. Phellis* 257 US 156; *Miles v. Safe Deposit & T. Co.* 259 US 247; *Irwin v. Gavit* 268 US 161; *Edwards v. Cuba R. Co.* 268 US 628.

Paine vs Oshkosh, 190 Wis. 69 (1926), on page 72,

". . . an income tax is not levied upon property, funds, or profits, but upon the right of an individual or corporation to receive income or profits."

IX

TAX ON DEFENDANT'S WAGES IS A CAPITATION TAX

As pointed out earlier, the Plaintiff is attempting to levy a direct tax on the wages of the Defendant; such direct tax is forbidden by Ar-

ticle 1, Section 9, Clause 4 of the United States Constitution, the Sixteenth Amendment notwithstanding.

Defendant's position is dealt with at length by Adam Smith in *The
Wealth of Nations* (1776), in volume three, pages 281 through 289; a copy
of which pages are marked pages 4 through 8 of Defendant's Exhibit "I-
1" attached hereto [2] and made a part hereof as if fully set forth herein.

X

DEFENDANT'S WAGES NOT TAXABLE UNDER INTERNAL REVENUE CODE

Lastly, Defendant would point out that Commerce Clearing House,
in its explanation of gross income, notes that the Congress relied upon
Eisner vs Macomber 252 U.S. 189, verifying the fact that Defendant's
wages are *not* taxable under the Internal Revenue Code. A copy of the
explanation of gross income by Commerce Clearing House is marked
Defendant's Exhibit "I-2" and is attached hereto and made a part hereof
as if fully set forth herein. [3]

WHEREFORE, PREMISES CONSIDERED, Defendant moves the
Court to dismiss, with prejudice, the charges pending against him in
this action as, contrary to the Plaintiff's claim, Defendant's wages for
1974 and 1975 are not subject to tax under the Internal Revenue Code
and/or the Sixteenth Amendment, hence the Defendant is not required
to make a return for 1974 and 1975.

[2]This is not included in this book.

[3]This is not included in this book.

DATED this 20th day of December, 1978.

Respectfully Submitted,

_____

IRWIN A. SCHIFF, Defendant

by Raymond W. Ganim,
Attorney for the Defendant [4]
2192 Main Street
Stratford, Connecticut

While this brief was submitted explaining why "wages" are not "income," it actually establishes why nothing — dividends, interest, rent, alimony, etc. — can be forcibly taxed as "income."

_____

[4]This motion was submitted to Judge Daly on my behalf by Mr. Ganim, my court appointed attorney, and resubmitted by me at my trial before Judge Clarie.

APPENDIX E

Briefs Exposing Government's Illegal Monetary Policies

This appendix contains

PART I:
1. my memorandum of law opposing the government's motion to dismiss my lawsuit that requested that it be restrained from further prosecuting me for not filing tax returns and opposing their request for attorney's fees;
2. my appeal to the Second Circuit Court of Judge Ellen Burns' dismissal of the above mentioned lawsuit ordering penalties to the government in the amount of $468.75 for reimbursement of legal fees;
3. the government's answer to that appeal;
4. my reply to its answer;
5. a letter to the court requesting additional oral argument time (they were only going to allow me *five* minutes); and
6. the Court's opinion.

The lower court had ordered me to pay a court fine (actually a reimbursement to the government for legal fees) in non-redeemable notes (i.e., Federal Reserve notes). In its reply brief the government was only able to cite lower court case law wherein lower courts deliberately disregarded and distorted all of the Supreme Court cases (both the majority and dissenting opinions) regarding the legal tender cases that had a bearing on the lawful nature of paper currency especially the *Knox vs Lee* and *Juilliard vs Greenman* cases. The government also completely misstated the *Juilliard* case.

In its opinion the Second Circuit judges affirmed (contrary to the clear holding of the Supreme Court that it cannot make that "which has no [intrinsic] value — money") the lower court's ruling that something other than lawful U.S. money could be used to pay a fine set by a District Court. By its action (contradictory to the Supreme Court, the U.S.

Constitution, and all relevant statutes) it, in effect, held that "Congress may make anything "which has no value — money" and, in so doing, surrendered any pretense that it is a legitimate Federal court.

PART II:

1. my appeal to the Second Circuit Court of Judge Clarie's refusal to grant me a *habeas corpus* hearing pursuant to Title 28, Section 2255.

PART I

MEMORANDUM OF LAW IN SUPPORT OF PLAINTIFF'S ANSWER TO DEFENDANTS "MOTION TO DISMISS" AND "REQUEST FOR ATTORNEY'S FEES"

The Defendants in their Motion To Dismiss make no attempt, whatsoever, to refute either the statute or case law offered by Plaintiff indicating that the Defendants conspired to deprive Plaintiff of his constitutional rights, nor why they should not be permanently enjoined from again prosecuting the Plaintiff in violation of his constitutional rights because:

1. The Plaintiff is not a person required either by statute or the United States Constitution to file an income tax return.
2. The Federal income tax is an excise and thereby, the attempt on the part of the Defendants to enforce such a tax upon him as a direct tax is in violation of the United States Constitution and the Plaintiff's constitutional rights, and
3. That the Defendants, individually and collectively violated the Plaintiff's constitutional rights while purporting to act under color of law.

Instead of dealing with these issues, the Defendants resort to name calling and a meaningless rehash of the events connected with Plaintiff's illegal prosecution as a smokescreen behind which to hide their failure to address the substantive issues of law raised by the Plaintiff.

The Defendants suggest that Plaintiff seeks to prevent them from prosecuting him for his "tax protest activity"; and further, that the Plaintiff is a well-known "tax protester." The "tax protester" label, of course, is a term used by the Federal government and its agents to enable them to avoid addressing the legal issues being raised by knowledgeable, private citizens, who insist that the Federal government collect taxes in accordance with the United States Constitution. If the Plaintiff "protests" anything, it is the unconstitutional activities engaged in by the Defendants, under the color of law.

If, on the other hand, insisting that the Federal Government collect taxes in a constitutional manner makes one a "tax protester," then, of course, the Plaintiff is a "tax protester." But, a continual insistence, on the part of the Plaintiff, that the government collect taxes in a constitutional manner cannot, in any manner, shape or form, constitute "recidivist criminal behavior" as the Defendants allege. Yet, the Defendants specifically asked the Court not to grant "injunctive relief preventing the Defendant prosecutors from further 'seeking to prosecute' him for his tax protest activity." Obviously, the prosecutors want a free hand to prosecute the Plaintiff, and perhaps others, for "tax protest activity" when such activity, even if engaged in, does not constitute criminal behavior." Obviously, therefore, the powerful prosecutorial prerogatives of the Defendants must be enjoined, because an apparent deepseated, jack-boot mentality (already admitted) prevents Defendant-Prosecutors from distinguishing between behavior that is criminal and behavior that is lawful and specifically protected by the United States Constitution.

How did the Defendants answer the Plaintiff's charges? Did they offer one shred of evidence indicating that the Plaintiff is a person required to file a tax return as the United States Attorney alleged in his Information of April 19, 1978 — and for which the Plaintiff was prosecuted and jailed?

Did the Defendants offer one shred of evidence to refute the some 50 (fifty) legal authorities cited by the Plaintiff that prove that the income tax is being unconstitutionally enforced as a direct tax; contrary to the apportionment clauses of the United States Constitution, and the Sixteenth Amendment? No, the Defendants avoided these substantive issues like the plague.

Instead, the Defendants state that the Plaintiff's conviction in his second trial was affirmed without an opinion. This admission, of course, merely affirms the Plaintiff's claim that he was tried not before judges (who must be impartial) but before agents of the Federal government.

Attached please find Plaintiff's Appeal Briefs,[4] covering some 17 (seventeen) areas of reversible error claimed by the Plaintiff, along with the government's evasive and vapid response. The Court will note that many of the issues raised by the Plaintiff were not even answered by the government. Yet, the Appeals Court affirmed Plaintiff's conviction without a written opinion. The Appeals Court affirmed Plaintiff's conviction *orally* because it could not formally address the issues raised without either: 1) reversing the Plaintiff's conviction, or 2) establishing a new legal precedent in tax law — that taxpayers can be held to an objective, rather than a subjective standard.

So the Appeals Court, in the interest of its principal the Federal government, disregarded the legal issues raised on appeal and summarily affirmed the Plaintiff's conviction, thus making a mockery of both the appeals process and the Plaintiff's right to due process.

Next, the Defendant states that the Plaintiff's Motion To Set Aside Conviction, pursuant to 28 U.S. 2255 was denied. It was not "denied," it was *disregarded* on the specious grounds that the issues raised were either raised at trial or should have been raised on appeal. Thus, the Trial Court illogically and hypocritically asserted that regardless of how valid were the appellant's allegations, the Court would not, under any circumstances, consider them. Thus, Judge Clarie barred the Plaintiff any access whatsoever (during his incarceration) to 2255 protection while, at the same time, rejecting the Second Circuit's own decision in *Grimes vs United States* 607 F.2d 6, wherein the Court clearly ruled that issues attacking "jurisdiction" or claiming significant denial of "constitutional rights" are validly raised under Section 2255, "even though prisoner could have raised the point on appeal, and there was no sufficient reason for failing to do so."

The Defendants also allege that "Plaintiff's substantive points were raised at, or prior to trial." They might have been "raised," but they were *never answered* at trial — but merely disregarded by the Court. Attached please find a copy of Plaintiff's Motion To Dismiss on the grounds that the Plaintiff was not subject to an income tax. *This Motion was never answered by the Government at either trial!* I would request that the Court ask the Defendants to produce their answer to this Motion, as an indication of whether "Plaintiff's substantive points" were considered at his trial." The Plaintiff was never afforded pre-trial hearings where these issues could be argued. When Plaintiff reurged these issues prior to the commencement of his trial, the Trial Court did not even ask the Defendants to respond, as the attached copies from the Plaintiff's trial transcript will confirm.[5] So any such constitutional issues raised were never "distinctly raised and determined" at Plaintiff's

[4]These are not included in this Appendix.

[5]These are not included in this Appendix.

trials, as alleged by the Defendants. If any such issues were raised, they were merely *avoided* and not "determined, " while the specific issue of "jurisdiction" was never raised!

The Defendants ask the Court to dismiss this action based on five grounds:

1. That Plaintiff seeks to block Defendants from prosecuting his "criminal conduct" and "from further prosecuting [his] recidivist criminal behavior."
2. That jurisdiction under 28 U.S.C. 1361 "does not lie to compel a discretionary function."
3. That the prosecutors' decision to prosecute is "largely immune from Judicial control."
4. That because in "an action for damages, the prosecutorial function is protected by absolute immunity [that] accordingly [there is] no basis for the exercise of the Court's mandamus power." And finally,
5. That it is "not the Court's function to anticipate and rule on points of law in a criminal prosecution, which may or may not take place."

The Court should reject all of the Government's arguments as specious and inconsequential on the following grounds:

I

The Plaintiff does not seek to block prosecution of his "criminal conduct" or "recidivist criminal behavior" as the Defendants allege. The Plaintiff merely seeks to enjoin the Defendants from prosecuting "as criminal behavior, " *behavior which is not criminal at all* — and that is a big difference. Filing a tax return is voluntary, and not filing one *does not constitute criminal behavior!* It is obvious, from the Defendants' Motion To Dismiss, that they somehow regard not voluntarily filing a tax return as "tax protester activity, " which constitutes "recidivist criminal behavior" and subjects Plaintiff to prosecution. It is precisely because the Defendant-Prosecutors cannot distinguish between criminal and non-criminal behavior that their prosecutorial functions must be restrained by a Federal Court that can perceive the difference.

II

The Plaintiff does not seek to restrain a discretionary function, but a nondiscretionatory **duty**. The Defendants, individually and collectively, have a **duty** to uphold the United States Constitution, and a

duty not to prosecute the Plaintiff for merely standing on his constitutional rights. The Defendants have a **duty** not to prosecute the Plaintiff in violation of the United States Constitution, and it is that constitutional **duty** that the Plaintiff seeks to compel. As the Court ruled in *Brown vs Schlesinger* et. al, (1973 DCUA) 365 F. Supp. 204, "that suits by those who seek performance of constitutional duties owed them by defendants who have a clear duty to perform said duties and where no other relief is available are within the scope of 28 U.S.C. 1361." Further, that Court stated (in a situation similar to the instant case): "Plaintiffs do not ask the courts to require the various defendants to perform a discretionary act; rather they ask that the defendants be required to recognize a constitutional right of the plaintiffs which the defendants threaten to disregard. The Court of Appeals also stated in *Burnett* (*Burnett vs Tulson* 474 F. 2d 877) that 'mandamus jurisdiction under 28 U.S.C. 1361 permits flexibility in remedy,' so that the injunctive and declaratory relief sought here is not inconsistent with this jurisdictional basis."

Also, in *White vs Matthews,* et. al. 420 F. Supp. 882, the Court stated: "Yet, the substance of plaintiff's complaint is that a nondiscretionary duty to provide care is owed. It is the opinion of this Court that this is sufficient for jurisdiction under 1361. For jurisdictional purposes it is not necessary that the duty be clear before the analysis begins; in other words, we take jurisdiction to determine whether there is a duty owed.

Moreover, this section granting jurisdiction to issue writs of mandamus is flexible and can also encompass declaratory relief if this remedy is deemed proper. . . Constitutional obligations as well as statutory duties are included within the perimeters of 28 U.S.C. 1361" [*Holmes vs United States Board of Parole* 541 F. 2d 1243 (1976) citing *Burnett vs. Tolson* 474 F 2d 877 (4th Cir. 1973) *Mead vs Parker* 464 F. 2d 1108 (9 Cir. 1972)]. *Holmes* also stated: "In cases charging a violation of constitutional rights mandamus should be *construed liberally*." (Emphasis added) Citing *Richardson vs United States,* 464 F 2d. 844 (3rd Cir. 1972) also stated *Holmes* that cases involving complex constitutional issues "do not effect jurisdiction" under 28 U.S.C. 1361.

III

The Defendants' claim that their decision to prosecute is "largely immune from judicial control," but admit that this does not hold where prosecution is based on an "arbitrary classification." Plaintiff submits that a classification arbitrarily charging "tax protesting" falls into such a category. Additionally, this claim fails on other grounds. "Where the manner in which public officials exercise their authority is challenged as contrary to constitutional and statutory mandates, the doctrine of soveriegn immunity may not prevail." *National Association For The Advancement Of Colored People vs Levi* 418 F. Supp. 1109 (1976) citing *Larson vs Domestic & Foreign Commerce Corp.* 337 U.S. 682, 702, 69 S. Ct. 1457, 93 L. Ed 1628 (194). Further, the Court held: "There is no sound basis for this Court to deny subject matter jurisdiction and sovereign immunity may not be asserted to avoid a hearing on the merits."

IV

The Defendants allege that because in "an action for damages, the prosecutorial function is protected by absolute immunity" that somehow this implies that "accordingly [there is] no basis for the exercise of the Court's mandamus power." This has absolutely no bearing on this issue whatsoever. "The Plaintiff's right to declaratory relief is not dependent upon showing that he is entitled to injunctive or monetary relief." *Mattis vs Schnarr* et. al (1974, C.A. 8 Mo) 502 F. 2d 588.

V

Lastly, the Defendants allege that it is "not the Court's function to anticipate and rule on points of law in a criminal prosecution which may or may not take place." In *Rowland vs Tarr* 378 F. Supp. 766 (1974), a case right on point, the Plaintiffs sought to restrain the government from prosecuting them for their failure to register under the Selective Service Act, while the Defendants argued that because the Act had, in fact, lasped and plaintiffs were no longer subject to induction, the action was moot "for want of actual case or controversy." The Court ruled, however, that the government ignored "the fact that under the Act, that any of the named plaintiffs may still undergo prosecution and severe criminal penalties for failure to perform certain affirmative duties. The threat of prosecution is real [the Court then stated in a footnote that it took judicial notice of the frequency of Selective Service prosecutions which had come before it in recent years]. This is not the situation where a statute has laid dormant and unenforced. *There is a real and current threat to them* and is by no means moot. In addition, there are potential class members who may still be inducted under current authority. Thus, there is an actual case of controversy over which this Court may exercise jurisdiction." Further, the Court stated: "We hold that being required to perform such affirmative duties under threat of criminal prosecution is proper" — and the government's attempt to dismiss the motion was denied. This action, of course, is precisely similar to *Rowland vs Tarr* wherein the Court rejected a similar Motion To Dismiss which asserted that it did not have the right to grant declaratory relief covering *possible* criminal prosecutions.

Thus, all of the Defendants' arguments to dismiss are fallacious and a hearing on the merits of Plaintiff's Motion should be granted for the reasons stated in his initial Motion, in this Reply to the Government's Motion to Dismiss and for the following observation by Chief Justice Burger in *Sheuer vs Rhodes* 416 U.S. 232.

> When a federal court reviews the sufficiency of a complaint before the reception of any evidence either by affidavit or admission, its task is necessarily a limited one. The issue is not whether a plaintiff will ultimately prevail, but whether the claimant is entitled to offer evidence to support the claims. Indeed it may appear on the face of the pleadings that a recovery is very remote and unlikely but that is not the test. Moreover, it is well established that, in passing on a motion to dismiss, whether on the grounds of lack of jurisdiction over the subject matter or for failure to state a cause of action, the allegations of the complaint should be construed favorable to the pleader."

The Defendants request for legal or "attorney's fees" is, of course, patently absurd. What statute provides that private citizens attempting to enjoin the Federal government and its agents from engaging in unconstitutional acts must reimburse said agents for the legal expenses involved in showing why their unconstitutional acts should not be enjoined? The Plaintiff notes that such legal fees were requested on the pretext that the Plaintiff's action was done "frivolously" and in "bad faith." The Plaintiff suggests that the Defendants (especially Mr. Blumenthal) will sing an entirely different tune when they are required to make responses under oath.

Respectfully submitted,

Irwin A. Schiff, *Pro Se*

Despite my answer — which I believe established my right to a hearing — District Court Judge Ellen Bree Burns (in a six page decision) denied my claim to a hearing on the merits and fined me $468.75 to cover the government's time and costs in defending the case which I appealed to the Second Circuit.

2. The Appeal

Irwin A. Schiff, *Pro Se*
60 Connolly Parkway
Hamden, Connecticut 06514

July 15, 1982
Docket No. 82-6015

UNITED STATES COURT OF APPEALS
FOR THE
SECOND CIRCUIT

IRWIN A. SCHIFF   *Appellant*

vs

UNITED STATES OF AMERICA   *Appellee*

ON APPEAL FROM THE UNITED STATES DISTRICT COURT
FOR THE
DISTRICT OF CONNECTICUT
DENYING APPELLANT'S MOTION FOR RELIEF OF
JUDGEMENT B
COURT PURSUANT TO FED. R CIV. P. 60 (b)

ISSUES PRESENTED

I

Whether the Federal government has the authority to make "that which has no value — money."

II

Whether currency claiming to be a note, but containing no promise to pay a sum certain either to the bearer of his order is, in reality, a note or simply blatantly unconstitutional fiat currency.

III

Whether a district court can order one party to pay to second party fiat currency in lieu of lawful money.

IV

Whether the monetary provisions of the United States Constitution have any relevance whatsoever in today's Federal courts.

V

What is the lawful meaning of a dollar and where can it be secured by American citizens?

CONSTITUTIONAL PROVISIONS AND STATUTES CONSTRUED

ARTICLE I, Section I, Clause 5 of the United States Constitution

> Congress shall have the power. . . to coin money and regulate the value thereof. . .

ARTICLE I, Section 10, Clause 1 of the United States Constitution

> No State shall. . . make anything but gold and silver coin a tender in payment of debts. . .

TITLE 31 U.S.C., Section 314

> STANDARD UNIT OF VALUE — the dollar of gold nine-tenths fine consisting of the weight determined under the provisions of Section 821 of this title shall be standard unit of value. . .

TITLE 31, U.S.C., Section 371

> The money of account of the United States shall be expressed in dollars or units. . . and all accounts in the public offices and all proceedings in the courts shall be kept and had in conformity to this regulation.

TABLE OF CASES

1. *Hepburn vs Griswold* 8 Wall. 513
2. *Juilliard vs Greenman* 110 US 421
3. *Knox vs Lee* 12 Wall. 281
4. *Ogden vs Saunders* 12 Wheat 214

STATEMENT OF THE FACTS

The Appellant was tried by two Connecticut district Federal courts (Bridgeport and Hartford) and incarcerated in a Federal institution for 4 months and 9 days for allegedly failing to file a tax return, despite the fact that there is no law requiring anyone to file a tax return.

Indeed, how can anyone be required to file a tax return when the Supreme Court ruled in *Garner vs The United States* 424 US 648, that "the information revealed in the preparation and filing of an income tax return is, for the purpose of Fifth Amendment analysis, the testimony of a 'witness' as that term is used herein"; while Section 6020 of the Internal Revenue Code establishes without question, that the furnishing of tax information to the government is a voluntary act.

Even the presiding Judge T. Emmet Clarie ruled at the Appellant's second trial that the filing of a tax return is voluntary. Judge Clarie's ruling enabled the government to introduce and use against the Appellant, the Appellant's 1973 tax return, which the government had to introduce in order to establish the Appellant's alleged "willfulness." So Judge Clarie ruled that the Appellant filed his 1973 return "voluntarily, " and then sent the Appellant to jail for similarly not "voluntarily" filing his 1974 and 1975 tax returns. The Second Circuit Court of Appeals apparently subscribed to this legal "logic" since it affirmed the Appellant's conviction orally on January 28, 1981.

Since the Appellant was prosecuted and incarcerated for the "crime" of not voluntarily submitting tax returns for the years 1974 and 1975, Appellant had a real fear of being similarly illegally prosecuted for the years 1976, 1977, 1978, 1979, and 1980 — years which he similarly had not filed tax returns.

Thus to protect himself from the possibility that a false information might again be filed against him by a U.S. Attorney, or false statements made to a grand jury to secure an illegal indictment, the Appellant on July 15, 1981 asked the Federal court in New Haven, Connecticut to permanently enjoin the Federal government from attempting to again illegally prosecute the Appellant for doing something that was obviously not a crime. The government responded to the Appellant's request asking this Court to dismiss Appellant's request, and in addition, asked to be reimbursed $468.75 for "legal expenses" which the Court dutifully granted.

On November 28, 1981 the Appellant filed a motion explaining why the Appellant could not possibly pay to the U.S. government the *468.75 dollars* that had been awarded — and in answer to the Appellant's motion, the court ordered the Appellant (in its order of December 8, 1981 — see attached marked Exhibit A) to pay "$(468.75) payable in legal tender, namely, federal reserve notes." In response to this order, appellant submitted a Motion For Relief Of Judgement by Court Pursuant To Fed. R. Civ. P. 60 (b), which was denied (see attached marked Exhibit B). It is the denial of this motion which the Appellant now appeals.

ARGUMENT

If there is anything that can be said with certainty about the United States Constitution it is that its monetary provisions were designed to prevent fiat paper currency from ever again being introduced into the American economy. The colonies had just experienced the horrendous economic consequences of "Continentals," irredeemable paper money issued by the Continental Congress, and our Founding Fathers sought to ensure that the citizens of this nation would not again be swindled by any future government seeking to issue fiat currency.

Justice Field's dissenting opinion in *Juilliard vs Greenman* 110 US 421, page 454 makes this clear:

> And when the Convention came to the prohibition upon the States, the historian says that the clause, "No State shall make anything but gold and silver a tender in payment of debts," was accepted without a dessentient State:
>
> "So the adoption of the Constitution," he adds, "is to be the end forever of paper money, whether issued by the several States or by the United States, if the constitution shall be rightly interpreted and honestly obeyed."
>
> Id. 137.

The court should also take judicial notice that Justice Field points out that the framers of the Constitution specifically denied to the Federal government the power to issue bills of credit (i.e., note currency). When such a grant of power was proposed, nine states voted against it and only two states voted for it. Commenting on this vote, Justice Field notes in *Juilliard vs Greenman*, supra, page 54:

> It was Madison, who decided the vote of Virginia, and he has left his testimony that "the pretext for a paper currency more particularly for making the bill a tender, either for public or private debts, was cut off."

Further, Justice Field quotes extensively from the Senate speech of Daniel Webster, recognized constitutional authority, who, in part stated:

> The States are expressly prohibited from making anything but gold and silver a legal tender in payment of debts, and although no such express pro-

hibition is applied to Congress, yet, as Congress has no power granted to it in this respect but to coin money and to regulate the value of foreign coins, it clearly has no power to substitute paper or anything else for coin as a tender in payment of debts and in discharge of contracts.

Juilliard vs Greenman, supra, page 455

This clear statement by Daniel Webster merely reflects the obvious intent of the framers of the Constitution as demonstrated by such statements as those made by James Madison in *Federalist Paper #10* where he termed the "rage for paper money. . . [as an]. . . improper [and] wicked project"; while in *Federalist Paper #44* he observed that "the prohibition to bills of credit must give pleasure to every citizen in proportion to his love of justice and his knowledge of the true springs of public prosperity."

Madison further referred to "the pestilent effects of paper money" and noted that government "ought not to be at liberty to substitute a paper medium in the place of coin." And that "The power to make anything but gold and silver a tender in payment of debts is withdrawn from the States on the same principle with that of issuing a paper currency."

In *Hepburn vs Griswold* 8 Wall. 513, the constitutionality of note currency first came before the Supreme Court. After noting "the long train of evils which flows from the use of irredeemable paper money. . . ," the Court held that

. . . we are obliged to conclude that an act making mere promises to pay dollars a legal tender in payment of debts previously contracted is not a means appropriate plainly adopted and really calculated to carry into effect any express power vested in Congress and such an act is inconsistent with the spirit of the Constitution and that it is prohibited by the Constitution.

I ask the Court to take judicial notice that the issue before the Supreme Court in *Hepburn vs Griswold* was the monetary legality of actual notes issued by the United States government itself, containing a promise to pay money (i.e., dollars) but still the Supreme Court held that such note currency was "inconsistent" with the Constitution. How much more inconsistent, therefore, is fiat currency, not even issued by the United States government, but issued by a private banking syndicate? I ask the court to take judicial notice that the Federal reserve is not even a part of the Federal government, but is owned by independent banks (who own stock in the Federal Reserve) and that the Federal Reserve itself pays a franchise tax to the Federal government. The independent nature of the Federal Reserve was clearly explained in a recent news article which the Appellant has marked (Exhibit A-1) attached hereto.

In a five to four decision, the Supreme Court in *Knox vs Lee,* reversed the decision it had reached in *Hepburn vs Griswold,* and held that the Civil War notes issued by the United States government were legal tender for debts contracted prior to the War. However, in reaching its decision, the majority conceded that there was no constitutional authority, either expressed or implied, which authorized such notes and justified their issuance solely on an implied wartime power, having nothing whatsoever to do with the government's legitimate monetary powers. The Court stated on page 306 that the Constitution "certainly was intended to confer upon the government the power of self-preservation." Here we see that the majority in *Knox* based the constitutionality of U.S. note currency on a non-enumerated constitutional power which it associated with the neccessity of preserving the Union itself in time of war.

To support its position, the majority in *Knox* relied solely on *McCulloch vs Maryland* 4 Wheat 416, and the principle laid down by Chief Justice Marshall as cited on pages 308 and 309 of the *Knox* decision:

> Let the end be legitimate, let it be within the scope of the Constitution, and all means which are appropriate, which are plainly adapted to that end, which are not prohibited, but consist with the letter and spirit of the constitution, are constitutional.

The Court went on to describe in extended detail the extreme conditions that then prevailed and which had created the need for the new Legal Tender law (pages 308 and 309):

> . . . We do not promise to dictate at length upon the circumstances in which the country was placed when Congress attempted to make Treasury Notes a legal tender. . . Suffice it to say that a Civil War was then raging which seriously threatened the overthrow of the government and the destruction of the Constitution itself. . . The necessity was immediate and pressing. The army was unpaid. There was then due to the soldiers in the field nearly a score of millions of dollars. The requisitions from the War and Navy Departments for supplies exceeded fifty million, and the current expenditure was over one million per day. . .

> . . . Now, if it were certain that nothing else would have supplied the absolute necessities of the Treasury, that nothing else would have enabled the government to maintain its armies and navy, that nothing else would have saved the government and the Constitution from destruction, while the Legal Tender Acts would, could anyone be bold enough to assert that Congress transgressed its powers.

Yet four Justices, including Chief Justice Chase, dissented — in a scathing and extended dissent.

Appellant would put the court on judicial notice that the majority in *Knox vs Lee,* supra, went to great lengths to explain that it was to save the Union in time of war that moved the Court to hold that these wartime notes were constitutional. Appellant wishes to put the court on judicial notice that the Supreme Court in *Knox vs Lee* never stated that the legal basis for note currency rested on any express or implied constitutional monetary power, but found these notes to be constitutional solely on the basis of a non-monetary, implied wartime power designed to save "the government and the Constitution from destruction." This is, of course, in sharp contrast to comparatively recent lower court decisions wherein Federal judges, blind to these decisions and constitutional provisions, have erroneously held that the issuance of Federal Reserve notes fall directly within the Federal government's express or implied constitutional *monetary powers.* No justice in any Supreme Court legal tender decision ever implied or suggested any such thing.

Quoting further from *Knox* on this issue, on page 313 we find

> The Legal Tender Acts do not attempt to make paper a standard of value. We do not rest their validity upon the assertion that their emission is coinage, or any regulation of the value of money; *nor do we assert that Congress may make anything which has no value — money.* What we do assert is that Congress has power to enact that the Government's promises to pay money shall be for the time being equivalent in value to the representative of value determined by the Coinage Acts or to multiples thereof. (Emphasis added)

Here the Supreme Court clearly states that fiat currency is unconstitutional and this holding by the Supreme Court has never been challenged or reversed.

Quoting further on the same theme, the Court in *Knox* held that in conveying legal tender status to U.S. notes (page 315) was

> not an attempt to coin money out of a valueless material [such as paper]. . . it is a pledge of the national credit. It is a promise by the government to pay dollars; it is not an attempt to make dollars.

Well, do currently issued Federal Reserve "notes" contain a promise to "pay dollars"? No, they obviously constitute an illegal attempt by the Federal government to "make dollars, " directly *contrary to the very principle cited here in the Knox decision,* and any Federal judge, who would cooperate with the Federal government in allowing them to get away with this blatantly unconstitutional scam should be ashamed to call himself a Federal judge, or even admit to graduating from law school.

Another Supreme Court case that the Federal government likes to cite as furnishing a legal basis for its fiat currency is the *Juilliard vs Greenman* decision (110 US 421). However, the issue before the Court in that case was clearly stated (page 437) as follows:

> The single question, therefore to be considered, and upon the answer to which the judgement to be rendered between these parties depends, is whether notes of the United States, issued in time of war, under acts of Congress declaring them to be a legal tender in payment of private debts, and afterwards in time of peace redeemed and paid in gold coin at the Treasury, and then reissued under the act of 1878 can. . . [be legal tender, and the Court held that they were].

But *Juilliard* cannot furnish any lawful basis for any sort of fiat currency which is not "notes of the United States"; not "issued in time of war"; never declared to be legal tender by any act of Congress "declaring them to be legal tender in payment of private debts"; and not redeemable in "gold coin at the [U.S.] Treasury." So any Federal judge that would accept *Juilliard vs Greenman* as furnishing a legal basis for currently circulating fiat currency is obviously admitting that he has not the foggiest notion of what *Juilliard vs Greenman* is all about.

Prior to the aforementioned three legal tender cases, the Supreme Court had (in *Ogden vs Saunders* 12 Wheat 214) clearly ruled that the constitutional prohibition which denied to the States the right to make anything but gold and silver coin a tender in payment of debt extended to the Federal government as well. Extended excerpts from this case are included in Appellant's Motion For Relief Of Judgement By Court Pursuant To Fed. R. Civ. P. 60(b) which is included in the Appendix, so I will only cite brief quotes here.

The constitutional prohibition of issuing "bills of credit, or making anything but gold and silver coin a tender in payment of debts, " said the Court (page 216), "was intended to cut up paper money by the roots." What could be plainer than that? And that statement was made by the Supreme Court, not some so-called tax protester. Further, the Court observed (page 265) that the United States Constitution

> . . . declares, that "no state shall coin money, emit bills of credit, make anything but gold and silver coin a tender in payment of debts." These prohibitions, associated with the powers granted to Congress "to coin money, and to regulate the value thereof, and of foreign coin, " *must obviously constitute members of the same family*, being upon the same subject, and governed by the same policy.

... it is for this reason. . . that the prohibition, in regard to state tender laws, will admit no construction *which would confine it to state laws* which have a retrospective operation. (Emphasis added)

It should be obvious to this court (given the clear interpretation of the monetary provisions of the U.S. Constitution by four Supreme Court cases) that fiat currency of the type currently being circulated as Federal Reserve notes is blatantly unconstitutional and cannot be the basis of any lawful judgement of any court, or substituted by a Federal court in lieu of lawful money (i.e., gold or silver coin) or lawful legal tender such as United States notes redeemable in lawful money (i.e. gold coin).

It is clear that the unchanged standard unit of lawful monetary value in the United States is still the gold dollar as referred to in 31 U.S.C., Section 314. It is further clear that the money of account of the United States as specified in U.S.C. 31, Section 371 is a standard gold dollar — and that Federal courts are not at liberty to award judgements in other than the lawful money of account of the United States.

It should also be clear from the face of currently issued Federal Reserve fiat currency that it is substantially similar to the "Continentals" that the Constitution was designed to prevent. It is also clear that any judge who would refer to currently issued "fiat currency" as "note currency" obviously does not understand the legal meaning of a note. It is also clear that note currency is no longer issued by the Federal Reserve, and since note currency is no longer issued by the Federal Reserve, no lower court decision having to do with Federal Reserve note currency can have any bearing on the instant case since we are not dealing here with note currency but, rather, with fiat currency. It should also be clear that a Federal court has no constitutional authority to compel payment in unconstitutional fiat currency simply because lawful money, or lawful legal tender note currency is not currently being provided by the Federal government since such an order would obviously be repugnant to the Constitution and thus null and void. This principle seems so obvious that it cannot be seriously challenged on any legitimate basis.

WHEREAS PREMISES CONSIDERED: Appellant prays for an order of this court staying the execution of the attached judgement of the District Court of Connecticut directing the Appellant to pay fiat currency and for such other further relief that the court deems just and proper.

Respectfully submitted,

Irwin A. Schiff, *pro se*

3. The Government's Answer

Irwin A. Schiff v. *United States of America, et al.*

United States Court of Appeals   August 9, 1982
for the Second Circuit
United States Courthouse   Docket No. 82-6015

Irwin Schiff appeals from a decision by the District Court for the District of Connecticut (Ellen Bree Burns, D.J.) denying Schiff's motion for relief from judgement pursuant to Rule 60(b)(4) and (6) of the Federal Rules of Civil Procedure.

On June 6, 1980 Schiff was found guilty of willful failure to file personal income tax returns for 1974 and 1975. He was sentenced to one year imprisonment with six months suspended and fined $10,000. The conviction was affirmed in an oral opinion by the Second Circuit Court of Appeals on January 28, 1981 (647 F.2d 163) and a writ of certiorari was denied by the Supreme Court on October 5, 1981 (U.S.   ,[1] 102 S.Ct. 137). A motion to set aside Schiff's conviction pursuant to 28 United States Code Section 2255 was denied by the trial court on April 10, 1981 and that decision was affirmed by the Second Circuit Court of Appeals on November 2, 1981.

On July 16, 1981, Schiff filed a complaint against the United States, Richard Blumenthal (then United States Attorney) and Michael Hartmere (Assistant United States Attorney) seeking declaratory relief and to enjoin the defendants from potential prosecution of Schiff for failure to file income tax returns for the years 1976–1980 (26 U.S.C. Section 7203). The defendants moved to dismiss and filed for an award of attorneys' fees on September 16, 1981. On November 9, 1981, the District Court granted defendants' motion to dismiss and, citing Schiff's "contumacity indicative of bad faith", awarded attorney's fees in the sum of FOUR HUNDRED SIXTY-EIGHT DOLLARS and SEVENTY-FIVE CENTS ($468.75) to the Government. (Record on Appeal, Document No. 12.)

On November 21, 1981, Schiff moved "to correct an ambiguous and therefore illegal fine", claiming that no "lawful" dollars existed with which he could pay the attorney's fee award. (Record on Appeal, Document No. 14.) In an opinion dated December 8, 1981, the District Court characterized Schiff's claim as "wholly without merit", denied his motion and again ordered him to pay "FOUR HUNDRED SIXTY-EIGHT

---

[1]This is exactly how the government submitted their answer — they did not even bother to find out the case number for inclusion!

DOLLARS and SEVENTY-FIVE CENTS ($468.75), payable in legal tender, namely, federal reserve notes." (Record on Appeal, Document No. 15.)

On December 24, 1981 Schiff moved for relief of judgment pursuant to Rule 60(b) based on his claim that because Federal Reserve Notes are unconstitutional, they could not be the subject of a valid judgment. That motion was denied without opinion on December 28, 1981. Schiff filed a notice of appeal for denial of his motion for relief of judgment on January 20, 1982. Attached to the notice of appeal was an affidavit asserting that Schiff did not have 75 "lawful dollars" with which to pay the filing fee for the appeal nor did he know where "lawful dollars" could be secured. (Record on Appeal, Document No. 18.) On May 14, 1981 Schiff filed a motion with the Second Circuit Court of Appeals "for determination of how appellent can lawfully pay filing fee in connection with appeal." The Second Circuit denied this motion on June 1, 1982 stating that the appeal would be "dismissed unless the filing fee is paid within seven days after the issuance of this order." (Appendix A.) Irwin Schiff paid the filing fee for this appeal in cash on June 4, 1982. (Appendix B.)

Argument

The District Court Properly Denied Irwin Schiff's Motion For Relief From Judgment Because The Monetary System Of The United States Is Constitutional.

The crux of this appeal is Irwin Schiff's claim that the currency presently being issued by the Federal Reserve is unconstitutional. Schiff further claims that Federal Reserve Notes cannot be the subject of a valid judgment and therefore the award of attorney's fees in this case should be vacated. This argument was twice rejected by the District Court. In denying Schiff's November 21, 1981, motion to correct an ambiguous and, therefore, illegal fine, his assertion that he was "unable to comply with the judgment. . . because no lawful dollars circulate in the United States" was characterized by the District Court as "wholly without merit." The court did not further comment on Schiff's claim that the currency is unconstitutional when it denied his December 24, 1981 motion for relief from judgment under Rule 60(b) of the Federal Rules of Civil Procedure — the denial which is the subject of this appeal. That denial should be affirmed because the currency presently being circulated by the Federal Reserve is constitutional.

Schiff bases his argument primarily on the theory that the United States Constitution requires currency to be redeemable in gold or silver. To support this proposition he relies heavily upon two Supreme Court opinions: the majority in *Hepburn v. Griswold*, 75 U.S. 603 (8 Wall.) (1870) — which Schiff acknowledges was reversed in *Knox v. Lee (The Legal Tender-Cases)*, 79 U.S. 457 (12 Wall.) (1871) — and Justice Field's dissent in *Julliard v. Greenman (The Legal Tender-Cases)*, 110 U.S. 421 (1884). Both opinions construe Article I, Section 10, Clause 1 of the United States Constitution, which provides that "No state shall. . . make anything but gold and silver coin a tender in payment of debts, " to be a prohibition applicable to the federal government as well as the states. Schiff attempts to limit the decisions in *Knox* and *Julliard* by arguing that they uphold the constitutionality of currency not redeemable in gold or silver only when issued during the exigencies of war. Contrary to Schiff's asserted limitation, the Court in *Julliard* specifically held that Congress' authority to issue currency not redeemable in gold or silver was not dependent solely on emergency wartime powers.

> Whether at any particular time, in war or in peace, the exigency is such, by reason of unusual and pressing demands on the resources of the government, or of the inadequancy of the supply of gold and silver coin to furnish the currency needed for the uses of the government and of the people, that it is, as matter of fact, wise and expedient to resort to this means, is a political question, to be determined by congress when the question of exigency arises, and not a judicial question to be afterwards passed upon by the courts.

110 U.S. at 450. Thus, the Constitution "prohibits the states from declaring legal tender anything other than gold or silver, but does not limit Congress' power to declare what shall be legal tender for all debts." *United States v. Rifen*, 577 F.2d 1111, 1113 (8th Cir. 1978) (per curiam).

As another ground for finding the presently circulating Federal Reserve Notes unconstitutional, Schiff suggests that even if Congress has the power to make notes not redeemable in gold or silver, the Federal Reserve, as a private institution, does not. Despite Schiff's contentions, Congress clearly delegated its power to issue such currency to the Federal Reserve System under 12 U.S.C. Section 411 and that delegation has been consistently upheld as constitutional. *E.g., Mathes* v. *C.I.R.*, 576 F.2d 70, 71 (5th Cir. 1978), *cert. denied*, 440 U.S. 911 (1979); *United States* v. *Anderson*, 584 F.2d 369, 374 (10th Cir. 1978); *Milam* v. *United States*, 524 F.2d 629, 630 (9th Cir. 1974) (memorandum).

The District Court's characterization of Schiff's constitutional claim as "wholly without merit" is well supported by other courts which have found such challenges to the monetary system to be frivolous. *See e.g., Birkenstock* v. *C.I.R.*, 646 F.2d 1185, 1186 (7th Cir. 1981) (per curiam) ("wholly lacking in merit"); *United States* v. *Moon*, 616 F.2d 1043,

1047 (8th Cir. 1980) ("there is no merit"); *United States* v. *Anderson,* 584 F.2d 369 (10th Cir. 1978) ("contentions. . . are without merit"); *United States* v. *Whitesel,* 543 F.2d 1176, 1181 (6th Cir. 1976), *cert. denied,* 431 U.S. 967 (1977) (quoting *United States* v. *Daly,* 481 F.2d 28 (8th Cir.) (per curiam), *cert. denied,* 414 U.S. 1064 (1973), for finding the contention "frivolous"); *United States* v. *Schmitz,* 542 F.2d 782, 785 (9th Cir. 1976) ("summarily found . . . to be without merit"), *cert. denied,* 429 U.S. 1105 (1977); *Hartman* v. *Switzer,* 376 F. Supp. 486 (W.D. Pa. 1974) ("clearly spurious").

In light of this precedent, the District Court properly denied Schiff's motion for relief from judgment under Rule 60(b)(4) and (6) of the Federal Rules of Civil Procedure. That rule reads in pertinent part:

> On motion and upon such terms as are just, the court may relieve a party or his legal representative from a final judgment, order, or proceedings for the following reasons: . . . (4) the judgment is void; . . . or (6) any other reason justifying relief from the operation of the judgment.

Under 60(b)(4), constitutional infirmity would certainly require the court to find the judgment void and to grant the motion (*see V.T.A, Inc.* v. *Airco, Inc.,* 597 F.2d 220, 226 (10th Cir. 1979)); but in this case the District Court properly found that the currency was constitutional and the judgment therefore valid.

Under 60(b)(6), the court may exercise its discretion in granting relief from judgment where exceptional circumstances make such relief appropriate to achieve justice. *Rinieri* v. *News Syndicate Co.,* 385 F.2d 818, 822 (2d Cir. 1967). On appeal, the denial of a Rule 60(b)(6) motion will only be reversed if there has been an abuse of discretion. *E.g., Altman* v. *Connally,* 456 F.2d 1114, 1116 (2d Cir. 1972) (per curiam); *Sampson* v. *Radio Corp. of America,* 434 F.2d 315, 317 (2d Cir. 1970); *Nederbandsche Handel-Maatchappij, N.V.* v. *Jay Emm, Inc.* 301 F.2d 114, 115 (2d Cir. 1962). Given the substantial precedent that characterizes as meritless the claim that the currency is unconstitutional, the District Court acted well within the limits of its discretion by denying Schiff's Rule 60(b)(6) motion.

CONCLUSION

For the foregoing reasons, Irwin Schiff's motion for relief from judgment was properly denied. It is respectfully requested that the District Court's decision be affirmed.

Respectfully submitted,

ALAN H. NEVAS
United States Attorney

By:
JOHN B. HUGHES
Assistant United States Attorney
P.O. Box 1824
New Haven, Connecticut 06508

On Brief:

Marilyn B. Fagelson
Law Student Intern

4. My Reply to the Government's Assertions

IRWIN A. SCHIFF, *pro se*
60 Connolly Parkway
Hamden, Connecticut 06514

Irwin A. Schiff v. *United States of America, et. al.*

United States Court of Appeals   Docket No. 82-6015
for the Second Circuit
United States Courthouse
Foley Square
New York, New York 10007

Gentlemen:

This is in reply to the government's answer of August 9th, 1982 to my appeal for Relief From Judgment Pursuant To Rule 60(b)(4) and (6). The government's answer is a conglomeration of false, irrelevant and idiotic assertions which cannot refute my contention that the District Court for the District of Connecticut (Ellen Bree Burns, D.J.) erred in

ordering the Plaintiff to pay to the United States government "fiat currency," as the money of account of the United States as an award for attorney's fees in her order of December 8, 1981. Such an award, the
Plaintiff contends, is contrary to the monetary provisions of the United
States Constitution, and all Supreme Court cases bearing on coin and
currency and also shows a distain by Ellen B. Burns of Sections 314 and
371 of Title 31.

I will refute the government's assertions page by page:
        1) The government claims (pg.4, lines 1 and 2) that,
"Schiff bases his argument primarily on the theory that the
United States Constitution requires currency to be redeemable in
gold and silver." I never argued or suggested any such thing. To the
contrary, I have always argued that the United States Constitution
never gave the Federal government any authority, whatsoever, to issue currency of any kind. But in this claim I am also joined by
every Supreme Court judge who ever sat in on any of the legal
tender cases both in the majority and in the minority. The United
States Constitution gives to the Federal government certain powers over money, while denying certain monetary powers to the
states. But currency is not money, and the granting of power to the
Federal government over money is not the granting of power of the
Federal government over currency. Currency is a money substitute,
and the Constitution leaves to the private sector the right to create
and handle its own money substitutes. (For an understanding concerning these differences, I suggest the first chapter of *The Biggest
Con: How The Government is Fleecing You* entitled "The U.S.
Money Swindle." The book is written by the Plaintiff and published
by Freedom Books, Hamden, Connecticut.)
        The Constitution in Article I, Section 8 gave the Federal gov-
ernment the power to "coin money, regulate the value thereof, and
of foreign coin. . ." There is nothing in that section giving the Federal government the power to issue paper currency *of any kind*. As
a matter of fact, such a power was contained in the first two drafts
of the Constitution, but was specifically eliminated from the final
draft as explained in my appeal brief. The Constitution obviously
did not have to specifically deny *currency powers* to the Federal government since the function of the Constitution, with respect to the
Federal government, was not to deny it power, but *to grant it power.*
And powers not granted are *automatically* denied. (See Amendment 10 to the United States Constitution.) The states, on the
other hand, were denied in Article I, Section 10, power to coin
money, as well as the power to issue paper currency, and they were

further denied the power to "make anything but gold and silver coin a tender in payment of debt."

Some states had at various times made other forms of money (i.e. wampum, furs, and tobacco) legal tender, but the Constitution established that states could not make these commodities legal tender. Article I, Section 10 clearly established that henceforth only gold and silver coin could be the lawful money of the United States since it was the only type of money allowed by the Constitution as legal tender. Since the Federal government *was never given the power to make **anything** legal tender,* the only thing that can be legal tender under the Constitution is gold and silver. This principle is so clear that one would have to be a blithering idiot not to understand it.

2) The government next contends that Plaintiff relied heavily upon two Supreme Court opinions which the government states are *Hepburn vs. Griswold,* and *Knox vs. Lee.* Why does the government totally disregard my reliance on another Supreme Court case — *Ogden vs. Saunders* 12 Wheat 214? Why does the government avoid this case like the plague? And how does the government deal with the Supreme Court's contention in that case that the monetary restrictions imposed by the Constitution were "intended to cut up paper money by the roots"?

3) The government continues its specious arguments with "Schiff attempts to limit the decision in *Knox* and *Juilliard* by arguing that they upheld the constitutionality of paper currency not redeemable in gold and silver only when issued during the exigencies of war." The government erects one strawman after another! I never, for a moment, contended that either *Knox* or *Juilliard* ever upheld the issuance by the Federal government of *fiat currency* as lawful because such currency was issued during the exigencies of war, or at any other time. First of all, the government conveniently forgets that I had made repeated attempts to distinguish in my brief that in both *Knox* and *Juilliard,* the Supreme Court was dealing with *redeemable note currency*, specifically note currency issued by the Federal government itself, and that *in addition,* it was issued during an exigency — the Civil War. But at least in that case it was *redeemable* currency and not *fiat* currency, *as we have here in the instant case.* In the instant case, I am being ordered by the District Court of Connecticut to pay the government *fiat* currency on the outrageous pretext that fiat currency issued by a private banking corporation can be the lawful money of account of the United States. If the Supreme Court had trouble constitutionally justifying the issuance *even in time of war* of redeemable Federal

government note currency, how does this Court think the Supreme Court would have reacted to a claim that *fiat* currency, issued by a private banking corporation, without any exigency whatsoever, was constitutionally authorized? "No one supposes, " said the Supreme Court in *Knox* (on Pg. 315)

. . . that these government certificates are *never* to be paid — that the day of specie payments is never to return. And it matters not in what form they are issued. The principle is still the same. Instead of certificates they may be Treasury Notes, or paper of any other form. And their payment may not be made directly in coin, but they may be first convertible into government bonds, or other government securities. Through whatever changes they pass, *their ultimate destiny is to be paid.* (Emphasis added)

Here we find a capsulization of the thinking that produced the majority decision in the *Knox* case. U.S. notes were merely ". . . a pledge of the national credit." They were "a promise by the government to pay dollars. . . not an attempt to make dollars." It was only an attempt "to make the government's credit. . . accepted and received by the public and private creditors during the pending exigency." (Pg. 315)

But even on this issue — the government itself has proved my case from its quote from *Juilliard* (on pg. 4) wherein the Supreme Court acknowledges that the issuance by the government of even *redeemable note currency* must be based on *some* "exigency" either in "war or peace, " but argued that the "question of exigency" is a "political question to be determined by Congress when the question of exigency arises, and not a judicial question to be afterwards passed upon by the courts."

But such Federal Reserve notes as were formally issued (and currently issued Federal Reserve *fiat* paper) were both circulated not as a result of any congressionally claimed "exigency" — either during *war* or *peace* — but their circulation was and is justified (lower courts would have us believe) as a normal and legitimate extension of the government's constitutionally granted monetary powers. Such a claim, this *very* passage proves, is preposterous.

4) The government's next judicial gem (Pg. 5) is the opinion of judges of the 8th Circuit, who, oblivious to the law of the land, ignominiously contend (the government claims) in *United States vs. Griffin* that "The Constitution 'prohibits the states from declaring legal tender anything other than gold or silver but does not limit Congress' power to declare what shall be legal tender for debts."

Obviously the judges of the 8th Circuit have to have pointed out to them that the function of the Constitution was not to ascribe limits to Federal power, but only to set specific limits over the power of the states as clearly explained in the Tenth Amendment. The Federal government only has those powers given to it — so it is nonsense for any jurist to claim that the Federal government *has powers* simply *because such powers were not "limited"* by the Constitution. But if the Constitution did not limit the government's monetary powers then why were there any legal tender cases at all? I would, therefore, ask of this Court to tell me if the Constitution does indeed set limits to the government's monetary powers and, if so, what those limits are. Please tell me what the legal tender cases were all about if the Constitution does not set limits to the government's monetary powers. The total absurdity of this quote from *Griffin* is, I suggest, satisfactorily answered by Daniel Webster as quoted on pg. 4 of my appeal brief.

In addition, if the 8th Circuit Court in Griffin was correct then the majority in *Knox*, who asserted that "Congress may [not] make anything which has no value — money, " is incorrect. So who is correct — the 8th Circuit Court in *Griffin,* or the Supreme Court in *Knox?*

Next the government contends that "Despite Schiff's contentions, Congress clearly delegated its power to issue such currency to the Federal Reserve System [and that delegation has been] consistently upheld as constitutional." First of all, Congress was never given the power to "issue such currency, " and so it cannot delegate powers that it does not have. But even given the government's legitimate power "to coin money and regulate the value thereof, " the assumption that such a power can legally be delegated is simply nonsense. Since the Federal government's power to "coin money and regulate the power thereof" is contained in Article I, Section 8 (along with such other powers as the power to raise and support armies, to make rules for the government and regulations of the land and naval forces, to provide for calling forth the militia, and to provide for the punishment of counterfeiting) can the government delegate all of these powers to private corporations? The fact that the government cites lower court decisions supposedly upholding such a preposterous assumption is merely an indication of the confusion that now exists among appellate courts — not only with respect to the government's monetary powers, but with respect to other constitutional matters as well.

But even 12 U.S.C., Section 411 can be of no help to the government in the instant case, since this Section provides that Federal Reserve notes shall be "obligations of the United States, [and that] they shall be *redeemable in lawful money* on demand at the Treasury Department of the United States in the City of Washington, D.C. or any Federal Reserve Bank." Thus this Section itself, *admits* that Federal Reserve notes are not lawful money, but must be **redeemable** in lawful money. Since currently issued Federal Reserve *fiat* paper is *not redeemable* in "lawful money on demand" it does not even fall within 12 U.S.C., Section 411. Further, currently issued Federal Reserve *fiat* paper is obviously not "obligations of the United States" since the wording on its face does not obligate even the Federal Reserve Bank (the private banking corporation that issued them) – let alone the United States – from having to pay *anything at all* to the holder of its phony paper. (I should only be able to get away with a scam like this.) Thus if the Court were to sustain the order of the lower court, it would obviously be ordering me to pay a substance that violates 12 U.S.C., Section 411, the very section that the government uses to bolster its hopeless case.

Therefore, the Supreme Court's decision in *Juilliard* can have no bearing on currently issued Federal Reserve *fiat paper* since such paper is not issued by the United States government; is not issued in time of war, or because of any claimed "exigency"; is not an "obligation of the United States"; and contains no promise to pay gold coin or any other kind of lawful money to the bearer or his order either currently or at any time in the future.

If the Court of Appeals for the Second Circuit does not overrule Judge Burns' preposterous order, then the prestigious United States Court of Appeals for the Second Circuit will have affirmed and proclaimed to all the world that in its considered judgment:

1. Promissory notes do not have to contain a *promise* of any kind; that anything can legally be a note as long as it *claims to be a note*, regardless of the terms appearing on its face; and that notes do not have to contain an unconditional order to pay a sum certain to anyone's order or to the bearer. Thus the adoption of this *new legal doctrine*, I suspect, might conflict with certain provisions of The Uniform Negotiable Instruments Act.
2. That fiat currency, issued by a private banking corporation, is the lawful money of account of the United States, and that Section 371 of Title 31, requiring the money of account of the United States be expressed in "dollars, " is in error; and that "accounts" [and] "proceedings in the courts [can be] expressed" in Federal Reserve *fiat* units and need not be kept or expressed in dollars

— the former "standard unit of value" as defined in Title 31, Section 314.

3. That the United States government can (regardless of any of the limiting provisions in the Constitution and the considered judgment of the Supreme Court as expressed in numerous legal tender cases) make anything it wishes (presumably, even bundles of garbage stamped "legal tender") legal tender in payment of debts.

WHEREAS PREMISES CONSIDERED: Appellant prays for an order of this Court staying the execution of the attached judgment of the District Court of Connecticut directing the Appellant to pay fiat currency and for such further relief that the Court deems just and proper.

Respectfully submitted,

Irwin A. Schiff, *Pro Se*

Let me remind this Court that "the intent of the legislatures constitutes the law of the land" (*Steward vs Kahn* 78 US 504). The intent of the framers of the Constitution with respect to fiat currency is clear: *They intended to stamp out fiat currency forever from these United States.* They knew the economic ravages that such a monetary scam creates since a number of states, as well as the Continental Congress itself, had attempted to employ a form of paper money (albeit note currency) and not as we have in the instant case — *naked fiat currency.* This is clear from all that transpired at the Constitutional Convention and from all of the writings that we have from those who wrote our Constitution and who guided its adoption.

For example, George Washington in his circular letter of June, 1783 to the governors of the several states wrote that

Honesty will be found on every experiment to be the best and only true policy. [being convinced that] arguments deduced from this topic could with pertinency and force be made use of against any attempt to procure a paper currency." (Washington to Theodoric Bland, August 15, 1786.)

"To emit an unfunded paper as a sign or value ought not to continue a formal part of the constitution, nor ever hereafter to be employed; being, in its nature, pregnant with abuses, and liable to be made the engine of imposition and fraud; holding out temptations equally pernicious to the integrity of government and to the morals of the people (Hamilton's Works, II, page 271.)

I never have heard, and I hope never shall hear any serious mention of a paper emission in this state. Yet ignorance is the tool of design, and is often set to work suddenly and unexpectedly. (Washington to R.H. Lee, Mount Vernon, August 22, 1785, in Sparks, IX, page 120.)

They may pass a law to issue paper money, but twenty laws will not make the people receive it. Paper money is founded upon fraud and knavery. (George Mason to George Washington, *Letters to Washington,* IV, page 190.)

Other states are falling into very foolish and wicked plans of emitting paper money. (Washington to Jefferson, August 1, 1786, in Sparks, IX, page 186.)

Paper money is unjust; to creditors, if a legal tender; to debtors, if not legal tender, by increasing the difficulty of getting specie. It is unconstitutional, for it affects the rights of property as much as taking away equal value in land. It is pernicious, destroying confidence between individuals; discouraging commerce; enriching sharpers; vitiating morals; reversing the end of government; and conspiring with the examples of other states to disgrace republican government in the eyes of mankind (Writings of Madison, I, pages 255, 256.)

And lastly, I attach as Exhibit (1) pages 18, 19, and 20, which were taken from George Bancroft's, *A Plea For The Constitution Of The United States,* in which George Bancroft (the leading American historian on the United States Constitution) in a book written to refute the errors committed by the Supreme Court in *Juilliard vs. Greenman* quotes at length from Roger Sherman's *A Caveat Against Injustice,* a treatise written by that great statesman from New Haven, Connecticut, concerning the evils of paper money.

I again would like to remind this Court, to take judicial notice that the government cannot use *Juilliard vs. Greenman* 110 US 421, as providing any legal basis whatsoever for establishing the legal basis of currently issued Federal Reserve "notes."; since the question before the Court in that case was clearly stated on Pg. 437, to wit:

The question, therefore, to be considered. . . is whether notes of the United States issued in time of war under acts of Congress declaring them to be a legal tender in payment of private debts, and afterwards in time of peace redeemed and paid in gold coin at the Treasury, and then reissued under the act of 1878. . . were constitutional.

EXHIBIT (1)

after the payments due them for their extraordinary services in the war were remitted to each one of them in coin, enacted that "no paper currency, or bills of credit of any kind issued in

EXHIBIT (1) (continued)

any of the said colonies or plantations, shall be a legal tender in payment of any private dues whatsoever within any of them." "No law," writes Adam Smith, "could be more equitable."

Roger Sherman, the great statesman of Connecticut, gave his mind to the questions about money and mediums, commerce and exchanges, and having mastered them, in 1752, under the name of Philoeuonomos, "the lover of just laws," he addressed to the men of Connecticut "A caveat against injustice, or an inquiry into the evil consequences of a fluctuating medium of exchange." These are some of his words: "The legislature of Connecticut have at length taken effectual care to prevent a further depreciation of the bills of this colony; the other governments," (meaning New Hampshire and Rhode Island) "not having taken the like prudent care, their bills of credit are still sinking in their value." . . . "Money ought to be something of certain value, it being that whereby other things are to be valued." . . . "And this I would lay down as a principle that can't be denied, that a debtor ought not to pay any debts with less value than was contracted for, without the consent of or against the will of the creditor." . . . "If what is used as a medium of exchange is fluctuating in its value, it is no better than unjust weights and measures, both which are condemned by the laws of God and man; and, therefore, the longest and most universal custom could never make the use of such a medium either lawful or reasonable.

"We, in this colony, are seated on a very fruitful soil; the product whereof, with our labor and industry and the divine blessing thereon,

EXHIBIT (1) (continued)[3]

would sufficiently furnish us with and procure us all the necessaries of life and as good a medium of exchange as any people in the world have or can desire. But so long as we part with our most valuable commodities for such bills of credit as are no profit, we shall spend great part of our labor and substance for that which will not profit us; whereas if these things were reformed we might be as independent, flourishing and happy a colony as any in the British dominions."

In May of the same year, the famous traveller, John Ledyard, and twenty-five other merchants of Connecticut caught up the theme, and in a petition to their legislature said: "The medium of trade whereby our dealings are valued and weighed ought to be esteemed as sacred as any weights and measures whatever, and, to maintain justice, must be kept as stable, for as a false weight and false balance is an abomination to the Lord, a false and unstable medium is equally so, as it occasions as much iniquity and is at least as injurious."

The Connecticut assembly supported the memorialists, excluded the bills of paper money of Rhode Island, and overcoming every embarrassment, at last, like Massachusetts, redeemed every nine shillings of its paper money with one shilling in specie. After the first day of November, 1756, all accounts in Connecticut were kept in lawful money.

---

[3]*A Plea For The Constitution of The United States,* (Spencer Judd, Publishers Edition, 1982) by George Bancroft, pages 18, 19, 20.

[2]But in 1982 a Federal District Court Judge wants to make, in Connecticut, fiat paper issued by a private banking corporation legal! Obviously there was greater financial sanity in Connecticut in 1756 than there is today.

5. Letter to the Court Re Additional Oral Argument Time

November 1, 1982

U.S. Court of Appeals   Re: Docket No. 82-6016
1702 U.S. Courthouse   Calendar No 244
Foley Square
New York, New York 10007

Gentlemen:

I note that the Court has only allocated five minutes for oral argument
which involves substantial constitutional issues as follows:

1. Whether Federal courts are at liberty to ignore the restrictions
   that the Constitution imposes on the Federal government's monetary powers and,
2. Are Federal courts at liberty to impose fines and levies in fiat
   currency.

The Connecticut District Court in the instant case has chosen to ignore
no less than four constitutional provisions which set limits to the federal government's monetary powers, as well as Title 31 USC, Section
371, and has acted as if there were no constitutional, and statutory restrictions *whatsoever* to the federal government's monetary powers.
This issue presents the Court with an example of a federal court totally
disregarding its constitutional responsibilities with respect to enforcing the monetary laws that apply to the federal government, and I am
prepared to offer no less than four Supreme Court decisions that support
my contention.

In addition, the question of whether the federal courts are free to impose
fines and levies in fiat currency is an issue that has never before been
argued before an appeals court.

In addition, I would like to challenge the government's position in a
more extensive manner than five minutes would permit since I plan to
appeal this matter to the Supreme Court, if need be, and I would like
the record to reflect responsible oral argument.

For all of the above reasons, I respectfully request that the Court grant me twelve minutes for oral argument, and three minutes for rebuttal.

Respectfully yours,

Irwin A. Schiff

6. The Court's Opinion

UNITED STATES COURT OF APPEALS
For the Second Circuit

At a stated Term of the United States Court of Appeals for the Second Circuit, held at the United States Courthouse in the City of New York, on the 17th day of January, One Thousand Nine Hundred and Eighty-two.

PRESENT:

HON. WILLIAM H. TIMBERS,
HON. ELLSWORTH A. VAN GRAAFEILAND,
HON. LAWRENCE W. PIERCE,
                         Circuit Judges

UNITED STATES OF AMERICA,
                                        Appellee,

v.   ORDER
                                                            82-6015

IRWIN A. SCHIFF,
                                        Appellant.

Irwin Schiff appeals from an order by the United States District Court for the District of Connecticut (Burns, J.), denying his motion for relief of judgment brought under Fed. R. Civ. P. 60(b)(4) and (6). We affirm.

Denial was proper under Rule 60(b)(4) because appellant failed to establish that the district court lacked power to issue the attorneys' fees order, or that the district court abused its power so as to offend principles of due process. *See In re Texlon Corp.*, 596 F.2d 1092, 1099 (2d Cir. 1979). Denial was also proper under Rule 60(b) (6). The arguments presented in the motion were substantially the same arguments raised by Schiff and considered by the district court on the November 21, 1981 motion. No appeal was taken from the denial of the November 21, 1981 motion. In view of this history, it is apparent that Schiff is attempting to use Rule 60(b) (6) as a substitute for an appeal, and that no exceptional or extraordinary circumstances are present that would warrant vacatur of the judgment. *See House v. Hogg,* F.2d   , 82-6034, slip opinion, at 4543-44, (2d Cir. August 30, 1982). The district court did not abuse its discretion in denying the motion.

Order affirmed with double costs to the Government.

PART II

1. My Appeal Re Judge Clarie's Refusal to Grant a Hearing Pursuant to Section 2255, 28 U.S.C.

The following is a copy of my appeal to the Second Ciruit Court of Appeals regarding Judge Clarie's unlawful and arbitrary refusal to grant me a *habeas corpus* hearing while I was imprisoned, pursuant to Title 28, Section 2255. Despite the obvious lawlessness of Clarie's action, he was nevertheless sustained by an equally lawless panel of appeal "judges" consisting of Chief "Judge" Wilfred Feinberg, "Judge" Henry J. Friendly, and "Judge" Lawrence W. Pierce.

These Second Circuit "judges" sought to escape making any semblance of a ruling on the issues using the lame excuse that since I failed to appeal a similar lower court holding (raised in connection with another matter) I could not appeal it later. In the following brief I explained fully why I did not attempt to appeal or argue that issue at the time, but this did not matter to the appeal "judges." This is further proof that those sitting on the Second Circuit Court of Appeals have little or no interest in protecting the constitutional rights of American citizens.

Irwin A. Schiff, *Pro Se*
144 Shepard Knoll Drive
Hamden, Connecticut 06514   Docket No. 81-2154

UNITED STATES COURT OF APPEALS
FOR THE
SECOND CIRCUIT

IRWIN A. SCHIFF,

Appellant

v.

UNITED STATES OF AMERICA

Appellee

ON APPEAL FROM THE UNITED STATES DISTRICT COURT FOR THE DISTRICT OF CONNECTICUT DENYING APPELLANT'S PETITION FOR A WRIT OF HABEAS CORPUS

I

ISSUE PRESENTED

That the incarceration of the Appellant in a Federal prison and his fine of $10,000 (for which the District Court of Connecticut illegally compelled the Appellant to pay, under duress, 10,000 non-redeemable notes issued by various and sundry Federal Reserve Banks in lieu of the $10,000 ordered by the Court) was illegal since the Trial Court had no jurisdiction.

CONSTITUTIONAL PROVISIONS AND STATUTES CONSTRUED

Fifth Amendment to the United States Constitution:

. . . nor shall be compelled in any criminal case to be a witness against himself.

Title 26 U.S.C. Section 6103(h):

. . . a return or return information shall be open to inspection by or disclosure to officers and employees of the Department of Justice (including United States attorneys). . . for their use in any proceeding before a Federal grand jury or any Federal or State court. . . in connection with determining the taxpayer's civil or *criminal* liability. (Emphasis added)

Title 26 U.S.C. 6103(i):

A return or taxpayer return information shall. . . be open to officers and employees of a Federal agency. . . in preparation for any administrative or judicial proceeding (or investigation which may result in such a proceeding) pertaining to the enforcement of a specially designated Federal *criminal* statute (not involving tax administration) to which the United States or such agency is or may be a party. (Emphasis added)

Title 26 U.S.C. Section 6103:

Par. (a):
If any person shall fail to make a return. . . but shall consent to disclose all information necessary for the preparation thereof. . . the Secretary may prepare such return. . .
Par. (b):
If any person fails to make any return. . . the Secretary shall make such return from his own knowledge. . .

Title 26 U.S.C. Section 6201:

The Secretary is authorized and *required* to make the. . . assessments of all taxes. . . imposed by this title. . . (Emphasis added)

Title 26 U.S.C. Section 6203:

The assessment shall be made by recording the liability of the taxpayer in the Office of the Secretary. . . Upon request of the taxpayer, the Secretary shall furnish the taxpayer a copy of the record of the assessment.

Title 26 U.S.C. Section 6303:

. . . the Secretary, shall as soon as practicable, and within 60 days, after the making of an assessment. . . give notice to each person liable for the tax. . .

TABLE OF CASES

1. *Flora vs United States*, 362 US 145, page 176
2. *Garner vs United States*, 424 US 648
3. *Grimes vs United States*, 607 F.2d 6
4. *Harris vs State*, 46 Del 111
5. *Maxfield's Lessee vs Levy*, 4 Dall (4 US) 330, 334 (1779)
6. *State vs Slorah*, 118 Me 203
7. *Stilwell vs Markham*, 135 Kan 206
8. *United States vs Choate*, (CA5) 276 F.2d 724
9 *United States vs Hall*, 98 US 343
10. *United States vs Hudson*, (1812) 11 US 7
11. *United States vs Schiff*, 612 F.2d 73

STATEMENT OF THE FACTS

An information was filed at Bridgeport, Connecticut against Appellant on April 18, 1978 charging him with two counts of willfully failing to file personal income tax returns for the calendar years 1974 and 1975. He was convicted on both counts on February 13, 1979, which conviction was reversed by the Court and a new trial granted. *United States vs Schiff*, 612 F.2d 73 (1979)

On remand, a jury of 12 and 2 alternates was selected and sworn on April 21, 1980, before Judge T. Emmet Clarie, Chief Judge, at Hartford. The trial began on May 27, 1980, and after 5 days of testimony, went to the jury on June 5, 1980. After 2 days of deliberation, and 17 minutes after the Allen charge, the jury returned and the verdict of guilty as to both counts on June 8, 1980.

On June 23, 1980, Judge Clarie sentenced Appellant to 1 year imprisonment and a committed fine of $10,000 on each count, execution of sentence to be suspended after 6 months. The sentence on each count to run concurrently. On Wednesday, January 28, 1980 a 3 judge panel of the Court Of Appeals affirmed in open court and without opinion Appellant's conviction as to both counts, thus, making a mockery of the appeals process and the Appellant's right to due process.

While the Appellant was incarcerated at Lewisburg Prison Camp, he filed a "Motion To Vacate Sentence" pursuant to Rule USC 2255 raising the issues that his incarceration was illegal on the following grounds:

1. The Court was without jurisdiction;
2. his incarceration violated his Fifth and Ninth Amendment rights;
3. his incarceration violated his constitutional right not to be subject to a direct tax which had not been apportioned; and
4. his incarceration violated his right to have the assistance of counsel at his trial.

Judge Clarie denied the Appellant's 2255 Motion without answering or requiring the government to answer any of the allegations raised by the Appellant. He did so on the specious grounds that the issues raised 'were raised before or during trial" or that "they could have been raised on appeal." Thus, the Court illogically asserted that regardless of how valid were the Appellant's allegations, the Court would not, under any circumstances, consider them. Thus, Judge Clarie effectively barred the Appellant from any access to or any relief under 28 USC 2255 and for all intents and purposes illegally denied 2255 protection to the Appellant.

In this connection, Judge Clarie's decision totally disregarded this Court's own decision in *Grimes vs U.S.* 607 F.2d 6, wherein the Court Of Appeals For The Second Circuit specifically ruled that issues attacking "jurisdiction" or "claiming significant denial of constitutional rights" are validly raised under Section 2255, even though the issues could have been raised on appeal and there was not sufficient reason for doing so.

II

ARGUMENT

THE TRIAL COURT WAS WITHOUT JURISDICTION:

Jurisdiction of the subject matter is derived from the law. It can neither be waived nor conferred by consent of the accused. Objection that the Court does not have jurisdiction of the subject matter may be made at any time, and the right to make such objection is never waived. *United States vs Choate* (CA5) 276 F.2d 724; *Harris vs State,* 46 Del 111; *Stilwell vs Markham,* 135 Kan 206; *State vs Slorah,* 118 Me 203.

It is hornbook law that before a Federal Court can have jurisdiction, there must be a Federal statute capable of being violated:

The legislative authority of the Union [Congress] must *first make an act a crime* (2) affix a punishment to it and (3) declare the court that shall have jurisdiction of the offense. (Emphasis added)

U.S. vs Hudson, (1812) 11 US 7

Before an offense can be cognizable in the Circuit Court, Congress must first *define or recognize it as such,* fix a punishment, and confer jurisdiction upon some court to try the offender. (Emphasis added)

U.S. vs Hall, 98 US 343

Section 7203, the statute which the Appellant was charged with violating, neither makes "an act a crime," nor does it "define or recognize" a crime. And, thus, Section 7203 cannot confer jurisdiction on any court. Section 7203 provides in relevant part:

. . . any person *required* under this Title to . . . make a return. . . who willfully fails. . . to make such return. . . shall be fined not more than $10,000. or imprisoned not more than 1 year or both together with the cost of prosecution. (Emphasis added)

However, Section 7203 does not state exactly who, IF ANYBODY, IS REQUIRED TO FILE FEDERAL INCOME TAX RETURNS. But, not only does Section 7203 not allege that anybody is required to file a tax return, but the Appellant is specifically not required to file a tax return for the simple reason that:

Our system of taxation is based upon *voluntary* assessment and payment, not upon distraint. (Emphasis added)

Flora vs U.S. 362 US 145, page 176

Thus, it should be obvious that if our tax system is based upon **VOLUNTARY** assessment, a tax return cannot be **REQUIRED** to be filed, and thus, the Appellant could not be subject to any charge under Section 7203.

This principal of the **VOLUNTARY** nature of filing a tax return was even recognized by the Trial Court, when (Pg. 98 of Appellant's trial transcript) Appellant objected to the introduction of his 1973 tax return to be used against him, on the grounds that he believed that the information it contained was "REQUIRED." The Court overruled the Appellant's objection (Pg. 99) and ruled as follows:

The Court will rule that the income tax return was filed voluntarily.

Well, if the Court allowed Appellant's 1973 tax return to be used against him on the grounds that the information was not compelled, that it was not **REQUIRED** to be filed, then the Appellant is not required to file and thus, not subject to 26 USC 7203, the statute he is charged with violating.

One doesn't have to be a legal genius to figure out that if Appellant's 1973 tax return was required to be filed (under threat of statutory punishment) then it could not have been admitted into Appellant's trial and used against him. Appellant's 1973 tax return was clearly admitted on the grounds that tax returns are not required, but are filed **VOLUNTARILY** as clearly stated in *Flora vs U.S., supra*.

Indeed, how can tax returns be "required" when under Section 6103 (h) and 6103 (i) of the Internal Revenue Code, return information can be turned over to the DEPARTMENT OF JUSTICE and used against taxpayers to determine their "civil or criminal liability," and for use in connection with "the enforcement of a specially designated Federal criminal statute [not involving tax administration] to which the United States or such agency is or may be a party to." Does the Court of Appeals for The Second Circuit believe that the Appellant can be required by law to furnish such information, via his tax return, to the DEPARTMENT OF JUSTICE?

If the Court of Appeals for The Second Circuit is going to hold that the Appellant is required to file tax returns, then the Court of Appeals is going to hold that the Appellant can be required by law to furnish the Department of Justice with testimony that it can use against him, and such a holding would, of course, be ludicrous.

Further, The United States Supreme Court held in *Garner vs U.S.*
424 US 648 that:

> . . . the information revealed in the preparation of the filing of an income
> tax return is, for the purpose of Fifth Amendment analysis, the testimony
> of a "witness" as that term is used herein.

Does The Court Of Appeals for The Second Circuit believe that a
citizen can be compelled by law to be a witness against himself? If it
does, it is probably because the Court confuses a citizen's constitutional
right, not to be a witness against himself, with the claim of a privilege
against self-incrimination, if one's testimony is compelled. The Court of
Appeals' confusion in this area was clearly evident in the *United States
vs Schiff, supra,* (at Pg. 76) when the Court stated that:

> Schiff's basic themes apparently were. . . that compelling him (to file a
> tax return) compels him to be a witness against himself in violation of the
> Fifth Amendment privilege against self-incrimination.

Thus, the Court Of Appeals illogically twisted the Appellant's
clear claim to a basic constitutional **RIGHT** into a supposed claim of a
less significant "privilege." This is, therefore, to inform this Court that
the Appellant does not at all contend that the **REQUIRED** filing of a
tax return violates his "privilege" against self-incrimination, but it
most assuredly would VIOLATE HIS RIGHT AGAINST BEING COM-
PELLED TO BE A WITNESS AGAINST HIMSELF. And, in the face of
Garner, supra and 26 U.S.C. Section 6103, how can this Court contend
otherwise? I would, also, respectfully request of this Court that it, not
again, twist, mangle, and distort the Appellant's clear claim and assertion of a constitutional "RIGHT, " which is relevant to this issue, into
a supposed claim and assertion of a "privilege, " which is not relevant
to the issue presented here.

It is evident that Title 26 does not **REQUIRE** citizens to file tax
returns since the Government is **REQUIRED** to assess all taxes based
upon its own determination (see Section 6201), record the citizen's tax
liability (see Section 6203), and give notice "to each person liable for the
unpaid tax" (see Section 6303).

A citizen can **VOLUNTARILY** cooperate in the preparation of his
tax return, as provided in Section 6020, by consenting "to disclose all
information necessary for [its] preparation"; but if he fails to do this,
"the Secretary shall make such return from his own knowledge." Thus,
it is clearly provided by statute that it is the Government that is **RE-**

QUIRED to determine and individual's income tax liability and citizens are not **REQUIRED** to file tax teturns, but they can **VOLUNTARILY**, provide such information if they choose.

In addition, Public Law 93-579, The Privacy Act, requires that each Federal agency that asks for information must inform individuals of:

> (D) the effects on him, if any, of not providing all or any part of the requested information. . .

In this connection, The Privacy Act Notice as contained ïn the 1040 Booklet which accompanys a tax return states in relevant part:

> If a return is not filed and if we don't receive the information we ask for, the law provides that a penalty may be charged. And we may have to disallow the exemptions, exclusions, credits, deductions, or adjustments shown on the tax return. This could make the tax higher or delay any refund, interest may also be charged.

There is nothing in the Privacy Act Notice that states that individuals face criminal prosecution under 26 USC 7203, "if a return is not filed." If criminal prosecution were lawfully provided as a consequence of not filing a tax return, THIS FACT WOULD HAVE TO BE INCLUDED IN THE PRIVACY ACT NOTICE. The fact that such a statement is not included in the Privacy Act Notice is proof that Appellant's prosecution and imprisonment under Section 7203 for "willful failure to file a tax return" was the result of a "legal fiction." During the regime of Lord Manfield, the English Common Law Courts defined and developed the practice of taking judicial notice of a legal fiction to gain jurisdiction. However, there is no evidence to support the contention that the "legal fiction" was embraced by our Common Law Courts when the Constitution was ratified, and it is absolute certainty that the United States Courts cannot employ a legal fiction to gain criminal jurisdiction. In the foregoing connection, the Supreme Court in *Maxfield's Lessee vs Levy* 4 Dall. (4 U.S.) 330, 334 (1779) is quoted as follows:

> It is true, the courts of law in England have countenanced and supported some fiction. . . It is sufficient to say of all these, that they originally took place, when very dark notions of law and liberty were entertained; . . . No court in America ever yet thought, nor, I hope, ever will, of acquiring jurisdiction by a fiction.

Obviously, the Supreme Court's early faith that American courts would not sink so low as to employ legal fictions to gain jurisdiction proved to be unduly optimistic, as is so clearly demonstrated by the instant case.

Thus, it is evident that Section 7203 did not confer any jurisdiction on the Trial Court since Section 7203 did not allege a crime, nor did it allege that Appellant was **REQUIRED** to file a tax return, nor is such a requirement contained anywhere in Title 26. If Title 26 did, in fact, require citizens to file tax returns then, given Section 6103, such a requirement would make the entire Internal Revenue Code unconstitutional as it would be repugnant to the Fifth Amendment to the United States Constitution.

CONCLUSION

Despite the fact that the Appellant is now no longer in physical custody, he should not be further punished because of this, nor should the government be allowed to benefit because of the dereliction of one of its own judges. The Appellant insists that he be allowed to prove that his incarceration was unconstitutional so that he can clear his name and, in addition, recover the 10,000 Federal Reserve Notes that were extorted from him. While the other issues raised in Appellant's 2255 Motion concerning his illegal incarceration and illegal fine are equally valid, he feels to argue them in this appeal is unnecessary, since if the Court will not be moved based upon the Trial Court's obvious lack of jurisdiction (the evidence for which is clear and overwhelming) than to argue any other point would prove equally futile.

Therefore, based upon the Trial Court's arbitrary refusal to either grant the Writ, or to issue an Order To Show Cause to the Appellee why the Writ should not issue, the Appellant now demands that the District Court be reprimanded for trifling with the Writ, and that this Court issue that Writ Of *Habeas Corpus* forthwith.

Submitted by,

Irwin A. Schiff
Pro Se

Appendix F

Miscellaneous Correspondence and "Court" Decisions

Part 1

On September 12, 1984 I sent a Privacy Act Request to the Secretary of the Treasury, Donald Regan, asking for a copy of the record of my Federal tax assessments for 1972 through 1984 (Exhibit 29). For 1972 and 1973 I filed traditional income tax returns; for 1974 and 1975 I filed Fifth Amendment income tax returns (for which I went to jail); and for 1976 through 1974 I filed no income tax returns at all. Under the Privacy Act the government is *required* to provide individuals with copies of requested documents as long as such documents are not exempted from disclosure. The Act does not require that agencies create documents that do not exist only that they send copies of those that do. Whenever an agency receives a request which would result in the creation of a document where none exists it will respond by stating that it is not required to create documents.

The government's answer to my request (dated October 11) is shown in Exhibit 30. Notice how the government had no problem locating certified copies of my assessments for 1972 and 1973 (the years I filed traditional returns). In addition, the government admits that for 1979 through 1984 no assessments were made. But note the government's response for 1974 through 1978: it informed me that its records indicated that I had previously received statutory notice of my tax liabilities for those years. But what does that have to do with my request? Obviously if I requested the documents I must have needed them. Even if the government *did* send me notices in the past (which it did not) I might have lost them. If such documents existed the government was *required by law* to supply them (as it did in the case of 1972 and 1973), or

EXHIBIT 29

Irwin A. Schiff
P.O. Box 5303
Hamden, Ct. 06518

September 12, 1984

Mr. Donald T. Regan
Secretary of the Treasury
Main Treasury Building
15th St. & Pennsylvania Ave. N.W.
Washington, D.C. 20220

RE: Privacy Act Request

Dear Sir:

Under the provisions of the Privacy Act, U.S.C. 552a, I hereby request that in accordance with IRC Section 6203 you furnish me with a copy of the record of my federal tax assessments for the years 1972 through and including 1984.

I agree to pay any fees for searching for, or copying the records I have requested, but if such fees exceed 10 dollars, please inform me before you fill the request.

If all or any part of this request is denied, please cite the specific exemption(s) which justify your refusal to release the information, and inform me of the appeal procedures avaiable to me.

In order to expedite consideration of my request, I am enclosing a copy of my drivers license.

Thank you for your prompt attention to this matter.

Sincerely
Irwin A. Schiff
Irwin A. Schiff

inform me that no such documents existed (as it did for 1979 through 1984).

It is obvious from the government's response that no such records existed. It is also obvious that the government did not want to admit this because it had already produced what its attorneys claimed were copies of my assessment at my "hearing" on June 20 and had already taken close to $200,000 from me for those years. If it now admitted that no taxes were ever assessed, it would prove that the documents previously produced were phony and that the $200,000 was taken illegally. Based

EXHIBIT 30

Internal Revenue Service   Department of the Treasury

District
Director

William R. Cotter, Federal Building
135 High Street, Hartford, CT 06103

OCT 11 1984

Mr. Irwin A. Schiff
P.O. Box 5303
Hamden, Conn. 06518

Dear Mr. Schiff:

I am writing in response to your correspondence to Mr. Donald Regan,
Secretary of the Treasury, dated September 12, 1984, which has been
forwarded to my office for reply.

Enclosed you will find certified transcripts of your U.S. Individual
Income Tax accounts for the years 1972 and 1973. Our records indicate
you have previously received statutory notices of your 1974 through 1978
liabilities. In respect to the years 1979 through 1984, our records do
not reflect any assessments.

Please contact the District Disclosure Officer at 722-2669 if you have any
further questions about your request.

Sincerely yours,

JAMES E. QUINN
District Director

Enclosure

(Continued next page)

on this I would have no trouble recovering such amounts in District
Court.[1] My request presented the government with an insolvable problem so it contrived a response hoping to pacify me.

When I received that letter I promptly sent a reply (Exhibit 31) and
the government responded (Exhibit 32) by forwarding what were pur-
portedly my assessments for those years. Compare these to the docu-

---

[1] I filed a suit to recover all of this money (plus interest and damages) in February,
1985.

EXHIBIT 30 (Continued)

Form FC-4 (1-79)   Departme   Treasury - Internal Reven

TRANSCRIPT OF ACCOUNT

DATE   04-16-84

IRWIN A SCHIFF
PO BOX 5303
HAMDEN CT 06518

1975-1994   5678901234567890 1234
RA FILING   00000000000000000000

EIN-SSN   047-16-2491
PERIOD ENDING   72-12
TYPE OF TAX   INCOME
FORM FILED   1040
NAME CONTROL   SCHI
CAF OR B TR   O 00

SPOUSE-RRB NO.
FREEZE-STATUS CODE   -Z
PRIOR NAME CONTROL

TRANSCRIPT TYPE   COMPLETE
SORT DLN   08299-080-10101-4
CONTROL DLN   06247-080-61424-6
LOCATION CODES   08-06-01
CURRENT
TDA (IF DIFFERENT)
PRINT CONTROL No   0000270
ADJ CONTROL NO.

EXPLANATION	TRANSACTION DATE	23C DATE OR MEMO ENTRIES	AMOUNT	CYCLE	TRANSACTION DOCUMENT LOCATOR NUMBER	COMP. CODE	REMARKS
RET FILED-150	04-15-73	05-28-73	1,754.00	7320	06221-111-12907-3	3	
CR W/HELD FICA-806	06-11-73		6,002.00-	7322	06221-111-12907-3		
RFND & INT-846	06-11-73		4,279.71	7322	06221-111-12907-3		
INT DUE TP-776	12-04-73		31.71-	7550	06229-333-10008-5		CNTL NO 65338-01050
AUDIT IND-420	03-30-78		.00	7614	06247-080-61424-3	X 32	
RV AUDIT 1-421			.00	7810	06254-461-15007-3	3	
TAX ADJ-290		03-20-78	.00				
R OF CR PD-12	05-28-73						
MODULE BAL			.00				
ACCRD INT	04-16-84		.00				
ACCRU PEN	04-16-84		.00				

"I certify that the foregoing transcript to the account
of the taxpayer named above in respect to the taxes
specified, is a true and complete transcript for the
period stated, and all assessments, credits and refunds
relating thereto as disclosed by the records of this
office as of the date of the certification are shown
therein. It also contains a statement of all unidentified
or advance payments, if any, made by the above taxpayer
for the period(s) stated."

Alvin H. Tanner

4-16-84

For taxable year 1972

(Continued next page)

EXHIBIT 30 (Continued)

Form FC-4 (1-79) Departm'ent · Treasu'y - Internal Rever

TRANSCRIPT OF ACCOUNT   DATE 04-16-84

IRWIN A SCHIFF
PO BOX 5303
HAMDEN CT 06518

1975-1994   5678901234567890123
IRA FILING 0000000000000000000

EIN-SSN	047-16-2491	
PERIOD ENDING	73-12	
TYPE OF TAX	INCOME	
FORM FILED	1040	
NAME CONTROL	SCHI	
CAF OR B TR	0 00	

SPOUSE-RRB NO.

FREEZE-STATUS CODE   -2

PRIOR NAME CONTROL

TRANSCRIPT TYPE   COMPLETE
SORT DLN   08299-080-10101-4

CONTROL DLN .   06247-080-60144-6
LOCATION CODES
CURRENT   08-06-01
TDA (IF DIFFERENT)
PRINT CONTROL NO   0000271
ADJ-CONTROL NO.

EXPLANATION	TRANSACTION DATE	23C DATE OR MEMO ENTRIES	AMOUNT	CYCLE	TRANSACTION DOCUMENT LOCATOR NUMBER	COND. CODE	REMARKS
RET FILED-150	04-15-74	06-03-74	851.00	7421	59221-131-19741-4		
AGI		10,380.00					
CR WT&FICA-806			3,917.00-				
EXT FILING-460	04-15-74		.00	7417	59217-103-02854-4		EXTN DATE 06-15-74
RFND & INT-846	06-03-74		3,066.00	7421	59221-131-19741-4		
AUDIT IND-420	01-29-75		.00	7506	59277-029-00000-5		CNTL NO 15029-77506
RV AUDIT I-421	04-02-76		.00	7615	06247-080-60144-6	X 32	
TAX ADJ-290		03-20-78	.00	7810	06254-461-15008-9	3	
EXT FILING-04	05-06-74						
R OP OR PD-12	06-03-74						
MODULE BAL			.00				
ACCRD INT	04-16-84		.00				
ACCRD PEN	04-16-84		.00				

"I certify that the foregoing transcript to the account of the taxpayer named above in respect to the taxes specified, is a true and complete transcript for the period stated, and all assessments, credits and refunds relating thereto as disclosed by the records of this office as of the date of the certification are shown therein. It also contains a statement of all unidentified or advance payments, if any, made by the above taxpayer for the period(s) stated."

4-10-84

For taxable year 1973

EXHIBIT 31

                                                    Irwin A. Schiff
                                                    P.O. Box 5303
James E. Quinn   Hamden, Ct. 06518
IRS, Disrtict Director, Hartford
135 High St.
Hartford, Ct. 06103

RE: Privacy Act Request

                                                    October 15, 1984

Dear Sir:

Your response to my Privacy Act request dated Sept. 12 1984 is incomplete.
In that letter I specifically requested copies of the records of my federal
tax assessments for the years 1972 through 1984. With regards to the years
1972 and 1973 I was supplied with the appropriate records. For the years
1979 through 1984 I was informed that your records "do not reflect any
assessments". and therefor no such records obviously exist. However, with
regards to the years 1974 through 1978 I was neither supplied with the
requested records, nor informed that no such records exist. I was merely
informed that I had "previously received statutory notices of my 1974
through 1978 liabilities". However, this has absolutely nothing to do with
my request. I did not ask whether or not I received any statutory notices,
but requested to be supplied with the record of my federal tax assessments
as provided by IRC section 6203.

I therefor reassert my request, and under the provisions of the Privacy Act,
U.S.C. 552a, request that you furnish me with copies of my federal tax
assessments for the years 1974 - 1978. If no such records exist (i.e. no
assessment has been made), then please inform me to that effect.

I agree to pay any fees for searching for, or coping the records I have
requested, but if such fees exceed __*10*__ dollars, please inform me before
you fill the request.

If all or any part of this request is denied, please cite the specific
exemption(s) which justify your refusal to release the information, and
inform me of the appeal procedures avaibable to me.

Thank you for your prompt attention to this matter.

                        Sincerely
                        Irwin A. Schiff

Enc.

EXHIBIT 32

Internal Revenue Service   135 High Street
                                      Hartford, CT 06103

                                      Date:
                                      Nov. 6, 1984

Dear Mr. Schiff:

    In accordance with your request dated

October 15, 1984, I am forwarding to you

transcriptions of your income tax accounts

for the years 1974, 1975, 1976, 1977 and 1978.

These documents were provided to this office by

our North Atlantic Regional Service Center.

                                      Sincerely yours,

                                      [signature]
                                      FREDRIC MEASER

                                      District Disclosure Officer

Attachment

Form 5260 (6-74)   Department of the Treasury

(Continued next page)

EXHIBIT 32 (Continued)

Internal Revenue Service Center   Department of the Treasury
North-Atlantic Region

Date: OcT. 31, 1984   Name of Taxpayer
                                                      (If Other than Addressee):

                                                      Social Security or
                                                          Employer Identification Number:
                                                      047-16-2491

Irwin A. Schiff
P.O. Box 5303
Hamden, CT. 06518

The record of accounts you requested is furnished on the attached transcript.

We are glad to be of assistance in this matter.

Sincerely yours.

Alvin H. Tanner

Supervisor, Account Unit

(Continued next page)

---

ments I received for 1972 and 1973. First, the assessments for 1972 and 1973 came from the Office of the District Director (where all such records are required to be recorded by law). For 1974 through 1978 the District Director did not have these documents so he had to write to the North Atlantic Regional Service Center for them. *This means that no such records existed at the time of my original request!* Why did Mr. Quinn not inform me of that?

Second, the papers I received in connection with my 1972 and 1973 assessments were *photocopies* of documents that already existed at the time of my request. Those which I received in connection with 1974 through 1978 were *not photocopies,* they were *hand written originals.* From looking at the handwriting and the ink it is obvious they were all written by the same person at the same time. Obviously *there was nothing to photocopy!* This is proof that as of that date I still had not been assessed though the government had confiscated some $200,000 from me for those years. (If assessment documents existed — as they did for 1972 and 1973 — photocopies would have been sent.) In addition, the Privacy Act did not require them to *create documents that did not*

EXHIBIT 32 (Continued)

Record of Accounts

			Tax Form Number		Social Security or Employer Identification Number	Sheet _1_ of _6_
			1040		047-16-2491 N	

Tax Period Beginning or Ended	Date of Credit or Assessment	Assessments	Credits	Account Balance	Remarks
12-31-74	04-20-83	14,406.25			Additional Tax assessed by audit
	"	8,203.13			Fraud Penalty
	"	525.00			Failure to Pay Estimated Tax Penalty
	"	17,562.54			Interest
	08-14-84		176.68		Payment
				43,460.24	

For taxable year 1974 — note *no* certification.

(Continued on next page)

EXHIBIT 32 (continued)

Record of Accounts

Tax Period Beginning or Ended	Date of Credit or Assessment	Assessments	Credits	Account Balance	Remarks
			Tax Form Number: 1040	Social Security or Employer Identification Number: 047-16-2491 N	Sheet 2 of 6
12-31-75	04-30-83	3,226.39			Additional Tax assessed by audit
	"	1,613.20			Fraud Penalty
	"	139.68			Failure To Pay Estimated Tax Penalty
	"	3,138.24			Interest
				8,117.51	

For taxable year 1975 — note *no* certification.

(Continued on next page)

EXHIBIT 32 (Continued)

Record of Accounts

Tax Period Beginning or Ended	Date of Credit or Assessment	Assessments	Credits	Account Balance	Remarks
12-31-75	05-17-84		6,927.08		
				6,927.08 CR	Payment

Tax Form Number: 1040

Social Security or Employer Identification Number: 047-16-3491

Sheet 3 of 6

For taxable year 1975 — note *no* certification.

(Continued on next page)

EXHIBIT 32 (Continued)

Record of Accounts

Tax Form Number: 1040   Social Security or Employer Identification Number: 047-16-2491   Sheet 4 of 6

Tax Period Beginning or Ended	Date of Credit or Assessment	Assessments	Credits	Account Balance	Remarks
12-31-76	12-27-82	.00		← This is a lie!	Return Filed
	04-01-83	19,006.00			Additional Tax Assessed
	"	9,503.00			Fraud Penalty
	"	709.00			Estimated Tax Penalty
	"	13,619.35			Interest
	02-25-83		5,400.00		Payment
	"		4,700.00		"
	08-01-83	18.00	4,631.61		Fees and Collection Costs
	08-08-83		1,161.91		Payment
	08-15-83		5240.00		"
	12-23-83		28,525.29		"
	02-06-84	3,669.10			"
	12-23-83	34.36		.00	Interest overpayment Transferred To 1978-1040

For taxable year 1976 — note *no* certification.

(Continued next page)

EXHIBIT 32 (Continued)

Sheet 5 of 6

Record of Accounts

Tax Form Number: 1040

Social Security or Employer Identification Number: 047-16-2491

Tax Period Beginning or Ended	Date of Credit or Assessment	Assessments	Credits	Account Balance	Remarks
12-31-77	12-27-82	-.00		↑ This is a lie!	Return Filed
	04-01-83	18,478.00			Additional Tax Assessed
	"	9,339.00			Fraud Penalty
	"	663.00			Estimated Tax Penalty
	"	11,080.99			Interest
	12-23-83		6,448.71		Payment
	01-05-84		37,355.30		"
	03-06-84	3,998.65			Interest
	01-05-84	44.97		-.00	Overpayment Transferred To 1978-1040

For taxable year 1977 — note *no* certification.

(Continued next page)

EXHIBIT 32 (Continued)

Sheet ___6___ of ___6___

Record of Accounts

Social Security or Employer Identification Number: 047-16-2491

Tax Form Number: 1040

Tax Period Beginning or Ended	Date of Credit or Assessment	Assessments	Credits	Account Balance	Remarks
12-31-78	12-27-82	.00			Return filed
	04-01-83	53,447.00		This is a lie! ➤	Additional Tax assessed
	"	26,724.00			Fraud Penalty
	"	1,706.00			Estimated Tax Penalty
	"	28,370.89			Interest
	01-05-84		44,009.70		Payment
	12-23-83		34.34		overpayment applied from 1976-1040
	01-05-84		444.97		overpayment applied from 1977-1040
	01-31-84		14,031.00		Payment
	03-01-84		4,670.00		"
	04-17-84		4,078.00		"
	04-26-84		148.96		"
	05-28-84	18.00			Fees and Collection Costs
	05-17-84		39,258.17		Payment
	06-11-84	13,009.27		-.00	Interest

For taxable year 1978 — note *no* certification.

exist, but since the government did not want to admit this, it *created* phony assessments in an attempt to comply with my request.

Third, the assessments for the years 1972 and 1973 contain *certifications of their accuracy,* correctness, and truthfulness — and *no such certifications* appear on the purported "assessments" for 1974 through 1978.

The government also indicated that income tax returns were *filed* for 1976 through 1978. That is a lie! *I filed no income tax returns for those years.* By comparison the government does not indicate that returns were filed for 1974 and 1975 — the two years for which I filed Fifth Amendment returns. The government indicated that income tax returns were filed for 1976, 1977, and 1978 because (according to Section 6201 of the Internal Revenue Code) no assessment can be made unless a return is filed — which is why no assessments could exist for me for any of those years. *The government also could not maintain that returns were filed for 1974 and 1975 because those were the years for which I went to jail for not filing.* The only records the government really had were for the years I did file — 1972 and 1973.

After receiving that information I sent another letter on November 9, 1984. On February 1, 1985 I finally received a reply. That reply was a stamped notice on the bottom of my original letter that stated:

INDIVIDUAL INCOME TAX RETURNS PRIOR TO 1977 HAVE BEEN OFFICIALLY DESTROYED BY AUTHORIZATION OF THE U.S CONGRESS. SUBSEQUENT YEARS, IF REQUESTED, ARE BEING PROCESSED.

The bottom line is this: the IRS has taken approximately $200,000 of my money (about half of which was for interest and penalties) yet after five months it still cannot produce a valid assessment to support its actions!

PART II

How Federal "Judges" Disobey Law and Fact

The following is the complete text of "Judge" Ellen Burns' ruling on my Motion for a temporary restraining order.

UNITED STATES DISTRICT COURT

DISTRICT OF CONNECTICUT

IRWIN SCHIFF   :

V.   :   CIVIL NO. B-83-289

UNITED STATES OF AMERICA,   :
INTERNAL REVENUE SERVICE AND
JAMES QUINN, District Director   :

RULING ON MOTION FOR PRELIMINARY INJUNCTION

Plaintiff in this action **is a zealous tax protester,** who claims that the federal tax system is unconstitutional as presently administered. He filed this suit seeking relief in the nature of mandamus and an injunction to prevent the collection of federal income tax, interest and penalties which have been assessed against him for the taxable years ending December 31, 1976, December 31, 1977, and December 31, 1978. A hearing on plaintiff's motion for a preliminary injuction was held on May 20, 1983.

For the reasons stated in defendants' brief, plaintiff's motion for a preliminary injunction must be denied and the complaint must be dismissed.

Plaintiff failed to file federal income tax returns or to pay income tax to the Internal Revenue Service for the taxable years 1976, 1977, and 1978. The Commissioner of Internal Revenue determined that he had income sufficient to require him to pay tax for each of those years and notified him, on December 2, 1982, of his tax deficiencies. Plaintiff failed to exercise his statutory right under 26 U.S.C. §7422 to contest the determination of the deficiencies in the Tax Court. On April 1, 1983 the Internal Revenue Service made an assessment against the plaintiff for unpaid federal income tax, penalties and interest and, on April 18, 1983, sent him a final notice advising him of the delinquent status of his 1976, 1977, and 1978 accounts. Plaintiff filed suit here on May 4, 1983.

It is fundamental tenet of the American legal system that federal courts are courts of limited jurisdiction. U.S. Const. art. III §2. Congress has explicitly limited the extent to which courts may intrude upon the assessment or collection of federal taxes. *See* The Anti-Injunction Act, 26 U.S.C. §7421.[1] Congress designed a procedure whereby an aggrieved party, challenging the Internal Revenue Service's *assessment* of income taxes, may petition the Tax Court to review the assessment. Alternatively, the petitioner may pay income taxes and, after exhausting the Service's internal review procedures, sue for a refund in *district court. See Bob Jones University v. Simon,* 416 U.S. 725, 746 (1974).

The Supreme Court has repeatedly upheld the Anti-Injunction Act's limit on federal court jurisdiction, by referring to the "Government's need to assess and collect taxes as expeditiously as possible with a minimum of pre-enforcement judicial interference." *Bob Jones University v. Simon, supra* at 736. *See Enochs v. Williams Packing & Navigation Co.,* 370 U.S. 1 (1960). An exception to the operation of the statute is found only if irreparable injury, a prerequisite for injunctive relief, and certainty of success on the merits are found. *Enochs v. Williams Packing & Navigation Co., supra* at 6–7.

Plaintiff has not shown either of the two prerequisites for a judicial exception to the Anti-Injunction Act. Payment of the assessed taxes imposes a financial burden on plaintiff, but does not rise to the level or irreparable harm.[2] Moreover, plaintiff has an adequate remedy at law, either through challenging the assessment in Tax Court or through suing in district court to recover any tax paid which he may allege was illegally or erroneously assessed. In addition, not only is there no certainty that plaintiff will succeed on the merits, but there is little likelihood that he will do so. Cf. Schiff v. United States, No. N-81-316, slip op. (D. Conn. Nov. 9, 1981).

Plaintiff, also, seeks relief in the nature of mandamus directing defedants to comply with the provisions on the Privacy Act, 5 U.S.C. §5529(e)(3), by indicating whether he must file an income tax return and whether such a filing is voluntary or mandatory. The Internal Revenue Service Privacy Act Notices have been held to satisfy the requirements of 5 U.S.C §552a (e)(3). See *United States v. Annunziato,* 643 F.2d 676, 678 (9th cir. 1981); *United States v. Rickman,* 638 F.2d 182, 183 (10th Cir. 1980); *United States v. Karsky,* 610 F.2d 548, 549 n. 2 (8th Cir. 1979), *cert. denied,* 444 U.S. 1092 (1980). In any event, the Privacy Act provides for relief only to amend an individual's record or to order that the records be provided the individual. 5 U.S.C. §552a(g)(2)(A) and (g)(3)(A). See *Hanley v. United States Department of Justice,* 623 F.2d 1138, 1139 (6th Cir. 1980); *Parks v. Internal Revenue Service,* 618 F.2d 677, 684 (10th Cir. 1980); *Cell Associates v. National Institute of Health,* 579 F.2d 1155 (9th Cir. 1978). There is no provision for injunctive relief of the kind plaintiff is requesting. Plaintiff's request arising out of the Privacy Act is denied.

Plaintiff's request for a copy of the record of assessment, to

which he is entitled under 26 U.S.C. §6203, has been granted.

Plaintiff's motion for a preliminary injunction is **denied** and his complaint is dismissed **for lack of subject matter jurisdiction.**

SO ORDERED

ELLEN BREE BURNS
UNITED STATES DISTRICT JUDGE

Dated at New Haven, Connecticut, this *27th* day of June, 1983.

FOOTNOTES

1. 26 U.S.C. §7421(a) provides in relevant part:

   [N]o suit for the purpose of restraining the assessment or collection of any tax shall be maintained in any court by any person, whether or not such person is the person against whom such tax was assessed.

2. Plaintiff's claim that his ability to earn a living as a publisher and a professional writer would be undermined, should an injunction not be granted, is unpersuasive. Plaintiff, also, claims that the assessment of taxes and fraud penalties against him is totally arbitrary and without any basis. He has provided no evidence to support this claim.

(Emphasis added)

PART III

The Second Circuit Strikes Again!

UNITED STATES COURT OF APPEALS

FOR THE SECOND CIRCUIT

Cal. No 439 — August Term, 1984
(Argued: Nov. 27, 1984   Decided: Dec. 20, 1984)
Docket No. 84-4082

IRWIN SCHIFF
Petitioner-Appellant,

v.

COMMISSIONER OF INTERNAL REVENUE,
Respondent-Appellee.

RAYMOND HEPPER, Tax Division, Department of Justice, Washington, D.C., (Glenn L. Archer, Jr., Assistant Attorney General, Michael L. Paup and Ann Belanger Durney, Attorneys, Tax Division, Department of Justice, Washington, D.C., of Counsel), *for Appellee.*

Before:

TIMBERS, VAN GRAAFEILAND, and PIERCE, *Circuit Judges.*

Irwin Schiff appeals from an order of the United States Tax Court (Hamblen, J.) dismissing his petition for redetermination of income tax deficiencies for the years 1974 and 1975 and upholding the Commissioner's assessment of additions to tax for failure to pay estimated tax and underpayment of tax due to fraud. **Affirmed with double costs and damages.**

PER CURIAM:

Irwin Schiff appeals from an order of the United States Tax Court (Hamblen, J.) which dismissed his petition for redetermination of income tax deficiences for the years 1974 and 1975 and upheld the Commissioner's assessment of additions to tax for failure to pay estimated tax, 26 U.S.C. §6654, and fraudulent underpayment, *id.* §6653 (b).

Appellant essentially urges this Court to reverse the decision of the tax court because it did not accept his arguments that he could not be penalized for fraudulent underpayment of taxes when he, in fact, made no payment, that the tax on wage income is unconstitutional, and that the Commissioner is not authorized to assess a deficiency if no return was filed. **We see no need to elucidate our reasons for dismissing these arguments.** Suffice it to say that **each is wholly lacking in merit,** is **without any logical basis,** and **has been rejected countless times** by this Court and others. Accordingly, **we affirm Judge Hamblen's well-reasoned decision.**

We now turn to the Commissioner's request for costs and damages. Where an **appeal** is completely frivolous, the **courts of appeals are authorized to award damages and single or double costs to the appellee.** Fed. R. App. P. 38. *See also* 28 U.S.C. § § 1912, 1927. This is so even where the Commissioner is the appellee. *Crain v. C.I.R.*, 737 F.2d 1417 (5th

Cir. 1984) (per curiam); *Beer v. C.I.R.*, 733 F.2d 435 (6th Cir. 1984) (per curiam); *Lamb v. C.I.R.*, 733 F.2d 86 (10th Cir. 1984) (per curiam).

Appellant is not, as his attorney maintained at oral argument, *exercising his right to voice conceivably meritorious claims*. His understanding of our federal tax system is such that **he must have known his claims would be rejected** by this Court. Indeed, **the tax court told him in no uncertain terms that his arguments were frivolous and that he was "engaged in a 'folly' which [would] be costly to him."** We can only conclude, therefore, that appellant brought this appeal either to delay the ultimate judgment against him or to make public his radical views on tax reform. We will not allow this Court's appellate processes to be misused for such purposes. **Both damages and costs are appropriate sanctions against "those who would persistently raise arguments against the income tax which have been put to rest for years."** *Parker v. C.I.R.*, 724 F.2d 469, 472 (5th Cir. 1984). Accordingly, we grant the Commissioner's request and award the Commissioner double costs and $2500 in damages.

Affirmed with double costs and $2500 in damages against appellant.

(Emphasis Added)

PART IV

Attempts To Determine My Legal Liability Under The Internal Revenue Code

In early 1979 I submitted a nine page **Petition for Redress of Grievances** to the IRS, the Supreme Court, and President Jimmy Carter. In that Petition I raised the following issues:

1. As currently imposed, is the income tax a direct or indirect tax?
2. If it is a direct tax, how can it be levied without apportionment? If it is an indirect tax, why are wages subject to it?
3. Am I a person required to file an income tax return?
4. Since an individual cannot be compelled to waive his constitutional rights, how can I be *required* to file an income tax return when, in so doing, I am compelled to be a witness against myself—in direct violation of the 5th Amendment?
5. If I still possess my 5th Amendment right not to be compelled to be a witness against myself, how can I file an income tax

return without waiving that right?

6. I asked for clarification of my rights under the 1st, 4th, 9th, and 13th Amendments as they related to the filing of an income tax return.

7. I asked five questions regarding the Privacy Act Notice and its ramifications with respect to the filing of income tax returns.

Exhibits 33 through 39 illustrate the futility of my efforts to have such seemingly simple issues clarified. My Petition was originally sent to the Commissioner of Internal Revenue, Jerome Kurtz. It was relayed to James Quinn, Acting District Director for Connecticut, who replied on June 7 (Exhibit 33). On June 14 I met with Quinn and Assistant District Director, Albert Shuckra, in Hartford, Connecticut. On June 18 I sent a letter to Shuckra confirming our conversation (Exhibit 34) and again asked for answers to the questions I raised in my Petition and at our meeting. In a letter dated August 21 I received a reply to the letter I sent Shuckra from Robert B. Dugan, District Counsel for the North-Atlantic Region (Exhibit 35). On September 7 I wrote to Dugan (Exhibit 36) and asked, once again, that my simple questions be answered. On September 10 I sent a letter to Shuckra (Exhibit 37) and to Kurtz (Exhibit 38) together with a copy of the September 7 letter to Dugan. I never received a response to either of those letters. Dugan responded on September 25 (Exhibit 39) but still **did not answer even one of my simple questions.**

So, after numerous and detailed attempts on my part to have important issues clarified for me with respect to filing income tax returns, the only issues clarified were

1. **The government refused** to identify the constitutional basis of the income tax;

2. **the government refused** to provide me with instructions on how to file an income tax return without waiving any constitutional rights; and

3. to all questions regarding statutory proof of the legality of its actions with respect to income taxes the government's lackeys tell citizens to "contact an attorney of your choice" for the answers.

If the individuals involved in the enforcement of Federal "laws" cannot — or will not — answer legitimate questions raised by citizens regarding those "laws," how can anyone be expected to understand them or be bound by them?

EXHIBIT 33

Internal Revenue Service   Department of the Treasury

District   P.O. Box 959, Hartford, Conn. 06101
Director
                                  JUN 7 1979

▷Mr. Irwin A. Schiff
2405 Whitney Avenue
Hamden, CT 06518

CERTIFIED MAIL

.Dear Mr. Schiff:

I am in receipt of your PETITION FOR REDRESS OF GRIEVANCES, which was
delivered to the Commissioner, Internal Revenue Service, on April 13,
1979.

As to your concerns regarding waiver or infringement of certain
constitutional rights, I enclose a copy of the opinion in James Randall
Holt v. Commissioner, T.C. Memo 1977-365, wherein the Court deals with
issues which you cite. If you have further concerns in this regard, I
suggest that you consult with an attorney of your choice to assist in
determining your course of future action.

                              Sincerely,

                              Al Shuckra

                          ⨍— JAMES E. QUINN
                              Acting District Director

Enclosure

EXHIBIT 34

 Freedom Books

P.O. BOX 5303   HAMDEN, CONNECTICUT 06518   PHONE (203) 281-6791

*If a nation values anything more than freedom, it will lose its freedom; and the
irony of it is that if it is comfort or money that it values more, it will lose that too.—Somerset Maugham*

June 18, 1979

Mr. Albert Shuckra
Assistant District Director
Internal Revenue Service
P.O. Box 959
Hartford, CT

Dear Mr. Shuckra:

This letter will confirm our conversation of June 14 held in the
office of the Acting Director of Internal Revenue for the State
of Connecticut, James E. Quinn, relating to my Petition for Redress of Grievances; his response to it; and my desire to pay
any lawful taxes due - without surrendering any of my constitutional rights.

First, his letter dated June 7, 1979 was totally unresponsive to
the questions raised in my Petition. The case he cited, <u>James
Randall Holt vs Commissioner</u> T.C. Memo 1977-365, was a decision
of an administrave "court," not a real court of law. This decision, therefore, can have no bearing on questions of <u>criminal
law</u> so it cannot be cited as settling any relevant constitutional issue. Even if the "court" were a <u>proper</u> authority (which it
is not), the case itself does not address itself to any of the
issues raised in my Petition.

The Petitioner in that case apparently raised "numerous constitutional objections" to the filing of an income tax return and
even raised the issue of whether "the payment of Federal income
taxes is valid." My Petition raises no such issues. I do not
for a moment contend that a Federal income tax is not lawful.
What I do contend, however, is that a direct tax based upon income must be apportioned, while an excise tax related to one's
income must be levied on the basis of geographic uniformity.

My petition simply asks the government on what basis it is levying the Federal income tax. Is it levying it as a direct tax
or as an excise tax? To date the government has evaded answering this question - and <u>Holt vs Commissioner, supra,</u> does not
answer it either.

(Continued on next page)

EXHIBIT 34 (Continued)

Additionally, Mr. Holt states that giving answers on a tax return might be "self-incriminating." My Petition did not raise the issue of self-incrimination but, rather, the far broader issue of whether a citizen can be compelled to be a witness against himself. I offered two Supreme Court cases which clearly stated that the preparer of a tax return is a witness within the meaning of the Amendment - and the Holt case does not address this question.

Finally, the tax court refers to Mr. Holt as some kind of a "tax protester." I, of course, do not protest the payment of taxes at all. I do, however, insist that the Federal government collect. them constitutionally while allowing me to preserve - intact and undiminished - all of my constitutional rights. Note I said rights, not privileges.

My letter also raised the question of whether the Privacy Act Notice on page (3) of a 1040 is complete since it does not state that if one does "not file a return or give us the information we ask" one would be subject to criminal prosecution as I recently experienced. The question, therefore, is whether or not the Privacy Act Notice on the return is complete and whether it conforms to the Privacy Act Law of 1974.

I, therefore, ask you directly: will my failure to give information - which you tell me you will be free to turn over to the Justice Department - subject me to criminal prosecution?

You realize that I have filed no tax returns for 1976, 1977, and 1978. I am asking the Internal Revenue Service to simply provide me with proof that it is levying the Federal income tax a) in a constitutionally lawful manner, and b) to explain to me how one files an income tax return without waiving one's constitutional right not to be compelled to be a witness against oneself.

One thing further - I will not give the Federal government any information to show how my tax was calculated without prior written assurances from it that any such information will not be turned over to the Department of Justice, to the State of Connecticut, other states, foreign governments, or any other department or agency of government. The Federal government was given no constitutional authority to serve as a conduit for such personal information.

Unless I receive answers to these questions and the assurances I seek you will receive no tax information from me for 1976, 1977, 1978, or any other taxable year.

Very truly yours,

Irwin A. Schiff

EXHIBIT 35

DISTRICT COUNSEL

Internal Revenue Service

NORTH-ATLANTIC REGION
100 Summer St.
Rm. 1728
Boston, Massachusetts 02110

CC:BOS-CT-075-78
JABoyce

AUG 2 1 1979

Irwin A. Schiff
c/o Freedom Books
P.O. Box 5303
Hamden, Connecticut   06518

Dear Mr. Schiff:

This refers to your letter of June 18, 1979, to Albert Shuckra, Assistant District Director of Internal Revenue, Hartford, Connecticut. Your letter has been forwarded to this office for a response.

In view of the numerous concerns you expressed in your June 18, 1979 letter, we must reiterate the advice we gave you in our May 21, 1979 letter. We suggest that you contact an attorney of your choice in order to discuss your concerns and to assist you in determining your course of future action.

Sincerely yours,

ROBERT B. DUGAN
District Counsel
Boston

By:

PETER J. PANUTHOS
Assistant District Counsel

Department of the Treasury

EXHIBIT 36

 Freedom Books

P.O. BOX 5303   HAMDEN, CONNECTICUT 06518   PHONE (203) 281-6791

*If a nation values anything more than freedom, it will lose its freedom; and the
irony of it is that if it is comfort or money that it values more, it will lose that too.—Somerset Maugham*

September 7, 1979

Mr. Robert B. Dugan, District Counsel
Internal Revenue Service
North-Atlantic Region
100 Summer Street
Room 1728
Boston, Massachusetts 02110

CC: BOS-CT-075-78

Dear Mr. Dugan:

Your letter of August 21st sent to me in response to the questions
that I was asked by Mr. Shuckra to submit in letter form is totally
unsatisfactory. My letter did not contain "numerous concerns", but
relate basically to four simple questions, which I will simply re-
state here (perhaps viewing them in this manner will help clarify the
questions for you).

1. Is the Federal income tax being levied as a direct or indirect tax?
2. Since both Sullivan vs. The U.S. 15F 2nd 809, P.112 and Garner vs.
The United States 424 U.S. 648, P.656 admit that "...one who files a
return under oath is a witness within the meaning of the Amendment".
Please send me instructions as to how I can complete a 1040 without
waiving my 5th Amendment right, which guarantees that I do not have
to be a witness against myself. The 1040 booklet furnished to me by
the government only contains instructions for those people wishing to
waive this right. Certainly there must be instructions for people who
do not wish to waive this right.

(Continued next page)

EXHIBIT 36 (Continued)

3. Will my failure to supply the IRS with a tax return or information, which the Privacy Act Notice informs me they will be free to turn over to the Justice Department, subject me to criminal prosecution, even though the Privacy Act Notice itself contains no such warning?
4. Am I required to furnish the government with information from which a tax can be computed and are such disclosures essentially "compulsory testimony"?

I don't see why you have any trouble answering these questions since No's 1, 3 and 4, only require one or two words apiece. Question No. 2 might require a somewhat longer answer, but even that should not involve anything complicated.

As to your suggestion that I "contact an attorney"; every attorney that I have contacted cannot even understand why I was charged <u>criminally</u> for my 1974 and 1975 returns. They are at a loss to offer me any advice with respect to these questions, and why or how I should file my 1976, 1977 and 1978 returns. Why should I presume that lawyers, who are confused and perplexed by the government's actions with respect to my 1974 and 1975 returns will advise me correctly concerning my 1976, 1977, and 1978 returns?

But, your suggestion that I should see an attorney contradicts the letter from Commissioner, Jerome Kurtz which appears on the front page of Form 1040, where he states, "if you need help, please call us at the number listed for your area on Page 46, or visit an IRS office." By your not answering the questions contained in my letters, both you and Mr. Shuckra will be guilty of violating the clear instructions of the Commissioner as quoted above.

All that I am trying to do is to pay any taxes that I may lawfully owe the government, while at the same time preserving for myself all of my constitutional rights and privileges. Is there anything wrong in this? Why won't you help me? Is it because these objectives are mutually exclusive?

Very truly yours,

Irwin A. Schiff

EXHIBIT 37

 Freedom Books

P.O. BOX 5303   HAMDEN, CONNECTICUT 06518   PHONE (203) 281-6791

If a nation values anything more than freedom. it will lose its freedom; and the irony of it is that if it is comfort or money that it values more, it will lose that too.—*Somerset Maugham*

September 10, 1979

Mr. Albert C. Shuckra
Assistant District Director
Internal Revenue Service
P.O. Box 959
Hartford, Connecticut 06101

CC: BOS-CT-075-78
JA Boyce

Dear Mr. Shuckra:

Attached please find my reply to Mr. Dugan's letter to me in reply
to my letter to you of June 18th. So far I have not as yet received
the reply to my letter of July 17th.

When I met with you on June 14th, you stated that <u>if I wanted</u> the
<u>answers</u> to the questions. I raised at that meeting, I would have to <u>submit</u>
<u>them in letter form.</u> This I did; however, the subsequent correspondence
will bear witness to the fact that <u>I still did not receive any answers</u> to
the questions I raised with you in Mr. Quinn's office.

I suggest to you that as long as the government <u>refuses</u> to clearly identify
for me the constitutional basis of this tax and <u>refuses</u> to provide me with
instructions as to how to complete a 1040 in a manner that preserves for me,
intact, all of my constitutional rights and privileges, it can have no claim
upon me for this tax or any of the paperwork that goes along with it.

Very truly yours,

Irwin A. Schiff

EXHIBIT 38

Freedom Books

P.O. BOX 5303   HAMDEN, CONNECTICUT 06518   PHONE (203) 281-6791

If a nation values anything more than freedom, it will lose its freedom; and the irony of it is that if it is confort or money that it values more, it will lose that too.—Somerset Maugham

September 10, 1979

Mr. Jerome Kurtz
Commissioner of Internal Revenue
1111 Constitution Avenue, N.W.
Washington, D. C. 20024

Dear Mr. Kurtz:

The attached correspondence is self-explanatory. <u>I have not filed any income taxes since 1975</u> and apparently neither you nor any of your underwings are prepared to advise me how this can be done without my surrendering any of my constitutional rights or privileges.

Neither the Internal Revenue, nor any other branch of government, it seems, is prepared to identify for me the constitutional category of the income tax that is, whether it is being levied as a direct or indirect tax.

Thus, I trust this correspondence has reached it's final ending, and our relationship with respect to the Federal income tax is severed.

Should you have any further questions or comments on these matters, please do not hesitate to contact me.

I am

Constitutionally yours,

Irwin A. Schiff

IAS/cr
enc. (2)

EXHIBIT 39

DISTRICT COUNSEL

Internal Revenue Service

NORTH-ATLANTIC REGION
100 Summer St.
Rm. 1728
Boston, Massachusetts 02110

CC:BOS-CT-075-78
JABoyce

Irwin A. Schiff
c/o Freedom Books
P.O. Box 5303
Hamden, Connecticut 06518

Dear Mr. Schiff:

In response to your September 7, 1979 letter to
this office and prior letters to the District Director's
office, Hartford, Connecticut, we can only reiterate our
suggestion that you contact an attorney of your choice
to discuss the concerns that you have raised in your
correspondence. This office is unable to provide you
with such legal services.

Sincerely yours,

ROBERT B. DUGAN
District Counsel
Boston

By: PETER J. PANUTHOS
     Assistant District Counsel

Department of the Treasury

PART V

Federal "Judges" — Criminals In The Courtroom

"Judge" Warren Eginton's arbitrary ruling dismissing my lawsuit against *Simon & Schuster* (without giving any reasons and **against all law**) proves that when Federal "judges" are issued their black robes they should also be issued black masks!

UNITED STATES DISTRICT COURT

DISTRICT OF CONNECTICUT

IRWIN SCHIFF
V.   **CIVIL N-84-9 (WWE)**
SIMON & SCHUSTER, INC.

JUDGEMENT

This cause came on for consideration of the defendant's motion to dismiss by the Honorable Warren E. Eginton, United States District Judge, and

The Court having considered the defendant's motion and all the papers submitted in connection therewith granted the defendant's motion,

It is therefore ORDERED and ADJUDGED that judgment be and is hereby entered for the defendant and the complaint is dismissed.

Dated at Bridgeport, Connecticut, this 6th day of November, 1984.

KEVIN F. ROWE, Clerk

By: Joanne E. Downs
Deputy-in-Charge

Reference Materials: Books, Reports, And Tapes By Irwin Schiff

BOOKS and REPORTS:

The Schiff Report

An indispensible publication for those who want detailed instructions on how to protect themselves from the IRS. Provides information nowhere else available including documents, sample legal instruments, and procedures to use against the IRS. Many subscribers report that each issue is worth the price of the subscription. Also contains Irwin Schiff's economic and political commentary. 8 issues per year. Newsletter format, ∅75.00/Volume III subscription. Special offer: Volumes I, II, and III -∅150.00. Single issues, ∅10.00.

How Anyone Can Stop Paying Income Taxes, by Irwin Schiff

Published in 1982, this book became the nation's best-selling hardcover book on Federal income taxes. Now in its fifth printing it has sold over 185,000 copies and neither the IRS nor any tax attorney has ever attempted to refute one word of it. It includes detailed instructions on how to stop paying income taxes, how to avoid audits and personal summonses, an analysis of the Privacy Act Notice, and much, much more. An indispensible companion to *The Great Income Tax Hoax*. Hardcover, ∅12.00

The Social Security Swindle - How Anyone Can Drop Out, by Irwin Schiff

An explosive exposé of Social Security - the biggest chain letter of them all. This book reveals in vivid detail all the underhanded practices employed by the Federal government to foist this swindle on the American public. It also provides readers with all the necessary documents and step-by-step procedures so that everyone (employees, employers, and self-employeds) can drop out of the social security scam. Hardcover, ∅13.00.

The Biggest Con: How the Government Is Fleecing You, by Irwin
Schiff

With over 100,000 copies in print this book provides a complete and en-
joyable education in economics and includes irrefutable evidence of the
criminal and destructive nature of the Federal government. "The single
most important book on the status of this nation I have ever read," said
Howard Ruff, editor of *The Ruff Times*. Softcover, ⌀8.00.

The Kingdom of Moltz, by Irwin Schiff

A delightful tale of our monetary system written so that even a child of
ten can understand it. "I laughed so hard I cried. Schiff's book is the
greatest thing since sliced bread," commented Dr. Camille Castorina,
economics professor at St. Johns University. Softcover, ⌀3.00.

How An Economy Grows And Why It Doesn't, by Irwin Schiff and
Vic Lockman

While only 108 pages, this humorous, fully illustrated book provides
readers with a thorough and fundamental understanding of what
makes an economy grow and the reasons why it doesn't. Subjects include the causes of inflation; how capital is created, discouraged, and
destroyed; and the use and misuse of commercial and consumer credit.
A delightful political and economic satire. Softcover, ⌀7.00

AUDIO/VISUAL MATERIALS:

1.   Over the last eight years thousands of Americans have been en-
     lightened and entertained by Irwin Schiff's famous Untax Semi-
     nars. His latest lecture is a series of three, one-hour video cassettes
     professionally filmed in Boston in 1984 that allows you to conduct
     your own seminars. Included is information on how not to pay Fed-
     eral income and Social Security taxes as well as advanced tech-
     niques that can be used in fighting the IRS and the government.

     Part I... ⌀39.00
     Part II.. ⌀39.00
     Part III... ⌀39.00
     SPECIAL - all three parts .... ⌀99.00

Please specify VHS or BETAMAX when ordering.

2. New, 50 minute television show that was produced in Hollywood is now available. Suitable for airing on local/cable TV, it is also available on standard VHS or BETAMAX cassettes. An excellent educational tool, this show is also entertaining and will quickly convince viewers that no one is required to file Federal income taxes.

    50-Minute TV Special .... ⌀75.00

Please specify VHS or BETAMAX when ordering. For Information and pricing on tape for TV airing, contact FREEDOM BOOKS.

3. Based on Irwin Schiff's *How Anyone Can Stop Paying Income Taxes*, these two, 90-minute audio tapes are convenient for use while driving or at home. An invaluable learning aid regarding "voluntary compliance."

    Two Audio Tapes (C-90) .... ⌀15.00

ALSO RECOMMENDED:

The Complete Internal Revenue Code

The best weapon against the IRS is the law itself — in order to effectively fight the IRS each citizen should have a copy of the Internal Revenue Code since the IRS misleadingly states the law and attempts to confuse individuals regarding IRS regulations (which are not binding when they conflict with the law — as many of them do). Soft cover, ⌀18.00.

Handbook For Special Agents

The Internal Revenue Service's handbook for its Criminal Investigation and Intelligence Divisions. Provides detailed information on the internal methods employed by the IRS in its illegal enforcement of the "income" tax. Softcover, ⌀20.00 (the government charges ⌀75.00 for this book).

Prices are denoted by ⌀ which refers to Federal Reserve units — fiat currency now fraudulently circulating as U.S. dollars — and include postage and handling.

Please use the card at the back of the book to order any of these materials.

INDEX